MW00737163

The Young Exceptional Child

Early Development and Education

The Young Exceptional Child

Early Development and Education

John T. Neisworth
Pennsylvania State University
Division of Special Education and Communication Disorders

Stephen J. Bagnato
Pennsylvania State University College of Medicine
Division of Pediatric Rehabilitation

MACMILLAN PUBLISHING COMPANY
New York
COLLIER MACMILLAN PUBLISHERS
London

Copyright © 1987, Macmillan Publishing Company,
a division of Macmillan, Inc.

Printed in the United States of America

All rights reserved. No part of this book may be reproduced or
transmitted in any form or by any means, electronic or mechanical,
including photocopying, recording, or any information storage and
retrieval system, without permission in writing from the Publisher.

Macmillan Publishing Company
866 Third Avenue, New York, New York 10022

Collier Macmillan Canada, Inc.

Library of Congress Cataloging-in-Publication Data

The Young exceptional child.

   Bibliography: p.
   Includes index
   1. Exceptional children—Education.   2. Child
development.   I. Neisworth, John T.   II. Bagnato,
Stephen J.   III. Title.
LC3965.Y68   1987   371.9   86-16364
ISBN 0-02-386300-5

Unless otherwise noted, all photographs are by Robert Neisworth, Pittsburgh, Pennsylvania.

Printing: 1 2 3 4 5 6 7   Year: 7 8 9 0 1 2 3

ISBN   0-02-386300-5

Contributors

L. Gayle Barney
Department of Speech and Language
Elizabethtown Hospital and Rehabilitation Center
Elizabethtown, PA

Nancy B. Burdg
Alabama Institute for the Deaf and Blind
Talladega, AL

Mary Ann Demchak
School of Education
Lehigh University
Bethlehem, PA

Eleanor G. Hall
Alabama Institute for the Deaf and Blind
Talladega, AL

Verna L. Hart
Department of Special Education
University of Pittsburgh
Pittsburgh, PA

Frances M. Hunt
Center for the Study and Treatment of Self-Injury
The Kennedy Institute
Baltimore, MD

Connie Kasari
Department of Psychiatry
University of California, Los Angeles
Los Angeles, CA

P. David Kurtz
School of Social Work
University of Georgia
Athens, GA

Gail L. Kurtz
Southeastern Network of Runaway Youth and Family Services
Athens, GA

Cynthia L. Landis
Department of Speech and Language
The Pennsylvania State University
Elizabethtown Hospital and Rehabilitation Center
Elizabethtown, PA

Michelle A. Larson
Department of Special Education
University of North Carolina
Chapel Hill, NC

Joseph H. Lasley
Department of Child Development and Family Studies
Purdue University
West Lafayette, IN

Robert H. MacTurk
Center for Studies in Education and Human Development
Gallaudet College
Washington, DC

Mary E. McCarthy
Maryland Schools
Headstart Program
Rockville, MD

Mary Beth McLean
Department of Rehabilitation and
  Special Education
Auburn University
Auburn University, AL

Donald Moores
Center for Studies in Education and
  Human Development
Gallaudet College
Washington, DC

Susan Munson
Exceptional Education Division
University of Georgia
Athens, GA

Patrick J. Schloss
Division of Special Education and
  Communication Disorders
The Pennsylvania State University
University Park, PA

Robert Sheehan
Department of Curriculum and
  Foundations
Cleveland State University
Cleveland, OH

Maureen A. Smith
Division of Special Education and
  Communication Disorders
The Pennsylvania State University
University Park, PA

Joseph D. Stedt
Department of Speech and Hearing
Cleveland State University
Cleveland, OH

Preface

Designing, developing, and delivering a textbook for publication is a challenging and arduous job, fraught with difficulties along many steps of the way. The task is made much easier and meaningful, however, when there exists a distinct mission, professional collaboration, and encouragement.

Indeed, our mission provided the primary basis for the book: we wanted to make available a useful and engaging introductory text in early childhood that emphasized not only the problems but also the possibilities of the young exceptional child. Using a developmental/behavioral approach, the various exceptionalities in early childhood are described and related to normal development. A Diagnostic/Prescriptive Model is then used to present overviews and close-ups of early childhood assessment and clinical instruction. Several topics are included to provide the comprehensiveness we sought: working with co-professionals, infants and toddlers, child abuse and neglect, chronic illness and hospitalization, and program evaluation.

The professionals who worked with us contributed superb chapters with the depth and currency that only specialists can bring. Their contributions are gratefully acknowledged.

Hopefully, certain features of the book will assist the student in using it: outlines for each chapter, numerous headings, vignettes on special-needs youngsters, highlighted terminology, and comprehension check points.

To be sure, our mission was speeded and our task made lighter through the help of some exemplary students and office professionals. Glenda Carelas took our sometimes rough and confusing manuscripts and always managed to iron out problems and turn out a polished document. Other office colleagues who directly helped to fashion the manuscript include Janis McWilliams (and child), Suanne Wilson, and Leslie Stewart. We were continually pleased and impressed with their professional participation.

Our "exceptional students" helped in two ways: topic and literature research, and manuscript evaluation. Part of Lori Amos' life has been spent within these pages; she certainly deserves a new car, a degree, or something grand. Mary Jean Dark, Colleen Martin, Kathy Trump, and Laura Waitz will no doubt for years remember (as we will) their participation. Finally, we are pleased to thank Angela Capone, Sue Gorniak, and Donna Hickey for their help in evaluating portions of the book.

We sincerely hope that our readers will find The Young Exceptional Child to be a valuable resource in learning about the exciting and expanding field of Early Childhood Special Education—a profession that brings together special education, early childhood education, child development, psychology, medicine, and allied health disciplines. Our multidisciplinary profession invites students with various interests to learn about and, if possible, choose a career in working with the young exceptional child.

J.T.N.
S.J.B.

Contents

X

THE PROFESSION

1

Introduction to the Young Exceptional Child

John T. Neisworth
Stephen J. Bagnato

CHAPTER OUTLINE

Randy and Linda leave their house at 7:30 A.M. every weekday, taking their lunches and two children with them. Keri is 4 years old and gets dropped off at the church day-care center. Maggie is almost 3 now and enjoys her day at the New Day Preschool. They're not alone. Seven million children are enrolled in some sort of early childhood care or education program, and the need is growing rapidly. In 1975, about one half of American mothers of school-age children worked outside the home. Today, the figure exceeds two thirds. The sharp increase in single-parent families has heightened the need for day-care service as has the rapid climb in employment.

Randy and Linda had no trouble finding a quality day-care center for Keri. It is not only safe and pleasant, but it offers a program of planned developmental activities. Keri learns something new every day. She's reading now and is excited at her new skill. Even more, Randy and Linda are grateful for the nearby New Day Preschool Center. It is operated by the local special-education agency especially for preschoolers with problems.

Maggie was identified in a community screening campaign as a special-needs child. She showed serious delays in language and motor development and has occasional seizures. Her parents were bewildered at the results of the developmental assessment. They didn't want to believe it. But that was more than a year ago. Now, Maggie is talking, enjoys being with other children, and seems to be doing better all the time. Her preschool enrolls 12 exceptional children. They all have different problems, but the teacher has had special training to work with handicapped and at-risk youngsters. Both Randy and Linda get together with Maggie's teacher about once a month. They are learning how to use toys and other materials to help Maggie learn at home. These parents are relieved and grateful that the center is there to permit them both to work. They are most happy, however, at the early help Maggie is getting—help that is improving the quality of life for them and for Maggie.

In the past, parents of handicapped children had to send their children to private schools (if they could afford it) or just keep them at home. America's preschoolers, children up to 5 or 6 years of age, are not presently served by the public schools in any systematic or unified fashion or on as national a scope as are school-age children. The picture is changing, however, and gradually more children who are in need of early education are being enrolled in programs designed to accommodate special needs. Some of these programs are private, some are federally sponsored projects, some are operated by school districts that have the money and staff, and many are offered by agencies with established funding. Head Start, for example, has been helping handicapped youngsters who come from low-income homes for more than a decade. More than 400,000 youngsters are now enrolled in Head Start.

The need for early-childhood education is becoming widely recognized as research, logic, and social planning point to the benefits of early intervention to prevent or remedy development problems (Anastasiow, 1983). The early education of youngsters who are handicapped or at risk for developmental problems will become not only a national priority but also a reality.

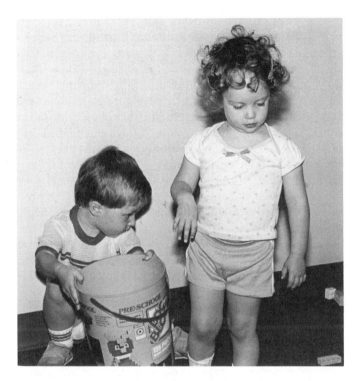

Learning to play together is an important step towards the development of social skills such as sharing and taking turns.

SURVEY OF YOUNG EXCEPTIONAL CHILDREN

Life's early years are marked by rapid changes in both body and behavior. *Physical growth and maturation* move ahead on a predetermined plan and pace characteristic of the species. The body grows, and distinctive physical features become established. Height and weight and nerve, muscle, and bone growth all follow predictable courses. *Behavioral* development also evolves rapidly, with competencies in various areas of functioning showing up at fairly predictable ages. The child's *nature* (heredity and constitution) and *nurture* (environment and child-rearing practices) interact to produce a unique human being that usually is in harmony with society's norms and exceptations.

But nature and nurture do not always produce the "standard" or "average" child. Many differences in the child's constitution are produced by hereditary variation, nutrition, and complications during pregnancy and delivery. Likewise, there are wide differences in children's environments. Social and economic factors provide a spectrum of possible environments that can influence the child's development (Anastasiow, 1983). In particular, the kind of upbringing provided by parents has an impact on the child's learning of skills and the age at which these skills are established (Richardson, 1976; Werner and Smith, 1981).

The mixture of hereditary and environmental influences produces an array of differences across individual children. Some children show marked differences in some skills whem compared with their peers. They are different from the "average" for their age. These *interindividual* differences show up early in life. Martha walked before her brother Bobby; Jimmy talked later than Joey; Beth seems curious about everything while Arnold does not appear to be interested in much. Children do indeed differ from one another on a host of dimensions. Likewise, a child may show wide discrepancies across different areas of development. Charley is 4 years old; his motor skills are age appropriate, but his language is only at a 2-year-old level. Such *intraindividual* differences can also be a serious developmental problem. Educators and therapists are interested in and concerned about these differences, especially when such deviation is substantial and constitutes a continuing problem for the young exceptional child. These and other issues are the concern of special educators, early-childhood educators, school psychologists, child-development specialists, social workers, and various therapists who work with the exceptional preschooler.

"Types" of exceptional preschoolers

Exceptional refers to a condition that is so different from the average or the expected that special methods, materials, and settings must be employed to promote child progress. *An exceptional child* is one who deviates to a marked degree from the average or normal child. "Such deviation must be of such an extent that the child requires a modification of school practices, or special educational services, to develop to maximum capacity" (Kirk and Gallagher, 1983, p. 3).

Preschooler usually refers to children between the ages of 3 to 5, although *early childhood* (birth through 8 years of age), with its more inclusive definition, is a preferred term.

Some children (for developmental or social reasons) do not enter the first grade until they are 8 years old, but many children are in need of developmental help as soon as they are born. More and more, early education is seen as important for any preschool child who evidences significant problems in development or who seems *at risk* for such problems.

Many terms are used in connection with the exceptional child—"special," "handicapped," "disabled," "abnormal," "deviant," "developmentally delayed," and "atypical." *Deviant, atypical,* or *abnormal* all technically refer to any significant departure from the average or typical, and do not necessarily mean the child is handicapped. John is 14 years old and 6 feet tall; he is "deviant," "atypical," or "abnormal"—but not handicapped.

Disability is used to indicate an actual loss of function resulting from physical disorder. Martha was born without normal arms or hands (a "thalidomide baby"); she has a *disability*, as well as being deviant.

Handicap refers to the burden imposed on a child as a result of the interaction of a deviant characteristic with an environment. Charlie is legally blind; he is deviant, disabled, and handicapped in the usual setting. His disability or deviation interacts with the environment to produce a handicap. If the demands of the setting change (i.e., if vision were not important), then there would be no handicap. Charlie is not handicapped in a dark room or in other circumstances where sight is not demanded. Thus, handicap does not refer to the person, but rather to the difficulty a person has when required to function in the (usual) environment. The distinctions among deviancy, disability, and handicap are useful; sometimes we need to describe a child's *difference* (deviancy) without implying a handicap or disability. Loretta is a black child in an all-white neighborhood. She is deviant, but her skin color is not a disability—she has no loss of function because of a physical disorder. Her skin color, however, *may* result in a handicap in the all-white context. We see, then, that *deviancy is a social or statistical judgment, disability is an actual physical disorder, and handicap is situational.*

Whatever terms are used, they usually refer to a negative deviance (i.e., a difference that is undesirable from the standpoint of optimal development). (Perhaps the only exception to this is the "gifted" category, where the exceptionality is a positive or desirable deviance.)

COMPREHENSION CHECK 1.1

How "different" must a child be before special intervention is warranted?

Can a child be handicapped without having a disability?

Other terms are used to identify specific handicapping conditions. Following is a listing of categories of exceptionality frequently used to classify children who show serious problems in development. These terms will be discussed in greater detail in Part Three.

Conventional Categories of Exceptionality

Speech and language disorders
Mental retardation
Learning disability
Emotional disturbance
Physical handicap
Hearing impairment
Visual impairment
Multiple handicap

Problems with categories and labels

Conventional categorical labels have come in to use from several sources—medicine, psychology, education—and are the subject of much professional debate (e.g., Hobbs, 1975). Objections to the use of categorical labels center on the negative bias they can create, the lack of educational information they carry, and the fact that children do not fit neatly into a single category. Early childhood special educators do not usually use handicap labels for youngsters, but prefer the term *special-needs children* to refer to all those children who are experiencing problems or who are at risk for problems.

Labels can bias social judgments

Handicapped children are as individual as any other children. However, children often become identified by their handicap. "Billy is the blind boy" may be used to designate Billy who is also blond, tall for his age, Catholic, and a good singer. His visual impairment is only *one* feature of his total being, yet it gets the most attention and becomes a label, a dominating characteristic.

When people know what categorical label is attached to a child, their judgments, ratings, and interactions with the child can be altered (Salvia and Meisel, 1980). Often, people tend to "see" traits characteristic of the category even if these traits are not really there. A child labeled "hyperactive" will be seen as exhibiting excessive activity even though his behavior may be normal (Neisworth, Kurtz, Jones, and Madle, 1974). In other words, labels can, themselves, impose additional handicap on the child.

Categorical labels do not provide developmental descriptions

Traditional disability labels—such as mentally retarded, emotionally disturbed, learning disabled—are based on the presumed cause of the child's difficulties or the "condition" that the child supposedly *has*; they describe what the child allegedly *is*. Charlie *is* crippled, and Martha *has* emotional disturbance. These labels do provide some information but not enough specificity to permit any kind of real program planning. For developmental/educational purposes, a much better approach is to describe what the child *does* (or does not do).

To know that Charlie has cerebral palsy (brain tissue damage) does not provide much information to the educator. A description of what Charlie *can do* or *not do* in each area of development is much more useful for program planning and treatment. Charlie cannot stand, walk, or run, but he has some use of his arms and hands (he can hold most things and write with special help); his speech is defective and most people cannot understand him, but his receptive language seems normal. Charlie seems to learn new material at a normal or superior rate. He gets along with peers and adults well and is able to develop relationships with others. He does not evidence mood swings and is generally happy. Such descriptions of what a child *does* are clearly more instructionally useful than categorical names for what a child allegedly *is*.

Children can belong to more than one category

A child who displays problems characteristic of one category (e.g., mentally retarded) can also exhibit difficulties associated with other categories (e.g., emotionally disturbed, physically handicapped). Seldom are children pure examples of a single clinical category.

The assignment to a diagnostic category is especially difficult—if not impossible—when dealing with preschoolers. Very young children have not developed a stable repertoire of skills, are difficult to test, and change rapidly. To be sure, *early detection* of developmental difficulties is crucial. However, this type of problem detection (e.g., assessing the child's language level) is not the same as assigning the child to a category of handicap. It is more useful to assess, describe, and report a child's current developmental capabilities than it is to diagnose an "underlying (categorical) condition."

Despite the widespread and continuing arguments against the use of categorical labels for children, such usage is firmly entrenched within the profession. At the preschool level, however, emphasis is on identifiable developmental difficulties. Part Three includes separate chapters on the developmental problems.

Exceptional preschoolers are deviant in at least one major area of child development—deviant enough to experience significant handicap in the usual environment. The basic areas or domains of development are described next.

COMPREHENSION CHECK 1.2
Do diagnostic labels describe a child? What use do they have?

Developmental domains

Experts in child development have organized human capabilities into several domains or areas of functioning. Although there are various names for them, we have identified the following as four major developmental domains: communication, affective-social, cognitive, and sensorimotor. These four domains include most of the skills and capabilities that children normally acquire. Children with handicaps show *delays*, *deficits*, or *distortions* in one or more of these four domains.

Communication

Children receive and express information in verbal and nonverbal ways. Speech (verbal expression) and language (nonverbal as well as verbal) competence are primary areas closely related to the development of intellectual or cognitive capabilities. Obviously, cleft palate or other oral malformations can impede language development. Significant problems in seeing and hearing can also delay the development of communication skills. Milder degrees of these sensory deficits among preschoolers often go undetected. Sometimes teachers and parents misinterpret the behavior of a child who has an unrecognized hearing or vision limitation. "He won't pay attention," "She disobeys," "He is unmotivated," and "He is a little slow," are remarks sometimes made about a child whose real problem is a sensory deficit. Children who experience delays or distortions in communication (regardless of the cause) may also suffer problems in other areas of development because of the important role of language. Not communicating with others can lead to problems in socialization and learning about what is going on around you. Deviations or exceptionalities in communication are important to detect and work with as soon as possible. Early detection and treatment of communication disorders often can prevent or remedy a more general developmental "slowdown" or distortion.

Affective-Social

The process of socialization becomes most evident after the age of about 2. This is a time when skills for getting along with others, with oneself, and with the surroundings begin to be demanded. Dependence versus independence is a struggle that begins soon in the child's life. Gradually, most children develop affective (emotionally based) characteristics. They learn to smile, giggle, coo, frown, cry, and in general display pleasure and displeasure. They become curious and motivated. Affective *reception* refers to the child's emotional sensitivity to or awareness of the environment; affective *expression* becomes part of the child's way to control the environment. (Crying and laughing can alter parent behavior so that a child's needs are usually met.) Many children develop some fears (e.g., of strangers, darkness, separation from parents), but these tend to disappear before they become developmentally disturbing. As children interact with other children and adults, they learn various social and emotional competencies. Important socioemotional capabilities include acceptable ways of eating and dressing, requesting help, making friends, competing and cooperating, managing emotional concerns (such as fears), delaying gratification, and developing a positive view of oneself.

Socioemotional development is crucial in itself, and disorders in it can—and do—impinge on other areas of development. Children who are socially incompetent or annoying may get fewer opportunities for learning, may evoke hostility from other people, and may develop abrasive ways of communicating their wants. The identification and treatment of social and affective disorders is an important part of the job of the early-childhood special educator and therapist.

Cognitive

The development of "the intellect" has been a primary concern of education for centuries. "Cognition" refers to thinking or reasoning and other mental operations. Of course, we cannot see or assess mental skills, but we can evaluate observable skills related to what we refer to as "intellectual functioning." Skills that contribute to cognitive development include paying attention to relevant stimuli, organizing and reorganizing information, short- and long-term memory, rote and concept learning, application of principles, problem solving, and creativity. Tests of "intelligence," which attempt to assess children's abilities in these (and other) cognitive areas, have been used widely in special education with school-age children. At the preschool level, however, there does not appear to be great use for general measures of intelligence. In fact, such measures are quite unreliable during the early years, showing marked fluctuations in scores. Rather, specific capabilities that seem important—such as concept development—can be assessed to estimate what concepts a child has and does not have and whether he or she is learning concepts at a normal rate.

School-related learning is heavily tilted toward cognitive (rather than motor or social) tasks. Reading, writing, and arithmetic are all school areas that demand cognitive skills. As with the domains of communication and socioemotional development, cognitive development interacts with the other domains and cannot be separated from them. The optimal growth of communication and social competence relies somewhat on cognitive development. Language development is an obvious example of an area that straddles the cognitive and communication domains. Frequently, problems in cognitive development can produce social and emotional problems. When children do not *understand* rules and policies, they are more apt to violate them. Consider, too, the child who does not pay attention to instruction, is easily distracted, or is punished or not rewarded. Such a condition encourages the growth of asocial and antisocial behavior. Thus, problems in cognitive development can induce difficulties in socioemotional development as well.

Sensorimotor

The sensorimotor domain includes both gross and fine motor development, as well as the interrelationships between sight, hearing, and these motor skills. "Motor" refers to muscular functioning. Terms such as "perceptual motor," "psychomotor," "sensorimotor," and "visual motor" all essentially refer to competencies contained in the motor domain. *Gross* motor usually relates to large-muscle functioning, such as rolling over, crawling, creeping, standing, walking, running, and other such activity. *Fine or skilled* motor, on the other hand, refers to more precise motions such as those involved in grasping, examining, and manipulating objects, eye-hand and eye-foot coordination, and other musculoskeletal movements that involve vision, hearing, or cognitive aspects. Again, development in this domain influences progress in others. Consider, for example how cognitive learning might be hampered when the child has restricted motoric abilities. The child confined to a wheelchair is not likely to command the same array of learning opportunities. Deficiencies in motoric functioning also limit the ways a child is able to respond. Both learning materials and methods must often be adapted to provide alternative means of expression and manipulation for the motorically limited child. Various devices and strategies are available to help children achieve learning objectives despite motor impediments. Walkers, wheelchairs, braces, prosthetic limbs, special furniture, and teaching machines are available.

It should be pointed out, too, that *assessment* of children's communication, socioemotional, and cognitive development often involves the use of motor skills. Youngsters are frequently asked to "point to the picture that is different from the others," "put the shapes in the right holes," or "put these in order." Difficulties in psychomotor skills can contribute to deceptively low attainment on developmental measures. Again, because motor skills are important in securing and participating in learning opportunities, deficits in motoric functioning can impose delays and distortions in the other domains of development.

COMPREHENSION CHECK 1.3

What developmental domain is most important during the first few years of life?

Is there a "most important" domain?

Compounding of handicap

Not only can the *environment* restrict development, but many handicaps produce restrictions that in turn generate further handicap. Being born blind or deaf does not automatically mean that the child will be intellectually or so-

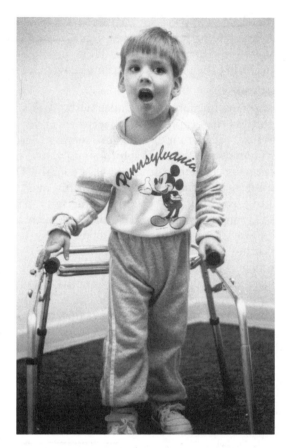

Neuromotor difficulties place restrictions on the child's opportunities to explore and manipulate. Early childhood education offers special arrangements and strategies to circumvent disabilities.

cially retarded. But, in the absence of compensation, not seeing or hearing is equivalent to not having things to see or hear. Orthopedic (physical) handicaps also provide an obvious example of restrictions on learning opportunities. Inability to get around or manipulate the environment clearly limits the range of opportunities for receiving and reacting to stimulation. Thus, *sensory and motor limitations can result in intellectual and social difficulties if nothing is done to offset the handicaps.*

There is yet another major factor that can limit the child's chances for optimal development: physical appearance. Cute, attractive children enjoy much social attention. Consequently, they are apt to receive more opportunities for learning, more attention for acquiring new skills, and less punishment or neglect for undesirable behavior. Many handicapped youngsters simply do not look or act like "regular" children. When the child is judged to be ugly, smelly, dirty, troublesome, or in other ways undesirable, he or she will not have the same social opportunities for development and may be devalued in various ways (Neisworth, Jones, and Smith, 1978).

Clearly, when children are socially unappealing, we must work to improve their appearance as well as to increase social toleration of differences. Cosmetic surgery for facial and other deformities illustrates one way children can be helped. There are other things that teachers and parents can do to improve the child's social interactions. Good hygiene, more flattering hairstyles, better looking glasses, and appropriate clothing are relatively simple devices that can yield great developmental benefits for the child. Indeed, professionals and parents must do all they can to "contain" a handicap so that it does not indirectly thwart other areas of development.

COMPREHENSION CHECK 1.4

Can a child's rate of learning be delayed simply because he or she does not bathe often?

HANDICAPPED CHILDREN: FROM ANTIQUITY TO THE TWENTIETH CENTURY

Historically, handicapped children have been subjected to extremes of treatment. Practices have ranged from killing and abandonment in ancient times, special status within certain religions in the past, to advocation of their individual and collective human rights in present times. How handicapped children were cared for (or not cared for) seems strongly related to at least three major factors: (1) the society's available resources and economic ability to provide for the handicapped, (2) prevailing philosophies and religious beliefs of the society, and (3) existing level of knowledge of the handicapping condition in addition to the skills for the management and treatment of persons in need.

Antiquity through the sixth century A.D.

In primitive societies, infants born with disabilities that reduced their social usefulness were frequently killed. Often these handicapped infants (disabled, sick, blind, etc.) were abandoned in the wild to die of starvation or animal attack. These infants were unwanted because they added a dangerous burden on a tribe whose resources were already marginal.

In the Greek city-state of Sparta, infants who were judged by a special committee to be "defective" were thrown over a cliff and "left to the fates." If the Gods decreed it, the baby might live. This "Spartan screening test" eliminated the physically weak but certainly did not indicate a high level of compassion.

During the fourth through sixth centuries, exceptional individuals seemed to be treated with more compassion. Free food for some handicapped and public pensions for blind citizens became law in Greece.

Throughout this period there was the recurring belief that disabilities had some connection with evil or bad luck. Many religious and superstitious practices were developed in attempts to avoid producing a handicapped infant or to seek a cure for the "afflicted."

Middle ages

Religion dominated the culture during the Middle Ages. Attitudes toward exceptionality were still based on superstition, and disability was viewed as the result of Divine or demonic forces. Some regarded the mentally retarded as "heavenly infants" that God sent to special families for care. Exceptional individuals were sometimes deliberately used for entertainment. Court jesters were often retarded or disturbed young people who were kept as fools or pets by the nobility. Christian teachings promoted by certain religious leaders (some who later became Saints) advocated compassionate care for the lame, weak, blind, and poor. Because of the religious support of the handicapped, beggars sometimes actually gathered up stray or abandoned children and deliberately maimed them in order to use them to collect charitable donations, as is still done in some regions of the world today.

Sixteenth and seventeenth centuries

Superstition continued to play a dominant role. The mentally retarded or emotionally disturbed were often viewed as "possessed." This resulted in some strange and cruel treatment practices. One treatment involved covering the person with blood-sucking leeches. Cutting the person's wrists to "let blood" and beatings were also common methods of "help." The intent of these "cures" was to force the evil spirit out of the body. Still another treatment involved lowering a person into a pit filled with snakes. This was designed literally to "scare the hell" out of the person and to force the evil spirits to take up residence elsewhere. Of course, infants seldom survived these "treatments."

In the 1690s, John Locke made the first attempts to distinguish between mental retardation and mental illness. He also promoted a "blank slate (*tabula rasa*)" conception of child development. Unlike previous philosophers, Locke did not believe that people are born with ideas of right and wrong, truth, or beauty. He represented a movement know as *Sense Empiricism* that emphasized the role of the environment in shaping our destinies. The "blank slate" is written on by the environment through the senses.

In summary, although there were some humane efforts, the history of the handicapped from antiquity to the mid-1700s was rather grim and marked by cruelty.

Eighteenth-century humanitarianism

The first glimmerings of hope for humane treatment of the handicapped began to appear during the eighteenth century. After the French Revolution, Phillippe Pinel, a physician, unchained several insane patients who had been confined for years in the Bicetre Hospital. Pinel taught the personnel of the hospital to treat the patients in a humane manner. This event is usually recognized as a major turning point in the treatment of the mentally handicapped.

Education of the deaf was greatly advanced through the elaboration of the finger-spelling system previously developed by Bonet and through the development of a lipreading system. Also during this era, Dr. Benjamin Rush, an American, wrote one of the first comprehensive volumes on psychiatry, which recognized the need for the special educaton of the disturbed.

Nineteenth century

Near the beginning of the nineteenth century, a boy of 11 or 12 years was found in the forest of Aveyron in southern France. This "Wild Boy of Aveyron," later named Victor, had lived most of his life as a forest creature. He was animal-like in appearance and behavior and vocalized only guttural sounds. Jean-Marc Gaspard Itard, a French physician, was convinced that Victor was capable of learning if the right sense-training methods were used. Using an intensive program, Itard worked with the boy for 5 years. Although Victor did show important progress, Itard was disappointed in the outcome and finally gave up working with the boy. However, Itard was the first to describe the use of an individualized program with a child. Through his work with Victor, Itard created great excitement about the prospects of changing a child's course of development through instruction and sensory input. He created a basis for the contributions of other pioneers.

Edward Sequin, a French physician and student of Itard, established the first school specifically intended to educate the mentally retarded. He later emigrated to the United States and was instrumental in establishing the first state residential facility (Vineland Training School in New Jersey) for the mentally retarded. Other reforms were simultaneously occurring in the United States. Samuel Gridley Howe, a physician, founded the Perkins Institute for the Blind. He became famous for the effectiveness of his techniques in working with the blind.

In the 1890s, Dr. Maria Montessori, influenced by the work of Sequin and other Sense Empiricists, organized a school for retarded youngsters in the slum sections of Rome. She trained teachers to be supervisors of the students in her "autoeducation" program that stressed sensory and motor training. Montessori, remarkably successful in teaching some mentally retarded children to read and write, began a training program for young normal children. Her preschool techniques continue to be popular and, indeed, have become fashionable among middle-class families.

Institutional treatment for the retarded began in the 1800s. Rehabilitation and integration into society were the objectives of such institutional efforts. Poor treatment, crowded conditions, entrenched handicaps, and untrained staff contributed to the failure of institutions; the aim changed from rehabilitation to custody. The institutions became warehouses where society stored the handicapped and kept them out of sight and out of mind.

COMPREHENSION CHECK 1.5

Early-childhood special education attempts to prevent, remove, or reduce developmental problems; how does this relate to John Locke's philosophy?

Twentieth century

At the turn of this century, the French public minister of instruction appointed Alfred Binet to discover ways to determine which students could benefit from public schooling. Binet devised a scale to identify specific ages at which children master particular skills. To Binet, the scale assessed achievement and not "potential." The test was brought to the United States by Goddard, and in 1916 it was revised at Stanford University by Lewis Terman. Since that time, the scale has gone through other revisions and continues to be widely used and is the standard against which newer intelligence measures are compared.

During the early twentieth century, the eugenics movement gained support among some intellectuals. A study conducted by Goddard was interpreted as supporting the view that mental retardation was hereditary. He reported on a family he named Kallikak. While a soldier in the Revolutionary War, Martin Kallikak had an illegitimate son by a retarded barmaid. He later became more "proper" and married a girl from a "good family." The descendants of the illegitimate son showed a high incidence of mental retardation, as well as a high number of criminals, prostitutes, and other "degenerates." On the other hand, the offspring of Martin's marriage were normal, some becoming doctors, lawyers, or teachers. This study lent support to the prevailing notion that if the mentally retarded stopped having children, the problem would disappear. In the United States, even up to the 1960s, numerous states had mandatory sterilization laws for the retarded as a means of eventually eliminating those believed to be inferior. Sterilization laws were upheld as constitutional by the Supreme Court until recently.

In the United States, institutionalization became increasingly popular as a method of separating the mentally retarded from the public, as well as a way of preventing the retarded from reproducing. The rights of the public were primary whereas the rights of the mentally retarded were virtually nonexistent.

COMPREHENSION CHECK 1.6

What was wrong with Goddard's conclusions based on his study of the "Kallikak" family?
Do intelligence tests measure native ability?

The treatment of the handicapped from the 1960s to the 1980s is characterized by legislative and judicial actions to promote optimal treatment and social integration (see Table 1.1).

GROWTH OF EARLY-CHILDHOOD EDUCATION FOR THE HANDICAPPED

In the United States, early-education programs for children with sensory impairments were the first to become widely established. Deaf and/or blind children were among the first children to receive the benefits of planned pro-

TABLE 1.1
History of Legislation and Litigation for the Handicapped

1954   BROWN V. THE BOARD OF EDUCATION
        Supreme Court ruling under the fourteenth amendment that it was
          unlawful to discriminate against a class of persons for an arbitrary or
          unjustified reason.

1958   PUBLIC LAW 85–926: NATIONAL DEFENSE EDUCATIONAL ACT
        Provided funding for training teachers of the mentally retarded.

1961   PUBLIC LAW 87–276: SPECIAL EDUCATION ACT
        Provided funds for training teachers of the deaf.

1963   PUBLIC LAW 88–164: MENTALLY RETARDED FACILITY AND
          COMMUNITY CENTER CONSTRUCTION ACT
        Provided funds for research centers, health centers, and teacher-training
          programs for the retarded.
        University affiliated facilities funding and coordination established.

1966   PUBLIC LAW 89–750: AMENDMENTS TO THE ELEMENTARY AND
          SECONDARY SCHOOL ACT
        Established the Bureau of Education for the Handicapped.

1968   PUBLIC LAW 90–538: HANDICAPPED CHILDREN'S EARLY
          EDUCATION ASSISTANCE ACT
        This legislation increased the number of young children receiving new or
          improved services.

1970   DIANA V. THE STATE BOARD OF EDUCATION
        A class action suit ending in a consent degree that ordered all children to
          be tested in their native language prior to placement in special classes.

1971   WYATT V. STICKNEY
        A court ruling that children be provided with adequate and appropriate
          programs regardless of the level of mental retardation.

1971   PARK, BOWMAN ET AL. V. THE COMMONWEALTH OF
          PENNSYLVANIA
        The consent decree for this case included a search for the students
          requiring special education, a provision for periodic reevaluation at least
          every 2 years, a provision for notification of change in placement, and the
          right to a due process hearing.

1973   PUBLIC LAW 89–750: AMENDMENTS TO THE ELEMENTARY AND
          SECONDARY SCHOOL ACT
        This act encourages states to obey federal laws governing the education of
          the handicapped or else the funding will be cut off.

1975   PUBLIC LAW 94–142: EDUCATION FOR ALL HANDICAPPED
          CHILDREN ACT
        The law states that all handicapped children, ages 3 to 21, are ensured a
          "free and appropriate" public education. The law provides for an
          individualized education program, the least restrictive environment,
          nondiscriminatory testing, confidentiality, and due process for each
          handicapped student.

1979   ARMSTRONG V. KLINE
        The court ruled that for some handicapped students an appropriate
          education may need to consist of an education program in excess of 180
          days a year. As a result, extended school-year programs are presently

TABLE 1.1
History of Legislation and Litigation for the Handicapped (cont'd)

being provided for severely handicapped students who exhibit regression and limited recoupment capacity in skills and behaviors related to self-sufficiency and independence from caretakers.

1982 YOUNGBERG V. ROMEO
Supreme Court ruling that a person may not be deprived of liberty through involuntary commitment and physical restraints without also providing adequate training to ensure freedom from undue restraint.

1982 BOARD OF EDUCATION OF HENDRICK HUDSON CENTRAL SCHOOL DISTRICT V. ROWLEY
Supreme Court ruling that an appropriate education, as mandated by PL 94–142, does not mean an optimal education. Ordinary, not extraordinary, opportunities are legally mandated.

1983 PUBLIC LAW 98–199: EDUCATION OF HANDICAPPED ACT AMENDMENTS
PL 94–142 was amended to add an emphasis on preschool, secondary, and transitional programs for handicapped children, parent education, and an improvement in personal preparation.

1984 ECONOMIC OPPORTUNITY AND COMMUNITY PARTNERSHIP ACT
Mandated head start programs to enroll at least 10% handicapped children. It established 14 resource access projects to give training and consultive assistance to head start programs to optimize the integration of handicapped and nonhandicapped children.

grams in a preschool setting. The availability of services was at first almost entirely limited to residential schools. Today, services are widely available for children with sensory impairments and other handicapped children in much less restrictive environments such as the public schools, the child's home, and clinical settings. No longer do these children have to be separated from their families for long periods of time to receive appropriate services.

The federal government had no involvement with the education of handicapped children until 1930. In that year, a Section on Exceptional Children and Youth was established within the Department of Education. The government role was limited, providing some support for research, graduate fellowships, and matching funds for states for some services. The 1965 Elementary and Secondary Education Act (ESEA) together with its subsequent amendments, is recognized as the major landmark for national involvement in special education. ESEA (and amendments) provided generous support for research and demonstration projects and for public school programs designed for handicapped and disadvantaged children from ages 3 to 21. The act also created the Bureau of Education for the Handicapped (now replaced by the Office of Special Education).

It should be emphasized that early preschool services were not mandated or even specifically targeted until 1968. That year saw the passage of the Handicapped Children's Early Education Assistance Act. Through this legislation and funding, more than 450 demonstration projects have attempted an array of models and materials with children having a variety of handicaps. This "first chance" network of projects continues to be a basis for extending services to preschoolers while expanding research evidence. The 1984 Economic Opportunity and Community Partnership Act mandated Head Start programs to enroll at least 10% handicapped children. It also established 14 Resource Access Projects to provide training and consultative assistance to Head Start programs to optimize the integration of handicapped and nonhandicapped children.

By 1975, amendments to the Education For All Handicapped Children Act and the passage of PL 94-142 mandated states to devise plans to identify and serve *all* handicapped children, 3 to 21 years old. This federal law, however, does not apply if it is in conflict with existing state law. Most states have existing laws that use an older age for mandatory public education, thus excluding infant and preschool services from the mandate. Nevertheless, this legislation did list preschool education as a priority that states must address, but only after provision of service to neglected school-age children and more appropriate placement for more severely impaired children.

PL 94-142 contains several provisions that benefit all handicapped children, including preschoolers. Major aspects of the law include requirements that local education agencies must identify and assess all children in need of services. Assessment must be comprehensive, involve several sources of information, and be repeated at least every 3 years. An Individual Education Plan (IEP) must be prepared each year for each child enrolled in special education. The IEP is intended to be the "blueprint" for guiding the child's program and must include parental participation (or at least consent). The law specifies that children must be placed in the least restrictive environment and be integrated with nonhandicapped children when and where possible.

Furthermore, parents are guaranteed certain rights, including access to their child's records, the right to seek an independent educational assessment of the child, consent for the child's placement, active participation in the development of the child's IEP, and the right to challenge program placement through an impartial hearing.

Finally, PL 94-142 offers supplemental funding to states for the early education of preschoolers who have been identified as needing services. These Preschool Incentive grants encourage states to conduct public awareness campaigns and community screenings and to plan for service delivery to special-needs preschoolers. As of 1985, every state and territory of the United States has a federal planning grant to develop and coordinate services for handicapped preschoolers.

The Handicapped Children's Early Education Program (HCEEP) is active in awarding grants for model demonstration (First Chance) and outreach projects. Outreach efforts extend the demonstration projects to new sites and attempt to create replication of the model. As mentioned already, more than 450 demonstration projects and 2,000 replications have been funded. Currently, there are more than 130 active demonstration and outreach projects (Black, 1985). In addition to model preschool projects, four Early Childhood Research Institutes have been established. These institutes are funded for 5 years and are designed to study specific dimensions of importance: the family context, program evaluation (especially cost effectiveness), social development and integration, and longitudinal socially relevant impact. HCEEP also funds the Technical Assistance and Development System to foster collaboration and provide training and consideration to funded projects.

To this point, then, federal policy encourages rather than requires states to provide *early-childhood* special education. Each state must develop its own legislation to establish preschool services for handicapped or at-risk youngsters. As of 1985, 24 states now mandate such services, with legislation pending in several more states.

COMPREHENSION CHECK 1.7

Does your state have a First Chance project?

EVIDENCE FOR THE EFFECTIVENESS OF EARLY-CHILDHOOD EDUCATION

Pioneer work

All through the Middle Ages and up to about the mid-1700s, the prevailing belief was that children were born with fixed developmental destinies. This view, known as *preformationism*, placed excessive importance on biological inheritance and gave no role at all to the environment.

The mid-1700s saw the rapid growth of a philosophical movement that emphasized the possibilities for releasing and encouraging human potential. This was a giant step for society and was in great contrast to the previous view that people were born into castes or social situations and were destined to stay there. John Locke, Jean-Marc Itard, Edward Sequin, Maria Montessori, and other pioneers shared this optimism regarding human capabilities. They were convinced that Sense Empiricism could be used to correct poor development. They proposed that a child's development could be altered by providing information about the world through the child's various senses. Indeed, these pioneers were experimenting with principles that today form the foundation for much of our current teaching techniques.

It was not until the mid-1900s, however, that the old beliefs regarding fixed development (including intelligence) really gave way to the contemporary view of *Interactionism*. This position holds that a child's biological inheritance can be shaped, for better or worse, by the experiences of the child.

About 50 years ago, a startling discovery was made. Two 1 1/2-year-old infants, tested and classified as moderately to severely retarded, were placed in a facility for mentally retarded adults. Both children were born of unmarried retarded mothers, were orphaned and were scheduled for placement in an institution for children. Because these facilities were crowded, they were enrolled in the adult institution. The infant's reported IQs were 35 and 46. Instead of being just more children in the crowded facility, they were somewhat star attractions among the women in the adult institution. Because their placement was unusual, those responsible felt that closer monitoring of their condition was important. Consequently, they were tested after 6 months and revealed a dramatic increase in scores—now estimated to be 77 and 87! Before the end of a year, the IQs were both in the normal range (Skeels and Dye, 1939).

What could account for this dramatic reversal of mental retardation—a condition that at that time was considered irreversible? Had the children been incorrectly assessed in the first place? Were they not really retarded? Was there some improvement in an unusual medical problem associated with retardation? Skeels and Dye were intrigued by the "accidental" changes and requested permission from state authorities to remove youngsters from understaffed children's facilities and place them in alternative settings designed for older retarded girls. After 2 years, the results were consistent and dramatic. Children who were placed in the more stimulating setting gained an average of 27 IQ points, whereas comparison youngsters left in the children's institution lost an average of 26 points. Thus, the apparent difference in IQ–test performance was more than 50 points!

In a follow-up study by Skodak and Skeels (1949), results showed that after 21 years the experimental children had maintained their "normalcy" and were self-supporting adults. One-third of the comparison children were still institutionalized. These and other findings lead Samuel Kirk (1958) to suggest that not only can we raise intellectual performance through environmental changes, but that perhaps much of mental retardation is *caused* by poor environmental circumstances. Other past and current reports attest to the positive impact that early stimulation can have on preventing and reversing developmental deficits (Dennis and Najarian, 1957; Garber and Heber, 1981; Heber and Garber, 1975; Kirk, 1973; Masland, Sarson, and Gladwin, 1958; Ribble, 1944; Scarr-Salapetek and Williams, 1973; Skeels, 1966; Spitz, 1945).

Collectively, the reported studies tell us that children from certain environmental situations can show remarkable improvement when placed in better circumstances. But what really makes the difference? Is it simply *more* stimulation, better *kinds* of stimulation, increased personal attachments, or other situational factors? Although we cannot answer these questions with confidence, it appears safe to say that three factors may be important: increased *range* of stimulation, quality *social* stimulation (early attachment and meaningful interactions with caregivers), and availability of opportunities to sense and respond during optimal developmental periods (see Neisworth and Smith, 1978, for a review).

Today, there is fairly convincing research that *intelligence and other characteristics are not fixed at birth but are shaped by the quality of the early environment* (Bloom, 1964; Heber and Garber, 1975; Hunt, 1961; Kirk, 1958, 1973; Skeels and Dye, 1939; Sontag, Baker, and Nelson, 1958). Hunt's book, *Intelligence and Experience* (1961), and Benjamin Bloom's *Stability and Change in Human Characteristics* (1964), marshaled theory and evidence and provided compelling arguments concerning the great potential for change of intelligence and other personal traits. Both past and current philosophy, theory, and research sound out this conclusion: *Development is not predetermined and fixed, but flexible and responsive to variations in child-rearing practices and environments* (Bradley and Caldwell, 1978; Sameroff, 1979; Werner and Smith, 1981).

Not only is development much more changeable than previously thought, but it appears that certain negative features of an environment are definitely linked to handicaps, especially intellectual and social dysfunctions. Generally speaking, *severe restrictions in experience can have disastrous effects on a child's development* (Goldfarb, 1945; Provence and Lipton, 1962; Spitz, 1945). It appears that a wide range of stimulation is desirable for early intellectual and social development. Opportunities to *receive* stimulation through the various senses seems most important for the infant. Later, it also becomes crucial for the child to have opportunities to *respond* and manipulate the environment. Children who have been locked in attics, hidden away in the woods, kept in austere institutions, or in other ways deprived of a normally stimulating environment fail to acquire normal intellectual and social skills. Redundant stimulation, a restricted range of opportunities, crowded living arrangements, poor parenting, and marginal nutrition all contribute to limiting developmental progress. It is no wonder that children from low socioeconomic circumstances are at much greater risk for retardation and other problems (Deutsch, Katz, and Jensen, 1968; Hess and Baer, 1968; Ramey and Finkelstein, 1981). The economic and educational status of a family can have much to do with the quality and range of stimulation made available at

Barren and restrictive environments can limit a child's achievement and motivation; impoverished stimulation can be as handicapping as a physical impairment.

home. There is no doubt among professionals that early environmental circumstances and parenting have a dramatic influence on the child's development.

COMPREHENSION CHECK 1.8

Can an infant diagnosed as "mentally retarded" achieve normal intellectual functioning? Specify circumstances that might contribute to a substantial shift in IQ.

Contemporary research

"Early intervention" includes an array of efforts designed to prevent, remove, or reduce handicap. The effectiveness of early intervention may be related to numerous factors: basis of handicap (biological or environmental), Indeed, these pioneers were experimenting with principles that today form the foundation for much of our current teaching techniques.
age of onset, the timing, scope, duration, and quality of intervention, and the outcome measures selected (Zigler, 1978, 1983).

Regardless of the complicating variables, the trend of research findings supports much of the theory and optimism of child- development specialists.

Efforts at *prevention* of handicap have produced substantial immediate results. Head Start was launched in 1965 in an attempt to offset the developmental delay and deviations associated with low socioeconomic circumstances. Initially, it enrolled only 4 to 5 years olds, not younger and more "developmentally flexible" children. First reports on Head Start were disappointing (Ciccirelli, 1969). Now, however, Head Start enrolls younger children, has better staff training, and has greater program structure. Furthermore, Head Start includes, as at least 10% of its enrollment, children with recognized handicaps. Later reports revealed that many Head Start programs can register impressive developmental improvements (Bronfenbrenner, 1975; Lazar and Darlington, 1978). Through a variety of programs and approaches at centers, in homes, in hospitals, and with multiprofessional and parent involvement, a convincing intervention effect is generally shown in contemporary studies. (Greenspan, Wieder, Lieberman, et al., 1985; White and Casto, 1985).

It must be pointed out that most of the research from Head Start and other programs involves children with delayed development from disadvantaged economic circumstances. The effects on specific and established handicapping conditions are less clear and uniform. There are numerous difficulties in evaluating early intervention for this group: lack of comparison groups, small sample size, brief and noncomprehensive intervention, and vague treatment procedures are some of the problems cited (Umansky, 1985). Nevertheless, reports coming from HCEEP and other sources support the value of early intervention (ERIC, 1985). Even children with clear biological disorders can show improvements resulting from environmental intervention (Bagnato and Neisworth, 1985; Simeonsson, Cooper, and Scheiner, 1982).

The *durability* of improvement is yet another issue related to evaluating effectiveness. Given that handicaps can be prevented, removed, or reduced through early programming, are the developmental gains maintained? Are there durable effects with at-risk and/or handicapped youngsters? And what measures should be included in assessing long-term impact? Longitudinal studies are rare, and often do not exceed a 3-year follow through. The preponderance of such studies have not reported maintainence of gains and, thus, the durability of intervention. Most of the studies, however, have used restricted measures (e.g., intelligence and developmental quotients) and have used weak research designs. Several major longitudinal studies, however, show clear and promising results (Consortium for Longitudinal Studies, 1978; Gray, Ramsey, and Klaus, 1982; Lazar and Darlington, 1978). The Perry Preschool Project (Epstein and Weikart, 1984; Schweinhart and Weikart, 1980) is exemplary in its research following children up to 18 years. This project reported substantial differences for enrolled versus comparison youngsters. The project uses ecological measures that reflect children's success in society—school graduation, teenage pregnancy, steady employment, and need for support services. The Perry Preschool Project provides clear evidence that early intervention to prevent handicap has a durable effect on socially important dimensions (Greenspan and White, 1985).

Among the socially significant findings emerging from long-term studies is the cost-effectiveness of early intervention. The earlier intervention begins, the lower is the cumulative cost of providing services through age 18 (Wood, 1981). Children in early-intervention programs, for example, are less likely to require institutionalization—which often costs society $30,000 to $50,000 a year for each child. They are also less likely to draw on public funds because of delinquency, unemployment, or dependence on welfare (Weber, Foster, and Weikart, 1978).

Long-term intervention effects for children with established handicaps cannot be reported at this time. There are no well-designed studies that have followed handicapped children for more than a year after intervention (White and Casto, 1985). Clearly, there is a great need for follow-through research that uses socially relevant measures with handicapped youngsters; such research is underway but premature to report.

COMPREHENSION CHECK 1.9

Suppose a friend or neighbor asked you if their tax dollar should go to handicapped preschoolers. Does early intervention make a difference? Does it "work" with at-risk children? With children born with handicaps?

DIAGNOSTIC-PRESCRIPTIVE MODEL IN EARLY-CHILDHOOD SPECIAL EDUCATION

Although there are exceptions, many if not most early-childhood special-education programs attempt to:

1. Identify children with developmental problems as soon as possible.

2. Assess each child's strengths and weaknesses.

3. Prescribe special instruction to reach specific developmental objectives.

4. Evaluate program effectiveness so that adjustments can be made.

To accomplish this full scope of activities, a *diagnostic-prescriptive* sequence of steps is used: screening and identification, developmental assessment and prescription, program delivery, and child progress and program evaluation.

Screening and early identification

Once children are enrolled in school, it becomes relatively easy to observe and test them. But how can we discover which children—not yet enrolled in school—are having developmental problems, are handicapped, or are headed for problems?

First, children must be *screened*. This refers to a global process of surveying the behavior of children in an attempt to detect the existence of general developmental problems (Neisworth et al., 1980). Screening is accomplished through observing and testing preschoolers and interviewing parents about their children. Some handicaps are obvious from birth, for example, deformities, many mental retardation syndromes, and other clearly medical problems. Many handicaps, however, are not reliably detectable at very young ages. Researchers are trying to discover ways to detect children who may be at risk for a handicap (i.e., those children who show signs that are predictive of future handicap unless intervention takes place). Screening can also consist of gathering information about the child's circumstances. Knowing characteristics of the parents—especially the mother, gauging the home environment, or other information is predictive of handicap (Ramey, Farran, and Campbell, 1979). The outcome of screening is a sorting of children into two groups: those who *may* deviate significantly in their development, and those who do not show any problems. Screening devices are helpful in discovering which children need a closer look but are not to be used for pinpointing problems or prescribing instruction.

A variety of screening devices are available (see Chapter 5). Many of these, with some training, can be used by paraprofessionals and parents. To screen children, it is, of course, necessary to have access to them. Investigators have tried various approaches for finding children to screen. Approaches include seeking referrals from physicians, community awareness campaigns, and child "roundups" through community action (Kurtz, Neisworth, and Laub, 1977; Zehrbach, 1975).

Developmental assessment and prescription

Screening establishes a likelihood that a child may have an emerging or existing handicap. *Assessment* is a process of analyzing, describing, and profiling a child's range of developmental skills to provide a basis for individualized educational planning (Neisworth et al., 1980). Assessment instruments usually require specialized training for their proper administration and interpretation. School psychologists and other appropriate experts trained in early childhood can administer and report results of formal, standardized developmental assessment. The early-childhood special educator relies on comprehensive assessment to determine the child's current levels of functioning in the various developmental domains. Assessment must be precise enough to permit clear linkages between assessment findings and specific instructional objectives (Bagnato and Neisworth, 1981). (See Chapter 5 for details about the assessment process.)

Types of programs

Programs offered to exceptional preschoolers differ in a number of ways. Some programs such as Head Start promote *developmental integration* (i.e., combine handicapped with nonhandicapped children) (HEW, 1980). Many compelling arguments in favor of integration have been offered (Guralnick, 1978), although with the exception of Head Start, the majority of early programs designed for handicapped youngsters do not yet include nonhandicapped children (DeWeerd, 1983).

Programs also differ with respect to the curriculum and methods used (see Chapter 4). The theoretical approach or model adopted by a program influences the choices of curriculum, materials, and instructional methods (Mori and Neisworth, 1983; Peters, Neisworth, and Yawkey, 1985; Peters, 1977). Three major models or approaches (described next) are widely employed in early education, although most programs do not strictly adhere to a "pure" model and many are really hybrid approaches.

Developmental enrichment approach

Traditional nursery schools have employed the developmental enrichment approach in the hope of encouraging normal development (e.g., Hymes, 1974). The basic mission is to provide an enriched and interesting environment so that children will socialize, explore, and learn in a permissive, play-oriented setting. Group games, learning activity areas, and much spontaneous teaching and learning characterize this approach. Teachers usually move about the room, coordinate activities, but do not engage in planned direct, individualized instruction. Such programs have general goals but no specific instructional objectives or specialized instruction. Few programs for exceptional preschoolers employ this approach because it is not prescriptive, data based, or focused enough to remedy problems.

Behavioral approach

Based on an environmentalist conception of development (Bijou and Baer, 1978), behavioral approaches stress providing stimulus and response opportunities, contingent reinforcement, and data-based direct instruction. Teaching methods which come mostly from operant psychology, include task analysis, shaping, prompting, modeling, rehearsal, and related techniques (Allen and Goetz, 1982; Peters et al., 1985). Within this preschool model, the chief goal is *repertoire expansion*, (i.e., teaching, generalizing, and maintaining skills across developmental domains) (Mori and Neisworth, 1983). Curricula (program objectives) are highly structured, offering hundreds of specific and sequenced developmental objectives and ways to track child progress.

Many early-childhood special education programs adhere to some version of a behavioral model. Aspects of the model help to comply with legal requirements (PL 94-142) associated with the early education of exceptional children. Emphasis on specific objectives and systematic data collection for accountability are aspects important in this regard.

Cognitive-developmental approach

Jean Piaget is the name most associated with the cognitive-developmental model for early education. Emphasis is on sensorimotor and cognitive development, with social and gross motor development getting considerably less attention. Children are provided with situations and events to explore and are allowed to be curious and spontaneous learners. Children are viewed as active learners who seek stimulation and whose intellect develops according to sequential stages (e.g., Weikart, Bonn, and McNeil, 1978). Teaching materials and methods have been devised to match the child's inferred cognitive stage. Language expansion is a prominent goal of many American programs because language is a dominant feature of the preschool years and a useful tool in cognitive development. Through language, the child communicates and negotiates with self, peers, and adults. According to Piaget's theory (1952), mental representatives of the world are constructed and reconstructed as information is assimilated and accommodated. Teaching methods and experiences have been developed that are theoretically consistent with Piaget's theory (Kamii and Radin, 1970; Lavetelli, 1968; Weikart, Rogers, Adcock, and McClelland, 1970), and many preschools employ some aspects of this approach. Applicability of this model for the early education of the exceptional child will depend on the handicaps and "developmental age" of the child. The cognitive-developmental approach would seem attractive to programs for gifted children, although it is also employed in programs where the children are intellectually normal but otherwise handicapped.

COMPREHENSION CHECK 1.10

What is the difference between screening and assessment? How does program evaluation differ from these?

Service delivery modes

Early-childhood special-education services can be offered in centers, the child's home, or in hospitals (see Chapter 4 for more detail). *Centers* bring children together for regular sessions, usually a few hours a day for 3 to 5 days a week. Youngsters, especially handicapped, can benefit from these socialization opportunities. Other desirable aspects of a center-based program include opportunities for staff members to work closely with one another, parents to observe and work with their own and other children, meetings among parents for emotional support, and other group interventions (e.g., testing, immunizations, special events).

Home-based programs bring the teacher into the home to promote parent and child participation. Instruction is provided by the itinerant teacher or the parent. Most programs provide parent education and involvement so that the parent may become the child's principle teacher as well as a more effective parent. Special toys and materials are often left in the home to facilitate parent-child interaction. Unlike center-based services, home-centered programs do not involve transporting children (especially a problem in rural areas). Children do not have frequent planned socialization experiences and are seen by the teacher perhaps only once a week. There are, however, theoretical and practical reasons why home-based education can have advantages (Brocler and Caruso, 1979; Shearer and Shearer, 1977). Familiar surroundings and materials, greater parent involvement, no school-to-home slippage in learning, and extension of benefits to siblings are some bonuses of a home-based program.

Combined center and home-based programs use the home for instruction in basic and preacademic skills and a center for socialization and other group purposes.

Hospital programs are often available to provide infant education. Increasingly, early-childhood special educators are conducting hospital programs for handicapped infants as well as for other chronically ill and partially hospitalized preschoolers. Parent training and close liaison between education and medicine are desirable features of a hospital-based program. (See Chapter 4 for more detail on programs.)

Child progress and program evaluation

Once identified as needing help (screening) and examined for specific strengths and weaknesses (assessment), children can then be enrolled in programs that respond to their developmental needs. Testing, observation, and further assessment is done *while the child is enrolled* to determine if the program is making any difference. *Accountability* is a term frequently used to refer to the responsibility that programs have to prove their usefulness or impact. Program evaluation is done to help adjust the program to improve its effectiveness, to estimate cost effectiveness, to test specific aspects of the problem, and to measure client and staff satisfaction (see Chapter 15).

COMPREHENSION CHECK 1.11

Explain why the traditional developmental enrichment approach is not popular with early-childhood special educators.

SUMMARY

The young exceptional child faces a far different future than would have been the case even a generation ago. Today, a number of forces have combined to produce a steady trend toward earlier and better childhood treatment education. Medical procedures, improvements in early detection, comprehensive developmental assessment, individualized instruction, specialized and adaptive materials, meaningful parent involvement, and program and child progress evaluation are a few areas where research, demonstration, and dissemination have had great benefit.

We are learning that early childhood problems necessarily involve the family; that the client is not the child *in vacuo*, but the child in the family. Furthermore, we are learning that assessment and treatment must be comprehensive—medical, psychological, educational, and social. Professionals from relevant disciplines now work with the teacher to plan and deliver earlier and better programs. We are also learning that our programs for training early childhood educators must change with the times to include the new dimensions of treatment.

As the evidence builds an ever stronger case for early intervention, our nation will move closer to providing specialized early-childhood education to handicapped and at-risk youngsters. In centers, homes, or hospitals, *all* of America's children deserve an even start, if not a head start.

SUGGESTED READINGS

Guralnick, M. (Ed.). (1978). *Early intervention and the integration of handicapped and nonhandicapped children.* Baltimore University Park Press.

Peters, D., Neisworth, J., and Yawkey, T. (1985). *Early childhood education: From theory to practice.* Monterey, CA: Brooks/Cole.

Ramey, C., and Trohanis, P. (1982). *Finding and educating high-risk and handicapped infants.* Baltimore University Park Press.

Spodek, B., Saracho, O., and Lee, R. (1984). *Mainstreaming young children.* Belmont, CA: Wadsworth.

Careers and Co-Professionals in Early-Childhood Special Education

John T. Neisworth
Stephen J. Bagnato

CHAPTER OUTLINE

Employment Opportunities
Preschool Centers
Developmental Day Care
Hospital Programs
Parent Programs
The Rise of Early-Childhood Special Education
Union of Early-Childhood and Special Education
Social and Legal Support for Early Intervention
Advances in Early Identification of Potential Handicap
Roles and Responsibilities of Early-Childhood Special Educator
Education Assessment Expert
Prescriptive Programmer
Educator/Therapist
Parent Consultant and Educator
Program Evaluator
Working With Co-Professionals
Need for Team Collaboration
Team Membership

Three Team Models
Multidisciplinary Teams
Interdisciplinary Teams
Transdisciplinary Teams
Co-Professionals on the Team
Developmental Pediatrician
Pediatric Nurse
Social Worker
Developmental Psychologist
Neurodevelopmental Therapist
Communication Specialist
Nutritionist
Liability in Early-Childhood Education
Rule of Seven, the Reasonable Man Doctrine, and Defamation
Problems of Special Concern
Summary
Suggested Readings

VIGNETTE

Five people are seated at a table in the conference room of the local Easter Seals Society to discuss Janis. Each has a report to share with Mrs. Bixby, the early-childhood special-education teacher who is Janis's case manager. Janis is 3.5 years old and was referred to the local Easter Seals center by the family's doctor. She is an exceptional child, with complex neurodevelopmental problems. Diagnosed as having cerebral palsy, Janis experiences frequent seizures involving blank staring and unresponsiveness. She has limited use of her arms and legs and has not yet learned to walk. In addition, she is not able to speak; she uses inconsistent gestures to express her needs. Frustrated at her inability to communicate, Janis has frequent tantrums. As a result of all these complications, her rate of learning is about one half of what would normally be expected. She functions intellectually like a 20-month-old child.

Because her problems are complex and overlapping, no one professional can adequately assess and plan an appropriate program for Janis. Fortunately, the multidisciplinary team employed by Easter Seals can provide the comprehensive assessment and program planning needed. Dr. Berlin, the developmental pediatrician, consults one day a week for the Society. He is adjusting the dosages of medication used to control seizures. Mrs. Wilkin (the physical therapist) and Mr. Forsberg (occupational therapist) will take a detailed look at Janis's use of her arms and legs. Mrs. Wilkin will plan activities to foster head and trunk control and motor patterns prerequisite to walking. Mr. Forsberg wants to promote eye-hand coordination and plans to focus on toy play and feeding skills. Ms. Gorman (speech and language therapist) wants a thorough assessment of Janis's speech and language—how capable is she of understanding and using language? Will a communication board be useful? The psychologist, Dr. Lewellyn, is working together with the teacher to normalize her play skills and social interactions. The teacher meets regularly with Janis's parents to plan home activities and to develop realistic goals and methods for parent-child interaction and instruction. The team will meet again next month to review Janis's progress and to make revisions in her treatment plan.

Early-childhood special education is an emerging profession dedicated to working with youngsters who are handicapped or at developmental risk. Its missions are to reverse, remedy, or prevent developmental delay and deficits in all areas of a child's functioning.

Careers in early-childhood special education are demanding, fulfilling, varied, and socially respected. The early-childhood special educator may work in a variety of settings including public, cooperative, and private schools; public, corporate, and military day-care centers and clinics; agencies devoted to helping children with specific problems (e.g., United Cerebral Palsy, various parent organizations); hospital programs (both inpatient and outpatient); and private industry (e.g., toy and baby product manufacturers). Students wanting careers in early-childhood special education may focus on infancy (birth to age 3), preschool (ages 3 to 5), or early childhood (ages 5 to 8). In addition, professionals in early-childhood special education use developmental theory and scientific tools and procedures (e.g., developmental assessment, behavior analysis, direct instruction, and special materials) to help establish and achieve humane goals for young exceptional children and their families. Most frequently, they work with other professionals on teams that plan and evaluate child programs.

EMPLOYMENT OPPORTUNITIES

Increasingly, handicapped youngsters are being enrolled in early-childhood programs alongside their nonhandicapped peers. Placing children of differing developmental levels together, termed *developmental integration*, is the preschool application of the least restrictive environment, mainstreaming, and normalization concepts. Employment settings for the early-childhood special educator include preschool centers, developmental day care, hospital programs, and parent programs.

Preschool centers

Both segregated and integrated programs are available for the handicapped youngster. Head Start has included special-needs preschoolers since 1973. These programs are enrolling children with distinct handicaps as well as at-risk youngsters from low-income families. At present, between 10% and 15% of Head Start children have special needs.

Specialized preschools have been developed for specific handicaps. Thus, there are segregated programs for mentally retarded, speech-impaired, emotionally disturbed, physically handicapped, and sensorily impaired children. Many of these programs are sponsored by private agencies; many are provided through state-sponsored early-childhood efforts. These segregated programs may soon be replaced by mainstreamed ones; more severe levels of handicap, however, may require the continued use of segregated facilities.

Developmental day care

Traditionally, day-care centers have provided custodial services for children of parents who cannot be with their children during the day. More and better day-care services are becoming available in response to social demand. There are several reasons for new and better day care for more families. Increased economic necessity, women's liberation, and other social factors have contributed to the movement for *developmental* as opposed to *custodial* day care. Some developmental day-care programs enroll not only at-risk but also handicapped children. Parents of handicapped children are especially grateful for a sound program that offers developmental help and mainstreams their child, and that gives them free time to pursue employment or just some freedom for at least part of the day.

Day care can be center- or home-based. Day-care homes are, in fact, the major form of day care. Day-care homes offer services to small groups of neighborhood youngsters, usually no more than six children per home. Although day-care homes have not been affiliated with special-education agencies or public schools, at-risk and special-needs children (often undiagnosed) have been enrolled in homes simply because they are neighbors. Currently, there are federally sponsored projects designed to train day-care providers to include handicapped children in their center- or home-based programs (see Gil, 1985; Kontos, 1985).

Preschool and daycare centers promote early socialization among children of varying developmental levels.

Hospital programs

Many hospitals now offer child life-education programs for youngsters who must remain in the hospital for a prolonged time or who frequently return to the hospital for health and developmental therapy. The young exceptional child is especially in need of services to promote development and to minimize developmental losses.

Hospitals frequently provide early-detection services, infant stimulation programs, clinic facilities, and formal preschool programs. Increasingly, hospital child programs include a professional early-childhood special educator. This is an exciting employment option for the early educator who prefers this setting and strong interdisciplinary involvement.

Parent programs

Sometimes a special-needs preschooler remains at home instead of going to a center. Excessive distance from a center, cost, or unavailability of a center are frequent reasons for home-based programs. Special-education state agencies often provide *home visitor* services to the youngster and family. Home visitors usually work for a regional agency and visit families each week. During the visits, the teacher and parent review the child's progress, discuss problems, and plan activities for the upcoming week. The teacher may do

Home-based early education is important for children who cannot be accommodated by a center or for parents who want to keep their child at home.

direct teaching with the parent looking on. This not only serves as immediate instruction for the child, but models desirable procedures for the parent to imitate. If the parent is capable and motivated, the home visitor and parent can achieve great progress with the child. With a constructive partnership between the teacher and parent, the benefits extend to the child through the week, to siblings, and after home-visiting is terminated. Home-based programs have the advantage of using the child's natural setting and, thus, minimizing problems in school-to-home carryover, parent cooperation, and relevance to family needs.

Many early-childhood special educators prefer to be home visitors. Their job includes travel throughout the region, working with a variety of parents, teaching on a one-to-one basis, and frequent interdisciplinary contacts.

COMPREHENSION CHECK 2.1

Would you rather work in a preschool center, hospital, or home-based employment situation? What are the reasons for your choice?

THE RISE OF EARLY-CHILDHOOD SPECIAL EDUCATION

The early-childhood profession is undergoing rapid expansion, with new training programs being developed within colleges of education, human development, home economics, and others. At least three factors are responsible for the dramatic progress of early-childhood special education: (1) the merging of the disciplines of early-childhood education and special education; (2) the social-legal support for early intervention; and (3) the development of tactics to make early identification and, thus, early treatment possible (Mallory, 1983).

Union of early-childhood and special education

Early-childhood special education is a hybrid profession, strongly rooted in the philosophies and content of child development and the special concerns and techniques of special education. Although not all professionals would agree, it appears that the disciplines of child development/early-childhood education primarily provide us with the goals and objectives for children, whereas special education provides both the actual technique and the precision necessary for special-needs children. Within early-childhood special education we see an alliance between cognitive-developmental and behavioral psychology. However, this is not to say that there is complete harmony between Piagetians and Skinnerians! There are common grounds and conflicts between traditional developmentalists and contemporary behaviorists; these issues are discussed in detail elsewhere (e.g., Peters, Neisworth, and Yawkey, 1985). The special needs of exceptional youngsters require the precise assessment, individualized instruction, and progress tracking typical of many special-education programs. At the same time, developmental theory and the nursery-school tradition offer developmental norms, principles, and models that emphasize not only the products of development (e.g., major developmental landmarks) but also important developmental *processes* (e.g., mastery, habituation). Furthermore, although special education traditionally has been preoccupied with what is *wrong* with children, remedying special deficits, and clinical segregation of children, early-childhood specialists have stressed *prevention* of problems through promoting *whole* and *balanced* general *development* in a *normal* setting. Some of the best early-childhood special-education programs express a child-development approach that focuses on the child's *total* development, including prevention or remedying of handicaps.

Social and legal support for early intervention

This appears to be a time when our society is deeply concerned with helping the handicapped, elderly, and others in need—but with accountability and cost effectiveness. Early-childhood special education, with its possibilities for preempting later problems, has the support of our citizenry and many if not most elected officials. College training programs for preparing preschool specialists are proliferating, with more than 100 programs funded in 1984 by the Federal Special Education Program's Division of Personnel Preparation.

TABLE 2.1
Evolution of Legal Bases for the Education for Preschool Children

1940   LANHAM WAR ACT
        Nurseries established for children of mothers employed in world war II
            defense plants.

1965   ELEMENTARY-SECONDARY EDUCATION ACT
        Launched head start program for underpriviledged preschoolers and
            provided funds for initiating programs for handicapped youth, ages 3
            through 21.

1966   BUREAU OF EDUCATION FOR THE HANDICAPPED
        Stimulated planning for preschoolers.

1967   EARLY AND PERIODIC SCREENING, DIAGNOSIS, AND TREATMENT
            (EPSDT) AMENDMENT TO THE SOCIAL SECURITY ACT, TITLE 19
        Provided hospital-based developmental screening for children from low-
            income families.

1968   HANDICAPPED CHILDREN'S EARLY EDUCATION PROGRAM
        Began to support development of model preschool programs or first chance
            projects; university affiliated facilities established to promote
            interdisciplinary training and collaboration.

1972   ECONOMIC OPPORTUNITY AND COMMUNITY PARTNERSHIP ACT
        Mandates at least 10% handicap enrollment in head start programs; 1974,
            redefined "handicap" to include more severe levels of developmental
            problems.

1975   PL 94–142, THE EDUCATION FOR ALL HANDICAPPED CHILDREN
            ACT
        Established major provisions for school-age children and initiated programs
            for some handicapped preschoolers through incentives to states that serve
            handicapped preschoolers.

Congressional action and judicial decisions have provided the legal basis
for the delivery of special provisions for special-needs youngsters. The key-
stone of the current legal structure is, of course, PL 92-142. Table 2-1 lists a
number of laws and judicial decisions that came before and after PL 92-142.
This table overlaps with Table 1.1, but it includes and emphasizes the national concern for *preschool* children in need of services.

Advances in early identification of potential handicap

Once a youngster is in school, significant problems in reading, writing, and
arithmetic become clear. However, detection of infant and preschool developmental delays and deviations is a more difficult matter. Passage of PL 93-380
provided a legal mandate to locate these children. Before this, the Early and
Periodic Screening, Diagnosis, and Treatment (EPSDT) Amendment (1967,
Social Security Act, Title 19) provided screening for children from low-
income families with medical coverage. Referrals from physicians and others,
community awareness and screening campaigns, and parent education efforts are used to locate children for developmental checkups. Furthermore,
new and more sensitive screening and assessment devices have been devised

that make early detection possible. Many of the new instruments are easy to use and do not involve much time. Paraprofessionals, parents, and professionals outside of special education or psychology can easily be trained to use these screening procedures (see Chapter 5 for further discussion of screening/assessment materials).

COMPREHENSION CHECK 2.2

More and more cases of early-childhood handicap are being identified; is this a result of improved detection or actual increases in incidence?

ROLES AND RESPONSIBILITIES OF THE EARLY CHILDHOOD SPECIAL EDUCATOR

In carrying out the major mission of promoting child development, today's early-childhood special educator serves not only as a teacher, but also in several other roles. These roles and related competencies have been described by The Council for Exceptional Children (1983) and other teacher educators (Stedman, 1973; Walker and Hallan, 1981). Although differing descriptions are presented by various sources, most authorities agree on certain common roles and competencies for the early-childhood special educator (Table 2.2).

Education assessment expert

School psychologists, educational diagnosticians, and child-development experts are professionals who usually carry out psychological and developmental assessment. Often, such assessments are too focused on the child's general condition or are couched in language of little use to teachers. The educator can play an important role as *interpretor of assessment* reports coming from noneducational sources. *Interpretation* refers to converting or translating behavioral, Piagetian, Freudian, or other theory-based terms into specifics for guiding instructional activity. This process greatly increases the report's instructional utility. In addition to translating reports from others, the educator can use a number of standardized and informal assessment tools to pinpoint developmental strengths and weaknesses. Delays and problems in development can then be described in terms of specifics, which then become objectives within Individual Educational Plans (IEPs).

Finally, continual measurement of child progress (formative evaluation) is valuable feedback that can be used by the teacher to adjust program methods, materials, and objectives. Clearly, educationally relevant assessment is a major duty of the early-childhood special educator. Teachers can assess child progress within the program through use of checklists, observational samples, and other informal techniques. Teacher-conducted assessment does not replace developmental evaluations conducted by trained developmental psychologists or other professionals; it supplements and enlarges these findings.

TABLE 2.2
Prominent Roles and Responsibilities of the Early-Childhood Special Educator

Assesses educational /Developmental levels	Translates reports from others, and uses selected developmental measures.
Prescribes programs	Links assessment to curriculum, writes clear and relevant objectives, selects or adapts appropriate materials, and includes prosthetic devices when appropriate.
Provides instruction/therapy	Designs and uses behavior-management strategies, conducts direct instruction, uses contemporary principles of learning, and evaluates program impact.
Consults with and Educates parents	Keeps parents informed, obtains appropriate parent consent, advocates and maintains parent rights, helps parents to understand and work with the child, and provides useful referrals.
Evaluates programs	Keeps records of child changes, reports curricular progress, evaluates family involvement, and adjusts program with formative and summative data.

Prescriptive programmer

Through observation, parent interview, information from co-professionals, and direct testing, the early-childhood special educator can design or prescribe developmental educational programs. The early-childhood specialist is in an excellent position to prescribe child programs with knowledge of a child's developmental status, what materials are available, and what techniques might be successful.

Specific instructional objectives are not familiar (nor particularly useful) to traditional early-childhood educators, but these specific targets are important when working with exceptional children. Clearly written and individualized educational goals and objectives are derived from specific assessment information. Delays and problems in development become special curricular objectives along with the goal of general developmental progress. Instructional objectives must be written in ways that permit measurement of progress. "Will learn to appreciate art and music" is a fine goal, but it is too vague to permit evaluation. Translating this goal into specific instructional objectives that can be measured is an essential step in designing a child's educational program.

Usually, a child's program will include objectives in all major areas of development: speech and language, cognitive, social, self-care, and motor development. Selection and creation of instructional materials and circumstances is certainly of major importance. The right materials, used properly, help the child reach developmental objectives. Often, materials will have to be modified or adapted to suit the needs of a child. Sequencing of tasks and effective design and use of space are other decisions that must be made (e.g., the content and arrangement of activity/learning centers).

Sometimes an exceptional youngster will require a prosthetic device; that is, equipment that replaces or supplements a child's sensory or response capabilities. Glasses, hearing aids, braces, wheelchairs, adaptive utensils, toys, and learning materials are examples of frequently employed prosthetics. Teachers must be familiar with the use and maintenance of many such devices because they are part of the child's necessary program of developmental progress.

Educator/therapist

The difference between education and therapy is often not clear, and this is certainly the case when working with exceptional youngsters. *Clinical teaching* (Smith, 1974) is a term that has been coined to refer to instruction that is not solely educational (i.e., school-related), but that also corrects behavioral/developmental problems; helping William to name the basic colors is teaching, working with William to correct a speech problem ("wed" instead of red) is speech therapy. Rather than force a distinction between education and therapy, it is more useful to consider these two roles as overlapping and complimentary. In carrying out the educator/therapist role, the early-childhood special educator must be skilled at group and individual behavior management, as well as at techniques for direct instruction on a one-to-one and small group basis. Behavioral psychology has contributed heavily to the storehouse of techniques available to today's educator (see Chapter 4). The expert and proper use of behavior techniques for both management and instruction can produce gratifying child progress, not to mention reinforcement for good teaching!

When youngsters have trouble in learning, teachers must take a closer look to determine where the weakness in the teaching-learning process may exist. Trouble may arise in any one of several phases of the learning process (Gagne, 1974). Contemporary early-childhood special educators rely on a variety of proven strategies to help children through their learning difficulties. Table 2.3 gives an overview of the several phases of learning and some strategies for correcting problems in each stage.

Regardless of the theoretical learning of the teacher, expert and consistent use of a particular set of strategies is preferred over a hodge-podge of techniques. Teachers must be trained to provide a sound, theory-based approach to instruction. The works of Piaget, Skinner, Bandura, Rogers, Erikson, and others are often used as the theory base for preschool approaches (see Chapter 4).

Parent consultant and educator

Parents are central to the young child's development. Practically all theories of child development acknowledge the crucial role of parenting in nurturing

TABLE 2.3
Phases of Learning and Related Strategies

Phases of Learning (After Gagne, 1974)	Importance	Instructional Strategies
Motivation	Children must be interested in learning, must expect some rewarding outcome (intrinsic or extrinsic).	Reinforcement, novelty, meaningfulness, high-interest activities.
Attention	Without selective attention, children will not learn what is intended; attention is prerequisite to direct learning.	Novelty, figure-ground contrast, prompting for attention.
Aquisition	"Latching on" to new concepts, words, and so on is the core of learning; new experience must be incorporated into the child's repertoire.	Meaningfulness of new material and its connection with what is already learned; proper organization of new material; coding; task-analysis; proper sequencing of skills.
Retention/Recall	Without maintenance of learning and recall when needed, new learning becomes fleeting and of minimal value.	Meaningfulness; overlearning; various memory strategies.
Generalization	Usually we want learning to be useful across a variety of situations, rather than situation-specific; transfer of learning is crucial for normal functioning.	Training in a variety of situations; common stimuli in learning environment and other relevant circumstances; reinforcement for transfer.
Feedback	Children need information about the adequacy of their behavior in order to adjust it if necessary; feedback is both informational and motivational.	Social reinforcement, programmed materials; self-instructional and corrective learning materials.

development. Indeed, it is the law that parents of exceptional preschoolers *must* be involved in deciding on educational objectives and placements. Parents must be viewed as *partners* with the teacher; each can learn from the other for mutual benefit and the child's progress (see Chapter 4).

Early-childhood special educators can provide several professional services to parents of handicapped youngsters. They should be able to communicate effectively, avoiding terminology unfamiliar to the parents. Communication ensures that the parents' knowledge of their child becomes a crucial element in planning the educational program. Parents are a valuable source of information about the child, and the family is the fundamental context for child development. It is also essential that this parent-educator communication remain both private and confidential, as required by law. Specific services provided by early-childhood special educators include informing parents of educational rights for themselves and their children, providing parent education and training, and providing information about, and referral to, other service professionals. (This relationship with co-professionals is the focus of the next section of this chapter.)

Program evaluator

Teachers want to know if the instruction they are providing is really making a difference. To assess child progress, the educator again uses assessment procedures and materials that provide feedback on the utility of instructional methods and materials. Teachers can evaluate their instruction by collecting child progress information on a daily or instructional session basis. This kind of *formative* evaluation is a way to supply the direct, rapid, and continual feedback needed to adjust instruction. *Summative* evaluation, conducted at fixed intervals (e.g., every 3 months), provides summaries of the child's progress. This information supplements formative data and supplies periodic overviews of how the program is influencing the child's development.

Involving parents in the education of their child is so important that many educators also wish to evaluate their effectiveness in this role. Often, teachers use methods and materials to assess parent satisfaction with their child's program. This can be done with simple questionnaires or interviews. Additionally, the educator may also seek to help parents to improve their skills and knowledge concerning child development. Because the role of parents in early childhood education is so crucial, early-childhood special educators must pay serious attention to evaluating their effectiveness with parents.

COMPREHENSION CHECK 2.3

Are any of the described roles of the early-childhood special educator different from those of the special educators of school-age children? Are any roles more important for the early-childhood special educator?

WORKING WITH CO-PROFESSIONALS

Even nonhandicapped children sometimes have developmental difficulties. Children at all developmental levels can experience problems in speech and language acquisition, nutrition, socialization, toilet training, separating from parents, and a host of other difficulties. Usually, the problems are transitory, not developmentally serious. Sensible parenting, patience, and a satisfactory preschool program are usually sufficient to offset most problems. Young exceptional children, however, present developmental complications that demand greater precision, diversity, and intensity of professional effort. Often, exceptional youngsters are medically involved, requiring surgery, drugs, specialized nutrition, prosthetic devices, and physical therapy. In addition to medical problems, there are frequently complications and delays in behavorial development. Inability to play, deficient communication skills, abnormal or delayed motor skills, and retarded cognitive development are problems often experienced by special-needs youngsters.

No one professional can be an expert in all possible areas, thus the need for collaboration with other professionals in related fields. A sharp distinction must be made between the *paraprofessional* and the *co-professional*. *Para* means "along side of "; paraprofessionals work beside, assist, and are subordinate to a designated professional. The teacher aide, dental assistant, and paramedic are common examples of such assistants. Co-professionals, on the other hand, are experts in their own professional discipline who have knowledge and skills needed but not possessed by the professional with whom they collaborate. The pediatrician, psychologist, nutritionist, and audiologist are examples of co-professionals who work with the educator.

Need for team collaboration

When a child's development creates concern, which professionals should become involved? Even when a problem seems specific, there may be several professionals who may provide necessary services. As an example, extreme shyness, excessive crying, and related socialization problems might be seen as demanding the services of a pediatrician, child psychologist, social worker, special educator, or communication specialist.

Sometimes the assumed cause, or *etiology*, of a problem dictates or at least suggests which professional should be contacted. Causes for delayed or deviant socialization, for example, can include general emotional disturbance, mental retardation, chronic health problems, poor parenting, hearing difficulties, and child abuse. Choice of a single professional in these instances is difficult when a specific cause cannot be determined. Even when a specific disorder can be identified (e.g., cerebral palsy) and a specific professional (e.g., pediatrician) is contacted, a child's developmental difficulties are seldom professional-specific.

The central point is this: No one professional can hope to deal competently with all the complexities of exceptional development. Collaboration among experts provides the integration of information and professional skills necessary to help normalize development and family functioning. The professional *team* is the chief way to bring about systematic collaboration (see Fewell, 1983).

Team membership

At the infant and preschool level, collaborative teams may include a diversity of professionals: pediatrician, nurse, nutritionist; developmental, physical, occupational, and/or recreational therapists; social worker; psychologist; audiologist; and speech pathologist. Exactly who is on a team will depend on the child's needs, availability of professionals, and philosophy of the agency or team organizer. Professionals who participate on teams are well advised that consistency of philosophy or theoretical orientation is not only desirable but a must (Holm, 1978). An expert in behavior modification will not be comfortable with a group of devoted Freudians and vice versa. A group of professionals with dissident and conflicting theories will certainly not function smoothly and will most likely provide conflicting information to parents. Although complete theoretical/philosophical uniformity is usually not the case, team members should at least share several common beliefs: (1) The child's problems can be detected and assessed; (2) treatment can be planned based on the assessment; (3) treatment can prevent, remedy, or reverse developmental difficulties; and (4) comprehensive assessment and treatment necessarily involve a multiprofessional approach.

THREE TEAM MODELS

Any group (two or more) of professionals who get together on a project may be considered a team. *How* the team operates and the degree of real collaboration varies considerably. Three levels of team collaboration are summarized here, from the least to the most interprofessional collaboration.

Multidisciplinary teams

The team leader, in this case the early-childhood special educator, draws on the expertise of the pediatrician, nutritionist, psychologist, social worker, audiologist, speech/language therapist, parent, and others. Input from these multiple sources is used to assess the child's developmental status and to help design program objectives, strategies, and needed services. A *multidisciplinary team* refers to multiple professional *input*, but not real professional exchange. Usually, the co-professionals supply their information to the team leader. The leader may be the early-childhood special educator, pediatrician, or other specialist. Each professional may also supply reports to the parents. The "team" members do not really interact, collaborate, or record their findings in ways that link with one another's reports. Sometimes, reports can even be contradictory, although team members may not even be aware of this. Despite the independence and separateness of the input, with an effective leader the multidisciplinary team does provide a wide professional base on which to build and operate a child's developmental program.

Interdisciplinary teams

Interdisciplinary teams take the idea of team membership one step closer to true collaboration. Whereas the multidisciplinary team simply channels the various professional's insights and comments to the team leader, interdisciplinary team members talk directly to one another in regular joint planning sessions. At these meetings team members are encouraged to interact with and substitute for one another (Holm and McCartin, 1978). Professional roles are not rigidly defined, but instead team members openly share information gathered in areas not directly related to their specific field. For example, the pediatrician may suggest that a child's failure to thrive be looked into by the team's nutritionist or nurse, or that they look into it together to see how various factors interact to cause the problem. This type of teamwork hinges on the team's belief in one another's professional competency. Professionals involved in this type of team must be aware not only of their own and their discipline's strengths, but also its limitations. Thus, the skills exhibited by the team members complement one another by building on each team member's strengths. Each member brings an element of expertise in child development, and interaction between team members ensures a comprehensive, integrated approach to educational intervention.

Transdisciplinary teams

In a transdisciplinary team, team members not only cooperate and exchange ideas but also train other team members in their own specialty areas. Thus, team members actually cross disciplinary borders, gaining knowledge and skills from other fields. An additional benefit is the incorporation of new skills from other disciplines into one's own professional practices. Also, this type of team has the added advantage of clearer communication, because of the interchange of profession-specific terminology during the training sessions. However, one caution must be stated. It is essential to remember that all the knowledge and skills available in the child-development field cannot be offered by a single person (Holm and McCartin, 1978). Thus, the team interaction is still the most essential part of the process. The experiences and training in field's other than one's own should help to increase communication, cooperation, and understanding among team members, not create "super professionals" versed in all aspects of child development and related fields. The true transdisciplinary team is a highly cooperative, harmonious group that thrives on integrating information and skills across disciplines. Such teams, unfortunately, are rare at present, but they are increasing in frequency.

COMPREHENSION CHECK 2.4

Summarize the essential differences among the multi-, inter-, and transdisciplinary team.

It can be argued that the central members of the interdisciplinary team are the early-childhood special educator and the parents. Valerie Caplan's training and experience with handicapped infants and preschoolers has convinced her of the importance of this role. Although she wears many hats in the preschool—teacher, diagnostician, case manager, community liaison, and advisor—she views her relationship with parents and their children as most crucial. If she can encourage the parents to trust her skill and sensitivity, then she is convinced that her recommendations on how to teach and manage these young exceptional children will be implemented outside the preschool. Valerie believes that she can most effectively teach special skills to parents by demonstrating them and then by guiding the parents in trying the techniques themselves. These techniques include ways to reinforce or eliminate behavior, plan developmentally appropriate teaching goals, monitor changes in skills and behavior, prompt the learning of new skills, and encourage the transfer of these skills to many different situations. Trust is very important here, because parents must always feel that they are competent and effective in managing and teaching their children, who have been dependent on them for so long. Valerie also believes that she can be effective as a type of facilitator for parents—helping them to express their feelings and to understand that sensitive professionals understand their hurt and can help them to cope; coping can also mean encouraging the parents, particularly mothers, to allow their children more independence and to practice separation so that they are more likely to function independently as they mature. This is a sensitive area that only a trusted and experienced teacher can accomplish. Mrs. Caplan is one of those teachers.

CO-PROFESSIONALS ON THE TEAM

In this section, the major professionals involved in developmental team work will be reviewed. These professionals include the pediatrician, pediatric nurse, social worker, developmental psychologist, neurodevelopmental therapist, audiologist, speech/language therapist, and nutritionist. Although these are the professionals most often involved on the team, others, such as nurses, recreational therapists, family counselors, and dentists, may be involved when considered necessary.

Developmental pediatrician

The pediatrician is probably the professional best known to the family of the child. The child's doctor is often the most influential as well as the first person to see the young handicapped child when abnormalities are observed or suspected. As a child specialist, a pediatrician must know a great deal about growth and development, as well as simply knowing about childhood diseases. Pediatricians are also often the source of guidance for parents on the basics of child care.

The nature and severity of a child's problem will determine the number and variety of services needed, as well as the necessity of consultation with other medical specialists. Pediatricians frequently consult other specialists, especially those in the fields of allergy, neurology, or genetics. The more complex the child's problems, the more specialists are required. When this is the case, the pediatrician serves as a medical services coordinator as well as performing customary roles of interpreting results for parents and setting medical priorities.

In relation to the professional team, the pediatrician serves many functions: coordinates both the medical evaluation and other medical consultants and discusses the etiology of the problem, the specific effects of certain disabilities, and the long-range prognosis. The physician may also report to the team on the effectiveness of medical treatments or possible side effects and is often instrumental in setting up referrals to other professionals on the team. The teacher, pediatrician, and parent may, for example, collaborate on evaluating the effectiveness of child medications at home and in the preschool or day-care center. Tracking the effects of drugs to control hyperactivity, for example, is frequently required to adjust dosages.

Pediatric nurse

Child development teams are fortunate when they include a nurse clinician or pediatric nurse. A professional nurse who specializes in young children holds a bachelor's degree with 4 years of preparation before licensing. The pediatric nurse has training in developmental screening, health assessment and care, family evaluation, and counseling in relation to child rearing and management.

Because of familiarity with the disciplines of medicine, child development, psychology, and social work, the nurse is a generalist who is frequently selected as the liaison between the pediatrician, family, and other team members. Pediatric nurses often work in a hospital setting, community health department, regional mental health/mental retardation facility, local agency (e.g., United Cerebral Palsy, March of Dimes), or a university nursing program.

Pediatric nurses often participate in community-based screenings. They may conduct both developmental and health screenings (when screening detects a child with possible developmental delays or problems, more detailed assessment is left to the developmental psychologist; see Chapter 5). The nurse also collects valuable information on the family situation. Through observation, interviews, and certain standardized instruments, the nurse can report to the child's team any family factors that may contribute to planning the child's developmental program. (More detailed family assessment and help can be provided by the social worker.)

Treatment and services may include helping parents with typical caregiving issues (e.g., feeding, toilet training, sleeping), and home-management concerns (e.g., self-help skills and compliance). A valuable function of the nurse is explaining medical information and treatment and assisting parents and teachers in the proper administration of drugs or other intervention. Help in monitoring the effects of drugs is especially important. Of course, the nurse can be relied on to monitor the health status of the child. Sometimes, developmental treatment may include procedures and activities that could negatively affect the child's health. Certain educational objectives involving motor activities, for example, might stress the child's endurance or in other ways be contraindicated.

The pediatric nurse is, indeed, the co-professional on the team who is in an ideal position to help the teacher plan, coordinate, and monitor an interdisciplinary treatment program (Bumbalo, 1978).

VIGNETTE

The tandem services of the developmental pediatrician and the pediatric nurse are invaluable to the early intervention team. Dr. Wilkins and Mrs. Semple, R.N., are aware of their pivotal roles and have purposefully forged a working relationship that is sensitive both to child care and to family needs. They are concerned about how the family understands and accepts their child's developmental difficulties and responds to their child's overall medical and developmental needs.

Dr. Wilkins helps to coordinate the team's initial perception of each child in the program by carefully identifying each child's physical and developmental needs that must be addressed during intervention. However, often the first view of the child's condition has been conducted by Mrs. Semple, who has visited the parents in the home and assessed both the global needs of the infant as well as the family's response to them.

Dr. Wilkins and Mrs. Semple direct their attention to such factors as the nature of specific developmental complications (e.g., prematurity, genetic factors, failure to thrive) and disabilities (e.g., cerebral palsy, spina bifida, cardiac problems), feeding disorders, chronic health problems, and the contribution of hereditary issues that may signal the need for genetic counseling with the parents. Recommendations to conduct specific medical diagnostic tests are also outcomes of their assessment. These may include CT scans, EEGs, and measures of brainstem auditory and visual-evoked responses to assess the transmission of electrical impulses along these nerves. The child's needs for medication to control conditions such as seizures may also be a part of the treatment plan. Mrs. Semple is the one medical professional who ensures that the parents are able to detect problems and to carry out various recommendations in the home; in this respect, she is one of the principle parent-team liaisons that allows the entire intervention plan to work most effectively.

Social worker

The social worker is the team member who works mainly with the child's parents or caregivers in addressing family needs and facilitating services across several agencies. Social workers are trained in human development—in understanding social, economic, religious, and political systems, in making decisions that affect children and their families, and in helping to create positive relations between families and the agencies that serve them. The social worker must also have skills in interviewing, child observation, and evaluation of the family's intellectual, emotional, and financial resources. All these skills are designed to facilitate social functioning for all family members. Activities undertaken by social workers include counseling, financial planning, securing services, advocacy, and providing information and referral.

In the team setting, the social worker is often the advocate for the child and the family. This co-professional focuses on giving the team information on family functioning, attitudes toward the handicapped child and community resources, and the possibility of the family's support for various recommended interventions. Finally, most teams view the social worker as the source of information on the "climate" of the home, and the religious, cultural, and social factors related to the family's child-rearing practices.

Although the social worker's role on the interdisciplinary team is often, unfortunately, taken for granted, it is one of the most essential. Brenda Johnson's wide experience with various community agencies and with many types of family circumstances allows her to fill her role most effectively. Brenda is the community liaison with the team and the child and parents. She is very concerned about the family's financial, insurance, and other economic resources—complicating factors that can determine whether or not a family will be able to focus on the essential needs of their child. Similarly, Brenda is a trained counselor who provides emotional support to the parents by helping to determine their social support network; this includes grandparents, child-welfare agencies, Big Brothers/Big Sisters, and an extended array of family members and friends who can help them cope with the stresses of managing a handicapped child. Much of Brenda's work occurs in the home, where she can assess and target family needs most accurately. The team depends on her to help design a total intervention plan that has the greatest chance of success, particularly for parents who are highly stressed by personal and socioeconomic hardships.

Developmental psychologist

The developmental psychologist is knowledgeable in the various areas of development. The main job of a developmental psychologist is conducting comprehensive assessments, which include child observation, gaining family input, giving and interpreting psychological tests, and deriving educational diagnoses and programs from the results. These assessment results are most often concerned with the child's intellectual and behavioral functioning. To assess intellectual functioning, the psychologist will select appropriate tests, administer and score the tests, and interpret the findings. In behavioral assessment, the psychologist will observe the child in a variety of situations, note the behaviors the child exhibits, use standardized checklists, and request input from the parents and teachers. Obviously, the developmental psychologist must have extensive training in child development, the use of tests, and observation skills. The psychologist must also be able to interpret the results received from many measures and sources to provide comprehensive assessment.

In the team setting, the psychologist provides precise information that helps to guide instruction. Like other members of the team, the developmental psychologist is expected to share and compare observations of the child with the team members, attempting to develop a clear, accurate picture of the child. Usually, the developmental psychologist also must explain assessment results to the team and share knowledge of such areas as behavior, management, counseling, or structuring the child's educational program.

Psychologists can help the teacher to develop and evaluate individual treatment and instructional programs.

Dr. Mayes has always been interested in the development of infants, toddlers, and preschool children. Her wide experience with developmentally delayed and handicapped preschoolers has convinced her that early treatment is the key to promoting the long-term growth of handicapped children before they enter school. In addition, she has a special sensitivity to the needs of parents of young handicapped children. So, her approach as a developmental school psychologist is to assess and describe the capabilities of these special youngsters so that she can design individualized plans of developmental and behavioral goals for each child. Moreover, she has special expertise in teaching parents how to teach and manage the behavior of their infants and preschoolers. Yet, she believes strongly that parents must develop a trusting relationship with team members and have their own emotional needs understood through empathetic counseling. This allows parents to adjust more adaptively to having a handicapped child so that they have greater "emotional energy" to devote to helping their child.

Finally, Dr. Mayes is a pivotal member of the early-intervention team. Other members rely on her to provide in-service training on such topics as behavior management, family stresses with handicapped children, diagnostic assessment and cirriculum planning, infant temperament and parent-child attachment, and the impact of developmental disabilities on all areas of functioning. She also helps the interdisciplinary team to monitor accurately the progress of children during treatment.

Neurodevelopmental therapist

The neurodevelopmental therapist is an occupational or physical therapist working with handicapped children in the area of sensory and motor skills. The main duties include assessment, treatment, and working with support personnel in these areas. This category of therapist has arisen because, in many areas, the work done by physical and occupational therapists has overlapped to the point where previous distinctions are no longer relevant. This merging of responsibilities has been facilitated by the understanding that the sensory and motor systems are, like the head, trunk, and extremities, all interdependent. In general, neurodevelopmental therapists work under the referral and guidance of a physician. Their goal is to make the child as independent as possible by teaching basic mobility and living skills such as locomotor skills, dressing, fine motor, manipulation, feeding, grooming, and sensory integration.

In a team setting, the neurodevelopmental therapist is primarily concerned with the child's gross and fine motor development and sensory skills. When both an occupational and physical therapist are on a team, they usually divide their responsibilities in keeping with their specific training. The physical therapist focuses on the child's gross motor capabilities, including locomotion, trunk movements, posture, and general coordination. The occupational therapist stresses fine motor skills and promotes the capabilities needed for independent functioning, such as eating, grooming, manipulating, and using the environment. The neurodevelopmental therapist must work closely with other team members in both planning and implementation. Objectives in this area must reflect the team's, child's, and parent's concerns, as well as being as normative and socially acceptable as possible.

Michael Zook has been a physical therapist for 14 years and specializes in serving young children who have suffered brain injuries resulting from meningitis, hemorrhages, or traumatic events such as automobile accidents. As a physical therapist, he is concerned with limiting the effect of impairments in various areas of gross motor functioning. This means developing the infant's skills in head control, balance, weight-bearing, trunk support, and general control of the large muscles of the body. These skills underlie various components of movement that enable a young child to roll, crawl, stand independently, and walk. Much of Mike's work occurs in a hospital setting, although he also works 1 day each week at the local Easter Seals early intervention program.

He prefers to work with infants and their parents, particularly mothers, so that he can demonstrate specific techniques of handling and body positioning; in this way, the mothers develop a trusting relationship with him when they observe that the therapy helps their child and causes much less upset than they expected. Mr. Zook also uses this time to explain neuromotor development to the mothers and fathers so that they can better understand the goals of therapy. Michael's main objective is to train the parents so that they can become their young child's "therapist" at home; this will enable the infant to develop skills in the best manner possible. His approach to physical therapy ensures that the parents are partners in their child's therapy and progress.

As an occupational therapist, Amy Trump is interested in many of the same neuromotor development factors as is Mr. Zook, the physical therapist, in her work with young exceptional children. These include body control, balance, weight-bearing, head control, and the interconnection between senses and motor control. However, as children mature, Amy narrows her treatment focus much more on the development of eye-hand coordination skills and such adaptive capabilities as feeding, dressing, and grooming. It is typical for the teacher and the developmental psychologist to seek advice from both professionals on the proper positioning of cerebral-palsied and other brain-injuried children. Their recommendations are essential for modifying the presentation of testing and teaching activities so that the young child can attend to and respond in the optimal manner. In fact, Ms. Trump often conducts her therapy activities within the preschool classroom so that both the teacher and the parents can see firsthand how they are directly incorporated into the child's daily actions and self-care routines.

Communication specialist

Among school-age children, communication disorders are at the top of the list of handicapping conditions. Schools focus on spoken and written communication, so problems in receiving and expressing information become highlighted. At the preschool level, communication disorders include not just verbal reception and expression, but other capabilities that precede and contribute to later communication skills.

The speech/language therapist is concerned with the child's physical and behavioral characteristics that may contribute to disorders in verbal expression, use of grammar, voice quality, spontaneous social communication, and articulation. The audiologist focuses on the child's awareness, discrimination, and comprehension of sound.

Communication is a complex process, involving hearing, cognition, and responding. The speech/language therapist and audiologist must work closely together because the child's problem may be in hearing and/or vocal production. General developmental delay, mental retardation, emotional disturbance, or other problems often include dysfunctions that must be considered when assessing communication.

The mission of the communication specialist includes screening for early detection of disorders, assessment of receptive and expressive capabilities, and planning therapy to prevent or remediate disorders.

Many preschool and day-care programs routinely conduct speech and hearing screenings so that problems can be identified before they are developmentally harmful. When a child has a communication problem, the specialist can conduct a more thorough assessment. Assessment can take between 1 and 2 hours and includes use of standardized measures (see Chapters 5 and 11), observation, and informal procedures. Children may be asked to point to, select, or sequence items. Books and toys are used to promote speech. Spontaneous speech samples provide good measures of articulation, voice quality, and communication apprehension and comprehension.

The communication specialist can readily work with parents and provide specific suggestions and materials. Parents can extend therapy to the home and actually see rapid improvements in the child's skills. Often, parents are advised to refrain from overprotecting their child, from anticipating needs. Sometimes delaying help until the child attempts a verbal request is the first step in promoting independent communication. Certain toys and books can be used in the home to provide communication opportunities. Without doubt, the communication specialist is a central member of most child program teams; communication is fundamental to learning and socialization, and, communication disorders are frequently preventable or reversible.

One of the central concerns of early-intervention programs is the young child's acquisition of speech and language skills. Development of these skills are dependent on many factors, but particularly the young child's reception and perception of sound. Barbara Phoneme is the early-intervention program's speech/language specialist who works closely with John Moores, the audiologist with the local children's hospital. Because a common problem among special-needs preschoolers is otitis media (see Chapter 14), their working interrelationship is essential to the team's programming for such children.

Barbara is skilled in working closely with both the preschool teacher and the parents to assess communication disorders and to plan practical treatment strategies that will encourage the child's comprehension, production, and use of language through workds, gestures, and even alternative systems for severely impaired children. However, Barbara is especially interested in ensuring that young children develop a "sense" of the value of communication with other children and adults. Many of her recommended activities are designed to encourage language development within a social situation such as snack time, group circle time, and reciprocal games at home. Barbara is skilled also in designing alternative systems of communication such as language boards for wheelchairs and computer-based methods to promote language skills for severely handicapped preschoolers; her work with John Moores is essential here because some of these multihandicapped children require hearing aids as the first step in acquiring functional communication skills.

Nutritionist

The nutritionist is concerned with the child's and family's dietary habits and the body's use of food elements. The major job of the nutritionist is to perform an intense specific evaluation of the family's eating habits. This is done through interviews, parent records, and observations. All these techniques give the nutritionist information about the child's food intake, habits, nutrient intake, typical eating patterns, and mealtime atmosphere.

Often, however, some pediatric nutritionists work directly with the child in teaching feeding skills, swallowing, and such. Usually, however, the nutritionist has little contact with the child, working behind the scenes with parents or other professionals. In fact, after initial evaluation of the child, the nutritionist's main job is to counsel parents and provide information to the other team members. Whereas parents usually require specific information in the form of recipes and suggestions, the team needs to hear the nutritionist's impressions regarding the child's developmental status and the family's needs. The nutritionist is also responsible for developing a nutritional plan for the child and ensuring that team members are aware of it and are supporting it in working with the child. This is especially important when the child is on a specialized diet (e.g., low in sugar, certain proteins, or artificial additives).

VIGNETTE

Many young handicapped children experience feeding disorders related to their developmental disabilities. In fact, failure to thrive both physically and emotionally can be a common but very serious problem in early intervention centers. Mr. Forsey is currently developing a diet and management method to ensure proper feeding for Toshua, a 3-year-old cerebral-palsied child who is not gaining weight as expected. Besides not eating enough, Tosh ruminates or vomits back food already eaten. Mr. Forsey works closely with the developmental pediatrician, nurse, occupational therapist, and parents often on "feeding teams." The team's objective is to manage feeding problems and to ensure adequate intake of nutrients so that the child has the strength and endurance to participate in therapeutic activities and to progress. He counsels the parents on the types and textures of foods that are most appropriate for Tosh's stage of oral motor development. With the occupational therapist, he models specific feeding techniques for Tosh that will allow her to feed in a nonstressful manner and then to gain more independent skills later.

COMPREHENSION CHECK 2.5

What three or four professionals might be most readily accepted by parents? What professionals might be included on a team that is not discussed in this chapter.

LIABILITY IN EARLY-CHILDHOOD EDUCATION*

Like any professional who interacts with children, the educator must take certain precautions to safeguard the child's safety and legal rights. Failure to provide reasonable care and treatment may result in legal problems. Fortunately, early-childhood special educators are usually not beset with lawsuits or other legal actions. About 2000 suits are brought against teachers each year, but only about one third of these actually go to court (Connors, 1981) and few of these end in prosecution of the teacher. The professional early-childhood special educator should be knowledgeable about the law and how to avoid complications. Standards of professional responsibility are more stringent for teachers of young children, because preschoolers are more dependent and vulnerable to mistreatment and environmental hazards. Increased community awareness and action regarding child abuse and molestation heighten the need for knowledge of the law and essential legal processes.

*This section is adapted from an original article by James K. McAfee (1985), Liability in early childhood special education. *Topics in early childhood special education*, 5, 1, 39–52.

Rule of seven, the reasonable man doctrine, and defamation

Three legal concepts help to guide decisions of courts. The legal concept of *Rule of Seven* states that children under the age of 7 are not responsible for their own actions. Teachers cannot claim that the child should have known better or in other ways blame the child for injuries. Teachers must *never* leave preschoolers unattended; accidents might happen and a case of negligence might be claimed.

The *Reasonable Man Doctrine* simply means that the teacher is expected to act in a dependable, reasonable way in an emergency and to exercise appropriate professional skills in crucial circumstances. Educators are not expected to be all-wise and powerful, but only to anticipate reasonably dangerous situations and to act reasonably in such circumstances.

Finally, *defamation* is a legal concept that refers to damaging a child's or family's character through false written (libel) or spoken (slander) communication (Talbutt, 1983). Teachers must take care not to ridicule or disgrace youngsters, even casually.

Confidentiality is certainly a major concern. A child's assessment results, family circumstances, and developmental progress are private matters to be shared only with the parents and appropriate professionals.

COMPREHENSION CHECK 2.6

Why is the Rule of Seven especially pertinent in early childhood education? Who determines what is "reasonable" and what constitutes "defamation"?

Problems of special concern

Malpractice

We have all heard of malpractice suits against physicians, dentists, and other health professionals. Such suits are brought by clients who allege that the treatment they received was inadequate or incorrect and that injury or financial loss resulted.

So far, the courts have not awarded damages to students who have brought suit against special-education teachers. The courts have maintained that there are no generally accepted standards for practice in special education and that treatment (instructional) failure may be the result of numerous causes. (It appears that education's lack of accountability has some advantages!) As instruction becomes more prescriptive and reliable, there may be malpractice suits against teachers who fail to use or improperly use some of the more proven and effective techniques (programmed materials, positive reinforcement, adequate assessment, and referral).

Behavioral techniques have come under attack partly because they involve clear procedures, permit observation, and data collection on effectiveness. The courts generally give teachers broad authority in working with children but have ruled that behavior modification programs must be *indivi-*

dualized and that certain limitations be placed on the use of *time-out* (Wyatt v. Stickney, 1971; Morales v. Turman, 1973).

The early childhood special educator should not be intimidated about using effective behavior change techniques because that is precisely what teachers and therapists are supposed to do. Proper use of techniques (following procedural standards) and involvement of parents can preempt most legal problems. Educators should obtain parental consent, closely *monitor* programs, individualize them, and minimize the use of aversive procedures (Wherry, 1983). Again, close involvement with the parent will usually preclude misunderstandings or the use of objectives or strategies not approved by the parents, and subsequent legal complications.

Child abuse

(See Chapter 7 for a full discussion.) Like anyone else, teachers must not abuse children in any way—even under the rationale of a treatment. Corporal punishment should be avoided, because many courts view this as abusive (Connors, 1981). Preschoolers should never be subject to physical punishment; other means for changing behavior are available, so physical punishment is not warranted.

The concept of child abuse also includes passive abuse (i.e., neglect). Early-childhood special educators may be liable if they lock up children in closets or rooms if they detain children so that they are subject to harm because they missed their usual transportation home.

Negligence also includes failure to supervise children in potentially dangerous circumstances. When danger is *foreseeable* and not corrected, and a child is injured, courts have awarded damages to the child (Dougherty, 1983; Potter, 1983; Thurston, 1982). Access to swimming pools, lawn tools, weight rooms, and such must be controlled to prevent children from exploring these areas and harming themselves.

Teachers must supervise volunteers, practicum students, and other assistants in order to safeguard the child. Harm to the child resulting from the action or inaction of an individual subordinate to the teacher may result in a negligence suit against the teacher.

Forcing children to use certain playground equipment or other physical tasks that are not ability-appropriate may result in injury and thus legal action. For example, a child with a heart condition should not be expected or required to exhibit the same physical activity as other youngsters; to do so could result in a lawsuit (Potter, 1983).

One final point with respect to child abuse: Courts have ruled that teachers are required to report suspected cases of child abuse (Knapp, 1983). Chapter 7 (Child Abuse and Neglect) summarizes the signs of abuse to which teachers must be alert. When failure to report is followed by significant child injury, the professional who should have detected and reported the abuse is liable.

Defamation

The Buckley Amendment (1974) sets out clear requirements for confidentiality and access to child records. Educators may not provide confidential information to anyone who does not have a justifiable role in the treatment of the child. Even divulging information to the police can be construed as a violation (Blair v. Union Free School District Number 6, Hauppauge, 1971).

In addition to confidentiality, educators must avoid nonobjective negative statements (written or spoken) about children. Records must not include material that reflects personal malice or conjectures that might be harmful or handicapping to the child.

COMPREHENSION CHECK 2.7

Describe a teacher's action that might qualify as "malpractice"; do the same for "defamation."

Many of us are terrorized at the very thought of a lawsuit and will avoid any involvement that has potential for legal trouble. The early-childhood special educator should not be disuaded from using the most effective techniques appropriate to the child. A competent professional usually has nothing to worry about. The best general advice is to plan, carry out, and monitor individual programs with parent involvement. Specific suggestions are listed in Table 2.4.

TABLE 2.4
An Early-Childhood Educator's Checklist for Preventing Liability

POLICIES—Is there a written policy and procedure for
    Suspected child abuse?
    Adequate class supervision?
    Inspection of equipment?
    Inspection of grounds/building maintenance?
    Supervision of professional trainees?
    Protection of confidentiality?
    Medical emergencies?
    Corporal punishment?
    Suspension?
    Aversive-behavior modification?
    Reporting potentially dangerous situations?

STAFF TRAINING—Do you provide staff training for
    Emergency medical procedures?
    Negligence?
    Writing objective educational reports?
    Implementing behavior modification plans?
    Adaptations for physically limited children?
    Planning and conducting field trips?
    Proper handling of aggressive students?
    Communicating with parents?
    Do you have immediate access to emergency first aid through a school nurse or an employee who is trained as an emergency medical technician?

TABLE 2.4
An Early-Childhood Educator's Checklist
for Preventing Liability (cont'd)

SELECTION, MAINTENANCE, AND INSPECTION OF EQUIPMENT
  Is equipment selected to be age-appropriate?
  Is equipment inspected on arrival for potential danger?
  Is equipment routinely reinspected?
  Is dangerous equipment locked up when not in use?
STUDENT TRAINING
  Are students provided with specific guidelines on conduct in potentially dangerous
    areas (e.g., swimming pools)?
  Are students carefully trained and evaluated before undertaking a new, physically
    demanding activity?
PARENTAL NOTIFICATION
  Are parents regularly informed of ongoing and special school activities?
  Are parents informed when a child is sent home early or kept late?
Identification of responsible persons—For each of the preceding items, is (are) the
  responsible person(s) specifically identified (e.g., who inspects equipment)?

Source: James K. McAfee (1985), Liability in early childhood education. *Topics in early child-hood special education, 5,* 1, 39–51. Reprinted with permission.

SUMMARY

Early-childhood special education is devoted to the prevention, early detection, and treatment of developmental problems of preschool children. Careers in early-childhood special education include teaching young children in center-based programs (public, private, hospital, or corporate), working with parents in home-based programs, and working in private industries concerned with child development.

The new professional early-childhood special educator has roots in both child development and special education. Philosophies and principles from both disciplines form the professional foundation for the educator of special-needs youngsters. Advances in national policies, social recognition of the importance of early treatment, and improvements in techniques for the early detection of handicap or risk factors all contribute to the expansion of the profession.

The several roles performed by the early-childhood special educator demand thorough training and an ability to relate to parents and key co-professionals. The integration of assessment findings from several sources and the orchestration of the efforts of varied professionals are key duties of the early-childhood special educator.

With appropriate training, parent involvement, and professional conduct, the special educator of young children can be pivotal to the future of the handicapped or at-risk youngster.

SUGGESTED READINGS

Fewell, R. R. (1983) "The Team Approach To Infant Education." In S. G. Garwood and R. R. Fewell (Eds.). *Educating Handicapped Infants*. Rockville, MD: Aspen Systems Corporation.

Allen, K. E., Holm, V. A. and Schiefelbusch, R. L. (1978). *Early intervention- a team approach*. Baltimore: University Park Press.

Golin, A. K., and Duncanis, A. J. (1981). *The interdisciplinary team*. Rockville, MD.: Aspen Systems.

PART II

PERSPECTIVES AND PRACTICES

3

Normal and Exceptional Early Development

Stephen J. Bagnato
John T. Neisworth

CHAPTER OUTLINE

Rachel was born 6 weeks prematurely but experienced none of the often serious complications suffered by many such infants. However, her low birth weight and episode of jaundice placed her at some slight risk for later developmental difficulties. Anticipating this, her mother and pediatrician agreed that it would be a good preventive measure to enroll her in the local infant intervention program at the hospital now that she is 4 months old. The goal is to support the natural development of her many behaviors and to highlight areas in which special treatment may be needed to prevent blocks in her progress.

Most of her developmental milestones are emerging just as expected. She is a social child who attends well to faces and objects and who tries to get adults to respond back to her; in fact, the frequency of her cooing seems to increase when others attend to her face. She is also able to reach toward objects that hang on her crib and to watch back and forth movements with her eyes. She often seems to startle when she hits a toy too hard and makes its bell ring loudly. Despite these skills, Rachel is an infant with low muscle tone. This condition makes it difficult for her to develop her motor skills in bearing weight on her forearms and rolling.

Her mother and teacher also work with a physical therapist who is showing them specific activities that can be used both at home and in the infant program to promote better muscle tone. In addition, specific toys are used to motivate Rachel to use her motor skills to move toward the toys; such toys as rattles, chime balls, and music boxes are appealing to Rachel at her stage of development and were chosen for this purpose. The toys reinforce or reward her attempts to roll and move with her arms and legs. With these methods, Rachel's less well-developed skills can be increased so that her overall development can keep on track.

Young children develop abilities and learn skills through a universal set of principles and operations. Research in early intervention strives to determine those principles so that specialists and parents can understand young handicapped children more sensitively and can plan treatment programs more effectively. Many early-intervention programs merge two sets of principles and methods to propmote gains for handicapped infants and preschoolers: *developmental* and *behavioral*. A combined *developmental-behavioral approach* recognizes that children's capabilities emerge in an invariant, sequential manner that is directly linked with neurophysiological factors. However, developmental capabilities, particularly for handicapped children, emerge only when specific environmental opportunities to practice, learn, and generalize these skills in interaction with others are provided. Thus, various early-intervention programs hold that developmental principles provide the *content* (e.g., developmental curricula and toys) of their program whereas behavioral principles provide the *methods* of teaching complex patterns of skills. Such behavioral principles will be discussed in Chapter 4 (e.g., reinforcement, shaping). In a complementary manner, this chapter reviews two major aspects regarding infant and early childhood development: (1) principles and assumptions within a developmental approach, and (2) normal and atypical developmental patterns in infants and young children.

PRINCIPLES AND ASSUMPTIONS OF A DEVELOPMENTAL PERSPECTIVE

Development is an orderly and sequential process of increasing refinement of the child's neurological, sensorimotor, and cognitive-behavioral capabilities. However, development is not an isolated process or series of events that occurs only *within* the child. Rather, it is the outcome of the child's continuous interactions with people and events in the immediate environment. These reciprocal interactions are important opportunities for the child to activate and practice emerging abilities. Developmental perspectives that stress the crucial importance of the child's environmental transactions for promoting progress are called *developmental interactionist* theories (Sprinthall and Sprinthall, 1981).

Parents learn to read their child's unique signals, which helps babies learn that they can influence events around them.

Principles and characteristics of normal and atypical development within these theories are summarized here and discussed more broadly in the following brief sections (Hetherington and Parke, 1979; Sroufe, 1979; Thomas, 1981):

1. The child is an *active* participant in promoting development.

2. The child is increasingly *competent* in using adaptive abilities to change the environment.

3. Development is *interactive,* it depends on reciprocal exchanges between the child's neurodevelopmental functions and the social and physical aspects of the world.

4. The child's developmental course involves highly *organized* patterns of sensorimotor and cognitive-adaptive processes.

5. Development is *multidimensional,* it reflects the emergence of interrelated cognitive, sensorimotor, and social processes.

6. Development is characterized by the emergence of invariant and *sequential* stages or patterns of behavior.

7. Development, although lawful, proceeds according to *individual* rates.

8. Development consists of *variable* behavioral patterns of plateaus, regressions, and accelerations.

9. The child's behavior proceeds from undifferentiated toward highly *specialized* clusters of developmental skills.

10. Development, although involving "sensitive" growth phases, is *flexible;* alternative routes lead to the acquisition of the same basic adaptive skills.

11. Development and dysfunctions are caused by the interplay of multiple personal and environmental variables—*multicausal.*

12. The child's neurodevelopmental system is highly *sensitive* in responding to appropriately timed opportunities to practice and learn adaptive skills involving thinking, communicating, and socializing.

Active

Development used to be viewed narrowly as the result of the impact of environmental and/or innate biological factors. In contrast, child development specialists today emphasize that each child is an active agent in promoting his/her own course of progress. Children both create and react to situational events. Their own behaviors initiate and maintain reciprocal "give-and-take" interactions with adults. In turn, these reciprocal interactions, created by each child, become further opportunities for learning. Infants gradually learn that crying, cooing, smiling, body activity, and direct eye gaze make adults come to them in a regular manner. They begin to understand their own competence in shaping events in their world. It is certainly true that environment and heredity are the raw materials for development, but the *interaction* of the child with the environment is the crucial factor.

Competent

Infants display a wide range of sensorimotor and adaptive skills at an early age. These abilities involve skills in such areas as visual-motor coordination, cognition, language use, and social attachment. As abilities in different processes become coordinated, children gain the capacity to exert greater control over their world. For example, with more refined coordination of visual and motor functions, infants can grasp and manipulate rattles and bells and learn that their movements make toys move and sound. This skill not only fosters a sense of mastery but also enhances attention, memory, and the capacity to form intentions to guide goal-directed behavior. Similarly, infant vocalizations and smiling also encourage social interactions with caretakers.

Interactive

Development and learning proceed because children, whether normal or handicapped, engage in reciprocal interactions with their world. The most basic adaptive act of the infant and young child is initiating and responding to changes in this environment. Thus, interactions with people and objects serve as continuous opportunities for the young child to activate and practice emerging abilities. Most major theories of child development stress the central role of the child's environmental exchanges in fostering growth and pro-

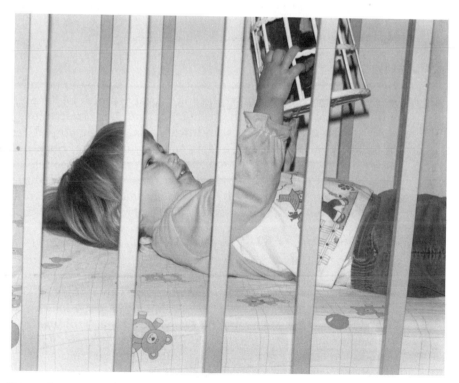

Many developmental skills, such as visual tracking, eye–hand coordination, and the concept of cause–effect, can be promoted with colorful and responsive crib toys.

gress. Behavioral perspectives refer to these transactions as *stimulus-response opportunities* (Bijou and Baer, 1981) whereas Piagetian views talk of "co-occurrences" (Brinker and Lewis, 1982).

Essentially, regular interactions with the environment enable the developing child to be continuously aware of a variety of events that are associated and occur in a related manner. These related events involve such contiguous chains of behavior as the visual appearance of the mother and mother's vocal sound; moving the hand and touching a rattle that sounds; crying and mother's approach to end crying. The child's ability to detect and remember such related events greatly influences the course of language, social, and cognitive development. Similarly, children with sensorimotor impairments have a reduced probability of experiencing connections between their own actions and the environmental changes that they can produce. Developmental intervention, in its most basic sense, must design natural but alternative experiences that increase opportunities or co-occurrences for the handicapped child.

Organized

The emergence and refinement of neurodevelopmental skills in children is a highly organized process. This process encompasses many areas of behavior (e.g., cognition, language, affective, social, sensorimotor) that develop simultaneously and in a sequential fashion according to age and individual readiness. Transformations in developmental skills occur as children grow. These transformations take place when abilities merge, as seen in the influence of language on memory, reasoning, and self-regulation.

Multidimensional

Development consists of processes that have multiple functions that must be monitored separately. These processes involve multiple domains such as cognition, imitation, language comprehension and expression, gross motor skills, perceptual-fine motor abilities, social and emotional responses, self-care skills, self-regulation, and temperamental style. Such a breakdown is somewhat artificial but is a necessary basis for detecting developmental problems and planning individual learning experiences. Moreover, each of these general developmental processes consists of sequenced subskills that serve as the building blocks for acquiring more specialized competencies.

Sequential

Children do not pass through stages of development at the same age; however, most children attain these substages of cognitive, language, sensorimotor, and affective development in the same order. The acquisition of skills or abilities at earlier stages is a crucial prerequisite for the learning of more complex skills at later stages. In one sense, there is a "building block" character to skill development. Nevertheless, the process is gradual and relies on subtle quality changes in the individual child's perception of how behavior influences people and objects.

Individual

Despite the fixed order of growth in stages, each child develops specific skills at an individual rate. Furthermore, each child displays a unique tempera-

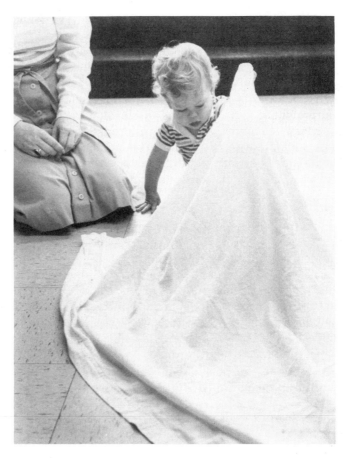

Hidden toy games are fun and also develop the youngster's sense of object permanence.

mental style (e.g., content, difficult, hypersensitive, active, slow to adapt) that is partly innate and that influences the child's readiness to develop skills and to interact with people and objects (Thomas and Chess, 1977). For example, the notion of individual rates and styles of development can be seen in the ages at which children typically acquire basic behavioral skills. By 8 months of age, 50% of children develop the ability to understand that an object still exists, even when it is hidden (object permanence). However, some children acquire that capacity as early as 6 months of age, still others as late as 15 months of age. Individual variations, whether involving normal differences or atypical deficiencies, must be considered in assessing and programming for young children.

Variable

A particular child does not always attain abilities in the areas of cognitive, language, motor, social, and self-help skills at the same time. Advances in one domain with slight lags in others are not uncommon. This pattern of variable rates of development is magnified in young children who experience sensorimotor and cognitive disabilities. For example, Martha is a 3-year-old child who shows average cognitive skills for her age but an immature style of playing with other children, adapting to strange situations, and separating from her mother. This behavior is more often typical of 2-year-old children. Similarly, some 3-year-old cerebral-palsied childred may show nearly average learning abilities but severely impaired expressive language and upper limb motor skills because of their neurological dysfunctions. Also, severely and profoundly retarded children develop cognitively according to the same invariant sequence as normal children but differ in terms of a slower and more variable rate of skill attainment. Down's syndrome children differ in their highly variable rate of mastering such thinking skills as object permanence, spatial relations, imitation, and causality (Rogers, 1977).

Specialized

As children grow and develop, their behaviors become much more specialized in form and function. During the first 3 months of life, children's behavior is characteristically imprecise and uncoordinated, owing to the immaturity of the nervous system and the global and undifferentiated quality of sensory abilities (vision, hearing, touch) and motor functions (grasping and trunk control). However, with experience and maturation, children learn to coordinate different behavioral functions so that their use becomes much more specialized. Thus, the ability to track objects visually and to focus enables the young infant to attend to rattles and rings placed in the hand and to follow the movements of people and objects. Soon, the child's sense of spatial relationships enables the coordination of vision with reaching and grasping to obtain toys that dangle out of reach. Thus, different behaviors with separate functions are coordinated to form more specialized behaviors, with unique functions.

Flexible

Hierarchical sequences of behaviors are characteristic of normal child development. Nevertheless, research with groups of developmentally disabled children (blind, deaf, physically handicapped) indicates that the process of development and learning is *plastic* (i.e., it is possible to have alternative pathways and sequences for acquiring the same adaptive skills) (Thomas, 1981). Despite "sensitive" growth periods when learning has its greatest impact, alternative, adaptive developmental experiences can help infants and young children acquire basic skills necessary for later learning. Thus, blind children can acquire an understanding of the independent existence of hidden objects by learning to use their channels of hearing and touch. Similarly, the cerebral-palsied child's understanding of objects is developed more through focused experiences in hearing and seeing rather than through motor and tactile processes.

Multicausal

Current perspectives emphasize that multiple factors operate in shaping the course of both normal and atypical development. Biological-genetic variables (prematurity, nutrition, family medical problems) and situational-environmental variables (poverty, lack of appropriate learning experiences) interact to determine the child's future development and behavior.

Sensitive

Two interrelated concepts underly the interactionist approach to developmental psychology: sensitive growth periods, and "the problem of the match." The concept of *sensitive periods* refers to the belief that there are certain times when the child's neurobehavioral system is most receptive to stimulation and change. Thus, during these phases, appropriately timed learning experiences can have their greatest and most lasting impact (Scott, 1968). "We must hope to catch the child at exactly that time when environmental encounters will most effectively allow his or her hereditary potential to flourish" (Sprinthall and Sprinthall, 1981, p. 94).

Bound with the concept of sensitive periods is the strong belief that *stimulus variety* is essential for optimal development (i.e., providing diverse and frequent experiences that involve all sensory systems in encounters with people and objects). These opportunities are "peak" learning experiences that allow the child to understand how objects and events are related.

The crucial factor in effective learning during sensitive developmental phases is the "problem of the match" (Hunt, 1961). This concept, also called "goodness of fit" (Thomas, 1981), emphasizes that the type and amount of stimulation must be matched with each child's readiness to receive, integrate, and use it. Too much stimulation causes the child to be overwhelmed and frustrated, too little causes the child to become uninterested.

Learning experiences must take into account the child's behavioral style (e.g., quiet, content, active, irritable). The child's capacity to profit from different amounts of stimulation is influenced, for example, by poor attention, fear of loud noises, resistance to changes, and ability to understand new experiences. Between 5 and 8 months of age, an infant has the greatest readiness to learn about how objects are related. Simple informal games such as hiding toys under cloths, dropping objects into containers, and activating a jack-in-the-box toy are well suited during this stage. However, toys such as puzzles, telephones, and hammer-peg sets do not match with the child's interests, or developmental readiness, at this time.

A variety of well-timed learning opportunities matched with the child's needs and capabilities are the essential ingredients for developmental progress.

Three characteristics or principles regarding normal development are particularly applicable for understanding atypical development in young exceptional children: individual rates, multiple processes, and sensitive learning. In essence, each child's disabilities influence development in an individual manner. Similarly, because all areas of development are interdependent, functional disabilities in one area have an impact on the acquisition of skills in other areas. Nevertheless, our experience with young children has demonstrated that structured learning experiences provided during sensitive periods of growth can help each child to compensate for limitations and thus enhance developmental progress.

It is important to maintain the perspective that all developmental functions mature and emerge in an integrated fashion. It is not surprising that disabilities or dysfunctions in one area seriously influence the emergence of adaptive capabilities in other areas. The devastating impact of multiple disabilities on overall adaptive functioning is most evident, for example, in the areas of blind-deaf, cerebral palsy-developmental retardation. Table 3.1 presents information compiled from a variety of resources to illustrate the comparative impact of developmental disabilities on the timely emergence of cognitive, adaptive, and affective processes. The normal emergence of various capabilities is contrasted with the typical span of skill acquisition in blind and cerebral-palsied children. An analysis of such interrelated *dual* functions as reach-grasp and intentional actions, object constancy and separation anxiety, object constancy and reciprocal games, and smiling and approaching adults emphasizes the profound impact of physical and sensory impairments on cognitive and affective development.

Perspectives on assessing and educating young handicapped children are intimately affected by these developmental principles. In particular, recent trends in special education emphasize a *functional* rather than a *categorical* approach to serving handicapped children. Rather than viewing developmentally disabled children as occupying certain distinct categories (mentally retarded, neurologically impaired, emotionally disturbed), a functional perspective recognizes that children with different problems share dysfunctions across their behaviors and areas of developmental functioning. For example, Barry is mentally retarded and Martha has cerebral palsy, but both may have severe deficits in their abilities to understand and use language. A functional description of the developmental skills that a particular child has or has not acquired in each behavioral area forms an accurate and practical basis for early intervention. Understanding normal developmental sequences in children, and how developmental disabilities inhibit and distort these sequences, enables early-intervention specialists to serve handicapped infants and preschoolers most effectively.

Recently, a few excellent narrative reviews have been published covering the "typical" developmental progressions of children suffering multiple disabilities (Langley, 1980; Ludlow, 1981). Yet, DuBose (1981) has strongly asserted that few specialists have undertaken systematic research studies,

TABLE 3.1
Developmental Disabilities and Infant's
Dual Cognitive-Adaptive and Affective Milestones

Process	Normal (months)	Blind (months)	Cerebral Palsy (months)
Reach and Grasp	3 to 5	10	14
Tactile-Auditory Patterns	4 to 6	9 to 12	15 to 20
Repeats Purposeful Acts	4 to 8	14	18
Extends Arms to Mother	3 to 5	8 to 12	18
Spontaneous Smile	1 to 2	12	4
Object Constancy	6 to 8	15 to 20	18
Separation Anxiety	8 to 12	24 to 36	24
Word/Object/Person Matches	12 to 14	20	18
Self-References (I-Me)	30	36 to 54	42
Actual Object Representations	24 to 30	60	Incomplete
Reciprocal Games (Peek-A-Boo)	6 to 8	14	12 to 14

rather than anecdotal reports, to chart the atypical behavior patterns from birth onward of developmentally disabled children. "The shortage of documented developmental information on impaired children is one reason examiners are poorly prepared to assess such children" (DuBose, 1981, p. 9).

The following capsulized overview of developmental processes and disabilities in young handicapped children is intended to provide substance to the "what" of developmental assessment and intervention and to highlight the complex interrelationships among emerging behavioral functions (Cohen and Gross, 1979).

COMPREHENSION CHECK 3.1

Give some examples to illustrate that infants and their parents influence each other's behavior in a reciprocal, "give-and-take" manner.

Is it possible for an infant of 3 to 4 months of age to understand or "realize" that when he cries, his parents will come to him?

How can motorically impaired children ever learn concepts of purpose, shape, and size about objects if they cannot use their hands to explore and manipulate toys?

NORMAL DEVELOPMENTAL PATTERNS

Reflecting a functional orientation, this description will detail normal child developmental patterns across the areas of cognition, communication, sensorimotor, and affective-social development in young children. Then, atypical patterns will be discussed by referring to selected disabilities (autism, retardation, neurologically impaired) and to the distortion of normal developmental processes by these dysfunctions.

Cognitive patterns

Definition

Cognitive developmental skills are a complex system of evolving problem-solving behaviors. These skills enable the developing child to understand complex interrelationships among people, objects, concepts, and events in the world—to comprehend, remember, compare, use, and master skills and experiences (Garwood, 1983; Hetherington and Parke, 1979). One of the most important cognitive skills is the ability to integrate and apply clusters of related competencies in order to understand and solve problems in novel situations. This skill is the ability to transfer or generalize learning.

Perspective

Theories regarding cognitive skill development and learning come from Jean Piaget (1952) and Robert Gagne (1970). They add scope and substance to our view of emerging problem-solving abilities in young children. Piaget's cognitive developmental approach details the emergence and refinement of intellectual capabilities or styles of thinking in children; Gagne's focus on the learning process identifies the conditions under which behavior change and transformation in problem-solving occur.

Piaget advances the view that children learn by active sensory and motor play with objects and people in their world. Through this active, reciprocal partnership between the child and the environment, the child begins to form expectations about how objects and people behave. Each new experience adds to the child's perceptions of how behavior can influence events in the world (i.e., cause objects to move and people to come when the circumstances are right). In this evolving process, infants and young children modify their expectations about the world (*schemata*) and their ways of responding (*operations*) based on how events happen as previously expected (*assimilation*) or when they require adjustments in typical behavior (*accommodation*). Discrepancies between old ways of behaving and the additional requirements of new situations cause uncertainty in the child (*disequilibrium*). This discrepancy serves as an incentive to promote a transformation in the quality of more effective ways of perceiving and responding.

The four major stages, or phases of change, in the development of thinking skills according to Piaget are outlined with examples in Table 3.2. Two of these stages apply most readily to both normal and handicapped infants and preschoolers: sensorimotor phase (0–24 months), and intuitive or preoperational phase (24–84 months).

The salient feature of the *sensorimotor phase* is the child's exploration of the world through the combined use of the senses and fine and gross motor capabilities. The infant's activity is practical because it involves visual inspection, tactile manipulation, and responses to a variety of sounds. Reaching, grasping, mouthing, banging, and searching serve as the primary methods of beginning to understand objects and events. Each experience is novel and stands as an incentive and an experential base for subsequent ones. Children in this phase gradually learn to coordinate sensory and motor functions to promote their continuing expansion of memories and knowledge about objects, people, and events. The results of learning in this phase include how objects move, how objects are obtained, the properties of objects, the emerging separation of self and environment, and the beginnings of language and communication.

The *preoperational phase* signals a change in the child's style of learning (i.e., language processes gradually replace immediate sensorimotor experience as the primary method of thinking about the world). Children make rapid progress in the ability to label objects and communicate. Memory skills increase, and concept knowledge expands. Imitation, fantasy play, and an increasing understanding of the properties of objects are the hallmarks of this stage. The use of language for self-regulation is also a major achievement (Kopp, 1982).

Gagne's perspective, on the other hand, emphasizes the importance of identifying individual child characteristics (internal) as they match with environmental characteristics (external) to promote thinking and learning. External conditions for learning include the timing and mode of presenting developmental tasks to children. Similarly, internal child characteristics necessary for learning to occur include attention, motivation, and memory. *Learning* is a change in the child's behavior, or way of interacting with the world, that occurs because specific environmental conditions are present.

TABLE 3.2
Characteristics and Achievements in Stages
of Intellectual Development According to Piaget

Stage	Approximate Age Range, Years	Major Characteristics and Achievements
Sensorimotor period	0 to 2	Infant differentiates himself from other objects; seeks stimulation and prolongs interesting spectacles; attainment of object permanence; primitive understanding of causality, time, and space; means-end relationships; beginnings of imitation of absent, complex nonhuman stimuli; imaginative play and symbolic thought.
Preoperational period	2 to 6	Development of the symbolic function; symbolic use of language; intuitive problem solving; thinking characterized by irreversibility, centration, and egocentricity; beginnings of attainment of conservation of number and ability to think in classes and see relationships.
Period of Concrete Operations	6 or 7 through 11 or 12	Conservation of mass, length, weight, and volume; reversibility, decentration, ability to take role of others; logical thinking involving concrete operations of the immediate world, classification (organizing objects into hierarchies of classes), and seriation (organizing objects into ordered series, such as increasing height).
Period of Formal Operations	11 or 12 on	Flexibility, abstraction, mental hypotheses testing, and consideration of possible alternatives in complex reasoning and problem solving.

Source: Hetherington, E. M., and Parke, R. D. (1979). *Child psychology: A contemporary viewpoint* (2nd ed.). New York: McGraw-Hill. Reprinted with permission.

This match between child and conditions influences the quality of development. Pivotal to this view is the notion that structured stimulation (educational intervention) fosters effective learning. Similarly, the acquisition of more complex skills is dependent on prior learning of sequences of more rudimentary, prerequisite skills. Thus, a hierarchy of learning and developmental processes from basic to complex is fundamental. Table 3.3 illustrates the progression in this learning hierarchy. Basic skills in attending, object-

TABLE 3.3
Stages in the Attainment of Object Permanence

Approximate Ages	Search Behavior
0 to 4 months	Nonvisual or manual searching
4 to 8 months	Searches for partially concealed objects
8 to 12 months	Searches for completely concealed objects
12 to 18 months	Searches after visible displacements of objects
18 months and older	Searches after hidden displacements of objects

Source: Hetherington, E. M., and Parke, R. D. (1979). *Child psychology: A contemporary viewpoint* (2nd ed.). New York: McGraw-Hill. Reprinted with permission.

searching and memory recall enable the child to perform behaviors that produce effects. These behaviors are used continuously because they are effective. Finally, such skills become useful in new circumstances that are different from the ones under which they were initially learned (generalization).

Normal developmental patterns

Throughout the early months, an infant's cognitive development is characterized by a variety of combined perceptual and sensorimotor strategies to explore the world rather than by mental or symbolic strategies typical of later years. The young infant displays various motor patterns that demonstrate recognition and anticipation of selected people, objects, and events. ". . . he behaves toward these objects and events with predictable, adaptive, and organized movements of his eyes, hands, and mouth which suggest that he 'knows' certain things about them" (Cohen and Gross, 1979, p. 66). The phases of behavioral organization achieved within the first 24 months are increasingly sophisticated and enable the child to develop more effective strategies to understand and deal with the world. A gradual progression is observed from predominantly sensorimotor patterns in the first 24 months to verbally mediated behavior from 2 to 6 years of age (McCall, Hogarty, and Hurlburt, 1972).

During the first 4 months (0 to 4 months) infants display behavior that is largely reflexive and that undergoes refinement and integration. Through repeated use, such patterns as sucking, visual tracking, visual focusing, auditory responses, grasping, and head control are stabilized. These form the foundation for coordinated behavioral functions that are the prerequisites for cognitive development. Thus, visual and auditory functions become integrated as the infant achieves the ability to turn the head and eyes toward sound sources. Similarly, sucking and eye-hand coordination gradually emerge as the infant mouths objects, focuses on the hand and the object held, and then reaches for and grasps dangling objects. Nevertheless, some research demonstrates that the infant's ability to attend to and process auditory and visual information is relatively well developed early and is not wholly dependent on the refinement of reflexive motor patterns. For example, studies by Eimas (1975) with newborns in the first 3 weeks of life reveal that they can accurately discriminate between speech versus nonspeech sounds and show a preference for human vocalizations.

Finally, in this phase, the infant begins to develop a rudimentary sense of an ability to attain and move objects. Therefore, random contacts with objects, such as rattles that produce sounds and dangling mobiles that swing, become more frequent and goal-directed as the infant attempts to repeat these interesting and pleasurable movements. This pattern of random to "intentional" contacts with toys is referred to as *primary and secondary circular reactions,* respectively.

In the following phase (4 to 8 months), previous patterns emerge under greater voluntary control. Children begin to behave toward toys in a manner that shows an understanding that objects are separate and constant (i.e., *object permanence,* see Table 3-3). Thus, reflexive responses are replaced by such goal-directed strategies as banging, throwing, and shaking as the child begins to explore individual objects in terms of their physical properties (texture, sound, color, movement) rather than solely the motor strategy available for such play. In addition, the infant will begin to reach and search for objects that are partially hidden by cloths and cups. The infant will anticipate the path of a moving ball that is screened in midroll. Peek-a-boo games begin to generate interest at this stage. The infant grows in the ability to imitate motor and vocal patterns that already exist in the repertoire of skills.

At 8 to 12 months, the infant's behavior toward objects reveals a much greater goal-directed character. The infant is able to use new motor strategies to achieve desired results such as pulling a cloth to reach a doll resting on it, pulling an adult's hand to sustain an action, or reaching behind a plastic screen to retrieve a toy. In addition, the infant will now search for toys that are completely hidden and will imitate verbal and motor behaviors that are novel (e.g., tapping the head, wiggling the nose). The beginning ability to consistently apply sound labels to objects and people also advances thinking and concept development.

The 12 to 18-month phase stands as a transition point in which the infant depends less and less on sensorimotor means and begins to increasingly use perceptual thinking skills and language to deal with the world. Search behavior changes so that the child understands that if a toy is not under the first cup it must be hidden under the second. Although problem solving is still primarily trial-and-error in nature, the infant can begin to correct imitations that do not match an adult's.

At 18 to 24 months, the end of the predominantly sensorimotor phase is apparent as the infant begins to solve problems by "visualizing" solutions rather than by only using trial-error motor manipulation.

The first 24 months of life are characterized as the *sensorimotor period* of cognitive development because of the necessity of immediate sensory input and motor manipulations for solving problems. The developmental phase from 2 to 7 years (24 to 84 months) is referred to as the *preoperational period* and represents a significant change in the child's thinking style and use of strategies. Specifically, language and conceptual knowledge allow the child to use symbols in place of actual objects or events in thinking and solving problems. The use of language to label, describe, explain, and indicate thoughts and wishes allows the child greater range in thinking style. Memory skills increase as the child is able to label objects and events to facilitate recall of them when they are absent. Perceptions of past, present, and future time also form. Because of the development of complex language abilities, children are capable of such intellectual strategies and symbolic operations as fantasizing through play, counting, sorting, sequencing, measuring, classifying, matching, recalling, explaining, and reasoning logically. However, much of the child's progress through this phase is a function of the nature of selective attention and the inability to view a problem from an alternative perspective.

COMPREHENSION CHECK 3.2

What changes in cognitive skills must occur before the toddler is able to "think" about the way to solve a problem without manipulating objects to solve it first?

Communication patterns

Definition

"Language is a system of communication that allows two or more persons to exchange meaning" (Cohen and Gross, 1979, p. 1). This simple definition highlights the critical dimensions of the development of language capabilities. First, the development of language, thinking, and social skills is inextricably related. Meaningful use of language to express thoughts and feelings occurs only within a social context. Despite early prelanguage behaviors such as babbling, the use of language to convey *meaning* depends on the attainment of certain cognitive prerequisites (e.g., object permanence and imitation). Next, language is a complex symbol system involving elements of content and form. Thus, language consists of a child's expanding knowledge of objects, actions, descriptions, and concepts and their relationships to one another. Similarly, language has a form consisting of sounds, words, and grammatical structures used to express the content. Finally, language expresses meaning, one's understanding of the essential concepts that underly each word and enable words to be related. The development of language is an amazingly complex process that has biological, cognitive, and social learning bases. Dysfunctions in any one system disrupt the course of functional communication skills in children.

Perspective

Research that describes, charts, and explains language development in children has greatly expanded in the past decade (Bloom and Lahey, 1978; Dale, 1979). The complex interrelationship between language, cognition, and self-regulation has been one of the most extensively studied areas (Michenbaum and Goodman, 1971; Vygotsky, 1962).

Currently, the most influential theory regarding language acquisition centers in a field called *developmental psycholinquistics.* This area of study concentrates on the achievement of competence in language and communication. In the developmental psycholinguistic view, language competence is seen as the ability to understand, formulate, and use a symbolic communication system and is believed to be primarily a biologically determined process (Lenneberg, 1967). Although young children learn to use language for the purpose of social communication through pragmatic, learned interactions with others (McCormick and Scheifelbusch, 1984), the ability to understand and use language is presumed to have a neurological basis. At birth, children have the natural capacity to develop language as they interact with their world and gain information about how words are used, sentences formed, and meanings changed.

Within a psycholinguistic perspective, children are neurologically "programmed" to extract rules and regularities from the language that they hear spoken in order to form a *surface structure* of language. The surface structure is the orderly syntactic relations between classes of words. Similarly, children learn that words and sentences have a *deep structure* in which meanings change depending on the context in which they are used, for example, "a blind Venetian" and a "Venetian blind." Children develop a functional communication system both through an active process of making deductions about language from that which is heard and through modeling and being reinforced for the language used. Functional use of language can occur only within a social context.

Normal developmental patterns

The development of a system of communication entails three features of language: form, content, and use. According to the view of Bloom and Lahey (1978),

> *Infants perceive and produce sounds (form); infants know about events in their immediate environments (content); at the same time, infants interact with other persons and objects in the context (use). . . . It appears that content, form, and use represent separate threads of development in the first year of infancy and begin to come together only in the second year as children learn words, sentences, and discourse. (pp. 69–70)*

Most evidence to date indicates that language development is both biologically and environmentally determined. Certain language processes are linked closely with patterns of neuromotor development (see Table 3.4). However, children are active in processing language and making decisions about how words are used and sentences are formed. The process of *pragmatics* enables a young child to learn that language has a social communication function that allows one to convey meaning to other children and adults (see Chapter 13).

Early language development consists of a variety of preverbal behaviors that involve both cognitive and social aspects. The formation of a meaningful communication system depends on the reciprocal relationship between mother and infant. The two most important dimensions for initiating early social communication are the transactional gaze patterns and smiling behavior. Consistent, maturationally determined patterns of crying (i.e., differentiated versus undifferentiated), pleasure-related cooing, and babbling (i.e., sound repetitions and intonations) predominate during the first 12 months of life.

TABLE 3.4
Synchronized Motor and Language Patterns in Early Child Development

At the completion of	Motor Development	Vocalization and Language
12 weeks	Supports head when in prone position; weight is on elbows; hands mostly open; no grasp reflex.	Markedly less crying than at 8 weeks; when talked to an nodded at, smiles, followed by squealing-gurgling sounds usually called cooing, which is vowel-like in character and pitch-modulated; sustains cooing for 15–20 seconds.
16 weeks	Plays with a rattle placed in hands (by shaking it an staring at it), head self-supported; tonic neck reflex subsiding.	Responds to human sounds more definitely; turns head; eyes seem to search for speaker; occasionally some chuckling sounds.
20 weeks	Sits with props.	The vowel-like cooing sounds begin to be interspersed with more consonantal sounds; labial fricatives, spirants and nasals are common; acoustically, all vocalizations are very different from the sounds of the mature language of the environment.
6 months	Sitting: bends forward and uses hands for support; can bear weight when put into standing position but cannot yet stand without holding on; reaching: unilateral; grasp: no thumb apposition yet; releases cube when given another.	Cooing changing into babbling resembling one-syllable utterances; neither vowels nor constants have very fixed recurrences; most common utterances sound somewhat like "ms," "mu," "da," or "di."
8 months	Stands holding on; grasps with thumb apposition; picks up pellet with thumb and fingertips.	Reduplication (or more continuous repetitions) becomes frequent; intonation patterns become distinct; utterances can signal emphasis and emotions.
10 months	Creeps efficiently; takes side-steps, holding on; pulls to standing position.	Vocalizations are mixed with sound-play such as gurgling or bubble-blowing; appears to wish to imitate sounds, but the imitations are never quite successful; beginning to differentiate between words heard by making differential adjustment.

82

TABLE 3.4 (cont'd.)

12 months	Walks when held by one hand, walks on feet and hands—knees in air; mouthing of objects almost stopped; seats self on floor.	Identical sound sequences are replicated with higher relative frequency of occurrence, and words ("mamma" or "dadda") are emerging; definite signs of understanding some words and simple commands ("Show me your eyes").
18 months	Grasp, prehension, and release fully developed; gait still, propulsive, and precipitated; sits on child's chair with only fair aim; creeps downstairs backward; has difficulty building tower of three cubes.	Has a definite repertoire of words—more than 3, but less than 50; still much babbling, but now of several syllables with intricate intonation pattern; no attempt at communicating information and no frustration for not being understood; words may include items such as ' ' thank you" or "come here," but there is little ability to join any of the lexical items into spontaneous two-item phrases; understanding is progressing rapidly.
24 months	Runs, but falls in sudden turns; can quickly alternate between sitting and stance; walks stairs up or down, one foot forward only.	Vocabulary of more than 50 items (some children seem to be able to name everything in environment); begins spontaneously to join vocabulary items into two-word phrases; all phrases appear to be own creations; definite increase in communicative behavior and interest in language.
30 months	Jumps into air with both feet; stands on one foot for about 2 seconds; takes few steps on tiptoe; jumps from chair; good hand and finger coordination; can move digits independently; manipulation of objects much improved; builds tower of six cubes.	Fastest increase in vocabulary with many new additions every day; no babbling at all; utterances have communicative intent; frustrated if not understood by adults; utterances consist of at least two words, many have three or even five words; sentences and phrases have characteristic child grammar, that is, they are rarely verbatim repetitions of an adult utterance; intelligibility is not very good yet, though there is great variation among children; seems to understand everything that is said to him or her.

TABLE 3.4
Synchronized Motor and Language Patterns in Early Child Development (cont'd.)

At the completion of	Motor Development	Vocalization and Language
3 years	Tiptoes 3 yards, runs smoothly with acceleration and deceleration; negotiates sharp and fast curves without difficulty; walks stairs by alternating feet; jumps 12 inches; can operate tricycle.	Vocabulary of some 1000 words; about 80% of utterances are intelligible even to strangers; grammatical complexity of utterances is roughly that of colloquial adult language, although mistakes still occur.
4 years	Jumps over rope; hops on right foot; catches ball in arms; walks line.	Language is well-established; deviations from the adult norm tend to be more in style than in grammar.

Source: Lenneberg, E. (1967). *Biological foundation of language.* Copyright 1967. Reproduced by permission of John Wiley & Sons, Inc.

Patterns of jargon emerge as a form of transition in which the child plays with personal sound patterns and intonations that approximate adult speech.

At approximately 12 months of age, children begin to attach selected sounds to specific people and objects as the first words emerge. These sound-object matches focus on immediate wants (e.g., cup, ball, juice, mama). In addition, children tend to use the same sounds with different intonation contours to express several distinct wants or feelings, depending on the situation. They begin to use single words as if they were whole sentences (holophrases).

The *holophrase* marks a transition point in language development. Toward the end of the second year (18 to 24 months), true *syntactic* dimensions begin to appear in the child's language (i.e., the orderly pairing of two or more words to express thoughts). Comprehension of objects and pictures has increased rapidly. Thus, the content available for language use is magnified. At this point, children begin to understand regularities or rules regarding the relation of words in sentences. Two-word duos emerge that have a characteristic *pivot-open* form consisting of combinations of action, or indicator, words and nouns or adjectives. Early syntactic patterns combine form, content, and use in such constructions as "there book," "want milk," "hit ball," "baby fall," "where ball," and "give candy." Unique constructions such as "all gone sticky" to convey the message that the food is gone and the hands are messy show that the child is actively processing the rules and meaning of language independent of direct imitation. Also, *telegraphic* patterns such as "where Daddy coat?" with omitted words and features represent the further extension of syntax.

Finally, from the third to the fifth years, expressive language expands greatly. Sentences increase in grammatic complexity, although one major idea dominates each sentence. Future tenses become widely used, and questions resemble adult forms. At 60 months of age, children have developed an adult linguistic form that can relate two or more ideas through relative clauses.

Parallel with syntactic development, children acquire an understanding of the *semantic* features of language. Semantic features are the meanings of individual words and surrounding words in sentences. Children initially comprehend that words are defined by their perceptual and functional features (i. e., the smell, look, feel, and sound of objects and what objects do). Children learn that a dog is shaggy, barks, has four legs, licks you face, and can run fast. Yet, as children learn specific features of specific objects, they begin to overgeneralize them to other objects. Thus, children initially begin to call all four-legged animals *dogs*. Gradually, children make more finely differentiated distinctions between objects and their features. The development of the understanding of meaning is intimately bound with conceptual development as children begin to group objects into generic categories (e.g., things we ride, things that jump, things we eat) and begin to understand that certain words cannot be paired with other words because their meanings clash, for example, "bachelor's wife." Finally, children's understanding of meaning expands as they learn that meaning varies with the context in which words appear.

Another language process, pragmatics, emerges concurrently with syntactic and semantic processes. In fact, pragmatic and semantic skills are firmly related. Pragmatics refers to the evolving use of language for social communication. It is a reciprocal, two-person operation in which young children learn the functional meaning of words (semantics) as well as nonverbal behaviors (gestures) to express thoughts and intentions (McCormick and Scheifelbusch, 1984) (see Chapter 13).

COMPREHENSION CHECK 3.3

Explain how the early face-to-face play between mothers/fathers and infants begins the complex process of language learning.

Affective—social patterns

Definition

The development of affective and social capabilities in children entails a complex cluster of interrelated dimensions including attachment, behavioral style, personal identity, self-regulation, and social and object play. Each of these bahavioral processes plays a significant role in shaping the young child's sense of personal and interpersonal competence. Through early attachment bonds with caregivers, infants and young children develop a secure expectation about the regularity of people and events in their world. The loving and consistent nature of this affective bond allows children to model and develop a range of effective interpersonal behaviors. Yet, each child's unique behavioral or temperamental style, which has some hereditary basis, influences the course of social and emotional development (Thomas and Chess, 1977). Early play experiences with people and objects serve as the "proving ground" for children to model appropriate social interaction patterns, to test individual competencies, to learn compliance with rules and limits, and to develop skills for self-regulation.

Perspective

Several related viewpoints help to shape our knowledge about the substance and process of development in the affective and social area. One view is that of Bandura (1977), who maintains that much of our repertoire of interpersonal skills and personal competencies (e. g., self-efficacy) is developed through a process of social modeling. Simply stated, children imitate social behaviors that are valued and reinforced by adults; in addition, these behaviors (e.g., compliance, sharing) become self-perpetuating as they are effective in initiating and maintaining interactions with others. Nevertheless, cognitive and developmental readiness factors also exert a large influence.

Erikson (1959) offers a developmental perspective on psychosocial growth that emphasizes that passage through successive stages in forming one's identity is influenced by the quality of parenting (see Table 3.5). In this process, it is assumed that children learn a basic sense of trust about the caring and constant nature of their world. Trust forms the basis for the child to successfully resolve other developmental tasks (e.g., conflicts) involving separating from parents, testing one's skills, and forming an individual sense of self.

Researchers believe that the process of *attachment* and *bonding* between caregiver and child, whether normal or handicapped, forms the solid base for future affective and social development (Ainsworth, 1973; Ludlow, 1981; Mordock, 1979). Attachment behavior, such as mutual smiling, touching, and talking between parents and young children enables enduring interpersonal bonds to be established. Disruption or misinterpretation of these "signaling" behaviors, particularly with handicapped children, distorts growth in this area. Nevertheless, it is believed that each child's innate temperamental style (e.g., attention, mood, activity level, sensitivity) has an impact on parents' behaviors while providing care.

Much attention has been addressed to the issue of attachment and bonding with normal children, but little clinical research has focused on the attachment/bonding process with parents and their handicapped children (Blacher, 1984). A sensitive or "critical" period for the occurrence of the attachment bond between mother and child has been postulated, but some critics suggest that professionals have overemphasized the importance of this process and have, in the process, made parents feel anxious and guilty. Work with severely handicapped children suggests that their sensory, motor, cognitive, and affective disabilities make them incapable of supporting the emerging attachment bond so important with their parents. Because of this, mothers often feel unusually stressed and discouraged by their seeming inability to engage their infants in interaction. This may contribute to the early "burnout" of parents as caretakers and teachers of their children. Child abuse can also be an outcome of such frustration. Nevertheless, research studies do show that even severely impaired infants have some adaptive responses that can be promoted in the development of the attachment/bond (Blacher, 1984). Early intervention specialists must emphasize the teaching of certain skills to parents to help them to identify, anticipate, respond to, and elicit these subtle behavioral cues that can form the basis of the affective bond. Thus, such parent-child interactive therapy should be a major part of every program.

Finally, much recent research has focused on the emerging refinement of self-regulatory behaviors in children. These behaviors include the infant's attempts at self-consolation when crying, the young child's ability to comply with rules and social expectations, and the child's ability to modify behavior to meet the demands of new situations (Kopp, 1982).

Normal develomental patterns

The stable course of children's emotional and social development is firmly rooted in the nature of the caregiver-child relationship. Within this interrelationship, characteristics of the child and characteristics of the environment provided by adults intertwine to influence such early developmental processes as attachment, social play, separation and self-identity, emotional responses, and self-regulation (Anastasiow, 1981). Individual differences in child temperament and the ability to respond to the overtures of caregivers also are major factors in early affective development. In fact, children with diverse neurodevelopmental disorders tend to have an increased incidence of emotional and behavior problems (Freidlander et al., 1982; Ulrey, 1981).

Table 3-5 presents one view regarding the general stages of socioemotional development during the birth to 6 year period (Erikson, 1959). The major achievements during these phases are early attachments to parents and the emerging capacity to separate oneself and become an individual.

During the initial birth to 18-month period, children gradually gain a sense of trust regarding the parent's ability to nurture and care for their needs. The process of attachment and bonding is central to this emerging sense. Cognitive, affective, and motivational aspects of an infant's behavior combine to influence the attachment process. Factors such as the infant's ability to recognize the major caregiver, to respond actively to caring behaviors, and to smile are essential in the formation of optimal bonds. Mutual patterns of touching, smiling, cooing, talking with intonations, rocking, face-to-face visual contact, and rhythmic starting and stopping activity between caregiver and child encourage "learned" social interactions. Parental responses to smiling and crying that are dependent on the infant's state and needs allow the infant to experience the impact of their own affective capabilities as well as typical adult responses to them. A secure attachment bond, then, serves as the child's base to begin gradual separations from the mother.

At 8 to 10 months of age, fear reactions to strangers and new situations emerge and also signal the discriminations required developmentally to begin the separation process. Each child begins to explore the environment by looking, reaching, and crawling away from the mother for short periods of practice. These periods increase with the ability to walk independently. In

TABLE 3.5
Erikson's Stages of Psychosocial Development

Life Crisis	Favorable Outcome	Unfavorable Outcome
FIRST YEAR Trust-mistrust	Hope. Trust in the environment and the future.	Fear of the future; suspicion.
SECOND YEAR Autonomy- shame, doubt	Will. Ability to exercise choice as well as self-restraint; a sense of self-control and self-esteem leading to good will and pride.	Sense of loss of self-control or sense of external overcontrol; the result is a propensity for shame and doubt about whether one willed what one did or did what one willed.
THIRD THROUGH FIFTH YEARS Initiative-guilt	Purpose. Ability to initiate activities, to give them direction, and to enjoy accomplishment.	Fear of punishment, self-restriction or over-compensatory showing off.

Source: Erik H. Erikson. *Childhood and Society.* New York: W. W. Norton & Company, Inc., 1950, © 1963. By permission of W. W. Norton & Company, Inc.

turn, the child's cognitive maturity allows the retention of a mental image of the mother and a sense that "she is still there." Yet, the child returns periodically to her for close physical contact that "emotionally refuels" and enables continued exploration. This separation-individuation process is an extension of the child's attachment to the parents and signals the child's capacity to function with greater autonomy.

This phase of increased autonomy (18 to 36 months) marks the child's developing sense of self apart from others. Increases in cognitive, language, and motor skills enable the child to function independently and to increasingly test their own capabilities to achieve self-mastery. During this phase, oppositional behavior, tantrums, conflicts with parents regarding compliance with rules and limits are typical. Consistent limit-setting with flexibility by parents is necessary to allow the child latitude in exploring and experiencing. The major achievement of this phase is the child's knowledge of competency to interact with and influence objects, people, and events with purpose and self-direction.

Finally, from 36 to 72 months of age, children further establish a sense of their own strengths and weaknesses, which includes modeling appropriate sex-role behaviors. Mastering basic self-care activities (e.g., toileting, dressing, grooming) and fantasy play regarding adult jobs and roles are typical of this period of testing and practicing. Firmer understandings of acceptable and unacceptable behaviors are also outcomes of this period.

Play

Another dimension of development that shapes socioemotional growth is *play behavior* in young children.

For the child . . . (play) . . . makes it possible to relate to things that might otherwise be confusing, frightening, mysterious, strange, risky, or forbidden and to develop appropriate competencies and defenses. The active solution of developmental conflicts through play thus enables the young child to demonstrate and feel social competence. (Mindes, 1982, p. 40)

The process of play intricately involves the merger of cognitive, sensorimotor, affective, and social behaviors. Play is vital in facilitating the development of an understanding of social rules and limits, concepts regarding object relationships, personal preferences and competencies, and self-control. Patterns of cognitive play with objects proceed in order from: (1) early exploratory schemes of mouthing, banging, and throwing; (2) fine motor manipulation; (3) constructive and creative play (e.g., drawing, measuring, building); (4) dramatic play (e.g., fantasy role playing); and (5) games with rules. These patterns of play with objects also involve a strong social aspect. Early infant play involves solitary activities of manipulating objects, playing with vocalizations, and self-exploration. Gradually, young children begin patterns of parallel play with other children using toys similar to those used by others. Finally, group play patterns emerge from unorganized, but associative playing to more organized styles of cooperation, sharing, and adhering to rules. All these styles and patterns of play serve as an indispensible vehicle for the child to develop important concepts: personal competence and self-regulation.

Self-regulation

Self-regulation, the ability to monitor and control one's behavior in response to social expectations is one of the most important features of affective development (Kopp, 1982). With increasing age, control evolves from primarily external sources (e.g., parental consequences) to internal child factors (e.g., personal verbal constraints, knowledge of social rules). Children learn appropriate social behaviors by modeling adult patterns that adhere to social rules. These patterns are reinforced in interactions with parents, teachers, and others. Gradually, these patterns, and the rules and expectations that underly them, are internalized and form the basis for self-regulation.

Kopp (1982) has synthesized much of the recent research on self-control capabilities in children in order to formulate a developmental progression scheme for the emergence of self-regulatory processes from birth onward (see Table 3.6). This progression devolves through five phases: neurophysiological modulation, sensorimotor modulation, control, self-control, and self-regulation.

The *neurophysiological modulation* phase (0 to 3 months) is characterized by the activation of various reflex operations to modulate states of arousal in the infant. Such behavior patterns as nonnutritive sucking for consolation, hand-sucking to stop crying, withdrawing from intrusive stimuli (e.g., sounds, lights), and habituation are indications of the body's emerging neurophysiological capacity to maintain a steady state. As reflex patterns become

TABLE 3.6
Developmental Phases in the Acquisition of Self-Regulatory
Capabilities in Young Children

Phases	Approximate Ages	Features	Cognitive Requisites
Neurophysiological modulation	Birth to 2 to 3 months	Modulation of arousal, activation or organized patterns of behavior	
Sensorimotor modulation	3 to 9 months +	Change ongoing behavior in response to events and stimuli in environment.	
Control	12 to 18 months +	Awareness of social demands of a situation and initiate, maintain, cease physical acts, communication, etc. accordingly; compliance, self-initiated monitoring.	Intentionality, goal-directed behavior, conscious awareness of action, memory or existential self.
Self-control	24 months	As above; delay on request; behave according to social expectations in the absence of external monitors.	Representational thinking and recall memory, symbolic thinking, continuing sense of identity.
Self-regulation	36 months	As above; flexibility of control processes that meet changing situational demands	Strategy production, conscious introspection, etc.

Source: Kopp, C. B. (1982). Antecedents of self-regulation: A developmental perspective. *Developmental Psychology, 18*(2), 199–214. Reprinted with permission. Copyright (1982) by the American Psychological Association. Reprinted/Adapted by permission of the author.

organized, sleeping–awake states defined, and sensitivity to stimulation modulated, the basis for more voluntary regulation is established. Interactions with parents and caregivers further aid the infant in recognizing and adjusting to routines that support evolving internal control mechanisms.

The second phase is referred to as *sensorimotor modulation* (3 to 12 months) because the developing infant is able to generate voluntary motor functions such as reaching and grasping and to alter those patterns in response to events and stimuli in the world. These emerging abilities to coordinate sensory and motor functions help the infant to focus attention to objects; smile in response to caregiver approaches; to reach for, search, for, and obtain hidden objects; and to engage in reciprocal games (e.g., peek-a-boo).

Parents and caregivers play an important role in encouraging infants to act on objects and to sustain those patterns by modulating their behaviors. Then, these patterns make the child more aware of the impact of these actions in changing the world. True "control" capabilities are dependent on the child's ability to distinguish his/her own actions from those of others.

The third phase is one of *control* (12 to 24 months). During this time, the child becomes aware of social or task demands established by adults and alters behavior accordingly. A wider range of behavior such as initiating, sustaining, and ceasing activity is now available for modulation. The major milestones involve the ability to comply with commands ("Don't run!") and the beginning capacity to monitor one's own actions. However, control is highly dependent on external cues about the appropriateness of behavior in specific situations. Moreover, this element of control is facilitated by the child's ability to engage in goal-directed, purposeful behavior and the awareness of the consequences of his/her actions.

The emergence of *self–control* and its refinement into *self–regulation* (24 to 36 months +) involves the capacity to comply with a command, to inhibit or delay behavior on request, and to behave according to rules and expectations in the absence of adult monitoring. The child's increased cognitive capacities, particularly representational thinking and recall memory, enable the child to relate more firmly his/her own behavior to specific consequences and adult dictates. Self-control is "self–initiated modification of behavior as a result of remembered information" (Kopp, 1982, p. 207).

Self-regulation differs in the quality of self-control capacities. Specifically, the child is more adaptable, more able to delay and wait in response to the requirements of situations (e.g., crossing the street). The child's emerging self-identity and more mature ability to reflect on and think about actions, as well as to remember and repeat back rules or alternative ways of behaving, serve as the cognitive underpinnings of self-regulation.

COMPREHENSION CHECK 3.4

Describe ways in which early childhood special educators can teach "self-control" behaviors to preschool children. How is it possible for the mother of a blind infant to encourage a sense of attachment with her baby when the infant cannot see her facial expressions?

Sensorimotor patterns

Definition

Sensorimotor development refers to the continually emerging interconnections between multiple sensory and perceptual systems (e.g., visual, auditory, tactile, kinesthetic, olfactory) and motor systems (e.g., reflex, fine and gross motor control). The complex interrelationship between sensory and motor systems is important to the development of basic cognitive processes and prerequisite learning skills.

Perspective

The progression of sensorimotor patterns follows the same course and developmental principles reflected in other functional processes, namely, sequential growth, and gross to finely differentiated states of functioning (Connor, Williamson, and Siepp, 1978; Cratty, 1979; Langley, 1980). Certain fundamental principles about sensorimotor growth assume that sensory input serves to both initiate and guide fine and gross motor patterns:

1. Interconnections between visual, auditory, kinesthetic, tactile, and motor systems provide feedback about the manner in which the body moves and enables the brain to alter movement patterns to explore the environment.

2. Development of sensorimotor patterns proceeds in a *cephalocaudal* (i.e., head to foot) and *proximal-distal* (i.e., trunk to extremities) direction. Control of the head and trunk are fundamental to balance, which is essential to independent walking. Fine motor precision occurs also with head and shoulder stability.

3. Basic movement patterns emerge through the differentiation and refinement of gross, prerequisite postural reflex mechanisms. While in the process of refining and mastering a particular motor skill, children practice elements of more complex skills that are next in developmental sequence.

4. As the neurological system matures, children become capable of dissociating movements in a selective manner. For example, infants gain more precise skills in grasping and manipulating objects as visual-motor coordination matures and more independent use of the fingers emerges.

In general, the ability to right one's position in space and to balance are automatic body responses that are critical to more refined fine and gross motor functioning. The total integration of sensory and motor dimensions is completed by 6 to 7 years of age.

Normal developmental patterns

The integration between visual, auditory, manipulative, and locomotor systems stands as the basis for subsequent learning and cognitive development (Cohen and Gross, 1979).

Research indicates that the auditory system is one of the most well developed at birth. Regularities in the behavioral responses of infants provide evidence of distinct developmental patterns in this area (see Table 3-7). The newborn infant demonstrates ability to perceive sound by a range of reflexive patterns consisting of eye blinks, brightening and widening of the eye, startle responses, and diffuse whole-body movements. At 3 to 4 months of age, the infant exhibits emerging abilities to localize sound sources by turning the head in a general direction. From this point, infants begin to localize sounds at various directions from the body in a more selective manner. It is evident that reflex and motor response patterns are the vehicles by which the infant displays perception of sound.

In a parallel fashion, the newborn infant demonstrates a capable, yet less mature *visual system*. At birth (0–2 months) visual acuity, visual accommodation, and the ability of the eyes to move together to fixate on an object are

TABLE 3.7
Developmental Progression of Auditory Localization in Infants

Developmental Age	Localization Behavior
Newborn to 4 months	Arousal from sleep by sound signal.
3 to 4 months	Begins to make rudimentary head turn toward a sound.
4 to 7 months	Turns head directly toward side of a signal; cannot locate above or below him/her.
7 to 9 months	Directly locates a sound source to the side and indirectly below.
9 to 13 months	Directly locates sound source to the side and directly below.
13 to 16 months	Localizes directly sound signals to the side and below; indirectly above.
16 to 21 months	Localizes sound signal on sides, below, and above.
21 to 24 months	Locates directly a sound signal at all angles.

Source: Northern, J. L., and Downs, M. P. (1984). *Hearing in children* (3rd ed.). Baltimore: Williams & Wilkins. Reprinted with permission.

all very immature functions. These visual limitations restrict the infant's attention to the most salient features of objects (e.g., size, pattern, movement, density). In this respect, infants prefer and appear "neurologically programmed" to respond visually to ordinary but complex patterns such as human faces. From 2 to 6 months, the infant's ability to fixate and attend to objects and people increases dramatically. New and unfamiliar objects seem to command the most attention; yet, the movement of objects begins to lose its exclusive control of attention as infants focus on the details of objects themselves. As infants are ready to reach and grasp, their visual system shows a preferential focus on the features of objects that facilitate motor manipulation.

The importance of vision as an impetus to functional *fine motor and gross motor development* cannot be overstated. Visual focusing and tracking serve to guide such precise motor functions as reaching, grasping, manipulating, and releasing. Head and trunk control develops in parallel fashion to eye-hand functions and establishes a stable basis for reaching and grasping. Full head control usually emerges at 6 months of age as the child gains the trunk stability to begin sitting independently. At this point, eyes and hands can coordinate functionally to locate and explore objects within reach at the midline of the body. Grasping proceeds through the stages of (1) reflexive clutching of objects, (2) holding an object near the outer palm (ulnar palm), (3) holding an object near the palm between thumb and fingers (radial-digital),

Figure 3.1
Infant Grasping Behavior

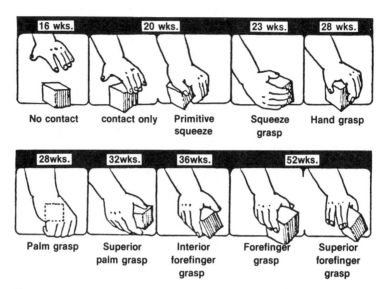

Source:
Wyne, M. D., and O'Connor, P. D. (1979). *Exceptional children: A developmental view.* Boston: D. C. Heath. (Adapted from Halverson, 1931)

(4) a scissoring motion of the fingers, and (5) a precise use of the thumb and index finger to obtain small objects (precise pincer). With these skills in grasping and holding objects, the base is set for such precision skills as container play, block play, and drawing (see Figure 3.1).

Similarly, gross motor patterns emerge (see Figure 3.2) and proceed toward independent locomotion. Such sequences as creeping, pull to stand, standing supported, cruising along furniture, independent walking, stair climbing, running, jumping, and throwing generally characterize these patterns and will be fully discussed in Chapter 11.

COMPREHENSION CHECK 3.5

Describe how a teacher can teach a blind 18-month-old infant to reach toward toys and to crawl or walk using both sounds and touch as cues.

ATYPICAL DEVELOPMENTAL PATTERNS

A variety of developmental disorders are responsible for the functional limitations that young handicapped children experience. These diverse disorders can be observed in the categories that are traditionally used to classify developmentally disabled children (e.g., Down's syndrome, cerebral palsy,

Figure 3.2
Developmental Progression of Gross Motor Skills

Source:
Wyne, M. D., and O'Connor, P. D. (1979). *Exceptional children: a developmental view.* Boston: D. C. Heath. (Adapted from Shirley, 1933)

blind, deaf, autistic, language-impaired). However, any dysfunction that involves the central nervous system and sensorimotor processes exerts a significant negative impact on the acquisition of neurodevelopmental skills across all *interdependent* functions (e.g., cognition, language, play, social communication, sensorimotor exploration, self-care, and self-regulation) and transcends the narrow boundaries that attempt to characterize a particular disorder as unique and homogeneous. To illustrate this interdependent quality, a final discussion of atypical developmental patterns will blend selected information about the early cognitive, affective, and sensorimotor deficits of young children suffering various developmental disabilities.

Sensory disabilities

Children who suffer visual, auditory, or multisensory (deaf and blind) impairments are at a profound disadvantage in their efforts to understand and respond to environmental stimuli. The lack of intergration between sensory and motor functions inhibits and distorts the full range of cognitive, affective, and communication processes in development.

Object constancy

The coordination of visual and motor functions forms the basis for subsequent cognitive development in normally functioning children. Visual impairments highlight the need for dual auditory and tactile stimulation, whereas auditory deficits necessitate a focus on exaggerated visual cues. Multiple impairments point to the tactile mode as the alternate channel for information. The blind child reveals dysfunctions in visual attention, tracking, and discrimination of light sources, depending on the severity of the deficit. Thus, spontaneous search behavior for objects out of reach is precluded, as is the child's understanding of the permanent nature of contacts with people and objects. The child must be afforded experiences in which sounds can be used to direct reaching for toys that make noise or music. The child fails to search for a lost object because there are no natural cues to its position in space and little basis for believing that, once it is not felt or heard, it still exists. Moreover, the child fails to develop a sense of connection between self and reaching, finding, grasping, and losing objects.

Means-ends

Without visual cues, the blind child fails to develop an understanding of the use of hands as functional tools for obtaining objects. Frequently, hands are held in an elevated, shoulder-high position, unprepared for contacts with or manipulation of toys. Self-stimulatory patterns of waving the hands over the eyes, rubbing the eyes to experience light sensations, and slapping the face become persistent if not interrupted and directed into purposeful tasks.

Causality

Visual impairments block children's understanding that their behavior causes objects to move or people to interact with them. Their inability to process and compare visual information impairs trial-and-error learning as well as intentional goal-directed behavior. Motivation is limited, and passivity and dependency are promoted by the fact that others must intrude to elicit behavior from the child. The establishment of auditorially directed reaching (i.e., the coordination of hand-arm extension to a sound source) is a prerequisite to independent creeping and motor movements in blind children.

Object relations and concepts

The absence of understanding the purpose for reaching and grasping limits the blind child's experience with objects. In turn, the ability to recognize different objects and understand their functional interrelationships (spoon, dish) is limited. Blind children develop a belief that objects materialize within their physical space by accident. According to Fraiberg (1977), visual functions serve to connect sound and touch in normal children before 4 months of age. Blind children display a 6 to 8 month lag in relating tactile and auditory attributes of objects. Therefore, without distinct concepts regarding the dimensions and attributes of whole, real-life objects, these children perceive large objects, such as chairs, as isolated parts that they sometimes experience. Similarly, the severely physically impaired child's understanding of objects, attributes, functions, and names of functions are distorted, which influences the pace of linguistic and conceptual development.

Social communication

The formation of enduring attachment bonds between the severely handicapped child, the parents, and other individuals is seriously influenced by the absence of visual responses and cues. Blind infants lack the capacity to extend their arms to reach for the mother to initiate a pattern of reciprocal interactions. Also, spontaneous and responsive affective behaviors, such as smiling, are often delayed until 12 months of age. In this context, caregivers tend to invest extraordinary energy in encouraging mutual responses but are faced with a frustrating and unrewarding style of detachment from the child who cannot receive and respond to social cues (e.g., facial grimaces, gestures, smiles). Similarly, deaf children are often quiet and seemingly preoccupied while signaling little need for adult attention. The lack of reaction to adult contacts, such as calling the child's name, may be personalized by the caregivers as "tuning out" or oppositional behavior directed against them. Moreover, the associated absence of give-and-take verbalizations is detrimental to the emerging interaction between the adult and the deaf child.

Neuromotor dysfunctions

The foundation for the development of cognitive-adaptive abilities is the integration and refinement of reflex motor patterns and their coordination with vision, touch, and hearing. "Thus, from the consolidation of early sensory and motor behaviors evolves the basic building blocks for subsequent learning" (Langley, 1980, p. 24). Whereas normal children create their own experiences to integrate these patterns, children with severe sensory and neuromotor impairments must have such opportunities created for them. The task experiences contained in developmental curricula provide specialized opportunities for sucking, grasping, visual-auditory attending, and movement to facilitate this learning for the child with cerebral palsy and other neurological impairments.

Object constancy, causal, and means-ends relations

In the cerebral-palsied child, abnormal tone and posture interfere with the integration of sensory and motor functions. The child demonstrates an inability to hold the head erect at the midline of the body as a result of the persistence of primitive reflex patterns that would have disappeared in normal children. This abnormal posture distorts visual attention and the localization of sound sources. In turn, problems with visual attention and auditory localization, coupled with dysfunctions in motor stability and equilibrium reactions, inhibit the child from reaching, grasping, and searching for toys. Moreover, absent or distorted experiences make the child unable to comprehend cause and effect relationships such as pushing a ball or repeating a motor response. The physical involvement of the arms and hands prevents the child from actively uncovering objects to discover and explore hidden toys. This inability precludes firsthand information gained through actual sensory and motor experiences; so, the information base, memory, and knowledge of objects and their attributes is diminished, and the sense of personal competence in causing objects to move is limited.

Object relations and concepts

Severe physical impairment inhibits shifts of attention from object to object, movement toward sound sources, and tracking and locating objects out of view. Similarly, this lack of direct motor experience affects both a knowledge of the physical properties of objects and the child's awareness of his own body's position in space in relation to objects. The absence of control over arms, hands, and legs fosters a sense that these body parts are detached objects not under personal control. Poor motor control and distorted experiences with objects lead to a limited knowledge about the properties of objects (texture, dimension, shape, manipulation). Thus, language and conceptual development are affected by the child's poor perceptions about objects and their uses.

Imitation and social communication

Severe neuromotor dysfunctions prevent the child from engaging in early reciprocal games such as peek-a-boo and pat-a-cake and matching and imitating adult gestures. Gestural and vocal imitation are blunted, which limits the child's sense of modeling such self-care behaviors as pulling off and putting on shoes and feeding with a spoon.

Abnormal body postures complicate the process of adequate bonding between caretaker and child. Cuddling produces body extensions and increased muscle tone, which the caregiver may interpret as rejection, irritability, and resistance. Moreover, hypertonicity and neurological difficulties prevent adequate respiration for sound production as well as prevent the ability to form fine mouth movements for vowel and consonant sounds. Absent is a sense of the communication value of sounds or fine motor gestures. Gross, whole body movements and behavior problems become the child's mode of indicating wants or discomfort. Furthermore, a limited experiential base and poor sound-word-object correspondences impair language development.

Affective-behavioral disorders

Two aspects of the development of children with severe affective and behavior disorders inhibit and disrupt the acquisition of adaptive capabilities: (1) neurological deficits that distort sensory input, and (2) a socially detached self-stimulatory style. Autism, and the various forms of self-injurious behavior (e.g. Lesch-Nyhan syndrome), include these neurodevelopmental deficits.

Object constancy and behavior-object relations

A child's understanding that objects exist independently depends on memory, visual representation, and visual attention. The autistic child's dysfunctions in regulating sensory (visual) input interfere with these processes. Poor attention, self-involvement, and frequent overreactions to sounds, sights, and textures inhibit the child from developing anticipatory behaviors and the ability to scan the environment to search for objects in an organized fashion. Perseverative behaviors, such as hand flapping, twirling, face slapping, touching, and smelling, prevent wider experiences in exploring the environment. Vision and hearing are used inappropriately and infrequently by autistic children as primary methods of exploring objects. Repetitive spinning and manipulation of tops and objects, such as cubes, offers increased sensory feedback but does not allow the chid to attend to, remember, and discriminate the physical attributes and useful functions of objects. This style of behavior limits concept formation.

Social communication

The autistic child's extreme lack of social responsiveness and failure to recognize and comprehend the value of the communication process are serious obstacles to the formation of attachment bonds. Such children show no desire for cuddling or interpersonal affection; instead, their bodies become tense and unresponding. The lack of eye contact, absence of crying when hurt, and failure to display a pleasant social awareness of others provide no reinforcement to caregivers. Moreover, the child's self-involvement and deficits in gestural communication, as well as idiosyncratic use of words and sounds, make social communication and concept formation a tenuous process. The most intrusive behavioral strategies are required to interrupt these detached patterns and to promote the acquisition of basic adaptive and social skills.

Developmental retardation

Severely and profoundly retarded children develop cognitively according to the same invariant developmental sequence as normal children, but they differ in terms of a slower rate of overall skill acquisition. Although mental age matches the progressive attainment of sensorimotor abilities (language, grasping, manipulating) retarded children differ in the variable rate of attaining such parallel subskills as the recognition of object permanence, spatial orientation, imitation, and causation (Rogers, 1977). Children with Down's syndrome display this pattern.

Object constancy and causality

When the profoundly retarded child cannot attain an upright posture, visual and motor exploration of the environment and the ability to form concepts of body image and person-object relationships are limited. Moreover, research (e.g., Fantz, Fagan, and Miranda, 1975) demonstrates that children with Down's syndrome show significant lags in their visual-perceptual development for the recognition of faces and novel stimuli. This may influence their ability to understand and complete a search for hidden objects and to respond to people socially.

Many severely retarded children show an inability to regulate responses to stimuli. Under and overresponsiveness to various stimuli are common, which prevent the formation of selective reactions to pleasant and unpleasant events. Thus, intentional motor acts may never develop and memories regarding the relationships of actions and consequences may never form.

Social communication

Deficits in the child's ability to smile responsively and to maintain eye contact with the caregiver seriously impede the development of social communication. Responsive smiling is a subtle indicator of cognitive ability. Down's syndrome children differ from normal children in the onset, frequency, and duration of smiling and eye contact with mothers. Therefore, the sustaining cues for social interactions are reduced. The brain-damaged, severely retarded child lacks the cognitive capacity to interpret visual and gestural cues from the mother, and if multihandicapped, the motor ability to respond to and maintain the interaction. The capacity of such children to respond selectively and to show acceptance or rejection of people is seriously impaired.

SUMMARY

The use of a developmental perspective is indispensible for thoroughly understanding the behavioral progress of both normal and handicapped children. A developmental approach establishes expectancies for the emergence of a variety of abilities in children; it enables us to understand the complex interconnections among cognitive, language, social, sensorimotor, and affective processes; it reveals how disabilities distort the emergence of important adaptive skills in children; however, its most vital function is in establishing an operational base to blend assessment, intervention, and progress evaluation. With this effective mixture of philosophy, purpose, and practice, early developmental programs can be designed that will enhance the adaptive functioning and learning of young exceptional children.

SUGGESTED READINGS

Cohen, M. A., and Gross, P. J. (1979). *The developmental resource: Behavioral sequences for assessment and program planning* (Vols. 1 and 2). New York: Grune & Stratton.

Garwood, S. G. (1983). *Educating young handicapped children: A developmental approach* (2nd ed.). Rockville, MD: Aspen Systems.

Garwood, S. G., and Fewell, R. R. (1983). *Educating handicapped infants: Issues in development and intervention.* Rockville, MD: Aspen Systems.

Hanson, M. J. (1984). *Atypical infant development.* Baltimore, MD: University Park Press.

CHAPTER
4

Programs for Parents and Children

John T. Neisworth
Stephen J. Bagnato
Mary Ann Demchak

CHAPTER OUTLINE

Early life is a crucial period for development; the amount and quality of experience during this time makes a lasting impact. The preschool years are especially critical for children with diagnosed handicaps and for youngsters at risk for developmental problems. Serious delays and deviations in language acquisition, motor skills, and intellectual and socioemotional development rarely ever "just get better." In fact, failure to provide early intervention programs for children with handicaps can have an adverse impact in that a "cumulative developmental deficit" can result (Bloom, 1964).

On the other hand, early identification and appropriate treatment can alter the child's "developmental destiny." Existing handicaps can be removed or reduced, and potential handicap can be prevented. But simple custodial care, concern, or compassion is not enough. Treatment must include careful assessment of the child's developmental state and early provision of planned, structured experiences to offset complications and to optimize development.

A variety of characteristics have been identified as common to successsful early-intervention programs (Bronfenbrenner, 1975; Filler, 1983; Karnes, 1977). One factor that seems to be critical is the involvement of parents in the planning and delivery of their child's educational program. Early-intervention programs can provide services and involve parents whether they are home-, center-, or hospital-based.

Another characteristic common to exemplary programs is a structured cur-

Parents can be helpful volunteers in the preschool and they can learn how to teach and play with their child at home.

riculum and a consistent program philosophy. In general, the curriculum should cover all developmental domains, permit individualization, allow integration of handicapped and nonhandicapped students, and provide for easy tracking of child progress. The choice of a curriculum is a vital part of the early-childhood special education program because it influences all aspects of the program—instructional objectives, teaching strategies, and materials.

Because of their importance to quality programs, this chapter emphasizes basics of parent involvement, service-delivery models, and program planning. Program planning further includes individualized educational programs and close-ups of preschool curricula, instructional strategies, and instructional materials.

COMPREHENSION CHECK 4.1

Attempt to list the characteristics of exemplary programs in order of importance.

PARENT INVOLVEMENT

Early-intervention programs should not focus exclusively on the child; family involvement is essential. A child does not exist in isolation, but within the context of a family. If a child is to achieve maximum gains, it is imperative that the family, especially the parents, be involved in the child's educational programming (Welsh and Odum, 1981). During the early years of a child's development, the family is the main influence on the child's development. It runs counter to common sense to exclude parents, and it makes great sense to build a strong working relationship with parents. Through a professional-parent partnership, the child's developmental and educational goals can be stressed in both the school and home. Because cooperation with parents is so important, it is emphasized in the following section.

Basic reasons for parent involvement

Various authors (Bailey and Simeonsson, 1984; Lerner, Mardell-Czudnowski, and Goldenberg, 1981; Linder, 1983; Welsh and Odum, 1981) have reviewed the several factors that support parent involvement in early-childhood special-education programs.

First, by law (i.e., PL 94-142) parents have the right to be involved in the identification, diagnosis, placement, and programming of their child. However, the rationale for involving parents in educational programs goes beyond a legal imperative.

Second, parents know their child better than anyone else and thus possess valuable information that professionals can use when planning instructional programs. In addition, parents often state their preferences for the skills to be taught to their child to ensure their child's needs are met. Thus, parent involvement may enhance the likelihood that parents and professionals will have similar expectations for the child.

Third, good parenting and good teaching for the young exceptional child are similar. Parenting and teaching are overlapping roles, and both involve individualized concern, consistency in encouraging and discouraging selected behavior, establishment of child routines and patterns, rewarding improvement, providing and requiring reasonable limits to conduct, and other similar skills in adult-child interaction. When parents are competent at parenting skills, they can readily assist in the teaching effort.

But sometimes parents, themselves, need help in using good child-rearing practices, in avoiding child abuse, and in using various community resources. Then, the teacher can offer advice and instruction in improving parenting capabilities. This must be done with sensitivity to the authority of the parent and in the interests of improving family functioning.

Members of the interdisciplinary team can act as consultants to parents to assist parents in being more effective parents and teachers of their own child (Ehly, Conoley, and Rosenthal, 1985). The basic steps in behavioral consultation are: (1) identify problem, (2) analyze problem, (3) design and implement intervention, (4) evaluate outcomes, and (5) fade intervention or try again (Ehly et al., 1985). Thus, teachers are supporting parents *as parents* by providing assistance concerning appropriate responses to child behavior. At the same time, teachers are helping parents develop skills that may enable them more effectively to teach their child. Because parents must cope with emotions such as stress, anger, guilt, and grief, they may require support in the form of counseling.

There are also several practical reasons for including parents in educational programs. If parents volunteer in the classroom, it reduces the adult-child ratio while keeping costs down. If the family lives in a rural area and transportation or distance to a center-based program is a problem, parents can become trained to teach the child. Thus, the child is not denied the benefits of receiving early-education services.

There are, then, strong reasons for involving parents in early-childhood programs. The trend toward increased parent and family involvement represents a growing realization that parent involvement is essential (Bailey and Simeonsson, 1984).

COMPREHENSION CHECK 4.2

Summarize the reasons for parent cooperation.
Describe an instance when parent involvement might be almost impossible or not beneficial.

Parent roles

Given that parent involvement in early-childhood special education programs is essential, there are various ways in which parents can become involved. Turnbull (1983) identified four basic parental roles: (1) parents as educational decision makers, (2) parents as parents, (3) parents as teachers, and (4) parents as advocates.

Parents as educational decision makers

PL 94-142, the Education for All Handicapped Children Act of 1975, requires that parents be involved in identification, evaluation, placement, and programming for their child. When a child is evaluated for special-education placement, the parents should be consulted for relevant information. In addition, parents can challenge the results of the evaluation and request an independent, private evaluation of their child.

The Individualized Education Program (IEP) is the primary means of assuring that each child receives an appropriate education. The IEP is a written document that is developed by a team. PL 94-142 requires that the parents are members of this team. Thus, they play an active role in planning their child's educational program. (The IEP will be discussed in more detail in a later section of this chapter.)

Other provisions of the law ensure that parents participate in the education of their child. Parental consent is required before an evaluation can be conducted. Parents have the right to examine all relevant records. They must receive written notice before a child is placed or moved to another program or facility. If the parents are unknown or unavailable or the child is a ward of the state, a surrogate parent must be assigned to ensure that the child has an advocate and receives a free, appropriate public education. If the parents are dissatisfied with the child's identification, evaluation, placement, or programming, they may initiate a *due process hearing*. All these requirements of PL 94-142 serve to make the parents active partners in the educational process instead of passive recipients.

The child benefits most when the parents are an integral member of the team that plans the individualized education program.

Parents as parents

Parents are mothers and fathers; other roles should not be overemphasized at the expense of this one (Turnbull, 1983). To be effective in this role, parents may need support as they proceed through a variety of reactions when they realize that the ideal child they expected is actually handicapped (Blacher, 1984). They may first go through a period of grief or disillusionment. A subsequent phase may involve anger, which can be self-directed or directed at the doctor, other professionals, or the child. Another parental reaction may involve denial that any impairment exists. The parents may experience guilt if they think they did something wrong or failed to do something and thus caused the child's handicap. This is a frequent concern; sometimes it requires counseling by a professional family counselor or psychologist. The final phase, adaptation, or acceptance, involves forming an accurate perception of the child's condition. The parents may still experience sorrow, guilt, and anger at times, but for the most part they accept and deal with the child's condition. (See Gargiulo, 1985, for a detailed discussion of parental reactions.) A universal process of moving through these phases does not exist; the adjustment process is unique for each parent.

Staff of an early childhood special education program will encounter parents at various phases of the adjustment process. If professionals are aware of the feelings and reactions experienced by parents, recommendations of the professionals regarding programming and placement may prove to be more beneficial to and better accepted by parents than the recommendations of professionals who are unaware of parental reactions (Blacher, 1984). Although teachers are not trained as counselors or therapists, they can act as listeners and can provide practical assistance and referral information in an attempt to make it easier for parents to cope with physical demands, financial difficulties, and behavior problems. Other types of assistance the teacher can provide include informing the parents about respite care or babysitters, providing training in behavior-management strategies, suggesting home activities, teaching instructional strategies, obtaining services from additional agencies, and explaining evaluation data.

Parents as teachers

Parents can successfully teach their own child, as well as other children, if they receive appropriate training (Welsh and Odum, 1981). Parents can act as teachers of their child either in a home-based or a center-based program as a paid assistant or a volunteer.

For parents to be successful teachers of their child, they need to achieve competencies that are similar to those required by any teacher: instructional strategies, behavior-management strategies, data collecting and record keeping, and participation in an interdisciplinary team (Karnes and Teska, 1980). However, not all parents will achieve these competencies to the same degree and some parents will not even be interested. It is essential that parents are involved in an individualized manner and to the fullest extent possible.

Parents as advocates

Advocacy refers to "advancing or securing the rights and interests of a client" (Turnbull, 1983, p. 39). Parent advocacy efforts, often directed at laws, regulations, or local school policies with which the parents disagree, can be in the form of litigation, legislative lobbying, or due process procedures. These types of efforts were effective in right-to-education litigation and in the passage of the Education of All Handicapped Children Act of 1975. Legal advocacy of this nature must continue in order to ensure that educational programs provided to handicapped children are meaningful. For example, in PARC v. Scanlon (1979), a parent organization successfully challenged the education provided to severely impaired students as inappropriate and unmeaningful. The Court ordered the school district to improve the educational programs provided to these students. Parents and professionals can combine efforts as legal advocates to influence legislators and administrative decision makers in producing policies beneficial to hanidcapped students.

Advocacy extends beyond legal interests; parents may require advocacy efforts in obtaining or initiating community resources and services. Parents may require recreational services and religious opportunities for their handicapped child, babysitting and respite care, as well as assistance in securing financial aid. Educators might assist parents in obtaining these services or they might refer them to other parents for assistance. Parent groups can be organized to help with advocacy efforts, to offer support during the adjustment process, and to provide training for parents. Table 4.1 presents a summary of parent involvement in the education of the young exceptional child.

TABLE 4.1
Components of Parent Involvement

Parents as Educational Decision Makers
  Involvement in identification, evaluation, placement, and programming of their child
  Member of the IEP committee
  May examine all relevant educational records
  Consent prior to evaluation and initiation or change in placement of their child
  May initiate a due process hearing
Parents as Parents
  Proceeding through various phases of adjusting to the child
  Copying with daily demands

Parents as Teachers
  Instructional strategies
  Behavior management
  Data collecting and record keeping
  Participation in an interdisciplinary team

Parents as Advocates
  Litigation
  Legislative lobbying
  Due process procedures
  Obtaining community resources and serivces

COMPREHENSION CHECK 4.3

If parents are so crucial and can play several roles, why do many parents avoid involvement?

EARLY-CHILDHOOD SPECIAL EDUCATION PROGRAMS

Service-delivery models

Early-childhood special-education programs differ in the way they deliver services and in the way they involve parents. *Service-delivery models* are defined as "replicable patterns or designs of getting assistance to those who need it, such as families of young children with handicaps" (Bailey and Wolery, 1984, p. 14). As mentioned in Chapter 1, service-delivery models include home-based, center-based, a combination of home-based and center-based, and hospital-based programs. The home-based model refers to programs delivered principally in the child's home; center-based models bring children together at a center or school for instructional sessions. Combination home- and center-based programs provide service in a center and include periodic home visits. Hospital-based programs are offered to infants and chronically ill or hospitalized young children. These programs, often called "child life programs," usually include an actual child center where a child specialist directs the developmental acitivities. Each of these models has advantages and disadvantages. The optimal model depends on family and child characteristics and the geographic location of the families.

The center-based and combination models permit handicapped and nonhandicapped children to receive educational service within an integrated setting. More and more frequently, young handicapped children are receiving services in concert with their nonhandicapped peers.

Home-based models

In the home-based model the child is taught at home with the parents acting as the principle teacher. Home-based services are often provided in rural areas where transportation for children involves an excessive amount of time or where there are very few children who require services. Typically, a teacher will visit the home approximately once a week to establish and maintain rapport, collect data on child progress, plan activities for the coming week, and teach the parent how to implement the activities.

The teacher's most important responsibility is to train the parent by using instruction, modeling, behavior rehearsal, and feedback. The first step involves providing instruction to the parent while simultaneously demonstrating the activity with the child. The teacher then asks the parent to perform the activity with the child. The teacher than asks the parent to perform the activity with the child while the teacher observes and provides corrective feedback and encouragement.

Although parents provide most of the actual child instructions, the child still benefits from the services of an interdisciplinary team (see Chapter 2). In this model, the professional trains the parent to be the primary teacher of the child. The facilitator coordinates the information into an individualized program for the child and transfers this information to the parents who provide the direct services. Each team member is involved in assessing the child, determining instructional objectives, and examining data to determine child progress.

A number of advantages are associated with the home-based model. Because the services are provided in the home, transportation is not a problem for the family. Furthermore, the natural environment of the child and parent enhances the generalization of skills. The home-based model provides an opportunity for other family members to become involved in the intervention. If the child is frail, the child's health may be better protected by providing services in the home. Services provided through a home-based model are inexpensive in that a facility does not have to be built or maintained. The model provides the parent with individualized training and permits the parents to be actively involved in their child's education. Finally, because attendance is not a problem, instructional sessions can be conducted regularly.

There are, however, also a number of disadvantages associated with the home-based model (Bailey and Wolery, 1984). Because the parents are the primary teacher, the child's progress could be hindered if the parents are poor teachers or are unmotivated. For many parents, placing their child in a center provides an opportunity for a break from caregiving responsibilities; the home-based model does not allow parents this opportunity. It is possible that services provided may not be as broad as those through another model (e.g., the combination home- and center-based model). Because the child is educated at home, there are restricted opportunities for social interactions with other children; this lack of socialization opportunities may be of special concern with some children. A final disadvantage involves the teacher; much time is spent in traveling and dealing with assorted domestic concerns. Even though the home-based model has some disadvantages, there are times when it is the most appropriate method for providing early-childhood special education.

The Portage Project   The Portage Project, a home-based program serving rural Wisconsin, employs the behavioral approach of instruction (Shearer and Shearer, 1972). Portage materials are used by many programs throughout the nation. This program directly involves the parents by teaching them what to teach, when to reinforce, how to conduct obeservations, and how to collect data on child behavior. The children served can have behavior problems or be physically handicapped, retarded, visually or hearing impaired, culturally disadvantaged, or have difficulties in the speech or language.

Each home teacher spends approximately 1 1/2 hours 1 day each week with each child and family for a period of 9 1/2 months. On the other 6 days of the week, the parent is responsible for providing instruction and recording child progress. When the home teacher visits the family, the first task involves collecting data on the previous week's activities. Based on these data, programs are modified or new ones are written. The *Portage Guide to Early Education* (Bluma, Shearer, Frohman, and Hillard, 1976) was developed by program staff to assist in this instructional planning. Following this planning, baseline data are collected on the new programs to determine the child's current level of performance. After the home teacher demonstrates a lesson, the parent is observed working with the child. The teacher advises the parent concerning the manner of implementing the activities. Finally, the parent is shown how to chart the child's performance on the activity chart. Twice a year each child is evaluated with an intelligence test and a developmental scale.

Center-based models

Children may be transported to a center on a scheduled basis for a few hours a day for 2 to 5 days a week. In this type of program, professionals, not parents, are the primary teachers. Teachers conduct assessments, plan and implement instructional programs, supervise paraprofessionals, collect data on child performance, and maintain records. Parents can participate in the program as volunteers.

As with the home-based model, center-based team members provide information to the facilitator as well as have some direct contact with the child. Services are often extended to the home, and, of course, the parent is a member of the team.

The center-based model has several advantages. It allows team members to work together closely and permits a more efficient use of staff time. Children have an increased opportunity for social interactions with other children. When children are at school, parents receive respite from their daily

Developmental integration at an early age helps children to accept and appreciate individual differences.

caregiving responsibilities. The parents have an opportunity to seek support from and share experiences with other parents. Although parent involvement is extremely important in a center-based program, children can receive service even if their parents cannot be actively involved with the program.

The center-based model does include at least three disadvantages. Transportation must be provided for the children; this is often expensive and time consuming. The center-based program is more expensive to operate than the home-based program because of the cost of the constructing and maintaining a building. Finally, parent involvement tends to be less in a center-based program than it is in a harder to involve the parent and to establish a working relationship.

Down's Syndrome Program The Down's Syndrome (now called Programs for Children with Down's Syndrome and Other Developmental Delays) is located at the University of Washington's Experimental Education Unit (Hayden and Dmitriev, 1975). Children are transported to the center to receive instruction in all of the developmental domains.

The program, which serves Down's syndrome children from birth through age 6, is comprised of four classes. The classes are organized around age groupings as follows: (1) infant learning program (infants 5 weeks through 18 months), (2) early preschool (18 months to 3 years), (3) advanced preschool (3 years to 5 years), and (4) kindergarten program (4 1/2 to 6 years). The infant learning program meets once a week for 30 minutes during which the parents and child receive 30 minutes of individualized training in early motor sensory development. The other three classes meet 2 hours a day, four times a week.

When a child enters the Down's Syndrome Program, the child is assessed to identify target behaviors in the physical, cognitive, communication, and social areas. The intervention techniques used allow individualization and are based on task analysis, the use of prompting and fading, and reinforcement contingencies.

A strength of the Down's Syndrome Program centers around a parent involvement component that requires parents to participate in the classroom on a regular basis. The parent is taught to manage and supervise play activities, to prepare materials, and to observe and record behaviors. At least one individual parent-teacher conference is held each academic quarter, with frequent telephone contacts occurring between conferences. During an evening meeting held once each quarter, the parents share data they collect on their child(ren)'s behavior, viewed and discussed videotapes of the preschool, and talked among themselves about common concerns. The parents are viewed as a critical component of the program.

Combination home- and center-based model

There are two types of combination home- and center-based models: (1) younger children are served at home whereas older children are served at a center, and (2) children receive services according to their individual needs (Bailey and Wolery, 1984). One child may receive both center- and home-based services whereas another child might receive only home-based. The teacher's responsibilities will depend on whether the teacher's role involves the home- or the center-based aspect of the program.

The advantages of the combination model are similar to those of the center- and home-based models. In addition, there is a wider range of flexibility in determining how to meet the needs of the child and family. The disadvantages of the combination model are also similar to those described for the home- and center-based model.

San Francisco Infant Program   A combination center- and home-based programming, the San Francisco Infant Program provides services for handicapped and at-risk children from birth to 3 years (Hanson, 1981). Children in the program represent the various populations (e.g., white, black, Asian, and Latin) of San Francisco and are placed in one of two groups when they enter: (1) the infant group, which meets once a week for a 3-hour session attended by parent; or (2) a toddler group, which meets three mornings each week with the parents present for two of the mornings. All children have individualized education plans and receive periodic home visits from project staff.

Parent involvement is an important aspect of the San Francisco Infant Program. Parents receive classroom instruction concerning teaching and handling infants as well as home visits approximately once a month. Parents develop their own objectives for their involvement in the program by completing a parent involvement plan. Other services provided to the parents include counseling and evening workshops to discuss topics such as legislation, behavior management, and genetics.

Hospital-based model

Many large hospitals conduct educational programs for infants, young children, and parents to assure the provision of services that meet the educational as well as the medical needs of the infant. The emphasis is on both the child and the family (Badger, Burns, and DeBoer, 1982). The hospital-based model encourages the educational and medical members of the intervention team to work together closely to develop an intervention plan for the infant and family. Bagnato and Neisworth (1985) describe an interdisciplinary team approach for infants and young children in a pediatric rehabilitation program. The team consists of a developmental school psychologist, an early-childhood special educator, speech/language therapist, developmental pediatrician, occupational therapist, physical therapist, pediatric nurse, and recreational therapist. Each parent-child pair receives separate therapy sessions in each of the disciplines. The study demonstrates that intensive interdisciplinary intervention in the hospital setting can promote significant developmental and behavioral progress of the enrolled children.

A hospital-based program has various advantages and disadvantages. The parents receive individualized training and are involved actively in their child's intervention program. Parent groups can be formed so that parents meet with one another for support and discussion of common concerns. Transportation may be a disadvantage if parents need to travel long distances.

Although the cost of providing a program may be expensive, the potential benefits to the infants and their families may outweigh the costs. Hospital-based intervention is designed to increase an infant's responsiveness and interaction with the parents; this increased social interaction may lead to enhanced general infant development (Leib, Benefield, and Guidubaldi, 1980).

TABLE 4.2
Advantages and Disadvantages of the Service-Delivery Models

Model	Advantages	Disadvantages
Home-based	No transportation required Natural environment Whole family involved Frail health better protected Inexpensive Individualized parent training Parents actively involved	Parents may be poor teachers No respite for parents Narrow scope of services Limited social interaction Professional loses teaching time

Center-based	Efficient use of staff time
	Increased social interactions
	Respite for parents
	Parent support groups
		Transportation may be
		  expensive and time
		  consuming
		Construction and maintenance
		  of center
		Reduced parent involvement

Combination Home- and Center-based	Combined advantages of
	  home- and center-based
	  models
	Wide range of flexibility in
	  providing services
		Combined disadvantages of
		  home- and center-based
		  models

Hospital-based	Individualized parent training Parents actively involved Parent support groups Educational and medical professionals work together	Transportation Expensive

Table 4.2 presents a summary of the advantages and disadvantages of the various service-delivery models.

Project Pre-Start   Project Pre-Start provided an example of a neonatal intensive care unit in the Department of Pediatrics, Stritch School of Medicine, Loyola University in Maywood, Illinois (Karnes, Linnemeyer, and Shwedel, 1981; Karnes and Teska, 1980). The project included infants, birth to 3 years of age, at risk for developmental delays, child abuse, and socioemotional disorders. Karnes and Teska (1980) described the program as having three categories of services: caring, sharing, and daring. Caring referred to those supportive services a family received before, during, and after the birth of an infant. Sharing referred to the support parents gave one another by discussing common concerns as well as to the information the parents and the Pre-Start team shared concerning the infant. Daring referred to providing services that were not typically provided in a medical center.

After an infant was referred to the Pre-Start team, the parents were contacted and provided with the necessary information. A child-development specialist evaluated the infant to identify the infant's competencies and to form a basis for the care provided. The infant was assessed on entering the center, at term date, and at 1, 3, 7, 12, 18, 24, and 30 months by a follow-up team to plan the parent and infant activities to be implemented.

Parent involvement was a vital part of Project Pre-Start because the parents worked with their infant in the hopital's special care unit and , subsequently, at home. Parents completed a needs assessment and shared information with the Pre-Start team to develop an individualized developmental plan that was based on the child's and parent's needs, interests, and skills. Other services available to the parents included counseling, membership on an advisory board, and training in areas such as advocacy or assessment. A 10-week in-service training was available to parents who wanted to work in the parent-to-parent calling program in which parents who had children in Project Pre-Start contacted new parents concerning the program.

COMPREHENSION CHECK 4.4

If you were the parent of a handicapped preschooler, what type of service model would you prefer? Why?

PROGRAM PLANNING

The Education for All Handicapped Children Act of 1975 (PL 94-142) specifies that handicapped children's education be designed and implemented through the preparation and use of an Individualized Education Program (IEP). The mandated requirements of the IEP process, such as the content of the document and the participants of the planning team, have an important impact on the education of the child.

Instructional program planning (i.e., the IEP) is greatly influenced by the curriculum used in a particular educational program. The curriculum reflects the underlying philosophy (i.e., normal developmental, cognitive developmental, or behavioral) of the program and subsequently influences all aspects of the program: assessment, objectives, instructional strategies, materials, and parent involvement (Bagnato and Neisworth, 1981). A close-up of several early-education curricula will be provided shortly.

Also to be considered are the instructional strategies and materials used to achieve the child's individualized objectives. Basic strategies for managing behavior and providing instruction (to be discussed) are crucial to the early-childhood special educator.

The individualized educational program

Purpose and content

The purpose of the IEP is to assure that handicapped children receive an education that is appropriate to their unique needs and abilities. An IEP is a written statement, prepared by a committee, of the instructional program to be provided to a specific child. The IEP represents an ongoing diagnostic-prescriptive approach to educating handicapped children. The required participants of the IEP committee include a representative of the local school district (e.g., the principal), the student's teacher(s), the student's parent(s), the student (when appropriate), and a member of the evaluation team if the student was evaluated for the first time. The committee is responsible for writing the IEP, which must include these components:

1. A statement of the child's present levels of educational performance.

2. A statement of annual goals and short-term objectives.

3. A listing of the special education and related services to be provided and a specification of the amount of time the student will participate in regular education programs.

4. The projected date for initiating services and the anticipated duration of services.

5. Evaluation procedures for determining at least annually whether the short-term objectives are being achieved.

Present educational levels   The statement of present educational levels summarizes the diagnostic information collected during individual assessment and identifies the child's specific strengths and weaknesses in all developmental areas (i.e., cognitive, social, motor, and communication areas). The comprehensive assessment is conducted by a multi-, inter-, or transdisciplinary team that is comprised of such members as teachers, therapists, or parents. The information presented in this section of the IEP serves as the basis for the individualized instructional program.

Goals and objectives   The annual goals represent the broad targets of the student's educational program and are directly linked to skill weaknesses indentified in the statement of present educational levels. Annual goals should be identified for all developmental areas. Whereas an annual goal is a broad target, a *short-term objective* is a specific statement concerning the student behavior expected at the end of instruction. Each short-term objective should be stated in observable, measurable terms with a condition, behavior, and specific criterion (Mager, 1975). Short-term objectives can be obtained from a commercially produced curriculum or they can be developed by the IEP team. Table 4.3 provides an example of an annual goal and a related short-term objective.

Special education and related services   The IEP must also specify the special-education and related services to be provided to the student. PL 94-142 requires that a continuum of services be because there is no single type of program appropriate for all handicapped students. The types of service-delivery models that are available for preschool handicapped children include home-based, center-based, conbination home- and center-based, and hospital-based programs. The type of program provided depends on the unique needs of the student. Regardless of the service-delivery model used, the handicapped student often requires related services. Related services are defined as developmental, corrective, and other supportive services that are necessary to assist the handicapped student in benefiting from special education. Related services include transportation, speech pathology and audiolo-

TABLE 4.3
Sample Annual Goal and Short-Term Objective

ANNUAL GOAL = Broad target of the educational program
   Example: Child demonstrates independence in feeding with utensils.
SHORT-TERM OBJECTIVE = Specific statement of expected child behavior
                                  following instruction that includes a:

	Condition:	The circumstances or situation in which the child will perform the behavior, such as materials or prompts.
	Behavior:	The observable skill to be performed.
	Criterion:	The level of performance accepted as mastery of the skill.
Example:	Condition:	Given a spoon and spoon-appropriate food.
	Behavior:	The child eats using the spoon.
	Criterion:	Without spilling on 9/10 trials.
	Evaluation Procedure:	Teacher observation and record of the frequency of trials without spilling.

Source: Adapted from Pennsylvania Preschool Pilot Individualized Educational Program, Project CONNECT, 1976.

gy, physical and occupational therapy, psychological services, recreation, counseling, and medical services for diagnostic and evaluation purposes, early identification, school health services, social work services in the school, as well as parent counseling and training.

The dates for initiating and terminating the special-education program and each related service must also be specified. The amount of time (e.g., the number of days per week and the hours per day) that the student receives special-education services and participates in regular education programs must be stated.

Annual review Finally, it is required that the IEP include provisions for determining on at least an annual basis whether the objectives are being achieved. The student's progress is reviewed and recommendations are made to continue or to change the student's placement. If special-education placement is going to continue, the IEP committee develops a new IEP for the coming year by following the procedures used in the development of the first IEP. All components of the instructional program are updated, and implemention of the special program would begin according to the new information.

Using the IEP

The IEP is not simply a paper document that is completed to meet legislative mandates. The IEP serves as a diagnostic-prescriptive tool that forms the basis of an individualized instructional program. The IEP is also a tool for evaluating the effectiveness of special-education programs in that the IEP provides a means of monitoring student progress. The annual review of the IEP gives information regarding the child's achievement in the developmental domains.

COMPREHENSION CHECK 4.5

All special-education teachers have become familiar with IEPs. The advantages to the child are numerous. What may be some disadvantages to the child or teacher?

Curricula

A *curriculum* is a pattern of educational objectives, or the "what to teach" of the early intervention program (Bagnato and Neisworth, 1981). Because the choice of a curriculum determines what and, frequently, how the child will be taught, it is a vital part of planning the child's IEP. In general, a curriculum for an early-childhood special education program should reveal several characteristics. A comprehensive curriculum includes objectives for the various domains of development: cognitive, personal/social, motor, and language. Although a good curriculum allows a child to be placed at the level most appropriate for that child and permits the child to progress at his own rate, it also permits the teacher to conduct group as well as individual lessons. A curriculum should also permit a teacher to record easily each child's progress. Numerous curricula that exist have these characteristics, but these curricula can differ significantly from one another in content.

Content

Proponents of the normal developmental approach, the cognitive developmental approach, and the behavioral approach have developed and promoted curricula reflecting these theoretical positions. The theory adhered to by the curriculum somewhat determines the content of the curriculum.

Normal developmental approach   Most of curricula for early intervention are based on developmental milestones (Bailey, Jens, and Johnson, 1983). Although this approach is beneficial for guiding initial educational programming decisions, there are some basic problems with the approach (Bailey et al., 1983). First, it assumes that the competencies that differentiate between nonhandicapped children at different ages are critical skills to teach and these skills will develop in the same manner in handicapped children as in nonhandicapped children. Although the skills are observed to emerge in nonhandicapped children, it does not mean these skills are related to either current or future adaptive functioning. Problems are also evident when a child is not physically capable of demonstrating mastery of a skill, such as placing blocks in a cup. The second inherent problem with the normal developmental approach is that it may not allow items to be grouped into a logical teaching sequence. Although the objectives may be arranged in a hierarchy within developmental domains (e.g., motor, communication, social, and cognitive), the teacher may be given little guidance concerning how to move through the curriculum with any child, handicapped or nonhandicapped.

Cognitive developmental approach   The cognitive developmental approach to curriculum development is based on the work of Piaget and emphasizes conceptual development or the acquisition of knowledge. Typically, a cognitive developmental curriculum progresses from concrete to abstract, and from specific to general (Wolinsky, 1983). Three assumptions underlie the cognitive developmental curriculum (Guess and Noonan, 1982). If instruction is to be motivating, the objectives must be slightly ahead of the child's present level of cognitive development. Because the child is viewed as an active participant of the learning process, the child must interact with the environment if learning is to result. Thirdly, the level of cognitive development determines and limits objectives for the other developmental domains; the cognitive domain is interrelated with the other domains.

The main focus of this approach is on the cognitive, language, and social domains, with very little attention given fine and gross motor development (Bailey et al., 1983). Because instruction in all domains is essential to a successful program, program staff would need to use other supportive curricula if the cognitive developmental approach is emphasized.

Behavioral approach   The behavioral approach is more concerned with how to teach rather than what to teach. Often, normal developmental milestones or specific sets of objectives from a variety of sources are used. The instructional strategies employed are different from those of traditional approaches, however. A behavioral curriculum uses a carefully structured learning environment for teaching specific skills (Allen, 1981) and does not wait for learning to occur as a result of maturation (Bailey and Wolery, 1984). Aspects of a behavioral curriculum include observable and measurable objectives, specification of the steps of each behavior to be taught, and provision of reinforcement and corrective feedback to each child.

There are several underlying assumptions of a behavioral curriculum (Bailey and Wolery, 1984). Because learning is not an observable process, it is inferred by observing a child's overt behavior. Behavior is influenced by stimuli that occur immediately before a behavior (i.e., antecedent events) and immediately after a behavior (i.e., consequences). Thus, the environment can be manipulated to increase the probablity that desired behaviors will occur. The third assumption involves assessing the child's strengths and weaknesses so that instruction can be individualized according to a given child's abilities and needs. Instruction should not be aimed simply at acquisition of a skill but also at the maintenance and generalization of skills. Therefore, the teacher should manipulate the learning environment in a manner that allows the child to practice skills over a period of time and in different settings. Within a behavioral curriculum, the main emphasis is the teacher who assesses child performance; specifies behavioral objectives; breaks skills into small, teachable steps; and provides prompts, praise, and feedback.

COMPREHENSION CHECK 4.6

Can a teacher adopt both a cognitive developmental *and* behavioral approach? How might they coexist, and when would one apply instead of the other?

Considerations in selecting a curriculum

General characteristics of curricula have already been discussed in that they must include all developmental domains, allow for individualization, permit some group instruction, allow for easy monitoring of progress, and have a theoretical basis. However, there are other more specific standards that curricula may meet: (1) developmental balance and expansion, (2) normalization, (3) developmental integration, and (4) spiral organization (Mori and Neisworth, 1983).

Developmental balance and expansion Developmental balance and expansion refers to coverage of all developmental domains and objectives for all areas and subareas of each domain. Both vertical and horizontal expansion should be available through the curriculum (Mori and Neisworth, 1983). *Vertical expansion* refers to teaching a child new skills that were not previously in the child's repertoire. *Horizontal expansion* refers to developing behavior across various settings and materials after the behavior is acquired. That is, horizontal expansion refers to generalizing, or transferring, a skill to new situations. Thus, a good curriculum is one that provides a balance of objectives in all domains and encourages generalization across life settings.

Normalization Normalization refers to using methods that are as culturally normal as possible to establish behavior that is as culturally normal as possible (Wolfensberger, 1972). Thus, a curriculum should include objectives that allow a child to approach normalcy. Even though some children may not reach the norm, it is essential that they have the opportunity to work toward it. A child should be individually assessed to determine where in the hierarchy of curricular objectives the child should begin instruction. It is possible that one child could be at a different level in each of the developmental domains. The teacher must strive to bring the child to chronological age expectancy (normalization) within each of the domains.

Developmental integration Integration refers to providing instruction for both handicapped and nonhandicapped children within the same setting. A good curriculum facilitates integration if it permits handicapped and nonhandicapped children to work at the same task at different ability levels. For example, a teacher may be working with a group of children on following verbal directions. One student might be given one-step directions; another student is given directions with two steps; while a third student is given three-step directions.

Spiral organization A spiral curricular pattern means that objectives from different domains are taught and then repeated subsequently in a more detailed and complex fashion (Bloom, 1956). Thus, skills are introduced in a simple manner and later learned more thoroughly and related to more complex performance. Repetition of objectives in this manner facilitates maintenance and generalization. When learning to measure objects with a ruler, a student may begin by measuring to the nearest inch. Later, the student can return to the task to learn to measure according to half inch and quarter inch.

> COMPREHENSION CHECK 4.7
>
> How is normalization promoted by a curriculum?

Summary of curricula

Because the curriculum influences all aspects of an early-childhood special education program, each child's IEP will be influenced by the curriculum used in a particular educational program. Therefore, the teacher should follow certain guidelines when selecting a curriculum. The underlying philosophy of the curriculum is important; if a teacher is a proponent of the behavioral approach, a curriculum with a cognitive developmental approach probably would not be appropriate. In general, a curriculum should be comprehensive, balanced, normalizing, self-assessing, and permit developmental integration. Close-ups of four preschool curricula are provided in the next section. Table 4.4 provides an overview of several curricula for early-childhood special education.

Close-ups of preschool curricula

Learning Accomplishment Profile

The Learning Accomplishment Profile (LAP) uses a developmental task approach and was designed for both normal and developmentally delayed children. The developmental domains in the curriculum are gross and fine motor skills, social skills, self-help skills, cognitive skills, and language skills. The LAP is comprised of seven major products to be used directly with children: (1) Learning Accomplishment Profile, (2) A Manual on the Use of the LAP, (3) Diagnostic Edition Kit, (4) A Planning Guide: The Preschool Curriculum, (5) Early LAP, (6) Learning Activities, and (7) Planning Guide for Gifted Preschoolers.

Use of the LAP centers around the Learning Accomplishment Profile and the Manual on the Use of the LAP. Contained within the profile is a listing of the hierarchy of developmental behaviors from birth through 5 years of age for each of the major domains addressed within the curriculum. Suggestions for skill-sequence development and a means for recording a child's behavior on a specific task are provided. To assist in implementing the LAP, the manual specifies the criteria and demonstrable behaviors associated with the specific objectives listed in the profile. The Diagnostic Edition was designed to be used for assessment purposes by the same person who uses the profile and the manual. It permits a child to be assessed in a one-to-one situation in less than 1 hour.

Other supplementary products are available. A Planning Guide: The Preschool Curriculum, based on the topical units described in the manual, suggests materials and activities for the classroom. The Early LAP is designed for individuals who work with children from birth through 36 months of age. Learning Activities contains 295 activities for use with chil-

TABLE 4.4
An Overview of Selected Curricula in Early-Childhood Special Education

Title, Author Publisher	Developmental Levels	Target Population Areas	Content	Theoretical
Adapting Early Childhood Curricula R. Cook and V. Armbruster	3 to 5 year olds	Mildly handicapped children in mainstreamed settings	Language, cognitive, motor, and social/emotional skills	Behavioral
The Cognitively Oriented Curriculum David Weikart The High Scope Press Ypsilanti, MI	3 and 4 year olds	Culturally disadvantaged and mildly retarded	Language and cognitive skills	Cognitive developmental
HICOMP Preschool Curriculum S. Willoughby-Herb and J. Neisworth The Psychological Corporation San Antonio, TX	0 to 5 year olds	Handicapped and nonhandicapped	Cognitive, language, social, and motor skills	Behavioral
Distar Instructional System Engelmann et al. SRA, Chicago, IL	4 to 8 year olds	Mildly handicapped and nonhandicapped children	Language, reading, arithmetic	Behavioral
Fowler's Curriculum and Assessment Guides for Infant and Child Care William Fowler Allyn & Bacon, Boston, MA	0 to 3 year olds	Mildly handicapped and nonhandicapped children	Language, knowledge, and problem-solving skills	Cognitive developmental
Learning Accomplishment Profile A. R. Stanford Kaplan Press Winston-Salem, NC	0 to 6 year olds	Handicapped children	Motor, social, self-help, cognitive, and language skills	Behavioral
Learning Language at Home M. Karnes Council for Exceptional Children	3 to 5 year olds	Handicapped children	Language skills; kit to be used by parents	Behavioral

Reston, VA

Program	Age Range	Population	Skills	Type
Portage Guide to Early Education S. Bluma et al. The Portage Project	0 to 6 year olds	Multiple-handicapped children	Infant stimulation, cognitive, language self-help, motor, and socialization skills; to be used by parents and home-based teachers	Behavioral
Programmed Environments Curriculum J. Tawney et al. CEDAR Clinic Penn State Univ. University Park, PA, 16802	0 to 3 year olds	Moderately, severely, and profoundly handicapped children	Language, cognitive, motor, and self-help skills	Behavioral
Step-by-Step Learning Guide for Retarded Infants & Children V. Johnson and R. Werner Syracuse University Press Syracuse, NY	0 to 4 year olds	Moderately and severely handicapped children	Social, motor, self-help, language, perceptual skills	Behavioral
Teaching Your Down's Syndrome Infant: A Guide for Parents M. Hanson University of Oregon Eugene	0 to 2 year olds	Down's syndrome infants	Motor, social, communication	Behavioral
Wabash Guide to Early Developmental Training J. Tilton et al. Allyn & Bacon Boston, MA	0 to 5 year olds	Moderately and severely handicapped children	Motor, cognitive, language, self-help	Diagnostic/ prescriptive
Washington Guide to Promoting Development in the Young Child K. Barnard and M. Erickson C. V. Mosby, St. Louis, MO	0 to 5 year olds	Normal and handicapped children	Motor, feeding, sleep, play, language, discipline toilet-training, dressing skills	Behavioral

The *Learning Accomplishment Profile (LAP)* is an early childhood education program that includes specific objectives, activities, and an easy way to assess child developmental level.

dren aged 12 to 76 months. The Planning Guide for Gifted Preschoolers is useful with children who are being integrated into child-development centers, preschools, and kindergarten classrooms.

Strengths of the LAP include field testing and provisions for record keeping and assessment. Because neither suggestions for accommodating various handicaps nor for using behavioral strategies for teaching objectives are included, a consultant may be necessary to train staff members in these two areas (Bagnato and Neisworth, 1981).

HICOMP preschool curriculum

HICOMP (Willoughby-Herb and Neisworth, 1983) is an acronym for higher competencies in the four domains of communication, own care, motor, and problem solving. HICOMP is appropriate for use with nonhandicapped as well as developmentally delayed children from birth to a developmental age of 5 and can be used with groups of children or individuals. The four components of HICOMP are: (1) *the Curriculum Guide,* (2) *Assessment for Placement and Instruction* (API), (3) *Developmental Activities Handbook,* and (4) *HICOMP Track Record.*

The Curriculum Guide includes a listing of more than 800 developmental objectives for the four domains. Details concerning instructions for implementing the curriculum, using developmental assessment for entering a child into the curriculum, and evaluating child progress are provided. Basic behavioral strategies for teaching the objective are included.

The *API* is a quick method for determining where to enter a child in each of the developmental domains. The *Developmental Activities Handbook* provides more than 500 activities for facilitating progress in each of the four domains. The Handbook specifies the domain, objective, instructional strategy, and materials needed to implement each activity. The *Track Record* allows the teacher to "keep track" of each child's progress through the *Developmental Activities Handbook.*

HICOMP assists early-childhood teachers in several ways: the curriculum assists the teacher in planning both general educational programs and day-to-day learning experiences and in recording and evaluating children's progress.

Small wonder

Small wonder is designed for an infant's first 18 months, but handicapped and developmentally delayed children can use the program to up to 3 years of age (Karnes, 1979). The curriculum is appropriate for use in home- or center-based programs by professionals or nonprofessionals. Small Wonder is comprised of these products: (1) Activity Cards, (2) My First 18 Months, (3) Look Book, (4) Picture Cards, (5) Picture Card Stories and Ideas, and (6) Casper the Caterpillar.

The 150 activity cards are grouped into six units; each 3-month age unit covers physical, intellectual, emotional, and language development. Each card identifies the age range, the activity, necessary materials, and the skills emphasized. *My First 18 Months* is a diary to keep track of the baby's activities from the baby's point of view.

The Look Book, used to display the Picture Cards for story–telling activities, permits the pictures to be changed for various stories. The 64 Picture Cards show people and familiar activities, toys, clothes, animals, food, and utensils. On the back of each card are suggestions concerning what to say about the picture. The Picture Card Stories and Ideas contains stories for various ages, suggestions about how to arrange the Picture Cards for story

Small Wonder is a kit with "recipe" cards that describe parent–infant activities for promoting interpersonal attachment as well as specific areas of child development.

telling, and descriptions for all the Picture Cards. Casper the Caterpillar is a hand puppet that is used to motivate the infant.

Portage Guide to Early Education

The Portage Guide to Early Education is a product of the Portage Project to serve children in rural Wisconsin from birth to 6 years of age. The curriculum includes the following materials: (1) *The Manual,* (2) Card File Box, and (3) *Checklist.*

Often referred to as the "Portage," this curriculum uses a behavioral/developmental approach for its theoretical orientation. The developmental areas included in the curriculum are (1) infant stimulation, (2) socialization, (3) language, (4) self-help, (5) cognitive, and (6) motor. Within the *Card File Box,* which is actually the curriculum, are color-coded cards for each developmental domain. Each card states an instructional goal and suggestions for achieving that goal. In addition, behavioral methods for instructing the children are included in the manual.

The checklist is used to determine where instruction should begin for each student. Like the curriculum cards, the checklist is color-coded for each of the six developmental domains. The checklist also serves as a record of child achievement.

COMPREHENSION CHECK 4.8

What curricula might be better for a center? Which one(s) might work better in a home-based situation?

Instructional strategies and materials*

Strategies

After behavioral objective have been written or selected, it is necessary that instructional strategies be selected for teaching the skills targeted by the objectives. Willoughby-Herb and Neisworth (1983) and Fallen and Umansky (1985) identified numerous procedures, strategies, and tactics for teachers to use to assist a student in achieving objectives: (1) task analysis, (2) shaping and chaining, (3) prompting and fading, (4) modeling and imitation, (5) questioning, (6) activity pairing, (7) behavior rehearsal, (8) discrimination learning, and (9) positive reinforcement.

After a child has "learned" a skill, it is important to determine whether the skill has generalized. That is, can the child perform the skill with different people and in various settings? Because generalization does not automatically result as a by-product of learning, the teacher must plan instruction in a way that will enhance the likelihood for useful generalization (Stokes and Baer, 1977). Not every teacher will use all available strategies, nor will all the strategies be appropriate for all skills and all students; instruction should be an individualized process. Eleven fundamental strategies are described in this section.

*Much of this section draws heavily on materials included in the *HICOMP Curriculum* (Willoughby-Herb and Neisworth, 1983).

Task analysis   Task analysis refers to breaking down tasks into their component parts so that each skill involved in performing the overall task is specified. Task analysis provides a basis for sequential instruction. A teacher can precisely pinpoint a student's behavior, place the student at the appropriate level for instruction, and then assist the student in mastering the skill. Because the skill is broken into small steps, student error is reduced (Moyer and Dardig, 1978). Snell and Smith (1983) identified steps to follow when analyzing a task: (1) specify the target behavior, (2) state each step in terms of observable behavior, (3) write the steps with adequate detail, (4) be sure each step leads to a visible change in the product or process, (5) order the steps from first performed to last performed, and (6) construct a data sheet. See Table 4.5 for a sample task analysis.

Shaping   Shaping involves rewarding progressively closer approximations of a specified objective. That is, when a child makes even slight progress toward an objective, the behavior is immediately reinforced. For example, suppose a teacher would like the students to participate in a group activity for 10 minutes, but, the longest Jimmy participates is 4 minutes. The teacher can increase Jimmy's participation time by gradually increasing the time and by reinforcing involvement for doing better. The teacher might first reinforce 4 minutes, then 5 minutes, and so forth until Jimmy stays with the group for the full 10 minutes.

Sequencing behaviors   Some skills, such as washing one's hands, are sequences of behaviors; that is, the skill involves a series of steps that must be performed one after the other. Each step, or link, in the chain is usually a behavior that the child can already perform. Chaining teaches the right sequence of behavior in that the component behaviors are linked together to form more complex skills.

Behaviors can be chained in either a forward manner or a backward manner. If forward chaining is used to teach Sara to wash her hands, Sara would be taught the first step (e.g., turn on the water), and subsequent steps would be added until the whole sequence is learned. If backward chaining is used, the teacher performs every step of the sequence for Sara except the last

TABLE 4.5
Sample Task Analysis

1. Put toothpaste on toothbrush
2. Turn on water
3. Brush teeth
4. Rinse mouth
5. Rinse toothbrush
6. Turn off water
7. Put away toothbrush
8. Get towel
9. Wipe mouth
10. Throw towel away

one, which Sara performs. If the behavior were washing hands, the teacher would turn on the water, wet Sara's hands, pick up the soap, lather the soap, replace the soap, rinse Sara's hands, turn off the water, pick up the towel, and dry Sara's hands. The final step, put the towel down, would be performed by Sara. As the last step is mastered, the step immediately preceding it (i.e., drying hands) is added to that which Sara does independently. Backward chaining moves back through the steps until the child is performing the skill independently.

Prompting and fading   Prompting is a strategy that involves a visual-stimulus, sound, or touch that the teacher uses to set the occasion for a particular behavior. Thus, prompts may be visual, verbal, or physical. The prompt acts as a crutch that assists the child to perform a task that might otherwise be too difficult. Gradually, the prompt is faded until the child independently performs the skill (Goetz, 1982).

Visual prompting involves adding a visual cue to a stimulus to make that stimulus easier to discriminate from another one. The teacher, for example, may place the child's name, as well as a photograph of the child, on the child's locker. The photograph serves as a prompt to make it easier for the child to select the correct name. Other methods of visual prompting involve changing the color, size, location, or other dimension of the stimulus.

Verbal prompts tell the child what to do. When selecting verbal prompts, the teacher should keep them short, simple, and consistent. For example, a student can be prompted to use scissors by the teacher saying "open, shut." Another means of giving a verbal prompt is to provide the child with a hint. Suppose a child is shown a picture of a cat and asked to name the animal. If the child cannot name the animal, the teacher might provide a verbal hint, or prompt, by saying "This animal says 'meow'."

Physical prompts involve manually guiding the child to perform a skill; the child is "lead through" the task. Willoughby-Herb and Neisworth (1983) suggest two basic guideline to follow when using physical prompts: (1) only prompt the parts of the behavior with which the child has difficulty, and (2) try to prompt from behind the child so that the child looks at the task and not at the teacher. A teacher can physically prompt a child to "Raise your hand" by moving the child's hand. To physically prompt a child to self-feed, a teacher can put his hand over the child's hand to assist the child.

As the child masters the new skills, the prompts should be gradually removed (faded). Fading can involve reducing the intensity, magnitude, frequency, or duration of the prompt (Goetz, 1982). To teach the child to find his name, the teacher can place a red dot next to the child's name. To fade the intensity of the dot, the color is made lighter and lighter until it finally blends into the white paper. To fade magnitude, the dot could be made smaller and smaller until it is no longer used. To fade frequency, the name would occasionally be presented without the dot. An example of fading duration could involve using a light turned on under the paper. When the light is on, the dot appears; the length of time the light is on would be gradually shortened. Continued prompts should be faded as quickly as possible so that the child does not become dependent on them. Like a crutch, specially continued prompts are useful in establishing a behavior but should be removed in the interests of normalcy and independence.

Modeling and imitation   When teachers show or demonstrate an activity, they "model" and encourage imitation. A child is more likely to imitate a model if that model is reinforced for the demonstrated behavior, is similar to the observer, and is perceived by the observer positively. Playing a game such as "follow-the-leader" involves modeling and imitation. Demonstrating how to do various activities is, of course, not a new technique but good modeling includes reinforcement for the imitator.

Questioning   Questioning permits the teacher to guide child behavior toward a specified objective. If the child does not respond correctly to the question, the teacher can either tell the child the answer or provide verbal prompts. If the objective is to have the child identify a missing body part (e.g., an eye) on a picture, the teacher might begin by asking "What looks funny about this girl?" If the child does not know, the teacher could start with minimum verbal prompts and move toward stronger verbal prompts as necessary: (1) "Think of the body parts you have." (2) "Is the girl missing any body parts?" (3) "Look at the girl's face." and (4) "Look at the girl's eyes." The teacher proceeds toward the stronger verbal prompts only as necessary for the child to answer correctly.

Activity pairing   Sometimes a teacher wants a child to behave a certain way in a particular situation. To teach a child to laugh when played with, it

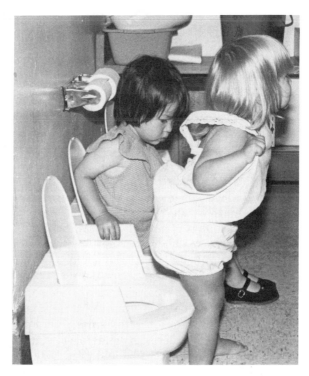

Modeling can be used to build many important self-care capabilities.

is suggested that the teacher pair something that already causes laughter (e.g., tickling) with play (Willoughby-Herb and Neisworth, 1983). Eventually, play itself will bring about laughter. In activity pairing a part of the environment (e.g., play time) becomes a conditioned event for a particular behavior (e.g., laughter). Music may be played, for example, to announce clean-up time. Eventually, merely putting on the music will cue the children to clean up.

Behavior rehearsal   Behavior rehearsal refers to having a child repeatedly practice a particular behavior. A teacher might have the child practice counting from 1 to 10 by providing various sets of objects to be counted. Sometimes the teacher may have a student rehearse a skill that is not usually practiced at school (e.g., placing an order at a fast-food restaurant). A variety of behaviors, such as walking up to the counter, placing an order, and paying the cashier, are "rehearsed, " or role played, in a classroom. After the student has mastered the behaviors in the role-playing situation, the teacher might take the student to a restaurant to use the behaviors that were rehearsed.

Discrimination learning   When using discrimination learning, the teacher attempts to teach children to differentiate behaviors of the students under the control of specific stimuli, or signals. Teaching a child to discriminate between his printed name and the printed names of the other children in the class is an example of such learning. The teacher teaches discrimination by following these steps: (1) give distinctive prompts for the correct behavior, (2) provide many opportunities to practice and be reinforced for the desired response in the presence of the prompt, (3) reduce opportunities for children to practice inappropriate behavior in the presence of the prompt, and (4) gradually fade any continued prompts that were used (Willoughby-Herb and Neisworth, 1983). Figure 4.1 presents an example of discrimination training.

Postitive reinforcement   In addition to planning instructional strategies for teaching skills, the teacher should also plan the consequences that will follow the child's behavior. Positive reinforcement refers to the contingent and immediate presentation of a reward of some sort after a behavior, which increases the future strength of that behavior. Reinforcers may be praise, food, attention, tokens, or favorite activities. Reinforcers are idiosyncratic in that what acts as a reinforcer for one child may not for another child and what is a reinforcer for a child today may not be tomorrow. It is important to remember that an event is defined as a reinforcer by observing its effect on behavior. If the event is a reinforcer, the future rate or probability of the behavior will increase.

Once it is determined what events are reinforcing to a child, the teacher can use these events when teaching the child. The reinforcers used should be as natural and as age appropriate as possible. For example, it is not acceptable always to reinforce a child's behavior with food. The teacher can pair the delivery of food with social praise and gradually decrease the amount of food given until praise alone maintains the child's behavior.

When a teacher begins teaching a new skill to a child, it may be necessary initially to reinforce every correct response. However, as the child masters

Figure 4.1
In this example of discrimination training, a child is taught to descriminate *between* his/her printed name and the printed names of the other children in his/her group.

A STEP-BY-STEP APPROACH IN DISCRIMINATION TRAINING

1. State the problem.
   Susan does not correctly identify her name tag on her chair and tooth-brush.

2. What do you want the student to identify?
   Susan

3. What other stimuli must the child be able to discriminate this from?
   All other names in her group.

4. List these stimuli in the order of maximum to minimum difference from the stimulus you are teaching (i.e., **Susan**).
   a. Joe b. Henry c. Marcia d. Sally

5. List some stimuli that would be even more different from the stimulus. **Susan** than are these names.
   Colored shapes, animal pictures, lines

6. Order these in terms of maximum to minimum difference from the stimulus **Susan.**
   a. animal pictures b. colored shapes c. lines

7. Next, think of stimuli that are not names of children in the group but are very close to the names. List these.
   Individual letters, nonname words, words of similar length, words of similar configuration, other words that start with capitals

8. Order these from maximal to minimal differences from the stimulus **Susan.**
   a. individual letters
   b. nonname words
   c. words of similar length
   d. words of similar configuration
   e. other words that start with capitals

9. Write a series of paired stimuli in which the child is to identify **Susan** by beginning with the order generated in Step 6, then going to the order in Step 8, and finally to the order in Step 4.
   Some examples of the actual discrimination materials follow. Just a few are given here, although you should have more than one example of each pairing.

What stimuli are being paired (easiest to hardest discriminations)?	What do the teaching materials look like?
1. Animal pictures, Susan	Susan "Show me your name."
2. Colored shapes, Susan	△ Susan "Show me your name."
3. Lines, Susan	< Susan "Show me your name."

Figure 4.1 *(cont'd)*

What stimuli are being paired (easiest to hardest discriminations)?	What do the teaching materials look like?	
4. Individual letters, Susan	Susan	**B**
	"Show me your name."	
5. Nonname words, Susan	dog	Susan
	"Show me your name."	
6. Words of similar length, Susan	jumps	Susan
	"Show me your name."	
7. Words of similar configuration, Susan (note shape of the words)	Beams	Susan
	"Show me your name."	
8. Other words that start with capital S, Susan	Short	Susan
	"Show me your name."	
9. Names of children in group, Susan	Susan	Joe
	"Show me your name."	

Source:
From Willoughby-Herb, S. J., and Neisworth, J. T. (1983). *HICOMP preschool curriculum*, pp. 17–18. Columbus, OH: Merrill. Copyright 1983 by Merrill. Reprinted by permission.

the skill, the teacher gradually decreases the frequency of reinforcement until it reaches a level that the child would receive in unstructured, nonteaching situations.

One method of reinforcing the child is to use *task-imbedded reinforcement* (i.e., with reinforcement built into the task). To make tasks reinforcing, teachers can (1) use content that is interesting to children, (2) build favorite activities into the task, and (3) create a game-type activity that involves the objectives (Willoughby-Herb and Neisworth, 1983). A storybook with the child's own name and friends in it is an example of immediate reinforcement. The hours of effort in playing video games is a prime instance of "task" imbedded reinforcement among school-age children. Ideally, education should involve much imbedded interest and reward.

Generalization A child learns a new skill and successfully performs that skill in the learning environment, but the mother states that the child still cannot perform the skill at home. The child has not generalized the skill from the school setting to the home environment. Instruction should include methods for enhancing the probability of generalizing so that the child competently performs the skill across settings, people, and time. What follows is a series of steps to facilitate generalization (Willoughby-Herb and Neisworth, 1983):

1. Observe the child with other people (e.g., parents, teachers, peers, and siblings) and in other settings (e.g., home, outdoors, speech clinics) to determine if the targeted behavior has generalized.

2. If the skill has not generalized, the teacher can facilitate generalization in a variety of ways (Stokes and Baer, 1977):
   a. Others can be prompted to reinforce the child's behavior.
   b. The behavior can be prompted in other settings (e.g., the teacher could send home materials so that the child can use the skill at home as well as at school).
   c. The teacher can "train loosely" (Stokes and Baer, 1977) by making the training conditions less specific and structured. For example, the teacher can vary the prompts (e.g., "Point to _____," "Show me _____") and the materials (e.g., trying the child's shoe, teacher's shoe, peer's shoe).

Observations and recording of the behavior shoud continue so that it can be determined whether the skill has generalized to other people and settings.

COMPREHENSION CHECK 4.9

Do teachers really use the strategies described in this section? What problems might exist that limit what techniques are actually employed?

Instructional materials

Materials are a critical component of the early-childhood special-education classroom because they are used in assisting the students to achieve various behavioral objectives. Instead of haphazardly selecting materials, a teacher should systematically evaluate materials to ensure their appropriateness. Neisworth et al. (1980) proposed four criteria for selecting instructional materials. The process begins by focusing on curricular appropriateness, then examines learner appropriateness, questions whether the materials are based on learning principles, and finally determines the cost and efficiency of the materials.

Curricular appropriateness The materials selected for instruction should match the theory of both the curriculum and the teacher (Ross, 1982). For example, a teacher with a behavioral viewpoint might prefer materials

Figure 4.2
Steps in the Decision-making Process

```
              Model for Materials Selection

                      Cost/Efficiency

                           Use of
                     Learning Principles

                  Learner Appropriateness

                 Curricular Appropriateness
```

Source:
From Neisworth, J. T., Willoughby-Herb, S. J., Bagnato, S. J., Cartwright, C. A., and Laub, K. W. (1980). *Individualized education for preschool exceptional children,* p. 112. Rockville, MD: Aspen. Copyright 1980 by Aspen Systems Corporation. Reprinted with permission of Aspen Systems Corporation.

that stress single concepts and provide immediate feedback, whereas a developmentalist might prefer materials that have several purposes (Ross, 1982).

Just as curriculum must represent a wide range of developmental domains, materials must also be relevant for various domains and ability levels (Neisworth et al., 1980; Ross, 1982). The teacher should choose materials appropriate for use in several curricular areas. The toys in Figure 4.3 are materials that are appropriate to help a child achieve more than one objective. For example, an infant can grasp or reach for the tracking tube; it can be used for teaching an infant to focus on an object and follow its movement; or it can be used to teach an infant to look toward a sound.

One curricular area should not be overrepresented with materials while another area has no materials. For example, the teacher should not select an abundance of language materials while the other domains have few or no materials. In addition, the teacher must avoid materials that are culturally biased (Ross, 1982) because even subtle prejudices can be depicted in story-books and flash cards.

Learner appropriateness   Learner appropriateness refers to selecting materials that meet the unique needs of the students. To select materials that meet students' needs, the teacher should identify student characteristics as they pertain to curricular areas. Table 4.6 shows a matrix that can assist a teacher in rating student behaviors across curricular areas. A zero rating means that the child is functioning at the expected age range for that particular curricular area; a rating of 1 refers to a functional level that is 1 year behind or ahead of the expected age range; and a 2 means a difference of 2 or more years. When the matrix is completed, the teacher can use it as an aid in selecting materials. Instructional materials would be selected for those areas in which it was indicated that students demonstrated aberrant functioning.

The teacher cannot simply attend to students' performance levels, but must also determine whether any students have sensory deficits or motor limitations. If the teacher identifies child characteristics that prohibit the use of the materials that the nonhandicapped children use, then the teacher will need to purchase special materials or adapt materials. Sometimes materials are actually adapted (e.g., pictures with raised objects on each page for visually impaired child to trace); at other times the type of child response is changed (e.g., the child can manually sign the name of a picture instead of verbally saying it).

Learning principles   If a material meets the cirteria of both learner and curricular appropriateness, then the material is examined to determine if it is based on learning theory. A variety of learning principles are relevant when examining instructional materials: concept learning, operational learning, overlearning, and imitational learning (Neisworth et al., 1980).

Figure 4.3
Examples of Adaptive Play Materials by Johnson and Johnson (1982)

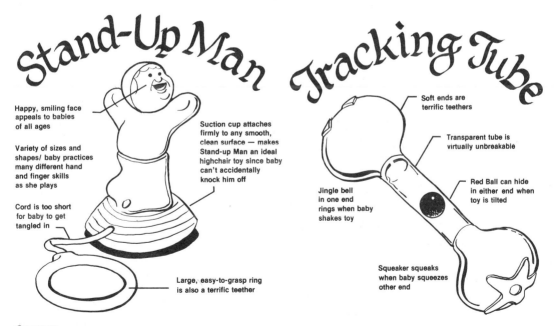

Source:
From Johnson and Johnson (1982). *Child developmental publications: Stand-up man and rattle.* Skillman, NJ: Johnson and Johnson Baby Products. Adaptive play materials manufactured by Johnson & Johnson.

TABLE 4.6
Relationship of Learner Behaviors to Curricular Areas

		Child		
		James	Jo-Ann	Janis
	Curricular Areas			
Communication:	Attention	1	0	1
	Imitation	1	1	2
	Responding	2	1	0
	Self-expression	1	0	0
	Play	2	1	2
Social skills:	Eating/drinking	0	0	2
	Dressing/undressing	0	0	2
	Cleanliness/health	1	1	1
	Social conventions	0	1	0
Motor:	Gross	0	1	2
	Fine	1	0	0
	Mouth and jaw control	2	0	2
Problem solving:	Attention	1	0	0
	Imitation	0	1	1
	Recall	0	2	1
	Concept formation	1	2	1
	Grouping	0	1	0
	Sequencing	0	0	0
	Application of principles	1	1	2
	Creativity	2	0	1

Source: From Forsberg, S. J., Neisworth, J. T., and Laub, K. W. *COMP-Curriculum.* By permission of the HICOMP Outreach Project, The Pennsylvania State University, 315 Cedar, University Park, PA 16802. Copyright 1974.

Young children learn many *concepts* such as colors, numbers, shapes, and animals. Materials that are used to teach concepts should follow specific guidelines: (1) prompts should focus on relevant attributes of the event, and (2) it should be possible to fade the prompts that are used to assist the discrimination.

Operational learning refers to manipulating objects in a manner that teaches operations such as buttoning, zipping, and latching. Materials should be selected that allow the child to progress from gross to fine motor controls and from simple to complex manipulations. For example, if a child were learning to button, the teacher would first provide buttons that were large and easy to grasp, then gradually move to smaller buttons.

Overlearning refers to providing opportunities to practice newly acquired behaviors so that the child maintains the behavior. The teacher could select materials that allow a child to practice skills during free play time. For example, if the child has just learned how to manipulate various types of latches, the child could practice opening latches on a toy cabinet during free play.

Although *imitational learning* will probably begin with live models, it does not necessarily continue to require live models. Teachers can provide children with pictured models that the children must follow to complete a task. For example, the teacher may present the child with a picture of six colored blocks that the child must match. Thus, the child can work independently.

Cost/efficiency   The last step in selecting instructional materials is a consideration of cost and efficiency. The teacher must examine all previous information gathered concerning the materials—curricular and learner appropriateness as well as use of learning principles. Based on this information, the teacher should rank materials from those that are absolutely necessary to those that would be luxury items. The teacher may want to select more efficient materials (i.e., those materials that have greater versatility). From this list of priorities, materials would be purchased for the preschool.

COMPREHENSION CHECK 4.10

Does cost really matter when dealing with a child's life? Why or why not?

SUMMARY

Effective early-childhood special-education programs have a variety of common characteristics. Parent involvement, an essential, includes the parents as educational decision makers, as parents, as teachers, and as advocates. Second, the program must be founded on an underlying philosophy of child development, include normalizing objectives, and employ proven instructional strategies. Based on the unique needs of the child and the parents, the educational services are provided in the home, center, or hospital. Finally, the actual educational program is planned for the child by the teacher and team members, including the parents. The curriculum used by the preschool program influences the instructional objectives, strategies, and materials. Although the underlying program philosophy, the service-delivery model, and the curriculum used can vary across early-childhood special-education programs, parent involvement is essential for any program if it is to be successful.

SUGGESTED READINGS

Berger, E. H. (1981). *Parents as partners in education: The school and home working together.* St. Louis: Mosby.

Cook, R. E., and Armbruster, V. B. (1983). *Adapting early childhood curricula: Suggestions for meeting special needs.* St. Louis: Mosby

Lerner, J., Mardell-Czudnowski, C., and Goldenberg, D. (1981). Curriculum strategies for preschool handicapped children. In *Special education for the early childhood years.* Englewood Cliffs, NJ: Prentice-Hall.

Neisworth, J. T. (Ed) *Developmental Toys,* issue 5:3 (Fall, 1985) of *Topics in early childhood special education.*

Thurnean, S. K., and Widerstrom, A. H. (1985). *Young children with special needs: A developmental and ecological approach.* Boston: Allyn & Bacon.

Developmental Diagnosis of the Young Exceptional Child

Stephen J. Bagnato
John T. Neisworth

CHAPTER OUTLINE

Mr. and Mrs. Allen brought Nicole to the child development center's interdisciplinary developmental disabilities (IDD) clinic because of concerns that their daughter was not gaining abilities at the same rate as other children. The Allen's had taken Nicole to the home of friends to play with their children and had become worried that her language, play, and fine motor skills were not as well developed as were those of their friends' children.

The Allen's have been somewhat concerned since Nicole was born 8 weeks premature and suffered birth complications, including hyaline membrane disease and two episodes of neonatal seizures (which were well controlled with antiepileptic agent). Nicole is now 28 months old and shows many apparent developmental delays compared with other children of similar age.

At the IDD clinic, a team of specialists worked with Nicole and her parents to diagnose and describe comprehensively her developmental skills and deficits in several areas of functioning with the objective of planning an individualized program of therapy to increase her functional capabilities and promote progress in these areas. Nicole's diagnostic team consists of a developmental school psychologist, pediatric nurse, speech/language clinician, occupational therapist, early-childhood special educator, and the developmental pediatrician. They used a battery of formal and informal scales and rating checklists, which include parent judgments, to assess Nicole in an accurate and comprehensive manner. Such scales as the Bayley Scales of Infant Development, the Early Intervention Developmental Profile, the Infant and Toddler Temperament Scales, and the Carolina Record of Individual Behavior were used in this evaluation. The results showed that Nicole, age 28 months, was functioning most like an infant of these developmental ages in the following skill areas: cognitive (20 months); language (16 months); perceptual/Fine Motor (18 months); socioemotional (26 months); gross motor (20 months); and self-care (18 months).

As can be seen, Nicole shows some significant delays or deficits within most developmental areas. She is using only a limited number of single words to label objects (but not pictures) and to express her wants. Her play patterns with toys are hindered somewhat by her uncoordinated and imprecise hand skills. She will will bang and toss toys unless more appropriate play skills are learned. Nicole's parents are now relieved to know her needs, but they are concerned about how she will develop. They are anxious to enroll her in the early-intervention program and her program of education and therapy so that she will have the best chance to mature and progress with the mildest possible problems.

Not every child has the same pattern of strengths and weaknesses or shows the same developmental progress. Billy's intellectual development is normal, but his social behavior is markedly below what is expected for his age. Again, his fine and gross motor skills are satisfactory, but his communication is like a child half his age. Billy's friend, Sally, shows development that is advanced. Her communication, social, motor, and intellectual capabilities are about 8 months beyond what is expected. Certainly, it seems clear that Billy's instructional program will not be the same as Sally's. Each child must be provided with individually tailored objectives and educational circumstances.

Developmental assessment provides us with a picture of each child's development, with details on delays and distortions in development. When developmental assessment is accurate and comprehensive, it can serve as a blueprint to guide educational and therapeutic efforts (Bagnato and Neisworth, 1981). The *developmental/diagnostic-prescriptive approach* refers to the series of steps or stages professionals use to (1) *detect* developmental problems, (2) *assess* the child's developmental status, (3) *prescribe* objectives and methods for treatment, and (4) *evaluate* treatment effectiveness.

The developmental/diagnostic-prescriptive approach is presented in detail in this chapter. The following steps are discussed:

1. *Screening and identification*—the detection process that highlights possible problems in development requiring more detailed assessment.

2. *Developmental assessment and linkage*—a comprehensive and detailed analysis of child-developmental capabilities that establishes goals for intervention.

3. *Developmental programming and intervention*—the design of individualized curricular activities and adaptive strategies for teaching young handicapped children.

4. *Evaluation of developmental progress*—the analysis of evidence regarding individual child progress and program effectiveness.

The following paragraphs provide a fuller picture of infant and preschool assessment with specific information on (1) early- identification instruments and child-find procedures, (2) comprehensive infant and preschool assessment techniques, (3) interdisciplinary child diagnostic teams, (4) adaptive assessment and curriculum strategies, and (5) methods of monitoring child progress.

THE DEVELOPMENTAL/DIAGNOSTIC-PRESCRIPTIVE APPROACH

Ultimately, assessment must lead to education and treatment or it has no practical or justifiable purpose. Assessment and intervention are inseparable processes. However, the approach (see Figure 5.1) includes a series of steps with overlapping purposes. These steps proceed from *screening* to *evaluation*. In addition, a distinction must be made between "testing" and "assessment" because such a distinction influences the purpose and scope of services to children. In *testing*, children's abilities are examined so that their performance can be compared with that of other children similar to them through a test score (e.g., mental age, IQ). The "score" is the end result of testing with no provision for planning educational programs. But, *assessment* involves not only a score, but, more importantly, gathering qualitative information about

Figure 5.1
Linking Assessment-Intervention Goals

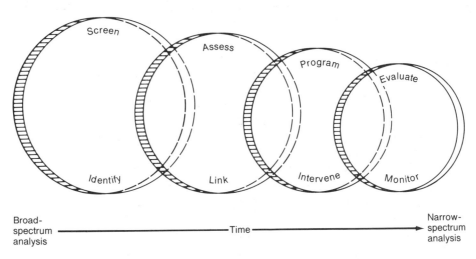

Broad-spectrum analysis ──────────────── Time ──────────────→ Narrow-spectrum analysis

how the child earned that score. Assessment produces a profile of each child's strengths and limitations with suggestions regarding the manner in which each child learns the best (Salvia and Ysseldyke, 1984).

Four stages of the developmental diagnostic-prescriptive sequence

The developmental diagnostic-prescriptive approach consists of four primary stages involving four overlapping purposes: (1) child screening and identification, (2) developmental assessment and linkage, (3) developmental programming and intervention, and, (4) evaluation of child progress and program efficacy. This sequence consists of assessment activities that are increasingly precise in defining a child's abilities and needs. Each goal serves as a prerequisite for the next goal in the sequence.

Perhaps the most effective way of understanding how the diagnostic process operates is to compare it with a series of wide- to narrow angle lenses. You would choose a wide-angle lens if you wanted broadly to scan or survey a landscape without attention to detail. In similar fashion, the process of *child screening* enables specialists broadly to survey multiple developmental functions (e.g., cognitive, language, social, sensorimotor) in order to *identify* or *detect* abnormal development. Screening usually locates areas of difficulty, but it does not provide specifics regarding that difficulty. Similarly, the College Board Examination screens or identifies those who may enter a college, but it does not help to decide what course of study a student should have.

Progressively narrower lenses are chosen to increase magnification (i.e., attention to detail) at the expense of broad coverage. To continue the analogy, *diagnostic assessment* more precisely analyzes developmental problems by focusing on the problem areas identified during the screening and then profiling the specific features in those developmental areas that require *individual goals* for intervention (e.g., visual-perceptual deficits that hinder the child's ability to imitate and copy drawn forms). An even more detailed focus is required to analyze the child's skills into subskills that can be more easily taught (i.e., developmental task analysis). *Developmental programming* establishes the objectives as well as the particular instructional strategies for *intervention*. Finally, *evaluation* couples the features of both lenses: wide-angle vision and attention to detail. For example, repeated assessment provides information on progressive developmental gains across time. Also, evidence of lack of child progress in certain curriculum areas enables specialists to analyze narrowly the strategies in the program that may be ineffective for a particular child and to modify them.

In summary, the primary developmental diagnostic-prescriptive operations are screening, assessment, programming, and evaluation. The respective purposes are to detect child problems, to profile and link the assessment findings into the curriculum, to design individualized intervention strategies, and to monitor child progress and program impact.

COMPREHENSION CHECK 5.1

What are the four stages in the developmental diagnostic-prescriptive approach?
Distinguish between "testing" and "assessment" of young handicapped children.

Selecting developmental measures

The notion of conducting one-time assessment or using only a single instrument is clearly inappropriate in the diagnosis of youngsters. Young handicapped children exhibit rapid changes in learning, depending on their handicap. Single assessments cannot capture these qualitative and quantitative changes and, thus, will foster inaccurate estimates about the child's abilities. Also, the behavior of young children is often so situation- and person-specific that one short evaluation session cannot accurately portray their adaptive skills. Finally, some instruments are so global in their survey of developmental skills that they lack a range of tasks that are functionally appropriate for multihandicapped children. A collection or *battery* of developmental measures must be used to assess the child's developmental status and progress over time and across different people and situations. To accomplish these aims, interdisciplinary teams of developmental specialists conduct assessments on developmentally disabled children by using a battery of specialized scales that have different purposes.

Several criteria must be observed in selecting a battery of developmental scales. The following criteria help ensure a better analysis of developmental capabilities and design of instructional goals and strategies.

Developmental base

The skills and processes contained in the assessment instrument are sequenced along a *developmental task analysis*. This means that developmental landmarks are arranged according to age level, level of difficulty (e.g., least difficult to most difficult), or adaptive stage (e.g., basic to complex). Child experts have worked long and hard to detail normal sequences of development. We now have a fairly clear picture of what children can do at different ages. In addition, the scales within the battery should provide information on emerging developmental *processes* (e.g., object permanence) as well as developmental skills (e.g., puts pegs in a pegboard). Finally, a good battery will generate both developmental *age scores* and ranges to describe child performance.

Comprehensive profile

Assessment scales must sample a broad array of developmental skills and processes rather than focusing on narrow aspects of development. A detailed survey allows specialists to profile the child's capabilities within and across important areas of development: cognitive, communication, perceptual-fine motor, socioemotional, gross motor, self-care, temperament, auditory, visual, and self-regulation. A variety of separate tests and observations can be used to ensure comprehensive coverage. Individualized intervention plans are designed using this *multidomain* approach. Global scores or descriptions of general functioning on isolated tasks is of limited use to teachers and therapists. *Comprehensive* (multidomain) analyses of specific developmental capabilities is a hallmark of useful developmental assessment.

Curriculum linkages

The items contained in the various instruments in the battery are often parallel with the curricular objectives in the infant preschool program. In fact, one of the most important instruments in the battery is the developmental curriculum itself. The common developmental landmarks contained in the assessment instruments and the curriculum (i.e., behavior/task sequence) provide the linkage between assessment and programming (Bagnato and Neisworth, 1981). Thus, sampled and predicted behaviors are the same (i.e., testing tasks and teaching tasks). Stacking three blocks, for example, is both an item in several assessment instruments and also a developmental objective included in curricula. "Assessment and intervention are linked through the evaluation of child progress" (Brooks-Gunn and Lewis, 1981, p. 88).

Multiple sources

The assessment battery should include the findings of several people who have observed the child's behavior across different settings. *Multisource* assessment helps to monitor capabilities that are inconsistent, emerging, or situation-specific. As we increase the number of sources of assessment, we increase the reliability or confidence we can place on the results. With assessment coming from several members of an interdisciplinary team (psychologist, speech/language specialist, physical and occupational therapists, teachers, and parents), we can more accurately estimate the developmental status and progress of young handicapped children.

Adaptive strategies

Assessment batteries should contain suggestions for modifying tasks so that handicapped children can demonstrate their knowledge and skills. Such adaptations as putting handles on formboard puzzle shapes for cerebral-palsied children and using eye localization, head pointers, or signing for language-impaired children are types of modifications that can be made. Recently, some commercially available developmental curricula have included "standardized" adaptive strategies in their testing and teaching activities for children with visual, motor, language, and auditory disabilities (DuBose and Langley, 1977; Moersch and Schaefer, 1981).

Technical adequacy

Assessment measures must consistently describe *(reliability)* the skills, processes, and behaviors that they say they measure *(validity)*. The use of only single measures often yields inconsistent and misleading estimates of child functioning. The use of several different measures tends to increase reliability and the confidence that can be placed in the validity of the results.

COMPREHENSION CHECK 5.2

Explain a *developmental task analysis*.
Give an example of an adaptive assessment strategy for use with handicapped children.

STAGE 1: CHILD SCREENING—DETECTING DEVELOPMENTAL PROBLEMS

Early identification of young handicapped children is crucial; intervention during the infant years can substantially reduce the negative effects of disabilities and facilitate developmental progress. However, many handicapping conditions that could be reduced or even prevented are not detected early enough (Aldrich and Holliday, 1971; Haynes, 1976; Werner, Bierman, and French, 1971).

Traditional early detection methods that rely on physicians, parents, and human service agency referrals are not sufficient to identify many existing and emerging dysfunctions.

Whereas serious and observable conditions, such as Down's syndrome and the aftereffects of rubella are identified at birth, less visible, but disabling neurodevelopmental difficulties (e.g., cerebral palsy, developmental retardation, communication disorders) may remain undetected for some time. Even the bizarre and disabling condition of autism often remains unidentified because of disagreements among specialists. The National Collaborative Infant Project surveyed thousands of infants and found that the time lag between parent suspicion of a problem and medical developmental diagnosis was 6 months for severe problems but up to 45 months for more subtle dysfunctions. Most parents (i.e., 75%) definitely suspect a problem by 6 months of age; however, the time lag between confirmation of that suspicion and placement in a program often approaches a year.

Because of this haphazard and inadequate identification process, federal and local programs have been started for the early identification of handicapped children including the Early, Periodic Screening, Diagnosis, and

Treatment (EPSDT) program (1967), a federally sponsored effort. These programs have resulted in the design of more creative mass methods for identifying exceptional children. Zehrbach (1975) reported a community roundup approach (i.e., Comprehensive Identification Process—CIP), in which mass community screenings of children resulted in the identification of many more children with mild to moderate problems than were identified by traditional physician or agency referral procedures.

An understanding of the nature and content of the early-identification process is an essential first step in diagnosing and intervening with young handicapped children.

Early-identification strategies

Determining risk status

Tjossem (1976) has proposed a model that allows specialists to categorize young children in terms of the type and degree of prospective developmental disorders. Three categories are described: (1) established risk, (2) biological risk, and (3) environmental risk.

Established risk   Children with an established risk are probably the most easily identified group of handicapped children. Their developmental disorders result from medically diagnosed conditions or syndromes, which may have specific causes. Genetic and metabolic conditions account for the major difficulties in this category, such as physical defects and marked developmental retardation. The physician can often diagnose such conditions prenatally. Recent advances through the use of amniocentesis allow medical specialists to diagnose such conditions as Down's syndrome and other chromosomal and metabolic disorders. Routinely, sound-wave outlines of the developing fetus can be achieved through ultrasound scanning techniques. More invasive and risky procedures such as surgical placement of an optical scanning device in the uterus can also help physicians detect physical and central nervous system defects.

During the early postnatal period, specialists can determine the scope of many developmental difficulties by examining physical evidence. Physical abnormalities referred to as "midline signs" guide specialists to determine the point during fetal development at which toxic or genetic insults became evident. Such signs as wide-spaced eyes, microencaphaly, cleft palate, webbing of feet and hands, dimpling on the chest and arms, and musculoskeletal abnormalities provide diagnostic evidence. A newborn screening procedure for detecting phenylkentonuria (PKU) allows physicians to prescribe a special diet to halt the progressive developmental retardation that otherwise results from this disorder.

Biological risk   Children with early developmental histories that suggest the strong probability for later neurodevelopmental problems fit in the biological risk category. Kessler and Newberger (1981) have summarized the long-term consequences of head trauma, toxic insults, diseases, infections, and pre- and post-maturity on later neurodevelopmental functioning. A combination of physical and behavioral assessment techniques and developmental history factors (prenatal, perinatal, postnatal) help diagnostic specialists to detect early disorders.

One of the most well-known physiological screening procedures is the Apgar test routinely employed to assess the status of newborns in the hospital. Conducted at intervals of 1 and 5 minutes, the Apgar scores (0, 1, 2) skin color, respiratory effort, reflex irritability, heart rate, muscle tone, and response to stimulation. The lower the total score (a score of 12 is perfect), the more at risk is the child's neurophysiological status. Similarly, new measures are being used to assess the status of premature infants and neonates (Brazelton, 1973; Tronick and Brazelton, 1975) and to teach mothers about the capabilities and care of their newborns (Brazelton, 1981). The Brazelton Neonatal Behavioral Assessment Scale is an instrument which analyzes the infant's interactive responsiveness to the environment as well as the ability to regulate, organize, and modulate his state. Children with immature or damaged central nervous systems display less capability in interaction or regulation of state. Various maternal, child, and environmental factors have been shown to be associated with later developmental problems in young children, (see Table 5.1).

TABLE 5.1
Factors Associated with Later Developmental Disabilities

MATERNAL FACTORS
  Diabetes
  Chronic kidney disease
  Rubella
  Toxemia
  Drug and alcohol abuse
  Exposure to radiation
  Poor nutrition
  Venereal diseases
  Multiple pregnancy
  Thyroid abnormalities
  Rh incompatibility

CHILD FACTORS
  Pre- and Post-maturity
  Low birth weight
  Complications during delivery
  Anoxia
  Seizures
  Meningitis and encephalitis
  Brain hemorrhage

ENVIRONMENTAL FACTORS
  Malnutrition
  Lead poisoning
  Severely limited sensory and response opportunities
  Impaired parent-child bonding

Environmental risk Often, children appear to be stable from a neuro-physiological standpoint but have impoverished environments which limit their ability to profit from important learning experiences. Poor nutrition and health care, child abuse, lack of stimulus and response opportunities, and poor mother-child interactions are the most prominent factors in this category of at-risk children, who suffer later developmental, educational, and psychiatric disorders. One approach to early diagnosis in these circumstances has been to assess the status of the home environment so that adjustments can be made. Caldwell (1970) developed the *Home Observation for Measurement of the Environment* (HOME) scale in order to evaluate the adequacy of such factors as emotional and verbal responsiveness of the mother, avoidance of restriction and punishment, organization of the environment, provision of appropriate play materials, maternal involvement with the child, and opportunities for daily stimulation. The adequacy of the child's early environment and adaptive behavior and intelligence at 3 years of age are highly related (Elardo, Bradley, and Caldwell, 1975).

The risk categories are not mutually exclusive but may occur in combination. For example, combined established and biological risk factors are often evident in children born into impoverished circumstances. Detailed knowledge of a variety of developmental risk factors enables specialists to organize the screening and identification process.

COMPREHENSIVE CHECK 5.3

Contrast established risk and biological risk in the screening of young children's problems.

Explain how environmental risk and biological risk factors can limit a child's developmental progress.

Implementing child-find procedures

Traditional early detection strategies tend to involve physician and agency referrals that result in the identification of young children with prominent disorders—the severely physically handicapped or retarded child. Yet, traditional methods are limited both in scope and precision. Because of time constraints and large client loads, physicians focus almost exclusively on physical development while ignoring or diminishing the importance of cognitive, language, and social dimensions. Thus, children with mild to moderate developmental/learning disabilities and behavior disorders often remain undetected (Meier, 1976).

As a practical alternative, many states have implemented community-based *child-find* procedures (Cross and Goin, 1977). Child-find or case-finding procedures are systematic activities within a community designed to locate handicapped or at-risk children for more detailed assessment and programming. These activities may include defining the sample of children to be studied, encouraging referrals from various community resources, media campaigns to increase community awareness, and door-to-door census-taking to register all children within the preschool age range.

The success of child-find efforts depends on the amount of interagency cooperation that is involved in the entire process of child-find-screen-assess programming (Kurtz and Laub, 1980; Zehrbach, 1975). Zehrbach (1975) recommends the use of a variety of information dissemination approaches for locating at-risk children. Mass mailings can be used to inform parents of the indicators of early developmental problems and the need for comprehensive screenings; follow-up telephone contacts to parents who did not respond can increase the yield from this approach. An open house or community health fair can be another child-locating source. Also, media campaigns can use radio and television spots, brochures, and announcements in local newspapers for substantially increasing the community's interest and cooperation in developmental screening. One of the most effective approaches is to send notices home with school-age children for parents to complete on their preschooler. In some settings, 40% to 60% of at-risk children were located using this simple method.

Conducting developmental screenings

Screening does not diagnose a condition, but rather it detects children who are *suspected* of having developmental difficulties. Screening sets the stage for more comprehensive assessment procedures that confirm or refute the screening results and that more precisely examine the child's needs.

Community roundups The concept of mass community screenings (i.e., roundups) has enjoyed increased popularity in recent years (Kurtz and Laub, 1978; Zehrbach, 1975). These screenings often take place in church basements, community recreation centers, or the meeting rooms of local shopping malls to screen groups of 700 to 1000 children over a 2-week period. Teams of well-trained developmental and educational specialists (e.g., teacher, speech/language therapist, psychologist, social worker) conduct the screenings, interview parents, or supervise the screenings of trained paraprofessionals (e.g., college students majoring in special education), in order to screen 50 to 100 children each day. In addition, certified state health agency workers are included to screen vision and hearing in a systematic manner to detect such difficulties as serious otitis media and various visual difficulties.

Once again, interagency cooperation in the community screening (e.g., Easter Seals, United Cerebral Palsy, Association for Retarded Children) is essential so that immediate follow-up for assessment and programming can become a reality.

Common developmental screening measures

The administration of developmental screening measures to individual children is the major event in the early-identification process. The child's ability to complete a variety of motivating "developmental milestones" or performance tasks helps to determine probable dysfunctions in development and learning. For this reason, care must be taken in selecting, administering, and interpreting developmental scales.

Various researchers have voiced cautions regarding the precision of available early-identification instruments (Gallagher and Bradley, 1972; Mercer, Algozzine, and Trifiletti, 1979). One major problem concerns the issue of false positives and false negatives in identifying handicapped children (see Table

5.2). False positives refer to patients identified as having developmental delays or deficits when in reality none exist. Similarly, false negatives refer to the failure to identify difficulties that really do exist. Mercer and coworkers (1979) acknowledge this problem in their review of 70 screening prediction outcome studies. An overall accuracy rate for all studies was between 70% and 90%. Multiple-instrument batteries showed greater predictive accuracy than did the use of single measures. The authors provide certain recommendations to increase the precision of individual child screenings:

1. Use multiple-scale batteries.

2. Select scales that are similar in content to the skills expected to be learned and taught in early-childhood programs.

3. Include physical indices, developmental histories, and socioeconomic status as essential screening information.

4. Emphasize teacher judgments of developmental readiness wherever possible.

5. Ensure follow-up services (i.e., assessment and programming) to defuse the issue of false positives and negatives.

Despite technical limitations, early-identification instruments and procedures allow earlier contact with children so that needed early treatment can be initiated. Early detection of atypical children is the essential first step in the treatment process (Frankenburg, 1977). Measures must be chosen that are rapid in administration, low-cost, objectively scored, reliable and valid, and acceptable to parents and professionals.

TABLE 5.2
**A Review of Child Performance-Prediction Outcomes
From Early Developmental Screenings**

| | | Performance on Criterion Measure | |
		Poor	Good
Prediction	Poor	Predicted to do poorly Performed poorly (valid positive) A	Predicted to do poorly Performed well (false positive) B
	Good	Predicted to do well Performed poorly (false negative) C	Predicted to do well Performed well (valid negative) D

Source: Mercer, C. D., Algozzine, B., and Trifiletti, J. J. (1979) Early identification: Issues and considerations. *Exceptional Children,* September 1979: 52–54. Reprinted with permission of the author and The Council for Exceptional Children.

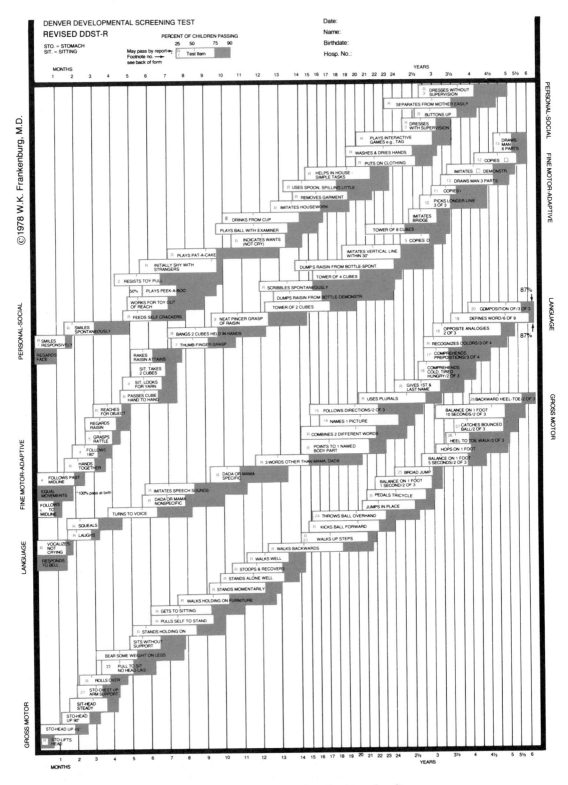

Test form from the *Denver Development Screening Test* (revised).
Source: Reprinted by permission from Denver Developmental Materials, Inc.

Many multidimensional screening tests are now available for early-childhood screenings. Frequently used instruments include the *Developmental Screening Inventory* (DSI) (Knoblock, Pasamanick, and Sherard, 1966), *Developmental Indicators for the Assessment of Learning* (DIAL) (Mardell and Goldenberg, 1972), *Boyd Developmental Progress Scale* (BDPS) (Boyd, 1974), *Comprehensive Assessment in Nursery School and Kindergarten: CIRCUS* (Educational Testing Service, 1974), *Denver Developmental Screening Test* (DDST) (Frankenburg, Dodds, and Fandal, 1975), and *Developmental Profile* (DP) (Alpern, Boll, and Shearer, 1981).

In addition, specialized screening instruments are available to detect specific developmental functions such as language and sensorimotor abilities. Examples include the *Receptive-Expressive Emergent Language* (REEL) scale (Bzoch and League, 1970) and the *Milani-Comparetti Motor Development Screening Test* (Milani-Comparetti, 1977).

The *Denver Developmental Screening Test* (DDST) is perhaps the most popular developmental screening measure. The DDST is administered to children between 1 and 60 months of age and surveys 107 landmark skills within four major developmental areas: fine motor-adaptive, gross motor, language, and personal-social. It was standardized on 1036 children and demonstrates adequate reliability and moderate predictive validity. The DDST identifies developmental delays signaling an "abnormal" performance requiring more detailed assessment.

Another frequently used multidimensional screening measure is the *Developmental Profile* (DP). The DP relies on a structured interview with

TABLE 5.3
The Communication Subscale from the Developmental Profile

COMMUNICATION DEVELOPMENTAL AGE SCALE
NEWBORN: 0–6 months
  1. Does the child use vocal noises for play? The child must *play* with sounds (not just cry or gurgle or laugh when something happens).

INFANT I: 7–12 months
  4. Does the child sometimes imitate spoken "words" such as "da-da" or "ma-ma?" The child may not know what these words mean.

INFANT II: 13–18 months
  8. Does the child say the names of at least five things (not in imitation and not including names of people)? The words must be said well enough to be understood by a stranger.

TODDLER I: 19–24 months
  12. Does the child put two or more words together to form sentences? "Me go," "You give," "Tom want," are all examples of passes. But, if the child *always* uses the same two words together (so that they are really one word to the child), that does not rate a pass.

TODDLER II: 25–30 months
  13. Does the child either repeat parts of nursery rhymes or join in when others say them?

Source: Alpern G. D., Boll, T. J., and Shearer, M. (1986) *The Developmental Profile II.* Copyright © 1972, 1980 by Psychological Development Publications. Copyright © 1985, 1986 by Western Psychological Services. Excerpted and reprinted by permission of the publisher, Western Psychological Services, 12031 Wilshire Boulevard, Los Angeles, California 90025.

parents and/or child observations to survey a child's range of developmental functioning. Normed on a sample of 3000 children between birth and 9 years of age, the DP covers 217 developmental tasks within five functional domains: physical, self-help, social, academic, and communication (see Table 5.3). Questions are clearly phrased in terms of "does" and "can" the child perform specific behaviors. Developmental age scores are derived for each domain, and the norm tables guide the interpretation of "developmental lags."

COMPREHENSION CHECK 5.4

What are "child-find" procedures?
Explain false negatives in the process of screening infants and preschool children.
Identify the most commonly used developmental screening test.

STAGE 2: DEVELOPMENTAL ASSESSMENT— CREATING PRESCRIPTIVE LINKAGES

Comprehensive developmental assessment is "a wide-ranging yet specific process of analyzing, describing, and profiling each child's range of developmental skills and deficits across multiple behavioral areas in order to determine levels of functioning and provide a basis for prescriptive developmental programming" (Neisworth, Willoughby-Herb, Bagnato, Cartwright, and Laub, 1980, p. 81). Developmental assessment "zooms in" with increased magnification of the problem areas detected during the screening process. This more precise assessment details the child's range of absent ($-$), emerging ($\pm$), and fully acquired ($+$) skills. This detailed developmental-behavioral analysis generates goal prescriptions to "link" into a program's curriculm. Also, the assessment precisely defines the degree and scope of the child's developmental dysfunctions in comparison with typical children of the same age. Variable profiles of different levels of performance in each developmental domain are generated for handicapped infants and preschool children through this diagnostic procedure.

Infant assessment: promoting early development (premature to 24 months)

The infant's limited behavioral repertoire, continuous state changes, and lack of self-regulatory abilities make assessment demanding. These same factors further complicate the assessment of infants displaying neurodevelopmental deficits.

Effect of infant behavior on assessment

The infant's partly innate behavioral style has been referred to as *temperament*. Such factors as distractibility, mood, activity level, persistence, intensity, and biological rhythms influence the infant's general style of interacting with events in his environment (Ulrey, 1982). Some infants are easily upset and difficult to console, whereas others are calm and adaptable. Infants with sensory and neurological dysfunctions have extreme difficulties in maintaining a steady temperamental state. The infant's *state* or level of arousal is related to and varies according to time of day and fatigue factors. Increases in the stability and regularity of both physiological and behavioral states (e.g., sleeping, feeding, attention, consolability, endurance) signal increasing levels of maturity. Infants show preferences for one type of activity involving a single *modality*. Repetitive or *perseverative play* with toys requiring repetitive visual and motor behaviors is also common. Similarly, the infant or handicapped preschooler often requires greater structure to maintain attention, motivation, and concentrated performance on a particular task. Finally, the effect of abrupt *separations* from mother for older infants, quick changes from task to task, and *unfamiliar environments* (i.e., people, settings, and stimuli) also influence behavior and need to be considered. The necessity for periodic, successive assessments of infants cannot be overstated given the fact that their behavior is so changeable. One-time assessment fails to provide a representative sample of the handicapped infant's capabilities. It is quite common for developmental specialists in an infant-stimulation or clinical-hospital setting to assess an infant daily at random times over a week's span.

The value of infant assessment

For handicapped infants, early intervention helps prevent the secondary complications (e.g., poor social responsiveness, poor object knowledge, self-stimulation, feeding and behavior disorders) that often accompany sensori-motor and neurological dysfunctions. Parent involvement on a continuous basis in early-intervention programs is essential. Early developmental assessment of infants establishes the "what" and "how" of infant-stimulation programs as it fulfills four major purposes (Brazelton, 1981), as described following.

Defines development Periodic assessments profile the unique dimensions of the infant's behavior. The infant's quality of performance, need to be aroused to optimal levels of behavior, and characteristic styles and rhythms in interaction all provide evidence of comparative functional levels and individual needs.

Enhances communication Conducting the assessment with the parents present establishes trust and builds a vehicle for communication about the infant. The infant's behavioral responses can be mutually observed and nonjudgmental descriptions can be given. Parents' feelings and reactions can be determined, and mutual goals can be set to promote the infant's future development. In the process, parent education, counseling, and infant stimulation are merged effectively and sensitively. "Having viewed it together (behavior), they would share a kind of communication about the baby. This kind of assessment would provide a window into the baby's performance, and by their reactions to it, uncover a window into the parent's feelings" (Brazelton, 1982, p. 6).

Evaluates progress   The assessment helps both the specialist and the parents to determine problems, current capabilities, and probable future courses to expect. Reassessments over a 3 to 6 month span document gains and highlight areas requiring more specialized help. Also, the assessment helps parents to learn about their developing infant and the child's special needs and also, to be more secure in their own judgments and styles of relating to their child.

Promotes learning   Each assessment session becomes a learning opportunity. Parents, particularly of infants with visual, auditory, and neuromotor impairments, will learn that they need to provide more distinct cues and to elicit behavior more actively from their infant. Abnormal posturing in the cerebral-palsied infant does not mean that he dislikes and rejects the mother but rather that a different manner of handling and positioning is required. Intervention-based assessment makes these insights and adjustments possible.

Four approaches to infant assessment

A variety of approaches and methods have emerged over the years for discovering the competencies of handicapped infants. Brief reviews of selected instruments that reflect each major approach will illustrate differences in both the content and the process of infant assessment.

Developmental task model   The Bayley Scales of Infant Development (BSID) (Bayley, 1969) and the Gesell Developmental Schedules (GDS) (Knobloch and Pasmanick, 1974) are the most prominent examples of the neuromotor or developmental task assessment approach. The BSID is the most technically adequate of the traditional developmental scales. It surveys the 2 to 30-month age range through 244 separate tasks and behavioral dimensions.

TABLE 5.4
Illustrated Sequence of Cube Tasks from the Bayley Scales of Infant Development (1969)

Item	Age and Range	Item Description
32T	2.5 (1–5)	Regards cube
49	4.1 (2–6)	Reaches for cube
51	4.4 (2–6)	Eye-hand coordination in reaching
54	4.6 (3–7)	Picks up cube
56	4.7 (3–7)	Retains two cubes

Source: Adapted from Bayley, N. (1969). *Manual for the Bayley scales of infant development.* New York: Psychological Corporation.

The mental and motor scales provide the framework for the sequenced developmental activities that emphasize the infant's fine-gross motor skills and visual-auditory responses (see Table 5.4). Language, cognitive, and social items are also assessed. The BSID was normed on 1,262 infants in a sample representative of the United States. Through "developmental quotients" (i.e., ratio of chronological age to developmental age) and developmental ages and ranges, the BSID defines the infant's status and degree of dysfunction by comparisons with normal infant expectancies.

Developmental process model   *The Infant Psychological Development Scale* (IPDS) (Uzgiris and Hunt, 1975) was designed for *qualitatively* assessing the infant's progression through Piaget's initial sensorimotor stage (i.e., approximately birth to 24 months). The scales are unnormed but provide specific problem-solving situations for the infant (see Table 5.5). Six scales form the structure of the IPDS:

1. Visual pursuit and object permanence

2. Means for obtaining desired events

3. Vocal and gestural imitation

4. Operational causality

5. Object relations in space

6. Schemes for relating objects

Performance on the scales provides evidence of the child's emerging ability to influence events as well as to understand the properties of objects. Although the IPDS does not offer specific scores regarding developmental delays, it does provide a logical sequence for planning stimulation activities.

Neurological model   Normal infants are born with a variety of readily observable primitive reflexes that result from the influence of "old brain" centers on neurophysiological functioning (e.g., brain stem, cerebellum, midbrain, basal ganglia). As development progresses, the "new brain" (i.e., cerebral cortex) takes on an inhibitory role by suppressing primitive reflexes and aiding the development of more functional motor behaviors. When children experience brain damage (e.g., as a result of cerebral palsy, head trauma, prematurity), this inhibitory system is disrupted and primitive reflexes reemerge. Thus, primitive reflexes are normal for the newborn but indicative of neurological dysfunction for older infants. Assessment techniques use these primitive reflexes as "neurodevelopmental markers" for cerebral dysfunction and neuromotor impairment (Capute et al., 1978; Dubowitz et al., 1970).

Interactive model   Greater emphasis is being placed on assessing the reciprocal interactions that occur naturally between the infant and people and events. The Brazelton Neonatal Behavioral Assessment Scale (BNBAS) (Brazelton, 1973) for premature infants and newborns represents the best of the "interactive" scales. The measures are based on the premise that one of the infant's critical developmental tasks is to learn to regulate, organize, and

TABLE 5.5
Infant Psychological Development Scale (IPDS)

SCALE I: THE DEVELOPMENT OF VISUAL PURSUIT AND THE
        PERMANENCE OF OBJECTS
Item 3: Finding an object which is partially covered

Location:	The infant must be in a sitting position with both hands free to manipulate objects. A young infant may be propped up in an infant seat or on a sofa using pillows. An older infant may be seated in a high chair or on a rug on the floor. A working surface must be available in front of and to the side of the infant; it may be provided by placing a board across the infant seat, by pushing the high chair against a table, or by using the rug-covered space around the infant, if he is sitting on the floor. An infant feeding table is also suitable.
Object:	Any object that the infant demonstrates interest in by reaching for it; and, for a cover or screen, a white nontransparent scarf. It is important that the object be unitary and that no portion of the object should look equivalent to the whole. A plastic doll or animal may be used, but an object such as a necklace would be unsuitable. Use of a white nontransparent scarf helps to minimize the interest of the infants in the screen.
Directions:	To ascertain that an infant desires the object, place it on the surface and observe that the infant reaches for it. Take the object, while making sure the infant is focusing on it, place it on the surface within his reach, and cover it with the screen in such a way that a small portion of the object remains visible (the feet of the doll, the tail of the animal, etc.). If, in his attempts to obtain the object, the infant covers it up completely, start a new presentation. If the infant's interest in the object becomes doubtful, interpose a presentation in which the object is left uncovered on the surface to determine if he will still reach for it.
Repeat:	3 times
Infant : Actions	a. Loses interest in the object once it is partly covered.
	b. Reacts to the loss of the object, but does not reach for it and does not obtain it once it is partly covered.
	c. Obtains object by pulling it out from under the screen or by removing the screen and picking up the object.

Source: Uzgiris, I., and Hunt, J. (1975). *Assessment in Infancy: Ordinal scales of psychological development.* Champaign: University of Illinois Press, 1975. Reprinted with permission.

modulate various states and behaviors. *State control* is viewed as an indicator of both developmental maturity and central nervous system integrity. The tasks on the scale also assess the infant's ability to *screen out* auditory, visual, and tactile stimulation during sleep or drowsiness. The ability to *habituate* quickly to repeated stimulation signals an intact system. Again, one of the major features of the BNBAS is the *analysis of interactive behavior.* Such tasks as visual focusing and tracking of people and objects, responses to sounds, and attention and search behaviors are included in this array (see Table 5.6). The scale shows promise both in predicting later developmental status and in clinical use as a parent-infant intervention tool.

Risk indicators for infants and young children

Comprehensive developmental assessment also requires that attention be directed toward specific physical, behavioral, and historical factors that could signal neurodevelopmental abnormalities. This brief summary is not intend-

TABLE 5.6
Summary of the types of behavioral processes sampled by the Brazelton Neonatal Behavioral Assessment Scale (BNBAS)*

Process	Description
Habituation	Decreased responsivity to repeated auditory, visual, and tactile stimuli over trials.
Orientation	Attention, alertness, response to people and objects within the child's visual and/or auditory field.
Motor	Muscle tone, neuromotor skill, and activity level.
State Variation	Changeability and intensity of behavior and temperament.
State Regulation	Capability to modulate behavior and temperament, to become calm and console.
Autonomic Stability	Physiological state indicated by changeability of skin color, startle response, tremors.
Other	Ability to sustain interaction with people and objects; several additional characteristics.

The revised BNBAS includes a total of 37 items that can be grouped as above.

*The Brazelton Neonatal Behavioral Assessment Scale (CDM 88). London: Spastics International Medical Publications.

ed to be inclusive but to highlight "markers" that can be indicative of difficulties.

Significant indicators of neurological dysfunction include such behaviors as abnormal alertness, movement disorders, abnormal crying, muscle-tone disorders, and dysfunctions in body axis and positioning (Dargassies, 1977). Infants judged to be at-risk for later difficulties exhibit poor attention and lack of alertness, overreaction to stimulation, fanning of the toes, hyper- or hypoactivity, poor muscle tone in arms and legs, and high-pitched crying.

A variety of events in the child's developmental history are important to consider. Such events include cerebral trauma (e.g., encephalitis, meningitis, head injury), problems with labor and delivery, respiratory distress, prematurity, and/or low birth weight.

Finally, Martin (1982) has discussed behavioral indicators of possible cerebral dysfunction that can be observed during the assessment of infants and young children. These behavioral signs involve early hand preference, poor coordination, suspected seizure activity, hand tremors, poor motor planning, poor visual-motor skills in writing and drawing, problems in auditory discrimination, speech and oral-motor difficulties, involuntary movements of the extremities, poor attention, impulsivity, distractibility, and perseveration.

COMPREHENSION CHECK 5.5

Give one example of how an infant's temperament can adversely influence behavior during assessment.

Explain how the Brazelton neonatal scale reflects the interactive model of infant assessment.

Early-childhood assessment: prescribing preschool programs (24 to 72 months)

Developmental and psychological assessment of handicapped preschoolers (i.e., ages 2 to 6) requires both a conceptual understanding of early-childhood development and a flexible, creative approach to diagnosis. A variety of variables influence the preschooler's ability to complete problem-solving tasks and, thus, to demonstrate a range of skills. Such issues as the child's rapidly changing styles of thinking and perceiving, language development and self-regulation, integration of related abilities, and social responsiveness must be considered in diagnosis. Similarly, comprehensive assessment of exceptional preschoolers necessitates a team approach to diagnosis that results in multiple strategies for developmental programming and treatment.

The effect of preschool behavior patterns on assessment

Young children make rapid changes in their abilities to perceive events and to reason. The emergence of language and the capacity to mentally visualize and remember events marks a major change from earlier motorbound immediate sensory experience and learning. Yet, the preschooler is said to have an "egocentric perspective"; that is, can consider situations from only a personal vantage point. Difficulties in understanding and complying with rules, and limits and even with reinforcement and praise are common. In addition, the preschooler is often distractible and impulsive and lacks the behavioral controls and sophisticated use of language to direct and limit his behavior. Thus, clinicians have to provide the external structure and controls in order to guide attention, motivation, and performance. Similarly, the preschooler's mood and behavior are often erratic and changeable. Accurate appraisals of skills and behavior require observations of the child in different situations with different people. Also, the child's ability to develop the capacity to relate socially to peers and adults must be judged as well as must cooperative play patterns in sharing and reciprocal games. Highly changeable mood states and negative and oppositional behavior are common and must be worked through.

Designing multidimensional assessment batteries

Diagnostic specialists on interdisciplinary teams are often frustrated by the challenging problems of selecting appropriate measures. Early-childhood specialists have attempted to resolve problems in developmental diagnosis by emphasizing team assessment batteries consisting of several scales designed to tap different aspects of child functioning. In general, two kinds of scales, according to how child information is derived, are combined in the team assessment battery: (1) *clinical judgment measures* (i.e., those that use the subjective, "gut-level" impressions and observations of team members), and (2) *child performance measures* (i.e., those that use the child's actual, elicited behaviors). The team assessment approach allows specialists to collect more accurate, descriptive, and broad-range diagnostic information. The different types of scales provide the handicapped child with alternative opportunities for circumventing sensorimotor disabilities. Table 5.7 illustrates one example of a team diagnostic battery for a 2-year-old handicapped child that integrates various types of measures (more fully discussed in the next section).

COMPREHENSION CHECK 5.6

Contrast clinical judgment and child performance measures for the assessment of exceptional preschoolers.

Who are the primary specialists most often found on community- based interdisciplinary teams working with young exceptional children?

Review of preschool scales

Prescribing preschool programs is the goal of early-childhood assessment. However, disagreement often arises regarding the most effective approach for achieving this objective. Several approaches are employed: norm-referenced, curriculum-referenced, and adaptive process (see Bagnato and Neisworth, 1981; Paget and Bracken, 1982; Simeonsson, 1977; Ulrey and Rogers, 1982).

Norm-referenced methods: comparative diagnosis Norm-referenced assessment (NRA) refers to measures designed to compare a child's skills and abilities with those of a "reference group" comparable in such aspects as age and socioeconomic status. Diagnostic analysis with NRA measures results in

TABLE 5.7
Team Developmental Diagnostic Battery for a Young Multihandicapped Child: Child Performance and Clinical Judgment Measures

Measure	Age Range	Type	Domain	Source
Bayley Scales of Infant Development (BSID)	2 to 30 months	Norm	Cognitive-motor	Child performance assessment
Early Intervention Developmental Profile (EIDP)	0 to 72 months	Adaptive curricular	Cognitive Language Perceptual-fine motor Socioemotional Gross motor Self-care	Team/child performance assessment
Callier-Azusa Scale for Deaf/Blind Children (CAS)	0 to 98 months	Adaptive	Socialization Daily living skills Motor development Perceptual abilities Language development	Parent-teacher skill judgment ratings
Carolina Record of Individual Behavior (CRIB)	Developmental Phases	Adaptive	State Social orientation Participation Motivation Endurance Communication Object orientation Consolability Activity Reactivity Frustration Attention Response contact Habit patterns	Parent-team behavior judgment ratings

scores that gauge the child's functional levels (e.g., mental age, developmental age, IQ, DQ, percentiles) in the several developmental areas. For example, Sammy is a 4-year-old cerebral-palsied child who displays knowledge and abilities that are typical of 2-year-old children; thus, he would be judged to be currently functioning at a rate that is one-half the rate expected given his chronological age. With a DQ (developmental quotient) of 100 considered average, his rate would be 50 [i.e., 24 months (DA) /48 months (CA)].

NRA is important in the process of determining levels of skill development; but used alone, it provides only general information for the initial phase of curriculum planning. Items within NRA instruments can often be matched to curricular objectives so that the relevance of these scales for planning is greatly enhanced (Bagnato, 1981). However, caution should be used with these scales because their activities often are inappropriate and unnecessarily limiting for children with certain impairments, and no handicapped children like them are included in the standardization reference group. (Adaptive procedures help to resolve this problem, as soon to be discussed.)

One example of a norm-based developmental scale is the *Gesell Developmental Schedules* (GDS) (Knobloch and Pasamanick, 1974), on which all other traditional developmental scales have been modeled. The GDS surveys the 1- to 72-month age range, analyzing functional skills across motor, adaptive (cognitive), language, and personal-social areas (see Figure 5.2).

Curriculum-referenced methods: skill-mastery diagnosis   Curriculum-based assessment measures the child's progress in learning by determining his initial level of functioning and skill development, setting goals or criteria to guide teaching that are based on initial skills, then teaching the unlearned skills toward mastery, and, finally, reevaluating the child to document evidence of behavior change and learning. Because of this procedure, curriculum-referenced assessment (CRA) has been referred to as the "test-teach-test" model. CRA scales survey precise, task-analyzed sequences of developmental skills whereas NRA scales assess a much more limited range of functional skills. Often, teachers prefer CRA because it more accurately measures child progress on actual program (curricular) objectives. Usually, NRA instruments contain developmental landmarks but not necessarily the specific objectives of a particular program.

The *Learning Accomplishment Profile-Diagnostic Edition* (LAP-D) (LeMay, Griffin, and Sanford, 1978) is a frequently used criterion-referenced developmental curriculum for handicapped preschoolers, covering the birth to 6-year age range. It assesses detailed sequences of developmental skills across five major functional tracts: fine motor, gross motor, language, cognition, and self-help. These five areas are then further subdivided into more precise subareas (e.g., writing, matching, comprehension, counting, manipulation) (see Figure 5.3). Diagnostic teaching is guided by the accompanying materials and instructional strategies. The LAP-D is a practical diagnostic (CRA) and program package.

Adaptive-process methods: functional diagnosis   Adaptive-process assessment (APA) incorporates features of NRA and CRA, but it is distinctive in that it stresses that systematic modifications in materials, response

Figure 5.2 An Illustration of Skill Analysis from GDS

Gesell Developmental Schedules

Age	Motor	Adaptive	Language	Personal-Social
2	Walks: runs well, no falling Stairs: walks up and down alone Large ball: (no dem.) kicks Cubes: tower of 6–7 Book: turns pages singly	Cubes: tower of 6–7 Drawing: imitates V stroke Formboard: places blocks on separately (G) Formboard: adapts after 4 trials Color Forms: does not identify any	Speech: jargon discarded Speech: 3 word sentence Speech: uses *I, me, you* Picture Vocabulary: 2+ correct	Toilet: may be verbalize needs fairly consistently Play: domestic mimicry Play: hands cup full of cubes Play: parallel play predominates Feeding: inhibits turning spoon Dressing: pulls on simple garmet Commun: verbalizes immed. experiences Commun: refers to self by name Comm: comprehends & asks for "another" Temperament: gentle, easy
2½	Stands: tries, on 1 foot Cubes: tower of 10 Drawing: holds crayon by fingers	Cubes: tower of 10 Cubes: aligns 2 or more, train Drawing: imitates V & H strokes Drawing: scribbles to circular stroke Inc. Man: adds 1 part Formboard: inserts 3 blocks on presentation Formboard: adapts repeatedly, error Color Forms: places 1	Interview: gives first name Interview: tells sex (G) Prepositions: obeys 1–2 Picture Vocab: 7 correct Action Agent: 3 correct	Play: pushes toy with good steering Play: helps put things away Commun: refers to self by pronoun "me" rather than by name Commun: repetition in speech and other activity Self help: can put on own coat (not necessarily fasten) Temperament: opposite extremes
3	Walks on tiptoe, 2 or more steps Stands on 1 foot, momentary balance Skips: tries Rides tricycle using pedals Stairs: alternates feet going up Jumps down: lands on feet (1) Broad jump: distance 12" Pellets: 10 into bottle in 26" (G); 24" (B)	Cubes: adds chimmey to train Cubes: imitates bridge Copy Forms: copies circle Copy Forms: imitates cross Inc. Man: adds 3 parts Formboard: adapts, no errors or immediate correction of error Color Forms: places 3 Counts with correct pointing: 3 objs. Pellets: 10 into bottle in 26" (G); 24" (B)	Speech: uses plurals Interview: tells age (G) Interview: tells sex (B) Prepositions: obeys 3 Digits: repeats 3 (1 to 3 trials) Picture Vocab: 11 correct Comprehension Question A: answers 1 Action Agent: 6–7 correct Picture Vocab.: 11 correct	Feeding: feeds self, little spilling Feeding: pours well from pitcher Dressing: puts on shoes Dressing: unbuttons front and side buttons Commun: asks questions rhetorically Commun: understands taking turns Commun: knows a few rhymes Temperament: cooperative

Source: Ames, L. B., Gillespie, C., Haines, J., and Illg, F. (1980). *Gesell developmental schedules* (Revised). Lumberville, PA: Gesell Institute for Human Developmental Programs for Education. Reprinted with permission.

Figure 5.3
A Subdomain Scale from the *LAP-D* Developmental Curriculum

Language/Cognitive: Naming

Developmental Age	Item	Behavior	1st +/-	2nd +/-	Comments
15	LN1	Imitates names			
15	LN2	Names 3 objects			
24	LN3	Names 3 body parts			
24	LN4	Names 3 pictures			
30	LN5	Names 6 body parts			
33	LN6	Names use of objects			
36	LN7	Names objects by use			
42	LN8	Names 3 actions			
42	LN9	Names 10 objects			
48	LN10	Names missing part			
48	LN11	Names 8 actions			
54	LN12	Names 18 objects			
54	LN13	Names activities recently performed			
54	LN14	Names cause of event			
54	LN15	Names consequence of action			

Figure 5.3

Language/Cognitive: Naming (cont'd)

Developmental Age	Item	Behavior	1st +/−	2nd +/−	Comments
54	LN16	Names activities he might soon perform			
60	LN17	Names differences among pictures			
60	LN18	Names picture removed from group			
66	LN19	Names source of actions			
66	LN20	Names who, what, where, why of story			
66	LN21	Names things needed for activity			
66	LN22	Names parts of items			
72	LN23	Uses analogies			
72	LN24	Names materials objects are made of			
72	LN25	Names opposites			
72	LN26	Names numerals/letters			
72	LN27	Names items in category			
72	LN28	Names category			
72 +	LN29	Names printed words			

Last Item Administered

Less Errors

Naming Score

Source:
LeMay, D. W., Griffin, P. M., and Sanford, A. R. (1978). *Learning accomplishment profile: Diagnostic edition* (Revised). Winston-Salem, NC: Kaplan School Supply. Reprinted with permission.

modes, and methods of presenting information to young multihandicapped children must be designed so that their "true" capabilities can be determined. The techniques of Dubose et al. (1979) and Haeussermann (1958) are most representative of this method. In this approach, diagnosis involves functionally evaluating the upper and lower limits of the child's ability to understand and complete problem-solving tasks. Then, adaptive modifications are introduced systematically to circumvent the child's disabilities (see Table 5.8). For example, handles are added to puzzle shapes for the cerebral-palsied preschooler; concrete objects or toys replace pictured objects; eye localization or flashlight head pointers replace gestures or language for the nonverbal, motorically handicapped child; and auditory and tactile cues are used to guide reaching for the visually impaired preschooler. With these modifications, it is determined whether a child actually understands a concept but cannot demonstrate knowledge because of disabilities or, rather, whether the disabilities have disrupted the opportunity to profit from critical learning experiences. Through this adaptive diagnostic-teaching "process," children gradually acquire skills and learn more functional behaviors (e.g., attention, orientation to a task, alternative forms of communication). The primary outcome is to suggest changes in the instructional environment.

APA not only involves the child's actual performance on structured learning tasks, but also systematic clinical observations of how different aspects of behavior change over time. These clinical judgments based on naturalistic

TABLE 5.8
An Example of Adaptive Modifications for Handicapped Preschoolers

*CHILD WILL FIND AN OBJECT HIDDEN UNDER ONE
OF THREE CONTAINERS ON THE FIRST ATTEMPT. OBJECT PERMANENCE*

Activities

  1. *Position the child so he can watch you hide a piece of cereal under one of three coffee cups that are turned upside down and lined up in a row. When he finds it, let him eat it.*

  2. *Move the hiding place to second cup. Draw child's attention to the place where you hid it. Initially, child will search under the first hiding place. Help him to look under appropriate cup.*

  3. *Continue to play the game until child goes immediately to correct hiding place.*

  4. *Now hide the item by pretending to place it under the first cup, then move it under the second cup, and then under the third cup, keeping the item visible between the placements. Leave it under the last one and encourage the child to find it. Repeat the game by hiding the item under the cups in a different order.*

  5. *Hide the item under one of the cups and then move that cup to a new location. Help the child find the hidden item.*

  Hearing Impaired: NC

  Motorically Involved: Spread cups farther apart. Have the child just look at the cup under which the object is hidden if he cannot remove cup himself. Then give him cereal to reinforce his successes.

  Visually Impaired: Encourage the child to search for and find noisemakers when they are sounded and then put in different locations within reaching distance.

Table 5.8 (cont'd)

CHILD WILL PLACE THREE SHAPES (ROUND, SQUARE, TRIANGLE)
CORRECTLY IN A FORMBOARD.   *FORM DISCRIMINATION*

Activities

1. Cut a circle and a square out of the center of a piece of heavy cardboard. Encourage him to feel the outline of each form and cut out with his fingers. Talk to him saying. *This one is round. This one is square. That one fits!* or, *No, not that one.* Show him how to place the pieces back into the cardboard. Encourage the child to imitate.

2. Make another puzzle, cutting out three pieces (circle, square, and triangle). Show him how to place the pieces in the appropriate holes and encourage imitation.

3. Allow the child to practice until he can place all three forms into the correct holes without assistance.

4. Remove pieces from puzzle and rotate form board so that the child must place pieces on the opposite side.

Note: Commercial wooden formboards are available, as well as a variety of shape discrimination toys.

Hearing Impaired: *MA*

Motorically Involved: *Begin activity by using materials which are easy to hold. If the child does not have enough fine motor control, encourage him to eye point to the appropriate holes.*

Visually Impaired: *Make several formboards using different textured materials (large flat sponges, sandpaper, plywood). Paint the puzzle background a highly contrasting color. Encourage the child to run his fingertips around the shapes and cut out spaces, and then match them.*

Source: Schaefer, D. S., and Moersch, M. D. *Developmental programming for infants and young children: Stimulation activities* (Vol. 3). (1981). Ann Arbor: University of Michigan Press. Reprinted with permission. Copyright © The University of Michigan, 1981.

observations can be important for understanding and programming for the severely disabled preschooler. *The Carolina Record of Individual Behavior* (CRIB) (Simeonsson et al., 1982) is one such measure that samples such emerging behavioral dimensions as attention, persistence, activity level, frustration, communication, social orientation, goal-directed behavior, and atypical habit patterns (e.g., head banging, rumination, rocking) (see Table 5.9).

Table 5.10 presents a comparison of selected preschool scales valuable to developmental programming for handicapped preschoolers.

COMPREHENSION CHECK 5.7

Explain the differences between norm-referenced and curriculum-referenced assessment methods.

What is the "test-teach-test" model of developmental assessment?

Explain why adaptive-process assessment methods are referred to as *functional diagnosis.*

TABLE 5.9
Sample Behavior Processes from the *CRIB*

OBJECT ORIENTATION

A7 Responsiveness to objects, toys, or test materials: Score behavior that is spontaneous rather than in direct response to demonstration or elicitation.

Rating

1 Does not look at, show interest and/or seem aware of objects.

2 Looks at and/or turns toward only if object attracts attention, e.g., makes noise, flashes light, etc. (high stimulus items only).

3 When presented with materials, turns to or looks at briefly but does not attempt to approach, reach for, or manipulate any object.

4 Sustained interest in objects as they are presented, e.g., turns to, looks at, smiles at, etc.

5 Does attempt to approach or manipulate objects: uses in same manner regardless of form of function, e.g., bangs all objects, mouths all objects.

6 Reaches for and manipulates objects in a variety of exploratory ways—holding, feeling, visual examination, shaking, etc.

7 Manipulates object with some regard to form (e.g., puts block in cup, peers into box, sticks finger in hole, etc.).

8 Manipulates object with appropriate regard to form or function (eg., rocks doll, pushes car, stacks blocks).

9 Plays imaginatively with materials, uses objects several ways.

REACTIVITY

B2 The ease with which the child is stimulated to react in general; his *sensitivity* or *excitability;* reactivity may be positive or negative

Rating

1 Only responds to physically intrusive and/or aversive stimuli, e.g., sudden change of position, pin prick, ice.

2 Reactive to strong and repeated non-intrusive stimulation, e.g., loud noises, bright lights. Doesn't habituate.

3 Periodic reaction to strong stimulation: Habituates rapidly.

4 Some tendency to be underreactive to usual testing stimuli and/or changes in environment.

5 Shows appropriate awareness to usual testing stimuli and/or changes in environment.

6 Some tendency to be overreactive to changes in environment and/or testing stimuli.

7 Overreactive to changes in immediate environment; alerts, startles.

8 Overreactive to selected stimuli enough to cry and/or withdraw, e.g., noises, lights, people.

9 Very reactive—every little thing causes child to startle, cry, and/or withdraw: reacts quickly.

Source: Simeonsson, R. (1981). *Carolina record of individual behavior: Experimental version.* Chapel Hill: University of North Carolina. Reprinted with permission.

TABLE 5.10
Comparing Preschool Assessment Methods that Guide Special Intervention

Norm-based Scales	Curriculum-based Scales	Adaptive-process Scales
Pictorial Test of Intelligence (PTI) (French, 1964)	*Early Intervention Developmental Profile (EIDP)* Schaefer and Moersch, 1981)	*Haeussermann Educational Evaluation (HEE)* (1958)
Ages 3 to 8 Six cognitive subscales Appropriate for physically handicapped children	Ages 0 to 6 Six developmental processes Team assessments Adaptations for handicaps	Ages 2 to 6 Developmental abilities Standard adaptations Strategies for cerebral palsy and response deficits
Hiskey-Nebraska Test of Learning Aptitude (HNTLA) (Hiskey, 1966)	*Project Vision-Up* (Croft and Robinson, 1976)	*Developmental Activities Screening Inventory (DASI)* (Dubose, 1979)
Ages 3 to 18 Twelve cognitive subscales Pantomine instructions Hearing and deaf norms	Ages 0 to 6 Six developmental processes Adaptations for visual impairments	Ages 6 to 60 months Developmental Teaching strategies Visual-auditory modifications

TABLE 5.10
Comparing Preschool Assessment Methods
that Guide Special Intervention *(cont'd)*

Norm-based Scales	Curriculum-based Scales	Adaptive-process Scales
Leiter International Performance Scale (LIPS) (Leiter, 1969)	*Uniform Performance Assessment System (UPAS)* (Haring et al., 1982)	*Callier-Azusa Deaf/Blind Scale* (Stillman, 1974)
Ages 2 to 18 Unrelated cognitive tasks Nonverbal matching response Deaf and language impaired	Ages 0 to 6 Five developmental and behavioral processes Task-analytic-behavioral Severe disabilities	Ages 0 to 9 Five developmental processes Observational judgments Behavioral
McCarthy Scales of Children's Abilities (MSCA) (McCarthy, 1972)	*HICOMP Preschool Curriculum* (Neisworth and Willoughby-Herb, 1982)	*BRIACC Autism Rating Scale* (Ruttenburg, 1977)
Ages 2½ to 8½ Verbal, memory, perceptual-motor, quantitative scales Highly motivating Learning disabilities	Ages 0 to 6 Five developmental processes Behavior strategies Normalized sequences	Ages 3 to 5 Seven behavioral scales Social and communication focus Diagnostic observations

Figure 5.4
A Sample Developmental Linkage Using the *GDS* and *HICOMP* Instruments

Child	Andy	Date	76-9-21
	Gesell Developmental Schedules	CA	43 months

PERFORMANCE CEILINGS	LINK #	CURRICULUM TARGET OBJECTIVES
DA = 9–12 Months	COMMUNICATION	
Orients to sounds consistently	C1-5.2	Head turn to sounds
Eye contact with speaker	C1-5.3	Gaze at speaker
Consistently repeats syllables	C1-1.8	Repeats syllables over/over
Gives objects on request	C1-3.9	Responds to request
Identifies objects when named	C2-3.1	"Show me the . . ."
Looks selectively at pictures	C1-5.6	Looks at pictures in book
Responds to name	C1-3.7	Responds with recognition to name
Imitates common words	C1-4.4	Imitates familiar words
Speaks 3 or 4 words	C2-2.4	Uses words in speech
Follows 1-level commands	C2-3.3	Follows simple commands
DA = 12 Months	OWN-CARE	
Reacts consistently to mirror image	01-1.7/.8	Smiles at mirror and reaches
Cooperates in dressing	02-5.1/.8	Helps—pants and limb in armhole
Cooperates in toileting	02-5.8	Helps push down-pull up pants
Indicates wet pants	02-2.5/.12	Indicates wet pants and need
Toliet/partial regulation	02-2.15	Attempts bowel/bladder control
Eats with spoon—spilling little	02-4.15	Spoon—food to mouth/no spilling
Drinks from cup—no spilling	02-4.9	Drinks from cup—unassisted
Cooperates in washing hands	02-2.3	Tries to wash hands
DA = 18(18–21) Months	MOTOR	
Kicks large ball	M2-1.12	Kicks large ball (stationary)
Stairs/updown—holds rail	M2-1.11	Stairs up/down—holds rail
Jumps both feet	M2-1.13	Jumps off floor/both feet
Attempts cube tower	M2-2.1	Stacks two cubes
Formboard/places circle	M3-2.9	Places round object in round hole

Figure 5.4 *(cont'd)*

Child Andy	Date	76-9-21
Gesell Developmental Schedules	CA	43 months

Imitates horizontal/vertical stroke M2-2.8		Imitates vertical stroke
DA = 11–15 Months	PROBLEM-SOLVING	
Finds hidden objects	P1-3.13/.14	Finds hidden object
Responds to directions "Look at me"	P2-1.1	"Look at me"
Attends to verbalizations	P2-1.6	Attends to verbalizations
Goes to correct location	P2-3.4	Goes where told
"Show me the . . ."	P2-4.2	"Show me the . . ."

Developmental linkages

As the developmental diagnostic-prescriptive model stresses, the purpose of comprehensive developmental assessment is to establish "developmental linkages" (i.e., individual instructional goals that will determine entry points for developmental programming and curriculum planning). Within the assessment process, a detailed profile of each infant's or preschooler's strengths (+), deficits (−), transitional or emerging abilities (±), and adaptive learning needs emerges. Because both developmental scales and developmental curricula have a common structural framework—the developmental task-analytic sequence—many linkages can be constructed between the child's performances on specific types of assessment tasks and initial activities within the sequence of curriculum tasks. This system of developmental assessment/curriculum linkages has been more fully explained by Bagnato and Neisworth (1981) and is briefly illustrated in Figure 5.4. Moreover, Bagnato (1981), in a study with 48 early childhood special education teachers, demonstrated that children's performances on the Gesell Developmental Schedules could be reliably matched with curriculum goals in both the *HICOMP Preschool Curriculum* and the *Memphis Comprehensive Developmental Curriculum*. Preschool teachers mutually agreed 87% of the time in linking assessment and curriculum tasks to form initial individualized instructional plans for a sample child while using a special "translated" diagnostic assessment report.

This general linkage procedure is supported also by other similar goal-planning methods. Schaefer and Moersch (1981) have recommended a procedure of planning stimulation activities within their infant curriculum, *Developmental Programming for Infants and Young Children*, based on levels of performance on their comprehensive scale, the *Early Intervention Developmental Profile* (EIDP). This system of matching assessment levels with stimulation processes is illustrated in Table 5.11.

TABLE 5.11
A Modified Sample of Matching Assessment Tasks and Stimulation Activities on the *EIDP*

±	Assessment Tasks	Cognitive Domain (9–18) mo.)	Instructional Processes
±	Finds completely hidden toy	Goal:	Child finds hidden toys and objects
±	Understands toy behind screen	Process:	Object constancy
±	Anticipates actions and events	Activity:	1. Hide cookie under one of three bowls in a row; child eats cookie if locates it after watching you.
±	Uses stick to retrieve distant object		
−	Understands cause-effect relationships		2. Change location to third bowl. Child searches and finds.
±	Imitates sounds and motions		
			3. Continue until child finds cookie consistently.
		Adaptive:	*Note:* For the *visually-impaired child,* prompt him to explore materials in front of him and find buzzers, bells, and clickers placed in different locations around his body when seated.

Source: Adapted from Schaefer, D. S., and Moersch, M. D. *Developmental programming for infants and young children: Stimulation activities* (Vol. 3). (1981). Ann Arbor: University of Michigan Press. Reprinted with permission. Copyright © The University of Michigan, 1981.

Meier (1976) suggested a practical format of sequencing developmental tasks from traditional scales such as the Bayley scales or Gesell schedules to form a task analysis of important infant behaviors to be stressed in programming. Thus, the traditional assessment scales were viewed as an important "profile and base for curriculum planning" (p. 190).

Any linkage procedure serves to provide the assessment process with *tangible* results. Based on the child's individual performance, specific instructional goals (i.e., curriculum entry points) are pinpointed. These entry points indicate levels at which developmental programming can begin. With these goals, the early special education teacher can then further define the child's adaptive learning needs through diagnostic teaching, and more detailed intervention plans can be formulated.

COMPREHENSION CHECK 5.8

What is the importance of making sure that assessment and treatment are closely connected in serving your exceptional children?

STAGE 3: DEVELOPMENTAL PROGRAMMING— DESIGNING INTERVENTIONS

Once a young child's developmental problems have been assessed, then the preschooler needs to be enrolled in some type of early intervention program sponsored by any of various community agencies (e.g., Head Start, United Cerebral Palsy, Easter Seals, public school special education programs). With enrollment in a program, developmental programming can begin. The third stage in the developmental diagnostic-prescriptive model involves a process of diagnostic teaching in which a child's adaptive learning needs are more precisely determined. The result is the design of an individualized program of instructional strategies, materials, and settings that will facilitate developmental progress. Simply, developmental specialists design tailor-made treatments for young exceptional children—the *Individualized Educational Program* (IEP).

Pinpointing developmental learning needs

Precision diagnostic teaching pinpoints a child's adaptive learning needs to guide developmental programming and intervention. It is a procedure that, like the adaptive-process assessment approach, blends diagnosis and intervention.

When children suffer visual impairments, hearing impairments, and/or neuromotor disabilities, various modifications must be made in the instructional process to set the conditions for developmental progress and learning. These adaptive modifications may involve any one or a combination of the following strategies.

1. Alter the children's response mode (i.e., method of indicating what is known).

2. Alter the input mode (i.e., method of presenting material or information to the child).

3. Modify learning materials (i.e., physical properties of toys, pictures, and objects).

4. Modify the learning environment (i.e., type of structure or setting in which instruction occurs).

5. Alter methods of eliciting responses (i.e., reinforcement contingencies to motivate the child to perform).

These strategies strive to alter two general aspects of the learning process: child characteristics, and environmental characteristics.

COMPREHENSION CHECK 5.9

What is the purpose of modifying methods of assessment and teaching for children with sensory and neuromotor impairments?

Designing developmental interventions

Hunt and Sullivan (1974) have presented a simple conceptual model that reminds us of important features in the learning process when planning individualized instructional programs. The *BPE model* stresses that Behavior (B) is the result of the Person (P) interacting with the Environment (E). In adaptive instructional terms, Developmental progress (B) results from pinpointing child characteristics and needs (P) and designing individualized instructional strategies (E), which are matched with these characteristics. This conceptual model is the basis for the Individualized Educational Program (IEP), which will be discussed in a later chapter. The IEP matches a child's developmental capabilities and needs with changes in instructional settings, materials, and strategies, as is illustrated in Table 5.12.

In practical terms, the BPE model could help us in planning an IEP for a 3-year-old visually impaired and cerebral-palsied child who demonstrates a cognitive knowledge of objects and functions that are more typical of a 1- to 1 1/2-year-old infant. Our goal becomes one of helping the child to independently explore objects in his world by using planned play activities, adaptive toys, and highly structured behavioral methods.

Child characteristics

The child's lack of ability to use his hands to play with toys at the midline of his body with head upright is a result of both his neuromotor problems (i.e., poor head and trunk control) and his mild visual limitations. Adaptations will be required to set the stage for teaching and learning. An adaptive wheelchair will be needed to support his/her head and body in an upright position with shoulder wedges to position arms and hands forward in a ready position to play with toys. Also, a tray on the wheelchair provides a stable horizontal surface for presenting toys in a stationary position or hanging mobile and suspended from a dowel-rod structure. The child will be able to indicate wishes by responding through head pointing or global gestures toward concrete objects placed on the tray or, later, pictures as symbolic representation is acquired.

TABLE 5.12
Conceptual Use of the BPE Model for Developmental Planning

Behavior (B) (Goals)	Person (P) (Developmental Level)	Environment (E) (Instructional Method)
Independent play in exploring objects in the environment	Cerebral-palsied–visually impaired infant Sensorimotor stage (12 months level)	Planned play Adaptive toys High structure

Source: Adapted from the BPE model described by Hunt, D. E., and Sullivan, E. V. (1974). *Between psychology and education.* New York: Dryden Press.

Instructional characteristics

At first, learning will occur on a one-to-one setting to reduce distractions and to maximize attention and performance. Special toys will be used such as objects with handles, various textures and high resolution color properties, that are capable of motion, manipulation, and sounds. These will increase motivation and provide easier methods of gaining attention, reaching, grasping, feeling, and manipulating. Social praise in the form of hand clapping, smiling, and verbal praise will reinforce appropriate exploratory responses by the child. Table 5.13 presents a sample adaptive instructional activity to illustrate how this exploratory-manipulative learning can be facilitated. In addition, Johnson & Johnson Baby Products Company (1982) has published

TABLE 5.13
Sample Adaptive Learning Activity from the Vision-Up Program

TITLE
Pulls string to secure object

BEHAVIORAL DESCRIPTION
When a piece of yarn or string is attached to a toy or object the child has indicated a preference for, he will pull on the string to obtain the toy.

PROGRAMMING
1. Repeat activities for Card No. 44FM5: Plays with String Exploitively.
2. Hold the child on your lap while seated at a table. Place one of his favorite toys on a piece of cloth. Guide the child's hand and help him pull the cloth so he can get the toy. If necessary, attach a light to the toy. Encourage the child to secure the toy by pulling the cloth strip without your assistance.
3. Place a toy attached to a string at one end of the table so that the child has to pull on the string to reach the toy. Have the child trace the path from the string to the toy. Tell or show the child how to get the toy by pulling the string. Try to let him do as much as possible for himself. Again, if necessary, use adaptation such as lights, as in item 2.
4. Experimentation also may be conducted by reversing the process; for example, by taking the toy from the child and letting him feel the string being pulled tight, or by letting the child feel the toy being pulled across the table.
5. Attach a balloon to a string and place it within the child's perceptual field. If he is not able to see the balloon, assure the child of its presence by moving his hand until he touches the balloon. Repeat items 3 and 4. Elastic may be used instead of a string.
6. Place the child on his back. Move a toy from a cardboard spool and a piece of string. Dangle the toy and tell the child to pull the spool.

MATERIALS
Child-preferred toy, lights, balloons, cloth strip, pieces of yarn or string, table, cardboard spool.

Source: Croft, N. B., and Robinson, L. W. (1976). *Project Vision-Up.* Boise, Idaho: Educational Products and Training Foundation.

an entire series of multisensory stimulus-response appropriate toys that can be effectively used in developmental intervention for handicapped infants and preschoolers.

STAGE 4: CHILD AND PROGRAM EVALUATION— MONITORING DEVELOPMENTAL PROGRESS

". . . assessment and intervention are linked through the evaluation of child progress" (Brooks-Gunn and Lewis, 1982). The final stage in the diagnostic-prescriptive model brings the assessment/intervention process full cycle. However, many programs omit this extremely critical stage. Child and program evaluation provide teachers, parents, and developmental specialists with quantitative and qualitative evidence that their adaptive plans and teaching strategies are effective. Evaluation serves to document developmental progress.

Program evaluation (see Chapter 15) highlights both changes needed in the child's program and evidence of overall developmental gains. *Formative evaluation* procedures are methods that chart each child's progress on a frequent (daily or weekly) basis. Objectives within a developmental curriculum provide the "items" for continuously monitoring skill acquisition. Also, formative evaluation alerts teachers to areas in which developmental progress is negligible and in which modifications in the instructional program will need to be made. In contrast, *summative evaluation* procedures "sum-up" child progress or lack of it only at the end of blocks of time (e.g., end of year achievement, quarterly assessment). Chapter 15 provides a detailed discussion of these major program evaluation methods.

COMPREHENSION CHECK 5.10

Explain why teachers and other team members must *regularly* and *frequently* monitor the behavior of children in their program.

SUMMARY

Designing strategies to assess and program for handicapped infants and preschoolers is a complex venture that requires a multidimensional team approach. Procedures that link diagnosis and intervention help to effectively stimulate developmental progress. Each sequential stage in the developmental diagnostic-prescriptive process is crucial to forge this systematic linkage. Developmental theory provides the base, and developmental methods provide the content and procedures. Philosophy, purpose, and practice are merged to initiate appropriate interventions for young exceptional children.

SUGGESTED READINGS

Bagnato, S. J., and Neisworth, J. T. (1981). *Linking developmental assessment and curricula prescriptions for early intervention.* Rockville, MD: Aspen Systems Corporation.

Neisworth, J. T. (Ed.) (1981). Assessing the handicapped preschooler. *Topics in Early Childhood Special Education, 1*(2).

Paget, K. D. and Bracken, B. A. (1983). *The psychoeducational assessment of preschool children.* New York: Grune & Stratton.

Exceptional Infants and Toddlers

Stephen J. Bagnato
Susan M. Munson
Robert H. MacTurk

CHAPTER OUTLINE

Mr. & Mrs. Gallop were worried because Brandon looked so small and helpless in his isolette, attached to a ventilator and so many electronic monitors. Because his breathing was assisted by a machine and his respiration and heartbeats were so fast, they feared the worst would happen. Brandon appeared to have no contact with people or events in this world. He weighed only 2 pounds when he was born 10 weeks too early. Like many premature, low birth weight infants, he suffers many complications because his physiological systems are not mature enough to function effectively on their own. His lungs are immature because of their lack of a surface chemical that promotes growth and elasticity; *hyaline membrane disease*, a disorder in breathing, is the result of this. Also, because his eyes were immature at birth, the oxygen used to assist his breathing had to be regulated very closely so that it would not damage his visual system; it is possible that Brandon has suffered some slight visual impairment known as *retinopathy of prematurity* because of the impact of too much oxygen on his eyes—an unfortunate, but common occurence in very low birth weight newborns.

Despite these difficulties, the nurses in the neonatal intensive care unit have observed that along with his gain in weight during the past 4 weeks, Brandon is much more alert and responsive for longer periods although he fatigues quickly. Brandon's parents seem to be unaware of just how much he is changing in a positive way; they talk only about his tubes and "that space capsule he's in." The nurses have asked the developmental psychologist to meet with the Gallops and to help them to view Brandon in a more positive and realistic light.

Dr. LeVan assessed Brandon's behaviors while the parents were watching to give them direct examples of positive changes in behavior. He used various toys and face-to-face smiling, cooing, and visual stimulation to increase Brandon's level of interest or arousal in the activities. When Dr. LeVan gently but firmly folds Brandon's arms across his chest and positions his head for midline gazing while he holds him, Brandon begins to look directly at a brightly colored pinwheel with some obvious interest in its spinning; next, when Dr. LeVan rings a bell sharply, Brandon widens his eyes and startles briefly. He reacts in a calmer, but interested, way each time the bell is rung as he seems to become used to its sound. When Dr. LeVan holds Brandon directly below his face and smiles, sticks out his tongue, and makes sounds, Brandon also looks intently, postures his own mouth in a disorganized manner as if trying to imitate Dr. LeVan, and sneezes as he loses his gaze and interest. When he recovers, Brandon seems ready for more face-face play as he makes some "mewing" sounds when the psychologist tries to "get him to talk."

Mr. and Mrs. Gallop have been watching this interaction with both excitement and disbelief. When Mrs. Gallop was able to get Brandon to do some of the same behaviors as Dr. LeVan did, she was even more excited and somewhat relieved; however, she stated that she was puzzled by what she had just seen. Dr. LeVan can now take this critical opportunity to teach the Gallops more about their high-risk but very capable infant, to counsel them about their feelings, and to capitalize on their readiness to know and understand Brandon now that he is changing.

Early-childhood special education is at its best when it focuses on infants and toddlers with special needs. In fact, "early intervention" reflects the belief that earlier is better in order to prevent, remedy, and/or compensate for early developmental disorders. Infant intervention is one of the most popular areas

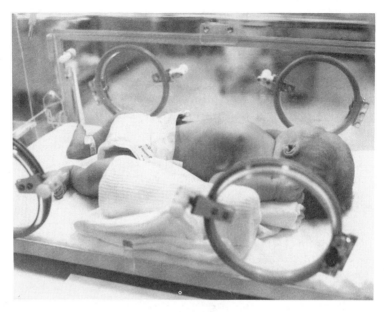

Neonatal intensive care units enhance the survival of premature, low birth weight infants.

of clinical service and research in the field of special education. It is one of the few instances in which theory and practice are so closely aligned. Specialists know that early developmental, medical, and behavioral treatment does alter the course of the disabled infant's functioning in significant ways. It is not surprising that many hospitals have implemented intervention programs in neonatal units as one strategy for helping the handicapped and high-risk infant to adapt to people and events in the world. Techniques and strategies of assessing and teaching infants are important; but one of the most critical dimensions of any comprehensive treatment program for special-needs infants is a focus on promoting the complex interrelationship between the infant and mother and father. Many parents need help in understanding and responding to their infant, who is often viewed as vulnerable and too immature-as was Brandon. This chapter surveys the field of infant intervention by discussing the types of problems observed in high-risk and handicapped infants, methods of assessing and treating these problems, the crucial involvement of parents in these programs, and evidence for the effectiveness of these early-intervention procedures.

DEFINITION AND PREVALENCE OF EARLY DEVELOPMENTAL DISORDERS

One of the wonders of neonatal medicine is its capability of promoting the survival of increasing numbers of very premature babies who would have died in earlier years. New medical diagnostic and treatment techniques have ensured their survival; yet this good news carries some negative aspects. Seven percent of the babies born in the United States each year are premature and suffer various forms and degrees of *developmental disabilities*. As more infants with low birth weights survive, greater numbers suffer such specific neurodevelopmental handicaps as brain injury, mental retardation, and motor and sensory difficulties. Special medical procedures, such as assisted mechanical ventilation for babies with underdeveloped lungs, can often contribute to permanent functional difficulties for the developing infant (Institute of Medicine, 1985; Rothberg, Maisels, and Bagnato, 1981, 1983). The Division of Maternal and Child Health in Pennsylvania estimates that in 1985 more than 10,000 infants were born weighing less than 5 1/2 pounds, with approximately 2000 babies weighing less than 3 1/2 pounds.

The Ross Conference on Pediatric Research (1982) reports the results of a longitudinal study to evaluate the impact of early developmental complications on later functioning in school. Three-hundred and thirty-five low birth weight infants were assessed on a regular basis until they were 6 1/2 years old. The results indicated that the incidence of abnormality in the sample was 42%. Many of these children showed multiple disabilities. Specific disabilities noted in the longitudinal study included learning disabilities (18%), mental retardation (9%), cerebral palsy (8%), major visual impairments (4.5%), sensorineural hearing impairments (3.6%), seizure disorder (3%), and pervasive neurodevelopmental deficits (7%). It is clear that a comprehensive approach is needed to aid parents in the care of their infants. A combined focus on preventive and treatment programs is necessary to reduce the disabling consequences of early-birth difficulties as well as to promote the progress of infants and the adjustments of parents.

COMPREHENSION CHECK 6.1

Why are premature, low birth weight infants "at risk"?
Even very premature neonates can now survive through medical and developmental intensive care techniques; what implications does this have for the special educator?

IMPACT ON THE FAMILY

The birth of a high-risk or handicapped infant has a profound effect on all family members. The family must be viewed as an interactive unit in which the special-needs infant plays a major role in how parents and siblings relate to one another (Belsky, 1981; Gabel, McDowell, and Cerreto, 1983; Thoman, Acebo, Dreyer, Becker, and Freese, 1979).

Parents may show a variety of psychological reactions in adjusting to a handicapped infant. The extent of the reaction varies according to many factors, such as the parents' general response to stress and the support of their network of family and friends. Many parents progress through various stages in their adjustment to the birth of their disabled infant. Mothers often sense early that their baby's movements, crying, and responses to sights and sounds are different. The subtle differences create a growing anxiety, although they may try to convince themselves that their worries are unfounded. However, their anxiety and fear and the concern of family and friends forces them to seek an evaluation to confirm or refute their suspicions. As discussed in Chapter 4, when parents learn that their infant is disabled, a period of mourning begins in which they must deal with the loss of the "perfect" child that they expected and must also ready themselves to care for their "real" handicapped infant. These stages are often followed by such reactions as shock, denial, grief, and anger. Many parents feel guilty that they are somehow responsible for their infant's disability and sift through memories of missed appointments with doctors and bumps to the stomach during pregnancy to find the answer. Eventually, after many months or years, many parents adjust to the demands of caring for and teaching their infant. However, families of handicapped children are vulnerable to repeated stresses, and their anger, fear, guilt, and sadness are constant events in their lives.

Brothers and sisters may show diverse reactions to the birth and development of a handicapped sibling. Some studies reveal that the incidence of affective and behavioral disorders appears to be higher in the siblings (particularly females) of handicapped children. In contrast, other studies suggest that siblings having a handicapped brother or sister in the family show greater degrees of empathy and a tolerance for individual differences in others. Obviously, families vary greatly in their adjustment and coping strategies.

Families with young handicapped children endure many personal and practical problems. Intervention programs need to emphasize the pressing needs of parents. Emotional support, counseling, and social and economic planning are often needed if parents are to adjust in a healthy manner and maintain enough emotional energy and persistence to provide the special care that their young child needs.

COMPREHENSIVE CHECK 6.2

Describe family characteristics that might contribute to minimal stress and a constructive adjustment to the presence of a handicapped infant.

IMPACT ON CHILD DEVELOPMENT

When newborns suffer either congenital or acquired brain injuries, every dimension of developmental and behavioral functioning is affected. The emergence of specific functions such as prelanguage behaviors (e.g., cooing, smiling, eye gazing), motor skills (e.g., reaching, grasping), cognitive, and social and objective play skills are delayed and often distorted in their timing and quality. (Chapter 3 describes specific ways in which overall development is influenced by such early developmental disabilities.)

Developmentally disabled and high-risk infants typically experience difficulties in attention and "state" control. Specifically, premature and older brain-injured infants are unable to console themselves when upset and are often highly reactive (startled) to even minor changes in sights, sounds, and body position. Poor muscle control makes it difficult for them to maintain head control and to focus on faces and objects for even short periods of time. Their lack of endurance often affects the ability to interact with people and objects. Signs of this lack of state organization and control are seen in sneezing, irritability, staring blankly beyond a person or object, and sudden startle reactions. Similarily, such infants, when even mildly stressed, show physiological changes such as tremors, breathing difficulties, and listlessness. Both parents and professionals need to be aware of the infant's stage of state organization so that the duration and intensity of therapy can be adjusted. Such a child-responsive approach can encourage the gradual development of self-control capabilities in infants. This may involve such activities as swaddling when upset, hand-to-mouth play, and vestibular stimulation (e.g., rocking, gentle bouncing).

Two other related areas that are inevitably affected by the infant's developmental dysfunctions (particularly neuromotor impairments) are a sense of personal competence and motivation or goal-directed behavior. Motor impairments interfere with the infant's emerging capability to grasp and explore objects and people. It is common for young children to develop a sense of *"learned helplessness."* They may learn after repeated failures that their actions have no immediate payoff in allowing them to secure or play with toys and other objects. They show signs of disinterest, passivity, and depression because, for them, their behavior does not produce results. This learned helplessness and lack of opportunity and experience limits contact with objects and events and so hinders the development of various cognitive concepts such as shape, size, weight, movability, and self-efficacy. Through therapy and adaptive play materials, parents and professionals can teach the infant to play so that their motor behavior contingently affects objects. This prevents the development of depression and also encourages the development of compensatory play patterns that will be vital to continued developmental progress.

COMPREHENSIVE CHECK 6.3

How do some parents unwittingly promote their child's development of learned helplessness? What should they do?

ASSESSMENT OF SPECIAL-NEEDS INFANTS

Because of their limited behavioral repertoires and inconsistent response to specific tasks, developmentally disabled infants require resourcefulness and patience by the observer if they are to be properly assessed. Accurate and functional assessment of an infant's capabilities is a complicated process that must involve many people and measures. It must also be conducted over time to detect emerging skills and complications. The developmental diagnostic-prescriptive model is important in this continuous process because it helps to ensure that assessment proceeds from general screening of strengths and weaknesses to multidimensional assessments of various developmental and behavioral dimensions that can serve as an individual guide for education and treatment. Several methods of comprehensively assessing high-risk and handicapped infants and toddlers are available to the early-intervention specialist.

Neurophysiological status

Evaluation of an infant's sensory, neurological, and motor capabilities should be one of the first series of assessments conducted. For infants and toddlers with neurological damage, the extent of the brain damage needs to be analyzed, especially to define whether *hydrocephalus* exists (i.e., an increase in cerebro-spinal fluid pressure in the brain). Detection of this condition can lead to a shunting operation that drains off excess brain fluid and decreases the risk of progressive brain damage resulting from the pressure buildup. Several tests are available to evaluate the extent and nature of brain damage. Computerized axial tomography (CAT scan) uses enhanced computer pictures of various portions of the brain to detect damage and changes to the brain such as cerebral atrophy. The PETT (Position Emission Topography Test) scan measures blood flow, heat patterns, and metabolic changes in the brain. Nuclear magnetic resonance is a new and expensive diagnostic procedure that involves a sophisticated process of photographing the brain while the cortical cells are aroused by their response to a magnetic field. With newborns and infants with a low threshold of response to sensory stimulation, specialists also use brain-wave tests to evaluate intactness of sensory systems. Diagnostic tests known as brainstem auditory evoked responses (BAER) and visual evoked responses (VER) measure the transmission of electrical impulses along the auditory and visual nerves into the brain to determine whether the infant's brain is receiving these impulses.

One of the least sophisticated but earliest diagnostic screening tests used with newborn and premature infants is the Apgar scoring system (Apgar, 1953). The Apgar is the pediatrician's method of rating the physiological condition of the infant at 5 and 10 minutes after delivery. The ratings of 0, 1, and 2 denote the quality of the infant's condition (high scores are best) in the following areas: appearance (color), pulse (heart rate), grimace (reflex to stimulation), activity (muscle tone), and respiration (respiratory effort). Moderate relationships between low Apgar scores and infant mortality (Serunian & Broman, 1975) as well as later cognitive functioning have been reported. Many developmental pediatricians and neurodevelopmental specialists use the Dubowitz scoring system (see Chapter 5) as a method of behaviorally analyzing an infant's neuromotor patterns and residual primitive reflexes.

Temperament, state, and behavioral organization

The terms temperament and behavioral style are often used interchangeably to describe an infant's individual pattern of personality characteristics and mood that influences interactions with people. Infant researchers have developed measures that allow caretakers and mothers to rate the temperament of infants. These measures attempt to determine and predict how infants typically respond emotionally to people and events. With handicapped infants, this assessment is important because it enables parents and therapists to adjust their own behavior and to organize the physical environment in such a way as to promote attention, steady state, endurance, and self-regulation in young children. Two of the most commonly used temperament scales are the Infant Temperament Questionaire (Carey and McDevitt, 1978) and the Toddler Temperament Scale (Fullard, McDevitt, and Carey, 1978). Both scales rate the young child's style of behavior along several dimensions: activity, rhythmicity, approach, adaptability, intensity, mood, persistence, distractibility, and threshold. Through subjective observation and judgments, to describe the infant as a difficult, a slow-to-warm, or an easy child. This description serves as a basis for adjusting parent-infant interactions and treatment planning. According to Carey (1985), temperament data can guide the specialist in promoting parent-child interrelationships on three levels: increasing the parents' awareness and understanding of their infant's unique differences, organizing more realistic perceptions by the parents of their child's individual style and needs, and setting general guidelines for alternative strategies of parent-infant behavior management.

Infants show early differences in interests, temperament, and achievement.

Simeonsson, Huntington, Short, and Ware (1982) developed the Carolina Record of Individual Behavior as a measure of the developmental capabilities and behavioral style and organization of severely handicapped infants and young children. The scale relies on parents and professional judgments of the young child's characteristics in such areas as social orientation, endurance, consolability, activity, reactivity, communication, response to frustration, and the presence of various rhythmic habit patterns (body rocking, head banging).

The Brazelton Neonatal Behavioral Assessment Scale–Revised (BNBAS-R) (Brazelton, 1984) was designed to assess the newborns responsivity to people, objects, and events in the environment. Although it is viewed as a measure of parent-infant interactions, the BNBAS-R is a valuable technique for describing the high-risk infant's behavioral style and level of behavioral organization. It covers such dimensions as habituation to auditory, visual, and tactile stimulation; orientation to animate and inanimate events, consolability, irritability, startle, and alertness.

Parent-infant interaction

One of the most important dimensions to assess with high-risk and handicapped infants is the quality of social interactions and, especially, parent-infant attachment. Early-intervention specialists realize that infants and their parents contribute reciprocally to social interactions. The attachment relationship allows infants to learn that predictable connections exist between their behavior and the behavior of others. This learning readies the young child to generalize behavior to other people, which promotes learning and developmental progress. For newborns and for severely handicapped young children, the BNBAS-R is the measure of choice for evaluating the interactive relationship between infant behavioral characteristics and the physical and social environment.

Child-development researchers are now developing scales that analyze the complex dual relationship between infant and caretaker characteristics. One such measure is the Mother-Infant Attachment Indicators During Stress (AIDS; Massie and Cambell, 1983). The AIDS scale is used with infants from birth to 18 months of age to detect atypical and distorted interactions in the behavior of mothers and their infants during stressful situations that are a stimulus for close bonding. The scale enables a pediatrician or developmental diagnostic specialist to assess various reciprocal behavioral dimensions evident in the interactions of mothers and infants. The following interactive patterns are observed and rated: gazing, vocalizing, touching, holding, affect, and proximity. Each behavioral dimension is operationally defined so that degrees of normal to abnormal responses in each of these areas can be determined and compared (e.g., 1 = always intensely anguished and fearful to 5 = always smiling). The scale serves four major purposes: to assess the adequacy of mother-infant dyadic responses; to highlight the need for psychotherapy and counseling to teach more sensitive and responsive patterns of interactions; to document the efficacy of treatment; and to teach observers the important features of maternal-infant interactions that are central to healthy psychological development.

Analysis of interactive relationships should also involve assessments of how the physical environment (especially home environment) affects infant development and learning. The Home Observation for Measurement of the Environment (HOME) (Caldwell and Bradley, 1979) describes aspects of the physical environment that contribute to quality parent-infant relationships: emotional and verbal responsivity of the mother, avoidance of restrictiveness and punishment, organization of the environment, provision of appropriate play materials, extent of maternal involvement with the child, and opportunities for a variety of stimulation. Assessment data are used to enable infant specialists to modify and plan home settings that foster development.

Developmental task performance

The most common infant assessment measures are those that analyze the child's ability to complete simple problem-solving tasks that require various combinations of motor, language, social, and cognitive skills. Two scales discussed previously are the best examples of norm-referenced child performance scales: Bayley Scales of Infant Development (Bayley, 1969) and the Gesell Developmental Schedules–Revised (Knobloch, Malone, and Stevens, 1981). Early intervention researchers have created expanded versions of these norm-referenced scales to serve as guides to individualized goal-planning and education. Examples of these criterion-referenced measures are the Early Learning Accomplishment Profile (Sanford, 1983), the Early Intervention Developmental Profile (Rogers et al., 1982), and the BRIGANCE Diagnostic Inventory of Early Development (Brigance, 1983).

COMPREHENSIVE CHECK 6.4

What is the difference between assessing infant "state" and assessing developmental task performance? Why are both important?

ASSESSMENT ADAPTATIONS FOR HANDICAPPED INFANTS

Increasing attention is being focused on alternative methods of assessing the cognitive capabilities of severely handicapped infants and toddlers (Bagnato and Neisworth, 1985; Brooks-Gunn and Lewis, 1981; Kearsley and Sigel, 1979; Simeonsson et al., 1980; Zelazo, 1979). These more sensitive, adaptive diagnostic strategies minimize or eliminate the need for responses that require motor or sensory capabilities of which some youngsters are incapable. Some of the more recent methods are more practical modifications of child-development research techniques. These strategies rely on the infant's intact visual skills to habituate to repeated presentations of a stimulus and to display emotional reactions (e.g., surprise, glee) to novel events that were not expected. Similarly, alternative communication systems and the use of eye localization allow infant's to demonstrate that they can comprehend and follow directions. Multidimensional assessment batteries are now being used to make such assessments more comprehensive and accurate. The Competency

Assessment Battery (Brooks-Gunn and Lewis, 1981) uses multiple measures to evaluate such dimensions as mother-infant interaction, visual self-recognition, temperament, visual-auditory attention, social/nonsocial attention, and mother-infant vocalization patterns. With further refinement, early intervention specialists will be able to use the results of such assessments for directly designing modified plans of developmental treatment that will specify the types of toys, activities, and methods of presenting information to young handicapped children that will most effectively encourage the learning of compensatory skills.

COMPREHENSION CHECK 6.5

Why might a child with *motor* problems (e.g., cerbral palsy) not do well on items that are supposed to measure *cognitive* capability? How does adaptive assessment attempt to minimize this problem?

EDUCATION AND TREATMENT OF SPECIAL-NEEDS INFANTS

Intervention with handicapped infants and their parents requires the coordinated services of a team of professionals who use specific integrated education and treatment techniques. The following sections discuss components of programs that most contribute to success.

Principles and goals of neonatal and infant intervention

Especially for handicapped infants, intervention during the neonatal period is vital in order to maximize the newborn's chances of developing effective adaptive behavior patterns that involve integrated skills from all developmental domains. Although controversy exists regarding the type of treatment that should occur during the neonatal period, research studies indicate that programs can have positive results for both infant and parents (Meisels, Jones, and Stiefel, 1983). The goals of neonatal and later infant-development programs should be viewed as occupying a continuum; the goals change as the infant's developmental and behavioral needs change. Because the high-risk neonate's systems are immature or damaged, the goals and related techniques of neonatal treatment should focus on readying the child's systems to meet the demands of the extrauterine world. Such programs help the infant to compensate for intrauterine experiences that were missed because of premature delivery. Also, they provide experiences that give the infant sensory stimulation, presumably to aid the growth of neurological and sensory systems (although the type and extent of such stimulation is debated). Neonatal programs use such strategies as tactile-kinesthetic stimulation (e.g., flexing, massage, rubbing, handling), vestibular stimulation, and visual-auditory practice with people and objects to promote sensory integration. A recently developed model (Als, Lester, Tronick, and Brazelton, 1982) advocates the following objectives and techniques:

1. Activities to regulate environmental stimulation (lights, sound, positioning) so that the infant maintains a steady neurophysiological state.

2. Activities to foster more organized patterns of state regulation and sensory and neuromotor behaviors.

3. Activities to help the infant maintain his state and behavioral organization when the environment becomes overstimulating and chaotic.

4. Activities to expand the infant's self-regulatory capabilities (console self when upset without adult holding, rocking, or swaddling).

5. Activities to encourage the development of optimal attention and social skills.

Some intervention specialists believe that a primary objective of neonatal treatment programs should be to facilitate attachment bonds between the mother and the high-risk infant (Goldberg, 1977). Specifically, such programs must increase the caregiver's ability to *read and respond* appropriately to the infant's behavioral signals, which are unique signs of his needs and capabilities. Similarly, therapists and caregivers must increase the "readability" and constancy of the infant's signals. Finally, the infants' endurance and state organization must be developed to promote social exchanges without harming other important developmental characteristics.

Treatment programs for older infants and toddlers with special needs share some of the same goals and principles as neonatal programs. However, as newborns mature, their neurodevelopmental skills across different functional areas become more integrated. At this point, infant programs begin to promote the development of specific patterns of "skills" in several interrelated areas—cognition, language, social, neuromotor, and self-care. Nevertheless, the focus of the programs should be on the integration of various capabilities that are considered to be "processes," such as eye-hand coordination, the components of gross motor movement, and responsive social communication with adults and toddlers. Finally, infant programs must continue the neonatal intervention emphasis on fostering parent-infant interactions. This takes the form of not only making parents more confident about their ability to understand their infant's capabilities and needs better, but also, helping parents to be effective teachers of their infants. They need to learn techniques that guide their infant to function more adaptively and independently and to understand that the infant has a direct impact on people and objects in his or her world (Garwood and Fewell, 1983).

COMPREHENSIVE CHECK 6.6

Why do professionals stress the importance of "bonding"? How can attachment or bonding be promoted?

Models for infant intervention

Services for developmentally disabled infants and their parents are provided in home-based, center-based, and hospital-based programs. The most effective early intervention models apply various combinations of these programs to meet the needs of individual infants and families. For example, newborn, premature infants that are discharged from the neonatal intensive care unit are initially best treated with home-based-only services provided by neurodevelopmental therapists, infant educators, and home health nurses. Older infants and toddlers can profit greatly from dual home- and community center-based programming that blends the advantages of social interactions with a variety of adults and children with personalized therapy in the home that is designed to teach parents effective care skills in a natural milieu. Finally, children with severe disabilities often progress best when they are admitted to a hospital-based program that provides highly intensive rehabilitation treatment services over a 2- to 6-week period; then, they are discharged into a community program with an updated treatment plan. A capsule overview of programs that exemplify each of these models will make their unique characteristics clearer.

Home-based services

Although the object of home-based treatment is the high-risk or disabled infant, the mother is the crucial vehicle through which home-based therapy is effectively delivered. Early-intervention specialists believe that treatment provided in the natural environment is most effective for mothers and their infants. With once or twice a week therapy from an infant special educator, a neurodevelopmental therapist, a home health nurse, or a trained paraprofessional aide, mothers learn to trust these professionals and their own competence and judgment about their child. Treatment techniques demonstrated and reinforced in the home are often more likely to be continued when the professionals are no longer present.

Various programs provide neurodevelopmental treatment services through a parent training, home-based model. Thompson and colleagues (1982) reported the results of a home-based early-intervention program for adolescent mothers and their infants who were at risk for medical, psychological, educational, and social problems. Monthly home visits were made by a nurse clinician who used the Carolina Infant Curriculum to foster developmentally appropriate physical, motor, language, perceptual, cognitive, and language skills in the infants by demonstrating play techniques to the mothers. Equally important, the nurse clinician helped the mothers to develop a positive and motivating style of interacting with their infants developmental needs and capabilities.

Center-based services

Center-based services for infants and toddlers are often provided by organizations such as United Cerebral Palsy, the Easter Seals Society, Association for Retarded Citizens, and regional child developmental centers. Parents and infants are treated in a setting with other parents where emotional support can be a natural outcome. Center-based services can occur more regularly with a greater number of staff; while infants can be treated individually, they also recieve the benefits of learning in an environment with the social and language stimulation of other youngsters. Bagnato and Neisworth (1980) reported results from a center-based early-intervention program for multihandicapped infants and preschoolers who were also integrated with normal preschoolers. The program focused on teaching functional skills in the areas of communication, socioemotional, motor, and problem solving. Results demonstrated that many severely handicapped preschoolers progressed at approximately a normal developmental rate during their 6-month period of special treatment.

Hospital-based services

Many infants require short- or long-term treatment in hospital settings during the infant and preschool years. Hospital-based services occur frequently for such developmental problems as failure to thrive, cerebral palsy, spina bifida and meningitis, encephalitis, and traumatic brain injury. Intensive programming by a team of neurodevelopmental therapists, infant special educators, developmental psychologists, and pediatricians can be very effective in organizing distorted developmental patterns and increasing social and object communication and play skills. Parent education is a crucial component of these programs as well as is demonstrating specialized treatment and behavior management techniques to community-program personnel. Hospital infant programs are crucial also for working with the parents of premature infants. Such early intervention can foster the emergence of social and self-regulatory capabilities and teach the parents techniques to enhance their attachment relationship with their infant.

The Infant Stimulation/Mother Training Program (Badger, Burns, and DeBoer, 1982) is a hospital-based intervention program that provides a comprehensive array of individualized services to infants in neonatal intensive care units (NICU) and their parents. NICU nursing staff are trained in infant stimulation techniques and parent involvement methods. The nursing staff then helps parents to develop their attachment bonds with their low birth weight infants; parent support groups are also formed to help the parents cope with the stress of having a high-risk infant. Finally, follow-up services are an integral part of the program once the child is discharged from the hospital NICU.

COMPREHENSION CHECK 6.7

What information would be needed about the child before a placement (center, home, or hospital) can be considered?

Parents as partners in infant intervention

The most critical time for initiating an early-intervention program is during the first 3 years of life, immediately after the birth or the identification of a handicapped child. The infant intervention models emphasize the central role of parents as primary caregivers and service providers. For two reasons, it is crucial that early-intervention professionals work cooperatively with parents of handicapped infants and toddlers. First, early intervention is necessary to facilitate the child's growth in cognitive, communication, social, and motor skills during the critical developmental period of birth to 3 years. Second, parents will need support and training in order to facilitate their emotional adjustment and to foster acceptance of their handicapped child.

Four approaches to parent-infant intervention

Bromwich (1981) describes four approaches for providing early-intervention services to parents and their handicapped infants. These approaches differ on the bases of the target of intervention. First, a *curriculum-based approach* that focuses on teaching the infant or toddler a prescribed sequence of skills may be used. The curriculum may be one of the models described in Chapter 4 (normal developmental, cognitive developmental, or behavioral). The parents' role in this approach to early intervention is that of teacher. Parents are trained in the home, hospital, or center to teach their child specific developmental skills. The Portage Project is an example of a curriculum-based approach to early intervention.

Parent therapy is a second possible approach. The focus of therapy is the parents, and the goal is to help the parents adjust emotionally to having a handicapped child. Individual or group counseling is used to provide an

Close and reciprocal parent–child relations promote strong attachments and secure social–emotional well-being later in life.

outlet for parents to work through their feelings of anger, guilt, or frustration that typically occur following the identification of a handicapping condition. The underlying assumption of this model is that well-adjusted parents will be more effective in coping and working with their handicapped youngster.

Parent-education programming, the third approach, is frequently employed in early-intervention services. Parents are given information on normal child development and the resulting impact of handicapping conditions, legal rights, and responsibilities, and community support services. They are also helped to use specific behavior management and instructional strategies with their child. The content of such programs is often determined by the parents' needs and is usually presented in a group instructional format. Bruder and Bricker (1985) used a parent-education program to train parents as teachers of their at-risk toddlers. These parents then trained other parents to select appropriate skills, to use effective teaching strategies, and to record the child's performance. This is a cost-effective approach for improving the skill level of both the parents and the at-risk child.

Parents of handicapped infants and toddlers are targeted for intervention because they have special needs for counseling or parent-skill training. Handicapped children are targeted for intervention because of their need for skill training in deficit developmental domains (areas). However, recent studies of the social interactions of infants and their caregivers have redirected the focus of early-intervention practices (Bailey and Simmeonsson, 1984). The *parent-infant interaction approach* (Bromwich, 1981) is based on the assumption that a reciprocal relationship exists between parent and infant; the behavior of one member of the dyad influences the behavior of the other member (Brazelton, 1976; Dunst, 1983). Thus, the goal of intervention in an interactional model is to change the pattern and quality of parent-infant interactions. Appropriate interactional patterns are critical for the optimal development of the child and enhancement of the parents' sense of competence (Bromwich, 1981; Ludlow, 1979).

Disturbances in parent-infant attachment

During appropriate interactions, both infant and parent behavior are positively reinforced. The parent responds to the mood or needs of the infant effectively and consistently; the infant responds positively and predictably to the parent. An emotional tie or bond develops between parent and infant when positive interactions such as these occur consistently over time. The child then begins to show a preference for the parent. During the first 2 years of life, the normal developmental process of emotional bonding and preference for the parent results in attachment. Given the security of this relationship, the youngster is free to explore the environment and learn (Bromwich, 1981).

Unfortunately, the attachment bond between parent and a handicapped infant is often disrupted and delayed (Odom, 1983). The infant may exhibit certain atypical behaviors owing to the nature of the handicapping condition. The infant may provide unclear signals for hunger, fatigue, or discomfort. Also, the infant may fail to respond to parent behaviors in a reinforcing manner (no smiling, laughing, or cuddling) (Brazelton, 1976).

An immediate result is decreased or unpleasant parent-infant interactions and parental feelings of inadequacy. The long-term effect of inappropriate interactional patterns is a negative impact on the child's overall development.

Bailey and Wolery (1984) and Ludlow (1979) provided examples of handicap-related behaviors that might interfere with the establishment of positive parent-infant interactions. Visually handicapped infants may not maintain eye contact and may require more tactile or auditory stimulation from parents. Hearing-impaired infants will respond inconsistently to verbal communications and may appear to be rejecting parental attempts to interact. Motorically impaired infants may be difficult to cuddle because of tense or limp muscle tone or may lack basic reflexes such as smiling or sucking. Autistic infants may avoid eye contact, fail to smile, or cry more often to signal their needs. Mentally retarded infants may be delayed in smiling or in responding to persons in their environment. Field (1978) observed that handicapped infants exhibited several of the aforementioned behaviors during play with their mothers. Handicapped infants cried more often, smiled and laughed less, and avoided eye contact more than did normal infants during play. The mothers of handicapped infants were more vocal, smiled less, and played fewer games with their handicapped infants than did mothers of normal infants. Decreased enjoyment in play activities may be due to the infants inability to respond to the parent. However, the parents may ineffectively read and respond to the infant's signals of displeasure.

It is critical that early-intervention programs focus on training parents to recognize the unique signals provided by their handicapped infant and to subsequently adapt their responses to the child (McCollum and Stayton, 1985). Parents must be encouraged to respond to three categories of infant cues (Bromwich, 1981). Biological cues will indicate the child's sleeping and eating cycles and states of distress and comfort. Parents must detect the infant's social-affective cues that indicate reactions to change in daily routine, response to other individuals, and mood. It is also important for parents to predict the infant's response to environmental changes within and out of the home and to noise level.

Atypical characteristics of parents also contribute to disturbances in the interactional pattern. Parents who are emotionally unstable, adolescents, or are from low socioeconomic environments are frequently at risk for establishing negative interaction patterns with their infants. In addition, infants are often at risk for developmental delays. Early-intervention programs have been designed specifically to work with these special parent-infant populations. Adolescent and low-income mothers, for example, can be trained to work with their infants (Field, Widmayer, Greenberg, and Stoller, 1982; Thompson, Coppleman, Conrad, and Jordan, 1982).

Awareness of cues will enable the parent to respond effectively and predictably to their child. This will enhance the positiveness of the interaction patterns, resulting in a competent parent and child.

In summary, early-intervention programs that have implemented a parent-infant interactional focus have clearly demonstrated several important program features. Parents must be taught to detect the subtle cues that their special infant is able to send; by their consistent and predictable response to this limited repertoire of subtle signals, parents gradually teach their infant those behaviors that help to initiate and maintain the interaction; the result of this sensitive training is that parents begin to realize that their special infant is competent and effective in meeting his needs. Infants benefit by developing those social behaviors that make them effective partners in the interactions. When this "well-orchestrated waltz" (Brazelton, 1982) is set in motion, parents are better able to adjust to their infant and the infant's developmental progress is ensured.

COMPREHENSION CHECK 6.8

How can parents be taught to "read" their child? Doesn't this skill "come naturally" with parenthood?

Parent-infant interactional model

The UCLA Infant Studies Project (Bromwich, 1981) was designed to provide comprehensive services (medical, social, educational) to families having preterm, high-risk infants. Diagnostic and intervention strategies are based on an interactional approach. The aim is to enhance the quality of parent-infant interactions to facilitate development of the at-risk infant (Bromwich, 1981).

Assessment procedures include three components: the *Developmental Screening Inventory* (DSI) (Knoblock, Pasamanick, and Sherard, 1966); the *Parent Behavior Progression* (PBP) (Bromwich, 1981); and the *Play Interaction Measure* (PIM) (Bromwich, 1981). Both the DSI and the PIM are used to estimate the infant's level in skills and play patterns. The PBP is designed to analyze parent-infant interactional patterns through interview and observation in the home. Six levels of parent behavior reflecting affective dimensions and skill dimensions are included within the levels (see Table 6.1). Results of the PBP are used to target intervention goals for each parent-infant dyad in the developmental areas of social-affective, language, and cognitive-motivational. The resultant guidelines for treatment provide practical strategies for the early-intervention specialist. Infant interventionists should ensure that parents remain in control during the period of teaching. The use of active-listening methods is encouraged as a way to develop parent trust, to respect the parent's goals for their infants, and to involve the parents in planning goals for their child. A focus on practical concerns is also maintained. While respecting individual styles of interaction, therapists provide corrective feedback and give alternatives about how to interact more sensitively with their infant. Stress is also placed on encouraging the parents to share experiences about how they deal with their high-risk infants.

Professionals working with parents of handicapped infants must support the parents during the initial stages of emotional adjustment while focusing the parent's attention on realistic goals for their infant. Bromwich (1981) suggests that this can be accomplished most effectively by beginning treatment guided by skill-development goals IV through VI (see Table 6.1). This directs the parent to very tangible behaviors and activities to use with their infant and thereby increases their sense of personnel competence. Once the

TABLE 6.1
Parent Behaviors in Affective and Skill Dimensions of the UCLA Model

Affective		Skill	
Level I	Enjoys infant	Level IV	Aware of age-appropriate activities, experiences, and materials for the infant
Level II	Observes, reads, and responds to infant's behavioral cues	Level V	Selects new activities for the infant based on training and experience
Level III	Engages in mutually satisfying interactions with the infant that facilitate attachment	Level VI	Independently provides age-appropriate activities for the infant in different developmental levels

Source: Bromwich, R. (1981). *Working with parents and infants: An interactional approach.* Austin, TX: PRO Ed. Copyright by the American Psychological Association.

parent begins to feel more in control, therapy can progress to goals in the affective-attachment realm, levels I through III.

The enduring strength of the UCLA parent-infant interactional model rests in its focus on both the infant and the parent in the interaction process. Parental emotional needs are addressed in a sensitive manner while they learn tangible skills to use to help their child developmentally and emotionally. Finally, the attachment bond is strengthened when the parents are emotionally available and confident enough to alter their interaction patterns to foster their infant's development further.

Curriculum materials and toys for infant intervention

One of the most important features of any infant intervention program is the selection of curriculum materials, including toys. Both high-risk and developmentally disabled infants require materials that are multisensory and multipurpose. Instructional materials and toys must stimulate and require the use of vision, hearing, tactile, olfactory, and kinesthetic senses; also, the materials should promote even and integrated skill development simultaneously across many behavioral areas. Infant toys can challenge the child to use and thereby develop cognitive-social and perceptual-motor skills; also, the materials must be capable of being modified or adapted for various handicaps or, at least, present qualities that allow the disabled infant to activate them with minimal effort. Model programs have devoted much time and effort to designing and producing curriculum sequences and materials for developmentally disabled infants and preschoolers. Curricula are available for specialized use with particular handicaps as well as for any child of a particular developmental range (Bailey, Jens, and Johnson, 1983; Fewell and

Sandall, 1983; Neisworth et al., 1980). It is important to recognize that an infant developmental curriculum should have a clear child-development theory base and display a direct relationship between *content* (what to teach) and *methods* (how to teach). A The following examples of infant and preschool curricula encompass these qualities.

A practical "process-oriented" curriculum that blends assessment and treatment goals and activities is *Infant Learning: A Cognitive-Linguistic Intervention Strategy* (Dunst, 1981). This Piagetian curriculum is based on the use of the *Uzgiris-Hunt Infant Development Scale*. It is intended for the young infant (0 to 24-month-old) and organizes instructional tasks into several developmental process (e.g., object permanence, means-end relationships, imitation). Methods of stimulating the emergence of each process goal are matched with assessment activities that tap those goals. The materials attempt to develop process skills simultaneously across several functional areas.

Developmental Programming for Infants and Young Children (Schafer and Moersch, 1981) is a curriculum focusing on both the 0- to 36-month and the 36 to 72-month age ranges. The sequence of tasks that comprises the assessment scale and forms goals for intervention blends recent trends in developmental research such as Piagetian theory, attachment theory, and primitive motor reflexes. The curriculum materials contain standardized suggestions for adapting the instructional presentation of each developmental task for young children with visual, hearing, and neuromotor dificits. This package is one of the most frequently and effectively used with developmentally disabled children. Recent research has demonstrated its capacity to reflect developmental progress of infants with both congenital and acquired brain injuries (Bagnato and Neisworth, 1985).

Another Piagetian-oriented curriculum that uniquely blends both developmental and functional approaches to intervention is the *Carolina Curriculum for Handicapped Infants* (Johnson, Jens, and Attermeier, 1979). The curriculum focuses on the 0- to 24-month period and organizes skills into a sequence of 24 domains (e.g., visually directed object manipulation, gestural communication, object permanence, vocal imitation) and cross-references these with the six traditional developmental areas evident in most other curricula. A strategy is provided for early-childhood special educators to select 8 to 10 objectives at any one time to be taught, while long-term goals consist of activities across all domains. This package includes instructional adaptations for blind and motorically impaired infants.

The *Hawaii Early Learning Profile* (Furuno, 1979) contains developmentally sequenced activities that cover the 0- to 36-month age range; the sequence of instructional tasks is organized into six developmental domains: cognitive, language, gross motor, fine motor, social, and self-help. A unique feature of the curriculum is the color coding of clusters of interrelated skills, which facilitates the selection of activities and behaviors that are integrated in a real way in the childs' developmental pattern. The curriculum has been field-tested in 35 states and has been used with both developmentally delayed and disabled young children.

"Curriculum materials" should also be broadly conceived as the appropriate selection of multisensory toys that can be used to stimulate the emergence of the types of skill clusters and sequences contained in each developmental curriculum. Many companies have produced commercially available toys for infants and preschoolers; however, Johnson and Johnson child development toys are particularly noteworthy as integral components of any set of curriculum materials. This line of toys was designed after extensive developmental research focusing on the physical features of toys that would make them most motivating at specific developmental levels. The toys were designed to accomplish several objectives when used in various ways. For example, the Stand-Up Man is brightly colored and contains a disjointed man form that is connected by a rope with a pull ring attached; by pulling the ring firmly, the infant begins to learn that his behavior has an impact on objects, he practices adaptive means-end behavior. The Piglet Crib Gym is composed of three connected pigs made of fabric; each form is filled with a different sensory experience (the sound of crinkling paper, a squeaker toy, and a rattle). The toy encourages reaching, grasping, and sound and perceptual skills. Finally, the Tracking Tube (depicted in Chapter 4) is designed to develop eye coordination and visual-pursuit skills in infants. The toy is composed of a clear plastic tube filled with a small red ball suspended in the liquid that fills the tube; the ends of the tube either squeak or rattle. The tube toy is designed also to stimulate object constancy skills in young children who intently watch the red ball disappear into the end of one tube and reappear when the rattle is tipped in the opposite direction.

Some toy companies are recognizing the need to produce play materials for developmentally disabled children. A limited number of toys are now being created or adapted so that children with sensory and neuromotor deficits can learn skills by playing with them. These toys often have pressure- or heat-

Shouldn't all children have toys? These toys are especially designed to be playful and educational for children with sensory and response limitations.

sensitive switches or plates that require only a small effort to produce an effect. Some European-built toys (Ambi and Havlakias) are designed with these same qualities (e.g., slinky toy with wooden balls suspended from wire coils that clack loudly when lightly touched). They can be effectively used with normal children as well.

COMPREHENSIVE CHECK 6.9

Are toys "instructional materials"?
Try to define "play."

EFFICACY OF TREATMENT WITH SPECIAL-NEEDS INFANTS

A significant body of research supports the view that early intervention is effective for high-risk and handicapped infants and young children. Nevertheless, evaluation of the efficacy of infant intervention is an incomplete technology that suffers from limitations in research design methods and lack of sensitive assessment of small increments of child progress. In addition, infant-program evaluation methods are only beginning to tap such important variables as changes in mastery motivation, affect, and social competence. In addition, more effective strategies of evaluating changes in parent-infant attachment relations are greatly needed. Yet, one of the most crucial questions concerns the determination of which features of an early-intervention program match best with which characteristics of both individual infants and groups of young developmentally disabled children (Sheehan, 1985). Although many more studies with larger groups of infants and toddlers are needed, efficacy studies have been conducted with both developmentally delayed and severely handicapped infants.

Parent-infant interaction disorders

Various treatment procedures have been designed to alter or enhance the ability of mothers and infants to respond reciprocally to each other in a "well-orchestrated waltz" (Brazelton, 1981). Once again, the intervention approach is designed to magnify the ability of infants to send clear signals and to promote the sensitivity of mothers to detect these cues and to respond to their infants' overtures.

Nurcombe and colleagues (1984) reported the results of a hospital-based intervention program designed to determine whether mothers of low birth weight infants can be coached to alter their interaction patterns with their infants. The intervention procedure applied a transactional model over a 6-month period to accomplish the program's goals with mothers and infants based on the work of Bromwich (1981) and Als (1976). The Mother Infant Transaction Program consisted of 11 intervention sessions with a trained pediatric nurse, 7 of which were conducted in the hospital 1 week before discharge and 4 were conducted at home during the 3 succeeding post-discharge months. The nurse coached the mother to identify signs of neuro-motor and physiological distress, to recognize state changes, to promote behavioral organization through consolation and soothing, and to foster the infant's attention and endurance in social play. Each mother and nurse maintained a log detailing the intervention experience.

A group of 78 infants weighing approximately 4 pounds at a gestational age of 37 weeks were assigned to an experimental or control group for purposes of determining treatment efficacy. The control received assessment services only. Multiple measures of mother and infant characteristics and functioning were included as dependent variables; for example, behavioral organization, temperament, cognitive and motor ability, maternal personality and adjustment, and maternal role satisfaction and attitudes about child-rearing. Results of the intervention study demonstrated that the program successfully increased mothers' capabilities to understand and respond to their vulnerable infants' cues. Treatment was also responsible for enhancing mothers' satisfaction with and confidence in mothering patterns. Changes were also observed in mother's perceptions of the degree of temperamental difficulty observed in their infants.

Developmentally delayed infants

Early-intervention specialists have targeted treatment programs to deal with infants who fail to thrive, premature babies with distinct neurological and physiological birth complications, and infants born to mothers from low so-cioeconomic circumstances who received no regular prenatal care. Many of these types of early intervention programs have been most successful when they combine both home- and center-based treatment strategies.

An interesting study focused on providing specialized parent training to 80 low-income black teenage mothers and their infants (Field, Widmayer, Greenberg, and Stoller, 1981). The mothers and their infants were randomly assigned to one of three treatment groups: home-visit, hospital nursery, and a no-treatment control group. The home-intervention program consisted of 6 months of biweekly visits in which mothers were instructed in how to care for their infants, to interact with them socially, and to promote the development of the infant's sensorimotor skills. Home visits were conducted by a psychology graduate student and a black teenage aide. Treatment involved giving the mother illustrated cards depicting exercises and toys to use with their infants. The mother observed and demonstrated her ability to conduct these activities. Treatment also involved daily practice and recording of how much time the mother spent daily with her infant working on these tasks and whether the infant successfully completed the tasks.

The hospital nursery program provided parent training, job training, and an income for the teenage mothers. Nursery school teachers were served by the mothers as teacher aides in the nursery. These mothers received the same child-intervention training as did the home-visit mothers, benefited from modeling the parenting and child-care methods of the professionals in the program, and reaped the advantages of job training and a regular salary. Regular assessments of infant development, mother-infant interactions, and maternal knowledge and care of their infants were conducted throughout the first year.

Results clearly demonstrated that the growth and development of infants in both home and nursery programs exceeded that of the control group infants during the first 2 years. Significant differences were observed in the greater weights of these infants, better social interactions, and stronger motor skills, with cognitive skills exceeding those of the control group after 12 and 24 months of age. Eventually, the infants in the nursery group demonstrated more highly developed motor and cognitive skills than did the home-visit group. The nursery program was observed to be most cost effective and resulted in greater benefits for mothers, as indicated in their higher work return rate, school attendance, and smaller incidence of repeated pregnancies.

Infants with severe neurodevelopmental disabilities

There are increased efforts to provide early intensive treatment for infants with severe neurological, developmental, and behavioral disorders. This group includes children with cerebral palsy; multiple neuromotor, visual, and hearing impairments; traumatic brain injuries; severe developmental retardation; autism; severe self-stimulation, and self-abusive behavior. Various researchers have been noteworthy in these specialized efforts (Bagnato and Neisworth, 1985; Brassell, 1976; Bricker and Dow, 1980; Bricker, Sheehan, and Littman, 1981). These intensive-treatment programs use an interdisciplinary approach to increase cognitive, social, and communication skills; foster more organized neuromotor patterns, promote object and social play skills; and increase self-regulatory and decrease self-involved/abusive behavior.

An intensive hospital-based rehabilitation program was provided to 17 infants and toddlers suffering either congenital or acquired brain injuries (Bagnato and Neisworth, 1985). The treatment consisted of 3 1/2 months of intensive therapy provided twice daily six times a week with the parents present. The therapy was conducted by an integrated team of physical and occupational therapists, speech/language therapists, early-childhood special educators, developmental psychologist, recreational therapists, and pediatric nurses, with the mothers and fathers observing and then eventually implementing therapy on their own. Regular assessments were conducted on a weekly basis to detect functional changes in developmental patterns as well as subtle alterations in various neurophysiological and behavioral processes.

Changes were recorded across 7 developmental and 15 neurobehavioral domains. Results clearly demonstrated that a uniform program of team-based neurodevelopmental therapy was effective in promoting the developmental and behavioral progress of brain-injured infants. Highly significant changes beyond gains expected because of maturation effects were observed in the areas of cognition, language, socioemotional, fine motor, and self-care functioning. The infants with acquired brain injuries showed no significant progress in gross motor skills during 3 1/2 months of treatment, which reflected the extent of their neuromotor damage. Significant behavioral gains were observed in various social communication areas, but few significant gains emerged in selected neurophysiological processes (e.g., consolability, reactivity, attention, activity level).

The program demonstrated that intensive treatment procedures can alter the functioning of severely handicapped infants in definite ways and that their status is not necessarily static as was once believed.

COMPREHENSIVE CHECK 6.10

Would infants with congenital or with acquired brain injury be more likely to reach normal developmental levels? Why might this be so?

SUMMARY

Both logic and data argue for developmental intervention as soon as possible for handicapped and at-risk infants. New medical procedures are now available to save infants who formerly would have died. The saved infants, however, are in special need of services to offset their initial handicap. Thus, growing medical technology produces new challenges for the early-childhood specialist.

Professionals are building a scientific base and body of practical procedures for work with special-needs infants. New screening measures—assessment of infant skills, temperment, and state—new teaching materials, and a strong emphasis on improving the mother-child relationship characterize some of the progress in the emerging field of infant intervention. No other area of special education and child development demands more multidisciplinary participation, more parent involvement, and more precision in assessment and treatment. Increased medical, psychological, and developmental research is crucial; it is the way to develop and evaluate efforts to help parents in meeting the responsibilities, challenges, and joys associated with improving the lives of children.

SUGGESTED READINGS

Garwood, S.G., & Fewell, R.R. (1983). *Educating handicapped infants*. Rockville, MD: Aspen Systems Corporation.

Bromwich, R. (1981). *Working with parents and infants*. Baltimore: University Park Press.

Hanson. M. (1981). *Atypical infant development*. Baltimore: University Park Press.

Bricker, D. (Ed.) (1982). *Intervention with at-risk and handicapped infants*. Baltimore: University Park Press.

Child Abuse and Neglect

Gail Kurtz
P. David Kurtz

CHAPTER OUTLINE

VIGNETTES

Melissa, age 4½, was taken to the hospital with multiple bruises and rope burns and suffering from dehydration. She went into a coma and died within 24 hours. A neighbor reported hearing a child crying and screaming. Police came and found the child naked and suffering from exhaustion. Further investigation revealed that the stepfather had caught her telling a "lie." He punished her by making her walk continuously around the room for several hours. He withheld food, water, and sleep and would whip her with a belt when she would stop walking. When she asked for water he made her drink tabasco sauce.

The Sampsons lived in a rural area and had up to 25 dogs in and around their poorly kept house. The dogs defecated in the house, and it was rarely cleaned up. They slept in the beds and had fleas and ticks. The dogs were not controlled, often barked, and would bite the children if they irritated them. The Sampsons' children, David age 4 and Amy age 2, were ill kept and dirty. They were unsupervised and had open sores on their bodies. They often went to neighbors for food.

A teacher noticed that one of her students, Jennifer, age 5, was going to the bathroom frequently. This behavior continued for several weeks. It was discovered that her mother's boyfriend had been sexually abusing her. He fondled her, came into her room at night and undressed her, and forced her to touch him and have oral sex with him. He threatened to kill her if she ever told anyone about their special secret.

The case descriptions you just read are illustrations of some of the more bizarre and dramatic occurrences of abuse and neglect in preschool children. Cases such as these do occur, and they occur with alarming frequency. In these types of cases the physical and psychological consequences of maltreatment are often readily apparent: bruises and burns, fear of adults, or excessive withdrawal. However, equally prevalent are cases in which the signs of abuse and neglect are much more subtle and difficult to detect. These are the children who, to the untrained eye, seem to be functioning in a relatively normal fashion. Yet, they may be in need of as much help as the obvious cases.

Educators are often reluctant to become involved, and statistics that they are less likely than other helping professionals to report suspected cases. But what helping professionals have more regular contact with a large segment of preschool children than do early-childhood educators? What professionals are in a better position to detect maltreatment of youngsters? What profession has championed the importance of the early years in children's development and the early identification and treatment of handicapped infants and preschoolers? Early-childhood educators.

Abused and neglected children are handicapped; their developmental progress is delayed or distorted by abuse and neglect. Clearly, child abuse and neglect fall within the domain of early-childhood educators, especially those educators working with exceptional preschool children. More importantly, you will learn what early-childhood educators can do to identify and assist in treatment of cases of abuse and neglect. You will also learn ways to work with children and parents to prevent maltreatment of children.

DEFINITION AND DESCRIPTION OF THE PROBLEM

There is no single, official definition of child abuse and neglect. To help describe what child abuse and neglect is and is not, try to decide which of the cases in the following list should be reported to authorities.

- A father always spanks his young son when he runs out in the street.
- A farmer takes his boy "to the woodshed" for leaving the door of the chicken coop open.
- A single parent allows her 9-year-old daughter to watch her 2-year-old son for 1½ hours after school.
- A very active 3-year-old often comes to school with bruises.
- A 6-year-old has rotting teeth, often falls asleep in school, and wears clothes that are ill fitting and inappropriate for the weather.

To be able to identify cases of child maltreatment, we must first be able to define it. What is commonly considered "proper child-rearing practice" may vary dramatically among families and be influenced by culture, socioeconomic class, ethnicity, location (urban/rural), age (of children and parents), religious orientation, beliefs about the rights and needs of children, and accepted community norms. Given these variations, it is often difficult to determine whether certain incidents are cause for alarm.

Children typically *need* certain circumstances to become productive human beings with respect for themselves and others. Primarily, children need to feel safe and secure. This means both physical and emotional safety and security. Physical safety and security includes freedom from bodily harm and pain, both intentional and accidental; emotional safety and security includes nurturance, stimulation, and opportunities for development of self-esteem. The consistent failure, either through neglect or abuse, to meet a child's needs should be viewed as possible child maltreatment.

Faller and Russo (1981) cite four conditions that must be met for a situation to be defined as child maltreatment: (1) existence of a definable parental behavior directed toward the child (omission or commission), (2) existence of observable harm to child, (3) establishment of causal link between parent behavior and harm to the child, and (4) sufficient seriousness to warrant intervention.

There are four basic categories of child maltreatment: physical abuse, neglect, sexual abuse, and emotional abuse and neglect.

Categories of abuse

Abuse is an active form of maltreatment where a child is injured by actions, regardless of whether or not the injury was intended. Children, especially preschoolers, are prone to be active, to experiment, and to explore. Increasing motor activity often naturally results in normal injuries such as cuts, bruises, occasional burns, and fractures. Although many of these injuries may occur from childhood accidents, the following list describes injuries that are *more likely* to be the results of child abuse.

Bruises, Scars, Cuts, and Abrasions
- Found in mouth, face, genital or rectal area, behind ears, on abdomen or chest
- Multiple bruises or scars in various stages of healing
- On infants
- Scars in shape of objects, such as belts or hands

Burns
- Round burns, such as those from cigarettes
- Found in facial or genital areas
- From rope
- From immersion in hot liquid

Fracture and Joint Injuries
- Multiple fractures
- Fractures of long bones, such as leg, arm, or ribs
- Fractures apparently caused by twisting or pulling

Head Injuries
- Subdermal hemorrhaging
- Jaw and nasal fractures

Neglect

Neglect is a passive form of maltreatment through which the child suffers from the omissions of the parent or caretaker. In many ways, neglect is even more difficult to define and identify than abuse. This is because it is less visible than the bodily injury of abuse and because the effects of neglect (harm to the child) may surface only after the neglect has taken place over a long period. It may also be difficult to tell the differencce between the impact of living in poverty and the effects of neglect.

Common examples of neglect are:

Abandonment
- Leaving child with no plans for return

Lack of Supervision
- Young children left unattended
- Young children in the care of other children

Inadequate or Inappropriate Nutrition
- Lack of quantity of food
- Lack of quality of food

Medical Neglect
- Failure to provide preventative medical care, including dental and eye care
- Failure to provide for hygiene of child

Lack of Adequate Education
- Failure to assure child's regular attendance at school
- Failure to send child to school

Lack of Adequate Housing
- Unsafe housing
- Housing that does not have adequate heating facilities
- Unsanitary housing

Sexual abuse

Sexual abuse is defined as "contact or interactions between a child and an adult when the child is being used as an object of gratification for adult sexual needs or desires" (Jones, MacFarlane, and Jenstrom, 1980, p. 1). Sexually abused children rarely sustain physical injuries, and the only indication of abuse is the report of the child.

Types of offenses against girls include exhibitionism, fondling, genital contact, vaginal, oral, and anal intercourse. Most male experiences involve fondling, mutual masturbation, and oral or anal intercourse. The use of children for pornographic purposes is also a common form of sexual abuse for males and females. Most childhood sexual abuse is committed by someone the child knows and trusts such as a parent, other relative, friend, neighbor, or babysitter. Some studies indicate that as much as 90% of such abuse is committed by these close acquaintances.

COMPREHENSION CHECK 7.1

Describe the factors that impede the establishment of a universal criterion in the diagnosis of child abuse. Identify four conditions that must be met for the situation to be defined as child abuse. Explain why neglect should be considered as a category of child abuse. How would you as a teacher differentiate normal injuries from those that result from child abuse?

Emotional maltreatment

Emotional abuse and neglect is the most difficult form of child maltreatment to define. Unlike physical abuse and neglect, the effects of emotional maltreatment are rarely visible on the child and often can only be determined by asessment of the behavior or development of the child. At least 45 states cite emotional maltreatment as a form of abuse and neglect and list such terms as "mental injury," "emotional abuse," and "impairment of emotional health" in their definitions.

The Draft Model Child Protection Act *(Resource Materials: A Curriculum on Child Abuse and Neglect,* 1979) lists four criteria to distinguish emotional maltreatment from ineffective parenting: (1) Emotional maltreatment is a parental pattern of behavior that has an effect on a child; (2) the effect of emotional maltreatment can be observed in the child's abnormal performance and behavior; (3) the effect of emotional maltreatment is long lasting; and (4) the effect of emotional maltreatment is a handicap to the child.

A typical example of a child exposed to emotional maltreatment is Sinclair, age 4, who had respiratory problems which required that he be hospitalized from time to time. Although his mother provided the needed medical attention, she openly and consistently blamed him and his illness for her husband's abandoning her. She also blamed the child for her subsequent economic problems. Furthermore, she made these statements in front of his brothers and sisters. Sinclair developed into a withdrawn younster who allowed other children to take advantage of him. His speech and cognitive development were noticeably delayed.

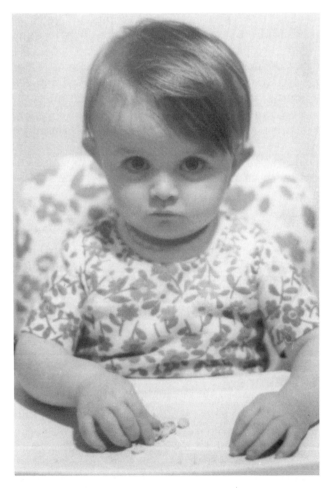

Handicapped youngsters are particularly vulnerable to neglect and emotional abuse.

IMPACT ON THE CHILD AND FAMILY

Children who are exposed to abuse or neglect may suffer biological, psychological, and developmental damage. Maltreatment does not result in a set pattern of problems but is made visible in a wide range of ways among children. The profile to be described identifies common themes found in maltreated preschool children. Delays in motor and social development may be evident as early as the first 6 months of life. Mistreated infants are overly alert to their environment, constantly scanning their surroundings, and ultrasensitive to loud noises and other hidden stimuli. Some infants avoid eye contact with adults and appear to be "shell-shocked." Often they are passively obedient, submissive, and accept whatever happens to them. Rarely do they show their feelings. They appear to be apathetic and listless (Jones, 1981).

With increasing age, the consequences of abuse and neglect become more evident. Between 6 to 12 months, children may display little reaction to being separated from their parents. Older children have difficulty forming healthy, age-appropriate relationships with adults. Such children tend to generalize their pattern of social withdrawal from abusive family members to other adults (Strain, Kerr, and Alpher, 1979). Delays in fine and gross motor development are common. From a review of the literature, Martin (1980) concluded that maltreatment of children increases the probability of retarded intelligence, learning disability, language delay, and perceptual-motor dysfunctioning. Two distinct patterns often emerge in maltreated preschool children. Some are submissive, compliant, and passive, whereas others are aggressive, unsettled, and negative.

COMPREHENSION CHECK 7.2

Is it correct to assume that an incident of child abuse will always result in observable physical symptoms?

Can emotional maltreatment be equated with traditional and primitive child-rearing practices?

Abused children learn to be untrusting in nature. How do you account for the development of this attitude?

Describe the long-term effects of abuse or neglect on the child.

Explain this statement: "An abused child is a handicapped child."

CAUSES OF CHILD ABUSE AND NEGLECT

How do we account for the causes of child abuse and neglect in families? Why, under stressful circumstances, do some parents abuse or neglect their children and others do not? What roles do children play in contributing to the problem? How do environmental factors such as inadequate housing and low income contribute to the occurrence of abuse and neglect? As these questions suggest, the causes of child abuse and neglect are many and varied. Each case has unique characteristics. There is no single factor in child abuse and neglect. Rather, a range of factors contributes to its occurrence. Causes of child abuse and neglect include parental, child, familial, and environmental factors. The interaction of two or more of these factors is common, and relative role of each factor varies from case to case. Treatment may involve individual, family, and environmental intervention.

Parental factors

Many abusive and neglectful parents develop inappropriate child-rearing behaviors and attitudes because of their own negative childhood experiences. Episodes of deprivation, abuse, excessive use of physical punishment, alcoholism, and mental illness are commonly found in their childhood histories. Parents reveal such themes as, "My parents never really seemed to care for me. I'm not sure they ever really loved me." "I guess I was sort of the black sheep . . . the one they picked on . . . always left out." "I never felt safe or secure. I was afraid to ask for things. I just sort of did what I was told. They didn't like to be bothered with me."

Because these parents seem to have been exposed to a punishing and neglectful home life, they have not had appropriate child-rearing practices modeled for them. They are often unaware of normal child-development patterns, developmental needs of children, child care and nurturing skills, and child-management skills. For instance, because of a lack of knowledge, some parents attempt to toilet train their youngster before he/she has sphincter control or may pressure the child to clean up his/her own mess. Impatient parents may interpret a toddler's lack of progress in controlling his/her bowels as a sign of defiance and use excessive force in a attempt to control the child.

> Larry T., age 26, freely admitted breaking the arm of his 2-year-old son during a hassle over a soiling incident. He thought his son's behavior was getting out of hand, and he needed to show him who was the boss. Larry also recalled that as a child he was taken down to the coal bin in the basement and was beaten until he was black and blue.

Parental inadequacies also operate in more subtle ways. Excessively high parental expectations can set up the child for failure. As a result of an infant's failure to respond appropriately to a mother's inept or ill-timed feeding attempts, the mother may grow to view the child as cold, negativistic, unresponsive, and not worth caring for. Some parents are unable to provide what Steele (1980) refers to as *empathetic caring* for their children. This term refers to a parent's sensitivity to children's needs and an ability to meet those needs. In times of stress, these parents place their needs ahead of the children. Steele stresses that empathetic caring is critical in the development of mother-child attachment and that "It is our strong belief it is the impairment of parent-to-child attachment that is most important in situations of abuse and neglect" (p. 55).

It is important to distinquish parents just described from parents who are psychopathic or seriously emotionally disturbed. Although only 5 percent of abusive parents are psychotic, children in their care are at high risk (Spinnetta and Rigler, 1972). Some parents, for instance, claim their infant is "out to get them" or must be cleansed of "bad blood" inherited from the other parent. Mentally retarded adults are capable of being nurturing parents, but frequently lack the "know-how" to care adequately for children. Thus, because of their limitations they may be abusive and neglectful parents.

COMPREHENSION CHECK 7.3

Each maltreated child presents a unique case regarding the etiology of child abuse. Give a clear explanation of this statement.
Would you consider a psychopathic personality as the fundamental reason for abuse and neglect by the parents? Justify your answer.

Fetal Alcohol Syndrome (FAS)

Nine-million people in the United States are alcoholic, two million of these are women, and half these women are of prime childbearing age (18 to 34 years old). Alcohol is a teratogen, an agent that disrupts fetal development. Alcohol abuse, even social drinking, can lead to complications in pregnancy because the placental barrier does not protect the baby from alcohol.

Fetal alcohol syndrome (FAS) is a recently recognized disorder. Prevalent characteristics of FAS include mental retardation, poor motor development, hyperactivity, and short attention span. There are extreme growth deficiencies both before and after birth. Those with FAS usually have atypical facial characteristics. Features such as short eye slits, low nasal bridge, short nose, narrow lips, small chin, and drooping eyelids are exhibited.

Both alcohol and drug abuse by pregnant women have been associated with damage to the fetus (Hanson, Jones, and Smith, 1976). Addicted pregnant women tend to neglect their own physical health and, consequently, the health of their fetus. Thus, their pregnancies are at considerable risk. Several states legally require reporting to the child protective services infants born addicted to opiates and the investigation of the adequacy of parental care. In a recent study, abuse and/or neglect of a child was found in 41% of the families with a parent addicted to alcohol or an opiate (Black and Mayer, 1979). The addiction interfered with the time, energy, and emotional stability necessary for adequately rearing children.

Social isolation of the parent(s) is another factor associated with child abuse and neglect. Abusive and neglectful parents often shun social contact and may not have telephones or transportation. They may resist help from education and human service agencies. As a result, they lack reciprocal relationships with resources such as friends, relatives, neighbors, churches, and other supportive agencies. These resources could relieve them of some of the daily burdens of child care and help them deal with problems in times of crisis. When parents are faced with the physical and psychological demands of child rearing without sources of social support, the likelihood that parents will abuse their children greatly increases.

COMPREHENSION CHECK 7.4

Explain why children with fetal alcohol syndrome are likely to be maltreated.

Child factors

In examining factors that make children prone to maltreatment, it is important not to blame the victim. Obviously, some children are difficult to nurture and manage. These children place a heavy burden on their parents.
However, maltreatment can never be condoned as an allowable or appropriate response to such children.

Circumstances of prematurity, low birth weight, perinatal illness, and
congenital defects place infants at risk. These conditions often require extended hospitalization that interferes with the bonding of the parent and
child and the development of attachment. Once at home, many of these infants require a great deal of parental attention.

Factors of temperament such as patterns of sleeping and wakefulness,
restlessness, responsiveness to parents, sensitivity to stimuli, and level of activity can be irritating to parents and may contribute to abuse and neglect.
Parents experience difficulty forming positive relationships with youngsters
who are fussy, hard to feed, have irregular sleeping patterns, or cry excessively. The circumstance of being born at an inconvenient time from an un-
planned pregnancy, being an unwanted child, resembling a hated person, or
being of the wrong sex may also place the child at risk.

Serious childhood disorders may impair parent-child relationships. In the
case of an autistic child, for example, parental attempts to provide nurturing
are not returned. As a result, parents feel rejected and the frequency of their
extending affection to the child can be greatly reduced. Parents may respond
to such atypical relationships in many ways, including maltreatment of the
child.

A growing body of evidence establishes a convincing connection between
child maltreatment and handicapped children. Are these children abused and
neglected because they are handicapped and thus inclined to invite abuse (as
suggested by Elmer and Gregg, 1967; Gil, 1969)? Or are handicapping conditions the result of maltreatment (as suggested by Brandwein, 1973;
Sandgrund, 1974)? These studies suggest that the answers to both questions
may be "Yes." Child abuse and neglect have been observed to occur far more
frequently in groups of neurologically handicapped (Martin et al., 1974),
behavioral disordered (Elmer and Gregg, 1967), and mentally retarded children (Martin, 1972). Clearly, the consequences of severe cases of abuse and
neglect appear to result in delays in children's psychosocial, cognitive,
language, and motor development. On the other hand, handicapped children
often present burdensome child-rearing demands and may not be responsive
to parents' attempts to nurture them. Such a relationship can increase the
likelihood of parents being abusive and neglectful.

Familial factors

Neglect and most cases of abuse are committed *by* family members and within the family environment. Family dynamics play an important role in the maltreatment of children. Typically, one parent functions as the active maltreater with the underlying approval of the other parent. For example, the parent identified as the disciplinarian has the unspoken permission of the passive parent to use abuse as a form of punishment for misbehavior.

The ordinary demands of child rearing require a marriage relationship in which the parents can routinely support and help each other. When there is marital discord, parents are not only unable to turn to each other to help, but the child may become entangled in the conflict. The hostility between the parents may be focused on the child. Marital relationships in abusive families are usually quite weak, and marital conflict frequently precedes the abusive act. One possible response of a spouse to provocation may be to punish the partner by hurting the partner's favorite child. This "displacement" enables the spouse to retaliate against the partner by harming the child. Stepparents and live-in partners who are not the parents of the children are overrepresented among abusive and neglectful parents. Apparently, they are usually less attached to children than are natural parents, and thus are more likely than natural parents to maltreat children under their care.

Single-parent families are more likely to mistreat children than are two-parent families. Several factors may account for this. Single-parent families tend to be poor, thus frequently they come in contact with human service agencies that are likely to report child maltreatment. Furthermore, the single parent carries the whole burden of child rearing and has few resources to turn to for regular support. Being a single parent can be stressful, but it is even more problematic if the single parent is an adolescent. The adolescent mother has her offspring during a developmental period in which she is struggling to throw off roles of childhood and move into the roles of adulthood. During this period, the adolescent's impulsiveness and irresponsibility combined with a lack of parental "know-how" heighten the risk of child maltreatment.

Environmental factors

High levels of stress in families are associated with child abuse and neglect. In some families a "life crisis" (such as a change of job, moving, or major illness) precipitates abuse. Violence is only one of many possible responses to stress. Why some parents respond to stress with aggression while other parents respond by coping, with passivity, resignation, or avoidance is not fully understood but is probably related to their own learning history.

Stress can be divided into two types: chronic and situational. When stress becomes a way of life for a family, it is *chronic*. Poverty is the most widespread chronic stress that can lead to child maltreatment. The lower a family's income, the more likely the parents are to be abusers. However, it is important to note that poverty alone is not a cause of abuse and neglect. Many poor families provide nurturing care for their children. A family member who has a long-standing physical or mental illness may drain the family's financial and psychological resources and be unable to consistently perform his/her share of the family responsibilities. Tension stemming from this chronic situation can lead to child maltreatment. Parenthood itself is a demanding role. The demands are increased by children who have special problems such as motor, social, and cognitive handicapping conditions. For some parents their child's problems can become a source of nagging stress.

Situational stress is caused by recent changes in the family's social circumstances. Loss of employment or housing, sudden illness, a domestic crisis, relocation, and change in family composition such as a new baby, the death of a family member, or desertion are common sources of situational stress. Virtually any environmental factor that arouses fear and tension, alters family member's roles, threatens the security of the family, or places overwhelming demands on family members can push parents to neglect and abuse their younsters.

Holmes and Rahe (1967) developed a Social Readjustment Rating Scale consisting of 43 of the most common life events reported. Hundreds of people were asked to rate the amount of social readjustment required for each of the events on the list, assigning an arbitrary value of 50 to marriage and comparing the other events to that standard.

Events that seem to produce stress for most parents include death of a spouse, marital separation, a jail term, death of a family member, and personal injury. Of course, many other cirumstances are stress-producing, and everyone reacts differently to life's events. There seems to be little question, however, that parental stress contriubtes heavily to child abuse.

COMPREHENSION CHECK 7.5

Why is the incidence of child abuse and neglect greater in handicapped children?

Why are children of single-parent families considered high-risk children for abuse and neglect?

PREVALENCE OF ABUSE AND NEGLECT

The reality is that the occurrence of child maltreatment is distressingly high and that our statistics only represent the tip of the iceberg. Child abuse and neglect occurs in all ethnic groups, educational levels, and economic classes.

Because reporting procedures vary from state to state, and because many cases are never reported, accurate records are difficult to obtain. We do not have accurate data on unreported abused and neglected children known to professionals and major agencies, those known to other individuals, and those to no one.

Some of the studies that give us specific indicators of the incidence of child abuse and neglect are:

• *Resource Materials: A Curriculum Guide on Child Abuse and Neglect* (1979) gives estimates ranging from a low of 41,000 cases of abuse (plus six times that number of neglect cases) a year to a high of 4.07 million abuse cases a year.

- American Humane Association (1980) shows 614,291 reports of abuse and neglect for a 1-year period.
- National Center on Child Abuse and Neglect conservatively estimates 200,000 cases of physical abuse, 800,000 cases of neglect, and 60,000 cases of sex abuse yearly.
- Straus (1978) reports that 6.5-million children are the victims of violence from being shot, stabbed, burned, kicked, punched, or hit with an instrument by their parents. These figures do not reflect the incidences of neglect, sexual abuse, or emotional abuse and neglect. It should be noted that this study was conducted among intact families. It is reasonable to assume that these statistics would be much high if this study had also included single-parent and blended families.
- National Center on Child Abuse and Neglect (1981) states that more than 1 million cases were reported to child protective service agencies during the last half of 1979 through the first half of 1980.

The indicators of the incidence of child abuse and neglect are sketchy, at best. What we do know, however, is that reporting procedures are inconsistent; reports only document a portion of the actual cases of maltreatment and the incidence of reported cases increases yearly.

Although we do not have accurate statistics on the incidence of child maltreatment, we do have some information to help us to know who are the abusers, who is most likely to be abused, and where they live. Some facts related to child abuse and neglect are:

- Boys and girls are equally likely to be abused.
- The highest incidence of abuse is found for boys during the ages 3 through 5.
- The highest incidence of abuse for girls occurs during the ages 15 through 17.
- Boys are more likely to suffer from neglect than girls during the ages 3 through 17.
- Half the reports of child abuse and neglect concern children younger than age 6.
- An only child is slightly more likely to be maltreated than is a child with siblings.
- Children of families with four or more children are more likely to be overrepresented in areas of physical neglect and emotional and sexual abuse.
- Preschoolers suffer more severity in abuse and neglect and more likely to sustain permanent damage than are older children.
- The greatest incidence of death from abuse and neglect occurs in children below school age.
- Mothers are more likely to abuse than are fathers.

- Homemakers with no additional employment are more likely to abuse than are women who have extra work.
- Unemployed fathers are more likely to abuse than are fathers who are employed.
- Parents in large cities abuse more; the highest incidence of abuse is reported in the Midwest, the lowest in the South.
- Emotional neglect is much more common in suburban areas.
- Sexual abuse is more common in rural areas.
- Abuse and neglect occurs in all ethnic and racial groups.
- Abuse and neglect is found more often in low-income families.
- Emotional abuse and neglect is found more in families with income greater than $15,000 a year.

COMPREHENSION CHECK 7.6

Outline sex differences in the maltreatment of children, taking into consideration all causative factors.

Research evidence indicates alarmingly high figures of child abuse and neglect. Do you think these figures represent an accurate estimate of the problem? Give reasons for your answer.

ASSESSMENT OF ABUSE AND NEGLECT

Legislation

Cases of child maltreatment have been documented for centuries; however, public and private agencies only became actively involved in intervention in the mid-1930s. It was not until the mid-1960s that states began to enact laws to address the responsibility of citizens to protect children from maltreatment and to report suspected cases of abuse and neglect. By 1966, 49 states had laws requiring professionals and citizens to report suspected abuse to public agencies (National Center on Child Abuse and Neglect, 1981); now, all states have such laws.

In cases where it is believed that a child is in too great a risk of danger in the home enviroment, the agency may temporarily place the child either in a foster-care family home, emergency shelter, or group residential home. Such placement is done through a court order. During the time the child is in temporary custody, personnel from an agency called the *child protective services* (CPS) work closely with the natural parents to help them make the necessary changes to provide for the return of the child. Parents may visit their child regularly during the period of custody. In some cases, where parents show no progress in their efforts to provide a safe home environment for their children, CPS may ask the court for a permanent termination of parental rights. If the request is granted, the child is then available for adoption and CPS tries to place the child with an appropriate adoptive family.

One common element of all laws of child abuse and neglect is that *all* suspected cases of child abuse and neglect must be reported. Many states have expanded that definition to include emotional harm and sexual abuse. None of the laws requires that the reporter know or be certain that the child is abused or neglected. "Reasonable cause to suspect" abuse or neglect is enough to justify reporting.

The most critical issue in the law is *who* must report. Early legislation indicated physicians as the group with the major responsibility. However, nearly all states now *require* other professionals who frequently come in contact with children to report suspected cases. These professionals include physicians, nurses, social workers, medical examiners, dentists, mental-health workers, teachers, counselors, law-enforcement officers, and child-care workers. Many states require "any person" who suspects abuse and neglect to report.

Failure to report is usually a misdemeanor ranging from 5 to 30 days in jail and/or $10 to $100 fine. Some states further provide that professionals who see child maltreatment and fail to report it may be held liable for damages cased by their failure to report. On the other hand, persons who do report suspect cases are protected from civil and criminal liability.

The following excerpts are taken from the Georgia law pertaining to child abuse and neglect and are typical of laws from most states.

(a) **Reports by Physicians, Treating Personnel, Institutions and Others.** *Any physician, including any doctor of medicine licensed to practice under Chapter 84–9 of the Code of Georgia of 1933, as amended, licensed osteopathic physician, intern, resident, all other hospital or medical personnel, dentist, psychologist, podiatrist, nursing personnel, social work personnel, school teachers and administrators, school guidance counselors, child care personnel, day care personnel or law enforcement personnel having reasonable cause to believe that a child under the age of 18 has had physical injury or injuries inflicted upon him other than by accidental or exploited by a parent or caretaker, or has been sexually exploited, shall report or cause reports to be made in accordance with the provisions of this section: provided, however, that when the attendance of the reporting person with respect to a child is pursuant to the performance of services as a member of the staff of a hospital, school, social agency or similar facility, he shall notify the person in charge of the facility or his designated delegate who shall report or cause reports to be made in accordance with the provisions of this section.*

Any other person who believes that a child has had physical injury or injuries inflicted upon him other than by accidental means by a parent or caretaker, or has been sexually assaulted, may report or cause reports to be made in accordance with the provisions of this Code Section.

(b) **Nature and Content of Report: To Whom Made.** *An oral report shall be made as soon as possible by telephone or otherwise, and followed by a report in writing, if requested, to a child welfare agency providing protective services, as designated by the Department of Human Resources, or, in the absence of such agency, to an appropriate policy authority or District Attorney.*

(c) **Immunity From Liability.** *Any person or persons, partnership, firm, corporation, association, hospital or other entity participating in the making of said report to be made to a child welfare agency providing protective services or an appropriate policy authority pursuant to the provisions of this section or any other law, or participating in any judicial proceeding or any other proceeding resulting therefrom, shall in so doing be immune from any liability, civil or criminal, that might otherwise be incurred or imposed, providing such participation pursuant to this Section or any other law shall be made in good faith. Any person making a report, whether required by this Section or not, shall be immune from liability as herein provided.*

(d) **Sanctions for Failure to Report.** *Any person or official required by this Code Section to report a suspected case of child abuse who knowingly and willfully fails to do so shall be quilty of a misdemeanor and upon conviction thereof shall be punished as for a misdemeanor.*

The effectiveness of a law is not determined by what it legally requires but by the extent to which it is carried out. The *National Study of the Incidence and Severity of Child Abuse and Neglect* (1981) revealed that only 21% of children suspected of being abused and neglected are reported to CPS. Because all children are required to attend school, educators come in contact with more suspected cases than personnel in any other agency. The national estimates for May 1984 to April 1985 indicate that 363,400 cases came under the heading of public education compared with 36,800 for hospitals, 29,100 for mental-health centers, and 53,900 for police departments. If educators had reported all the children they identified as possible victims of mistreatment, they would have accounted for 56% of all estimated referrals to CPS. The actual number of cases reported to CPS from all agency sources was 212,400. The public-education category accounted for 46,800 of the cases, which was more than any other agency. These agencies reported to CPS only about 25% of the cases they found. Public-school personnel reported only 13% of the cases they recognized. In fact, the estimated number of unreported children identifiable from public schools alone (316,000) was much larger than the total number of children reported to CPS by all sources combined (212,400). In summary, educators have the greatest opportunity to identify and report suspected victims of abuse and neglect. However, the vast majority of cases recognized by educators are *not being reported* to CPS.

Role of child protective services agency

The Child Protective Services Agency, which is part of the state welfare or human resources agency, has the primary responsibility for investigation of the delivery of services to the child abuse and neglect cases. Child Protective Services is required to investigate reports of child maltreatment, to assess the validity of the report, the severity of maltreatment, the possible need for immediate intervention to protect the child, and the need for supportive services. The primary goal of the agency is the protection of the child within his/her family through supplying supportive services. There are two types of support services offered: direct service in the form of casework, counseling, parent education, and homemaker services; and indirect services, which entail referral to other agencies providing day care, food stamps, mental-health, and public-health services. The purpose of these supportive services is to assist families to alleviate problems that have contributed to the child abuse and neglect.

COMPREHENSION CHECK 7.7

Discuss the implications for educators of the law requiring professionals and citizens to report suspected abuse to public agencies.
Educators can play the most prominent role in checking child abuse. Do you agree?

TREATMENT OF ABUSE AND NEGLECT

Role of early-childhood educators in intervention

About half the incidences of child abuse and neglect occur during the preschool years. Increasing numbers of children are enrolled in day care, nursery school, and home-care programs. Such preschoolers have no regular contact with helping professionals other than preschool personnel. Therefore, the role of the early-childhood educator is critical in the identification, treatment, and prevention of abuse and neglect.

Identification

In all states teachers and child-care workers are legally required to report cases of suspected child abuse and neglect. The *National Study of the Incidence and Severity of Child Abuse and Neglect* (1981) revealed two distressing findings. First, public-school educators reported only 13 out of every 100 suspected cases, a much lower proportion than other helping professions. Furthermore, nearly half the cases that educators *did* report were inappropriate or not serious enough according to CPS standards to warrant intervention. These findings suggest that teachers need training and motivation to reduce the number of inappropriate referrals and the nonreporting of appropriate cases.

Table 7.1 lists warning signs that may indicate that a child has been abused or neglected (*Resource Materials: A Curriculum on Child Abuse and Neglect,* 1979). Early-childhood educators can use this table in assisting them in checking the condition of children they suspect may be maltreated.

In reporting abuse and neglect, a major concern is how to distinguish between a vague and a reasonable suspicion. Many educators have legitimate reservations about reporting more subtle cases of suspected maltreatment. In such situations, it is important to collect additional information to document impressions. Observe the child in the classroom, using the indicators of abuse and neglect to assess the child. Consult fellow workers for their observation. In doing so, be certain to gather specific facts, which confirm or dispel impressions, rather than relying on rumors. Talk to the parents to

TABLE 7.1
Indicators of Child Neglect

ABANDONMENT
1. Children abandoned totally or for long periods of time.

LACK OF SUPERVISION
1. Very young children left unattended.
2. Children left in the care of other children too young to protect them.
3. Children inadequately supervised for long periods of time or when engaged in dangerous activities.

LACK OF ADEQUATE CLOTHING AND GOOD HYGIENE
1. Children dressed inadequately for the weather or suffering from persistent illnesses such as pneumonia, frostbite, or sunburn that are associated with excessive exposure.
2. Severe diaper rash or other persistent skin disorders resulting from improper hygiene.
3. Children chronically dirty and unbathed.

LACK OF MEDICAL OR DENTAL CARE
1. Children whose needs for medical or dental care or medication and health aids are unmet.

LACK OF ADEQUATE EDUCATION
1. Children who are chronically absent from school.

LACK OF ADEQUATE NUTRITION
1. Children lacking sufficient quantity or quality of food.
2. Children consistently complaining of hunger or rummaging for food.
3. Children suffering severe developmental lags.

LACK OF ADEQUATE SHELTER
1. Structurally unsafe housing or exposed wiring.
2. Inadequate heating.
3. Unsanitary housing conditions.

IN IDENTIFYING NEGLECT, BE SENSITIVE TO:
1. Issues of poverty versus neglect.
2. Differing cultural expectations and values.
3. Differing child-rearing practices.

INTERNAL INJURIES
1. Duodenal or jejunal hematomas—blood clots of the duodenum and jejunum (small intenstine) resulting from being hit or kicked in the midline of the abdomen).
2. Rupture of the inferior vena cava—the vein feeding blood from the abdomen and lower extremities (resulting from kicking or hitting).
3. Peritonitus—inflammation of the lining of the abdominal cavity (resulting from a ruptured organ, including the vena cava).

INJURIES CONSIDERED TO BE INDICATORS OF ABUSE SHOULD BE CONSIDERED IN LIGHT OF:
1. Inconsistent medical history.
2. The developmental abilities of a child to injure itself.
3. Other possible indicators of abuse.

QUESTIONS TO ASK IN IDENTIFYING INDICATORS OF ABUSE:
1. Are bruises bilateral or are they found on only one surface (plane) of the body?
2. Are bruises extensive—do they cover a large area of the body?
3. Are there bruises of different ages—did various injuries occur at different times?

TABLE 7.1
Indicators of Child Neglect *(cont'd)*

---

4. Are there patterns caused by a particular instrument (e.g., a belt buckle, a wire, a straightedge, coat hanger)?
5. Are injuries inconsistent with the explanation offered?
6. Are injuries inconsistent with the child's age?
7. Are the patterns of the injuries consistent with abuse (e.g., the shattered eggshell pattern of skull fractures commonly found in children who have been thrown against a wall)?
8. Are the patterns of the burns consistent with forced immersion in a hot liquid (e.g., is there a distinct boundary line where the burn stops—a "stocking burn," for example, or a "doughnut" pattern caused by forcibly holding a child's buttocks down in a tub of hot liquid)?
9. Are the patterns consistent with a spattering by hot liquids?
10. Are the patterns of the burns consistent with the explanation offered?
11. Are there distinct patterns caused by a particular kind of implement (e.g., an electric iron, the grate of an electric heater) or instrument (e.g., circular cigarette burns)?

Source: U.S. Department of Health, Education, and Welfare (OHDS), Publication 79–30221, September 1979.

determine their child-rearing practices and attitudes. Ask questions. Is the child perceived as giving parents problems at home? How do parents discipline their child? What arrangements do they make for the child's care when they are away from home? What type of medical treatment do parents provide for their child? Is the family experiencing an excessive amount of either chronic or situational stress?

Another major concern is distinguishing between parental discipline and abuse. What are the differences between a parent's acceptable use of corporal punishment to discipline a child and physical abuse? A young mother, recently divorced from her husband, lost her temper and beat her 5-year-old child when the child spilled paint on the new carpet. In deciding whether the case involves child abuse, keep in mind that a survey showed that 84% of parents use some degree of corporal punishment to discipline their children (Steinmetz and Strause, 1974) and that by law most schools have permission to use corporal punishment as a method of disciplining unruly students. Two criteria are essential in making a determination of physical abuse: severity and frequency. If a beating is inflicted with no apparent physical injury and seems to be an isolated incident, then it may be effective to work with the mother to show her alternative child-management skills. However, if another incident occurs, the teacher should report the case.

A comprehensive school referral or reporting procedure is critical to ensure that suspected cases receive proper services. The following steps are recommended for reporting cases:

1. Assistance should be sought from the school director or principal and school social worker before making the referral.

2. When in doubt whether or not to refer a case, the question should be resolved by a joint decision of the professionals involved in the case.

3. The designated school person, usually a school social worker, should contact CPS to make the written referral and cooperate with CPS to maintain and provide follow-up services.

Child abuse and neglect cannot be treated as a single entity existing in isolation from other problems. Treatment of child abuse or neglect cases is individualized to take into account the unique needs, composition, and interactions of each family, the specific factors that contribute to the problem, and the motivational level of various family members. Common forms of treatment include individual therapy for either parent or child, therapy focusing on parent-child interaction, marital treatment, family therapy, and group therapy. Many cases are, at least in part, a function of inadequate material resources. Services to meet concrete needs include financial assistance such as Aid to Families of Dependent Children, General Assistance, Social Security Insurance, employment and job-training services, medical assistance, housing services, and homemaker services.

Early-childhood educators can provide valuable support services in treating cases of abuse and neglect. One of the most common parent needs is for relief from child-rearing responsibilities. Correspondingly, the child needs to receive warm, consistent child care. Center-based early-childhood education programs play a significant role not only in providing a secure, nurturing environment but also in facilitating the child's development, which may have been stunted by exposure to neglect and abuse. An alternative to center-based preschool education is the home-based program. This is particularly appropriate for families in which it is advantageous for the maltreated child to stay at home and for the parents to learn more adequate child-management skills.

In caring for and teaching mistreated children, early-childhood educators need to be made aware that the child who has established a pattern of withdrawal from his/her abusive parents is likely also to withdraw from teachers. Even in circumstances where teachers are extremely nonpunishing, these children are less likely than their peers to engage in social interaction with teachers. By contrast, abused and neglected children often have positive social relationships with their peers. Thus, peer-tutoring may be more effective than teacher-controlled interventions with these children (Strain, Kerr, and Alpher, 1979).

Prevention

Teachers are the most important link in the detection and prevention of abuse and neglect. "No other single professional group is more likely to be exposed on a regular basis to the warning signals issued both by children and their parents" (Richey, 1980, p. 329). In addition to early detection, early-childhood educators are in a position to teach parents nonpunitive child-management techniques as well as methods for providing youngsters with nurturing, healthy care.

Because child abuse and neglect are vastly complex human problems, we have not been able to develop a perfect enough understanding to allow for successful prediction. At the moment we are unable to predict with accuracy who will abuse or not abuse. In developing a strategy for prevention, we clearly are concerned with certain characteristics or circumstances that increase the likelihood of abuse. We cannot, however, offer sources of support only to high risk parents, for we simply do not know for sure who they are. (Cohn and Garbarino, 1981)

Thus, it is important that preschool educators actively seek to engage all parents in parent-education programs. Fortunately, through the years, early-childhood education has had a history of working with parents. In some preschools, in fact, parent involvement is a required and integral part of the classroom program. Parents may acquire appropriate child-management skills through teacher modeling, incidental learning, and direct instruction. The parent can then try out the newly acquired skills under the supervision of the teachers. Other preschools offer parent-education classes such as Parent Effectiveness Training and behavior-modification-based child-management courses. Through these programs, parents develop more realistic expectations of their children, are able to make more informed decisions about their children's developmental needs, learn how to communicate with their children, and acquire a range of nonpunitive strategies for disciplining their children.

Parent-education programs are particularly critical for parents of handicapped children. Rearing a developmentally delayed child can present many problems ranging from unrealistic expectations and financial burdens to marital strain and role confusion. Parent education programs can help increase these parents' ability to cope with the stress often associated with caring for an exceptional child.

Although parents are the primary perpetrators of child abuse and neglect, Harper (1980) points out that "any adult who is responsible for the physical, social, or academic development of the child is capable of child abuse" (p. 322). He assumes that "bad teaching arises out of the same intrapersonal and environmental dynamics as child abuse. Poor teaching *is* child abuse . . . (persistent neglect of the physical, social or psychological needs of the child)" (p. 323). He argues that stress arises from overcrowded, noisy classrooms. The ill-prepared teacher often lacks classroom management skills and sufficient knowledge of child development necessary for setting realistic expectations and disciplining unruly children. Furthermore, teachers are not immune from persistent personal problems and stresses. When these conditions are present, there is an increased likelihood that some teachers may engage in verbal abuse and, when physical punishment is an accepted practice, they may misuse this method of discipline. These conditions point out the importance of teacher-preparation programs in preventing unprepared teachers from entering the field. In addition, school personnel must provide supportive environments to help reduce feelings of professional isolation and enable teachers to seek help in dealing with professional problems.

Children, themselves, can also be the focus of preventative efforts. Early childhood educators pride themselves on teaching children a range of cognitive, language, motor, social, and self-help knowledge and skills. Preparing children to be aware of and deal with harmful abuse and neglect situations should be a legitimate part of a comprehensive early-education curriculum. In recent years, a handful of materials has been developed that can readily be incorporated into a preschool lesson plan. For example, a coloring book, *Red Flag Green Flag People* (Williams, 1980), is designed to teach children about different types of teachers and how to prevent sexual exploitation. The first section enables children to identify people who touch them. The second part helps children identify the difference between positive (green flag) and exploitive (red flag) touches. The class discusses: What are ways various people touch you? How do certain types of touches feel to you? Is it a touch you like or dislike? The final part teaches children how to handle potentially harmful situations through verbally rehearsing "what if situations." Suppose a stranger said, "Your mother sent me to talk to you." What would you do? How would you feel? Name someone you might talk to about this.

Clearly, early childhood educators can and must play a siginificant part in the prevention, early identification, and treatment of child abuse and neglect. Their comprehensive knowledge of child development and their keen sense of observation provide them with the tools necessary for early detection. Their ability to facilitate children's development is a key ingredient in ameliorating developmental delays resulting from maltreatment, and their commitment to universal parent education can be a potent preventative service.

COMPREHENSION CHECK 7.8

Discuss the advantages and disadvantages of teacher consultation vis-a-vis peer tutoring as an effective intervention strategy with abused children.

What role should preschool teachers play in the prevention of child abuse and neglect?

SUMMARY

Child abuse and neglect cases occur with alarming frequency among all ethnic groups, educational levels, and economic classes. In some cases, the physical and psychological results of maltreatment are blatant. Equally common are those cases in which the indicators of abuse and neglect are hard to detect. Child abuse and neglect fall within the realm of early-childhood educators. There is no one official definition of child abuse and neglect. As a result of the variation in "proper child-rearing practices," it is often difficult to determine what incidents are cause for alarm. Children need both physical and emotional safety and security. If these needs are denied, it should be considered a warning signal of maltreatment.

There are four major categories of child maltreatment. The first is physical abuse. In this instance, a child is injured by actions regardless of whether or not the wounds were intended. Neglect is an inactive or passive form of maltreatment in which the child suffers from the omissions of the parent or caretaker. Abuse where there is contact or interactions between a child and an adult where the child is used to satisfy the adult's needs and desires is called sexual abuse. The fourth form of abuse is emotional abuse and neglect. This is the most difficult to define because its effects are rarely visible and they are hard to detect. Children who are exposed to abuse or neglect may experience biological, psychological, and developmental damage.

A range of factors contributes to the occurrence of child abuse and neglect. Causes include parental, child, familial, and environmental factors. There is usually an interaction of two or more of these factors. Treatment may involve individual, family, and environmental intervention.

Teachers and child-care workers in all states are legally required to report *all* suspected cases. "Reasonable cause to suspect" is enough to justify reporting.

Early-childhood educators can provide valuable support services in treating cases of abuse and neglect. They are also the most important link in the detection and prevention of child abuse and neglect.

SUGGESTED READINGS

Christiansen, J. (1980). *Educational and psychological problems of abused children*. Palo Alto, CA: Jossey-Bass.

Levin, P. (1983). Teacher's perceptions, attitudes and reporting of child abuse and neglect. *Child Welfare, 42*(1):14–20.

Skoblinsky, A., and Behena, R. (1984). The educator's role in prevention, delection, and intervention. *Young Children, 39*(6):3.

Tower, C. C. (1984). *Child abuse and neglect: A teacher's handbook for detention, reporting and classroom management*. Washington, DC: National Education Association Professional Library.

CHAPTER
8

Chronic Illness and Hospitalization

Mary McCarthy

CHAPTER OUTLINE

VIGNETTES

Vanetta is a small, attractive 4-year-old who loves going to her morning preschool class and especially enjoys painting and playing "grocery store" in the doll corner. Several times a year, however, she is unable to go to school; she grows tired and feverish, her hands and feet swell, and she suffers severe pains in her joints. The whites of her eyes turn pale yellow. Sometimes she must go into the hospital for several days. Vanetta has sickle cell anemia.

Mr. and Mrs. Ames worry about their 11-month-old son Jimmy. He is underweight and has been slow to sit up. Sometimes when he cries, his lips and fingertips turn blue and he loses his breath. Jimmy tires easily, and he still sleeps all curled up, his knees to his chest, like a much younger infant. When he is older and bigger, he will need to have surgery. Jimmy has a heart defect.

Of all the children in her preschool class, Karen is the most active. This 2 1/2-year-old loves to run and jump, and her teacher encourages her to do so. Everyday before lunch, Karen's teacher positions the little girl on her lap and "claps" her on the back and chest with cupped hands, occasionally stopping to tell Karen to cough. Karen is thin and her chest is shaped like a barrel. She must have a diet that is high in protein and calories and low in fat, with extra salt added. Karen has cystic fibrosis.

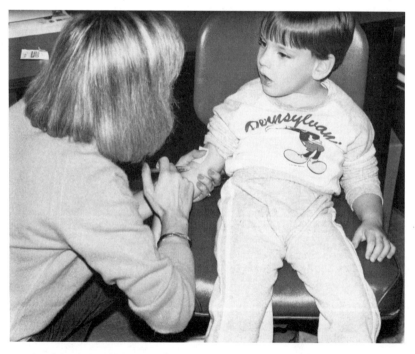

Getting a shot often frightens young children. Professionals can anticipate and allay such fears.

Many years ago, when he was 4 years old, John was admitted to the hospital with a severe case of pneumonia. Even today he remembers how scared he was. A lady in white took away his clothes and made him put on a nightgown that was open all up the back. Next, a man came and took some of John's blood with a needle. The man said that the needle wouldn't hurt, but it did. When John cried the man told him to stop, that big boys didn't cry. Things happened fast after that. John was given another needle, but this one stayed in his arm and had a tube that went up to a bottle on a pole above his head. He was put in a high bed with sides just like a baby's crib, and a clear plastic tent was put on a frame over his head and shoulders. The tent was full of cool fog and a low hissing sound came from one corner. The lady and the man in white were talking about him, but he didn't understand the words they used. Then the lady said that Mommy had to go home, but she could come back the next day to visit. John was left all alone. He was terrified. He worried that the needle would fall from his arm and all his blood would run out. He worried that the fog would get inside him and he wouldn't be able to breathe. He heard someone crying across the hall and worried that whatever was happening to that child would happen to him. But most of all, John worried that Mommy wouldn't come back and that he would have to stay in the hospital forever.

DEFINITIONS AND DESCRIPTIONS OF THE PROBLEM

Vanetta, Jimmy, and Karen all suffer from a chronic illness or health problem. As you can see from the vignettes, the term "chronic illness" does not refer to just one disease. Instead, it is used to talk about many kinds of disorders that have certain characteristics in common but vary in other ways.

General characteristics of chronic disease

What characteristics define a chronic illness? Various workers in the field have answered this question in different ways. For example, Pless, Satterwhite, and Van Vechten (1976) define chronic illness as "a physical or sensory disorder lasting 3 months or longer" (p. 38). This statement makes an important point: an illness or health condition must persist over time to be termed "chronic." Every definition includes this idea of a long-term condition. However, some researchers incorporate additional characteristics into their definitions. Travis (1976), for instance, maintains that an active disease process must be present in a chronic illness; such conditions as cerebral palsy do not qualify as chronic illnesses for Travis because there is no disease present.

For purposes of this chapter, *chronic illness* will be defined as a health problem that is long term; is not primarily an intellectual, sensory, communicative, or motor impairment; it requires some type of special care. Although all chronic illnesses share some characteristics (their long-term nature, for example), they can differ from one another in many ways. One such difference is evident in Mattsson's (1972) statement that chronic illnesses "can be progressive and fatal, or associated with a relatively normal life span despite impaired physical or mental functioning" (p. 801). Some illnesses, such as cystic fibrosis, always end in an early death, while others, asthma for example, may not significantly affect the life span. Chronic illnesses also vary widely in their causes, the severity of the symptoms, the organ systems involved, and the types of treatment required. These differences will become more obvious as individual chronic illnesses are discussed.

Descriptions of 10 chronic illnesses

CYSTIC FIBROSIS*

Background Information
Inherited disorder affecting one child in 1600 at birth
Far more prevalent in whites than in blacks or orientals
Equally common in boys and girls

Disease Process
Exact mechanism unknown
Certain glands produce abnormally thick and sticky mucus that prevents organ systems from working properly
Causes chronic infections of the lung, eventually resulting in tissue damage
Prevents digestive enzymes in the pancreas from reaching intestines so that food is not broken down and absorbed properly

Signs and Symptoms

Shortness of breath, coughing, repeated respiratory infections, thinness, barrel-shaped chests, bulky and foul smelling bowel movements

Treatment
No cure found yet
Attempt to reduce lung infections as much as possible by use of antibiotics, medications to thin mucus, loosening mucus by special positioning and "clapping" cupped hands on child's chest and back, encouraging child to breathe deeply and cough up mucus
Modify diet to ensure good nutrition: low fat, high protein, added vitamins, pancreatic extracts, and salt

Outcome

Disease is eventually fatal
Average life expectancy is 15 years

LEUKEMIA

Background Information
Accounts for approximately 40% of childhood cancer deaths
Boys more likely to be victims

*Information for this section was compiled from DeVita, 1982; Downey and Low, 1974; Kleinberg, 1982; LeBow, 1984; Taitz, 1983; Travis, 1976; Williams, 1981; Ziai, 1975.

Peak incidence occurs between 3 and 4 years of age

About 7000 cases diagnosed early in American children

Disease Process

Causes not well understood, although radiation, viruses, and genetic factors may be involved

Disorder of the blood system

Normal bone marrow replaced by abnormal white blood cells; healthy blood cells become reduced in number, resulting in anemia, increased vulnerability to infection, and decreased blood-clotting abilities

Signs and Symptoms

Paleness, fatigue, fever, joint and bone pain, excessive bruising and bleeding

Treatment

Specific therapy: drugs and sometimes radiation to destroy abnormal cells

Supportive therapy (to counteract effects of disease and drugs): blood transfusions to relieve anemia and encourage normal blood clotting; antibiotics and sometimes isolation to control infection

Side-effects of treatment include nausea, vomiting, diarrhea ulcers, and loss of hair

Outcome

Drugs often produce a "remission," or disease-free period that can last weeks, months, or years; however, most children eventually suffer a recurrence

Latest studies suggest that approximately 50% of children who develop leukemia will be long-term survivors

ASTHMA

Background Information

Most common chronic childhood illness, affecting about 2% of population

Typically develops in early to middle childhood

Boys twice as likely to be affected as girls

Genetic predisposition may exist for this disease

Disease Process

Thought to be caused by a heightened sensitivity (or allergy) of the lungs and breathing tubes to a variety of factors such as pollen, mold, dust, chemicals, cold, exercise, or emotional upset

An attack occurs when the smooth muscles of the breathing system go into spasm, linings of the lungs swell, and thick mucus is produced, so that breathing becomes difficult

Attacks can be mild or severe, develop gradually or suddenly, last for hours or days

Signs and Symptoms

Shortness of breath, coughing, wheezing, feeling of suffocation, blueness of lips and fingertips

Treatment

Prevent attacks by avoiding factors known to cause them and by temporary desensitization with allergy shots

Relieve attacks with medication to reduce swelling in lungs and to expand breathing tubes; severe attacks may require hospitalization with administration of oxygen and corticosteroid drugs

Outcome

Severity and frequency of attacks often decrease after adolescence

Lung damage may occur, but greatest health hazard is threat of death during a severe attack

Good medical care often results in an essentially normal life span

JUVENILE DIABETES MELLITUS

Background Information

Inherited through one or more recessive genes

About 10 of every 1000 people have diabetes; approximately 5% of these are younger than age 15

Can develop at any age, but most commonly appears abruptly and severely just prior to adolescence

Disease Process

For as yet unknown reasons, the pancreas produces little or no insulin, a hormone necessary for the proper breakdown of carbohydrates; this results in excess sugar in blood and urine

Because carbohydrates cannot be used for energy, the body burns fat and protein; by-products of this burning (keytones) build up in the bloodstream, causing prolonged loss of consciousness and eventual death when they reach the brain

Signs and Symptoms

Excessive thirst and urination, weight loss, decreased energy, and sometimes nausea and vomiting

Treatment

Insulin shots and diet must be carefully monitored in a very precise balance; urine is checked daily for sugar to determine whether more or less insulin is required

Too much insulin results in insulin shock; too little results in hyperglycemia (high blood sugar)

Outcome

Long-term effects may include kidney damage, numbness and pain in the extremities, and reduced vision or even blindness

Juvenile diabetics typically survive about 30 years from the time the disease is diagnosed

HEMOPHILIA

Background Information

Sex-linked, inherited disorder transmitted from mother to son

Affects less than 1% of males in the population

Disease Process

Disorder is characterized by sudden, uncontrollable bleeding

Blood lacks one of the specific factors that enable it to coagulate, or clot, resulting in excessive bleeding; this bleeding can be external, caused by a cut on the body surface, or internal, spontaneous bleeding into joints and the body cavities

Signs and Symptoms

Bleeding that cannot be stopped, excessive bruising, pain and stiffness in joints

Treatment

Bleeding episodes can now be controlled by the injection of the missing clotting factor, which has been synthesized in laboratories and is available for use at home

Outcome

Death may occur during untreated hemorrhages of the brain or throat

Although hemophiliacs still face a reduced life span, most now survive until adulthood, and their range of activities is far-less restricted

SICKLE CELL ANEMIA

Background Information

Predominantly found in blacks, of whom 1 in 400 suffers from the disease in the United States

Inherited through a recessive gene

Symptoms usually appear in the latter half of the first year of life

Disease Process

Disorder of the oxygen-carrying part of the red blood cell that results in anemia

During an aplastic crisis, or pain attack, the red blood cells become crescent or sickle-shaped and cannot flow smoothly through small blood vessels; these vessels become blocked, causing damage and death to the body tissue to which they usually supply oxygen

Crises last for hours, days, or even weeks, and can be caused by infections, excessive exercise, change in air pressure, or anything that increases the body's demand for oxygen

Signs and Symptoms

These vary widely, depending in part on the organ systems affected during a particular crisis, but can include paleness, fatigue, poor appetite, jaundice, fever, swollen and painful joints, nosebleeds, and bloody urine

Treatment

There is no cure for sickle cell anemia

Crises are treated by bedrest, forcing fluids, antibiotics, pain relievers, and sometimes by oxygen and blood transfusions

Outcome

Severity of the disease varies greatly

Lasting damage can occur in any organ system, but particularly in the bones, brain, and kidneys

Many children die in their late teens, but with earlier detection and improved medical care, more and more individuals are surviving well into adulthood

KIDNEY DISEASES

Background Information

Can be caused by congenital malformations of the kidneys and urinary tract or by infections

Severity and age of onset varies widely

Disease Process

Kidney disorders are characterized by a reduced ability to filter the blood properly, which allows waste and excess fluid to accumulate in the tissues and produces an inbalance among the chemical components of the blood

Signs and Symptoms

Abdominal pain, fatigue, fever, swelling of the face and other parts of the body, leg cramps, headaches, bloody urine, high blood pressure

Treatment

Varies according to the cause of the disorder, but can include surgical correction of malformations, antibiotics to fight infections, and dietary restrictions

Severe cases may require blood be taken from the body, filtered through a machine, and returned, taking several hours two or three times a week, or kidney transplant

Outcome

Varies greatly according to the cause of the disorder; however, these condition can be life-threatening

HEART DISORDERS

Background Information

Can result from congenital malformations of the heart or from heart disease

Six babies of every 1000 are born with heart defects; these can often be traced to maternal infections during pregnancy, radiation and other environmental factors, and chromosomal aberrations

Major cause of acquired heart disease is rheumatic fever, although this is becoming much less frequent than in previous years

Disease Process

These disorders have in common the impairment of heart function, that is, the heart is not able to pump blood efficiently

Results can include an inadequate supply of oxygen in the blood, an overload of blood in the heart chambers, insufficient amount of blood pumped through the body, or increased blood pressure in the blood vessels of the lungs

Signs and Symptoms

Shortness of breath, fatigue, lack of energy, bluish coloring of skin, heart murmur, failure to gain weight, rapid or uneven pulse, squatting

Treatment

Varies according to cause of disorder

Many congenital abnormalities can be corrected surgically

Good dental care and penicillin before dental work help to prevent infections that can harm an already damaged heart

Medications given may include antibiotics, heart stimulants, and diuretics

Depending on type of disorder, some degree of activity limitation may be required

Outcome

Varies greatly

Many infants with heart defects die in infancy

Disorders of the heart are potentially life-threatening

OBESITY

Background Information

Defined by many authorities as the condition of being more than 20% heavier than considered appropriate for age and height

Multifaceted problem probably affected by both genetic and environmental factors in different combinations for a particular child

Estimates of the number of obese children in the United States vary widely, depending on populations studied and definition of obesity, from 3 to 40%

Disease Process

Condition is characterized by an abnormal increase in the amount of fat tissue, owing to increased number of fat cells and/or increased size of fat cells

Causes are not clear, but possible factors may include some or all of the following: a lowered metabolic rate, limitation of activity resulting from illness or handicapping condition, compulsive overeating, dysfunction of the brain's feedback system affecting feelings of fullness and appetite control, problems in the endocrine system, the high calorie, low residue Western diet

Treatment

Main treatments are reduced calorie diets and excercise programs

Drug therapy with appetite suppressants is controversial and is currently indicated only in some cases because of the potential for abuse

Behavior modification programs, support groups, and psychotherapy are often helpful in combination with other treatments

Radical measures such as therapeutic fasting and surgical interventions are used only in extreme cases

Outcome

Life expectancy during childhood does not appear to be affected significantly by obesity, but there is evidence that obesity may be associated with increases in respiratory infections, diabetes, heart problems, high blood pressure, and susceptibility to disease

Obese children also have increased risk of social and emotional problems

Research is not clear, but some studies suggest that obese children have a greater chance of becoming obese adults than do children of normal weight

JUVENILE RHEUMATOID ARTHRITIS

Background Informtion
About 1 child in 5000 is affected

More common in girls than in boys, 2 or 3 to 1

Peak onset is between 2 and 4 years of age, again between 8 and 12

Disease Process
Cause of this condition is not known, although an infection or fall often occurs just before onset, this may be coincidental

Course of the disease is marked by alternating periods of remission and flare-ups; in most children, it eventually goes away by itself

If condition is not diagnosed promptly and treated successfully, complications can result; for example: serious inflammation of the eyes leading to loss of vision or blindness, retardation of bone growth, heart problems, or, most commonly, permanent distortion of bones or loss of mobility of joints

Signs and Symptom
Primary symptom is inflammation and swelling of one or more joints, accompanied by pain

There may or may not be fever, a salmon-pink rash, enlargement of liver, spleen, and/or lymph nodes, or redness and discomfort of the eyes

Treatment
Disease can be controlled but not cured

Aspirin recommended to reduce pain and, more importantly, decrease inflammation; steroids also used at times, but only in emergencies and with strict monitoring

Physical therapists often involved to provide range of motion exercises to maintain flexibility and muscle function; braces and splints sometimes needed to correct deformities

Surgery occurs in relatively few cases when other treatments have failed

Outcome
Difficult to predict outcome for individual children

Approximately 4% of affected children die from complications of disease or treatment

About two thirds of children eventually recover; of these, one third have a complete recovery, one third have mild to moderate crippling, and one third suffer severe crippling

COMPREHENSION CHECK 8.1

Given the long-term nature of epilepsy, can it be classified as a chronic illness? Give reasons for your answer.

IMPACT ON THE FAMILY

In considering the effects of chronic illness and hospitalization, two major points stand out. First, chronic illness is an ongoing condition; in most cases it cannot be cured and it will not just go away. Children must be helped to face the fact that they will always contend with a chronic disorder, year in and year out, and must plan their lives around it. For parents, the chronic illness of their child is a constant stress. They never know when the disease may flare up and must live in a constant state of tension. Especially in our society, where medical technology has provided the means to cure and eliminate many diseases, the constant and unending nature of chronic illness can be exhausting, frustrating, and discouraging for everyone.

The second point is that the impact of chronic illness is variable. It depends in large part on the age of the child, the type of chronic illness, and the unique characteristics of the family. As the child resolves the challenges of one developmental state and begins to face those of the next, the stresses and barriers imposed by the particular illness will change because the child has changed. Similarly, because families also grow and develop over time, the impact of chronic illness will be different from year to year. Just when a family has learned to cope with the problems of a chronically ill infant, the infant becomes a toddler and a whole new set of problems appear.

The whole family is disturbed by problems caused by the disease. Fleck (1972) defines five functions, or tasks, that the family must fulfill:

1. The forming of a coalition, or alliance, of the parents to meet their own needs and those of the children.

2. Providing the children with the physical and psychological "raw materials" that they need, such as food, trust, and learning experiences.

3. Teaching children the communicative styles that will enable them to participate in peer and other social relationships.

4. Weaning children away from the family by allowing them to experience increasing independence.

5. Coping successfully with the series of crises that constitutes the developmental course of family life.

Each of these tasks is made more difficult by the chronic illness of a child. The formation of the parental coalition may become more difficult because both parents are trying to cope with feelings of grief, often in dissimilar ways. In addition, parents may disagree about how to deal with the fact of the child's illness. One parent may want to pretend that the disease does not exist, while the other needs to discuss and carefully work out each part of the child's treatment. Feelings such as guilt, fear, anger, and depression may stand in the way of the establishment of a "united front" by the parents.

Parents may also find it difficult to take care of their children and provide for their needs. Obviously, the costs of continued medical treatment can be most burdensome to the family. This problem alone can devastate a family and distort the present and future plans of family members.

Not only can the parents not protect the child from the illness itself and the often painful medical treatments involved, but even supplying such a basic item as food may not be simple, because many children require special limited diets. Teaching children how to participate in peer and other social relationships becomes more complex, too. Other children may reject a chronically ill peer because the child looks or acts different. In addition, when children have had frightening, painful experiences with a series of medical personnel, they are likely to be wary of engaging in social relationships outside the family.

Chronic illness also interferes with the parent's attempts to help a child become more independent. As mentioned previously, many of the medical treatments required in chronic illness may necessarily increase a child's dependence on the parents. Parents, faced with the very real vulnerability of a chronically ill child may react with an overprotectiveness that is understandable, but not in the child's best interests.

Finally, the family may find it extremely difficult to cope with the series of crises that chronic illness often involves. Most parents and children are not faced with the potentially life-threatening situations that the family of a chronically ill child must encounter every day. The stress level of such a family is extremely high, and some degree of outside support is usually required to function successfully

The reactions of the siblings of a chronically ill child deserve special mention. Depending on their ages and temperamental characteristics, brothers and sisters may experience a variety of responses. For example, older children may be embarrassed or ashamed to admit the problems of their younger sibling. Younger children may not understand the illness and may fear that they will become ill, too. Sometimes, in the case of diseases with a genetic component, this may actually be a possibility. Children of all ages can experience jealousy and resentment that another child is receiving more of the parents' time and attention. This jealousy is often followed by guilt that they themselves are healthy.

COMPREHENSION CHECK 8.2

Does stress brought on by the presence of a chronically ill or handicapped child increase or decrease family (especially marital) bonds? Do parents in such families have a higher or lower divorce rate?

IMPACT ON THE CHILD'S DEVELOPMENT

Chronic illness can disrupt the developmental progression of the child at every age. As an infant, the child is developing a secure, trusting relationship with the parents and is learning about the world by exploring the environment. Chronic illness can interfere with both these processes. The separation of the infant from the parents during hospitalization may disturb the infant's growing sense of trust and distort the interactions with the parents. Opportunities for exploration may be limited by the infant's lack of energy, by medical restrictions on activity, or by the child's need to be protected from germs and infections.

As children get older, they begin to develop a sense of their own identity in which the appearance and functioning of their bodies play an important part. Chronic illness can cause children to be ashamed of or frightened by their bodies. At a time when most children are becoming more independent, those who are chronically ill may be discovering new areas of dependency. Children with diabetes may need an adult's help with insulin shots, whereas those with cystic fibrosis require adult assistance with loosening and dislodging the build-up of mucus in their lungs.

Problems in attachment

Hospitalization interferes with the development of attachment between parent and infant. The attachment process begins early. For parents, it can start even before the child's birth as they talk about and plan for their new son or daughter. Typically, once the baby is born, the new parents care for their infant, providing love and security. This caregiving is an important opportunity for parents to show affection to their baby in an explicit way and to gain a sense of confidence and competence in their new role as parents. Caregiving is a crucial factor in enhancing the bond that is growing between parent and child.

When a newborn is sick or handicapped and must stay in the hospital for an extended period, the parents lose much of the opportunity to take care of their baby's needs. Often the infant will be placed in an incubator and will require services that the parents are not trained to give. Doctors and nurses take over much of the primary caretaking responsibility. Parents may feel helpless and unnecessary, and the process of developing strong and secure positive feelings for their baby becomes much more difficult.

Normally, the growth of attachment on the part of the infant proceeds in a reciprocal, or complementary, fashion. As infants have the experience of being cared for, they learn that someone will feed and change them, hold them and rock them, and keep them warm. When this care is given consistently by only a few people, an infant begins to develop a warm, secure relationship with those persons. Over time, the infant comes to know the primary caregivers and responds to them in a positive manner. Mutual or interpersonal positive reinforcement or reciprocity is dominant.

Again, hospitalization disrupts this process. Not only are the parents unable to assume their role completely, but the hospital staff is large and constantly changing. Many people may care for the infant over the course of a single day, and it becomes impossible for the infant to come to know all of them. Thus, the infant may be unable to form a strong attachment to any one or two of the caregivers, including the parents. This early lack of attachment can cause difficulties in forming attachments and social interactions later on. Social and emotional disorders may originate in this manner. Also, mother may start out at a high level of nurturing, then burn out; for example, there are differences in maternal interaction when infants are full-term and when they are premature (Infant Behavior and Development, 1984).

An issue related to attachment is that of trust. As infants become attached to their primary caregivers (usually the parents), they begin to learn that their needs will be met— that they will be fed, clothed, and protected in certain consistent ways. In general terms, they develop a sense of trust that the world is a safe and secure place to be. For a normal infant, the development of trust usually occurs by 6 to 9 months of age. When infants have come to know and trust their parents, the separation that can occur during hospitalization is a violation of this trust. No longer can the infant or young child count on the caregiver or the type of care to which he/she has become accustomed. No longer does the world seem to be such a secure place. This can be extremely upsetting to the child and can have long-term effects. For children from late infancy through the preschool period, regardless of their handicap or developmental level, separation from the parents and the resultant violation of trust is a major concern.

Problems in independence

As most children get older and learn to do more things, they begin to venture out on their own more and more. The development of skills such as crawling and walking means that children can physically put distance between themselves and their parents when they want to. With an expanding vocabulary, children can verbally separate themselves by disagreeing with others and expressing their own sometimes contradictory wishes. Children begin to develop a sense of themselves as competent persons as they become increasingly able to perform their own self-care skills.

During hospitalization, children are returned to more passive, dependent roles. Often, because of sickness, weakness, or immobilization, hospital personnel must do things for children typically done by children themselves. Even when such total help is not really necessary, nurses and aides may choose to take over the child's care because it is easier, faster, and usually less messy than letting the child do it. Aggravating for any child, forced dependence can be especially devastating for handicapped children whose skills have often been acquired much more slowly and painfully. In addition, children are usually denied much choice in what happens to them, having no control over what they must do, or how and when they must do it. At all costs, parents and teachers must avoid "crippling the child to kindness" and let the child be shaped into *"learned helplessness."*

Increased opportunities for fears

The preschool period is a time of egocentric thinking. Because children of this age have not yet developed the capacity for logical and objective reasoning, they are at great risk for misinterpreting many of the things that happen to them in hospitals (Blos, 1978). For example, children are often afraid that they are to blame for their sickness or hospitalization: "I wasn't good so Mommy brought me to the hospital," or "I didn't do my exercises right so I have to have an operation."

Because children of this age normally have many fears (of unknown, pain, desertion, loss of control, monsters, witches, and boogiemen), the needles, treatments, and separations that they experience in the hospital merely heighten and reinforce their feelings of helplessness and make it more difficult for them to separate reality from their own fantasies. The inner workings of their own bodies are not understood or perhaps understood only in a distorted fashion. For children who do not realize why certain treatments must be given, it seems quite reasonable that they are being tortured and that worse torture may occur without warning at any time. In addition, hospitalization is usually a time of great stress for the entire family. Parents, themselves, may be frightened and upset. They may be unable or unwilling to communicate their thoughts verbally to their small children. The children can then become alarmed at the discrepancy that they perceive between their parents' words ("Everything is fine, Billy") and the fear and anxiety that is expressed in their behavior.

Decreased opportunities for learning

Restricted environment

As educators, we know that children learn by interacting with their environment. Infants learn in concrete ways by exploring both visually and manually the properties of the objects with which they come in contact. Very young children observe the ways in which objects and parts of objects can be combined and experiment endlessly to see "what will happen if I do this, or this, or this?" Most hospitals do not allow children to have the kind of experiences with the environment that will advance development (Beuf, 1979).

Learned helplessness

An important concept in understanding the potential emotional and intellectual hazards of hospitalization and chronic illness comes from the work of psychologist Martin Seligman (1975). Seligman found that in laboratory experiments where animals had no control over painful and upsetting experiences (being restrained and thus unable to avoid an electric shock, for example), they became passive and immobilized. Even later, when escape from the shock was possible, the animals did not attempt to run away and avoid the pain; they seemed to have lost their motivation to exert any effort on their own behalf, even though the shock was obviously upsetting to them. These animals had acquired a reaction that Seligman called "learned helplessness." Seligman believes that this reaction can occur in human beings also, when they are exposed to traumatic events over which they have no control. In addition to being emotionally devastating, this type of helplessness is thought to decrease motivation and to lead to a cognitive deficit that prevents a person from making connections between events and their consequences (Hall and Lindzey, 1978).

For chronically ill children, who are routinely subjected to traumatic events, "learned helplessness" can be a definite peril. Because they come to believe that they have no control over either the unpleasant aspects of their illness (sickle cell crises, for example) or the painful treatments that are necessary (e.g., physical therapy to maintain muscle and joint function), such children are at risk for "giving up" entirely and becoming passive and dependent. This situation can be avoided or improved by helping children find ways in which they can feel in control. Sometimes this can be done by allowing children to participate in the decision making surrounding their care, arranging choices within the constraints of sound medical practice. For example, when possible, children can be asked when and what they would like to eat, or in which arm they would like their shots. Although it is obviously impossible to give complete control to the child, even seemingly small concessions can help to allow the child to feel more powerful. Another tactic is to assist the child in learning to cope with things (such as pain or necessary treatments) that cannot be changed. For example, sometimes pain can be borne better when a child knows its course is limited; for painful procedures such as shots, the child can be told to count to 10 with the nurse or doctor and can be assured that when "10" comes, the shot will be over. Such techniques as progressive relaxation and guided imagery can also be used to give children more control over pain, but these techniques should be employed only by those professionals who have been well trained in their use.

A psychologist who directs the child-life department at a large children's hospital once stated that even if she sat down and tried, she could not design a less-stimulating environment than that of the traditional child's hospital room (Robinson, 1972). A very young infant who is at the stage of visual exploration will find nothing interesting to look at in a blank white room. A 3-year-old Down's syndrome child who recently learned to walk cannot practice this skill if he/she is confined to a crib all day. Hospital treatments and procedures often require children to be restrained and held in certain positions. Even the stimulation that comes from moving arms and legs may be denied for varying lengths of time. If an exceptional child is in an intervention program, hospitalization usually means missing out on the specific learning experiences that he or she needs and has come to expect.

Most chronic illnesses do not have a direct negative effect on the brain. Physiologically, at least, chronically ill children should be no more likely to have learning problems than are other children. However, there are aspects related to chronic illness that can indirectly influence a child's ability to learn. The side effects of the disease, medications, and other treatments and special fears can disrupt learning and development. Teachers must deal with these issues in order to promote the child's education and development (this is discussed in the treatment section).

COMPREHENSION CHECK 8.3

Jim is a 10-year-old handicapped boy. Explain how his growth and development in the early years has affected his functioning with his peers.

PREVALENCE OF CHRONIC ILLNESS AND HOSPITALIZATION

How many children suffer from chronic illnesses? This question is difficult to answer because the definition of chronic illness varies from survey to survey. In addition, only those children who are receiving some type of services, medical or otherwise, are counted; children who are undiagnosed or untreated are not likely to be included. These factors create problems in determining the actual number of children with chronic illness (Martini and MacTurk, in press); however, the best estimate seems to be that about 7% to 10% of children under age 18 suffer from conditions of this nature. Of these, asthma is the most common problem (2%), followed by cardiac conditions (0.5%) and juvenile diabetes mellitus (0.5%) (Mattsson, 1972). Thus, it seems warranted to estimate that about 5% to 7% of our nation's preschoolers suffer from a chronic health dysfunction that can have developmental implications.

TREATMENT OF CHRONIC HEALTH AND HOSPITALIZATION PROBLEMS

Changes in hospital treatment

In the past, as today, health-care professionals based hospital procedures on what they thought was best for their child patients. Their first goal was to treat and cure the child's physical ailment. Everything else was seen as secondary. Hospital rooms were relatively stark and bare so that germs would have fewer places to hide and breed infection. Children were not usually told in advance about what was going to happen because it was thought that they would not understand the medical realities and would only become unnecessarily frightened and upset. Parents were discouraged from visiting or allowed to visit only briefly at specified times because the staff observed that children clung to their parents when present and cried when they left. The staff wanted to avoid these painful scenes as much as possible. The general belief was that children's negative reactions to the hospital were only temporary and would disappear when they returned home.

During the 1940s and early 1950s, however, researchers such as Robertson (1952, 1953) and Bowlby (1961) became concerned about the emotional consequences of both short- and long-term hospitalization of children. They noticed in particular a characteristic progression in young children's reactions to being separated from their parents. First, the child protested the separation by crying, screaming, clinging, and attempting to follow the parents. Next came withdrawal; the child would refuse to interact with hospital staff or other children and would often curl up in bed with his/her face to the wall. The final stage was detachment; although the child seemed to have recovered from the previous withdrawal phase and would talk and play with other people, he/she was cold and remote to the parents when they returned. These negative reactions did not just disappear when the child left the hospital.

Problems such as nightmares, regressive behavior, temper tantrums, and excessive fearfulness were often reported after the child had been discharged and for some time thereafter (Douglas, 1975; Prugh et al., 1953).

After carefully examining the situation, health-care professionals began to experiment with ways of helping parents and children deal with hospitalization and avoid some of the negative effects. Interventions were planned and carried out based on an understanding of how hospital procedures could affect children at various ages, and it was found that some techniques were indeed helpful in preventing or minimizing adverse reactions to hospitalization (e.g., Hardgrove and Dawson, 1972; Skipper and Leonard, 1968; Visintainer and Wolfer, 1975).

Being hospitalized is still an upsetting and potentially traumatic experience for children and families. Fortunately, there are ways of minimizing psychological damage and of helping children and parents cope. Because young exceptional children have a much greater chance of being hospitalized than the average child, it is important for early-childhood special educators to be aware of the ways in which hospitalization can affect different children at different ages and to understand the specific techniques that can be used to lessen its impact. For an excellent, extensive review of the literature in this area, see Thompson (1985).

COMPREHENSION CHECK 8.4

Describe measures that parents can take to safeguard against the ill effects of hospitalization of their chronically ill child.

Techniques for intervention during hospitalization

The methods that have been developed to prevent and minimize some of the problems discussed can be grouped loosely into three categories: advance preparation, support during the time the child is in the hospital, and "debriefing" (Crocker, 1980) after hospitalization or specific procedures. Some of these techniques are appropriate for special educators to use with their young exceptional students, whereas others should be left to the highly trained members of the health-care team. For example, although a teacher can prepare a child (or a whole class) in a general way for the experience of hospitalization, explanations about a specific operation or procedure that a child is to undergo will best be done by the hospital staff, because they will know precisely what is planned and how to describe the events to the child.

Preparation

The role of early-childhood special educators in preparation for hospitalization can perhaps best be described as helping the child and parents become familiar, in a general way, with the concrete objects and experiences that they are likely to encounter in the hospital. Being examined with stethoscopes, electronic thermometers, and blood-pressure cuffs, eating in bed, using a bedpan, and seeing doctors and nurses dressed in a variety of special outfits are situations that most hospitalized children will experience. These are the events the teacher should attempt to describe to the child, not specific operations and medical procedures. Children who have heard about and seen these things previously, when they are not under stress, are apt to accept them relatively easily when hospitalized. Children to whom these events are totally new may regard them with suspicion and fear because these children are likely to be upset already about other aspects of hospitalization.

The process of familiarizing children with the hospital environment can begin even before a specific hospital admission is planned by encouraging children to learn about different aspects related to health care and the hospital. This can be done in a formal way by incorporating such topics into the cirriculum, or in a less structured fashion by making material available to the children so that they can explore it at their own pace according to their own interests and needs. Topics that lend themselves well to a traditional preschool approach include hospital helpers (occupations), hospital equipment, and functions of various body parts. Many art, science, and other learning activities can be planned around these themes.

Playing doctor has always been a favorite game of young children. Stocking the doll corner with operating room hats and masks, stethoscopes, empty syringes (with the needle removed), rubber tubing, bandages, and other medical paraphernalia allows children to gain familiarity with the equipment and to defuse some of their anxiety about its use. Children at fairly low developmental levels can often benefit from handling these materials even if

Pretend doctor and hospital toys help to prepare children for hospitalization. Role playing, rehearsal, and desensitization are useful strategies to decrease fears.

they do not appear to be engaging in fantasy play. Teachers should monitor medical play carefully to ensure that any misconceptions expressed by the children are corrected.

Many books that deal with hospitalization, illness, and health-care experiences are available. The classics are *Curious George Goes to the Hospital* (1966) and *Madeleine* (1939), but others of equal quality and more variety can also be found (Altschuler, 1974) that are suitable for the preschool level. For toddlers, or children functioning cognitively at about that level, a similar function can be served by cutting out and mounting simple pictures of medical personnel and equipment on plastic cards.

Recently, many hospitals have initiated tours of their facilities and other types of outreach programs. Teachers should call local hospitals to find out what is available in their areas. The hospital can be a fascinating, as well as frightening, place for small children to visit, so teachers should prepare the children carefully for what they will experience. However, being exposed to strange sights, sounds, and odors is much less threatening when one is a visitor surrounded by classmates and friends than when one is facing a hospital admission. In many cases, hospitals will now send a staff member to visit preschools and kindergartens with a special (often "hands on") presentation of information and equipment. This staff person is usually experienced at explaining health and hospital issues to small children and at responding to the spoken and unspoken fears that may surface during such a session.

When it is known that a child will be hospitalized in the near future, the parents should be consulted to determine the most appropriate way in which to discuss the upcoming hospitalization with the child. It is crucial that the information received by the child be consistent, whether it comes from parent, doctor, or teacher. Because young children do not have accurate concepts of time, it is likely that they will not be told far in advance about the coming hospitalization. Obviously, the teacher will not want to bring up the subject before it has been discussed between parent and child. However, because parents are often uneasy about explaining hospitalization to the child, they might welcome the teacher's participation in such a discussion. An ideal situation would be for the child's doctor, parents, and teacher to plan the preparation program together. In this way, the teacher's special knowledge of the child, together with experience in determining and teaching to the appropriate level of development, can make a valuable contribution to an individualized program of preparation. Standard preparation activities, such as preadmission tours given by the hospital, could then be incorporated into this plan.

It should be emphasized again, however, that teachers should not attempt to prepare a child for specific medical events without the express knowledge and cooperation of both doctor and parents, because inaccurate information can often be worse than no information at all.

The younger or more handicapped the child, the more the preparation process should revolve around the parents. All parents of soon-to-be-hospitalized children need to have information about the specific routines and procedures to which their child will be exposed so they can better support their child and help him/her cope with the experience of hospitalization. However, when the cognitive or communicative abilities of a child are limited, as is the case with infacts and many handicapped children, the parents must assume an even greater responsibility. Parents become, to a very large extent, their child's sole link to normality and security. If the parents are prepared and know what to expect of the hospital, they are much more likely to project a calm and matter-of-fact attitude that will be immensely reassuring to their child. In this case, the early-childhood special educator's most helpful role might be to assist the parents in any way possible to obtain the necessary information and resources.

Support during hospitalization

When children of preschool age or younger are admitted to the hospital, the most important support that they can receive is the presence of their parents. Hospitals are beginning to recognize this fact, and many facilities now allow the parents to visit when they choose for as long as they want. Some hospitals even encourage one parent to stay with the child most of all of the time by providing sleeping accomodations in or near the child's room. This situation allows the parent to participate actively in the child's routine of feeding washing, and toileting, which increases the child's sense of security by quieting fears of separation and the unknown. In the case of exceptional children, this participation is particularly important. Most parents can communicate with and care for their child better than can the hospital staff, who may have no experience with handicapped children.

Hospitals have also changed their policies in recent years to attempt to meet children's needs in continuity of learning experiences. Most pediatric facilities now provide some type of play or activity program for their patients. Special hospital staff members, variously called recreation therapists, activity specialists, or child-life specialists, plan and implement a diverse program of stimulating activities for children at various developmental levels. These professionals, in collaboration with doctors and nurses, also provide special kinds of carefully supervised "hospital play." Such activities help children to express their fears and concerns about illness and medical procedures and to work through their anxieties.

What can the early-childhood special educator do to support children in the hospital? Because the teacher is a familiar figure, visiting the hospitalized child often provides a much-needed link between the hospital and the outside world. Bringing reminders of school and classmates, such as artwork or tape-recorded greetings and messages, can reinforce the child's sense of normalcy and continuity. If the child happens to be admitted to a hospital without a child-life or play program, the teacher can work with the parents in supplying activities to occupy the child and allow the child to participate in developmentally appropriate, reassuringly normal pursuits. Teachers can also offer their experience and skills to the hospital staff to help in setting up the most suitable plan for the child, both during hospitalization and afterward.

Remembering the child's dependence on parents, the teacher can help to support the child by supporting the parents. Calling to inquire how the child is doing, offering help, and listening sympathetically if the parent needs someone to talk to, are all techniques that will assist parents in coping with hospitalization, and thus better enable them to help their children.

"Debriefing"

Once discharged from the hospital, the child will need help in working through the pain and fear that may have been experienced. Teachers can provide support and active assistance in this process. First, the teacher needs to know (and may have to help the parents understand) that children often deal with hospitalization by engaging in regressive behavior once they are home. This means that they return to earlier behaviors that they had outgrown prior to hospitalization. For example, a child who was potty-trained before going into the hospital may begin to wet his/her pants again, while a child who had learned self-feeding may again demand to be fed. Other reactions that may be expected include increased crying and whining, unusual fearfulness, temper tantrums, and aggressive behavior. The teacher can deal with these problems gently but firmly, sympathetically and consistently indicating what is expected of the child while patiently tolerating frequent relapses.

Children often need to defuse their fears and anxieties about hospitalization and medical procedures in a more specific way. By allowing them varied opportunities to do so, the teacher can help them cope with the aftereffects of the hospital experience. Some children may be able to work through their fears verbally. Talking about the things that happen to them with the teacher and other children seems to reduce their anxiety. Less-advanced or less-verbal children may need to express their fears symbolically. They should be encouraged (but never forced) to handle and play with safe medical equipment as described earlier, because this often relieves tension to some extent. Reading books and seeing films dealing with hospitalization and health care may also lessen anxieties and may encourage the child to express fears instead of denying them. Whenever teachers see or hear children communicating incorrect medical information or misinterpretations of what was done to them, correct explanations should be provided. Sometimes a teacher may need to consult the parents or doctor to find out what real treatment or procedure involved.

COMPREHENSION CHECK 8.5

State the rationale for acquainting preschoolers with information regarding hospitals and doctors. As a preschool teacher, describe the program you would develop and specify your objectives.

EDUCATING CHRONICALLY ILL PRESCHOOLERS

Side effects of disease

Two major consequences of chronic illness can contribute to a child's poor performance in a school or intervention program. The first of these occurs when a child misses sessions because of a flare-up of the illness or hospitalization for tests or treatment. Obviously, a child cannot benefit from educational services not received. Sometimes, if the child is well enough, the teacher can instruct the parents or hospital staff so that they can provide some activities for the child that will help maintain skills while absent from the program. In the case of hospitalization for tests or nonemergency treatment, the teacher could encourage the parents to delay the procedure until a regularly scheduled vacation arrived. Other than this, there is little that can be done to improve the situation.

Another negative effect on learning is the lack of energy or general malaise (not feeling quite well) that chronic illness can produce. Sometimes this condition can be improved by a change in medication or other treatment. The teacher should approach the child's parents about the problem to see if anything can be done. Often, however, no improvement can be made. In this case, the teacher must work around the problem by scheduling the most strenuous or demanding tasks at times when the child is usually the most alert and by alternating short periods of intense work with longer periods of more restful activities.

Medication

Two issues regarding medication are crucial in determining how effectively the chronically ill child will function in an intervention program: proper administration and proper prescription. The teacher is obviously more concerned with the first of these, but also has a responsibility to observe the child closely and talk to the parents and doctor whenever there is some doubt that the medication is doing what it is intended to do.

In most center-based intervention programs, teachers take on the task of administering medications that their students need while they are attending the program. This is a heavy responsibility, and teachers should be absolutely scrupulous about carrying it out. First of all, the educator must be certain that state law allows teachers to perform this function. Next, the educator should become an expert on the medication. What is the drug meant to do? What are the signs of too much or too little, and how can these effects be corrected? What is the exact dosage? What are the conditions of administration; that is, should the drug be given before or after a meal, with or without certain foods or activities? Over how long a time span should the medication be given? Three days? Two weeks? Or until it is all used up?

Finally, the teacher must draw up a strict plan to guide administration. The medications must be kept under lock and key to prevent mishaps from occurring. A master schedule should be developed to show which child gets what medication at what time. Such a schedule should include space for a daily check-off indicating that the child did indeed receive the medication, with the initials of the person who administered it. It is often a good idea to write a brief description of the medication on the schedule so that it is absolutely certain that the correct pill or liquid was administered. If the medication is one that the child must take on a continuing basis, the teacher should notify the parents when the supply is running low, allowing enough time for a refill to be obtained. Most important of all, no drug should be given without a *written* order signed by the child's doctor.

The second issue related to medication is appropriate prescription. The child's physician is, of course, the ultimate judge of what medications should be given to a child. However, teachers do have an obligation to speak up if they believe that a certain drug is not in the best interest of the child. For example, there was great controversy in the 1970s about the drugs given to so-called learning disabled children to control their hyperactivity. Some people argued that the medications were given to make the children easier to control by the parents and teachers, and that they improved a child's ability to learn. On the contrary, others said, the drugs put the children into a zombielike state in which learning was actually impaired.

Although it is not likely that a similar situation exists for medications commonly prescribed for most chronic illnesses (that is, that they are given to make the child easier to handle rather than for a valid physical reason), it is still possible that certain drugs may have side effects that detract from the child's ability to learn. These side effects include drowsiness, irritability, and impaired motor coordination. The teacher should always communicate this situation to the parents and doctor in an objective and nonthreatening manner. It may be the case that the child needs that particular medication, despite the side effects. The doctor may, however, be able to prescribe a similar drug that could perform much the same function without the side effects.

COMPREHENSION CHECK 8.6

Assume that you have two chronically ill preschool children in your class. What added responsibilities does this imply? Outline specific steps you would take to meet this responsibility.

Other treatments

In addition to medication, chronically ill children often require some type of special treatments, which may need to be done during the course of an educational session. These treatments may include special diets and eating routines, procedures such as *catheterization* (inserting a tube into the bladder for the release of urine), or *postural drainage* (putting a child into special positions to encourage the draining of mucus). Sometimes specific limits must be placed on a child's activities (no running, or no high swinging, for example).

When it is known that children must have these treatments, teachers should try to be as flexible as possible, either providing the treatments themselves or arranging for the school nurse, therapist, teacher aide, or parent to carry out the procedure. Although scheduling these necessary treatments may make the school day awkward, early-childhood special educators should take great care not to show anger or irritation in the presence of a child, because this could make the child self-conscious and anxious. Needless to say, anyone providing these special treatments would be rigorously trained in the correct procedures to follow.

Special fears

All young children have fears about pain, death, and separation, but in the case of chronically ill children these fears are often validated by reality. They are separated from their parents during hospitalization; they are subjected to painful medical procedures; and the threat of death often does hang over them. In addition, because of the characteristics of particular diseases, children may develop fears that are directly related to their own chronic illness. Many asthmatics and children with cystic fibrosis, for example, fear that they will suffocate. Hemophiliacs may be afraid that they will bleed to death. Almost all children dread the thought of being different from their peers, and this is another fear that can come true for chronically ill children. They may not be able to eat the same foods as the other children, or go to the bathroom in the same way, or engage in the same activities.

Being anxious and fearful takes quite a lot of energy and can seriously interfere with what a child is able to learn. Early-childhood special educators should be alert to indications that children are particularly worried and should attempt to discover what is frightening the child. Careful observation or gentle questioning (if the child is old enough) may be helpful. In some cases, teachers can take steps themselves to reassure children. For example, with a boy who is overwhelmingly frightened that he will die during an asthma attack at school, a teacher might emphasize all the things that are being done to help prevent an attack (avoiding certain foods, objects, or activities, for instance) and remind him of the medication and treatments that can quickly be given if an attack should occur. Or, with a small girl who is anxious about her partial baldness from cancer therapy, a teacher might work with the other children to educate them about the situation so that they will be less likely to make fun of the little girl.

When children have fears about certain medical treatments over which teachers have no control, such as needles or specific painful procedures, the teacher can make sure that the doctor knows about the fears. In addition, the teacher might try allowing the child to re-create the painful situation with safe medical equipment and dolls or stuffed animals. Often during this kind of play, where the child is in complete control, worries and anxieties can be defused. In severe cases, where the child seems completely immobilized by fears, the teacher should speak to the parents about obtaining professional mental-health care for the child.

The most important task of the teacher in these situations is to support the child emotionally in any way possible. Such support includes *always* taking a child's fears seriously, no matter how ridiculous or farfetched they may appear to an adult. With a warm, caring, and matter-of-fact attitude, a teacher is likely to help a child put his/her fears into perspective.

COMPREHENSION CHECK 8.7

Explain how the fears of chronically ill preschoolers affect their learning. As a preschool teacher, what measures would you take to reduce this interference with learning?

Working with health-care professionals

No magic rules will guarantee successful interactions between the teacher and the medical staff responsible for a chronically ill child's care. Communication in this case requires the same hard work and suffers from the same pitfalls as in any other professional situation. However, there are some considerations that may help teachers to approach doctors and nurses in ways that are maximally effective.

The first point for early-childhood special educators to keep in mind is that working with a chronically ill child can be an upsetting and frustrating task for anyone involved. This is especially true for doctors and nurses whose training has been to treat sick children and make them well. In the case of a chronic illness, the child can never be made completely well. Thus, medical and nursing staff may feel helpless and may resent the fact that they must subject the child to painful treatments while never effecting a cure. Sometimes health-care professionals may adopt what teachers view as a cool, overly detached attitude toward the child in order to cope with their own feelings of vulnerability. Educators should remember that almost all doctors and nurses, just like most teachers, have the best interest of the child at heart.

When it is necessary to communicate with members of the medical team, teachers should prepare their comments or questions carefully. Recommendations or observations should be presented objectively based on an examination of all the data that the teacher has available. The attitude of the early-childhood special educator should be that of a professional communicating with another professional. Just as the teacher would not like the physician recommending what teaching techniques to use, doctors will not appreciate statements that try to direct their actions. It seems almost unnecessary to add that verbal attacks or insinuations about the medical staff's competence or good intentions are totally out of place. By their calm manner and rational, realistic approach to the needs of chronically ill children, and with their understanding of the stresses that may be affecting doctors and nurses, teachers should be able to work collaboratively and effectively with members of the health-care team.

COMPREHENSION CHECK 8.8

How does a program of constant interaction between parents, teachers, and medical staff help the chronically ill child?

The dying child

At one time or another, many teachers may be faced with the tragedy of knowing that one of their pupils is dying. Death is always a devastating event, but the death of a small child, even one who has suffered from a chronic illness or handicap, seems to violate the natural order and thus is a particularly wrenching experience. Teachers will find that they need to provide support not only to the child, but also to parents, other members of the class, and, not least, to themselves.

Preschool children's conceptions of life and death are heavily dependent on their state of cognitive development. Because these children tend to be in what Piaget describes as the "preoperational" state, their mental processes are often characterized by animism and magical thinking: not only do they credit inanimate objects (the sun, for example) with life, but they also perceive life and death as alternating and therefore reversible conditions. Since a "dead" battery can be "brought back to life" with a jolt from a jumper cable, it must seem equally logical to a preschooler that a dead person can come back to life. These youngsters may know and use the word "dead," but they have no real notion of what death implies.

How does a teacher help a dying child? The most important way is to resist the very natural temptation to avoid or to distance oneself from the child, and to continue to be a friend and source of positive emotional support, even when the child is no longer in school. Because young children do not understand death realistically, their greatest fear may not be of dying, but rather of being ignored, deserted, or forgotten. Thus, continuing to keep in touch with the child, perhaps bringing notes, pictures, and messages from classmates, can help the child continue to feel loved and supported.

When told about a child's terminal condition, teachers should attempt to find out from parents what information the child has been given. Many parents feel that young children should not be told they are dying; issues of death aside, however, children are usually sensitive enough to realize that something serious is wrong with them, anda their feelings will be violated by parents who pretend that everything is just fine. Although teachers should never take on the responsibility of imparting information behind the parents' backs, they can and should encourage the parents to be as realistic as possible in what they tell their child. Sometimes sharing books that deal with children and death (e.g., Grollman, 1976; Hughes, 1978; Wass and Corr, 1984) will help parents with what to say to their own child.

Children who have been told nothing directly about their condition, and who feel subtly discouraged from questioning their parents, may sometimes try to gain information by sounding out a trusted teacher; this can put the teacher in the terrible position of wanting to help the child, but not wanting to upset the parents, or to say the wrong thing. Usually an oblique response to the child such as, "What have your mom and dad told you?" or "What is making you think about that?" will serve to keep open the lines of communication, and perhaps to elicit some of the child's fears and worries, which can then be routed back to the parents and medical staff.

With a terminally ill child, as with a hospitalized child, sometimes the best way to support the child is by supporting the parents. Allowing the parents opportunities to ventilate their feelings can often be a great service to them. However, teachers need to develop an exquisite sensitivity so that they can express their willingness to listen without imposing an obligation on the parents to repeat painful and upsetting stories to yet another person. Another way is which teachers can provide a crucial service to parents is by helping them to see glimpses of normality in their children, especially when the appearances of such children have deteriorated over the course of their disease. Comments such as "Jimmy still has that same sweet smile" or "I've always loved that sparkle in Jenny's eyes" may remind the parents of the essential qualities of their child even when they are less obvious because of illness.

The death of a classmate can be an upsetting experience to preschoolers, especially if some of them have the same condition as the dead child. Teachers need to provide information and activities that will help the other children cope with the event without forcing any of them into experiences for which they are not ready. Some of the books mentioned earlier can serve as good references for teachers as well as parents; often such stories will provide opportunities for children to hear about death in other contexts and give them words with which they can express their thoughts and concerns. Children, particularly those suffering from the same illness as the dead child, need to be reassured (as far as is honest) that death is not in their own immediate future.

Planning a special occasion or event to memorialize their classmate is another method of helping children cope with their loss. A quite time when each child can mention something he or she remembers about their friend, planting a seed, drawing pictures of shared activities—these are all ways in which teachers can place emphasis on the positive experiences that were enjoyed rather than on grief and loss.

Finally, teachers need to attend to their own feelings surrounding the death. Often by concentrating on ways in which the teacher was able to provide comfort and support for the child, rather than on the problems and pain encountered, the teacher can find consolation and satisfaction in a job well done.

SUMMARY

"Life is not a matter of holding good cards, but of playing a poor hand well" (Robert Louis Stevenson, as cited in Mattsson, 1972, p. 801). This might serve as an apt metaphor for the work of early-childhood special educators as they employ every bit of their wisdom and expertise to help exceptional children make the best possible use of their physical and mental capabilities.

Hospitalization presents problems for children that vary according to their level of development. Infants are at risk for disruption of the attachment process that should be developing between parent and child. All children of preschool age and younger can be adversely affected by separation from the parents and the violation of trust that this implies. As children progress in their development, hospitalization can have negative effects by forcing them to assume more passive roles and interrupting their slowly building sense of independence. Medical procedures may confirm and heighten preschool children's worst fears and fantasies about the unknown, pain, separation, and loss of control. Finally, at every level of development, hospitalization can interfere with the learning experiences that all children need to grow and progress.

Early-childhood special educators can become involved with children's chronic health and hospitalization problems in several ways. A preschool teacher may have one or more students in class whose exceptionality is a chronic illness rather than a motor disability. An infant stimulation specialist may find that many handicapped infants must be hospitalized for surgery or infections that are directly or indirectly related to their handicaps. Finally, an increasing number of early-childhood educators are choosing to enter the relatively new positions of hospital teacher or child-life specialist and are working directly and exclusively with children who are hospitalized.

SUGGESTED READINGS

Batshaw, M. L., and Perret, V. M. (1981). *Children with handicaps: A medical primer.* Baltimore: Paul H. Brooks Publishing Company, Inc.

Gadow, K. D. (1979). *Children on medication: A primer for school personnel.* Reston, VA: The Council for Exceptional Children.

Halsam, R. H. A., and Valletutti, P. J. (Eds.). (1975). *Medical problems in the classroom: The teachers role in diagnosis and management.* Baltimore: University Park Press.

Peterson, R. M., and Cleveland, J. O. (1975). *Medical problems in the classroom: An educators guide.* Springfield, IL: Charles C. Thomas.

Schultz, F. R. (1984). Respiratory distress syndrome. In J. A. Blackman (Ed.). *Medical aspects of developmental disabilities in children birth to three,* pp. 207–209. Rockville, MD: Aspen Systems Corporation.

PROFILES OF DEVELOPMENTAL PROBLEMS AND PROGRAMS

9

Developmental Differences in Communication

L. Gayle Barney

Cynthia L. Landis

CHAPTER OUTLINE

VIGNETTES

Ellen is a 2-year-old nonambulatory child with cerebral palsy. Because of her neurological and motor difficulties, the fine motor control of her right hand is significantly impaired; her left hand functions well. Also, although her visual acuity is normal, Ellen shows a congenital paralysis that affects the muscles in her left eye. As with most cerebral-palsied children, Ellen has significant problems in acquiring language and communication skills—she is nonvocal. Ellen communicates many meanings effectively with a wide range of gestures, facial expressions, and body movements. However, she understands much more than she can express verbally: She can identify pictures of basic objects and actions as well as follow simple directions about location.

Ellen is a smart child and interacts socially with many people. It is important that her social and cognitive development not be hindered by her lack of speech. This can be prevented by providing Ellen with an alternative communication system designed by a speech/language specialist in conjunction with her parents and her preschool teacher. Several basic communication boards will be designed. One will contain appropriate content for home, while another will include information in picture form about events and needs in school. Simultaneously, through therapy, vocalization will be promoted in the classroom and at home; prespeech skills will be emphasized through appropriate feeding patterns. It is difficult to predict whether Ellen will eventually become capable of speech for communication; however, early therapy now with an emphasis on alternative communication methods can prepare her and promote her developmental progress.

Michael is a 4½-year-old boy showing many characteristics typical of learning-disabled children. He is highly distractible, particularly in the classroom. His ability to attend and concentrate is greatly affected by seemingly minor events (cars passing on the road outside, children using the restrooms down the hall, and water passing through overhead pipes). Michael also has much difficulty following classroom routines. He frequently watches his classmates for clues in order to know when it is circle time, snack time, recess time, and time for working alone with his teacher. Moreover, Michael shows signs of subtle but pervasive language problems that affect his ability to learn independently and to express himself effectively. For these reasons, he receives language therapy twice each week with a classroom language program once a week. Michael understands many basic words and concepts, but his overall concept knowledge is about 8 to 12 months behind others his age. He has great difficulty following and even recalling from memory portions of directions that are given to him. Similarly, Michael has a "word retrieval" problem, an inability to recall exact labels for objects, actions, and events when asked questions. In his conversational speech, he often stalls for time when he cannot think of particular words by using filler words and phrases such as "that thing, that, you know, it is over there, ummm, that big thing, uh, oh, I forget its name." Finally, he often transposes syllables in speaking, as banana becomes "abana" or spaghetti becomes "busgetti," or has problems sequencing words in his speech such as "read to my book" instead of "read my book to me." The speech/language specialist can be a valuable ally in helping Michael's preschool teacher to use strategies and aids that will remedy his deficits. Through individual therapy, Michael can be taught to slow down, sequence his thoughts and words before answering, and learn techniques that will help him remember more quickly.

DEFINITION AND DESCRIPTION OF THE PROBLEM

As these vignettes illustrate, difficulties in understanding and using language are similar whether a child is mentally retarded or has cerebral palsy or is learning disabled. For this reason, it is more meaningful and practical to describe the characteristics of a child's language rather than to focus on the reasons why a child has not acquired language skills. Bloom and Lahey (1978) assert that there is a general lack of agreement on the terms used to describe or classify child language disorders. Nevertheless, a child experiences a language disorder if he fails to use language or if he has language behaviors that differ from those expected of the typical child his age. Disorders in comprehending (i.e., *receptive skills*) and in using language for communication (i.e., *expressive skills*) need to be identified.

Disorders in form, content, and use consist of distortions in various elements that make language possible. *Syntax* refers to the precise sequence in which words are ordered in a sentence so that they convey meaning. The elements of language that can be heard or seen in writing are referred to as the *surface structure* of language. *Semantics* refers most specifically to vocabulary development and the conceptual understanding of how different words relate to one another to express meaningful thoughts. This meaning depends on the context in which words appear (e.g., a playpen versus a fountain pen). Disorders in the use of language involve problems in *pragmatics* (i.e., understanding and using the purposes or functions served by language when communicating with others). Finally, *phonologic disorders* refers essentially to "speech" problems in how to produce and relate different sounds to produce words.

COMPREHENSION CHECK 9.1

What determines whether a young child has a language disorder? When does a child have a problem with pragmatics in language?

IMPACT ON THE FAMILY

When a child fails to acquire language and communication skills, the mixture of emotions that this event generates in parents is a major point of concern for early-intervention specialists. Language capabilities have great meaning for parents because they are taken as the most pronounced indicator of a child's intelligence. Parents often wait anxiously for the "first word" and often interpret the child's sound patterns as indicating a specific object or need. When their child fails to develop language at the age expected or when their child's peers do, parents often become fearful and anxious. In the past, their pediatricians have counseled them to "wait, he'll outgrow this stage." Despite this, parents still feel vaguely uneasy about the advice. When they later learn that their child has a language disorder or mixed developmental disabilities, they express a mixture of anger, frustration, anxiety, and sadness that their "intuition" about their young child was not taken seriously much sooner.

Parents often flounder in their efforts to help speed their child's language development; with the increase in anxiety, they often try to correct the child's speech and make the child give a correct pronunciation of a word rather than considering their child's current developmental capabilities. Often they fail to reduce the length and content of their directions to the child to compensate for his fleeting attention and immature memory capacity. Their increased vigilance about language makes them expert at deciphering the child's sounds to interpret his needs even though others cannot understand and his language skills are not functional.

Often parents need direction in how to encourage language use, but they become confused and exhausted by the language-disordered child's inappropriate behaviors that are inadvertently reinforced and used as a substitute method of communication. The behavior problems become the child's response to frustration at not being able to communicate. Thus, total body communication and inappropriate behavioral reactions become a form of self-expression. Moreover, language-disordered children often fail to develop a sense of the value of communication. Both siblings and parents frequently talk for the child and get him things without requiring him to communicate for them. This lack of demand and opportunity to initiate communication of wants and needs is often a difficult and intractable problem. Parents and brothers and sisters need counseling about appropriate ways to encourage communication to young children with both mild and severe language disabilities if progress is to occur and social and emotional adjustment is to be promoted within the family.

COMPREHENSION CHECK 9.2

What common mistakes do parents make with their language-disordered children? Why do children with language problems also develop behavior problems?

IMPACT ON THE CHILD'S DEVELOPMENT

Birth to three years

The development of communication skills depends on the emergence of parallel skills in several other developmental areas. The child must know what he wants to communicate, how to sequence that information linguistically, and how to communicate that information through speech. It is important to have a model of language acquisition that explains how this process occurs. The model must illustrate the domains in which a child must develop expertise in order to be an effective communicator. One such model, the *transactional model of language acquisition* was described by McLean and Snyder-McLean (1978) (Figure 9.1). The transactional model describes those areas in

Figure 9.1
A Transactional Model of Language Acquisition

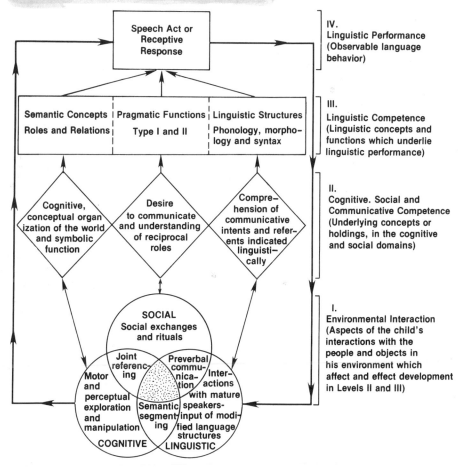

Source:
McLean, J. E., and Snyder-McLean, L. K. (1978). *A transactional approach to early language training.* Columbus, OH: Merrill.

which the child must develop prerequisite skills necessary for communicating thoughts and needs.

The strong relationship between cognition and language is evident in development. Early language acquisition has been described as a mapping of language onto already achieved concepts (Bowerman, 1978). Conceptual development must be intact for language learning to occur. However, the exact nature of this relationship remains controversial. Bowerman (1978) describes several phenomena in language acquisition that are not dependent on conceptual development. For example, a child may hve developed a concept but is unable at his linguistic age to express it adequately. Therefore, it appears difficult to draw a direct causal link between specific cognitive achievements by the child and specific language milestones.

The young child (Piaget's stages II and III, ages 1 to 8 months), interacts with objects in a limited motoric manner. Thus, he lacks knowledge about objects and their properties. Actions on objects such as banging and mouthing are random and not coordinated. Unusual and interesting behaviors are repeated.

At 8 to 12 months of age (Piaget's stage IV), actions are differentiated. The child explores the properties of objects and their relationships. Action now becomes more goal directed, for example, in using intermediaries to accomplish goals. The caretaker/teacher becomes instrumental in completing coordinated action sequences. For example, the child rolls the ball in anticipation of someone returning it. Prelanguage sound and motor imitation skills begin to occur at this developmental level.

At age 12 to 18 months, actions become more specific in terms of functional activity with a particular object. The child now begins to initiate action sequences that result in different reactions from the caretaker/teacher. Beyond 18 months, the child gains ability to better regulate actions. Anticipation of others and their actions is keener. Object permanence and an awareness of object identity are established. Here, many describe the child as "ready to learn language." Single words have begun to emerge. Beyond 24 months, the child exhibits symbolic behavior. The beginning of combining words to make utterances appears. So this early development relies heavily on the senses such as vision and hearing and their coordination with motor acts. Future development becomes more dominated by representational and symbolic activity. Language is that universal expressive medium for future thought and activity.

Child language is quantitatively and qualitatively different from adult language. Semantics, or word meanings and relations, provides a logical explanation of this difference and the child's first words and their ordering to produce two-, three-, and four-word utterances. It is more apparent that the young language-learning child neither comprehends nor is able to produce utterances of syntactical complexity. Likewise, the child appears to have little understanding of the logical ordering of words needed to formulate language as the adult does. Whereas the adult realizes that many parts of speech (e.g., subjects, verbs, pronouns, participles) can be sequenced to express abstract thoughts, the child's words and meanings are much more concrete. More importantly, these words and meanings are ordered according to the concrete, experiential relations they describe. For example, the young child may say "ball" to indicate knowledge of the existence of that object. Six months later, he may request "roll ball" (i.e., action-object). Major semantic-grammatical rules are now used to describe the young child's language. For the preschooler, more traditional syntactical terms become appropriate to use in analyzing the language.

Just as cognitive and language development are related, communication skill development also depends on social and behavioral capabilities. *Social interaction* between caretaker and child is the framework in which communication will take place. For the young child, that communication may take the form of a smile to indicate "tickle me again." In communicating with the child under 1-year-old, the caretaker often initiates the interaction. With developing linguistic structures, the child can more actively participate in communication. In this way, the child gains more control over his/her environment and is expected to be a willing participant in the "communication volley." Likewise, a reaching out and appropriate responding to other children are expected. Confidence in social behavior is necessary for the young child. Evaluation of this social interaction and the reasons why people communicate, or *pragmatics*, will be discussed later in this chapter. Figure 9.1 provides a visual representation of how each of these areas relate to one another in the communication process.

Not all interactions with young children are pleasant nor are they expected to be. Certainly, as young children play, one observes more than perfect "give and take." However, for many speech-and language-delayed children, *behavioral control* is a major problem area. For this reason, it cannot be deleted from the discussion of communication. For example, a child who cannot fully express need for a snack may obtain it by pulling the entire container onto the floor. The child who has not developed the linguistic markers to aid in describing what he/she is doing that morning in preschool may run around the room confused, causing disruption in the classroom. The child who can use well-formed words but refuses to do so when asked a question often complies with little else in the classroom. This whole issue of child behavior brings to light even further the caretaker/teacher's role in the communication interaction. So often the teacher/caretaker must take a careful inventory of how he/she behaves in reinforcing desired child behavior or in extinguishing undesirable behavior in the child.

Games such as peek-a-boo between mother and child are vital to the development of social communication, especially for mentally retarded children who do not initiate interaction.

COMPREHENSION CHECK 9.3

Give an example with a toddler to illustrate how language, social, and motor skills with toys are related. Explain the concept of "communication volley" involving infants/toddlers and their parents.

TABLE 9.1
Comprehension in the Intentional Sensorimotor Period (8 to 24 months)

Cognitive Level (Approximate Age range)	Development
Sensorimotor Stage 4 (8 to 11 months)	No lexical comprehension Context-determined responses: 1. Look at objects that mother looks at 2. Act on objects that you notice 3. Imitate ongoing action or sound if it is already within your repertoire 4. Laugh at familiar interaction sequences
Sensorimotor Stage 5 (12 to 18 months)	Lexical comprehension: 1. Understanding of one word in some sentences when referents are present Comprehension strategies: 1. Attend to object mentioned 2. Give evidence of notice 3. Do what you usually do in the situation

Sensorimotor Stage 6 (18 to 24 months)	Lexical comprehension:
	1. Understanding of words when referent is not present
	2. Understanding of action verbs out of routine context; carries out two-word commands, but often fails to understand three lexical elements
	3. Understanding of routine forms of questions for agent, object, locative, and action
	
	Comprehension strategies:
	1. Locate the objects mentioned
	2. Give evidence of notice
	3. Do what you usually do:
	  a. Objects into containers
	  b. Conventional use
	4. Act on the objects in the way mentioned
	  a. Child as agent

Source: Adapted from Chapman, R. S., and Miller, J. F. (1980). "Analyzing language and communication in the child." in R. L. Schiefelbusch (Ed.). *Nonspeech language and communication,* pp. 87–118. Baltimore: University Park Press.

Pragmatics and the development of language content

The developmental content of language refers to those areas that include semantics, morphology, and syntax. To appreciate language content, we can most comfortably think in terms of two broad categories: *language comprehension* and *language production*. In other words, one examines what a child understands and what language structures he can produce in a social context in order to detect how language disorders have affected his development, to outline language development using cognitive levels, and to approximate age ranges as reference points. Language comprehension and production skills in Piaget's sensorimotor period (8 to 24 months) are outlined in Tables 9.1 and 9.2. Lexical comprehension refers to an understanding of the

TABLE 9.2
Production in the Intentional Sensorimotor Period (8 to 24 months)

Cognitive Level (Approximate Age Range)	Development
Sensorimotor Stage 4 (8 to 12 months)	Precursors: 1. Differentiated cries 2. Syllabic babbling 3. Commmunication games 4. Intentional action

Sensorimotor Stage 5 (12 to 18 months)	First words:
	 1. Performatives (gesture accompanies vocalization or word)
	    a. Hi, bye routines
	    b. Comment
	    c. Request object or attention
	    d. Reject

Sensorimotor Stage 6 (18 to 24 months)
 Early
 	
 Later
 	
 20 months
	Transition to two-word combinations:
	 1. New semantic roles
	    a. Action-object relations: agent, action, object, recurrence, disappearance
	    b. Object-object relations: location, possession, nonexistence
	 2. Asks a What's that question
	 3. Answers some routine questions
	 4. Rapid acquisition of vocabulary
	 5. Successive one-word utterances
	 6. Increased frequency of talking
	 7. Onset of two-word utterances

Source: Chapman, R. S., and Miller, J. F. (1980). Analyzing language and communication in the child. in R. L. Schiefelbusch (Ed.), *Nonspeech language and communication,* Baltimore: University Park Press. pp. 87–118.

actual meanings of the words contained in a vocabulary. There is a theoretical distinction between comprehension strategies—behaviors children do indicating understanding (e.g., demonstrate the conventional use of objects) and lexical comprehension (e.g., understanding the meaning of an action verb out of context).

At the early sensorimotor stage 6 (18 to 24 months) the child begins to understand linguistically those meanings for which he has an experiential base. These include meanings such as object existence ("ball"), disappearance ("ball gone"), and possession ("me ball"). Language comprehension for the 2 to 3 year old begins to reflect their understanding of many "Wh- questions." This ability is critical, as so often one begins to assess the child's production ability by using such questions (Table 9.3). The 2 to 3 year old can now verbally elaborate, increasing the length of his utterances. He continues to talk about the present, immediate past, and imminent future (Table 9.4).

Finally, analysis of language content and use can be extremely difficult for the child whose speech is unintelligible. This involves *phonology* or the rule system that governs the actual ordering of specific sound units to form individual words. Phonologic process analysis is most appropriate for children with

TABLE 9.3
Comprehension in Early Preoperations (2 to 3⅓ years)

Typical Age	Development
	Lexical comprehension:
	Sequence for understanding of the meaning of WH-questions in nonroutine forms
2½ years	What for object What-do for action Where for location (place)
3 years	Whose for possessor Who for person Why for cause or reason How many for number
3 years	Understanding of gender contrasts in third person pronouns

2 and 3 years	Comprehension strategies:
	1. Do what is usually done
	    a. Probable location strategy for in, on, under, beside
	    b. Probable event strategy for simple active reversible sentences
	2. Supply missing information (2 years)
	    Supply explanation (3 years)
	3. Infer most probable speech act in context

Source: Chapman, R. S., and Miller, J. F., (1980). Analyzing language and communication in the Child, in R. L. Schiefelbusch (Ed.). *Nonspeech language and communication,* pp. 87–118. Baltimore: University Park Press.

TABLE 9.4
Production in the Preoperational Period (2 to 7 years): Semantice

Cognitive Level	Development	Example
2 years	Basic semantic relations	
	Agent-action	Boy run
	Action-object	Push truck
	Agent-object	Mom spoon
	Possessive	My shirt
	Entity-locative	Ball up
	Action-locative	Push down
	Existence	Blocks
	Recurrence	Want more blocks
	Nonexistence	All gone
	Rejection	Go way
	Denial	No cat
	Attributive	Red car
2½ years	Number (noun plural)	Dogs
	Locative containment and support (in, on)	In box
	Temporary duration (ing)	Boy playing
3 years	Immediate future	I gonna

Source: Chapman, R. S., and Miller, J. F. (1980). Analyzing language and communication in the child. in R. L. Schielfelbusch (Ed.). *Nonspeech language and communication,* pp. 87–118. Baltimore: University Park Press.

multiphonemic articulation disorders (i.e., many sounds in error) and is intimately tied to language and concept development. For example, a child may not produce a word correctly for which he has no meaning or a distorted meaning. For example, a child may have the same label "ba" for "ba*th*" and "ba*t*." He may not realize that the two items are different. Correction of this language concept is essential as part of the remedying of the phonologic disorder.

Three to five years

As young children develop, the link between sensory, perceptual, congnitive, memory skill, and language acquisition becomes stronger (Figure 9.2). *Cognition* can be viewed as the ability to relate bits of information implicitly or explicitly, to attend to information, to remember information, and to process it, organize it, and relate it to past information in an effort to reason and make appropriate judgments based on what is known. Attention, memory, auditory processing, and sequential organizational skill are four cognitive mechanisms having a profound developmental impact on a child's language acquisition.

Memory, or the capacity to recall and retain chunks of information for varying lengths of time, influences what the child will remember and also

Figure 9.2

The Relationships among Perceptual, Linguistic, and Cognitive Processing in Language Comprehension

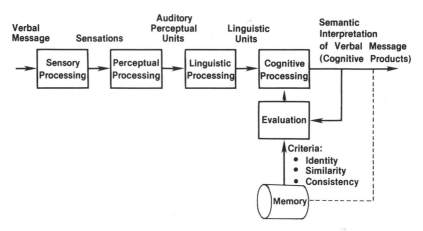

Source:
Wiig, E. H., and Semel, E. M. (1976). *Language disabilities in children and adolescents.* Columbus, OH: Merrill.

how well information will be recalled. As age increases, memory capacity increases as well. The preschool child displaying a memory deficit may display difficulty recalling instructions beyond a one-level command; the child may recall a portion of an instruction, but not in its entirety. The child at this young age may better remember information presented in one modality versus another (e.g., auditory versus visual) or may have to be "walked through" a task to accomplish it accurately. Expressively, the child with a memory deficit may be unable to formulate verbal responses to questions because of the inability to remember what was asked. The child may begin to withhold speech, thinking that no response is better than an incorrect one. In additon, the child with a memory deficit may also display a word-retrieval deficit. That is, the child may display an inability to recall exact word labels from long-term memory. This may make the child's conversational speech appear less fluent and organized than that of other normal preschoolers, and conversational speech may be laced with "empty space holders" such as, "um, err, m-m-m, uh, and uh."

To learn a task, one must first be able to *attend* to that task for a sufficient amount of time. Research has demonstrated that attention is developmental in nature and that as the child matures, attention becomes more refined and systematic. The child between the ages of 3 and 5 years will most likely first attend to eye-catching details such as shape and color. Other equally important aspects of the environment such as location and size will be ignored until the child becomes more mature.

The child aged 3 to 5 years displaying an attention deficit will display difficulty attending to prominent features within the environment. This child might be seen moving from one area of the room to another, briefly exploring items of high interest. In contrast, the nonambulatory child may display an inability to tune out background noise and may fail to respond to even simple tasks if placed in a less than quiet environment. Details in auditorially and visually presented information may be ignored as well. In terms of expressive language, the child displaying an attention deficit may fail to respond verbally to questions or may respond incorrectly. Verbal language may, at times, be unrelated to current information. This child may ask questions at an inappropriate time during the day (e.g., inquiring about going home during midmorning snack time) or may ask a question but continue on to another activity without waiting to receive a response.

Auditory processing, the ability to comprehend information presented auditorially, is directly influenced by syntactic complexity, semantic knowledge, contextual cues, and rate of presentation of information (Lasky and Chapman, 1976). T⋯ ⋯ars can more easily understand a simple noun⋯ ⋯ll the ball") than a complex noun phrase-auxil⋯ ⋯"The dogs are not running quickly"). Familia⋯ ⋯easily than unfamiliar ones. Processing can b⋯ ⋯f additional visual or kinesthetic cues and by ⋯ ⋯ rate of presentation of new material.

Preschool ⋯ ⋯rocessing deficits will most likely present the⋯ ⋯e children may require preparatory cues such⋯ ⋯to get ready to listen. They may display difficul⋯ ⋯ed directions and may even repeat or "reaud⋯ ⋯truction in an attempt to aid language proces⋯ ⋯play a significant latency when responding and ⋯ ⋯al time to process information. They may displa⋯ ⋯fatigue easily when presented with auditory infc⋯

Finally, *organi⋯ ⋯be viewed as the capability to synthesize, order, ⋯ ⋯n organized fashion to aid in problem solving. I⋯ ⋯lity to sequence motor movements to accomplis⋯ ⋯sing, eating, and walking, but also includes high le⋯ ⋯⋯⋯⋯such as temporal ordering (what happens first, second, etc.), categorization (grouping items according to prominent and salient features), and aproaching tasks in an orderly, sequential fashion to achieve success.

Preschool children displaying deficits within the organizational/sequential realm may display difficulty following the daily routine and may often rely on situational cues and observations of peers to carry out activities at an appropriate time. They may exhibit difficulty understanding "if—then" conditional concepts and may fail to understand instructions including temporal concepts (e.g., "Before you can play, you must eat lunch"). They may display difficulty following a story line or retelling even a simple nursery rhyme. In additon, they may exhibit an inability to classify items by size, or even color. Expressively, these children use inconsistent word ordering and may arbitrarily switch word order within phrases. Articulation disorders may persist, characterized by omission of final consonant sounds; in addition, articulatory precision will most likely deteriorate as the length of utterance increases.

Multisyllabic words such as spaghetti, or salami, are almost impossible for this child to pronounce; instead, the child may say "busgetti," or "maslami."

Deficits in any of these four cognitive mechanisms and their concomitant language disorders have significant implications for academic readiness in the child between the ages of 3 and 5 years. At this age, the child may be participating in a nursery school or may be involved in preschool programming and is expected to begin to perform some preacademic tasks (e.g., sitting in small group sessions, completing show and tell activities, attending to a processing auditory information of increasing length). Performance of even these preacademic tasks requires the processing of information that is primarily linguistically encoded; therefore, a child displaying deficits in auditory attention, memory, language processing, and the like, will indeed be more likely to display difficulty completing these preacademic tasks (Gerber and Bryen, 1981). With this introduction of preacademic skills, heavier linguistic demands are placed on the child and the child who has not acquired adequate knowledge of linguistic skills or use of language structure will begin to experience difficulty.

COMPREHENSION CHECK 9.4

Give an example of how memory and attention problems in preschoolers affect language comprehension and use. Define *auditory processing* and *organizational/sequential* skills in preschoolers.

Five to eight years

The effects of maturation outlined in the previous section clearly show that as the child approaches 5, 6, and 7 years of age, language problems similar in form to those of the younger child are perpetuated but at a more sophisticated linguistic and cognitive level. These older children continue to display deficits in language comprehension, language formulation, organization/sequencing, memory, and word retrieval. However, the most striking element of these deficits is that now these language-cognitive-perceptual deficits will clearly influence and interfere with the child's successful achievement of academic tasks. Indeed, many of the aforementioned deficits will be used to determine the child who may be "academically at risk" or learning disabled. As the child progresses into first, second, and third grades, he/she is faced with increasing demands for auditory processing of information and verbal recall of information. In addition, a new demand for oral presentation is now placed on the child. Wiig and Semel (1976) note that as a result of these increased demands language problems that existed in kindergarten and first grade tend to continue or even increase in severity.

Some of the most striking deficits noted in the child entering kindergarten or first grade is the limited ability to identify phonic sounds, to discriminate same or different sounds, and to analyze and synthesize phoneme and phoneme sequences. These deficits result in the development of poor sound-symbol associations and inevitably lead to poor academic achievement in spelling, reading, and mathematics (Wiig and Semel, 1976). Added to these deficits is the child's continued lack of organization when approaching and completing tasks, increased distractibility, and decreased attending skills, which only serve to magnify difficulties at the academic level.

It must also be noted that word-retrieval deficits, also termed *dysnomia*, continue to persist and significantly influence the young child's academic achievement. Current research has indicated that a positive relationship exists between dysnomia and dyslexia. Dyslexic children have been found to display significantly more naming errors than do their academically achieving peers (Wiig, Semel, and Nystrom, 1982). Children displaying word-retrieval deficits will most likely display deficits in several curriculum related areas. They may display an inability to complete tasks requiring silent picture naming and may do poorly on spelling tasks because they may inadvertently substitute an antonym or rhyming word for the spoken stimulus word (Wiig et al., 1982).

Wiig and Semel (1976) report numerous other correlations between language abilities and their effects on reading and mathematics. In particular, they report (1) reductions in mathematic abilities to be significantly correlated with deficits in linguistic processing, (2) correlations at low but significant levels between auditory-perceptual abilities and reading, (3) positive relationships between a child's knowledge of morphology and his/her reading achievement, (4) that error patterns in reading reflect transformation of syntactic structure and semantic information

Linguistic-cognitive deficits most definitely interfere with the child's ability to function adequately in the academic classroom, and this linguistic-academic link has numerous implications for classroom intervention.

CAUSES OF LANGUAGE AND COMMUNICATION DISORDERS

Language development is inseparably related to cognitive, social, and neuro-motor development. Dysfunctions in any of these developmental functions significantly affect the course of language and communication development and vice versa. For this reason, the causes of language disorders must be viewed in terms of how various communication processes are affected. These developmental disabilities naturally encompass the traditional categories of mental retardation, autism, neurological impairments, and learning and perceptual motor disorders.

Auditory impairments. Deficits in the child's ability to receive auditory input because of a hearing loss is a primary cause of language and communication problems. Serous otitis media, or fluid build-up in the ear because of ear infections, seriously hinders the child's capactiy to learn the content and purpose of language.

Expressive disorders. Children with various mild to severe neurological and motor difficulties have related problems in coordinating their oral muscles to produce fine movements required to form a variety of speech sounds. The problems can range from mild misarticulations and dysarthria to the absence of speech owing to the neuromotor impairments.

Learning and perceptual disorders. Often, children labeled learning disabled have problems developing an understanding of linguistic concepts because of their difficulties in perceiving and interpreting the speech of others. These children are presumed to have subtle evidence of brain damage that limits their ability to process and comprehend. Symptoms of these problems include a short memory for auditory information; inattention to auditory information; difficulties sequencing numbers, words, and information in phrases in sentences; and problems following directions and commands.

Cognitive disabilities. Mentally retarded children develop language in the same developmental sequence but at a significantly slower rate than do other children their age. With the young child, language emerges at approximately the same developmental level as their ability to solve nonverbal problems. Generally, they have difficulties understanding the complex symbol system of communication and do not have the ability to mentally represent objects and pictures in memory at 18 to 24 months as do normal children. Thus, they require a longer period of using "concrete" objects to label and understand the form and function of toys.

Affective and behavior disorders. Emotionally disturbed and behaviorally disordered children experience problems in comprehending and producing language and in understanding the communicative function of words and sentences. Their failure to develop interpersonal relationships with adults and other children hinders their growth in acquiring language skills. Autistic children, for instance, display ritualistic and repetitive behaviors and a self-involved style of attention that prevents communication from developing. Even communication through gestures is often impaired. Intensive shaping of language behaviors through behavior-management techniques and teaching the rewarding value of adult attention and contact is necessary to promote even the most rudimentary language behaviors.

ASSESSMENT OF LANGUAGE DISORDERS

The assessment of language disorders is a complex operation because language development and dysfunctions involve many interrelated skills that are intimately interwoven with all other developmental areas. Young children must have the oral-motor control to form and produce expressive speech. Language understanding and use relies on intact cognitive capabilities, particularly the ability to comprehend the functions and interrelationships between various common objects and pictures. Thus, cognition and language are inseparable functions. Finally, functional language only occurs within a social context—in the two-way communication process between individuals.

Thus, assessment of language skills must monitor form, content, and use as well as comprehension and production. This necessarily involves a comprehensive evaluation of the relationship between language and cognitive, motor, and socioemotional processes. For this reason, several measures must be combined in a diagnostic battery to describe multiple language abilities.

Specific language measures and strategies

Comprehensive language assessment entails a variety of evaluation strategies. Behavioral observation is a primary technique involving a description of the sounds a child produces, the average length of phrases or sentences, how the child uses language functionally to express wants to adults, and the child's understanding of what words to use in language structures.

Several developmental language and sentence scoring techniques that rely on systematic observation in naturalistic situations are available. Complementary strategies are available that assess a child in a controlled clinical situation and describe the language output by comparing it with that expected for the typical child of the same age. These are referred to as *norm-referenced* language measures.

For infants, few formal measures are available because early language consists of preverbal capabilities such as auditory orientation, cooing, babbling, echolalia, and jargon, which are only rudimentary precursors to more meaningful language forms. The *Receptive-Expressive Emergent Language Scale* (REEL) measures infant language capabilities throughout the birth to 36-month period. The scale measures prelanguage abilities by assessing both comprehension and production of language. Similarly, the *Sequenced Inventory of Communication Development* (SICD) was created to describe the communication skills of both retarded and normal children between 4 and 48 months of age. The instrument profiles various receptive and expressive language subskills such as awareness, discrimination, understanding, imitation, and motor, vocal, and verbal responsiveness in initiating communication with others. The SICD provides a developmental structure of goals and activities to guide classroom early intervention for young children who are suffering language disorders or who are sensorially impaired, retarded, or learning disabled.

The *Environmental Language Inventory* (ELI), though not norm-referenced, provides an excellent tool for examining those meaning units (semantic-grammatical rules) that comprise the child's first sentences. A complete training program for use in therapy, home, and the classroom called *Ready, Set, Go—Talk to Me*, accompanies the ELI.

For young children in the 36 to 84 month age range, various scales measure the child's understanding of various language concepts and forms. The *Assessment of Children's Language Comprehension* (ACLC) measures the child's ability to identify various "critical elements" in the child's understanding of language by selecting the correct picture from the array of five other pictures. These involve basic vocabulary concepts (e.g., shoe, bird, box, sitting) and the ability to retain increasing lengthy forms in memory (e.g., "horse standing," "ball under the table," "happy little girl jumping"). The child's ability to retain and identify increasingly complex syntactic units forms a basis for language intervention.

Similarly, the *Test of Auditory Comprehension of Language* (TACL) assesses the child's understanding of vocabulary, morphology (e.g., nouns, verbs, pronouns, adjectives, prepositions), and syntax through selection of the correct pictured form. The *Peabody Picture Vocabulary Test–Revised* (PPVT–R) also evaluates basic receptive vocabulary and may be a good general estimate of one aspect of verbal intelligence. The *Carrow Elicited*

Language delayed preschoolers can frequently demonstrate their receptive language long before they are verbally expressive.

Language Inventory (CELI) evaluates the child's emerging language competence by his ability to imitate increasingly lengthy and complex phrases and sentences modeling an adult.

One of the newest and most comprehensive language measures for children beginning their school experience (6 to 8 years) is the *Clinical Evaluation of Language Functions* (CELF). The CELF generates a profile of specific language functions such as phonology, syntax, semantics, memory, and word finding and retrieval. This is accomplished by requiring the child to process and produce various arrays of information such as oral directions, spoken paragraphs, word series, word classes, naming on demand, model sentences, word associations, and linguistic concepts. The diagnostic battery provides an invaluable profile for planning individualized treatment schemes for developmentally and learning-disabled young children.

Finally, *functional assessment* of a young child's communication skills should reach beyond the speech-language therapist's clinic room into the classroom and home. Home assignments can often be completed by the use of a questionnaire or interview. Classroom assessments can be completed in one classroom through a close, working contact with the classroom teacher who is trained to describe language behaviors. For the very young child, little is gained in an indivdual therapy setting. Rather, a teacher and child benefit best by having the speech-language pathologist working side by side with them in the early intervention program. Here the speech-language pathologist can continue to assess the child's and teacher's or caretaker's interactions and guide them appropriately by modeling appropriate behaviors. Assessment, then, becomes a functional guide to in situ programming.

The 3-year-old child may benefit from both the classroom group setting and time alone with the teacher and/or speech-language pathologist. Here systematic classroom programming is essential. For example, the teacher and speech-language pathologist working together may identify three specific situations where certain language requirements will be made on that child during the week. These situations and appropriate techniques could be posted on a card with that child's name on it so that the teacher and others will have a cue to which they can refer when interacting with the child. Classroom programming might include planning by the teacher and speech-language pathologist of a specific play situation when specific responses will be expected from each child as appropriate. For example, one child might be expected to ask for an object while another is expected only to point.

Likewise, this joint planning is necessary between teacher, parent, and speech-language pathologist. Short training sessions for parents in language facilitation techniques should be planned. An effective means of communication between school and home should be established. Remember, that children and parents talk about at home can be very different from what at school. Always modify the content of training as well as the facilitation technique for parents as appropriate.

Pragmatics: Functional taxonomy for describing language disorders

Pragmatics refers to the use of language for communication. Each person who communicates has reasons or intents for doing so. These intents are the overall determining factors of what (semantics) a person will say. Likewise, to define, describe, and use pragmatics in analysis and intervention for young children, some type of taxonomy is needed to describe all the reasons why children are talking or not talking. For example, they may ask a question (e.g., "Where's the ball?") or they may comment on an event (e.g., "Ball roll"). Developing such a taxonomy or classification system is a difficult and tedious task requiring many hours of observing and classifying communicative intents between caretaker/teacher and child. Once developed, the taxonomy must be examined again and again for its reliability, validity, and usefulness. Today a number of different taxonomies are available. Examples from a few of the taxonomies described by Chapman (1981) will be examined to increase the reader's understanding of pragmatics and its critical role in understanding the communication process and its disorders.

First, it is important to examine some nonverbal pragmatic behaviors that serve as precursors to later language development in children as well as early speech acts expressed by children as they begin to talk using one-word utterances (Tables 9.5 and 9.6). Others have begun to look more closely at actual discourse for the preschool-age child regarding the expectations and conditions that surround the social communication between people (Chapman, 1981). For example, when a child requests that an action be completed, there is an expectation that the listener can complete the task or have a good reason why he cannot do so.

The communication process

Communication is a two-person process. The importance of the caretaker/teacher's response to the child cannot be overemphasized, and this

TABLE 9.5
Pragmatic Behaviors in Nonverbal Children

Category	Definition
Object requests	Gestures or utterances that direct the listener to provide some object for the child
Greeting	Gestures or utterances subsequent to a person's entrance that express recognition
Showing off	Gestures or utterances that appear to be used to attract attention

Source: Adapted from Chapman, R. S. (1981) Exploring children's communicative intents. in J. F. Miller (Ed.). *Assessing language production in children*, pp. 39–61. Baltimore: University Park Press. Adapted from Coggins J. and Carpenter R., unpublished manuscript, 1978.

must be assessed in a natural context in a functional way. Knowing that a child does not respond to the teacher's direct questions makes a difference in how any person should approach that child. That child may only respond when others are responsive. For example, in play, the parent or teacher should only label the child's action rather than ask "What's happening?" six times over. The caretaker/teacher's style in communication should be examined also. An evaluator might ask questions about how the teacher continues a topic with a child. Does the teacher repeat what was said, acknowledge what the child said, or give additional information? If the teacher only repeats, should he/she be giving the child more information? Consider the following examples:

Example 1:	Child	"Roll ball"
	Teacher	"Roll ball"
	Child	"Roll ball"
Example 2:	Child	"Roll ball"
	Teacher	"Roll big ball"
	Child	"Roll big ball"
	Teacher	"Roll big ball again"

In Example 1, only repetition was used. In Example 2, the teacher provided additional information ("big") and used repetition ("roll big ball" again).

Likewise, these same questions should be asked about how the child interacts and communicates with peers. With whom in the class does the child communicate? Does the child ask questions? Can the child maintain a topic with another child? Do others comply with the child's requests? Does the child instruct others? Is the child able to produce three- to five-word sentences but unable to communicate effectively?

TABLE 9.6
Primitive Speech Acts—One-Word Level

Speech Act	Definition	Example
Labeling	Uses word while attending to object or event. Does not address adult or wait for a response.	C touches a doll's eyes and says "eyes."
Answering	Answers adult's question. Addresses adult.	Mother points to a picture of a dog and asks "What's that?" C answers "bow-wow."
Requesting	Asks question with a word, sometimes accompanying gesture. Addresses adult and awaits response.	C picks up book, looks at Mother, and says "Book?" with rising terminal contour. Mother answers "Right, it's a book."
Protesting	Resists adult's action with word or cry. Addresses adult.	C, when his mother attempts to put on his shoe, utters an extended scream of varying contours while resisting her.

Source: Adapted from Chapman, R. S. (1981). Exploring children's communicative intents. in J. F. Miller (Ed.). *Assessing language production in children.* Baltimore: University Park Press. Adapted from J. Dore. (1975). Holophrases, speech acts and language universals. *Journal of Child Language* 2:21–40.

If the answer to this last question is "yes," then you can be sure that a pragmatically disordered child has been identified. With this assessment of how a child and adult communicate, one might justifiably ask "How am I, the teacher, going to apply this information to the children I see?" Establish situations (e.g., request toy in play, request apple to eat) where one would expect the child to request objects. Does the child do so? Establish situations (e.g., the child does not want jelly on toast) where one expects the child to reject what is being done. Does the child do so? Examine the child's understanding of the rules and conventions that apply to communication. For example, does the child understand that he/she must have a good reason for why he/she cannot complete a task? Does the child follow the humor behind saying "bye" when in fact the person just arrived and one would be expected to say "hi" to a newcomer? Likewise, can a child demonstrate understanding of the conditions of communication by jokingly calling auntie "unk" (meaning uncle)? In these last instances, the child knowingly violated the convention, showing understanding.

COMPREHENSION CHECK 9.5

How is behavioral observation used to assess language? Define and give an example of norm-referenced language measures. How can a taxonomy help to describe a young children's language skills and deficits?

EDUCATION AND TREATMENT FOR LANGUAGE-DISORDERED CHILDREN

A practical, cooperative relationship among the early-childhood special educator, the speech-language specialist, and the parents is one of the most important keys to effective treatment for young exceptional children.

While the speech-language pathologist provides language training on an individual or small-group basis, the preschool classroom teacher becomes the medium through which these new language behaviors are carried over into the classroom. The classroom teacher's role expands to encompass language activities that will develop the child's total communication skills. With direction from the speech-language pathologist, the classroom teacher structures daily activities to facilitate language use among the children and to relate language usage to everyday functions. As more preacademic tasks become part of the curricula, and as expectations for children are increased, the preschool language-learning child's deficits become more apparent and more remediable by informal language-facilitation strategies.

Within the preschool language classroom, the teacher, with the assistance of the speech-language pathologist, defines major concepts to be developed. Classroom goals must be based on what is known about normal language development and the sequential development of language skills. Classroom intervention must be a continuous process of establishing immediate goals, evaluating the child's progress toward the goals, and revising the goals as necessary (Bloom and Lahey, 1978).

Involving the parent or caretaker in particular goal-directed activities is also essential for reinforcing the use of newly learned linguistic structures and to relate language to everyday functional activities. Too often it may happen that parents have expectations about their children's language skills that are unrealistic, thereby causing a discrepancy between what is required in the home and classroom and what the child is ready to display. Parental knowledge of their children's specific language capabilities, classroom requirements, and simple language-facilitation strategies can greatly aid the language-learning child's emerging skills. In addition, parents begin to feel confident of their expertise in stimulating their children's language development.

Thus, the preschool and home settings become the primary settings for successful language learning. A variety of guidelines and techniques are available to encourage the effective acquisition of communication skills in these settings when used jointly and consistently by the parent, teacher, and therapist.

COMPREHENSION CHECK 9.6

How are classroom language goals designed for young children? Explain the parent's role in stimulating language use in the classroom and at home.

Language facilitation strategies for the preschool child

Promoting the development of communication skills requires a consideration of several interrelated areas. For example, all persons working with the language-disordered child must simultaneously focus on three major dimensions: (1) building and maintaining rapport, (2) developing cognitive skills, and (3) structuring the environment (See Table 9.7).

Rapport

It is important for the teacher's interactions with the child to be positive. Being positive does not mean that the children should always get their way;

TABLE 9.7
Language Facilitation Strategies for Young Children

MAINTAINING RAPPORT WITH THE CHILD
Be positive, but set limits
Enter the child's world
Respect the child
Develop the child's respect of others
DEVELOPING COGNITIVE SKILLS
Maintain the child's attention to tasks and others
Establish a joint line of reference with objects by using:
Locational cues
Verbal markers
Noise cues
Physical prompts
Positioning of the child

Facilitate functional play
Help the child understand communication

Encourage turn taking
Facilitate reciprocity
Respond to the child
Encourage all communicative signs
STRUCTURING THE ENVIRONMENT
Provide areas for: "free communication"
Group listening
Language-experience stories
Expression of basic needs
Show and tell

Manipulate objects in the environment:

Place desired objects elsewhere
Mystify known objects
Introduce new objects

Direct people in the environment

Encourage interaction on a one-to-one basis
Encourage interaction among verbal and nonvocal children
Introduce a new person
Establish group experiences

Design events to encourage communication

however, instructional time should end on a positive note. The teacher may have to set limits on each child's behavior but should do so in a constructive manner. For example, when young children first enter an early-intervention program, they may need time to explore the surroundings with the teacher as a guide. This activity can be appropriate until the child insists on pulling all the adult cookware from the cabinet. The teacher's immediate identification of this behavior as inappropriate and substitution of a new behavior (e.g., playing with child's cookware in play kitchen) is a constructive way to continue the activity and interaction in a positive manner. An unproductive manner for handling this situation would have been to reprimand the child or drag him from the scene. Appropriate redirection of the child's behavior in this instance maintained the rapport between the teacher and child. Remember, the child must be comfortable with the teacher and vice versa for communication to happen and for the teacher to acquire positive reinforcing attributes.

Another issue in maintaining rapport with the child revolves around what the teacher and child use as a base of their interaction. The teacher must *enter the child's world*. Most of the child's early learning occurs through play. The implication here for teachers is that they must use that mode to teach the child. However, by using play that is geared to the child's developmental level, the teacher will be able to maintain rapport with the child. It is unlikely that the 3-year-old will tolerate formal testing and become very frustrated with the teacher unless testing is interspersed with play activities. Similarly, the teacher may learn much more about what natural communication the child can initiate in that play setting than could be learned through formal assessment.

Cognitive skills

Language techniques for developing cognitive skills include facilitating many prelanguage and precommunication skills. These include gaining the child's attention to the task. Listening to the teacher and maintaining eye contact with others and objects are basic skills that may need to be promoted. This can be done by excluding other "noise" in the environment. Placing a dressing screen in the classroom to separate the training area from the remainder of the room can be helpful. Working with a child here until the child is ready to handle more distraction and maintain attention can be advantageous. A child can be encouraged to establish a joint line of reference by the teacher giving cues. For example, a child may not focus attention on the ball until the teacher squeezes it, giving a noise cue in addition to pointing to it. Moving an object closer to the child may facilitate joint line of reference. Verbal markers (e.g., "Look over here") or physical prompts (e.g., turning the child's head or body) may facilitate the child's focus of attention.

In the play activities, facilitate the functional use of objects. Children should be using objects as adults would intend an object to be used. Show the child many and varied functional uses of objects. For example, a can serves as a container, a drum, a mirror, and an object to roll back and forth. Recall that the meanings the child later expresses are first experienced in play.

Just as the child must know about his environment, he must know about the communication process. Developing *communication sense* refers to the

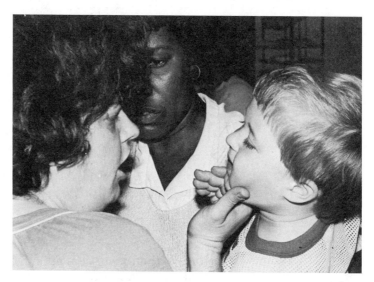

Many youngsters have attention disorders. When saying "Look at me" does not seem to capture the child's attention, physical prompting may be necessary.

child's beginning to show anticipatory behavior and reciprocity in interaction. For example, the young child lies on his back and giggles after being tickled, indicating "Do it again." This establishes a reciprocal routine between the two. Likewise, the next time the child is laid down, he may smile at the caretaker/teacher, showing an anticipation of the game. Teachers working with young children should establish as many events as possible where this reciprocal activity can occur.

If communication is to be learned, then it must be facilitated. Always respond to the child's communicative attempts or else the child cannot learn their value. Talk to and with the child even though the child may not always respond reciprocally. Talk as though one is conversing. This means comment on events (e.g., "Ball roll") and do not always ask questions. Often when an adult only seeks information (i.e., asks questions) without giving it (i.e., commenting), the child will not respond. Lastly, encourage all communicative signs such as gestures or vocalizations. The teacher's response to these will give meaning to *communicating*. In other words, the child will learn cognitively what it means to communicate. For example, encourage the child's clapping to indicate "Let's do it again."

COMPREHENSION CHECK 9.7

Explain how the teacher can use *play* to promote language gains in the classroom. Give an example to show that an infant or toddler has developed a "communication sense."

Environmental structure

The success of programming for the language-delayed child hinges most on the teacher's ability to structure the environment to facilitate language learning. The environment in this case includes the physical environment (the room, objects), the people in the environment, and the events that occur within the environment. Think of the classroom as a theater. In a theater one finds a stage with props (classroom, objects), actors (children and yourself plus aides), and events that occur (the routine activities of a day). The teacher can view herself/himself as director and an actor. The last critical element of a play in the theater is its script or what people say as they interact on stage. The teacher can control the script by knowing what language the child is capable of using and encouraging it. Any number of cues—events, people, objects—can facilitate communication.

First, examine the actual physical space in the classroom and structure it to promote interaction. Leave an area where the children can go freely to play with minimal direction from an adult. Establish another area used for group listening. Here certain restrictions are placed, and it is expected that the child will remain within these guidelines. This same area might be used for show and tell. An area for language-experience stories can be good. (The use of such stories will be explained later.) Likewise, some areas will be designated for basic needs such as eating and bathrooming. The child knows certain events within the social context are to occur in these designated areas. Particular social conventions are inherent in these specific settings. The environment itself cues certain communicative behaviors.

Placing objects in that environment out of reach can encourage the child to request that object or request that another person act to obtain that object. The teacher may hide Johnny's favorite truck just slightly out of his reach. This may encourage him to crawl to the teacher, tug on her leg, and point upward. For show and tell, the teacher may bring a windup toy to the classroom in a cake container. As it sits on the table in the listening area of the room, a child may ask "What's that?" When told that there is a surprise item in the container, the child may be prompted to ask more questions ("Where is it, What, When we see?") or make a demand ("Show me"). One new object in the room can prompt questions or comments from a child (e.g., "A pumpkin!"). Again, all these techniques are geared at structuring the physical space and objects in space.

Another area to be examined is the directing of people in the environment. Encouraging peer interaction is most effective. Get to know the children in the classroom in such a way that you can identify how they relate to one another. In other words, identify the *bully*, the *shy child*, and the *agreeable child*. Pair the child who is shy with the pleasant child in an activity. One may find that the child who rarely speaks because of being so withdrawn will respond to the pleasant child who has average verbal skill. Encourage a child who is verbal to also use a picture communication board with the child who understands language but cannot speak. Just as a new object was introduced to stimulate conversation, so can a new person be introduced into the environment. Make prior arrangements to have a visitor in the classroom during a specified time.

Establish group experiences to facilitate language. For example, this may

Teachers can give toys contingent on the child's use of progressively more appropriate verbal communication.

take the form of a "show and tell" time when a child brings a favorite toy from home to show and talk about. Others in the group might be encouraged to ask questions. Pass a box of items from child to child. Have each child take their turn and remove an item. Allow the child to label the object. Look for a volunteer to tell and demonstrate its use.

Another important type of group experience is the language-experience story. Tell a sequential story using pictures, such as the steps in washing a dog. Tell it again on the next day, but this time have the actual items and allow three children in the group to act out the story. On the third day, review the story but allow the children to complete the script. By this time, they should have thought of many two-, three-, and four-word phrases to generate regarding the story. We can hope that a similar real-life situation at home on some later date will cue this language.

Lastly, designing events to encourage communication will be examined along with "writing the script." It has already been established that routine events such as eating, listening time, and enjoying language-experience stories are to be established. In each of these events, manipulation of the subject material or people can facilitate certain types of communication. For example, in having a snack, a child may be required to ask for the food item. An interesting object used in the language-experience story (e.g., a cash register that takes money) may prompt a question such as "Where go?"

Again, the introduction of a new event, such as making a small garden outside in the spring, can prompt much conversation and fun. Such an event as this provides for long-term carry over of new language learned when the children talk about planting and tending to their garden. Making a new type of artwork using beans can be a new event. Events designed to encourage problem solving are probably most beneficial in stimulating communication. Giving the child everything he/she needs to make an art picture except for the glue will require language use to obtain his/her needs. Giving a child incorrect directions on how to put the train cars together may prompt the child to say "No, this way." This kind of facilitation, as well as the others discussed, requires the teacher to always be one step ahead in planning and structuring the environment, others in it, and what is to be said. This can seem like an unwieldly task, but it really is not. Often, the teacher can establish a set of cues for for herself/himself and aides. These cues might include an envelope for each child on the wall describing generally the child's communication profile. Another card might describe areas that need to be strengthened for that child (e.g., making more demands). The last card might describe some events/situations that will occur that week where the child will be encouraged to communicate (e.g., in this case, make demands). For example, an event might be planned where that child is excluded intentionally to encourage her demanding to be included in the group. These many specifics of structuring the environment should be worked out between the teacher and the speech-language pathologist.

Language comprehension and production

Foremost in encouraging *language comprehension* is facilitating the child's attending and listening skills (see Table 9.8). Use of visual input is necessary to facilitate comprehension. For example, showing a child how to play with a new toy can be much more effective than just telling her. Use gestures when speaking and pictures or objects if appropriate.

TABLE 9.8
Teacher Facilitation Strategies to Enhance Language Comprehension and Production

COMPREHENSION
Encourage listening behavior
Encourage attending behavior
Provide visual input
Use simple language when speaking
    Label the environment
    Give information
    Expand the child's utterances
    Rephrase utterances to the child
    Repeat information

PRODUCTION
Provide models
Encourage imitation
Allow repetition and practice by the child
Give evaluative feedback
Correct the child when appropriate

Teachers need to use simple language in terms of length and meanings. Speak in short phrases or sentences using a vocabulary appropriate for the child. Always label objects and events. For example, "There's truck; truck go." Continue to give the child simple information as well as more elaborate information. For example, a nod of the head can confirm "Yes, it's a ball." More complete information might be given by saying "It's a round, red ball . . . (pause) . . . roll ball." This second example shows how the teacher might expand on the child's question "ball?"

Rephrase what is said to the child. This should be done particularly if the child shows signs of not having comprehended what was said. Repetition of what was said is a good technique for facilitating language comprehension. In this way, the child is given a second chance to process the information. Again, look for signs from the child that he has comprehended what was said. Always incorporate comprehension tasks in all activities. For example, in the language experience story, the child might be asked to point out the appropriate items in the story picture. Comprehension is essential for the child to respond.

In facilitating *language production*, models by the teacher, aides, or other children are invaluable. The teacher provides models by using many of the same strategies already discussed in facilitating comprehension. Encouraging the child to imitate what has been said can be valuable. Allowing the child time to repeat and practice her own phrases without interrupting is essential in facilitating production. The teacher gives evaluative feedback regarding the child utterances. This may include acceptance ("That's right") or rejection ("No, dog go"). In this latter instance, the utterance was rejected, and a correction was given. The next step for the facilitator might then be to wait for the child to say "Dog go" rather than "Horse go." Enhancing specific language content and structures again varies with the specific toy, event, or activity. Language production target goals can be built into specific activities. For example, encouraging the use of certain action words in two-word sentences describing the body can be done by using a doll in show and tell time. Actual language production skills (i.e., learning how to structure a question) cannot be learned unless the child's environment is structured in such a way as to encourage question-asking behavior.

An assumption that has been made thus far is that the child's speech is at least understandable to a moderate degree. This is not always the case. Some children's speech is entirely unintelligible even though their comprehension skills are good. In this case, the teacher must rely on the child's being able to point out an object or gesture an appropriate action in response to the question. However, verbal approximations should always be encouraged. This particular type of child often needs successful talking time in a relaxed situation. Interpretation by the teacher of utterances the child initiates is essential but not always possible.

Another type of child is one whose speech is unintelligible and who has only moderate comprehension skills at best. This child might be using pictures on a communication board to supplement speech. Here again, speech and the communication board should be used concurrently. In both cases, where speech is poor, good models should be provided. However, it can become very frustrating for both teacher and child if correction of specific sounds is forced on the child. The specific mechanics of learning the sound

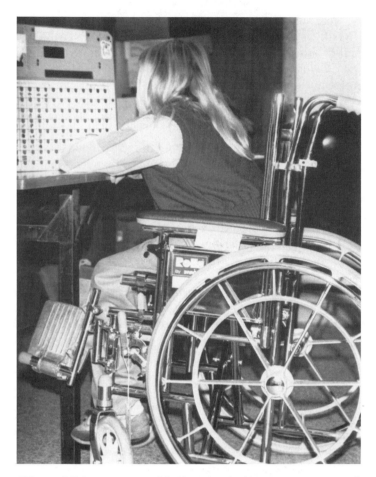

When children are unable to speak, they can communicate through the use of language boards and other adaptive aids.

production are probably best done with the therapist. However, once the sound or process is learned, carry-over should be encouraged by the teacher.

The last issue to be discussed with language facilitation techniques for young children is *behavioral management*. It is not uncommon to see a young child who has language but does not use it because his behavior prevents her from doing so. For example, the child may have found that throwing a tantrum is a much more effective way of fulfilling her needs than is using words. On the other hand, a significant portion of the child's behavior problem can result from her poor ability in using language to organize her life. In this case, the structure and organization of the classroom is essential. The child's awareness of this structure should be reinforced. Always verbally prepare this child for what is next. Some basic guidelines can be given to handle the behaviorally disordered child. These include:

1. Be sure the child knows what is expected. For example, prepare the child for what happens during "listening circle."

2. Redirect the child to behave more constructively. For example, supply the child with a piece of paper on which to draw rather than on the wall.

3. Teach new behaviors in small steps (i.e., shaping). For example, a child may be required to pat his/her tummy to signify "eat" rather than say the word. Compliance in the activity at this point may be more important than how the child complies.

4. Give the child *prompts* to aid in developing new behaviors. For example, show the child what he is to do. "The towel goes in the waste basket like this. Now you put your towel in."

5. Provide appropriate positive reinforcement (attention and praise) for those behaviors the child needs to increase. For example, telling two children that they are doing a nice job working on their puzzle will reinforce the children and they will continue. No reinforcement may result in one of them throwing the puzzle to get attention.

For the behaviorally disordered child, it is extremely difficult to facilitate appropriate language and communication until the behavior is managed more successfully.

COMPREHENSION CHECK 9.8

Explain how a teacher can modify the physical arrangement of the preschool to promote language learning. Give an example of how group experiences can help language growth in children. Explain how *prompts* can be used by the teacher to develop newly shaped language behaviors.

Language facilitation strategies for the early grades

For the school-age child, effective programming continues to require constant communication between the teacher, speech-language pathologist, and parents. Not enough time is allowed in many educational systems today for this communication. Quality programming is the end product of such group problem solving between all those intricately involved with the child. Pressure on the child, who is now school age and exhibiting specific learning and language difficulties and disabilities, is even greater with the demands of the classroom. This same child at a very young age (0 to 5) was, it is hoped, able to participate in appropriate early-intervention programs. Appropriate early intervention can significantly lessen the extent of the problems the child faces when school starts. Certainly, the emotional impact when starting school is less for the child and parent who have already begun to deal effectively with the learning and language problems.

The child at this age should continue to participate in individual therapy and group sessions designed to enhance language-learning skills in the classroom. In addition, the child will be expected to handle the academic curricula. Adaptation of the academic curricula to suit individual learning styles is a necessary element in classroom programming. For example, the child who is a visual learner may require pictures to understand fully what is being said. Giving auditory instructions without showing how to complete a task will be difficult for this child. Showing how to solve the problem on paper will be of greater value than telling the child how to do it. For another child, highlighting the critical elements of the story may assist the child in comprehending the story.

Many of the facilitation strategies already discussed for the child up to age 5 or 6 remain appropriate for the school-age child. The expansion and refinement of particular strategies is appropriate for the older children in the academic setting. Of particular concern are *listening skills*. Robinson and Smith (1981) have effectively summarized strategies the teacher can use to modify the message given to the child and strategies that can be used to modify the child's attention, language, memory, and comprehension or input (see Tables 9.9 and 9.10). Strategies described for attention and language are self-explanatory and have been addressed at various points in this chapter. Concerning memory, groups of words that are logically related are easier to recall than are those words that are not. For example, a group of words such

TABLE 9.9
Strategies to Modify Input (The Message)

Input	Intervention
Attention Focusing the listener's attention on the speaker	1. Give direct instruction (e.g.: "Listen to what I'm going to say") 2. Shorten input 3. Use visual aid 4. Reduce extraneous stimuli 5. Increase proximity of speaker to listener
Language	1. Simplify vocabulary 2. Restate message 3. Simplify syntax
Memory The speaker's facilitating listener recall	1. Use high-frequency words 2. Disseminate group information in easily associated categories 3. Use groupings categorized by semantic membership (what they are) rather than where or when 4. Control message length 5. Control linguistic (or surface) structure 6. Control restatements—should be exact or will confuse 7. Control serial position of information—information given last is remembered best, information given in the middle is forgotten most easily 8. Use careful phrasing—can group words or elements for listener 9. Increase relevance of material to listener—increases recall.
Comprehension	1. Provide practice at all levels of literal, critical, and appreciative comprehension.

Source: Robinson, S., and Smith D. (1981). Listening skills: Teaching learning disabled students to be better listeners. *Focus on Exceptional Children,* pp. 16–31. Denver, CO: Love Publishing Company.

as shoes, socks, shirt, and pants are more easily remembered than fork, hat, bus, and book. Wiig and Semel (1980) report that words grouped by semantic class membership (e.g., what: fruits—apples, pears, grapes) are easier to remember than words grouped spatially or temporally. For example, information grouped spatially would include things found in the garage such as paint, wrench, and auto. Examples of words related temporally might include morning—breakfast, toothbrush, and ironing.

Similarly, to enhance memory, the authors recommend the presentation of the most critical information last in giving directions. Careful phrasing or clustering of the words spoken is recommended. The teacher should pause naturally when speaking. Peer interaction as a way to model some of these listening strategies cannot be overemphasized. For enhancing memory, rehearsal of organized material is critical. Remember, many of the skills can best be actualized in highly motivating situations. Use of teaching material that is relevant and of high interest is important. Generalization of these skills in the group-communication process as well as in the strict learning

TABLE 9.10
Strategies to Modify Listening Behavior

Listening Behavior	Interventions
Attention	1. Peer modeling
	2. Teacher modeling
	3. Verbal rehearsal
	4. Reinforcement
	5. Physical guidance
Language	1. Increase in vocabulary
	2. Increase in knowledge of multiple-word meanings
	3. Increase in syntactic skills
Memory	1. Rehearsal during listening
	2. Clustering or chunking information
	3. Coding information (POP for people, organizations, populations, etc.)
	4. Visualization
	5. Question asking
	6. Identifying organizational cues (First . . . second . . . etc.)
	7. Rehearsal after listening
	8. Summarizing message after listening
	9. Comparing information received to develop categories
Comprehension	1. Practice at all levels of literal, critical, and appreciative comprehension
	2. Practice in identifying nonverbal messages

Source: Robinson, S., and Smith, D. (1981). Listening skills: Teaching learning disabled children to be better listeners. *Focus on Exceptional Children*, pp. 16–31. Denver, CO: Love Publishing Company.

setting is desirable. The child who is motivated to give information to another child will do so using strategies he/she has learned through modeling. However, it still remains that the situation must be structured to facilitate such an information-sharing interaction between two children.

SUMMARY

In this chapter, a wide range of facilitation strategies for young children with communication disorders have been addressed; however, the lists are not complete. For organizational purposes, chronological age markers have been used to group strategies. However, it should be noted that overlap can exist between strategies described as appropriate with the 3-year-old and strategies described as appropriate for the 5-year-old. Also apparent is the fact that each child is an individual; although strategies were grouped according to general types of children exhibiting language disorders. For example, the learning disabled child who is language disordered was discussed as well as the young child exhibiting a pragmatic disorder who may or may not have been identified as learning disabled.

No specific categories of language disorders are mutually exclusive. This assumption is inherent in discussing communication as a dynamic process. For the teacher who uses this chapter as a resource, it will be important for him/her to describe the behaviors that the child exhibits regardless of the child's age or labels that may have been placed on the child. In this way, the teacher will be able to select strategies that might be most appropriate to facilitate the child's language. For example, the teacher may be working with a 5-year-old who uses only one-word phrases for basic needs and does not have the concept of object constancy for many items in her environment. Strategies discussed in this chapter for the younger child would certainly be applicable for this 5-year-old.

Lastly, without appropriate facilitation by parents and caretakers, intervention for the child as a whole is meaningless. Facilitation is multiple settings and with several people determines whether or not the skill will be learned.

SUGGESTED READINGS

Bloom, L., and Lahey, M. (1978). *Language development and language disorders*. New York: Wiley.

Holland, A. L. (1984). *Language disorders in children*. San Diego, CA: College-Hill Press.

McCormick, L., and Scheifelbusch, R. L. (1984). *Early language intervention: An introduction*. Columbus, OH: Merrill.

Miller, J. (1981). *Assessing language production in children*. Baltimore: University Park Press.

Scheifelbusch, R. L. (1980). *Nonspeech language and communication*. Baltimore: University Park Press.

CHAPTER
10

Developmental Differences in Learning

Mary McLean
Nancy B. Burdg
Eleanor G. Hall

CHAPTER OUTLINE

VIGNETTES

Jennifer is a premature infant. She weighed only 3½ pounds at birth and suffered from a respiratory problem known as hyaline membrane disease. She was taken immediately to the neonatal intensive care unit (NICU) in a large hospital about an hour from her home-town. Jennifer is lucky to be in a special infant stimulation and parent involvement pro-gram that has recently begun at the hospital. Her NICU nurses have been specially trained in infant stimulation techniques. Her incubator has a colorful mobile hung above it so that she can visually focus on its parts. Now that she can be taken from the incubator for feeding and "play" times, the nurses rock her, talk to her, pat and rub her body and shake rattles for her to hear. Jennifer's mother and father have been to the hospital many times to be with her. They have received instruction from the nurses in feeding and stimu-lation techniques. Her parents are also taking part in parent support meetings held at the hospital weekly. Here they can talk with other parents of premature infants about their fears and concerns for their children.

When Jennifer is released from the hospital to go home, her parents will bring her back regularly for follow-up clinic visits where her developmental progress will be closely watched. Her mother and father will also be invited to go to parent-infant classes where stimulation activities for infant development will be demonstrated. At these classes, there will be a chance to discuss child-care or family adjustment problems that may occur. Jennifer's parents will also receive home visits from a hospital staff member. In this way, information from the parent class can be extended to the home situation. All these ser-vices have been offered by the hospital to make sure that premature infants like Jennifer receive physical and sensory stimulation, as well as social interaction with their caregivers in a manner as close as possible to that experienced by full-term infants. The hospital realizes the importance of early intervention with premature babies who are at risk for the development of learning problems.

Jonathan is 3½ years old and has Down's syndrome. He goes to a special class every morning in the elementary public school near his home. Because his mother works, Jonathan goes to a neighborhood day-care center in the afternoon. In his special class, Jonathan receives educational intervention in cognitive, language, fine and gross motor, socioemotional, and self-help skills. His teacher works closely with a speech and language therapist to plan Jonathan's educational program. Among other things, Jonathan is learning to put three and four words together in sentences, and he is learning to dress himself, including buttoning and snapping. He is also working on toilet training and is learning to play cooperatively with other children during playtime. Jonathan's teacher meets regularly with his day-care teacher so that his experiences in both settings will be coordinated.

Jonathan's parents have been active in his education since he was born. They meet often with his teacher to review his progress and learn about intervention techniques. They also attend parent meetings at school with the parents of Jonathan's classmates. Jonathan's parents are aware that he is mentally retarded and will not learn as readily as a normal child does. They want to help him grow to his fullest potential.

Heidi, a 4-year-old gifted child, attends a neighborhood cooperative nursery school. Her parents are interested in her development and want Heidi to be well adjusted and happy in school. They hope Heidi will have the friends and emotional support to reach her poten-tial.

In the nursery-school class, Heidi is a leader in the dress-up corner and is often the "mother" of the imaginative family. This sometimes results in conflicts with other children, as Heidi has strong ideas about how the others should behave. Heidi then withdraws from "playing house" and retreats to the book corner to read. Heidi reads at second-grade level and can read most of the books in her room by herself. Heidi also knows how to tell time, all the colors including various shades of colors, how to count to 20, and some simple addition and subtraction.

Heidi's parents are members of a parent advocacy program that meets to improve public understanding of the needs of gifted children. Heidi's parents hope that the school will be able to provide for her needs. In some areas, Heidi is very advanced, in other areas she is average, and in other ways she seems immature.

Providing for Heidi's needs requires the understanding of a teacher in education of the gifted. This teacher needs to nurture and foster her intellectual strength while at the same time providing emotional support and growth in social skills. An opportunity to interact with other gifted children would help her to learn to be a follower as well as a leader. She would learn communication skills with other gifted children that could be adopted for use with all children. If left on her own, Heidi might develop into either a disruptive child who does not get along well with other children or a withdrawn child who retreats into her own world of books and fantasy.

Exceptionalities in learning include the traditionally used categories of mental retardation, specific learning disabilities, and giftedness. The early-childhood special educator may work with children who exhibit a range of these exceptionalities together in the same classroom. Their problems are different, and their instructional programs will include different objectives, methods, and materials.

MENTAL RETARDATION

Definition and description of the problem

Mental retardation is officially defined by the American Association on Mental Deficiency as "significantly subaverage general intellectual functioning existing concurrently with deficits in adaptive behavior and manifested during the developmental period" (Grossman, 1973, p. 11). Mental retardation is further divided into four levels of functioning—mild, moderate, severe, and profound—as defined by performance on a standardized intelligence test. However, an IQ score alone is not enough to label a child as mentally retarded. A deficit in adaptive behavior must also be demonstrated. *Adaptive behavior* is defined as the extent to which a child demonstrates age-appropriate social and self-care skills.

COMPREHENSION CHECK 10.1

Why is it important to consider both the level of intellectual functioning and the level of adaptive behavior in the diagnosis of mental retardation in young children?

Impact on the family

The diagnosis of mental retardation usually causes major changes in the way a family functions. Parents and other family members may react to the diagnosis with shock, disbelief, grief, or a combination of these reactions. The parents of a mentally retarded preschool child may require professional help ranging from basic information about the condition itself to counseling. The family may also require practical help in dealing with basic day-to-day problems such as discipline, dealing with siblings, and financial matters. Parents of mentally retarded children must also be helped to accept their child's disability. Many parents of mentally retarded children cling to the hope that the condition is temporary, that their child will "grow out of it" or that the condition can be "cured." As a result, some parents go from professional to professional seeking a cure. However, it is only when the parent accepts the child and the problems that real help can begin. Parents must be encouraged to recognize and accept both the strengths and weaknesses in their child and to learn how to build on the child's strengths. This is expecially important during the preschool years in order to maximize the child's chances for early remediation and prevention of intellectual delay and deficiencies.

COMPREHENSION CHECK 10.2

How can parents be encouraged to accept a diagnosis of mental retardation in their child when they refuse to believe the assessment results?

Impact of the child's development

Mentally retarded children usually demonstrate delays in all developmental areas. Motor skills, speech and language skills, cognitive skills, perceptual-motor skills, and even social and emotional behaviors will be acquired more slowly than with the nonhandicapped child. *Developmental retardation* is really a more apt description than *mental* retardation.

In general, the mildly mentally retarded child functions at a developmental level that is approximately one-half to two-thirds of the child's chronological age. For example, a 6-year-old mildly retarded child might demonstrate behavior similar to that of a child between 3 and 4 years of age. The moderately retarded child functions at a developmental level that is approximately one-third to one-half of the child's chronological age. Betty is a 6-year-old *moderately* retarded child but behaves like a child between 2 and 3 years of age. Morris is a *severely* retarded 6-year-old whose behavior is typical of a child younger than 2 years or less than one-third of his chronological age. In many cases, mental retardation occurs along with other physical or sensory handicaps. The learning problems these multihandicapped children face are increased by the presence of more than one disability.

Causes

There are many identified causes of intellectual or mental retardation, although it may not be possible to specify the cause for each individual child. The following are some medical factors that can result in mental retardation (see Chapter 1):

This four-year-old Downs Syndrome girl is at the same developmental play level as her two-and-a-half-year-old playmate.

Prenatal infections (rubella, syphilis)
Postnatal infections (encephalitis, meningitis)
Birth trauma
Metabolism/nutrition problems
Cranial abnormalities (hydrocephalus, microcephalus)
Chromosomal abnormalities (Down's syndrome)
Gestational disorders (premature birth)
Accidents causing brain injury

Recent scientific advances in genetic counseling, virus vaccines, and early screening for metabolism abnormalities have helped to prevent mental retardation in many cases. Good prenatal medical care and education for expectant mothers can also significantly reduce the number of children who demonstrate learning problems caused by mental retardation.

Incidence and prevalence

The prevalence of mental retardation in the general population is typically stated as 3% (Heward and Orlansky, 1984). In relation to young children, however, the incidence varies depending on the identification procedures established in a given community. The percentage identified typically increases as children become school-aged. Infants and preschoolers who are identified are typically the moderately and severely retarded. Telford and Sawrey (1977) reported that 0.07% of children from birth to age 4 are identified as mentally retarded and 1.18% of children from 5 to 9 years of age are identified as mentally retarded.

COMPREHENSION CHECK 10.3

What cautions should be emphasized with diagnosing mild mental retardation in a 2-year-old child?

SPECIFIC LEARNING DISABILITIES

Definition and description of the problem

The official definition of *learning disabilities* currently used in federal legislation is:

> *Specific learning disability means a disorder in one or more of the basic psychological processes involved in understanding or using language, spoken or written, which may manifest itself in an imperfect ability to listen, think, speak, read, write, spell, or do mathematic calculations. The term includes such conditions as perceptual handicaps, brain injury, minimal brain dysfunction, dyslexia, and developmental aphasia.* The term does not include children who have learning problems which are primarily the result of visual, hearing, motor handicaps, mental retardation or cultural and/or economic disadvantages.

COMPREHENSION CHECK 10.4

How is a learning disability different from mental retardation?

Impact on the family

Parents of children with specific learning disabilities have somewhat different problems than do parents of children with other disabilities. One striking difference is that their children look "normal," both physically and developmentally. Often these children reach all developmental milestones but at a different pace. As a result, parents often feel that with the correct teacher or program, their child could catch up with their peers. Another problem faced by these parents is the apparent inconsistency in their child's behavior. In some areas, these children have average or above average abilities. Yet in other areas, they are significantly behind their peers. This variation can cause confusion and frustration.

Impact on the Child's Development

Hare and Hare (1979) list the following as the most frequently identified characteristics of the population of learning disabled children:

Near-average to above-average cognitive ability
Activity level either too active or sluggish
Problems in focusing attention
Poor fine and gross motor coordination
Visual perceptual problems
Auditory perceptual problems
Delayed speech or language development
Socioemotional behavior problems
Spatial orientation problems
Poor work habits
Problems in academic work

Of course, a child with a learning disability will not necessarily have all these problems.

The identification of learning disabilities in young children has been a problem for educators. In public school programs, the classification of a child as learning disabled usually depends on the discrepancy between achievement and ability in an academic area such as reading or math. Of course, this type of measurement is not easily applied to preschool children. Indeed, many professionals are hesitant to use the term "learning disability" with the preschool population (Lerner, Mardell-Czudnowski, and Goldenberg, 1981). At the same time, delaying intervention until a child reaches school may greatly reduce the effectiveness of intervention. This is true both in terms of the child's academic performance and self-concept. Teacher observation of a child's preschool performance becomes an extremely important element of identification. This is especially true for children who demonstrate developmental delay or the characteristics identified by Hare and Hare (1979), which may be distinct indicators for later problems. These children are considered to be "high risk" and may in the future be identified as learning disabled. Providing quality preschool intervention may correct mild learning problems so that intervention at school-age is not necessary.

Causes

No one is sure what causes specific learning disabilities. Researchers have speculated that certain factors may be related to later learning disabilities. (see Table 10.1). Remember that learning disabilities are really defined in terms of school-related content (i.e., reading, writing, and arithmetic). At preschool age, then, the effort is to try to find precursors or predictors of the full LD syndrome.

Incidence and Prevalence

Because the definitions of learning disability vary so much and because the problem is school related, estimates of the percentage of preschool children with specific learning disabilities either are not possible or are highly speculative. Approximately 10% of the school-age population have specific learning disabilities. It is probably safe to assume that at least 10% of our preschool population manifests some of the risk and/or behavioral factors that seem predictive of later learning difficulties.

TABLE 10.1
A Selective Review of High-Risk Indicators of Learning Disabilities

Poor prenatal care	Neuromotor dysfunctions
Pre- and Post-maturity anoxia	Parental history of reading problems
Maternal toxemia	Delayed language, motor, and social development milestones
Failure to thrive	Hyperactivity, impulsivity, and attention problems
Feeding disorders	Feeding problems
Seizure disorders	Difficulties in birth and delivery
Meningitis or encephalitis	Maternal use of cigarettes, drugs, and alcohol
Traumatic head injuries	

GIFTEDNESS

Definition and description

Giftedness is thought of by some educators as outstanding ability in various areas. In contrast, others see it as a more uniform trait such as superior intellectual ability. Definitions of giftedness range from "consistently remarkable performance in any potentially valuable area" (Witty, 1940, p. 516) to the federal definition (*Congressional Record*, 1978), which defines *gifted and talented* as:

> *Children and youth who are identified at the preschool, elementary, or secondary level as possessing demonstrated or potential abilities that give evidence of high performance capability in areas such as intellectual, creative, specific academic, or leadership ability, or in the performing and visual arts and who by reason thereof require service or activities not ordinarily provided by the school.*

The following list of characteristics of young gifted children should help to clarify one's perception of these children:

- Talent in music, drawing, rhythms, or other art forms
- Ability to attend or concentrate on complex tasks
- Asks many questions about topics about which young children usually are not interested
- Keen observation and retention of information about things observed
- An early interest in clocks and calendars, and an ability to understand their function
- The early accurate use of a large vocabulary
- The ability to tell or duplicate stories and events with detail

- Carries on a conversation with older children and adults
- Learned to read early, with little or no formal teaching.
- Can write short stories, poems, or letters

It should be remembered, however, that individual gifted children show great diversity with respect to every trait. However, as a group, gifted young children will exhibit these characteristics more frequently, to a higher degree, and at an earlier age than do other children.

Impact on the family

Parents of gifted children who were interviewed by Frinier (Hall and Skinner, 1980) concerning this list of characteristics often reported that when their children were in the primary grades they were bored, becoming behavior problems, or quiet and unhappy in regular classroom settings. Early identification of giftedness is suggested to prevent the boredom and frustration that is so frequently found among gifted children. This is especially true for those who have not had the benefit of identification and intervention.

Giftedness includes early talent in art, music, and other creative activities.

Therefore, parents of gifted children often spend a great deal of time trying to gain appropriate programs and materials for their children. In the preschool years, parents may also be active in setting up enrichment programs for their child.

COMPREHENSION CHECK 10.5

Identify ways that parents of intellectually gifted preschoolers can also promote the development of appropriate social skills for their children.

Impact on the child's development

Gifted youngsters are not handicapped—but they are exceptional. Because they are different, even in a positive way, they encounter problems and pressures. Most of the problems of gifted children probably arise from two major factors: (1) *interpersonal differences:*—wide discrepancies between gifted and normal age-appropriate behavior, and (2) *intrapersonal differences:*—discrepancies among the various levels of development within a given child.

Interpersonal differences

Gifted children often show interest and excell in a variety of activities, including areas considered "inappropriate" for age or sex. Thus a gifted young boy might become interested in cooking or sewing ("He's going to be a sissy") or in politics ("He's too young to understand all that"). The social pressure to conform to the group and to not be "weird" can obviously create real anxieties for children. Gifted youngsters are frequently quite sensitive and can accurately "read" the social situation—often a situation of rejection. Accelerated physical growth, larger size for age, greater physical attractiveness, and earlier onset of puberty are all characteristics that can earn rejection by the norm group. Of course, *preschoolers* do not encounter rejection for these reasons that arise later, but they begin to sense their differences during the early years. Early guidance in how to deal with "being different" is important, therefore, to gifted as well as handicapped children. Making and keeping friends is crucial to all children, and all preschoolers need help in learning how to cooperate with, tolerate, and accept the differences of others.

Intrapersonal differences

Although gifted children are often advanced in all areas of development, this is not necessarily the case with all such youngsters. Socioemotional problems may arise when one area of development, especially intellectual, is well advanced compared with the others. Self-doubt, frustration, and much introspection may result when the child's mental age is "out of sync" with the rest of development. Physical and social development, for example, can lag behind cognitive functioning. When unrealistic adult expectations of social behavior are based on IQ scores, there can be great pressure on the child and the beginning of a troublesome history of social conflict.

The early-childhood educator must be aware of the struggles of children as they attempt to learn who they are and how their differences can be tolerated, managed, and valued. Early-childhood experiences can help children to cope with the differences within and between them and can ease the difficulties associated with uneven development.

Causes

Many researchers stress the genetic or "nature" aspect of giftedness. This is consistent with the popular view of "God-given" (inborn) or innate talents that the environment can increase or hinder but not create. The thinking is that either one "has" the talent or not, that giftedness is not something that can be taught but that can be enhanced. Of course, approaches and theories that emphasize the role of the environment stress the shaping and strengthening of capabilities through favorable contingencies, modeling, and parenting practices.

Incidence and prevalence

Data on incidence and prevalence are affected both by the difinition used and by the means used to identify a child as gifted. However, Sisk (1978) states that it has been assumed in federal reports and legislation that 3% to 5% of the school-age population is gifted or talented. The figure in the preschool population should be theoretically about the same.

ASSESSMENT OF LEARNING

Birth to three years

Identification of children with learning problems is easiest for those children who have congenital disorders. These children include those with identifiable syndromes of mental retardation or who have undergone severe birth trauma. According to Scott and Hogan (1980), two-thirds of these children will be identified by their pediatricians during the first year of life. However, at this time, it is not possible to identify with certainty those children who will eventually demonstrate mild mental retardation or learning disabilities (Lewis and Fox, 1980; Turner and Wade, 1982). Professionals in early-childhood special education use the term "at risk" to refer to that group of infants who do not demonstrate delayed development at the present time but may in the future because of biological and/or environmental causes. One way of tracking such children so that information can be provided if needed is to establish a high-risk register. A register may be kept by a medical, social service, or educational agency. The purpose of such a register is to identify those children whose family history, home environment, or birth history suggests that learning problems may occur later on. For example, children who have been in a neonatal intensive care unit because of birth complications would qualify for such a high-risk register. Periodic developmental evaluations would then identify those children who do have learning problems as those problems become evident.

Referrals to intervention programs may come from neonatologists, pediatricians, or family practitioners who identify a handicapping condition in the infant. Referrals may also be made by public health nurses or social workers who visit homes of some low-income families after an infant is born. To maintain these channels of referral, the early-intervention program must communicate regularly with professionals. There are two reasons for this communication: (1) professionals will be aware of the program's existence and procedures for referral, and (2) medical or social service professionals will be certain that they are referring the family to a program that provides quality services. Publicizing the existence of an early-intervention program in the community through newspapers, radio, and television is also recommended, because many times referrals are made by ministers or teachers, friends, and family members who suspect that a young child may have a delay in development.

Not all children who need early intervention are referred for such services, however. Children from lower socioeconomic families are frequently not identified because of a lack of medical care. In fact, they may not come to the attention of professionals until they are school-age. In other cases, parents may suspect a problem, only to be told by a pediatrician that their child will "grow out of it" (Hayden and Edgar, 1977). A systematic screening program not only would reach more children but would give professionals a basis for determining whether or not a referral for further assessment is needed. Several easily administered screening instruments are available. These devices assess developmental milestones to help professionals make such decisions. Chapter 13 in this book presents an in-depth discussion of screening procedures.

COMPREHENSION CHECK 10.6

Design and describe a child tracking and screening system (flowchart) that a small *rural* community could use to identify at-risk infants. This system should describe working interrelationships between physicians, community programs, and even churches.

Three to five years

Most parents are aware early in their child's life that the child is not developing like other children of the same age. The clues to developmental delay or potential learning problems may be obvious. As described earlier, this initial identification may occur at birth. However, some learning problems that initially go undetected may surface as the child enters the preschool years. A parent or other individual who is frequently with the child may notice that the child has been slow at reaching developmental milestones that come easily to other children. The child may have begun walking or talking at a later age than his age group. He may display inappropriate social behavior, appearing to be a much younger child than his age. Indicators such as these become the basis for referral. Once a referral is received, early-intervention programs can provide an in-depth assessment of the child. The goal of this assessment is to identify the child's specific strengths and weaknesses. Assessment results provide the basis for intervention and preschool educational programming.

The ultimate goal of the assessment of the preschool child should be that of providing appropriate intervention and educational programming for the child. Developmental assessment, is the key to quality programming. Criterion-referenced measurement provides a way of identifying specific strengths and weaknesses within an individual. Once a comprehensive analysis of developmental skills is completed, appropriate individualized educational programs may be developed.

Several developmentally based assessment instruments for preschool-age children are available. Most of these assessments require no specialized training, other than a familiarity with the test and interpretation of the assessment results. Some examples of these tests are the Learning Accomplishment Profile (LAP) (LeMay, Griffin, and Sanford, 1977), the BRIGANCE Diagnostic Inventory of Early Development (Brigance, 1978), the Carolina Developmental Profile (Lillie and Harbin, 1975), and the Uniform Performance Assessment System (UPAS) (White, Edgar, Haring, et al., 1981). The first two are criterion-referenced measure. The third device is especially efficient for assessment in a preschool program that has limited resources. The last is a "curriculum-referenced" assessment instrument.

The four assessment instruments mentioned here include sections that assess cognition in young handicapped children. It must be stressed that assessment in the area of cognitive development is necessary and an essential component of a preschool assessment program. This is true despite the handicapping condition exhibited by the child. "Cognition" is a pervasive term involved in all areas of the preschool handicapped curriculum (Lerner, Mardell-Czudnowski, and Goldenberg, 1981).

Early identification and assessment
of gifted characteristics

Identification of gifted children is usually a two-step process. The first step is screening all candidates to find as many potentially gifted children as possible. The second step is selection to refine the choices to determine which children are the gifted ones in the group. The most effective identification systems use as many available measures and procedures as is practical and possible. This is limited by the amount of time and resources available. A good match between the identification method used and the anticipated program should be made. Because intelligence-test scores are not stable for younger children without extensive language, identification of young gifted children is a complex process. Children must be given wide opportunities to display a variety of intellectual skills. Thus, a child's best, rather than average, performance should be the primary selection criterion. Futhermore, children's parents should be encouraged to contribute their observations to the identification process.

Screening

Jackson and Robinson (1977) suggest using the short form of the Stanford-Binet Intelligence Test as a measure of general intellectual ability. They also recommend the Block Design and Mazes Subtest of the Wechsler Preschool and Primary Scale of Intelligence (WPPSI) (Wechsler, 1967). Whenever a child passes the most advanced items on a WPPSI subtest, parallel subtests of the Wechsler Intelligence Scale for Children–Revised (WISC–R) (Wechsler, 1974) can be used to continue the testing.

This combination of the short form Binet and Block Design and Mazes of the Wechsler Tests provides measures of both verbal and spatial ability. Also included in the screening process is a one-page reading inventory and the Peabody Individual Achievement Test (Dunn and Markwardt, 1970). These tests are used to measure preschoolers academic skill levels. This test is standardized for kindergarten age and older but has been found to be effective with bright preschoolers as young as 3-years-old (Shorr and McClelland, 1977).

To supplement the test results, it is always important to get descriptive information from the parents, as well as observational information. This is important because young children may refuse certain test items. Credit should be given for advanced skills observed during an interview or test session no matter how informal the context in which the skills are displayed (Jackson and Robinson, 1977).

Use of parent information is important in the identification of gifted children at any age, but it is especially important for screening preschool-age children. The Child Development Research Group of Seattle, a program associated with the University of Washington (Roedell, Jackson, and Robinson, 1980), has demonstrated that parents exercise considerable selectivity in responding to calls for intellectually or academically gifted children. The average performance level of each group is usually about 130 IQ. This is substantially above what would be expected even in a university community. This same tendency has been reported in other studies involving parent nomination of children for gifted programs (Jacobs, 1971). Parents who have the chance to recommend a child are usually realistic about their children's abilities. Thus, as Roedell, Jackson, and Robinson (1980) state, parent nominations can provide an efficient tool for identifying gifted children.

However, educators should keep in mind that some well-educated parents from middle-class communities tend to set extremely high standards in defining superior intellectual performance. One parent noted, "In our neighborhood almost every child is reading by age 4" (Roedell, Jackson, and Robinson, 1980, p. 56).

Despite the difficulties, researchers have found parent information about 2- and 3-year-olds more useful in predicting later performance than the child's test performance at the time.

Sample items asked of parents on these questionnaires include:

- Has your child drawn a person with at least some representation of legs, head, and eyes?
- Does your child recognize and correctly identify the numbers 1 through 9?
- Does your child comment on words that have two or more meanings?
- Does your child read, not listen to, books such as *Winnie the Pooh* or *Little House on the Prairie*, which contain long stories and few pictures? (Roedell, Jackson, and Robinson, 1980, p. 58)

Note the rather specific information requested from the parents on the sample items. This is the type of information that is most helpful in the identification of gifted children.

Studies from the literature suggest that kindergarten teachers are not as likely to be as effective nominators of gifted children as are parents (Jacobs, 1971). However, the preschool teachers in the Seattle Project (Roedell, Jackson, and Robinson, 1980) have become accurate judges of children's overall intellectual maturity. This result could occur because these teachers were more highly educated than many preschool teachers. They were also trained to be sensitive to individual children's abilities.

Another effective screening tool for identifying gifted children is the use of *product evaluation*. This technique has the potential for adding additional information about a child's creative ability and intellectual ability. Use of rated products may also help to clarify judgments about a particular child. This is especially true for children whose parents were too strict in their criterion for giftedness. These products may be drawings or paintings, poems, stories, or clay figures. The research of Martinson and Seagoe (1967) on product ratings demonstrated that these ratings discriminate between the most and least original and most and least expressive children.

It seems important that ratings be made on a variety of products rather than one product in one medium. However, it should be remembered that young gifted children sometimes make their products look like every other child's. Therefore, raters should try to make sure they are getting the most original, complex, and elaborate products. To increase the probability of this, children should develop the products by themselves and be encouraged to

Gifted preschoolers often show special talent in creative activities.

make them as unusual and elaborate as they possibly can. No opportunities to see what other children are doing should be allowed.

Selection

To make the screening process manageable, a matrix weighted-score method is recommended (Baldwin, 1977). Both test performance and parent and teacher information are given points for various degrees of superiority. Scores from standardized tests are also given values. These values are based on the most advanced performance demonstrated rather than the average performance usually used. This position is based on the experience of Jackson and Robinson (1977). Therefore, a preschool selection matrix for a preschool program for the gifted might look something like the one presented in Figure 10.1.

Once a group of children have been screened and identification matrices have been scored, children may be rank-ordered from highest to lowest. Whenever a child's highest performance is among the top scores for the group, the child should be considered gifted, regardless of the average scores. There is no way to avoid making some subjective decisions about children when it comes to the final selection process. However, children's IQs can change and any identification always leaves an opening for children to qualify as gifted later on.

The reason for identifying gifted children is to provide encouragement and to nurture and support their talent. It is also to avoid the loneliness, unhappiness, or personality change commonly found among children who have not had the opportunity of special intervention programs.

COMPREHENSION CHECK 10.7

Describe specific ways in which parents and teachers could use toys and other materials to assess a young gifted child's *creative* skills.

Figure 10.1
Preschool Identification Matrix for Gifted Children

Child's Name: _____   Address: _____
Date of Birth: _____   Today's Date: _____
Age: _____   Sex: _____

(Circle value that represents quality of performance.)

	Rating: highest				lowest
1. Parent questionnaire	5	4	3	2	1
2. Short-form Binet	5	4	3	2	1
3. Wechsler Subtest Mazes	5	4	3	2	1
4. Wechler Subtest Block Design	5	4	3	2	1
5. Product ratings	5	4	3	2	1
a. Drawing or block construction	5	4	3	2	1
b. Story or poem	5	4	3	2	1
c. Rhythms or clay object	5	4	3	2	1
Total score					

Models of service delivery: Birth to three years

Between birth and the age of 3 years, children identified for early-intervention services are those who show learning problems because of birth complications, environmental disadvantage, or identified syndromes of mental retardation. Early-childhood special educators work closely with the medical community in this age range because a primary means of identification is referral from doctors and public health nurses.

Services for children with complications such as prematurity often begin in the hospital at birth. Recently, there has been growing interest in providing sensory and physical stimulation for such infants by the hospital nursing staff (Brown and Hepler, 1976). Such stimulation is often accompanied by parent training in the stimulation techniques while the child is still in the hospital. This training may also include home visits after the child's release to assist in establishing satisfying parent-child interactions and continued developmental stimulation for the infant (Badger, Burns, and DeBoer, 1982; Bromwich, 1981).

Intervention for children younger than 3 years is often based on a model of teaching parents to carry out intervention procedures in the home. This may be done through periodic visits of the professional to the home or by asking the parents to bring their child into the intervention program. In this setting, instruction may take place individually or with groups of parents. Parents may be instructed in observation of their child's behavior, techniques for teaching their child new skills, and how to evaluate the child's progress. General information on child development, caregiving suggestions, and handicapping conditions may also be given.

Models of service delivery: Three to five years

Children from 3 to 5 years benefit greatly from interaction with both handicapped and nonhandicapped peers. For this reason, many early-intervention programs organize classroom situations for their 3- through 5-year-olds. Many early-childhood classrooms are noncategorical, serving all types of handicapping conditions within the same class. Some practice "reverse-mainstreaming" by also serving nonhandicapped 3- through 5-year-olds. Many classrooms follow a transdisciplinary model with special educators, speech and language therapists, occupational therapists, and physical therapists working together in the classroom. This allows these professionals to share their skills with one another.

For the child with mild learning problems, whether biological or environmental, preschool is an opportunity to "catch up" developmentally with his or her peers. Preparation for successful integration into a regular kindergarten program becomes very important. Such children may even be integrated into regular preschools with the special educator providing only consultation.

For the child with severe learning problems, preschool is a time to learn functional self-care, communication skills, and play skills. Severely handicapped children should also be prepared for the least restrictive public school program possible for them when they reach school age. According to Vincent, Salisburg, Walter, Brown, Gruenewald, and Powers (1980), "the most successful outcome of early intervention programs would be to prevent the handicapped child from entering the same special education program at age 5 that he or she would have typically entered without remediation" (p. 307).

Working with the family

Early-intervention programs place special emphasis on working with families. Most programs have some form of parent education, and many rely on the parents actually to carry out most of the intervention with their child. Programs may be *center-based* so that the parents and child come into the center for instruction or *home-based*, in which a professional is sent to the home to work with the child and family. Some programs use both center and home components.

The early-childhood special educator works with the parents of young children to help them see areas where intervention is needed. It is also important that parents learn strategies for intervention that can be carried out at home. Programs differ greatly in terms of how they approach involving parents in the education of their child. The program established by Bromwich (1981) emphasizes improving the quality of parent-child interactions. This program also emphasizes the importance of enhancing the parents' ability to provide an appropriate learning environment without direct supervision by professionals. Other programs train parents directly in teaching strategies used by special educators. One example of such a parent-education program is that developed by Hanson (1977). Hanson's program for Down's syndrome infants teaches parents to write behavioral objectives, use task-analysis procedures to break those objectives down into smaller steps for instruction, and identify criteria for determining when the objective has been learned. Table 10.2 presents an example of the procedures parents are trained to use in Hanson's program (Hanson, 1977, p. 22).

COMPREHENSION CHECK 10.8

Do some library research on the effectiveness of integrating young handicapped children with normal peers in the preschool. What are the pros and cons of this practice? To what extent should parents be participants in classroom learning activities or therapy with their children?

Working with gifted children

Gifted children have needs similar to all children in terms of social, physical, and emotional development. The difference between the average and the gifted is in the need gifted children have for intellectual and creative expression at an advanced rate. They also need greater depth and complexity of subject matter than is usual for their age. This intense desire for knowledge, understanding, and creative expression must be met. However, it is also necessary to nurture social, emotional, and physical skills in a manner similar to that for all children.

Intervention during the preschool years is often difficult to provide. Gifted

TABLE 10.2
Sample from Down's Syndrome Parent Training Program

To teach the behavior: Baby visually follows a moving object

A. Decide which behavior you want to teach:
   INFANT WILL LOOK AT AND VISUALLY FOLLOW A MOVING OBJECT
   WHILE SITTING SUPPORTED.

B. Decide on the cue you will use to tell your infant when to do the behavior:
   SAY, "LOOK, STEVEN," WHILE PRESENTING A FAVORITE OBJECT
   DIRECTLY IN FRONT OF HIM.

C. Break the behavior into small steps and order the steps:
   1. INFANT LOOKS AT OBJECT FOR A FEW SECONDS.
   2. INFANT LOOKS AT OBJECT AND VISUALLY FOLLOWS IT FROM
      DIRECTLY IN FRONT OF FACE TO 2 INCHES (5.1 cm) TO ONE SIDE.
      (Alternating sides each time done.)
   3. INFANT LOOKS AT OBJECT AND VISUALLY FOLLOWS IT FROM
      DIRECTLY IN FRONT OF FACE TO AS FAR TO THE SIDE AS INFANT
      CAN COMFORTABLY TURN HEAD. (Can do this going both directions.)
   4. INFANT LOOKS AT OBJECT AND VISUALLY FOLLOWS IT FROM ONE
      SIDE COMPLETELY OVER TO THE OTHER SIDE.

D. Decide how well the infant must do the behavior:
   1. The number of seconds you will wait following the cue.
      THE INFANT WILL LOOK AT THE OBJECT WITHIN 30 SECONDS
      AFTER THE OBJECT AND VERBAL CUES.
   2. The number of seconds or distance the child will do the behavior. (This will
      change for each teaching step.)
      THE INFANT WILL LOOK AT THE OBJECT AND FOLLOW THE OBJECT
      VISUALLY AS IT IS MOVED 2 INCHES (5.1 cm).
   3. The number of trials the child should correctly do the behavior.
      THE INFANT WILL DO THIS CORRECTLY 8 OUT OF 10 TRIES. WHEN
      THE INFANT DOES THIS 8 OUT OF 10 TIMES FOR 3 DAYS, HE CAN GO
      ON TO THE NEXT STEP.

Source: Hanson, M. J. (1977). *Teaching your Down's syndrome infant: A guide for parents,* p. 22. Baltimore: University Park Press.

children are seldom considered to have learning problems or to require inter-vention. Therefore, few preschool programs exist that truly meet the needs of this type of exceptional child. Gifted children require interaction with chil-dren of similar ability to develop communication skills in keeping with their potential. Thus, a preschool program with other gifted children is most effec-tive. Children should be positively reinforced for behavior that encourages them to build on their strengths and successes. Most psychologists and edu-cators agree that the most effective learning occurs when children have ex-periences that slightly challenge their capabilities. Children are more likely to be motivated by material that is appropriate to their competence level. Another challenge is to have enough material and activities to keep the child interested. Gifted children go through learning materials very quickly and will need advanced materials more rapidly than most teachers realize. The need for large amounts of material is also difficult because of the financial restrictions in many preschool programs.

Some programs for gifted preschool children do exist. These programs are often part of a larger program for gifted children that serves children through elementary school or high school. Young children are generally taught in an open-concept environment. In this environment, affective education is stressed along with academic pursuits, problem solving, and decision making. Children are encouraged to develop in social understanding as well as physically and mentally. A broad range of experience is provided through units of studies around central themes. Children participate in a variety of activities that encourage the development of their strengths. Teachers attempt to extend the children's learning in activities that the children choose themselves. Children are expected to use their time productively and to value learning. The classroom schedule is flexible. Children work either independently or in small groups. Parents are sometimes brought in and taught ways to encourage and help their child at home. Sometimes, parents volunteer their services in the program itself.

When gifted children have had the opportunity of a good preschool program, they are ready for the regular public school experience before the usual entrance age. Few schools will accept gifted children in public education until they have reached the legal age of school entrance for the state. However, early entrance directly to a higher grade can be done with a minimum of difficulty in most school districts throughout the country.

Early school entrance has been well researched and is a highly effective method of meeting the need of gifted children (Reynolds, 1962). In fact, studies show positive results in terms of greater success and more motivation in school. Early admission to school is preferable to other methods of acceleration such as grade skipping. This is because it is the least disruptive to the child's adjustment and to the continuity of education.

Some parents have found that entrance directly into first grade instead of kindergarten has been successful for particular gifted children even when preschool education was not provided. In any case, early entrance is most likely to be successful when done carefully. Especially in this case, the child must be assessed prior to the decision being made. Parents are most helpful in providing supplementary data concerning the child's ability to handle early entrance.

Once the child has gone from preschool to regular kindergarten or first grade, efforts must be continued to provide a match between mental age and learning opportunity. An environment similar to the one described for preschool is needed. A good gifted program provides many opportunities to structure the program as well as to be flexible and free. Choices are necessary, but so, too, are requirements. Gifted children, like all children, must develop responsibility. When assignments are appropriate and challenging, gifted children rarely neglect their responsibility to achieve and contribute. However, when lessons are too easy and too often repeated, gifted children tend to rebel against them. Conflicts between the child and the teacher can result.

SUMMARY

The early-childhood special educator may encounter a wide range of exceptionalities of learning in the classroom. Each child will display different problems and require different instructional programs. Mentally retarded children usually demonstrate delays in all developmental areas, and their learning problems tend to increase with the presence of more than one disability. The learning-disabled child usually displays a relatively normal developmental rate in most areas, but shows wide discrepancies in attainment of certain skills (e.g., ability to work with words or numbers). The range of definitions for giftedness is varied. It should be remembered that each gifted child shows great diversity with respect to every trait. Learning problems of congenital origin are generally the only ones identified at birth. It is usually not until the child reaches school age that the less physically noticeable learning problems are identified. Referrals and screening are two measures that are important to the identification of children with learning problems. Assessment of children should lead to an appropriate intervention and educational program.

To identify gifted children, a two-step screening and rank-ordering selection process is recommended. A wide variety of opportunities must be given for the child to display intellectual skills. Treatment for infants identified for early-intervention services includes physical and sensory stimulation and is often based on models of teaching parents to carry out the intervention. Programs during the preschool years are focused on remedying mild learning problems and preparing those with severe problems for integration into the least-restrictive public school program. The focus of preschool programs for the gifted is on ensuring that the children develop a positive attitude toward both learning and school situations, are socially and emotionally secure, and are motivated to achieve their maximum potential.

SUGGESTED READINGS

Clark, G. (1983). *Growing up gifted*. Columbus, OH: Merrill.

Coleman, L. (1985). *Schooling the gifted*. Menlo Park, CA: Addison-Wesley.

Garwood, S. G., and Fewell, R. (1983). *Educating handicapped infants: Issues in development and intervention*. Rockville, MD: Aspen.

Lerner, J., Mardell-Czudnowski, C., and Goldenberg, A. (1981). *Special education for the early childhood years*. Englewood Cliffs, NJ: Prentice-Hall.

Whitmore, J. (1980). *Giftedness, conflict and underachievement*. Boston, MA: Allyn and Bacon.

Differences in Neuromotor Development

Connie Kasari

Michelle A. Larson

Margaret A. Veltman

CHAPTER OUTLINE

VIGNETTES

Robbie is a 4-year-old child with spastic hemiplegia linked to birth complications. He has been receiving physical therapy services since he was 12-months-old. He attends a normal preschool and is of above average intelligence. The teachers describe Robbie as cooperative, talkative, and happy, as do his parents.

Robbie actively participates in group activities. He continues to prefer his right side, although he uses his left hand when encouraged to do so by his teachers. On the playground Robbie tries to keep up with his playmates, climbing the stairs to the slide, running, and kicking balls. Although Robbie is somewhat slower than the other children, they often wait for him or encourage him to keep up.

His parents wonder if Robbie's limitations, though mild, might affect his self-esteem as a teenager. In conversations with his teachers, they recognize that sometimes they are overprotective and worry that their fears may hold him back.

Twenty-two-month-old Meagan has a rare genetic syndrome. Her condition is marked by mental retardation and physical disabilities requiring special handling and care. Meagan has been in an early-intervention program since birth and has received special education, physical therapy, and occupational therapy on a regular weekly basis. Even so, she still lags far behind other children her age. Her physical limitations require special positioning for even usual activities, such as eating at the family table or riding in the car. Meagan's father, with instruction from her physical therapist, built her a special chair for use at home, in the car, and at school. The chair has helped her posture and allows her to interact with others.

Her parents realize that Meagan will never be like other children her age and will always need special training and supervision. However, through the efforts of her family and therapists, Meagan is making slow and steady gains.

Early childhood is a time when motor development is rapidly taking place. Even the casual observer can readily see the young child's intense attention to movement. It is obvious that children's actions are rich in variety, complexity, and intensity. Although the basic features of movement necessary for the development of higher level skills have begun by the end of the first year, the development and refinement of most motor skills continue for many years (Connor, Williamson, and Siepp, 1978). In contrast, the brain-damaged child will display delayed motor development. In addition, this child will exhibit motor patterns that are stereotyped and usually associated with an abnormal muscle tone (Bobath and Bobath, 1975). One of the most challenging

---

COMPREHENSION CHECK 11.1

Explain the importance of movement in the first year of a child's life.
As a caregiver and teacher, why is it essential to have knowledge about the pattern of normal motor development?

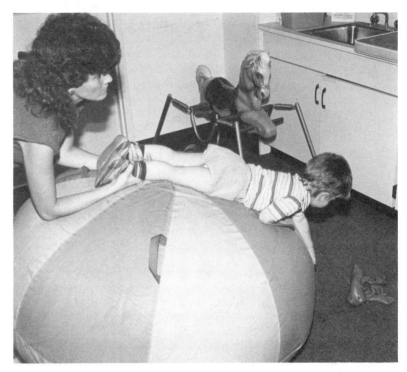

Here is a technique frequently used by physical therapists to facilitate children's development of balance, righting, and weight-bearing.

tasks given to early-childhood educators is that of helping children develop to the best of their physical abilities. Our purpose here is to provide teachers with a theoretical view of how motor control develops and what behaviors may occur when there is a problem with the central nervous system.

DEFINITION AND DESCRIPTION OF THE PROBLEM

Theory of motor control

There are many theories of motor control. For this chapter, *motor control* is defined as the process by which the brain and the muscles work together to produce coordinated, skilled movement. Some theories of motor control have emphasized sensations and muscles. Other theories focus on the role of the brain in starting and guiding movements. At present, the generally accepted theory is that it is the interaction between these two areas that should be the real focus of research and teaching. Following is a short explanation of how normal movements appear to be controlled.

The most basic of all motor acts is the reflex. A *reflex* is a stereotyped movement produced in response to a particular sensory input. Examples of reflexes are the blink of an eye when the cornea is touched, the jerk of the knee when the tendon is tapped, and the withdrawal of a limb when a sudden pain is felt. Touch, stretch, and pain are sensory experiences.

The simplest reflex involves only one muscle and one part of the spinal cord. Thus: sensory input = spinal cord = motor output. This simple reflex is known as the *stretch reflex*. More complex reflexes involving more than one muscle and more than one part of the spinal cord also exist at the level of the spine. Collectively, these spinal reflexes have an important role in the control of movement.

Lying above the spinal cord, but below the sensorimotor cortex, is an area of the brain known as the brain stem. This area is responsible for the *tonic reflexes*. These are the reflexes that are seen early in development. Later they are integrated and controlled by the cortex of the brain. Together, the spinal reflexes and the tonic reflexes contribute to muscle tone, determine posture, and allow the child to prepare for movement.

At the level of the brain stem known as the midbrain, the righting reactions are coordinated. These righting reactions are basic components of normal movement and provide the infant with normal alignment. This normal alignment includes the position of the head relative to the trunk, the trunk relative to the limbs, and rotation about the body axis. There are five righting reactions, which appear in the following sequence: neck righting, body on head, body on body, labrinthyine righting, and optical righting.

In neck righting, the reaction is reflected in log rolling. This refers to the fact that if the child's head is turned, his body will follow with no rotation. The second two righting reactions provide the infant with rotation around the body axis. The infant uses the labrinthyine reaction to raise his head and trunk automatically without visual input. All these reactions are coordinated in the normal infant by the age of 9 months. The only exception is the optical righting reaction. This reaction refers to the use of vision to maintain posture. Unlike the other righting skills, the optical righting reaction is used throughout development. It also dominates over all other righting reactions.

At the "highest" level is the motor cortex, basal ganglia, and cerebellum. Here movement is produced and coordinated. At this level, the equilibrium reactions, which coordinate muscle tone changes in response to a shift in the center of gravity, are coordinated. These reactions alter the righting reactions and help in maintaining the child's balance against gravity. The relationship of these structures in motor control can be represented as in Figure 11.1. The figure shows the interaction that occurs among sensations, muscles, and the brain. Although the diagram is presented as though the brain was a commander over all motor functions, it should be noted that there is an

---

COMPREHENSION CHECK 11.2

Which part of the central nervous system governs the reflex action? Enumerate the functions performed by reflex actions.

What do you understand by the term "righting reactions"?

Explain the role played by the cortical region of the brain in establishing motor control.

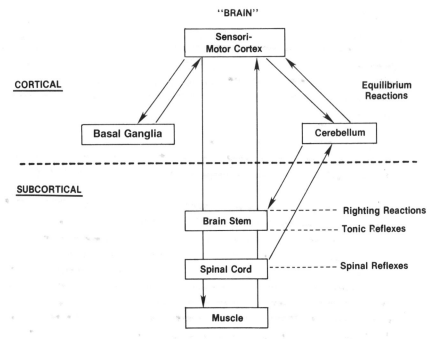

Figure 11.1
Structure of the Brain Involved in Motor Control

interrelationship among these elements. A break in any one of these connections can produce a physical or motor problem. Because of the close relationship of these elements, any injury to the brain will interfere with normal motor control. This is true whether the injury occurred early or late in development.

Components of normal motor control

An important concept emphasized by Bobath is that of components of movement. These components contribute to the quality of a motor act and consist of the righting reactions, equilibrium and protective reactions, and arm-hand support (Bobath and Bobath, 1975; Van Blankenstein, Welbergen, de Haas, 1975). These components are important in the acquisition of the motor milestones. These milestones include rolling, sitting, crawling, standing, and walking. Therefore, normal motor development is simply not progressing from one motor milestone to the next. Instead, it is the acquisition of components of movement that underlie the development of these milestones. For example, when coming to a sitting position from a supine position, the infant needs to first raise his head, rotate his trunk, bear weight on his arms, and balance in a transitional phase. This phase is between supine and sitting erect. The cerebral-palsied child can assume a sitting position in other ways and may use compensatory movements to achieve this and other positions. Therefore, it is important to note how a movement is accomplished. To do this, one must determine which basic components are present and which are absent.

Righting reactions

The early components of movement that assist in the control of the head and trunk are righting reactions. According to Connor, Williamson, and Siepp (1978) to "right" means to bring or restore to an upright position. These righting reactions permit the infant to maintain the position of his head in space. They also assist him in maintaining his head and body in alignment. In addition, they provide the infant with a means of breaking up the total patterns of movement that characterize the younger infant. That is, the newborn is predominantly flexed or curled up. As the child develops, he begins to demonstrate extension. *Extension* is the term used to describe the child's unfolding from this flexed position. This "breaking up" of total patterns into combinations of flexion and extension is accomplished by the development of rotation about the body axis.

Head and trunk control

There are three components to head control. The child must be able to (1) maintain the normal position of the head when the body is moved, (2) regain the normal position of the head after loss of control, and (3) achieve independence of the head from arm and trunk movement. Although head control is usually thought of as preceding trunk control, the child actually works on both simultaneously. The first component of trunk control is a vertical component of flexion and extension. The next to develop is a side-to-side component. Finally, the rotation about the body axis develops.

Rotation about the body axis

The development of trunk control provides the stability from which further movement is based. Initially, the child used his neck righting reactions to roll like a log from supine to prone and vice versa. At around 6 months of age, when the body-on-head righting reaction comes in, this log rolling is inhibited and rotation throughout the trunk begins to be seen. The ability of the child to have rotation about the trunk is critical to the development of further mobility.

Protective and equilibrium reactions

Protective and equilibrium reactions are more complex and variable than are righting reactions. Now there are actually coordinated muscle tone changes in response to a shift in the center of gravity. These muscle tone changes help to restore balance by pulling the center of gravity back to where it was.

Two important aspects of protective reactions are the ability to move a limb and the ability to bear weight on a limb. Development of these reactions begins at 2 months of age with the parachute reaction. This reaction consists of immediate arm extension when the body is thrust downward, head first.

The development of equilibrium reactions lags behind the acquisition of major motor milestones. There are two components to the equilibrium reactions: response to slow tipping and response to quick tipping. They first appear at 6 months in prone and supine positions when the infant is already sitting. Next, they appear in sitting when the infant is beginning to stand. Finally, they appear in standing when the infant is beginning to stand. Finally, they appear in standing when the infant begins to walk.

Equilibrium reactions are fully developed in the child at approximately 7 years of age. However, it has been noted that these reactions can be developed throughout life (Connor, Williamson, and Siepp, 1978).

Arm-hand support

Bobath and Bobath (1975) emphasize the importance of weight bearing as a prerequisite to upper extremity usage. The infant first bears weight with his hands fisted and his elbows flexed (prone puppy position). The next step progresses to weight bearing on extended arms. This progression of weight bearing helps to increase the hand opening that is important for later acquisition of fine motor coordination.

There is a normal range of variability in motor development. However, when development is abnormal, differences will not always be immediately evident at birth. Some become apparent only later in childhood. The most common neuromuscular disorders are outlined following.

COMPREHENSION CHECK 11.3

Normal motor development is solely concerned with the acquisition of milestones from rolling to walking. Comment.

Describe specific movements performed by the child that are indicative of the acquisition of head control.

Cerebral palsy

Cerebral palsy has been defined as a group of conditions characterized by motor problems that result from damage to the brain early in the developmental process. The term "early" is used to refer to damage that occurred before the age of 5. It is important to note that cerebral palsy is a nonprogressive condition, in that it will not become worse as time goes on. Cerebral palsy may result from lack of oxygen, prematurity, hemorrhaging, infection, trauma, or hereditary malformation of the brain (Bleck, 1975). Bobath and Bobath (1975) note that children with cerebral palsy display disturbances in muscle tone and in the smooth movement of a muscle around a particular joint. They also display abnormal or primitive patterns of movement. The problem with cerebral palsy lies in the brain's inability to control the muscles. The muscles themselves are quite normal.

Three major types of cerebral palsy are spasticity, athetosis, and ataxia. Spasticity is characterized by increased muscle tone, a limitation of movement, and abnormal movement patterns. Children with athetoid cerebral palsy display excessive movement in abnormal patterns. Their muscle tone fluctuates from too high to too low. Ataxia is characterized by problems with balance and posture. These problems, together with fluctuating muscle tone, cause the child to have irregular spatial relationships. The child falls frequently and is easily identified by a lurching gait.

Muscular and structural disorders

Children with muscular or structural disorders may also experience delayed or limited motor development. The most prevalent muscular disorder is *mus-*

cular dystrophy. The most common form of muscular dystrophy is the Duchenne, or childhood, form. This disorder is generally not evident at birth, but becomes noticeable around 3 years of age. At this age, the child may first exhibit the clumsiness that can be an indicator of problems. As the child gets older, his muscles weaken and characteristic behaviors become evident. These behaviors include toe-walking, frequent falling, and difficulty moving in and out of positions.

Common structural disorders include missing or malformed limbs, spina bifida, and osteogeneous imperfecta. The child with missing or malformed limbs will often require surgery, artificial limbs, or braces to gain the needed motor abilities to function optimally. *Spina bifida* is a hereditary problem in which the spinal column does not close properly. Disabilities associated with spina bifida may include weak or absent muscle function of the trunk and lower limbs, dislocation of the hip, clubfoot, and curvature of the spine. There may also be loss of sensation to pain, temperature, and touch, bowel or bladder paralysis, and increased fluid surrounding the brain (hydrocephalus). *Osteogenesis imperfecta* is often referred to as brittle bone disease. This disease is the result of loosely woven bone fibers and protein-deficient bones. Surgery is often effective in delaying breakage. Also, the condition generally stabilizes as the child grows older (Bleck, 1975).

Other deviations

A sensory disorder may also affect a child's motor development. For instance, children with severely limited vision are limited in their explorations of their environment. As a result, these children lack experiences with spatial relationships, which, in turn, affects their ability to gain motor skills. This is especially true of the child's ability to project his body into space, which includes being able to pull the body into a standing position, walking, jumping, and running (DuBose, 1979). Another sensory disorder is *tactile defensiveness*. This term refers to the child's inability to tolerate certain textures, touch, or stimulation (Ayres, 1972).

Deviations from the developmental sequence of motor behavior may occur for numerous other reasons. For example, Down's syndrome children are generally characterized by low muscle tone and general developmental delay in motor development. Likewise, children raised in deprived environments may show a lag in reaching certain motor developmental milestones (Rutter, 1972).

All the above conditions may contribute directly or indirectly to a child's

---

COMPREHENSION CHECK 11.4

State the causative factors of cerebral palsy.

Describe the behavioral manifestations of cerebral palsy.

Justify the inclusion of spina bifida in the category of neuromotor disorders.

Explain how sensory disorders can contribute to neuromotor dysfunctioning.

motor delay. However, these motor deficits are displayed in different ways and as a result are treated differently. The emphasis in this chapter will be on the child who shows patterns of motor development that are significantly different from those shown by normal children. Specifically, the chapter will focus on the patterns that result from problems in the central nervous system rather than on children who have a more general developmental delay.

Characteristics of children with neuromotor problems

The motor impairment demonstrated by children with neuromotor difficulties can best be described as incoordination of movement. Frequently, central nervous system (CNS) damage will be indicated through symptoms related to motor behavior. Various symptoms may appear as motor manifestations of CNS deficits.

Abnormal tone

One such indication of CNS damage is abnormal tone, which is organized in patterns. This tone may take the form of hypertonicity (increased tone), hypotonicity (decreased tone), or fluctuating tone (changes in tone from high to low). The various degrees of abnormal tone may range from mild to severe. Varying degrees may also be present in a combination of forms. For example, although a child may exhibit hypertonicity, this increased tone may actually be superimposed over a base of low tone. As a result, once relaxed the child may actually be "floppy." Therefore, it is important to note how the child's postural tone actively changes not only in different positions but with handling.

The organized patterns are usually seen as a flexor pattern and an extensor pattern. It is rare that young children display one pattern without the other. Rather, these patterns are variable, especially in the arms. The most typical pattern seen in the arms is flexion of the elbow and wrist with a fisted hand. However, the shoulder may be either forward or backward, elevated or depressed.

This tone, whether *hypertonic*, *hypotonic*, or fluctuating, can involve all or parts of the body. The extent to which the body is involved is defined by Bobath and Bobath (1975) as *quadriplegia* (total body involvement), *diplegia* (legs more involved than the arms), or *hemiplegia* (one side of the body more involved than the other). The quadriplegic child shows total body involvement and may be characterized by increased tone (*spasticity*) or fluctuating tone (*athetosis*). The diplegic child usually displays total involvement with the legs much more involved than the arms. The diplegic child generally shows good head control, whereas the quadriplegic child does not. Diplegics are characterized by spasticity. Although both sides of the body may be involved, the hemiplegic child demonstrates a greater involvement of one side of the body over the other. Hemiplegic children are also characterized by spasticity.

Usually, the hypotonic child is totally involved and assumes a position with the arms outward and flexed and the legs flexed and outwardly rotated (frog position). Whereas the hypotonic child demonstrates patterns seen in normal development, the hypertonic child demonstrates pathological patterns never seen in development.

Loss of selective movement

As a result of this abnormal postural tone, the child has a loss of selective movement at individual joints. Thus, the child is unable to raise his arm above the horizontal without the elbow and wrist also flexing. Similarly, the child cannot bend at the hip without the knee and ankle also bending. Thus, motor function is limited to these total patterns. This further reduces the child's degree of freedom for movement. Often the goal of treatment is to inhibit the child's abnormal posturing and tone while simultaneously helping to increase voluntary selective control.

Arrested or delayed motor development

In the case of arrested or delayed motor development, an insult to the immature CNS affects the child's normal progression of development. The acquisition of "motor milestones" is usually slowed or stopped. For example, the normal child begins to walk at the age of 11 to 14 months, but the cerebral-palsied child begins to walk on the average of 33 months (Connolly and Russell, 1976), the Down's syndrome child at 24 months (Hanson and Schwarz, 1978), and the blind child at 12 to 20 months (Fraiberg, 1974).

Associated reactions

With the presence of associated reactions, a strong effort of an uninvolved limb will increase tone in the involved limb or limbs. This increase in the postural tone and patterns already present in the affected limbs may further hamper control. The use of the associated reactions in treatment varies among the different approaches.

Sensory or perceptual distortion

The child learns from sensations of movement. Because the child with a CNS deficit experiences only abnormal muscle tone and patterns, he perceives these to be normal sensations of movement. In overusing abnormal movements in his early explorations, he is limited to basing future motor achievements on a foundation of abnormality. The continued use of these abnormal patterns of movement may cause the child's physical disability to become more severe as he grows older. This could, in turn, possibly result in secondary disabilities.

COMPREHENSION CHECK 11.5

What are the major symptoms indicative of abnormal motor development?

IMPACT ON THE FAMILY

When parents receive the diagnosis of a physical handicap, they often have a great need to make the child as normal as possible (Schlesinger and Meadow, 1972). The danger in this perspective is twofold. First, no intervention, no matter how effective, can remove the handicap. Second, in trying to normalize the child, the parents risk making the child feel rejected. Compounding ize the child, the parents risk making the child feel rejected. Compounding these problems is the fact that many parents of physically handicapped children find their children frightening or repulsive. The child may also seem unresponsive to the parents. This is often a function of the handicapping condition itself. If the child is severely physically handicapped, it may be difficult for the parent to understand the child's efforts to communicate. This, in turn, diminishes the social reinforcement the parents get for interacting with the child. Finally, the parents of physically handicapped children must cope with the added burdens of prostheses, accessibility, and learning proper handling and teaching strategies for their children, as well as with the economic strains of needed hospitalization, special services, and physical aids.

IMPACT ON THE CHILD'S DEVELOPMENT

Basic principles of development recognized by most theorists are the progression of motor control from head to toe (*cephalocaudal*), from *proximal to distal* (center of the body outward to the limbs), and from gross to fine control (see Chapter 3). Furthermore, development is sequential. This means that the infant uses components of movement he has already achieved and combines them in new forms. This combination produces a new motor act. Although the rate at which normal children develop varies, the sequence remains constant. For example, sitting with support generally occurs around 6 months. This skill rarely occurs before the child has developed head and trunk control in the prone position. Motor sequences are also overlapping. Thus, while mastering a particular motor act, the child is also experimenting with new components. For example, the child pulls to a stand and sidesteps around furniture while still working on the transition from prone to sitting.

Relationship of movement dysfunction to other areas of development

It is impossible to separate the effects of a motor disability from the child's overall development. A motor handicap tends to extend into areas beyond that directly affected by the handicapping condition itself (Robinson, 1982). For example, a restriction in movement also affects a child's ability to engage in problem solving, communication, and social interaction. This spreading of a motor disability has important implications for classroom teachers who are responsible for a child's total educational programming.

Cognitive development

The discussion of cognitive development and the physical capabilities that it may or may not require centers on several issues. Traditionally, our view of a child's cognitive ability has been based on the assumption that both handicapped and nonhandicapped children follow the same sequence of development (Robinson and Robinson, 1978), though the handicapped child's rate of development may be slower. This hypothesis has been confirmed in studies with children whose delayed motor development was the result of structural, sensory, or chromosomal deviations. Decarie (1969) found that children with missing limbs were able to make use of other parts of the body to perform sensorimotor activities. In an object permanence task, Decarie observed the children to use their toes to remove a cloth from a desired toy. Similarly, Fraiberg, Siegal, and Gibson (1966) noted that blind infants were delayed both in their physical exploration of the environment and in their sequence of searching behavior. This was true until they had developed the concept that a sound could indicate the location of a desired toy. Studies of Down's syndrome children have indicated that their motor and mental development are delayed. But the sequence of their development is comparable to that of normally developing children (Hanson, 1978; Harris, 1981).

Physically handicapped children whose postural tone restricts movement may differ from other types of handicapped children in their ability to influence their environments. As Piaget (1973) and others have noted, cognitive growth is heavily based on a child's opportunities to explore the environment. Indeed, most tests of early cognitive development rely on the child's nonverbal communication and motor skills to show understanding of basic concepts. However, if the child's ability to manipulate and explore the environment is stunted by abnormal tone and movement patterns, he may be less clear in demonstrating that he understands a concept. As a result, several authors have suggested changing the physical criteria used in determining a child's level of understanding (Haeusserman, 1969; Robinson and Robinson, 1978; Zelazo, 1982).

Haeusserman (1969) has presented a series of teaching procedures and material adaptations for preschool cerebral-palsied children. More recently, Robinson and Robinson (1978) expanded these forms to traditional sensorimotor tests. For example, they recommend accepting visual cues to indicate that the child knows where an object has been hidden. This would be used when the child cannot physically manage to uncover a toy in the traditional manner. Similarly, Bower (1974) suggests that visual searching for an object that just disappeared can be a reliable indicator of the object concept.

Nevertheless, there continues to be disagreement among researchers as to whether learning experienced directly or indirectly is actually equivalent. Fetters (1982) investigated the development of object permanence in motorically impaired infants aged 13 to 29 months. In the study she compared procedures involving direct and indirect participation. She reported that all the children scored higher when Bower's nontraditional criteria were used rather than a traditional test. This was true whether the children were classified as manipulators or nonmanipulators. Zelazo (1982) has further elaborated procedures for assessing how a physically involved child processes information from his environment. Such information is gained from measuring the child's affective and physiologic responses to a set of visual events that are repeatedly presented and then changed slightly.

There are several important considerations in teaching cognitive skills to physically handicapped children. Jens and O'Donnell (1982) support the idea of adopting an "as if " approach to interventions with handicapped children. This is, one should assume that applying knowledge about nonhandicapped people is appropriate if there is no evidence that this is not so. However, it may be necessary to adapt procedures or materials so that the physically handicapped child can accomplish a task. For example, the child may need built-up handles on pens or pencils, knobs on puzzle pieces, or a peg on his desk top so that he may reduce involuntary movements with one hand while he writes with the other. Similarly, procedures may be altered. For example, the teacher may allow a greater time between a request and the desired behavior or may use an audiotape for a child with visual difficulties. In cases where the handicapped child cannot perform physical tasks that are similar to the nonhandicapped child, the teacher may need to change the task requirements (Robinson and Robinson, 1978). These changes may include accepting an "eye-point" in a discrimination task or a smile as a positive response to a particular question.

Communicative development

Considering the problems in postural tone and movement patterns exhibited by motorically impaired children, it is not surprising that an estimated 70% to 95% of these children show disturbances in their abilities to communicate (Hagan, Porter, and Brink, 1973; Morris, 1978). The muscles of the face, mouth, and diaphragm, which are generally responsible for speech production, tend to be a reflection of the child's overall postural tone.

Several authors suggest that the child's delay in speech may actually be related to earlier disturbances in prespeech and feeding behaviors (Jones, 1975; Morris, 1978). Four sensorimotor behaviors that are necessary for the development of speech have been detailed by Morris (1978). These behaviors are the development of head and trunk control, coordinated respiration and sound production, normal development of feeding patterns, and babbling or automatic speech. The normal infant develops these sensorimotor behaviors that influence later speech by the age of 2 years. In contrast, the brain-damaged child will often have delayed or abnormal development of these prerequisite skills. This is largely a result of abnormal postural tone, uncontrolled movements and/or the lack of movement, and the failure to coordinate primitive reflexes (Morris, 1978). Even if the child does develop speech, he may exhibit difficulties in volume, pitch, variability, duration, and initiation of sound production (Connor, Williamson, and Siepp, 1978).

If a severely physically handicapped child is delayed in the development of speech, he may benefit from the use of a communication or language board. Such a device can help to improve the child's total language program and does not interfere with oral communication. Instead, it allows the child a means of communicating with those around him as he continues to work on oral speech. (For discussion of the factors involved in the choice of a communication board for severely handicapped children, see Morris, 1978, and Harris-Vanderheiden and Vanderheiden, 1977).

Because of the child's abnormal postural tone and patterns of movement, correct positioning and handling is essential. This is especially important in the design of mealtime or language interventions. (For reviews on normal and abnormal oral-motor function and intervention strategies, the reader is referred to Campbell, Green, and Carlson, 1977; Connor, Williamson, and Siepp, 1978; Morris, 1978; and Wilson, 1978).

Affective responses

Theorists have long believed that cognition and socioemotional development are inseparably linked (Piaget and Inhelder, 1969; Spitz, 1965). Indeed, many view them as twin aspects of the same process (Dunn, 1982). Studies have shown that the affective responses of Down's syndrome and nonhandicapped populations progress in much the same fashion (Cicchetti and Stroufe, 1978). However, affective responses of physically handicapped children may be inhibited by abnormal tone (Morris, 1978). The physiological component is an important consideration in the child's ability to respond affectively to his environment (Gallagher, Jens, O'Donnell, 1983). For instance, a child with low muscle tone may be identified by a droopy expression while a child with increased tone may be restricted in her ability to respond affectively.

Gallagher, Jens, and O'Donnell (1983) looked at the affective responses of 14 multiple-handicapped children. These children, aged 11 to 38 months, were exposed to a series of affect-eliciting stimulus items developed by Cicchetti and Stroufe (1978). Results indicated that a child's ability to express laughter was related to his physical status; that is, the more abnormal the child's postural tone, the harder it was for the child to express laughter. It appears that postural tone influences the child's ability to respond affectively. Consequently, this may impair the child's ability to signal, communicate nonverbally, or experience success in social interactions.

Social interactions

A child with a physical handicap is at risk for a variety of distorted social interactions. Child behaviors that are often interpreted as communicative signals in social interactions include smiles, looks, vocalizations, and gestures. These child behaviors are dependent on increasing flexibility and control over motor responses.

The specific influence of a movement disability has rarely been the focus of research in social interactions. However, two studies have looked specifically at cerebral-palsied children in interactions with their mothers and several studies have examined other disabilities characterized by delayed or aberrant movement abilities, for example, Down's syndrome.

Brooks-Gunn and Lewis (1982) found that when samples of developmentally delayed, physically impaired, and Down's syndrome infants were compared with normally developing infants of equivalent developmental age, all the handicapped infants exhibited less positive effect and more negative affect than did normal infants in interaction with their mothers. Of the three dysfunctional groups, the Down's syndrome infants showed the least amount of positive affect, and the physically handicapped infants showed the most. Buckhalt, Rutherford, and Goldberg (1978) also found that retarded infants showed less positive affect than did normal infants in mother-child interactions.

A movement dysfunction may affect the child's interactive behaviors in several other ways. Aberrant postural tone may be a contributing factor in a child's decreased activity level and failure to initiate interactions, thereby leading to a characterization of child passivity (Kogan, Tyler, and Turner, 1974). Additionally, it may affect the child's ability to respond to others in an expected period of time (Connors, Williamson, and Siepp, 1978) or to signal with gestures (e.g., pointing, reaching) (Walker, 1982).

Maternal behavior in interaction with cerebral-palsied children has been the focus of two separate studies. A very early study by Shere and Kasten-baum (1966) indicated that mothers of preschool cerebral-palsied children spent more time caring for their children's motor needs than for their psychological needs. As a result, the authors executed an intervention program that assisted the parents in providing levels of stimulation appropriate for the children's total developmental needs. Similarly, Kogan and her colleagues (1974) provided an intervention program to mothers following the results of their two-year longitudinal study with mothers and there cerebral-palsied youngsters. They observed that mothers of cerebral-palsied children exhibited greater assertive control when interacting with their children than did mothers of normal children. In addition, they found that mothers of cerebral-palsied children showed greater negative affect over the course of the study, and the degree of negative affect was greatest when mothers were performing therapy with their children. Consequently, the aim of their intervention program was to facilitate greater maternal warmth and enjoyment in interactions with their children.

One must consider, however, that children with physical handicaps do not inevitably have aberrant dyadic relationships. Although it may be more difficult for parents to interpret the communicative signals of their handicapped children, the majority of parents are able to alter their interaction style to accommodate the idiosyncratic nature of these behaviors (Sorce and Emde, 1982). For some parents to achieve a satisfactory relationship with their child, it may merely take experience with their child; for others, it may require intervention from trained professionals.

Any interactive difficulties the physically handicapped child experiences with adults are likely to be similar in interactions with peers or siblings. The difference, however, is that the adult commands greater sophistication in interactive skills and can compensate for abilities lacking in their young partner. A same-aged or younger child may not be aware of his partner's physical limitations and may be unable to spontaneously alter his typical interactive behaviors. Peers may need instruction in order to adapt their behaviors to the interactive needs of their partners. The early-childhood teacher is in a position to assist her students in successful interactions. For example, the teacher may need to position the physically handicapped child in particular ways. She/he may need to instruct the nonhandicapped child in waiting longer for a response from the disabled child, or in placing toys closer to the child. Careful observations of peer interactions will be necessary to plan appropriate interventions.

CAUSES OF NEUROMOTOR PROBLEMS

There are three major categories of physical handicaps: *neurological disorders*, *musculoskeletal disorders*, and *congenital malformations*. Each category has different causes, but each of these types of physical handicaps may be present at birth.

Neurological disorders are caused by damage to, or a defect or deterioration of, the brain or spinal cord (Cartwright, Cartwright, and Ward, 1981). Some of the more common causes of this class of physical handicaps are heredity, maternal infection, lack of oxygen to the fetus, Rh incompatability, prematurity, diabetes, toxemia, exposure to X-rays, and unknown causes (Bleck, 1975). A relatively common neurologic disorder is cerebral palsy.

Musculoskeletal disorders may be acquired or hereditary. These disorders usually affect the child's limbs (legs or arms), spine, or joints. There are many causes for these handicaps. Among the most common are infectious diseases, accidents, genetic defects, and developmental disorders. An example of a musculoskeletal disorder is muscular dystrophy.

Congenital malformations are those present at birth. Malformations of the heart and hips are the most common form of congenital malformations (Cartwright, Cartwright, and Ward, 1981). These defects may be genetic or they may result from complications during the pregnancy itself. These may be due to abnormal development of the fetus or disease or other conditions in the mother at the time of pregnancy.

PREVALENCE OF NEUROMOTOR PROBLEMS

Owing to the many causes of physical handicaps, and the range of severity in the handicaps themselves, exact prevalence figures are difficult to determine. However, it is estimated that 5 in 1000 school-aged children are physically disabled. This means that they have a physical disability severe enough to affect the child's performance in other educational areas (Hallahan and Kauffman, 1978).

ASSESSMENT OF NEUROMOTOR PROBLEMS

To get a realistic picture of the physically handicapped child's skills, it is important to observe the child's behavior across several situations. To assess the child's motor behavior, checklists of motor development skills are traditionally used by staff members. However, these lists merely indicate whether a behavior is present or absent. These assessments rarely reflect the underlying neuromuscular elements necessary for movement. They also fail to assess the quality of a particular movement.

If the reason for assessment is to gain information for planning individualized programs, then a checklist provides only limited information. Currently, there is a trend toward the use of data from several sources, rather than from a single test (Simeonsson, Huntington, and Parse, 1980). This type of testing is called *multisource assessment*. This approach to assessment may prove to be helpful by also providing information on how the child's physical handicap may be limiting the child's overall learning.

Several authors have also emphasized the importance of clinical judgment in the assessment of a child (Ellis, 1978; Rogow, 1978; Simeonsson, Huntington, and Parse, 1980). In many therapeutic settings, clinical judgment is the only procedure used to record the developmental changes of the child. Although we are not suggesting that clinical judgment be used alone, its ability to supplement other methods does deserve attention. For example, it is not uncommon to find teachers, therapists, or parents who say that they "feel" a handicapped child has made progress or "know" she understands more than she can show because to her handicap. This is particularly true of multiple or severely handicapped children, who often do not show gains on traditional or standardized tests.

In assessing muscle tone, the use of clinical judgment may be especially important. However, because clinical judgment is subjective, it is important to use it only as a supplement to the regular assessment process. Thus, it should only be used to support existing information.

In addition, information gained by observing the child may assist in planning interventions. This information is not traditionally included in motor-behavior checklists. Important information may be gained from asking the following questions guided by the use of *curricula* designed to appraise patterns of neuromotor development.

1. How does the child's posture and muscle tone change under different conditions and in different positions?

2. Which parts of movement are absent, and which contribute to the child's delay in gaining motor milestones?

3. In which positions is the child's postural tone most normal?

4. Which position helps the child to perform the greatest number of voluntary, self-initiated movements?

5. How does the child gather information from his/her surroundings?

COMPREHENSION CHECK 11.6

State the importance of clinical judgment as an assessment tool of neuromotor problems.

TREATMENT OF NEUROMOTOR PROBLEMS

Many methods and practices have been developed to help increase normal motor behavior in children with CNS deficits. How one sees the problem determines the aim of treatment, the emphasis, and the procedures used. Here we will discuss the various treatment approaches most commonly used with children with CNS deficits. The approach most familiar to teachers and most frequently used by physical and occupational therapists is the neuro-developmental treatment (NDT) or Bobath approach. The Rood, proprioceptive neuromuscular facilitation (PNF), and Doman-Delacato approaches are also discussed because they are often seen as supplements to other treatment. These several treatment approaches are similar in that all are based on normal child development and the concept that movements are organized in patterns.

Rood approach

A guiding principle of the Rood technique is that all functions and structures of the neuromuscular system can be related to one of two biological purposes. The first purpose is the survival of the individual through protection and mobility. The second purpose is the growth of the individual through pursuit and adaptation, called *stability* (Stockmeyer, 1967). The basis of this treatment approach is the use of touch, vision, and olfaction to facilitate, activate, or inhibit motor reactions. The types of stimuli used are icing, vibration, brushing, stretch, touch, and pressure. However, the techniques of this approach need to be used cautiously. Any use of stimuli, such as icing or brushing, needs to be constantly supervised by a knowledgeable therapist.

Proprioceptive neuromuscular facilitation (PNF)

The basis of PNF is helping to improve movement through sensory stimulation of the CNS. In this technique, reeducation is based on mass movements obtained through CNS stimulation. The muscle is encouraged to display its normal function in the performance of a particular movement. Thus, the muscle either relaxes to allow for a movement, performs the movement, or assists in a particular movement. All muscles work in combination with one another. The aim of PNF is to bombard the CNS with as many sensory stimuli as possible to encourage the muscle to work at its maximum (Knott, 1966; Showman, 1962).

Temple Fay: Doman-Delacato

The foundation of Temple Fay: Doman-Delacato approach is an evolutionary perspective of the individual. Thus, human movements are based on primitive patterns of responses that were evident in prehistoric evolutionary eras. There are similarities between the movement patterns of the infant and more primitive forms of life. Reflexes are viewed as fragments of ancient motor behavior that persist or emerge in human beings. This emergence depends on the degree of control that the more complex centers of the CNS exert. This technique emphasizes the use of passive exercises, and the use of existing reflexes. It also stresses the use of lower levels of mobility before attempting higher levels of function. The treatment program is called *patterning* and has been the focus of much controversy in recent years. In part, objections to this approach have stemmed from the lack of controlled studies supporting this treatment (Cratty, 1970; Freeman, 1967) and lack of any know validity of the test instrument, the Doman-Delacato Profile. The program also raises ethical issues in requiring a demanding and inflexible regime of both the family and the handicapped child. The American Medical Association has found this approach to be in serious scientific disrepute. For a detailed discussion of these problems, see Freeman (1967) and Sparrow and Zigler (1978).

Bobath approach (neurodevelopmental treatment approach)

The principles of NDT are developed from the concept of the normal postural reflex mechanism. This mechanism includes three fundamental factors

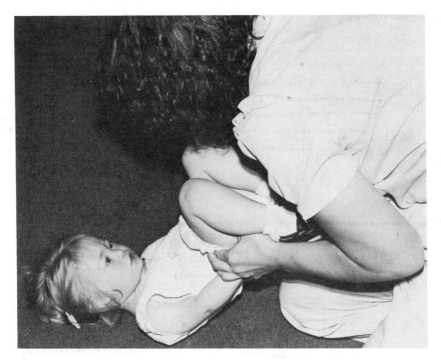

The neurodevelopmental techniques of Bobath are widely used to treat developmentally disabled preschoolers.

necessary for the performance of any skill. These factors are normal postural tone, varied degrees of smooth coordination of the muscles about a particular joint, and normal patterns of coordination.

The child with CNS dysfunction, as described by Bobath, has an abnormal postural reflex mechanism. It is this mechanism that is responsible for the abnormal tone and patterns of movement shown by the child. Bobath's techniques of inhibition, facilitation, and stimulation are used simultaneously to promote normal motor behavior (Bobath and Bobath, 1975; Semans, 1967).

Designing interventions

From the previous discussion it should be clear that the limited responses presented by a physical handicap reduces the child's ability to interact with people and the surroundings. The more limited the child's abilities, the more the child must depend on a caregiver to provide both his social and physical environments. However, the caregiver must realize that the environment he chooses for the child may not be the same one as the child would have chosen for himself. What are some guidelines for these decisions? Generally, the principles that could help to structure the environment for physically handicapped youngsters are similar to those principles common to traditional therapeutic intervention.

The first principle states that delayed or abnormal motor development will affect the child's functioning in other developmental areas. It is not uncommon to see a child whose restricted movement patterns delay his normal movements. This delay also hurts his development in speech and cognition. Thus, the task of the intervention team is to inhibit the child's abnormal patterns of movement and also to help the child learn more normal responses to his environment.

It should be clear that the handling and treatment of a physically handicapped child is complex and requires the skills of a number of people. As a result, the next principle concerns the role of the team in helping the physically handicapped child. The team may include teachers, physical and occupational therapists, speech therapists, psychologists, social workers, and nurses. Preferably, the team will be inter- or transdisciplinary (see Chapter 2).

In infant and home-based programs, the physical or occupational therapist is usually the team manager for a physically handicapped child. In the preschool or elementary school, the team manager is usually the classroom teacher. This is because of her responsibility for the child's overall classroom programming.

According to Bricker, Seibert, and Scott (in press), a teacher should assume a variety of roles, including those of evaluator, generator, and synthesizer. As a synthesizer, the teacher must pull together specific information and suggestions from a variety of people. As a generator, the teacher must creatively mesh these suggestions into a challenging and smoothly run classroom. Thus, the teacher is responsible for organizing the child's education by synthesizing information, coming up with creative adaptations, and testing the effects of the programs.

The transdisciplinary approach is the one we recommend. However, this approach does not succeed without cooperation of all team members. The team manager must be willing to take the responsibility of working in all educational areas. Also, the other staff members must believe that the team manager can do a good job on a variety of programs.

One approach to training staff members has been described by Brackman, Fundakowski, Filler, and Peterson (1977) and Filler and Kasari (1980). This approach suggests a way of tracing staff training across disciplines to ensure that all team members are working in the same manner.

The fourth principle is concerned with the child's role of active versus passive participation. From the viewpoint of these authors, the active involvement of a child is preferred to merely "doing to" the child. A professional preoccupied with the treatment itself may forget to notice how or what the child is contributing. Others may simply not require the child to participate, for example, in the performance of a passive range of motion exercises. These exercises involve moving a joint through its full range of movement. The procedure requires no active movement on the part of the child and is performed primarily to prevent a shortening of the muscles, which might further restrict movement. However, the same goal can be reached through activities that require activity from the child.

A related area is that of motivation. If the child cannot control outside events, she may risk developing "learned helplessness." Seligman (1975) noted that a child only believes she can control her environment if she has had the chance to control it before. Learned helplessness is the "expectancy that one's behavior is irrelevant to the environment" (Brinker and Lewis, 1983).

An ordinary tricycle has been adapted (with pillows and straps) to permit this child with cerebral palsy to participate in the fun with her peers.

The physically handicapped child can become a victim of learned helplessness. This is because he cannot adequately initiate movements that would affect his environment. If he is not allowed to experience the consequences of his actions, he comes to think that these things will simply occur. As a result, he may feel that he does not need to let anyone know what he needs. This reduces his own motivation to behave. For example, a child may have all the movements needed for walking, but if he does not know that he can control them, he will not walk. Furthermore, if the child is handicapped, his attempt to control his behavior may not be noticed by his environment. If the surroundings are not responsive, there is little opportunity to gain information about them. This may well interfere with further learning.

COMPREHENSION CHECK 11.7

In the context of the physically handicapped, explain how "learned helplessness" may impede further learning, and adjustment.

Another important principle in programs with physically handicapped children is the functional nature of a particular skill. It is important to teach the child the types of motor skills he really needs. These skills should give the child greater control over his physical or social environment. Therapists often worry about a child who uses an abnormal reflex to respond to his environment. However, there are times when the quality of a response is less important than for the child to have control over his environment. For example, a child may use an abnormal response to show where a toy has been hidden in a cupboard. This child is using some control over environmental events. But he is also practicing and reinforcing an abnormal movement. This will strengthen the movement. The problem for the early intervention team is to decide on the importance of the response to the child's continuing development. Then they must determine what the trade-offs are (Robinson, 1982).

To ensure that skills are practiced across a variety of settings, instruction needs to help the child's overall development. It must also be highly meaningful to those providing the services. When designing activities for parents, it is important to know about their individual family situation. Parents who are given instructional activities to do at home may be more likely to practice them if they are incorporated into routine activities. This has the greatest value for parents. For example, a busy mother with a physically handicapped toddler may find that the most free time she has with her child is during bath time. The teacher may suggest that activities be done while the child is in the bath. Some examples may include dropping objects into a floating bowl or finger painting with shaving cream in the bath. Once bathing is finished, the mother may be instructed to towel dry the child using rotation to reduce muscle tone (see Figure 11.2).

Using therapists in the classroom is one way of sharing information among all those working with a child. It also is a way of working on therapeutic objectives throughout the child's day. The teacher and therapist can creatively plan activities that combine objectives for a particular child or

Figure 11.2
Mother Incorporating Movement and Rotation in Towel-drying for Tone Reduction. Child Supported in Bath by Inflatable Swim Ring

group of children. The teacher may learn that simply positioning materials in particular ways can help to challenge the child to move correctly (see Figure 11.3).

COMPREHENSION CHECK 11.8

Explain what is meant by the transdisciplinary approach in the intervention of neuromotor dysfunctioning.

In the remediation of neuromotor disorders, testing, programming, and evaluation should constitute a continuous cycle. Explain with a specific example.

Describe specific steps that a teacher may take to minimize the impact of motor problems of the child.

After observing in the classroom, a therapist may suggest a different position for a child in a particular activity. This is simpler than thinking up an artificial situation for the child to practice the same position.

Testing, programming, and evaluation should not be isolated areas of a child's program. These areas should interact to a large degree. Indeed, a major goal of our programs should be to coordinate information from testing with treatment goals. For example, in working with a child the teacher and therapist should look at the child's state of arousal, his performance on particular tasks, and his response to instruction or treatment. The adult can then change either her own behavior or the treatment.

Figure 11.3
Positioning of Materials for
Trunk Rotation

A typical technique used by adults is to "up the ante" (Bruner, 1982). That is, as the child masters one part of a task, the adult expects a bit more of the child. This continues to challenge his ever-increasing abilities. If the child does not respond, the adult will give the child more information or support until he can. The creative adult can up the ante without the child knowing he is learning something new. For example, for a child who needs practice pulling to a stand, the adult may begin by putting a toy on a low table. Once the child has the toy, the adult may put another toy at the other and of the table. If the child reaches for the toy, the adult may help the child or prompt him to move toward the toy. The adult then removes support as the child takes over.

Data must be gathered to tell whether or not a behavior has been mastered or when an intervention approach is or is not working. Many approaches to the collection of data on children's behavior have been described (Filler and Kasari, 1980; Hanson and Bellamy, 1977; Haring, Liberty, and White, 1980). The defining of objectives related to less clearly seen neuromuscular aspects of a child's development have also been described (Rainforth and Thompson, 1978). It will be up to the intervention team to decide which method of data collection best fits into their setting. However, some form of data collection should be used. As data is used for purposes of accountability (Simeonsson and Wiegerink, 1975; Bagnato and Neisworth, 1980), they are also used as a basis for decisions on a child's individual program.

COMPREHENSION CHECK 11.9

Besides the traditional role of teaching, what are the other critical roles performed by the teacher of the physically handicapped?

Adapting the environment to provide support

Children with physical and motor problems often need unique and adapted furniture. This special furniture is unlike the furniture typically used in most nursery or primary-grade classrooms. The use of assistive and adaptive equipment can be important in assisting the child's overall educational program.

Selection of equipment must be based on its ability to increase an individual's potential for movement and opportunities for learning. The basic objective of any positioning device should be to eliminate maladaptive patterns of movement. Ideally, the device should provide enough support while still allowing active and purposeful exploration. It is important to think about several factors before buying or making equipment for specific children. First, the device should be selected by the entire team. At the very least, the physical therapist, teacher, and parent should be asked. Each team member should provide unique information regarding the child's therapeutic and educational needs. For example, the physical therapist may want the child to be positioned with hip extension in a weight-bearing posture. The teacher may ask that the child be in a comfortable position for hand activities. She may also ask that it be a mobile piece of equipment that can be used at a table with peers. In addition, the parent may want something that can be made easily and cheaply at home. The choice and construction of equipment will need careful team planning and ongoing sharing of information.

Second, it is important to remember that any device can only be used for a limited amount of time. This is due to growth and developmental changes in the child. Parents and staff may tend to use the device longer than needed because they want to get their money's worth from it.

Third, one must think about the child's social environment. The often strange appearance of adaptive equipment may separate the handicapped child from his peers even more than the handicap itself (Kasari and Filler, 1981). If the child is able to assume a correct posture independently, the use of adaptive equipment may not be necessary; instead, the child must be encouraged to remain in the posture (see Figure 11.4).

The typical preschool does not usually allow for a one-to-one relationship between adult and child throughout the day. Therefore, the child must spend some time in independent activities. When adaptive equipment must be used to help the child into an appropriate position, the teacher should think about the placement of the devices. This is especially true in relation to the child's peers. Certainly, there is more opportunity for enhancing social, communicative, and cognitive skills if the child is positioned close to peers (see Figure 11.5).

Another method to encourage peer interactions involves small groups or paired instruction. This targets individual goals for all who participate (see Figure 11.6).

Adaptive equipment most often found in preschool environments are wedges, kneel-standers, prone-standers, bolsters, and a variety of adapted chairs. This equipment has been used to help hold the child in a prone, kneeling, standing, and sitting position, respectively. This equipment can be purchased, constructed, and/or designed by parents, teachers, therapists, and others (Barnes, Murphy, Waldo, and Sailor, 1979; Bergen, 1974; Campbell, Green, and Carlson, 1977; Connor, Williamson, and Siepp, 1978; DuBose and Deni, 1980; Finnie, 1975).

Figure 11.4
Children in Independently Assumed
Therapeutic Positions

Figure 11.5
Equipment Placed to Facilitate Peer Interactions

Both the choice of design and the construction will depend on the child's needs. This adaptive equipment will be discussed in terms of the aim of positioning and the adaptive devices that have been used to accomplish these aims. The use of any positioning device should only be included with a good understanding of the child's problems and with advice from a physical or occupational therapist.

Prone

Positioning the child on his stomach (*prone*) is often used to encourage the child to raise his head against gravity (see Figure 11.7). This helps to develop extension in the body and weight bearing on forearms or extended arms. Assistive devices used to help achieve this position include wedges, bolsters, and inflatables. Sandbags placed on either side of the child may help main-

Figure 11.6
Children Therapeutically Positioned for Dyadic Play

Figure 11.7
Children Positioned Side-lying on Sidelyer and Prone on Wedge

Supine

Supine (back-lying) positioning of the child is often avoided because of abnormal posturing of many children in this position. These abnormal postures
include the total extensor pattern, asymmetry, or "frog" pattern. This position may be helpful for particular activities, such as visual tracking across
midline, bilateral reaching activities, or face-to-face interactions. To use the
supine position for certain activities, the child's abnormal posturing can be
changed by adaptive equipment. An inflatable swim ring (Kasari and Filler,
1981), hammock (Finnie, 1975), or pillows and sandbags may be used to help
achieve appropriate supine positioning (see Figure 11.8).

Side-lying

Side-lying is thought to be a good position for reducing abnormal posturing, and lateral head righting. A goal of side-lying is to maintain the child

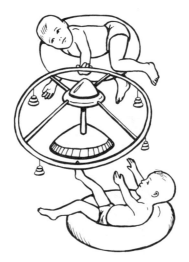

Figure 11.8
Babies Positioned Side-
lying and Supine in Inflatable Swim Rings

with neck flexion, body symmetry, and disassociation of legs. Several plans for the construction of side-lyers are available (Bergen, 1979; Connor, Williamson, and Siepp, 1978; DuBose and Deni, 1980). The position may also be maintained via an inflatable swim ring (Kasari and Filler, 1981) or by pillows or sandbags (see Figures 11.7 and 11.8).

Sitting

Depending on the child's needs, he may be asked to sit on the floor or sit in a particular chair. Many types of specialized chairs are available. These include corner seats, barrel seats, floor sitters, bucket chairs, and inflatables (Bergen, 1979; Connor, Williamson, and Siepp, 1978; Finnie, 1975). When purchasing an adapted chair, further changes may be necessary. These changes may be as simple as adding a footrest or tray to the more complicated addition of a pelvic tilt bar (Bergen, 1979).

Kneeling/standing

Both kneeling and standing are difficult positions to maintain properly. However, certain children have used these positions to successfully encourage weight bearing, upper extremity function, and extension. Devices used to help achieve these postures include kneel standers, prone standers, and standing tables (see Figures 11.5 and 11.9).

Any positioning device must be carefully selected and based on the child's current needs. Three general guidelines in the selection of equipment are:

1. The device should not lock the child into a position, but should provide enough support so that the child can gain some active control.

2. The goal of a device should be to break up total patterns of abnormal movement.

3. The position achieved with the device should facilitate the disassociation of movements.

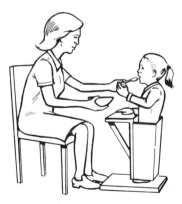

Figure 11.9
Caregiver Assisting Child with Feeding While Child is Positioned in a Prone Stander

In particular, when breaking up a total pattern of movement, it is important that you do not create another equally harmful total pattern. For example, if the child exhibits total patterns of flexion, it would not be helpful to place the child into a total pattern of extension.

COMPREHENSION CHECK 11.10

Outline the general principles that determine the selection of particular adaptive equipment for the physically handicapped.

SUMMARY

The child with CNS dysfunction displays characteristic patterns of motor control that may or may not be present in the normal progression of motor development. The child's motor deficits can best be evaluated in terms of areas of movement, such as righting reactions and head and trunk control. This is in comparison with evaluation based on milestones such as rolling, sitting, and standing. Abnormal characteristics of motor development most often involve abnormal tone organized in patterns, the loss of selective movement, associated reactions, sensory or perceptual distortions, and arrested or delayed motor development.

As a result of a physical handicap, a child also experiences delays in other areas, such as cognitive, communicative, or social development. Thus, a goal of intervention is to lessen the impact of the child's physical deficits on total learning. This can be done by inhibiting abnormal tone and patterns of movement while helping to encourage self-initiated movements.

Principles regarding the design of appropriate learning environments for physically handicapped children are: the involvement of the child into an active learning program that incorporates movement goals into other learning activities; the need for programming functional activities for the child and his family, basing these activities on individual needs; and the importance of the team in the management of a child with CNS dysfunction. Finally, testing should be linked to programming and evaluation.

Adaptive and assistive equipment should be used as an adjunct to the child's total educational program.

SUGGESTED READINGS

Bleck, E. E., and Nagel, D. A. (1975). *Physically handicapped children: A medical atlas for teachers*. New York: Grune & Stratton.

Bobath, B., and Bobath, K. (1975). *Motor development in the different types of cerebral palsy*. London: William Heinemann Medical Books.

Connor, F. P., Williamson, G., and Siepp, J. M. (1978). *Program guide for infants and toddlers with neuromotor and other developmental disabilities*. New York: Teachers College Press.

Finnie, N. (1975). *Handling the young cerebral palsied child at home.* New York: Dutton.

Kanor, S. (1985). *Toys for special children.* Hastings-on-the-Hudson, NY: Steven Kanor, Inc.

Neisworth, J. T. (Ed.) *Topics in early childhood special education: developmental toys.*

Pearson, P. H., and Wiliams, C. E. (1972). *Physical therapy services in the developmental disabilities.* Springfield, IL: Thomas.

12

Differences in Social and Emotional Development

Maureen A. Smith

Patrick J. Schloss

Frances M. Hunt

CHAPTER OUTLINE

VIGNETTES

Tammy is 5 years old. When her kindergarten classmates are playing group games on the playground, Tammy stays close to her teacher and merely watches. Her parents describe her as "shy." Even when she is with familiar people, she is quiet, rarely speaks above a whisper, and appears easily embarrassed when others talk to her.

Her teacher is concerned because Tammy does not seem to be developing friendships and does not seem to enjoy the same kinds of activities as do her peers. Her parents are wondering how she will adjust to first grade. Tammy is an "isolate," or socially withdrawn child.

Glen is a 6-year-old "bundle of energy," as his mother describes him. He does not seem to be able to sit still, play with anything for longer than a few seconds, and does not listen long enough to hear a complete set of instructions. He often awakens a few hours after bedtime and has trouble sleeping more than 5 hours at night. Glen is referred to as "hyperactive" or "hyperkinetic."

Five-year-old Angie refuses to go to school. Each morning her mother has to dress her and physically guide her through the morning routine. Because Angie is so disruptive, she cannot take the school bus with the neighborhood children. Instead, her mother drives her to school and sometimes even has to carry her to her classroom. Throughout the morning she cries and argues and complains that she does not feel good. She often refuses to participate in group activities. She suffers from fears and phobias.

I just turned my back for an instant and Amy's crying alerted me. Nathan wanted to play with one of her toys and when she resisted, he pulled her hair and hit her with the toy. Other children may occasionally push and shove, but with Nathan, this seems to be the only way he knows how to interact. Nathan's behavior is clearly aggressive.

Theresa was a very difficult infant to care for. She was never in good health and was frequently hospitalized for respiratory problems during her first 2 years. She began to have seizures when she was 18 months old, and it was about this time I began to suspect that she could not see well. Theresa is now considered extremely noncompliant; she refuses all commands and most requests. Her parents are bewildered about what to do.

At 11 months of age, Tonia was considered to be at-risk nutritionally. Bottle-feedings were becoming more and more difficult. Tonia often refused the bottle after drinking only a few ounces. What was especially upsetting to her mother, however, was that Tonia had recently been vomiting after each feeding. Although she was being fed up to 15 times each day, she was losing weight much too rapidly. Tonia suffers from somatic disorders associated with her emotional disturbance.

Johnny was always a difficult child. When he was newborn, he was very difficult to feed and did not seem to enjoy cuddling and playing simple games like "peek-a-boo." He was an early walker compared with my other boys, and for awhile I just thought he would outgrow his aloof behavior. By the time he was 2 1/2, however, we knew it was something different. He refused to be picked up, never interacted with other children, and spent hours rocking, shaking his head, and watching his fingers. Sometimes his rocking got so intense that he would bang his head on the wall or the side of his crib. Although Johnny can say many words clearly, he does not use words as a language: he cannot communicate. Johnny is "autistic."

In this chapter we will discuss seven classes or categories of behavior that reflect social and emotional problems exhibited by young children. These categories are social isolation/withdrawal, hyperactivity, fears and phobias, aggression, noncompliance, and severe problems including somatic disorders and autism. After brief descriptions of each problem, common concerns are addressed: the impact of the problems on family and the child, the causes, and assessment considerations. Then, for each problem area, treatment approaches and educational concerns are presented. Five major models used to explain, assess, and treat children's emotional disorders will be emphasized.

DEFINITION AND DESCRIPTION OF THE PROBLEMS

Children with social and emotional problems comprise perhaps the most diverse category of exceptionality. Unlike with other areas of exceptionality, it is difficult to specify when a social or emotional problem actually becomes extreme enough to require treatment. There are no clear standards against which problems can be compared and thus determined to be "abnormal." Often, what is judged by one observer to be "normal" is a serious concern to another.

The ambiguity in defining social and emotional problems becomes even greater when considering young children. Because youngsters develop at such different rates, only severe social/emotional problems are reliably identified.

Definitions of social and emotional disorders emphasize the effects of children's inappropriate behaviors on other students, teachers, and on the children themselves (Pate, 1963). Haring and Phillips (1962) note that these inappropriate behaviors can range from excesses such as hyperactive and impulsive behavior to deficits including depression and withdrawal. "Abnormal" can refer to otherwise typical behavior that occurs often or infrequently. It can also refer to otherwise normal behavior that does not take place in the right circumstances (e.g., changing clothes in the street). Sometimes, however, "abnormal" refers to behavior that is deviant in its own right and not because of sheer excess, deficiency, or situation appropriateness. Biting oneself and head banging are considered abnormal in absolute terms. It is generally recognized that children's emotional problems fall on a continuum ranging from mild to severe. We will discuss specific emotional disorders from this perspective.

Mild social and emotional problems

Social withdrawal

Children who have low rates of interactions are often described as *socially isolated* or withdrawn. Because "normal" levels of interaction are defined by culture and situation, there is no clear-cut criterion for determining when the rates of interaction are low enough to warrant concern.

Children who exhibit isolation and withdrawal may have skill deficits, motivational deficits, or both (Schloss, 1984). For example, the child may not know how to play popular games or may lack skills such as communication or motor skills necessary for the interaction. In other cases, the child has these skills but does not use them consistently. In the former situation, intervention involves training new skills. In the latter, altering the motivational conditions can help to increase rates of social interaction. Before implementing an intervention program, it is important to determine whether or not the low rates of social interaction are, indeed, having a detrimental effect on the child. As Shenfeld (1980) points out, "It is tempting to infer that the child who has few friends or is outwardly rejected by his peers must be sad and lonely" (pp. 5–6). Assuming that socially isolated children will have future adjustment problems has not been documented in the professional literature.

Hyperactivity

The label "hyperactive" may be the most readily applied among young children. *Hyperactivity* refers to overactivity—excessive talking, fidgeting, distractability, and almost continuous motor activity. Most "hyperactive" children evidence normal intelligence, but they are often easily frustrated and rejected by their peers. "Hyperactivity" is not a clearly identifiable problem, and, as with the case of most social and emotional problems, children

Even very young children can be depressed, lonely, and withdrawn; such quiet children often go undetected unlike their hyperactive peers.

who are labeled as hyperactive often exhibit varying levels of activity. It is estimated that approximately 5% of school-age children are hyperactive, most of which are boys.

Phobias

Fears are common among children and adults, and, in many cases, serve an adaptive function (e.g., it is wise to be afraid of snakes). When these normal responses to potentially threatening events become unreasonable, however, they are considered to be phobias. It is not uncommon for children to experience fears related to animals, medical or dental procedures, heights, storms, monsters, and the dark. About 10% of school-age children have fears and phobias related to school, although they outgrow them within a few years. When fears or phobias become debilitating, or when they reach "clinical duration" (i.e., they persist for more than 2 years), intervention is warranted (Graziano and Mooney, 1984).

Aggression

Some estimates indicate that almost one third of all parent and teacher requests for mental health services are for their aggressive children (Roach, 1958). These children's behavior becomes a concern when kicking, hitting, throwing objects, biting, verbal abuse, and other similar behaviors become frequent or intense. Early intervention for aggressive children is especially critical, because follow-up evidence indicates that these children are unlikely to "outgrow" their deviant behavior. Severe aggressive behavior in younger children typically becomes a serious problem throughout the child's life (Morris, 1956; Robins, 1966).

Noncompliance

The term "noncompliance" refers to a broad class of child responses including disobedience, refusal, arguing, teasing, and ignoring. It refers to a child's failure to initiate or stop a response when requested by an authority figure (e.g., parents or teacher) or when mandated to do so by rules. The following vignette describes a noncompliant child.

"Lauren, wash your hands for dinner." No response. "Lauren, did you hear what I said? It's time for dinner. Now turn the TV off and come in here." No response. Lauren's mother turns off the TV, "Stand up right now. Go into the bathroom and wash your hands." Lauren picks up a nearby toy and throws it on the floor. "I'm not hungry!" she cries. Her mother starts to physically guide her toward the bathroom sink. Lauren turns around and starts laughing. "Are you going to punish me? Why are we eating dinner now?" After washing her hands, with plenty of assistance from her mother, Lauren arrives at the table and begins to climb into her younger brother's highchair. "Get down and sit in your own chair." "But this is my chair," says Lauren.

It is not always clear that noncompliance poses a serious problem for children. In some cases, the expectations and values of the authority figures are unreasonable. In some situations it may be appropriate and justifiable for a child to be noncompliant.

COMPREHENSION CHECK 12.1

All children display behaviors that may be described as characteristic of children with mild social and emotional problems, yet they are never diagnosed and labeled as such. Why?

Severe social and emotional problems

Some preschoolers exhibit severe behavior problems that occur in only a very small percentage of the population. Intervention for these problems requires more elaborate efforts than do the problems just described. Some of these children have severe and multiple handicaps. All are the focus of continuing research involving many disciplines.

Severely, profoundly, and multiple-handicapped children have been described by Sontag, Burke, and York (1973) as:

> *Those who are not toilet trained; aggress toward others, do not attend to even the most pronounced social stimuli; self-mutilate, ruminate; self-stimulate; do not walk, speak, hear or see; manifest durable and intense temper tantrums; are not under even the most rudimentary forms of verbal controls; do not imitate; manifest minimally controlled seizures; and/or have extremely brittle medical existences. (p. 22)*

Often these children's handicaps are so severe that they are obvious at birth. Although estimates vary, severe, profound, and multiple handicaps are generally thought to occur in less than 0.5% of the population. For those individuals, modification of inappropriate social and emotional behaviors may be as much a focus of intervention as training of basic adaptive responses.

Autism

It is generally agreed that *autistic children* exhibit all or most of the following characteristics (Koegel, Egel, and Dunlap, 1980; Rimland, 1978):

1. *Lack of appropriate speech.* The child may be nonverbal or may exhibit echolalic speech.

2. *Lack of appropriate social behavior.* The child may be oblivious to others or relate in a bizarre manner.

3. *Apparent sensory deficit.* The child may be incorrectly suspected of being blind or deaf.

4. *Lack of appropriate play.* The child may ignore toys or interact with them inappropriately.

5. *Inappropriate or out-of-context emotional behavior.* Behavior may range from extreme tantrums, outbursts of hysterical laughter, or a complete absence of emotional responding.

6. *Self-stimulation.* The child displays high rates of stereotyped behaviors such as finger flicking, rocking, and self-injurious behavior.

7. *Isolated areas of high-level functioning—"splinter skills"*. Despite low functioning in communication of self-care areas, some children may exhibit relatively high-level abilities in music, number configurations, or manipulation of mechanical instruments.

Although many "normal" children exhibit one or two of these features, the prevalence of children who exhibit most of these and are later diagnosed as "autistic" is low—only 1 in 2500 (Koegel, Egel, and Dunlap, 1980). At the preschool level, most autistic children are likely to exhibit few functional skills and engage in high rates of inappropriate behaviors. Included in this class of behaviors are self-stimulation, such as rocking, head weaving, finger flicking, as well as more serious disruptive behaviors, such as self-injurious behavior, tantrums, and emotional outbursts. When these disruptive behaviors occur at high rates, the priority for intervention is to reduce them, not only because they may interfere with the acquisition of more adaptive responses (Foxx and Azrin, 1973; Koegel and Covert, 1972; Koegel, Firestone, Kramme, and Dunlap, 1974; Lovaas, Schreibman, Koegel, and Rehm, 1971; Risley, 1968; Solnick, Rincover, and Peterson, 1977), but because they may actually be physically harmful to the child or others in the child's environment.

Common to both of these groups are bizarre behavior excesses including self-stimulatory and self-injurious behavior. Although the research literature includes many reports of strategies that have been used to control these behaviors, most severely retarded and autistic children continue to exhibit high rates of these responses. This may be a consequence of few professionals being adequately trained to implement complex intervention procedures. In addition, the resources for such interventions are often limited and gains achieved are unlikely to generalize to new situations.

Self-stimulation

Behaviors such as rocking, finger flicking, rhythmic manipulation of objects, hand flapping, head weaving, teeth clicking, and any number of other similar, apparently nonfunctional behaviors have been described as one of the greatest obstacles to educating children with severe impairments. *Self-stimulation* rates may be so high that the child engages in little if any other type of activity, including those necessary for learning even rudimentary care, communication, and motor skills (Koegel, Egel, and Dunlap, 1980). Evidence seems to indicate an inverse relationship between self-stimulation and the acquisition of new appropriate behaviors (Epstein, Doke, Sajwaj, Sorrell, and Rimmer, 1974; Foxx and Azrin, 1973; Koegel and Covert, 1972; Koegel, Firestone, Cramme, and Dunlap, 1974; Lovaas et al., 1971; Risley, 1968).

Self-injury

Self-injurious behavior (SIB) includes behaviors such as scratching, biting, severe head banging, face slapping, and pinching. Some researchers suggest that 4% to 5% of the psychiatric population exhibits some form of self-injurious behavior (Frankel and Simmons, 1976). Although it is not clear why SIB occurs in the severely handicapped population, a number of hypotheses have been proposed. Carr (1977), for example, suggests several reasonable explanations:

Repetitive behavior such as hand-flapping is common among neurologically impaired and emotionally disturbed children when they are overstimulated during play.

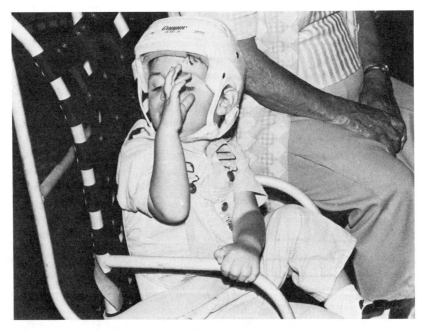

Neurologically impaired children unfortunately often display self-stimulatory and self-injurious behavior.

1. SIB is a learned response, maintained by positive reinforcement (e.g., attention).

2. SIB is a learned response, maintained by negative reinforcement or escape from unpleasant situations (e.g., to avoid changing clothes, bathing, or attending).

3. SIB is a means of providing sensory stimulation.

4. SIB is caused by or related to abnormal physiological processes (e.g., is related to abnormal levels of certain body substances, as in Lesch-Nyhan syndrome, a rare genetic disease).

COMPREHENSION CHECK 12.2

Explain how children with mild social and emotional disturbances differ qualitatively and quantitatively from children with severe social and emotional disturbances.

PREVALENCE OF SOCIAL AND EMOTIONAL DISORDERS

Although numerous authors have reported prevalence estimates of behavior disorders among primary and secondary grade students, there is a relative absence of reliable estimates for young children. The President's Commission on the Mental Health of Children (Rich, 1982) reported that 20% of all children and youth in this country exhibit mild to moderate behavior disorders. Of these, 0.6% exhibit severe emotional disturbances. Although 3% to 5% is the generally accepted prevalence rate among school-age populations (Rich, 1982), this estimate may be high for preschoolers.

It is generally recognized that mild and moderate behavior disorders are not evidenced until a child enters school. Peer pressure, competition for attention, separation from parents, and academic failure exacerbate behavior problems to the point that they are recognized by professionals. Also, before entry into school, parents have few opportunities to compare their child's social development with age-matched peers. Consequently, socially immature behavior may be recognized as age-appropriate responding. Finally, only more severe behavior disorders are identified during the first few years of life. Given these factors, it is reasonable to assume that the prevalence of severe behavior disorders among preschoolers is below 2%.

COMPREHENSION CHECK 12.3

How might fiscal concerns influence the percentage of emotionally disturbed young children identified by service providers?

IMPACT ON THE FAMILY

The relationship between a young child's behavior and his/her family's adjustment is extremely complex. A child's behavior disorder can cause or be caused by family influence. More likely, the disorder may result from the interaction of child and family variables.

Although some theorists place almost exclusive blame for children's behavior disorders on parenting practices (i.e., Bettelheim, 1950), there is little evidence that parents are directly responsible for children's behavior disorders. In a comprehensive review of literature pertaining to family factors, Kauffman (1981) concluded research has failed to link behavior disorders with family relationships. He suggested that, at best, family relationships contribute to social maladjustment. He argues that "Given what is known today regarding the family's role in children's behavior disorders, it would be extremely inappropriate for special educators to adopt an attitude of blame toward parents of troubled children" (p. 104).

Despite Kauffman's admonishments, parents continue to be a focal point of efforts to determine the origin of children's behavior problems. This effect has contributed to parents feelings of failure, guilt, and resentment. The parents' perceived role in contributing to the disability, coupled with the social stigma, produces a number of adverse consequences.

As discussed in earlier chapters, parents may move through various stages of acceptance. In the process they may remain excessively long in one or more stage, thereby threatening their own "adjustment" and interferring with professional efforts on behalf of the child. During the *denial* phase, for example, parents may be reluctant or unable to provide accurate information pertaining to the severity and nature of the problem. The absence of this information may result in faulty diagnosis and/or a misguided treatment plan. During the *recognition* phase, parents may be overwhelmed by the apparent magnitude of the problem. Confusion resulting in multiple explanations, anger toward professionals, frustration, and guilt may threaten the most carefully devised intervention plan. Parents may respond to appropriate treatment strategies with concerns for the amount of time and effort involved, the cost to other family members, disruptions in the family routine and so on. Finally, the *constructive action* phase may be characterized by parents being overly zealous to "do what is best for the child." In the process they may ignore responsibilities to themselves, their spouse, and other children.

In any case, it is not sufficient for professionals to recognize and wait for the stages to run their course. Professionals must be available to assist parents in resolving personal conflicts that arise as a consequence of having

---

COMPREHENSION CHECK 12.4

How can a preschooler's ability to engage in smiling, attachment, or play behavior influence his/her interactions with other family members? How do these interactions influence future development?

a disabled youngster. The goals of this assistance may be twofold. First, the professional may help the parent to resolve irrational feelings related to their child's behavior disorder. Second, assistance may be provided in helping the parents to understand the nature of the child's disorder as well as effective home-based interventions.

IMPACT OF EMOTIONAL DISTURBANCE ON THE CHILD'S DEVELOPMENT

The impact of emotional disturbance on other areas of a child's development has not been clearly documented. Emotional disturbance is often presumed to adversely influence development in a number of domains, including intelligence, achievement, social and emotional characteristics, communication, and motor skills. In addition, the degree to which emotional disturbance influences these domains is a function of the severity of the problem. Each of these domains will be considered separately, as a problem in one area is not necessarily indicative of a problem in another.

Intelligence

Research has demonstrated that emotionally disturbed children tend to perform less well than their nonhandicapped peers on standardized intelligence tests. Findings indicate that the majority of mildly and moderately disturbed children perform at levels that are only slightly below the average IQ (Lyons and Powers, 1963). However, as Kauffman (1981) notes, a disproportionate number of these children function in the dull normal and mildly retarded range of intelligence, with only a very small minority functioning in the upper ranges.

Data obtained on severely and profoundly disturbed children indicate they score in the moderately to mildly retarded range of intelligence (DeMyer, 1975), although a small number demonstrate normal or above average IQs. Kauffman (1981) hypothesized that these children demonstrate an average IQ of 50, with the majority of scores falling between 25 or 30 and 70 or 75. Therefore, although severe behavior disorders may be found at any level of intelligence, they occur more frequently in children with more severe levels of retardation.

In summary, evidence suggests that emotionally disturbed children demonstrate varying degrees of intellectual deficits. Although practitioners concerned with emotionally disturbed prescoolers are cautioned against inferring a causal relationship between low intelligence and emotional disturbance, it should be noted that IQ can be one of the best single predictors of educational achievement and later adjustment (DeMeyer, 1975; Garmezy, 1974; Robins, 1966; Rutter, 1972; Rutter and Bartak, 1973).

COMPREHENSION CHECK 12.5

Intelligence is usually measured by standardized tests. How can an emotional problem influence a child's performance on tests?

Achievement

The vast majority of studies relevant to academic achievement of emotionally disturbed children have been conducted with children of elementary and secondary school age. Obviously, little is known regarding the achievement status of preschool children because of the inappropriateness of both subject matter and testing instruments for this population. However, a brief overview of the academic status of older emotionally disturbed children will be presented in order to acquaint the reader with the achievement levels that could be expected from preschool-age children displaying various degrees of emotional disturbances.

A review of the literature leads one to conclude that academic achievement demonstrated by mildly to moderately emotionally disturbed children is inferior to that of their nonhandicapped peers. Typically, these children do not demonstrate achievement levels that are commensurate with their mental or chronological ages. Stone and Rowley (1964) used chronological age to gauge academic retardation and identified 59% of the population surveyed as academically delayed, 21% as at grade level, and 20% as academically advanced. By using mental age as a criteria, 52% were academically delayed, 19% were at grade level, and 21% were advanced. Achievement levels attained by mildly and moderately disturbed children have also been specified. Kauffman, Hallahan, and Gajar as reported by Kauffman (1981) surveyed mildly and moderately disturbed children enrolled in public schools and found an average academic retardation of 7 years in reading, 1.6 years in spelling, and 1.7 years in arithmetic.

Severely and profoundly disturbed children are rarely found to be as academically competent as their age-matched peers. In fact, academic instruction for these students may take a backseat to instruction in functional skills such as self-help skills, language, and play skills.

The preceding discussion highlights the relationship between emotional disturbance and academic achievement. At this point, however, it is unclear which causes the other. A child who is evidencing an emotional disorder may be unable to benefit from academic instruction causing achievement deficits. On the other hand, a child confronted with an academic task he/she is unable to complete may respond with inappropriate behavior. In either case, practitioners concerned with the future educational adjustment of emotionally disturbed preschoolers must be aware of this relationship and be prepared to address those behaviors that may preclude full participation in academic settings.

COMPREHENSION CHECK 12.6

Identify some readiness skills that may need to be developed during the preschool years to maximize a child's ability to benefit from academic instruction in the future.

Social and emotional characteristics

Social and emotional development of infants and preschool children generally falls into four areas: smiling and laughter, fear and anxiety, surprise, and the emergence of play behavior. Normal development will be briefly described in each of these areas in order to provide the practitioner with a basis for gauging when a child's responses may be indicative of a problem warranting further investigation.

Smiling and laughter

An infant's first social smile is considered a major milestone by parents and other family members. Early investigators believed smiles at 2 or 3 months of age were indicative of gas (Salzen, 1963), although more current research has refuted this assumption (Emde and Harmon, 1972)! Smiles at 6 to 12 weeks of age are generalized responses to auditory, visual, and tactile stimulation. Beyond this age, the infant responds differently to varying stimuli. Smiling progresses to chuckles and laughter in the 4- to 6-month-old infant in response to tactile and auditory stimulation. Visual and social stimulation elicit laughter from an infant between the ages of 7 and 9 months.

Fear and anxiety

Major indicators of fear and anxiety in infants and young children are separation from mother and meeting strangers. Separation anxiety occurs at approximately 10 months of age and is in response to the mother leaving the room for a short period of time. Stranger anxiety occurs between 8 and 10 months of age and is in response to the arrival of an unfamiliar person. Both are characterized by crying and attempts to reestablish contact with the mother (Johnson, Jens, Gallagher, and Anderson, 1980).

Surprise

Bower (1971) demonstrated surprise responses in infants as young as 16 weeks of age. This behavior occurred when an object was no longer in the place they last saw it.

Play behavior

Perhaps the single-most important evidence of social and emotional growth in young children is the development of play behavior. Weisler and McCall (1976) defined play as

> *Behaviors and behavioral sequences that are organism dominated rather than stimulus dominated, behaviors that appear to be intrinsically motivated and apparently performed "for their own sake" and that are conducted with relative relaxation and positive affect. (p. 494)*

Weisler and McCall (1976) also reviewed theories explaining why children engage in play behavior. Early theories emphasized genetic or physiological reasons such as the need to release excess energy. In contrast, more recent theories have concentrated on the function play behavior fulfills. For example, play affords children the opportunity to learn about people, animals, and objects. It also promotes independence from parents.

Two types of play behavior have been described in the literature: play that involves objects and play that involves peers. Play that involves objects has been grouped into six levels:

Level I: The child either repeats the same motor pattern with the toy or mouths it.
Level II: The child pounds, throws, pushes, or pulls the toy.

Level III: The child performs acts on himself/herself, using the toy (e.g., puts a ring on his/her arm).

Level IV: The child manipulates movable parts of toys.

Level V: The child separates toy parts.

Level VI: The child begins to use different play materials together in various combinations.

Similarly, Sutton-Smith (1970) has categorized toy behavior, using chronological ages, which may be useful to preschool educators. Between 12 and 24 months of age, children primarily engage in exploration and manipulations that involve banging, tasting, emptying, and filling objects. At 24 to 36 months, children enjoy building, painting, pasting, and working with clay and puzzles. Between 36 to 48 months, children draw, cut, color, and complete advanced puzzles. Finally, between 48 and 60 months, children enjoy making collages, painting, and working complex puzzles.

Play that involves peer interaction has also received a great deal of attention. Perhaps the most widely accepted description of peer interaction was presented by Parten (1932). She defined six categories of children's play behavior.

1. *Unoccupied behavior.* The child watches anything of interest. In the event that nothing interesting is happening, he/she is content to play with his/her own body, climb on furniture, or follow an adult.

2. *Solitary play.* This is the most common form of play behavior displayed by children between the ages of 24 and 30 months. During this time, the child plays with his/her own toys and makes no attempt to interact with other children who may be present.

3. *Onlooker.* The child watches other children and may engage in conversation with them. No attempt is made to enter into the play behavior of other children.

4. *Parallel activity.* Between 30 and 42 months, the child plays beside, rather than with, other children, using similar toys although in a manner of his/her own choosing. There is no attempt to modify or influence the behavior of nearby children.

5. *Associative play.* Between 42 and 54 months of age, the child plays with other children, sharing their toys, and making mild attempts to control their behavior.

6. *Cooperative play.* The child plays in a group engaging in a goal-directed activity, such as a formal game or the creation of a material product.

Although Parten's categories (1932) define play behavior of normal youngsters, they may prove valuable to the preschool educator who must describe and classify the social play of handicapped children before planning and evaluating intervention strategies.

When compared with age-matched peers, young children with mild and moderate emotional disturbances differ quantitatively in the behaviors they display. Their range of behavior is considered normal in that they display behaviors that are no different from those exhibited by all children. For example, they smile, laugh, cry, and progress through development stages of toy play and peer interaction, just as their nonhandicapped peers do. However, they may exhibit behaviors more often, longer, or with a greater intensity. For example, a moderately emotionally disturbed child may prefer solitary play behavior, even though he is 4 years old. Conversely, children with severe or profound emotional disturbances engage in behaviors that are qualitatively as well as quantitatively different from their nonhandicapped peers. For example, these children may fail to develop smiling behaviors or may consistently interact with toys in inappropriate ways (e.g., turning a truck upside down and spinning the wheels). In either case, standards of normal child development are valuable tools that assist the teacher in identifying, assessing, and modifying the behavior of emotionally disturbed preschoolers. These areas will be discussed in succeeding sections of this chapter.

Communication

Communication problems of emotionally disturbed children may be classified in two ways: behavioral excesses or behavioral deficits. Excesses are those behaviors that occur too frequently, whereas deficits are those behaviors that occur infrequently or not at all. The types of behavioral excesses or deficits vary as a function of the degree of emotional disturbance.

Children displaying mild to moderate emotional disturbances may display communication excesses that include talking out in class or swearing. Communication deficits typically include limited interpersonal skills, such as the lack of social amenities or inability to appropriately convey complimentary or critical remarks. Severely and profoundly emotionally disturbed children display communication excesses that include echolalia and repetitive verbalizations. *Echolalia* is defined as the meaningless repetition by the child of words or sentences initially spoken by other people. *Repetitive verbalizations* are repetitions by the child of an utterance he/she spoke. Communication deficits frequently found among severely and profoundly emotionally disturbed children include limited interpersonal skills such as those evidenced by less-involved children or an extreme delay or complete lack of speech and language development.

COMPREHENSION CHECK 12.7

Echolalia and verbal repetitions are behaviors characteristic of normal language development. At what point should their use by a preschooler be a cause for concern?

Motor skills

The development of physical and motor skills in emotionally disturbed children so closely resembles that of age-matched peers that they are virtually indistinguishable from other children. The exception to this generality is the severe or profoundly disturbed child who often evidences unusual motor behavior such as hand or finger flapping, rocking, or head banging.

CAUSES OF SOCIOEMOTIONAL DISORDERS

For the vast majority of children, the origin of emotional disorders is unknown. Unlike severe mental retardation, sensory impairments, and physical handicaps, where specific genetic and health factors are linked to the disorder, few, if any, objective variables are associated with behavior disorders. Consequently, much has been written to advance various theoretical views of the cause of emotional disturbance. The Child Variance Project, a program intended to integrate prominent definitions, causes, and treatments of emotional disturbance, highlighted five major orientations. These are biophysical, psychodynamic, sociological, learning, and ecological. Each of these views offers a complimentary or conflicting explanation for children's emotional disorders.

Biophysical

The biophysical model views emotional disorders as resulting from a physical disease, disorder, or dysfunction. Genetic, neurological, or biochemical pathology may all contribute to the emotional disorder. Several different biophysical explanations are currently being studied. These will be discussed separately.

Genetic influences

Genetic theories emphasize the role of hereditary endowment on behavior patterns. Proponents of this view assume that genes, passed on from one or both of the parents, may be expressed in the child's personality (Wilson, 1979). The degree of expression is dictated by whether the gene is dominant or recessive, whether one or both parents contribute defective genes, and the extent to which the environment supports the trait. Research supporting this view generally takes the form of studying the lineage of children with emotional disorders and comparing the characteristics of twins raised under separate conditions. Unfortunately, because of the methodological problems of this research, few definitive statements can be made about genetic influences on emotional disorders (Rich, 1982).

Temperament influences

Thomas and Chess (1977) propose temperament theory to explain emotional disturbance. This theory suggests that certain constitutional factors are inherited but that they must interact with environmental variables to be manifested. Thomas and Chess (1977) have described three temperamental types of characteristic ways of responding to situations: easy, difficult, and slow-to-warm-up. Easy children positively approach new stimuli, readily adapt to change, and have a high tolerance for frustration. Difficult children have irregular biological functions and demonstrate negative withdrawal, limited adaptability to change, and frequent negativism. Slow-to-warm-up children display a mixture of behaviors, but eventually they adapt satisfactorily. Theoretically, emotional disturbance develops as a function of the interaction between these temperament types and the demands and management techniques used by significant others in the environment.

Neuropsychopharmacological influences

Proponents of neuropsychopharmacological influences emphasize the role of neurological and chemical imbalances on emotional disorders. Support for these variables as the cause of emotional disorders generally results from studies in which psychotropic drugs are used as treatment agents (Paul and Epanchin, 1982). There is little doubt, based on current evidence, that drugs exert a powerful influence on childrens' emotional disorders. However, there is substantial debate as to the direct relationship between pharmacological agents and the origins of the disorder.

Nutritional influences

One of the more popular theories of causality over the past decade has focused on the role of diet and toxic substances. Some theorists have emphasized the role of vitamin deficiency, suggesting that elements necessary for the development of mental health are not being digested in sufficient quantities (Hawkins and Pauling, 1973; Pauling, 1968; Peterman and Goodhart, 1954). Other researchers have focused on chemical additives in food leading to allergic reactions that are manifested as emotional disorders (Abrams, Shultz, Margen, and Ogar, 1979). To date, neither of these views has produced well-controlled studies to support their claims (Siva-Sankar, 1979). Future research in these areas, however, may be promising.

Neurological influences

Damage to the central nervous system, when diagnosed through objective measures, may produce abnormalities in emotional expression. Cerebral palsy, epilepsy, and other neurological disorders often increase the likelihood of adverse emotional adjustment (Rutter, Tizard, and Whitmore, 1970). Consequently, some theorists have attributed emotional disorders not corresponding to major insult to the central nervous system to result from "undiagnosed" brain damage. Minimal brain damage, for example, has been proposed as an explanation for hyperactivity, impulsivity, and emotional instability. Owing to the very concept of attributing emotional disorders to "unknown" neurological causes, research supporting this view has failed to emerge.

COMPREHENSION CHECK 12.8

What impact will a biophysical model have on service delivery? On the attitude of the teacher?

Psychodynamic

Psychodynamic views of emotional disturbance result from the work of Freud (1979). Freud emphasized the evolution of personality through stages of psychosexual development, and his treatment paradigm was restricted to psychoanalysis. More recent proponents have minimized the role of sexual instincts and have become more concerned with interactions between internal personality dynamics and interpersonal relationships.

Two basic principles underlie modern psychodynamic theory. First, psychological/emotional development occurs over three district phases in childhood: early childhood, latency period, and puberty. Emotional reactions can only be understood with reference to the particular stage of development. Second, emotional adjustment is predisposed (or not predisposed) by internal personality dynamics. Three elements that comprise personality are the child's instinctual responses, or id; responses governed by reality, or ego; and responses that result from social awareness and conscience, or superego. The id is considered to be present at birth and motivates basic urges for satisfaction. In the first 2 years after birth, the child's ego develops. This facet of personality directs the child's urge for satisfaction to realistic, self-preserving ends. Finally, the child's superego evolves to ensure that the child's satisfaction is not obtained at the cost of others.

As may be apparent from these principles, emotional disturbance is caused by conflicts between the id, ego, and superego. These conflicts are inflamed by deficiencies in the child's interpersonal relations. Exemplifying this explanation, ego impulses may dominate the child's personality. Consequently, the child, motivated by his or her id, strives to maximize self gain to the exclusion of superego controls. Such a child may engage in aggression, noncompliance, hyperactivity, and other acting-out responses that evidence little regard for others in the environment. Conversely, children with overdeveloped superegos may be concerned excessively for societal reactions toward their behavior. Withdrawal, rigidity, or compulsive responses may result as the child attempts to comply with others' expectations.

Recent psychodynamic theorists have expanded Freud's views to emphasize relationships with others. Rogers (1961), for example, highlighted the discrepancy between children's self-concepts and their actual status in the etiology of emotional disturbance. Rogers suggested that children seek to conform to their self-concept. Consequently, they approach activities likely to result in self-actualization. Failure, authority judgments, and other events that are inconsistent with a child's positive self-concept are considered by Rogers to be emotionally provoking.

Finally, Erikson (1968) has elaborated on Freud's stages of psychosexual development by proposing eight stages of psychosocial development. He argues that the failure of a child to progress successfully through these stages is associated with emotional disturbance. Young children normally pass through the first four of these stages:

1. *Trust versus mistrust.* In the first year of life, the child should develop trusting relationships through the quality of care provided by the parents. Inconsistency, separateness, and generally poor care result in mistrust for others.

2. *Autonomy versus shame and doubt.* In the second year, the child develops a sense of autonomy through motor activities. Being deprived of motor opportunities results in expectations for defeat, shame, and doubt.

3. *Initiative versus guilt.* Before entering elementary school, the child develops initiative through fantasies, curiosity, and independent play. Guilt results from adults imposing values that limit initiative.

4. *Industry versus inferiority.* Once in elementary school, the child gains recognition for achievement. Inferiority results from failure.

COMPREHENSION CHECK 12.9

Do all children progress through various stages of psychsocial development at the same age? What implication does this have for diagnosis and intervention?

Sociological theory

Emotional disturbance, from a sociological perspective, results from the child's behavior conflicting with social norms. Sociologists emphasize that families, schools, churches, civic groups, and so on are established to teach and enforce the value system operating in the culture. Students whose behavior fail to conform to the standards exposed by these institutions are labeled as deviant. Five major sociological theories have been proposed to explain the origins of emotional disturbance. These are defined as follows.

Cultural transmission theory

The cultural transmission view holds that children are not innately normal or deviant. Rather, they learn a model of behavior typical of the group with whom they are associated. The acquired model of behavior may conform to the subgroup in which they were reared but be at odds with that of the majority culture. Dissonance between acquired values and the values of the dominant culture may be defined as deviance.

Functionalism

Society results from a balance between maintainence forces and disruptive forces. Forces that fulfill human needs are considered to be functional. Conversely, forces that interfere with human needs are deviant. Deviant behavior, therefore, is defined by society as responses that are not congruous with the general welfare. Children exhibiting these responses are considered to be sick or mentally ill and are isolated in special classes and institutions.

Labeling

Labeling theorists suggest that the major variables associated with emotional problems are the labels applied by society. The contend that all individuals to varying degrees exhibit norm-violating behaviors. What separates the emotionally disturbed is that they are labeled as such. Once labeled, children behave in a manner consistent with the label's designation.

Social disorganization theory

The social disorganization view emphasizes social interaction patterns with the community. The changing composition of a community, or an institution within the community, can result in a breakdown of communication.

Stress resulting from this breakdown produces increased rates of deviance among community members.

Theory of anomie

Social norms provide comfortable boundaries for personal expression. The evolution of society, however, produces vague areas in which norms are not clearly established. This results in personal judgments replacing clearly defined social rules. The greater the demand for individual community members to project their own norms, the greater the frustration that often results in deviant behavior and emotional disturbance.

COMPREHENSION CHECK 12.10

What implications does a sociological view of causality have for a preschooler whose background differs from that of his teacher?

Learning

Learning theorists suggest that behavior, both positive and norm violating, is learned. Children raised in environments characterized by appropriate peer and adult models, reinforcement for appropriate behaviors, and negative consequences for inappropriate behaviors are likely to develop positive emotional and behavioral features. Those frequently exposed to norm-violating models, who gain satisfaction for negativistic attitudes and behaviors, and who are seldom reinforced for positive responses are likely to develop emotional disturbances.

Although learning theorists all agree that learning is the basis of social adjustment, they differ on variables operating in the acquisition of positive and negative responses. Three major learning theory views are typically discussed. These are classical conditioning, modeling, and operant conditioning.

Classical conditioning

Classical or respondent conditioning is generally used to explain the acquisition and maintenance of emotional responses. Early in life an infant reacts to a small number of unconditioned stimuli. These stimuli elicit uncontrolled emotional responses. Warmth, food, the removal of irritants, and so forth produce satisfying, yet relatively undifferentiated, positive feelings and expressions. Over time, these stimuli are paired with neutral events and the neutral events eventually elicit the same emotional responses. These learned stimuli subsequently elicit a range of emotional responses. During normal development, unconditioned stimuli are consistently paired with parental attention, indicators of achievement such as awards and grades, and other events that typically produce positive responses in mature persons.

Some unconditioned stimuli elicit negative emotional reactions. Excessive heat, irritants, pressure, and so on produce pain. Just as positive emotional responses are developed through the pairing of unconditioned stimuli with neutral events, negative responses may be formed by pairing adverse unconditioned stimuli with neutral events. Consequently, rather than environmental events (e.g., going to school, earning good grades, participating in athletic competitions) producing satisfying emotional feelings, they may produce disruptive reactions.

Modeling

Other learning theorists emphasize the role of observational learning in the acquisition of positive and adverse emotional responses. Bandura (1969), for example, has argued that children develop positive social behaviors by observing and imitating others. This process is enhanced by the availability of high-status models who perform and are reinforced for behaviors that the child is able to emulate. As with other learning theories, modeling may be used to explain the genesis of both positive and negative emotional responses.

Operant conditioning

The final group of learning-theory principles emphasizes the role of positive reinforcement, negative reinforcement, and punishment. *Positive reinforcement* is defined by the increased likelihood that a child will exhibit a behavior that produces satisfying outcomes. *Negative reinforcement* is the response-contingent removal or avoidance of a dissatisfying event. Both positive and negative reinforcement strengthen or maintain the associated behavior. Punishment, on the other hand, involves the reduction of a behavior through the contingent presentation of an unpleasant event.

Positive social and emotional behaviors are developed through their consistent ability to produce satisfying outcomes (positive reinforcers) as well as their ability to remove or avoid noxious events (negative reinforcers). Norm-violating behaviors may develop through the same associations. Cheating, for example, may be positively reinforced by the presentation of good grades and the avoidance of failure. Similarly, a very young child may learn that biting is connected with the delivery of food (a positive reinforcer) or the removal of a competing youngster (negative reinforcer).

COMPREHENSION CHECK 12.11

Will children of the same age display similar behavior characteristics? Why or why not?

Ecological

The ecological model involves the study of relationships between children and their environments. Because each of the preceding perspectives includes either learner or environmental components, the ecological view is seen as reconciling the major orientations. Within-the-child aspects such as ego development, biological endowment, and so on are considered to be as important to understanding the child as are overt behavioral features. These variables are useful in recognizing and understanding the problem only to the extent to which they interact with the sociological and operant contexts. Consequently, causes of emotional disturbances from this perspective relate to a mismatch between the child and his or her ecosystem.

Exemplifying the ecological orientation, Paul and Epanchin (1982) suggest the following interactions that may lead to emotional disturbance:

1. Conditions in the classrooms. *Public school classrooms can contain conditions which promote negative feelings and behaviors . . . while most children are able and willing to tolerate these conditions, there are some children who are not. Many of these children are labeled emotionally disturbed . . .*

2. Dissonance between environments. *Children who are expected to adapt to radically different demands in different settings are in particular jeopardy. Sometimes the conflicting demands of the home and the school, or the regular class and the resource room, are too much for children to handle.*

3. Poor fit between the behavior and the environment. *Every child has a set of skills, attitudes, perceptions, and values. These attributes combine to produce characteristic ways of behaving—of dealing with others, reacting to conflicts, and responding to environmental forces. As long as the child is in an environment that is appropriate to his or her attributes and tolerates his or her behavior, there is a good fit and disturbance is minimized. In an environment that makes inappropriate demands upon the child, however, she may react negatively, through aggression or withdrawal, for example. (pp. 224–225)*

This section has presented the five major theoretical views surrounding the development of emotional disturbance. As the field develops, dysfunctional explanations may evolve from usefulness, leaving more unified explanations. Until then, practitioners must be guided by approaches most applicable to applied settings.

COMPREHENSION CHECK 12.12

Which theories of causality are compatible? Which are conflicting?

ASSESSMENT OF EMOTIONAL DISTURBANCES

Once the presence of an emotional disturbance is suspected, it is essential to evaluate the child's behavior so as to facilitate the development of an intervention plan appropriate for that child. This is accomplished through the assessment process. Assessment involves a precise determination of the nature and extent of the problem, identification of possible causes and contributing factors, selection of appropriate intervention strategies, and the monitoring of a child's progress after intervention has begun. In keeping with the previous discussion, assessment techniques will be presented in light of the five major theoretical views of emotional disturbance; biophysical, psychodynamic, sociological, learning, and ecological. These models differ with respect to the professional in charge of assessment, the nature of the assessment, the setting in which it is conducted, and the assignment of professional responsibility.

Biophysical

The goal of the biophysical assessment process is to identify physical abnormalities that may adversely influence a child's physical or emotional health. Assessment results will be used to advise intervention strategies that will either correct the problem or help the child compensate for it.

Typically, a biophysical assessment of an emotional disorder is conducted by medical specialists, including pediatricians, pediatric neurologists, nutritionists, allergists, ophthalmologists, and audiologists. Assessment procedures are conducted in a hospital, clinic, or doctor's office and typically include a complete physical as well as vision and hearing tests, a CT scan, and an EEG. Commercially available instruments may also be used, including the Denver Developmental Screening Test (Frankenburg, Dodds, and Fandal, 1975), the Carolina Record of Individual Behavior (Simeonsson, Huntington, Short, and Ware, 1982), and the Temperament Scales (Carey and McDevitt, 1978).

The teacher's participation in a biophysical assessment of an emotionally disturbed preschooler is limited because of its medical nature. However, the teacher can perform two important functions. First, the teacher serves as a screening and referral agent for students in the classroom. By using observation techniques, the teacher can identify symptoms and behavior patterns that may be indicative of a physiological problem. Symptoms that warrant further exploration may involve a child's physical appearance (e.g., infections, rapid weight loss), academic performance (e.g., inattentiveness to verbal or written instruction), or behavioral patterns (e.g., convulsive seizures, loss of consciousness). Second, the preschool teacher can monitor the child's behavior following medical intervention and report any improvement or deterioration of behavior to the supervising physician.

COMPREHENSION CHECK 12.13

Explain the statement: The biophysical method leads to both a removal of guilt and an abdication of responsibility.

Psychodynamic

The purpose of a psychodynamic assessment is to identify a behavior pattern that describes a child's developmental inadequacies, defense mechanisms, inadequate impulse control, and the lack of prosocial behaviors. Assessment must also address the child's inner dynamics, including self-esteem, motivation to learn, and independence.

A psychodynamic therapist conducts the assessment, usually in a clinical setting, and is aided by several professionals, including a psychologist, a social worker, an educator, and a neurologist. Data are obtained from school records, medical examinations, psychological tests (e.g., intellectual tests and projective personality tests), and interviews conducted with both the child and the parents.

The specialized training required to conduct a psychodynamic assessment of a child with emotional disorders limits the role of the preschool teacher. However, the teacher may provide observational data regarding the child's academic functioning and social relationships.

COMPREHENSION CHECK 12.14

What kind of information, if any, would be obtained from a psycho-dynamic assessment that would be useful to a preschool teacher?

Sociological

Sociological assessment of emotional disturbance focuses on the environment rather than on the child. It is conducted by a sociologist who studies all aspects of the environment in order to identify those conditions that promote deviant behavior. The health of society is based on an analysis of three areas: society, schools, and the relationship between them. To analyze the society in which an emotionally disturbed preschooler is expected to function, the sociologist identifies the values of the culture and their relative importance, the primary vehicles for socialization, and the agents of social control. To analyze the school, the sociologist identifies the agents of social control, formal/informal social groups within the school and the basis on which they are formed, and methods of transmitting cultural values. To analyze the relationship between school and society, the sociologist identifies racial, ethnic, and socioeconomic groups in the school and compares their proportion with that in the surrounding community. In addition, a sociologist may seek information from the preschool teacher about the child identified as disturbed. The preschool teacher can provide information regarding the child's ethnic subculture, socioeconomic background, and academic potential as compared with the majority of other students in the class.

COMPREHENSION CHECK 12.15

Sociological assessment is nonjudgmental. What other assessment model could be described this way?

Learning

Assessment of an emotional disturbance from the perspective of a learning model lends itself very easily to a preschool setting. It is ideally suited to the preschool teacher who already possesses the skills necessary to define all relevant aspects of the problem, including the target behavior, environment, and the individual.

The first step in the assessment process is the identification of the target behavior. To measure its occurrence accurately, a clear, complete description of the target behavior in observable terms is required. Practitioners are discouraged from using general descriptions of a child's behavior (e.g., unfriendly, inattentive) and to rely instead on terms that are observable and measurable. For example, a behavioral deficit such as poor interpersonal skills that may be targeted for development may state, "When Tom arrives every morning, he will greet his teacher by saying 'Good morning, Mrs. Jones'." Targeted behaviors defined in such a manner are valuable aids to establishing baseline rates of occurrence under conditions that currently exist in the classroom.

After defining the target behavior, the preschool teacher is ready to initiate the second step in the assessment procedure in which all relevant aspects of the environment are described. The teacher should measure how often the behavior occurs, using any one of three observation techniques; these are frequency recording, interval recording, and duration recording.

Frequency recording

The least amount of time is required for frequency recording, and it is often the most useful of the measurement techniques. The frequency of the behavior is recorded by counting each occurrence of the target behavior over a specified period of time. Frequency recording is appropriate when the start and stop time of the event is distinct and the event takes a relatively consistent amount of time.

Interval recording

When the behaviors vary in length or do not have discrete start and stop time (e.g., crying episodes, laughing episodes, discussions), interval recording is appropriate. A long period of time (e.g., 10 minutes) is divided into shorter periods (twenty 30-second intervals). Each of the intervals is scored on the basis of whether the behavior occurred or did not occur.

Duration recording

When the intervention focuses on increasing or decreasing the amount of time the child performs the target behavior, duration recording is appropriate. For example, the staff member may record the amount of time the child spends engaging in self-injurious behavior.

By collecting data using one of these three methods, the teacher will have an indication of the strength of the target behavior under normal environmental conditions. The reader is referred to the HICOMP Curriculum (Willoughby-Herb and Neisworth, 1983) for a comprehensive review of data collection strategies appropriate for handicapped youngsters.

In addition to measuring how often a targeted behavior occurs, the practitioner should consider other relevant aspects of the environment, including antecedent and consequent conditions. Antecedent conditions are those conditions that precede the target behavior and influence the probability of its occurrence. They can either cue an undesirable response, fail to cue a desirable response, or fail to cue an undesirable response. A consequent condition follows a target behavior and influences the probability of its occurrence. Consequences can either strengthen, weaken, or maintain the target behavior. Antecedents and consequences that are believed to maintain or strengthen disruptive behaviors will be identified and removed whereas antecedents and consequences that support positive social behaviors will be intensified.

The third step in assessment according to a learning model is a description of relevant individual characteristics. These characteristics are observed or inferred features of the child that mediate between the target behaviors and the antecedents. For example, if observation indicates that greeting by peers (antecedents) evokes no response (target behavior), the teacher may hypothesize that the child lacks interpersonal skills (individual characteristics).

A description of relevant characteristics also includes an analysis of the child's reinforcement hierarchy, that is, the identification of those consequent events that are satisfying and likely to promote behavior or dissatisfying and likely to suppress behavior. Reinforcing events can be *primary*, satisfying basic biological needs (e.g., food and warmth) or *secondary*, acquiring reinforcing qualities through frequent association with a primary reinforcer (e.g., social praise and money).

Various techniques can be used to assess the strength of potential reinforcers. These include:

1. Asking the child what he or she likes.

2. Observing how the child spends free time.

3. Observing what objects the child plays with.

4. Exposing the child to a variety of potentially enjoyable activities and asking him or her to identify the most pleasant.

Reinforcers should be ranked from least to most natural to the preschool setting. Using the most natural incentives available will enhance the durability of the behavior change.

To summarize, assessment of emotional disturbance within a learning model requires the preschool teacher to clearly define the targeted behavior and identify all relevant environmental and individual characteristics. This information is essential if the teacher is to design an appropriate intervention program.

COMPREHENSION CHECK 12.16

Learning theory requires that standards for assessment be clearly and consisely described. What implication does this have for evaluating the effectiveness of intervention?

Ecological

Because of the reconciliatory nature of the ecological model, assessment of an emotionally disturbed child is conducted through the cooperative efforts of many professionals using techniques appropriate to their settings. One technique is ecological mapping, which is completed by a family therapist. Ecological mapping results in a genogram that charts all the relationships between people who are significant in the child's life. A second technique is the heuristic case report (Cantrell and Cantrell, 1970). Information is gathered about the family, neighborhood, community, school, and classroom. The preschool teacher can contribute to this report by providing a detailed analysis of academic and behavior problems exhibited by the child in the classroom. A third technique was proposed by Kounin (1977) who recommends a detailed analysis of all dimensions of the school setting. Again, the preschool teacher can provide relevant information, including the physical characteristics of the setting, the child's pattern of behavior, and description of where and when activities take place.

After information is gathered by specialists within their respective settings, it is shared and compared. Differences between behavior at home, in the neighborhood, and in school are noted. This information is used to define the exact nature of the problem, target its source, and identify potential intervention procedures.

COMPREHENSION CHECK 12.17

An ecological assessment is a very broad approach requiring input from a wide variety of sources. What is the disadvantage of this approach?

TREATMENT OF SOCIAL AND EMOTIONAL PROBLEMS

As may be apparent from the preceding sections, a professional's orientation to early-childhood emotional disturbances will influence the selection of intervention procedures. Persons viewing the disturbance as a biochemical imbalance would suggest the use of medication, diet, or vitamin therapy. Those speculating that the child's behavior is a result of faulty learning environments would ensure that reinforcement is consistently available for prosocial behavior. Professionals emphasizing the role of the family, school, church, and community in originating and perpetuating the disturbance would seek to create change in these social systems. Each of the five major models of emotional disturbances propose complimentary, and sometimes contradictory, treatments. This section will review strategies associated with each of these orientations. Emphasis will be placed on strategies that may be implemented by teachers and parents.

Biophysical interventions

The biophysical model assumes that emotional disturbances results from physical disease, disorder, or dysfunction. Consequently, treatment involves altering the presumed internal pathology. Because biophysical interventions typically involves medical management, they are of limited value to direct-service providers. The major role of educators within this orientation is to monitor or assist in carrying out the biophysical intervention plan. The two prominent responsibilities are to monitor medications and to assist the child in following a prescribed diet.

Monitoring medications

Two types of drugs influence the behavior of emotionally disturbed children. The first are anticonvulsants, such as Dilantin. These have been traditionally used to control seizure disorders. The second are psychotropic drugs such as stimulants (e.g., Ritalin and Cylert), tranquilizers (e.g., Mellaril and Valium), and antidepressants (e.g., Tofranil). The use of these medications, particularly the psychotropics, is extremely controversial. Opponents cite negative side effects and limited long-term effectiveness as major reasons for avoiding the use of these chemical agents. To offset these problems, teachers must be alert to monitor and report behavior changes that may be associated with the drugs. As emphasized by Sleator and Sprague (1978), "We recommend strongly that monitoring of drug effects must include reports from the teacher if the physician hopes to effectively treat school children" (p. 579).

Assist with a diet

As is so far drug treatments, diet therapy is highly controversial. Despite the lack of evidence supporting the effectiveness of special diets, many parents have joined the bandwagon and implemented a restrictive diet with their child. It may be the teacher's responsibility to follow through with the diet in school. A variety of diets exist, ranging in complexity from the elimination of nonnutritional foods (e.g., caffeine and sugar) to highly specialized diets involving the removal of specific food additives. Therefore, it is important that the teacher recognize and comply with specific dietary recommendations established by the physician.

COMPREHENSION CHECK 12.18

Does the biophysical model provide intervention techniques for handling the crises that arise in the classroom every day?

Psychodynamic

Treatment within the psychodynamic model emphasizes hypothetical cognitive processes such as insight, awareness, and transference. Psychodynamic interventions typically involve the development of these processes in an effort to resolve internal conflict. In the purest form, psychoanalysis and insight therapies are reserved for specially trained therapists—typically psychologists or psychiatrists and sometimes counselors and social workers. Other psychodynamic therapies are often practiced by teachers. These will be discussed briefly.

Reflective listening

This strategy involves reflecting or restating the child's vocal expressions in a nonjudgmental manner. A teacher may say, for example, "You are saying that . . . ," "It really makes you mad when . . .," or "It sounds like you are happy with . . ." These reflective statements are intended to assist the child in clarifying his or her vocal message, thereby gaining insight into the related emotions.

Play therapy

Very young children are often unable to vocalize their underlying feelings. These feelings, however, are frequently reflected in their play behavior. Consequently, play therapy may use "fantasy" or "make believe" situations to work through internal conflict.

Life-space interviewing

This strategy, developed by Redl (1959), involves providing counseling in situations associated with emotional conflict. Life-space interviewing assists the child to work on long-term social-personal goals while encouraging an emphathetic teacher-child relationship.

COMPREHENSION CHECK 12.19

Psychodynamic approaches are often difficult to put into effect and clearly define. What implication does this have for demonstrating their impact on a child?

Sociological

Proponents of the sociological model emphasize the role of social systems in creating and maintaining emotional disturbance. Consequently, intervention within this perspective involves altering the social context of this disorder. Typical strategies include:

Involvement in the political process

Legislation and litigation is the basis for a number of our social policies. Although legislation and litigation do not ensure social acceptance and elimination of artificial barriers, they do force open the door of opportunity. President Johnson's War on Poverty making Head Start programs available for disadvantaged and handicapped children is one example of the value of political action.

Deemphasizing pejorative labels

As was discussed previously in this chapter, many sociologists believe that exceptional labels perpetuate emotional disorders. Teachers and administrators who advocate noncategorical programs seek to eliminate labels as a contributor to deviance.

Recognizing cultural uniqueness

Differences between a child's home culture and the dominate culture may be a major source of conflict resulting in emotional disorders. Teachers who recognize and accept cultural diversity help minimize this effect.

Modifying the learning environment

Many sociologists define emotional disturbance as a mismatch between social rules in the classroom and the adaptive capacity of the youngster. They recommend modifying the structure of the classroom to correspond with the child's characteristics.

COMPREHENSION CHECK 12.20

How functional are sociological intervention strategies for the preschool teacher?

Learning theory

The learning theory model, including operant, respondent, and modeling paradigms, offers the widest range of interventions. This model emphasizes that all persons involved with the child are in a position to teach and reinforce prosocial behavior. Therefore, treatment strategies are typically focused at enhancing the behavior-management skills of persons in the child's natural environment. Many commercial programs with a learning theory foundation are available to practitioners interested in promoting appropriate social and emotional development in preschool children. They include the Adaptive Behavior Curriculum (Popovitch and Latham, 1981), the Carolina Curriculum for Handicapped Infants (Johnson, Jens, and Attermeier, 1979), Facilitating Children's Development (Meir and Malone, 1979), and the HICOMP Curriculum (Willoughby-Herb and Neisworth, 1983). All present objectives for socioemotional development and methods for teaching that are based on learning theory. These methods will be reviewed in the following subsections.

Training social skills

It is not uncommon among preschoolers for withdrawn or isolated behavior to occur because of deficiencies in social skills. Often, children first entering preschool have had limited opportunities to interact with other young children. They have not had to share toys, take turns, compromise on which games are played, or communicate with individuals other than parents.

Occasionally, a child may lack these skills because physical or other impairments minimize opportunities to practice and develop them. A child with limited motor capabilities, for example, may not be able to manipulate toys or participate in movement games. A communication dysfunction may discourage a child from participating in fantasy games or expressing preferences. Although opportunities for normal interactions might have existed in the environment, it is likely that the child was not able to adapt his responses to participate effectively in social interactions. In these cases, intervention should focus on helping the child to overcome his deficiencies through a social skills training.

1. *Contingent reinforcement of social skills.* The training of any new skill requires the *reinforcement of closer and closer approximations of a response.* Desirable social responses that teachers and parents will want to reinforce include watching peers, eye contact with peers, moving closer to other children, offering toys, and speaking to peers using simple words such as "Thank you," "Hi," and "Bye-bye."

2. *Manipulating the consequences.* Careful application of reinforcement and punishment strategies can reduce obnoxious, annoying, and bizarre behaviors that deter normal social interactions.

3. *Changing the environment.* Simple modifications, such as changing seating arrangements or free play groups, can do much encourage desirable social behavior. One example is to rearrange squares at circle time so that a "withdrawn" child sits between two outgoing peers who are likely to encourage social interaction.

4. *Modeling.* Simply demonstrating the expected behavior is perhaps the easiest teaching strategy used to promote acquisition of new skills. Perhaps modeling may be an effective method for teaching appropriate interaction with toys.

Reducing excessive responses

A number of behavioral strategies can be used to reduce behaviors and establish more appropriate responses. The most effective ones combine positive reinforcement for appropriate behavior and punishment for specific aggressive responses. Response cost, overcorrection, and time-out are some of the approaches that can be used effectively with preschool children.

1. *Response cost.* This strategy involves the removal of some stimulus (e.g., a toy truck) contingent upon a specific aggressive response (e.g., throwing the truck). Simple response cost programs can use basic rules such as "When we hit, we lose our toys" to communicate contingencies to young children. Response cost programs can also involve more elaborate reinforcement systems such as token economies (e.g., throwing a toy truck results in the loss of a plastic chip; see, e.g., Spates, Alessi, Gutmann, Ellsworth, Mueller, and Ulrich, 1974).

2. *Overcorrection.* This procedure involves two components: restitution and positive practice (Foxx and Azrin, 1972). Restitution involves repairing the consequences of the inappropriate response. If a child kicks over a stack of books, for example, restitution would involve picking up all the books and rearranging them neatly on the bookshelf. Positive practice involves extensive repetition or practice of some "extremely appropriate" behavior. In the example above, the child would be required to "practice" picking up *all* the toys in the classroom (not just the ones he knocked over).

3. *Time-out.* Time-out procedures involves removing the student's opportunity to earn reinforcers for a specified duration. For example, as soon as aggressive behavior occurs, the teacher presents a signal that the child has lost access to reinforcement for a specific amount of time. Although the teacher can use signals, such as placing an "x" on the blackboard or setting a 2-minute timer, removal of the child from the setting for a brief isolation period is the procedure most often used.

4. *Extinction.* Extinction refers to withholding a consequence that previously followed a response. For example, crying may be reinforced if the teacher always attends to a tearful preschooler whose mother has just left. The teacher may reduce crying in this situation by no longer attending to the child until crying has stopped.

5. *Differential reinforcement of other behavior.* This procedure, referred to as DRO, involves the systematic reinforcement of behaviors other than the inappropriate behavior. For example, the child is reinforced only when he/she is *not* engaging in self-injurious behavior. The effect of DRO is to increase the frequency of nonself-injurious behaviors and reduce or eliminate the self-injury: The increase in "other" behaviors is said to "displace" the inappropriate responses (Kazdin, 1980). Spates et al. (1974) used DRO to reduce tantrum behavior in preschool children.

Application of aversive stimuli

One of the most controversial topics related to the use of behavior modifications centers on the application of aversive stimulation. Aversive stimuli may include verbal reprimands, mild taps, aromatic ammonia, or lemon juice. Ethical considerations in using painful stimuli to suppress inappropriate behavior have resulted in restrictions in the application of this procedure, particularly in the public schools. Teachers should be aware that punishment usually results in a number of undesirable side effects, including emotional outbursts, generalized response suppression, and avoidance of the situation in which it is administered (Kazdin, 1980). Aversive stimulation should be considered only when all other alternatives have been exhausted (Ross, 1981) and implemented only after careful planning based on empirically founded guidelines.

Social-learning packages

The preceding sections discussed potentially isolated intervention strategies; however, it is likely that parents and teachers will combine several social learning tactics. A combination of procedures, for example, may (1) teach a new response, (2) motivate the student to engage in the response at an acceptable rate, (3) reduce incompatible negative responses, and (4) alter the child's emotional reactions to the loss of the negative response. As may be apparent, reinforcement, punishment, and respondent conditioning elements must be present to achieve all these goals. Table 12.1 presents a par-

TABLE 12.1
Example of a social learning package

1. At bedtime, a doll, pacifier, and raisin were taken into the bedroom with the child.
2. The parents placed the pacifier's ring around the dolls arm and gave the doll to the child saying, "See the doll? It's time for her to go night-night."
3. The parents asked the doll if she wanted the pacifier, and indicated that the doll said no. The parents then removed the pacifier while placing a raisin next to the dolls mouth. The parents then told the doll that it could go to sleep and placed it in the child's bed.
4. The preceding procedures were repeated from three to five times. The child was encouraged to handle the doll as the parents spoke. Also, the parents encouraged the child to hug the doll when it went to bed without the pacifier.
5. Next, the child was offered the pacifier. The child was socially reinforced and given a raisin if she refused the pacifier.

Source: Schloss, P. J., and Johann M. (1982). A modeling and contigency management approach to pacifier withdrawal. *Behavior Therapy, 13:*254–257.

ticularly novel example from the early-childhood literature that incorporated such a treatment package.

COMPREHENSION CHECK 12.21

Explain this sentence: "Techniques suggested by a learning model will eventually evolve themselves out of usefulness."

Ecological

By its very nature, ecological interventions borrow heavily from each of the other intervention models. As discussed earlier, ecologists attribute emotional problems to a mismatch between the child and his·or her environment. Consequently, intervention approaches focus both on the child's characteristics and the social system. Depending on the precise nature of the problem, an ecologist may implement strategies designed to (1) alter physical/medical factors associated with the disorder, (2) alter the child's personality dynamics, (3) teach and reinforce prosocial behaviors, or (4) alter the social context in which the deviant behavior occurs.

The most widely recognized example of the ecological model is the Re Ed project (Hobbs, 1966). Within this model, a child is removed from the esosystem in which he/she is experiencing difficulty. Advocates of the model emphasize that removal is necessitated by the need to work with the child and social system independently before the two are reunited. Once the child is removed, social workers work in the school and/or home setting to adapt these environments to the child's characteristics. Similarly, mental health counselors, teachers, and others work with the child to assist him/her in developing characteristics that will facilitate the transition back to the original environments. Once the school, child, home, and other participants are reeducated, the child is gradually reintegrated.

COMPREHENSION CHECK 12.22

An ecological intervention depends on techniques derived from other models. How can this be an advantage? A disadvantage?

MODELS FOR SERVICE DELIVERY

A number of models for service delivery have been proposed to meet the unique demands of youngsters with social and emotional disturbances. They include preschool programs with a home-based approach, a center-based approach, a combination approach, day-care centers, and day-care homes. Placement in a setting should reflect the results of an in-depth assessment of the child's needs and the goals of intervention.

Home-based

The majority of preschool emotionally disturbed children are cared for in their homes by their parents. Therefore, a home-based delivery system focuses on training parents how to manage their child's behavior and manipulate the environment to maximize learning. For example, the Portage Model, one of the most widely used programs, trains parents to assess their child's behavior repertoire, target skills that need to be developed or modified, and effect changes through the use of behavior management and teaching strategies. "Home teachers" visit the homes for 90 minutes each week to train parents and help them develop the skills needed to manage their children (Shearer and Shearer, 1976). Kelly identified advantages of home-based programs including a more comfortable environment, more natural child behavior, better protection of the child's health, less disruption of parent and child routines, inclusion of other family members, regularly scheduled sessions, and training in the natural environment.

Center-based

Center-based programs are typically for older preschool children and associated with hospitals or child-guidance clinics. Although emotionally disturbed children receive intervention in a center, parents are strongly encouraged to participate actively in the activities as teacher aides or therapy assistants. This participation provides parents with the opportunity to acquire new skills to be used during follow-up activities conducted at home. In addition, center-based personnel schedule meetings with parents in which they share information, give support, and provide training in behavior-management techniques and other specific procedures for developing or modifying the child's behaviors. Additional advantages include the opportunity to share experiences with other parents, the opportunity for the child to be stimulated by other children, and reduced costs (Kelly, 1980).

Home- and center-based

The third approach affords the advantages of the previous two models by combining center-based activities with home visiting. During a home visit, the practitioner can observe the child in his/her natural environment, identify issues central to intervention, and enlist the support of family members to make necessary modifications. The practitioner is also better able to offer more personalized and private support to family members of an emotionally disturbed child. Center-based activities provide the child with high-quality specialized services and the opportunity to interact with peers. Classroom activities are complemented by follow-up activities conducted in the home.

Day-care centers

Many handicapped preschoolers are enrolled in traditional day-care centers where little or no modifications have been made in the curriculum or instructional strategies. These day-care centers offer a major advantage to emotionally disturbed preschoolers. They are provided with the opportunity to associate with nonhandicapped peers.

Day-care Homes

Many emotionally disturbed preschoolers receive day care in other private homes while their parents are at work. A new demonstration project may enhance the way in which handicapped preschoolers are served in this setting. Project Neighborcare, which is associated with The Pennsylvania State University, is training day-care providers to deal with handicapped preschoolers. Its purpose is to develop innovative methods to enhance the level and quality of day-care services currently available to special-needs preschoolers. Parent participation is encouraged by including parents in the development of individualized education plans for both the child and themselves.

Segregated preschool programs

A special program specifically designed for emotionally disturbed preschoolers offers many advantages over less restrictive placements. The segregation of a class allows the teacher to develop a more controlled, therapeutic environment that addresses the needs of the students. Classes for handicapped preschoolers are smaller, allowing the teacher to provide more attention to each child. Adult contact is further maximized by the presence of an aide. Finally, curriculum can be modified and intervention techniques selected to enhance the development of cognitive skills, verbal communication, self-help, and social skills. Day-care centers for handicapped youngsters have been described in detail by Cataldo and Risley (1974), who address environmental considerations, and Spates et al. (1974), who address program objectives and instructional procedures.

COMPREHENSION CHECK 12.23

Arrange the models for service delivery just presented on a continuum from least to most restrictive.

SUMMARY

This chapter described seven classes of emotional disorders that constitute a continuum from mild to severe disturbances: social isolation/withdrawal, hyperactivity, fears and phobias, aggression, noncompliance, somatic disorders, and autism. Impact of each of these disorders in the family was described. The family of an emotionally disturbed child is frequently the focal point of efforts to identify a cause. Practitioners are advised to avoid assigning blame and to assist family members in developing constructive methods of confronting the problems posed by an emotionally disturbed child.

The impact of emotional disturbance on other areas of the child's development was also discussed. It is presumed that emotional disturbance interferes with development of intellectual, academic, social, communication, and motor skills. In addition, the degree to which any one of thesee areas is effected is a function of the degree of emotional disturbance. Two other issues must be considered. First, there is no clear documentation of the impact of emotional disturbance on other domains. Second, the fact that a problem exists within one domain does not necessarily indicate a problem exists within another. Therefore, the practitioner is cautioned against making global assumptions regarding the characteristics of an emotionally disturbed child.

This chapter also described five major theoretical positions regarding causes of emotional disturbances as well corresponding assessment techniques and intervention strategies. The biophysical model emphasizes individual factors related to genetics, neurological influences, nutrition, and biochemistry. Assessment and intervention are conducted by medical personnel with teacher participation limited to monitoring and reporting classroom behaviors. The psychodynamic model links emotional disturbance to internal personality dynamics. Assessment and intervention are supervised by a specially trained therapist. In the sociological model, emotional disturbance is viewed as the result of a conflict between the child's behavior and social norms. The practitioner can contribute to the assessment process by providing the sociologist with information concerning the child's subculture, socioeconomic status, and academic potential. Intervention focuses on changing both the child and the environment.

Proponents of the learning model believe all behavior is learned, whether it is normal or abnormal. Assessment can be conducted by the preschool teacher and involves a description of the target behavior, including its antecedents and consequences, as well as a description of the individual child. Intervention is also managed by the teacher, and involves the systematic arrangement of environmental events to change behavior. Finally, the ecological model is an attempt to reconcile major orientations by describing emotional disturbance is terms of the interrelationship between the child and the environment. The practitioner contributes to the assessment by providing information regarding the school environment. Intervention focuses on both the child's characteristics and the social system.

Finally, this chapter described models for service delivery that comprise a continuum of services from least to most restrictive: home-based, center-based, and home- and center-based preschools, day-care centers, home day-care providers and segregated preschool programs.

Practitioners concerned with the education and treatment of emotionally disturbed preschoolers have no doubt recognized the variety of disturbed behavior as well as suspected causes and possible treatments. Such diversity may be confusing. Practitioners are advised to keep abreast of new developments in this field in order to better serve the emotionally disturbed preschool child in applied settings.

SUGGESTED READINGS

Apter, S. J., and Conoley, J. C. (1984). *Childhood behavior disorders and emotional disturbance.* Englewood Cliffs, NJ: Prentice-Hall.

Brooks-Gunn, J., and Lewis, M. (1981). Assessing young handicapped children: Issues and solutions. *Journal of the Division for Early Childhood* 2:87–94.

Garwood, S. G., and Fewell, R. R. (1983). *Educating handicapped infants.* Rockville, MD: Aspen Systems.

Gotts, E. E. (1979). Early childhood assessment. In D. A. Sabatino and T. L. Miller (Eds.). *Describing learner characteristics of handicapped children and youth.* New York: Grune & Stratton.

Hanson, M. J. (1984). *Atypical infant development.* Baltimore: University Park Press.

Sroufe, L. A. (1979). Socio-emotional development. In J. Osofsky (Ed.). *Handbook of infant development.* New York: Wiley.

Developmental Differences in Vision

Verna Hart

CHAPTER OUTLINE

John was a good baby, content to lie quietly in his crib, cooing. His mother noticed things, however, which began to worry her. John often startled and sometimes cried when she touched him. He did not turn to look at her when she spoke to him or came near, he did not reach out to touch a toy if she held it in front of him, and he did not seem to follow people with his eyes as they moved around him. He did not seem interested. John seemed content to coo and gurgle to himself but did not especially seem to enjoy such "talking" face to face with someone else. John's mother became convinced that her baby did not like her. He did not seem happy to see her. She knew her sister's baby always smiled and cooed when he saw his mother. What was wrong?

John's parents expressed their worries to a friend who worked at a local day-care center. The friend asked her supervisor about John, describing the parents' concern. Now the friend was convinced that all was not as it should be with John. She urged the parents to take him to a pediatrician for a thorough examination.

After their appointment at the clinic, they found that, although John was a healthy baby in all respects, his vision was extremely impaired. The exact extent of the impairment could not be judged until John was older.

Now John's parents are receiving help from a home visitor who has had special training in working with blind children. The visitor has shown the parents how to read the baby's cues and has helped them to know how to interact with John to help him "make sense" of his environment.

How many times have we been told that if we keep reading in dim light we will ruin our eyes or that we will go blind if we keep using our eyes hour after hour? These are common misconceptions that have existed for many years. At one time, even physicians and optometrists believed that if a child already had a visual impairment, using the eyes extensively would lead to blindness. In fact, the "sight saving" classes and schools of the past were built on this idea and were dedicated to saving what little vision those children had.

Late in the 1950s, it became clear that the use of vision would not result in total blindness. Ophthalmologists began to assure their young patients and their parents that it was all right to use their eyes as much as they wanted. Children with a low amount of vision would not harm their eyes by using them. In the early 1960s, a study (Barraga, 1964) showed that students could not only use their eyes, but many of those who previously had been trained to use braille as their manner of reading could be trained, through carefully sequenced steps, to use their eyes to read print. Some of the children had to use enlarged print to read while other children learned to read regular print. Since that time, children have been encouraged to use their eyes to read print, if possible. Modern technology, with the introduction of various types of reading magnifiers and other devices, has promoted this use of printed materials.

When we think about children who have visual impairments, their ability or inability to read regular print is not the only factor that must be considered. About 80% of learning takes place through the visual modality, and much cognitive development will be affected if there is defective input into that system. An inability to see the clouds, for example, means that all references to them will have to be explained. If we fail to see particular clouds, we may be unaware of an approaching storm or the glory of a coming sunset.

If we are unable to see well enough to imitate the actions of others, much of our incidental learning, that learning which does not have to be specifically taught, fails to occur. Because they fail to see people moving around them, totally blind babies often do not learn to creep unless specifically taught. The volume of voice we use, for example, is usually monitored by the manner in which others look at us. At parties we learn which behavior is considered "proper" by observing how others are behaving. Blind children lack ability for this type of learning. Visual impairment at an early age can limit and distort cognitive, motor, and social development.

DEFINITION AND DESCRIPTION OF THE PROBLEM

The use of the word "blind" may create misunderstandings, for a common myth is that blind children see nothing but blackness. In truth, about 80% have usable but defective vision. By learning to use efficiently the vision they have, these children can become more aware of their environments. They can have more accurate perceptions of the world around them and base their resulting ideas on concepts that are closer to reality.

The legal definitions for visual impairments are as follows: *legal blindness* is visual acuity of 20/200 or less in the better eye after the best possible correction with glasses or contact lenses; *partially sighted* is visual acuity of between 20/70 and 20/200 in the better eye after maximum correction.

There are many variations among children who have been labeled as *visually impaired*. There also are different conditions resulting in determination of a person as legally blind. Because the normal eye sees at 20 feet what it should see at 20 feet, it is stated that those who see normally have 20/20 vision. In comparison, the visually impaired person who has 20/200 does not see at 20 feet what the normal person sees at 20 feet. The visually impaired person sees at 20 feet what the nonimpaired person is able to see from 200 feet away.

The amount of remaining vision may vary from legal blindness, 20/200, to total blindness. Some children may be unable to distinguish form but may be able to identify objects by their color. However, these children may lack enough vision to determine particulars about the objects. Other children will have only enough vision to tell if something is moving in front of them. Even this amount of vision is useful, because the ability to see people moving can help the individual maneuver in the environment. Other children may only be able to tell the difference between light and dark. Although this amount of vision is not usually of much help in reading, it can be of great help in becoming familiar with the environment. Such things as open doors with light streaming out can be particularly helpful in assisting mobility. The amount of vision among those who are labeled legally blind varies considerably. Even a small amount of vision, however, can be used to aid these children in their education.

Because not all vision problems have to do with distance vision, there is another definition applied to legally blind individuals. Sometimes the vision is 20/20 in ability to see but the *field of vision may be restricted,* even after the best correction. These children may see only through the center of the eye. The picture they receive is small and only a part of the total—such as we might see when looking through a paper towel tube. Others may be able to see only the outer edges of what is viewed and miss the central part completely or have blurred vision. Because of a restricted field of vision, the ability to see only a part of a word or a single word when reading, or the necessity of moving the head back and forth and up and down when looking to see if a car is coming, is handicapping. Therefore, if the angle of vision is less than 20°, an individual is considered to be blind.

COMPREHENSION CHECK 13.1

Explain the difference between 20/20 and 20/200 vision. State which vision is considered normal.
Explain what is meant by "tube" or "tunnel" vision. How does this contribute to visual impairment?

IMPACT ON THE FAMILY

Visual impairments have the lowest incidence among the handicapping conditions. It is difficult to define or characterize those who have such handicaps because, even though it is a small population when compared with mental retardation, speech or learning disabilities, physically handicapped, emotionally disturbed, and deaf, it is not a homogeneous group. This heterogeneous group varies in the degree of remaining vision, the cause of the visual problems, the age of onset of the handicap, and the presence or absence of multiple handicapping conditions. Therefore, the impact on the family varies greatly with each particular case. At the preschool level, visual impairment is usually not casually detected unless it is severe.

Of particular importance is the family attitude toward a visual impairment. The mother who continues to call her 4-year-old son "My blind baby" instead of using his name, is telling us a great deal about how she feels. Families may believe that a visual loss is so handicapping that they must do everything for their children, even though those children are capable of doing much independently. Such treatment can affect the children's attitude toward themselves and toward the world in general. Many handicapped children with "the world owes me a living" attitude had this notion instilled in them during the preschool years. Other children who were expected to perform despite their handicaps have become productive, thoughtful, and competent individuals.

Accidents are a major cause of blindness; if the child or someone else has been careless or disobedient, this fact may be something that the child will always live with and blindness the price paid. Parents may look on accidental factors differently than they view the results of genetic problems. If both parents are blind, or if they are familiar with blindness in the family and are adjusted to it, they will react differently. Parents who are familiar with blindness will deal with their children's lack of vision in a much different manner than will sighted parents.

IMPACT ON THE CHILD'S DEVELOPMENT

Children who are visually handicapped suffer from conceptual and experiential deprivation. From infancy on, they have fewer perceptual experiences on which to base their ideas. Because so much of our learning is gained through vision, and so much is incidental in nature, children who have an inaccurate perception of the world will suffer. For these reasons, it is extremely important to have good preschool experiences. No group of children has a greater need for a good preschool teacher. Blind children can too easily become socially isolated, but a good teaching and learning environment can considerably influence whether the children will become contributing members of adult society.

The nature and degree of the visual impairment, as well as the age of onset and the severity of impairment, affect the functioning of the child. If the onset is sudden and the child previously had vision, the impact on the child will be much greater than if the child were born with the problem or if the condition had a gradual onset. The cause of the impairment can also affect the performance and attitude of the child. If the condition is caused by an uncontrolled glaucoma, a pressure within the eye, the relief from pain resulting from the removal of the eye may be so welcome that the trauma resulting from the loss of vision is small in comparison.

Blindness directly inhibits young children's learning in feedback from the environment, relationships with others, and mobility (Lowenfeld, 1971). Conceptual development is also often delayed or distorted. These problems are present from birth when the child is born blind.

COMPREHENSION CHECK 13.2

Describe how the development of visually impaired children is shaped largely by the interaction with parents during early childhood.

Feedback and socialization

Blind babies do not look at their mothers' faces, gaze at objects, or visually follow activities around them. They substitute sound for what they cannot see. Blind babies do not wiggle in anticipation when their caretakers approach to pick them up. Instead, they are quiet. A mother who has been reinforced by wiggling anticipation of her earlier baby is often concerned and sometimes upset because her baby is not responsive. She comes to believe that her child does not like her. Often such mothers are not aware that their babies must have some type of warning before they are picked up. When the babies are approached noiselessly and picked up, they set off a startle response and often cry. All these factors contribute to the mother's belief that her baby does not like her. Such infants are often content to lie still, perhaps listening to what goes on around them. They are content when not bothered by others. Mothers, in response to this behavior, often label their children as "good babies" and do little to intervene in their lives. Consequently, mother-infant emotional bonding may be affected. When a preschool teacher enters such a situation and begins to intrude on the solitude that the babies have come to expect, there may be frequent cries and temper tantrums from the little ones. It is important to explain what is happening to the parents. Without support at this critical time, parents may refuse to work with their children and will leave them alone. But, leaving them alone tends to perpetuate the problem and ensures that when someone does interfere with their solitude, there will be tantrums.

Blind children are cut off from much of their environment. If there is no intervention, their social development can suffer. Blind babies are not as able as their sighted peers to observe the effects of their behavior. Such children become demanding, and parents can be easily manipulated into a situation where their world centers on their children. These children command and the world is brought to them. They do not reach out to explore it as do seeing infants and toddlers. There is little opportunity for such children to test and refine their perceptions of the environment. Parental fear that their children might get hurt often adds to the problem. Thus, these children often become passive. Parents reinforce a passivity by making few demands on them.

Because much of our social learning is imitative in nature, there can be serious shortcomings in social development without early and appropriate intervention. These children do not have the opportunity to observe the social behavior of their peers and so have no models to copy. Blind children are unable to see the expressions on the faces of their peers in order to read responses of happiness, surprise, anger, or fear. Unless those feelings are interpreted for them, or they learn to interpret such feelings from voices, they may be self-centered and have inappropriate social skills.

COMPREHENSION CHECK 13.3

With reference to behavior, demonstrate how the parent-infant relationship is different if the child is visually impaired.

Outline the sequence of events that leaves the mother with a negative feeling toward her visually impaired infant.

Discuss the contribution of social learning in the development of sociomotional behavior. How does this apply to visually handicapped children?

Mobility

Several factors associated with poor vision can contribute to problems in mobility for the young child. Objects in the environment are not visually enticing, thus reducing encouragement to explore and move about. Furthermore, bumps and bruises encountered will punish mobility efforts. Another aspect of infantile blindness is significant: Such babies are often kept on their backs *(supine position)* in order to tend to their various needs. The development of head balance and control, however, is attained when the infant is in the *prone* (on stomach) *position.* When head control is delayed, general coordination may suffer. The prone position also aids in developing the muscles in the shoulder girdle concerned with reaching; such infants may fail to reach out to their surroundings. Early intervention can prevent such lags and allow earlier interaction between the child and the environment.

Early intervention can aid these children to develop their balance, which, in turn, helps them attain skills in reaching and walking. Such attention can assist children to creep. Without someone there to help them learn this skill, blind children frequently skip this step. Without assistance, parents have the tendency to put the children on their feet and teach them to walk rather than to creep. Creeping assists the development of reciprocal movements and rotation of the pelvic area, therefore creeping can aid these children in developing a more normal walk.

The development of a normal walk is important, for the loss of vision removes most of the cues that help us to attain normal movement. By seeing others walk, we want to walk, too. We want to interact and to move near to those we like. When normally sighted people begin to walk, they can see how far they are from the ground. Visual reference points assist us to right our bodies. Vision helps us to know when our heads are tilted. Blind children cannot do these things. They may be quite timid in their walking. They usually broaden their base of support so they will not fall, much like a baby walks with a broad base of support to maintain its balance. Blind children often shuffle with their feet, for their feet provide a major contact with their environment. They fear "stepping off into space." They also fear bumping into something and getting hurt. There is, therefore, a tendency on the part of blind children to protect their faces. We can see how natural all these actions are if we close our eyes and try to move around.

Because most blind children do not have cues early in life to get them to lift their heads, their early balance of the head is frequently learned with the head tilted down. When they attain sitting balance, it is frequently with this head down position. The head down position continues into attainment of walking balance. Therefore, it is important to help these children in infancy to attain head balance with a head up position. If proper help is not given early, the orientation and mobility instructors, who enter the children's lives at a later period, will have to assist the children to relearn all of their postural balance and reactions. By preventing the abnormal head balance while the children are infants, much can be done to assure normal adult posture.

COMPREHENSION CHECK 13.4

Why is the acquisition of head control delayed in some visually inpaired children?

Poor mobility and thus exploration of the environment contributes to a lack of information about the world. Blind children must be prompted to reach out and explore while still infants. They must be encouraged to move around in their environments. Parents must be advised to help their children to move about and to take them places. And above all, parents must accept the fact that their children, because of their blindness, will suffer frequent bumps and bruises. However, parents can do much to make home and yard safer and less conducive to falls. Only after parents accept that fact will they be able to encourage their children to brave such bumps and bruises as a part of life without making a great deal out of it.

Blind children's ability to reach out and grasp things is also affected by the lack of vision. Combined with the lack of development of the shoulder girdle is the lack of ability to know that there are things to reach out to. The children need to have many things touch their bodies, particularly their hands, so that they can learn about the objects by touching them. Once children have established a favorite toy, that toy can be used to develop searching and identifying abilities. Such activities can also help the children establish the hands-to-midline position. Lack of this ability has been noted by educators of young visually handicapped children as a weakness in their students. By varying the positions from which a familiar objects is handled to the children, they can be stimulated to explore the space around them. By widening the circle in which this activity is carried out, these children can be encouraged to bring their hands to midline and then to cross the midline.

Even with good tactual skills, touch does not permit the same perceptions that vision allows. The wholeness or visual integration is missing. Children could explore, foot by foot, the outside of the house in which they live and still be unable to integrate that information into a meaningful whole.

Concept formation

The concept of *object permanence* causes difficulty for young visually impaired children. For these children to have an understanding of the permanence of an object, they must know that an object exists even though that object can be neither seen nor heard. This concept is an important one for blind children to attain. The idea that things exist "out there" is an essential one—because all their learning is based on what they cannot see. Many objects make no noise (clouds, towels, milk) and others are not tactually available (roofs, treetops, flying kites). Object permanence is a crucial conceptual ability to develop.

One characteristic attributed to blind children is that of *verbalism*. Verbalisms result when children are taught words but have little experience on which to base the concepts concerning the meaning of those words. Two examples illustrate this point. One preschool teacher introduced her lesson with the question, "How many of you boys and girls help your mothers to cook?" One totally blind child, who did nothing for herself and even had difficulty finding her way around the classroom after months of daily attendance, raised her hand. The teacher continued, "How many of you help your mothers clean?" The child raised her hand. "And how many of you help your mothers do the laundry?" Again the hand went up. "How about ironing? How many of you help your mother iron your clothes?" Her hand was the only one that was raised, but she waved it vigorously, stating, "I do! I do it all the time." Knowing she could not possibly have done all the things that she had just indicated, the teacher questioned the girl's mother when she came to pick her up. The mother indicated that whenever she had a lot of work to do, she asked her daughter if she would like to help her cook, clean, iron, or whatever the particular task was. When the girl answered that she would like to help, the mother told her that she could help by sitting in a chair and staying there until the work was finished! Because she never saw the mother doing the tasks, the daughter thought she was helping and really believed she could do all the things that were mentioned by the teacher.

A second example: A gifted blind preschooler was talking with his teacher before coming into the school building. Wondering if his precocious vocabulary had firm concepts behind it, the teacher asked the child if he knew what a tree looked like. He responded that he did and asked the teacher if she meant evergreen or deciduous. When the teacher said she meant deciduous, the student went on to say that a tree was big. It had green leaves that changed color in the fall and then fell off. And trees had black, rough trunks at the bottom. While he was describing the tree, the teacher gently steered him into a small deciduous tree. She apologized for bumping him into something and then asked if he could identify what he had touched. She pulled the leaves down so that he could feel them and let him tactually explore all around the tree. She helped him feel where the roots were protruding from the ground. The youngster finally gave up, saying he had no idea what they were examining.

These are good examples of verbalisms that blind children sometimes have. The words are a part of their vocabularies by not a part of their concepts. Without good practical experiences as well as lots of directions, questions, and verbal descriptions, these children attain words and integrate them so that they really believe they know what they are talking about. Verbalisms may be a result of poor teaching. Thus, any type of service-delivery system must have good teaching as its basis.

People who have worked long with the visually impaired population have learned about their mannerisms, or *"blindisms."* These mannerisms include such things as rocking, eye poking, and finger flicking. Several theories have been advanced to explain these behaviors. One theory is that the mannerisms are developmental stages through which all children move. Visually impaired children seem to be "stuck" at one or more of those developmental levels. (An older and more Freudian theory is based on an abnormal mother-child relationship.) Another belief is that these children are lacking stimulation from their environments and these mannerisms are their attempts to provide that stimulation. Still others believe mannerisms are learned behaviors that occur because of a nonstructured environment.

There are other theories, but the theories are not as important as the knowledge that there are few normal mannerisms in children that have had early and effective intervention. The best way to deal with mannerisms is to prevent them from occurring; establishing things that the children like to do and keeping them busy carrying out those tasks. If hands and body are busy doing things, they cannot at the same time be involved in self-stimulatory behavior.

Dealing with mannerisms that have already been established is a different matter. Often the behavior has become so habitual the child is not aware of it. Merely bringing the mannerism to the child's attention and then reminding when we see the behavior occurring is all some children need. Children who are less aware of their environment are not as easily broken of these habits. All types of behavior management have been tried to eliminate blindisms. The most effective techniques seem to be those that involve teaching skills that the child finds rewarding that are incompatible with the mannerisms. Whatever their cause, it is clear that parents and children must avoid encouraging blindisms. Paying attention to them strengthens them and makes them useful to the child. Caregivers must be advised to put such behavior "on extinction" and, instead, reward more developmentally constructive behavior (differential reinforcement). This can involve reinforcing a response that competes with the behavior that you want to eliminate or reduce. For example, a child will not concurrently poke his eyes with his hands and play appropriately with toys.

Correcting blindisms at the preschool level is important because such behaviors make the children who have them appear different from their peers and thus less likely to fit in with them. Parents need to be involved in attempts to eliminate blindisms so that the program can be carried out at home as well as in the classroom.

COMPREHENSION CHECK 13.5

What contributes to the development of "verbalisms" in visually impaired children?

Using the differential reinforcement of incompatible behaviors approach, explain how you would help a visually impaired child overcome his blindism of finger flicking.

CAUSES OF VISUAL IMPAIRMENTS

Visual impairments are often caused by infection, disease, poisoning, accidental injury, muscle deficits, tumors, or perinatal conditions. In the past, premature births have produced large numbers of infants suffering from a condition known as *retrolental fibroplasia* (RLF). This condition was linked to the administration of high concentrations of oxygen to a child at birth. This abnormal eye condition can result in complete blindness. In the 1950s, researchers found a relationship between high levels of oxygen present in the incubators that held premature infants and this condition. For a time, more precise monitoring of the oxygen supply in incubators reduced the number of cases of RLF. However, recent advances in medical technology allow survival of numbers of children who are born 3 to 4 months prematurely. These children are often handicapped with RLF, now more accurately termed *retinopathy of prematurity* (ROP).

Another common cause of visual impairment occurs when the expectant mother contracts rubella (German measles) during the first 3 months of her pregnancy. In the rubella epidemic in 1964 and 1965, almost 40,000 children were affected by rubella before birth. One of the common results of rebella is the formation of congenital cataracts. Many of today's multihandicapped young adults were conceived during the rubella epidemic. In addition to a loss of vision, they may also suffer from deafness, mental retardation, heart conditions, and neurological impairments.

Still another cause is the failure of the optic nerve to develop. The number of children with this condition is increasing.

COMPREHENSION CHECK 13.6

List and explain several major causes of congenital and early childhood blindness.

PREVALENCE OF VISUAL IMPAIRMENTS

Worldwide estimates place the visually handicapped at 15 to 25 million. The National Society for the Prevention of Blindness estimated that there were 437,000 legally blind persons in the United States in 1970 and about 519,000 in 1980 (Dickman, 1977). In 1979, research from the National Center for Health Statistics indicated that 1 in every 1000 persons under the age of 45 will be severely visually impaired. The National Society for the Prevention of Blindness estimated that 10% of all legally blind individuals (20/200 or less) will be under 20 years of age. For every 10 severely visually handicapped individuals, only 1 will be totally blind.

ASSESSMENT OF VISUAL CAPABILITIES

Assessing the visual capabilities of young blind children is a complex activity involving visual acuity, perception, and the functional use of residual vision for exploring and understanding objects and people. Early-childhood special educators and diagnostic specialists must be aware of considerations and problems that influence the assessment process with young visually impaired children. Similarly, they must have a practical understanding of various scales that are available for comprehensively evaluating the capabilities of these children.

Considerations in early developmental assessment

The type and cause of a visual impairment can make a difference in the amount of vision particular children have as well as their reaction to the impairment. It is necessary to know whether the eye condition is stable, deteriorating, or operable. It should also be determined whether the lens prescriptions are up-to-date and effective for the children. Have other types of optical aids been tried? Are they useful? If the children have had such aids prescribed for them, for what purpose were they given? These facts can be obtained by talking with the vision consultants assigned to the children or by going through the children's records. Other factors may also contribute to the effects of a visual impairment. Teachers should know as much about these factors as they can in order to provide a good environment for children with impaired vision.

Visually impaired children will usually arrive at the preschool with an estimate of visual acuity that has been obtained by an eye doctor. The doctor will be either an ophthalmologist or an optometrist. The former is a physician who has taken further training in diseases of the eye. For this reason the *ophthalmologist* assesses vision and fits corrective lenses and is also allowed to prescribe medication and to perform surgery. An *optometrist* has completed a prescribed course in refraction and fitting of corrective lenses. Some optometrists have particular interest in low-vision aids. Both types of doctors are allowed to fit lenses, but medical or surgical treatment must and should be handled by the ophthalmologist. The ideal type of formal visual assessment takes place in a clinic specializing in assessing individuals with low amounts of vision. In such clinics, both types of eye doctors work cooperatively with every patient. They examine their patient's eyes and try different types of refractions and low-vision aids to ascertain the best possible correction.

Because the doctor's office is an artificial setting, a good correction there may not mean that the child will be able to use the aid in less-structured settings. For this reason, it is important for teachers to observe children carefully to see how much and how well they are using their vision.

As stated previously, it is not the amount of visual acuity that children have but how well they are able *to use* that vision that determines their visual functioning. Some children learn to do this quite naturally, particularly if they have perceptive parents who encourage them to use their vision. Most children must be taught to use the vision they have to the maximum extent. Visual training can result in significant gains in visual efficiency (Barraga and Morris, 1980).

Before determining visual functioning, children's medical records should be examined to determine the cause, nature, degree of loss, age of onset, prognosis, and implications of their visual problems. Other medical conditions that may affect vision should also be considered. Assessment should be scheduled for the time of day when children are most alert and at their optimal level of functioning. When setting up such a schedule, it is important to note if and when a child has taken medication. Many medications affect not only the alertness of children but their short-term memory spans as well.

The way in which the room is set up as well as the types of surfaces on the walls and on the floor can influence the way the children respond. Outside distracting noises and the noise level within the room can also affect the results. The size and type of stimuli that are being used can have different results. A favorite toy or food can result in a different response than can an object that the children care nothing about. The amount of light can also be a big factor. Because many eye conditions cause different reactions to light, knowledge of the condition and its cause can be helpful in determining the amount of light under which the testing should occur. Because some eye conditions result in a sensitivity to light and other conditions need an increase in the normal amount of illumination in order to see; lighting must vary based on the individual needs of these children. The conditions surrounding the children during their testing situation should always be considered because different environmental conditions may result in different findings.

When the children are taken to a specific area for assessment, they should be oriented to their surroundings. Because many of them have had traumatic medical experiences, they may be frightened by testing situations. A long period of time may be needed for these children to establish rapport before actual testing begins.

Many preschool blind children also have accompanying handicaps. It is necessary to position these children in the manner that will best allow maximum functioning. Finnie (1975) is recommended for explaining in nontechnical terms the manner in which neurologically impaired children should be positioned. The chapter on movement and appendix on adaptive equipment in Connor, Williamson, and Siepp (1978) can also aid the teacher, for it is necessary to position many of these children because their extension patterns prevent them from turning at will to respond to the various types of stimuli presented. We must make sure the reason that these children are not responding is because they are unable to see the objects rather than that they cannot move to indicate tracking or following various items.

Several aspects of the children's vision need to be assessed. [For more information, Smith and Cote (1982) not only gives specifics, it also includes a brief description of the anatomy of the eye, several definitions of the most common eye conditions, and procedures for assessing visual functioning.] Langley (1980) carefully outlines materials and methods for assessing low-functioning children. Several of these aspects already will have been examined by more formal procedures in the doctor's office. The doctor is mainly interested in acuity level so that adequate and optimal corrections can be made. After correction has been made, the level of visual functioning becomes important. To obtain the type of information we will be able to use to set up learning situations that will help the child, we need the information below.

Is there a pupillary response? Lack of a response does not mean that the child cannot see. However, the presence of a pupillary response tells us that there is response to light. The blink reflex can let us know that the child may see movement. Muscle imbalance needs to be examined to make sure the eyes are working together. Otherwise, double vision may occur and *amblyopia,* a type of blindness, may result. The field of vision needs to be determined to see if there are spots where there is reduced vision or lack of vision, either in the center of the field of vision or in the periphery. The area of the visual field that the child prefers is important, too. If an object is placed in a position where the children are more likely to be able to see it and they are comfortable looking at it, they are more apt to respond to it. What is the eye preference? Can the children visually follow objects? If they can, are they able to shift their attention from one subject to another as both come into their field of vision? Are they able to scan their visual field? Because we constantly scan our visual field when we are outside and observing safety and orientation factors, this ability is important. We frequently scan the page while reading to locate where we are, to find our place, or to gain information quickly.

Each of these questions can help us gain a picture of what children respond to when using the visual modality. The information is not obtained in one trial or setting but through careful observation over a period of time. This assessment, then, provides basic information about how and to what extent a child can accomplish various developmental tasks that represent an understanding of the world.

COMPREHENSION CHECK 13.7

Summarize the aspects of vision that should be assessed in estimating the child's visual modality.

Strategies for educational and developmental assessment

Few specific assessment measures have been developed for the visually impaired child. Those that are available are either adaptations of various scales for normal children (i.e., items requiring vision are excluded) or curriculum-imbedded scales with skill sequences appropriate for such children.

Adapted versions of some traditional instruments are useful for assessing the global capabilities of young visually impaired children. The Maxfield-Buchholz Scale of Social Maturity for Preschool Blind Children is an adaptation and expansion of the Vineland Social Maturity Scale that excludes items requiring prominent visual skills. By interviewing parents, teachers, and caretakers about children's abilities to demonstrate specific skills on tasks, an assessment of their capabilities is obtained. However, the standardization group used in the development of the Maxfield-Buchholz no longer typifies present visually impaired preschoolers. That fact, along with a lack of reliability and validity data make the test results questionable for most evaluation purposes with the current population.

The Boehm Test of Basic Concepts has been modified using raised dots on plastic cards to evaluate the visually impaired child's knowledge of concepts regarding size, number, position, shape. For older children, the verbal subtests of the Wechsler Intelligence Scale for Children–Revised have been used to assess general intellectual functioning. Adaptations of the Stanford-Binet Intelligence Scale are available through the Hayes-Binet and Perkins-Binet versions. However, administration of traditional global scales is not sufficient because much of children's development across domains will be overlooked (e.g., socioemotional, play styles) or will not be validly assessed because of to these modifications that violate standardized procedures. Yet, when "functionally" appropriate scales are employed and/or adapted, the environmental circumstances for the assessment must be carefully prepared and reported.

Because of the need for specific and individually appropriate scales to assess the wide-range developmental skills of young blind children, professionals have begun to develop curriculum-based measures that blend assessment, goals, and teaching strategies. Although such scales need validation, they have great promise. Two examples of such curriculum scales are the Project Vision-Up developmental scale and the Oregon Project developmental sequence for visually impaired and blind preschool children. Both scales contain task-analyzed sequences of skills that visually impaired children may be expected to demonstrate across the 0- to 72-months of age range within several developmental areas (i.e., communication, cognition, gross/fine motor skills, social skills, and self-help skills). Individualized goals and teaching strategies accompany specific developmental tasks.

COMPREHENSION CHECK 13.8

Explain why the features of the Vision-Up curriculum are especially important to the visually impaired child.

TREATMENT OF VISUAL IMPAIRMENTS

Many visual aids are available for severely impaired youngsters. These include eyeglasses, contact lenses, magnifiers (hand held and on stands), telescopic lenses, and optical enlargers. Contact lenses do not supply sufficient magnification for most severely handicapped children. Eyeglasses are usually worn by these children. For safety reasons, many visually handicapped children wear eyeglasses that have unbreakable plastic or case-hardened lenses.

Low-vision aids and other new technology are helping visually handicapped youngsters to learn through their residual vision and/or their other sense modalities.

Visually handicapped children also benefit from the use of special equipment. These devices enable them to increase their reading, writing, and mobility skills. Among the more commonly used pieces of equipment are tapes and cassette recorders, record players, talking book machines, large print materials, tactile pictures, braille (a system for reading and writing based on a combination of six dots within a cell two dots wide and three dots high), and electronic reading devices (machines that convert print to intelligible English speech). Complete listings of aids and appliances for the visually handicapped are available from the American Printing House for the Blind and the American Foundation for the Blind (see Appendix).

EDUCATION OF VISUALLY IMPAIRED CHILDREN

Goals

There is more to producing competent blind persons than just academic aspects. All children must be helped to attain the skills needed to perform in the "real world." Many visually impaired individuals who have been able academically to complete college degrees were than unable to become gainfully employed. Thus, it is important to teach all aspects involved in being a productive person.

Completing tasks that are started is one capability that should be begun in the preschool years when children's attitudes are forming. Following directions is important. If children are excused for not following directions because they are blind, they soon learn that they do not have to follow directions. We must not bring the world to the children. We may do it initially when infants are not aware of the world around them, but we should teach so that children go out into their environments and learn from them. Teach children how to organize their environments, make good use of time, and sequence their activities. They should gradually learn to delay reward in order to finish activities and should not be encouraged to be impulsive. Sometimes simply "prematching" activities helps children to enjoy their less-preferred activities when they are followed by more preferred events. Let them quickly experience a treat or special event after they pick up their toys, finish a lesson, or such. Of course, all children can benefit from this discipline, but handicapped youngsters are sometime "corrupted" by overindulgent albeit well meaning adults; they are often in need of special management techniques to offset misguided social attention and doting. They need to be encouraged so that they will develop perseverence. It takes longer for the visually impaired to do many of the things that seeing individuals perform effortlessly. It may also take a lot more energy. The children must learn to persevere if they are to survive in a competitive society. Independence must be fostered.

Attention must also be given to appearance. Those who are not familiar with blind individuals tend to stare at them. Blind persons will be the center of attention when they enter restaurants, busses, and planes. They need to learn early to ignore the attention they get, to accept it for what it is, and to try to educate the public by being as competent as they can be.

Personal interactions must be developed so they become skillful in such relationships. They need to learn these skills in one-to-one relationships and extend them so that they can hold their own in group settings. Nowhere is this easier to learn than in a preschool setting where all the children are learning these skills.

Only by attending to all the needs of each individual with impaired vision will they become capable, productive adults. The preschool setting is the place where such attention can provide optimal results.

COMPREHENSION CHECK 13.9

Discuss how your own study behavior might be improved through "prematching."

Service delivery systems

The heterogeneous group of visually impaired children have as great diversity among them as exists among other children. There is no such thing as *the* visually impaired preschooler. Consequently, there must be a diversity of programs to meet all needs. Throughout the country various types of programs have been undertaken for this purpose. Although some are less than optimal, the low incidence of this handicapping condition often results in children being served in programs where they would not be placed if the incidence were higher and more effective groupings could be made.

Some children who have no other handicapping conditions are frequently mainstreamed into classes with their normal seeing peers. In fact, such children have been mainstreamed for decades—long before current attempts to place handicapped children in the least restrictive environment. Such integration with their peers has worked satisfactorily for many of these children. A major factor regarding the successful placement of children has been the teacher of the group in which the children are placed. Because the children do not see much of what goes on around them, it is essential that the teacher fosters a hands-on approach. The children need the freedom to climb, touch, handle, and get dirty. If a teacher is not willing to allow the children to have these experiences, that classroom is an inappropriate setting for children who have impaired vision.

Most infants who are identified at birth begin their training as soon as they are identified. In areas where there is a large enough population of visually impaired children to have a class, the children may be brought to a center by their parents and taught in group or individual sessions. In more sparsely populated areas, there may be an itinerant teacher who travels to children's homes and works in that setting. Some systems are structured so that teachers work in the homes with only the children, only the parents, or with both the parents and the children. Some programs are structured so that teachers go into the home and then the parents bring the children into the center at specified time periods; once a month, once a week, or as determined.

In areas where there is an even smaller population of visually impaired youngsters, children may be served by special-education teachers who are trained broadly in special education but have no particular expertise for teaching children with vision impairments. Unfortunately, because they have no background in recognizing the implications of specific visual problems and their resulting difficulties, such teachers may not be able to serve these children appropriately.

As children reach the toddler stage, they may be placed in part-time or full-time center-based activities, in itinerant home programs, or in settings with their seeing peers. If served in the last type of facility, the children may or may not have an itinerant vision specialist who can help the preschool teacher with specific information and materials that have been developed for the visually impaired. If no teacher is available who has been trained to meet the specific needs of the preschool visually impaired children, again, the special needs of the children may not be met.

Some children are served in the preschool years by those whose background is not in special education. Nurses, child development specialists, occupational and physical therapists, social workers, and others may be delivering the services for this population. Again, effective preschool education demands expertise in the area of preschool visual impairments because the needs of the children are such that mobility skills, habits, and concepts gained during the preschool years greatly influence their later lives. Some older children may have few skills but have been in preschool classes from the time of birth. It is the quality of such programs that is the critical variable, not necessarily the length of time spent in them.

Deciding on the educational placement

In response to the question of whether a visually impaired child is ready to move into an integrated setting in a preschool program designed for sighted children, Heiner (1982) recommends that both the home teacher and the parents consider together the child's ability to function in a large group setting, interaction with other children, level of independent self-care skills, effective use of remaining vision and other senses, adjustments to new situations, communication with others, and free movement in a familiar environment. Positive responses in each of the areas probably indicates that a child can be successfully mainstreamed. Negative responses usually indicate a need for further work in those areas before mainstreaming is attempted.

Before beginning the new integrated program, Heiner recommends that the parent and vision teacher visit the program to: (1) learn about the physical setting; (2) determine what will be expected of the children in that program; (3) observe the daily routine; (4) determine information the new teacher will need, including appropriate records; and (5) decide on skills the children will need to acquire before attending the new program. The parents, children, and vision teacher should then visit the new program to introduce the children to the new teacher, help them learn to travel and get about in the new setting, and allow them to become familiar with the school before other children are present.

These are procedures that all children who attend preschool programs could follow. The difference in applying them to visually handicapped children is that these children will probably need a longer time to orient themselves by walking around the school to become familiar with it. Visually impaired children must become familiar with each section of the school so that they can get a total picture of the environment.

Educational materials and tools

The American Printing House for the Blind has previously been mentioned as a resource for obtaining materials for visually impaired children. Although they formerly did not have specific materials developed for the preschool level, the current population of multiple-handicapped children and the mandates of law for preschool education has thrust them into developing materials for this age group. There is a research staff involved in this development. Catalogs of materials are available by writing to the American Printing House.

The American Foundation for the Blind is another resource for information about and materials for blind and visually impaired persons. They have a preschool consultant who can answer questions, direct a teacher to services, and recommend materials. The foundation is also a source for balls, watches, games, and other devices adapted for use by the blind. Free catalogs and publications are available as well as other published materials for parents, teachers, and other professionals.

Also of help to those dealing with preschool visually impaired children is the National Association for Parents of the Visually Impaired, Inc. This group welcomes as members both parents and professionals and publishes a newsletter with information that appeals to both groups. The International Institute for visually Impaired 0–7, Inc. is another group that welcomes both parents and professional members. The latter group addresses the needs of the preschool age child whereas the former encompasses the total student age group.

A source of useful information for both parents and teachers is a newsletter, *The National Newspatch*. Published in a residential school for the blind by teachers who have had experience working with preschool visually impaired children, the newsletter contains concrete suggestions for meeting some of the needs of the children of that population.

Current addresses for each of these groups can be found in the Appendix. In addition, children who are eligible for services can obtain materials from their local or regional library or Library for Blind and Physically Handicapped. Although more appropriate for older children, there may be talking book machines, records, and tapes appropriate for loan for certain younger children.

Three curricula have been used extensively with blind children of preschool age. All three are based on a developmental approach to learning. O'Brien (1976) describes in book form the program that she developed in Montgomery County, Maryland. It contains useful information about setting up a program, assessing children, and carrying out intervention strategies. It lists specific activities for developing the use of vision, as well as other areas, to specifically meet the needs of preschool children.

A curriculum that was developed by teachers of visually impaired preschoolers comes from the Oregon Project for Visually Impaired and Blind

Preschool Children. The curriculum provides for assessment and instruction for teaching of specific tasks. This specificity is most helpful when planning instructional objectives.

The third curriculum, the Vision-Up Program (Croft and Robinson, 1976) (also called "Growing Up: A Developmental Curriculum"), was developed at the Idaho School for the Blind for use in that state. That curriculum contains materials for parents to use to help assess children's current level of functioning. There are also lesson plans that can be used with children. There is a graph on which teachers can plot skills matched to determine the gains and developmental levels of children.

All three curricula contain task-analyzed sequences of skills that visually impaired children may be expected to demonstrate across the 0- to 72-month age range within several developmental areas (i.e., communication, cognition, gross/fine motor skills, social skills, and self-help skills). Individualized goals and teaching strategies accompany specific developmental tasks.

New materials that were developed for those working iwth visually impaired infants are the Reach Out and Teach (1985) books. Although designed especially for parents, all working with such infants will find them useful. A series of slide tapes and teacher's manual are also available. The slide tapes are particularly effective with parent groups.

Although there are many other curricula that may be adapted for use with preschool visually impaired children, these three are mentioned because they were developed by teachers of preschool visually impaired children especially for use with that group.

COMPREHENSION CHECK 13.10

Outline the various educational delivery systems for the visually impaired. Which would you consider most appropriate and why?

Visually imparied children in the preschool

It is important to remember that visually impaired children are first of all children with the same needs as their seeing peers. They should be a part of the everyday activities. In addition, visually impaired children have distinct needs that must be met because of their visual problems.

These children should be treated as other members of the class with the same exceptions and the same rules of discipline that apply to all children. If the children infringe on those rules, the consequences should be similar and to the same degree that they would be for all class members.

Visually impaired children should be encouraged to take part in all the activities in the classroom. If they have some remaining vision, such activities may motivate them to use as much vision as possible. If they have no vision, activities such as finger painting can be enjoyed. Whereas children with vision may enjoy the colors, those without vision can enjoy the feeling of the paint.

Never do for the children what they are capable of doing themselves; too often the dependence of the preschool years is carried over into the school years with the children sitting in their seats and the teacher getting them their Braille writers, paper, and aids. Once children have learned to become independent in activities, they usually do not want to lose that independence. Thus, preschool settings are the ideal places to build up that independence. As these children become capable of doing things independently, their classmates will begin to see them as more competent, more like themselves, and will begin to treat them more normally—expecting more give-and-take from them.

Youngsters need to develop tolerance for some frustration and learn how to deal with it in solving their own problems. Let them struggle a bit before intervening. On the other hand, the situation should not continue so long that children become discouraged. Watch to determine the right moment when these children may need that extra boost.

Safety consciousness is a must, but we should not become overprotective. Visually impaired children must learn safety rules. At the same time they must recognize that their lack of vision means that they will be prone to develop bruises from running into unexpected barriers. However, they need to be encouraged to move and explore within those rules, not becoming so fearful that they are unable to function within the normal range. These children need help to overcome effects of overprotection and the resulting experiential deprivation. Such effects usually result in a lack of confidence and many fears and anxieties about traveling alone, even in familiar environments. Overprotection may produce a lack of stamina, lowered endurance, and lowered expectations on the part of the children and their families.

All who work with visually impaired children must learn to identify themselves to the children until the children can identify their voices in unfamiliar settings. "Good morning, Johnny, it's Miss Gregory," can be a model statement for the whole class. Classmates of blind children must also give their names when first speaking. Sighted people often take some time to identify those who come up to them and begin talking as if they were readily known. Most people have had the experience of spending several minutes trying to search their memories for any clues to the identity of the speaker and find they have not been following the conversation closely. It becomes even more difficult for a blind person, for there are no visual clues to aid in the identification.

Not only is it necessary to identify oneself when first approaching these children, it is necessary to let them know when you leave them. Blind children will not know you have gone unless you give some indication. They may be left talking to themselves or reaching out to hand something to someone who is no longer there. Classmates of blind children should also be taught to let their blind cohorts know when they are leaving.

People have a tendency to speak in louder tones when addressing blind persons. Blindness does not affect hearing. It is particularly important to provide a good model for other children when addressing the blind child. Blind children, themselves, need help in talking at an appropriate level. Because blind children do not have the visual feedback to determine if they are talking too softly or too loudly, we will have to provide this information for them. They can learn to monitor their own voices by learning what is and what is not appropriate in various noise settings.

Answer any questions about blindness and visual impairment openly and with truth. Both the children themselves and their peers with normal vision may ask questions about the degree of vision, why the children cannot see, whether the condition is catching, if the children were bad and that caused the condition, and so on. Both the visually handicapped and their seeing peers need to hear the answers in order to clear up any misconceptions they may have about visual handicaps and blindness.

Be prepared for all the children in the class to "play blind" when the first blind child is admitted to the class. This stage does not usually last long. It is one way for the children to learn some of the limitations blind children must overcome. They learn that they can still walk around the room and school, go up and down stairs, and eat without seeing. Such experiences often result in the establishment of more normal peer relationships among all the children.

For those children who have low vision and must wear thick glasses and/or use other visual aids, acceptance can usually be enhanced if all the classmates are given a chance to use those aids or look through the glasses. The visually impaired children themselves can often explain the use of aids or glasses effectively. By openly discussing their aids, many taboos can be removed. These discussions show the other children that it is permissible to ask questions about the aids, and they are not a forbidden topic of conversation. By discussing this, much of the fear and aura of mystique disappears.

When talking with visually impaired children, people should feel free to use sight-oriented words. When asking a blind child to look at something, the child learns that to look means to take something into the hands, tactually explore it, and listen to see if it makes any characteristic sounds. Colors and color-oriented words are so common in our conversations that blind children need to learn them and their meanings. The children can relate to others that they feel blue without ever having perceived the color blue.

When carrying out activities in the classroom, it is necessary to verbally describe what we are doing and identify sounds that are occurring within the classroom. Pencil sharpeners, drawers closing, fans humming, water running, and many other sounds occur regularly in the room. Such sounds can be used by the blind children not only for identification, but for orientation purposes. By hearing certain sounds come from specific location, the children learn to orient themselves in respect to those sounds. Practice in these skills is a good basis for more formal orientation and mobility skills.

Not only should these activities be described, but any tests, or use of objects also should be described. This is important for children with low vision. Too often a good job is done with totally blind children, knowing that they need all the information. Children with low vision may need the information even more because we think they see more than they do see and have more realistic concepts than they possess. One boy, who had a lot of useful vision although he more than met the requirements of legal blindness, expressed great gratitude following a movie when the teacher sat beside him and described what was taking place. He related that he had never enjoyed a movie so much and that no one had ever done that before. He asked if he could sit next to the teacher the next time a movie was shown.

A multisensory approach to teaching must be used in any classroom where visually handicapped children are enrolled. Because these children cannot learn by imitation or by observation, they need to feel, touch, smell, taste, and handle objects to get the real perception of those objects. Because the hearing aspect has such significance, it is particularly important to teach the selection of auditory clues, so that processing, retention, and use of auditory information is developed.

A good environment is important for visually limited children. It should be interesting, manipulable, meaningful, and diverse in order to motivate the children to explore and learn from it. Such an environment does not have to be expensive. Objects such as boxes, material scraps, and carpet remnants all meet these requirements. In addition, it is helpful if there are places for children to sit, lie, crawl, and stand where they can compare their bodies with the spaces around them. Sound and odor clues are also important parts of the enviornment. If smells are coming from something cooking, they should be mentioned. All odors should be brought to the children's attention and then identified. This identification of odors can be developed and will prove helpful in independent mobility.

The children should learn that their environment is a *predictable* place in which they can find their way around. Until they learn to move with ease, everything should remain in the same place. Once the children orient themselves to the room and become familiar with it, changes should be made. Through gradual changes, the children learn that certain things are predictable, but they cannot be rigid in their expectations. Changes do occur. When changes are made, such as relocating a table, the children should be advised of these changes when they first enter the room. Independent mobility is important, and children should be made comfortable enough in their surroundings that they feel free to move within them.

Once blind children learn the location of doors in and out of the room, including doors to cupboards, they will more freely move toward them if they are not confronted with bumping into a half-open door. By completely and consistently opening or closing all doors, children will learn to trust the environment.

"Messy" activities are important for the visually impaired child's growth. If children are afraid to get their hands messy or dirty, they become restricted in their exploratory behavior. Because much of their learning must, of necessity, come through this means, it is important that they learn to use their hands to explore freely in their environment.

When the children are engaged in exploratory behavior, teachers should connect and expand the new to what they already know and to verbally and tactually assist them at appropriate times. Teachers must help children develop systems of exploration so that when they explore they will increase their awareness rather than confuse it. Once we believe that they have assimilated and accommodated the new information, opportunities should be provided to see if the information can be generalized to new materials and new settings. Such activities are necessary for the development of good concepts. By beginning with concrete, relevant situations that are meaningful to the children within that environment, they can learn to identify objects, obtain spatial relationships among and between them, gain the concept of directionality, and develop awareness of their own body, image, self-concept, and schema. Tactile exploration needs to be constantly encouraged and verbal reinforcement given for both the activity and the identification of the concepts to be learned.

A good knowledge of task analysis is necessary when teaching the skills needed by visually impaired children (Hart, 1974). Sometimes a complete task is so overwhelming that children need more assistance. When they become stuck at a certain level while learning a task, teaching by using task analysis can help them progress beyond that stage.

Prereading skills are particularly important at the preschool level. The children need to develop the use of the vision they have. They must develop their tactual skills as well. Proper use of lighting is particularly important and may vary with the individual child. Natural and artificial lighting need to be examined to determine the maximum use of light. Glare should be avoided, both in overall lighting as well as on the surface on which the children are working, even on the paper on which they write or read. The children will have individual needs. Other prereading activities should help determine the best color contrast between print and paper, the size of print that is most comfortable, and the best spacing between the printed lines. Purple and blue ditto papers should usually be avoided because most of them do not offer enough contrast between the paper and ink to be readily seen. If it is necessary to use such papers, the lines should be gone over with a black felt-tip pen to deepen the contrast.

When examining materials to be used in the preschool setting, it is important to look at their tactual quality. Good tactual characteristics will help the children to recognize the material. It should also help them to go from the parts to the whole to see their relationship. This part to whole relationship is important in learning shape conception and recognition. Children need that information in order to go from a three-dimensional to a two-dimensional representation of various items. If not sure of the tactile quality, close your eyes and explore the items tactually. If still not sure, the best way of determining the appropriateness of an item is to have visually impaired children examine the item. Instructional materials centers that lend are often a good source from which to get materials because they can be tried for effectiveness before an actual purchase is made.

Once teachers believe that children have gained valid concepts from the environment, have oriented well, and have social competencies within that environment, opportunities should be given to try out those same skills in new settings. These children will still need to be oriented to the settings, but such change in environments provides a real test as to whether the children have attained the skills that we want them to have. Many opportunities are needed to show that the children can anticipate and imitate. Opportunities are also needed whereby children can develop and exhibit the short-term memory that is necessary for good braille and tactual reading skills. The ability to integrate all that they have learned must be offered in many different situations. Change in schedules and ways to interact with different people, toys, and environments must be extended.

Above all, teachers must talk and keep talking all the while when they have visually impaired children in their classrooms. Everything must be named and identified. Real objects must be used to help children identify what the words mean so that verbalisms are avoided. Incidental learning should be a part of every classroom. However, if the children fail to pick up the information, it should be specifically taught. Only when such care is taken will these children be able to become capable, competent blind students.

COMPREHENSION CHECK 13.11

Because of their handicap, visually impaired children should be treated differently in the class setting. Express your reactions to this statement. Overprotective parents and teachers do more harm than good for the visually impaired child. Explain.

Explain how a multisensory approach to teaching contributes to independent mobility of the visually handicapped child.

Enumerate general principles that should be considered in teaching concepts to preschoolers. Do these principles apply in the case of visually impaired children?

SUMMARY

Most visually impaired children can learn to use the residual vision they possess and thus become competent, capable, independent adults. The legal definition of visual impairment is visual acuity of 20/200 or less after the best possible correction. Partially sighted children have vision between 20/70 and 20/200. In addition to distance difficulties, visual impairment can result from a restricted field of vision. Blindness deters a child's development in three areas: mobility, relationships with others, and feedback from the environment. Causes of visual impairment fall under several categories, the most common being prenatal. Teacher assessment and intervention with the visually impaired should be done in conjunction with medical treatment. All visually impaired children must be helped to acquire the skills needed to perform in the real world. They are children with the same needs as their seeing peers. Both in the classroom and at home, visually impaired children should be treated equally and should be encouraged to take part in all activities, chores, and games.

SUGGESTED READINGS

Barraga, N. (1983). *Visual handicaps and learning* (rev. ed.). Austin, TX: Exceptional Resources.

Brown, D., Simmons, V., and Methvin, J. (1978). *Oregon Project for Visually Impaired and Blind Preschool Children*. Medford, OR: Jackson County Education Service District.

Hart, V. (1974). *Beginning with the handicapped*. Springfield, IL: Thomas.

Warren, D. (1977). *Blindness and early childhood development*. New York: American Foundation for the Blind.

Developmental Differences in Hearing

Joe D. Stedt
Donald F. Moores

CHAPTER OUTLINE

Brandon is a 5-year-old boy born profoundly deaf. Although most children start saying words when they are about a year old, Brandon never did. By the time he was 2 years old, Brandon was still not talking, still not responding to his mother's vocal communication. Because Brandon had two older brothers who had both started talking before they were 2, Brandon's mother suspected that something was wrong.

A series of tests determined that Brandon had a profound hearing loss. He was fitted with hearing aids to amplify his residual hearing and now attends a preschool exclusively for deaf children.

Brandon now communicates fluently using sign language. His family has learned sign language to communicate with him as they now realize that he will never hear and will never have normal speech. In most ways, however, Brandon is just like any other 5-year-old boy. He fights with his brothers, loves his dog, and likes to play catch. Brandon's family does believe that his deafness is sometimes a bother, but they do not view it as a handicap.

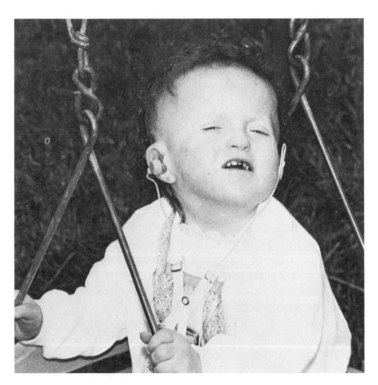

This preschooler benefits from wearing a hearing aid that allows her to make use of her residual hearing.

DEFINITION AND DESCRIPTION OF THE PROBLEM

Hearing impaired is a generic term that includes both deaf and hard of hearing individuals. Billy and Martha are both called "hearing impaired," but Billy has a slight difficulty in understanding the speech of others, whereas Martha cannot understand any speech even when using a hearing aid. Obviously, the term "hearing impaired" is so vague that it offers virtually no information about how the child behaves and reacts within his/her environment.

A loss of hearing sensitivity is often measured in decibels (dB). The *decibel* is a standard unit that measures sound intensity. Based on a logarithmic scale, zero decibels represents the point where a normal hearing person can begin to hear a sound. A 10-dB sound is 10 times greater than a 0-dB sound and a 20-dB sound is 100 times greater than a 0-dB sound. A whisper has a sound intensity of 20-dB, a conversation has a sound intensity of 60-dB and a sound of 120-dB produces a painful sensation (Rose and Tompkins, 1978).

One way to classify hearing losses is to create two categories: the *hard of hearing* and the *deaf.* Specifically, the Conference of Executives of American Schools for the Deaf has developed the following definitions:

A hard of hearing person is one whose hearing is disabled to an extent (Usually 35 to 69-dB) that makes difficult, but does not preclude, the understanding of speech through the ear alone, without or with a hearing aid.

A deaf person is one whose hearing is disabled to an extent (usually 70-dB or greater) that precludes the understanding of speech through the ear alone, without or with a hearing aid. (Frisina, 1974, p. 3)

Classifying hearing impairments in terms of dB losses is the job of *audiologists,* those professionals who measure and study hearing and develop remedial procedures, such as prescribing hearing aids. The audiologist measures hearing using an electronic instrument called an *audiometer.* The child's hearing level is then graphically represented on an *audiogram.* An audiogram gives precise information regarding the hearing loss of an individual.

It should be explained that classifying hearing loss is a complex task. People who have hearing losses often encounter distortions in the sounds they can hear in addition to having a diminished level of hearing sensitivity. The effect is that hearing-impaired people hear sounds in a form that is greatly distorted compared with what is heard by a normal-hearing person. Amplifying sounds, through the use of a hearing aid, merely intensifies already distorted sounds. The hearing impaired person may not gain *normal* hearing by using a hearing aid. You can see then, that children might have the same dB hearing loss but different amounts and kinds of distortions. Some persons with a loss of 75-dB, for example, will understand very little speech even when using a hearing aid. In contrast, other persons with a hearing loss of 75-dB will be able to hear well enough to comprehend speech over the telephone with the help of a hearing aid.

It is difficult to predict the effects of hearing loss given just the hearing loss in dBs. Audiologists have not yet perfected technology to a point where they can predict the effects of hearing loss. On examining a child, an audiologist cannot give precise information regarding how well that child will be able to respond to a hearing aid and auditory training or how well that child will progress in school.

In defense of audiologists, it must be remembered that the audiologist tests the child in a clinical setting in a sound-treated room under optimal conditions. The child's ability to use residual hearing in a classroom, playground, or home situation may be much different.

Bearing in mind these cautions, we have taken the four categories of hearing loss, as given by Newby (1979), and added explanations that are general in scope. These categories are described next.

COMPREHENSION CHECK 14.1

Name and define two categories under which all hearing-impaired children can be accommodated.

Degrees of hearing loss

1. *Mild hearing loss (30–40-dB)*. Mild losses are often undetected in a preschool population because the problems manifested are generallly not severe. These losses are often caused by acute problems such as middle ear infections. Mild hearing losses are often detected in school when the child has problems responding to the teacher in noisy situations.

2. *Moderate hearing loss (50–70-dB)*. Children with moderate losses are more likely to be detected than those with mild losses because there are more behavioral manifestations. These children usually have some speech problems and some language delay. Still, many of these children will go undetected until the beginning of school years. Some of these children benefit from the introduction of a manual sign-language system. Many children with moderate losses will need additional help to be successful in school.

3. *Severe hearing loss (70–80-dB)*. Children with severe losses are often identified early in life. Speech and language processes are virtually always delayed. These children, in most cases, should learn a manual sign-language system as well as oral communication.

4. *Profound hearing loss (85-110-dB)*. These children are sometimes referred to as deaf. Most parents recognize within the first 2 years of their child's life that something is wrong with their child if a profound loss is present. A profound loss affects virtually all aspects of a child's life: social and cognitive, as well as language. These children usually require some type of sign language for communication.

Types of Hearing Loss

Conductive

Hearing losses can be either *transitory* or *permanent.* Severe and profound losses are always permanent. Some mild and moderate losses, on the other hand, can occasionally be alleviated by drugs or surgery. Many mild and moderate hearing losses are *conductive.* A conductive hearing loss is one that consists of a problem in the middle or outer ear. The outer ear consists basically of the ear canal and the visible portion of the outer ear. If there is some type of obstruction in the ear canal, such as excessive earwax or foreign objects, a hearing loss may result. The eardrum serves as the outside border for the middle ear. Within the middle ear is a cavity containing three small bones called *ossicles.* These bones, the hammer (malleus), anvil (incus), and the stirrup (stapes), vibrate in sympathy with sounds that enter the ear canal and impinge on the eardrum.

The most common type of conductive hearing loss is caused by the buildup of fluid in the middle-ear cavity caused by infection. This condition, *otitis media,* has been estimated to have caused conductive hearing losses in 25% to 65% of the population of children under the age of 2 years (millions of children). The effect of the infection is to impede the movement of the ossicles, which results in reduced sensitivity to sound. Such a problem can be eliminated through the use of antibiotics. It must be stressed that when fluid is in the middle-ear cavity, hearing sensitivity is decreased. This transitory hearing loss can become severe enough to effect a child's ability to function in a normal hearing environment. Some children experience chronic otitis media that can, in turn, cause a hearing loss that will lead to language, speech, and possibly academic problems. It is possible for an audiologist to discover such problems through a procedure called *impedance audiometry,* which produces a tympanogram. A *tympanogram* is a graphic record of the ear pressure of the middle ear. When the middle ear has a buildup of fluid, the pressure will be different from the pressure in a normal ear.

Sensorineural

Any hearing loss that is not a conductive problem is a *sensorineural impairment.* A sensorineural loss is one that affects the inner ear (cochlea) or the eighth cranial nerve. Simply stated, the job of the inner ear is to take the sounds from the outside world and translate them into electrical impulses that are sent to the brain. The eighth cranial nerve carries the impulses from the inner ear to the brain where the sensations are decoded as sounds.

It should be stressed here that hearing losses that are sensorineural in nature cannot be restored by drugs, medical procedures, or therapy. During a person's life a sensorineural loss may become worse, but it will never become better. There are, however, experimental procedures being developed to combat hearing loss. A cochlear implant is one such procedure in which an artificial cochlea is surgically implanted. These procedures are still in the experimental stage, however, and have yet to restore normal hearing to a profoundly impaired ear.

A third type of hearing loss consists of a combination of conductive loss and a sensorineural loss. This is called a *mixed hearing loss.*

COMPREHENSION CHECK 14.2

Explain the condition otitis media. What symptoms in the child would suggest the prevalence of this condition to the preschool teacher?

In the process of hearing, what is the function of the cochlea? What is the impact of damage to this part of the ear?

Differentiate between conductive and sensorineural hearing loss. In your opinion, which condition would impede language and speech development to a greater extent? Give reasons for your answer.

Onset of loss

In addition to the severity of a hearing loss, another factor that is important is the *time of onset* of the hearing loss. The longer a child retains hearing, the more likely that the child will have normal speech and language. Children who become deaf *before* acquiring speech and language (sometime between the ages of 2 and 4 years) are referred to as the *prelingual* deaf. *Postlingual* deafness means that the hearing loss was suffered after speech and language were obtained. Those children who are postlingually deaf often need fewer educational adjustments than those children who are either prelingually or *congenitally* deaf (born with the hearing impairment).

You can appreciate the greater difficulties in educating children who have never learned what the world sounds like. Thunder and babbling brooks, for example, have no meaning. On the other hand, the child who becomes deaf after the establishment of spoken language (postlingual) can use all the auditory referents acquired before deafness.

COMPREHENSION CHECK 14.3

The number and kind of educational adjustments needed for a child is related to the time of onset of hearing loss. Explain this statement.

IMPACT ON THE FAMILY

Reactions to hearing loss in children are as many and varied as parents themselves. Some parents are perceptive enough to understand the remifications of hearing impairment with little or no explanation from outside sources. Other parents are not so fortunate. Some parents spend the first several years of a child's life denying that there is a problem. It is not uncommon for parents to profoundly hearing-impaired children to exhaust all resources in looking for a cure that will restore hearing to normal. There simply are no cures for profound hearing losses. (Some mild and moderate losses can be remedied; others cannot.) There are many reports of parents in desperation resorting to faith healers, vitamin injections, acupuncture specialists, cochlear implants, home remedies, and even electric shock to restore the hearing of a child. With the exception of middle ear problems, however, most of the cures that are proposed to heal those with hearing problems only make the parents' and the child's frustration worse. The parents must be helped to accept the fact that their child has a hearing loss that is permanent and will not go away. They must realize that the deaf child will become a deaf adult.

Of great importance is the undiagnosed infant in whom mother-child interactions and reciprocity are impaired. Even in diagnosed hearing loss, the infant's interactive process of language acquisition can be altered.

Maternal interactions

Mothers of hearing impaired children have not been thoroughly studied at this time. In fact, it has been pointed out by Moores (1982) that little work of a developmental nature has been done on a real family with a deaf child. Some of the information that is available, however, indicates that the mothers of hearing-impaired children tend to be more dogmatic, more manipulative, and less encouraging toward their deaf child as compared with mothers of hearing children; in addition, parents of deaf children are more likely to spank their children (Schlesinger and Meadow, 1972). These parents were concerned about being either overprotective or underprotective with their children.

The problems of interaction with the deaf child can be improved under certain circumstances, however. Greenberg (1983) has studied the effects of a comprehensive program working with families of deaf children under the age of 3. By working with families having deaf children, it was found that mothers were more consistent in their use of praise, less directive, and enjoyed interacting with their deaf children more than mothers in the control group. Therefore, it appears that more work is needed to help mothers deal with the stress of having a deaf child in the family.

It must be emphasized that deaf children, like other children, can suffer from a variety of handicapping conditions. A deaf child may also be visually impaired or mentally retarded. A deaf child could even be visually impaired *and* mentally retarded. In a similar vein, a deaf child may exhibit learning disabilities, socioemotional problems, or orthopedic problems. Depending on definition, deaf children with another handicap (also called multihandicapped deaf children) comprise from 11% to 33% of the total population of deaf children (Moores, 1982).

Families who have a hearing-impaired child encounter many stresses that are unknown to families with hearing children. One obvious problem is the hearing aid. Because most children with significant losses need hearing aids, families must invest both time and money to ensure that hearing aids are properly fitted. Because there are no simple answers for selecting the proper hearing aid, parents should rely on a certified audiologist for help.

The purchase of a hearing aid places stress on the family for several reasons. One reason is that the purchase of a hearing aid is often the first event that forces parents to confront the problems of having a child with a hearing loss. Another reason is that parents must learn how to assist the child with putting on the aid, setting it at the proper level, keeping active batteries inside the aid, and cleaning the molds. Parents may also find it frustrating if the child does not help in the maintenance of the aid and, further, insists on such things as bathing while wearing the aid.

Parents will also encounter stress when seeking appropriate school placements for their child. Because not all communities have services to meet the needs of a hearing-impaired child, parents are sometimes forced to transport their child to an appropriate preschool. Some parents actually move to another town or even state to be closer to appropriate services. These extra burdens and frustration focus the family's attention on the hearing loss of the child, causing the child to be even more closely identified as "handicapped."

The parents may not be the only members of the family to experience difficulty. When there are other siblings in the family, they often experience various forms of stress because of the hearing-impaired child. The siblings are often expected to help the younger hearing-impaired child to adjust and not become "picked on." Also, the time required for a parent to care for a hearing-impaired child may take time away from the child's brothers and sisters.

Most families, of course, do adapt and cope. Their deaf children, like hearing children, grow up to be competent, independent adults who contribute to society. Meadow (1981), in a book entitled *Deafness and Child Development*, has produced an excellent text in this area for the interested reader. Freeman, Carbin, and Boese (1981) have written a highly readable and helpful book for parents of deaf children called *Can't Your Child Hear?* The book *A Deaf Adult Speaks Out* by Leo Jacobs (1980), a deaf man, has also proved to be a rich source of information to hearing parents of deaf children (see, the Appendix for additional resources for parents of a deaf child). In addition, the International Association of Parents of the Deaf has been a powerful and effective advocate for deaf children and their families.

COMPREHENSION CHECK 14.4

Describe the reactions of parents when hearing loss is first confirmed in the child. How do these reactions affect the child?

IMPACT ON THE CHILD'S DEVELOPMENT

It must be stressed that a profound hearing loss has a pervasive effect on virtually every aspect of a child's life. Some of the areas of functioning that can be affected in a deaf child are the following: communication (speech, written and spoken language), education, self-image, and independence.

Communication is undoubtedly the major area of concern for children with large hearing losses. Speech is the most disrupted form of communication in deaf children in that it is difficult for a deaf person to develop speech that is intelligible and functional (Conrad, 1979; Moores, 1982). A manual sign-language system for deaf children is usually a necessity for communicative survival. Without the input of signs, children with profound hearing loss develop little, if any, effective coommunication.

When a child does learn a manual sign-language system, it is important for all members of the family to learn the system. When only one family member learns to use sign language that person is often forced into the role of interpreter. When the parent allows one of the children to act as an interpreter for the deaf child, the communication becomes less personal and less effective.

A young deaf child is often delayed in other areas of communication, such as writing skills. The result is that a family may not be able to communicate with the child in written form for the first 8 or 9 years of the child's existence. Clearly, waiting that long for communication is not desirable.

Research has shown that deaf children are less socially mature than their hearing counterparts (Meadow, 1981). Most social skills are learned through language; because deaf children usually have poor language skills, it follows that they would have problems in social areas. A deaf child, for example, cannot be expected to have good manners unless someone teaches and models the manners.

Meadow (1981) found that deaf children may have inaccurate and inflated self-images and act more impulsively than do hearing children. Additionally, teachers tend to complain that deaf children are less independent than are hearing children and need more constant attention.

Hearing-impaired children encounter a unique social situation. There is a great deal of social isolation that is experienced by profoundly hearing impaired individuals when interacting with groups of hearing people. However, young deaf children, under the age of 5 years, are often able to relate well to other children of similar age because much of their communication is not based on language. Instead, young children can interact with their peers through nonverbal play. Sometimes young children make their wants and needs known through pushing and grabbing. Such communication is commonly nonverbal in nature and within the realm of all deaf children. As children grow older, however, communication becomes more verbal. People are more likely to make their wants and needs known through speech rather than by pushing and shoving. The older the deaf child, the harder it becomes to communicate with peers.

As a deaf child matures, therefore, communication problems often become more pronounced. Even if the child has excellent speech-reading skills, which is usually not the case, group situations are difficult. When several people begin talking, the hearing-impaired child has problems knowing when one person stops and another person starts to speak. As the deaf person is scanning the room to discover who is talking, another person may begin to speak. The deaf child may be quite lost in the conversation. Eventually, the child may not even bother to try to listen.

It must be emphasized, however, that deaf people are not social isolates. Deaf people do spend time interacting with hearing people, but their social interactions many times may take place predominantly with other deaf people and hearing people who know sign language. Sign language becomes more than a system of communication for deaf people—it becomes a common ground on which to meet and establish a self-indentity. This socialization occures at an early age for those children who have deaf parents. There is an active deaf culture in the United States, and deaf people may be seen as comprising an ethnic group in much the same way as do black, Hispanic, Irish, or Jewish Americans. The major difference is that most deaf children have hearing parents. Therefore, the process of acculturation into a deaf community usually occurs after childhood.

The lives of deaf individuals are greatly influenced by daily contact with hearing people. Not only do most deaf children have hearing parents, but most deaf parents have hearing children. Deaf people live, work, shop, and play in areas where the hearing predominate. There are no separate towns or neighborhoods for deaf people in America. Their success in dealing with a larger population having little understanding of their needs is a tribute to the human spirit. This is not to say that deaf adults live in an insolated world of their own. Deaf people must shop in stores run by hearing people, deaf people must buy gas from stations run by hearing people, and deaf people must live in a world that is largely inhabited by hearing individuals. It is of interest, however, that the vast majority of deaf adults marry other deaf adults.

COMPREHENSION CHECK 14.5

Explain the reasons for poor social development in severely hearing impaired children.

Outline certain steps that a family can take to increase communication with the hearing-impaired child.

CAUSES OF HEARING IMPAIRMENTS

In many cases, the cause(s) of childhood deafness cannot de determined. Currently, five major causes of deafness have been identified.

Heredity

In about half of all hearing-impaired children heredity is the cause (Moores, 1982). Deafness can "run in the family." The hereditary link could be directly from the parents or from other family members, for example, a distant aunt. Also, certain syndromes, including Down's syndrome, have high incidence of hearing impairments.

Rubella

If an expectant mother contracts rubella (German measles) in the first trimester (3 months) of pregnancy, it is possible that the child will be born deaf. A nationwide epidemic of rubella in the early 1960s caused a sharp increase in the number of deaf children.

Blood incompatibility

When Rh factors are different in the mother and the baby blood incompatibility occurs. Commonly, this occurs when an Rh-negative mother gives birth to an Rh-positive baby. "The mother's antibodies cross the placenta and enter the bloodstream of the fetus destroying his red blood cells and leading to a severely jaundiced baby . . . of those who survive, a large proportion are deaf " (Mindel and Vernon, 1971, p. 28).

Meningitis

Meningitis is a bacterial infection of the membranes encasing the brain and spinal cord. About 10% of childhood deafness can be attributed to meningitis. Three to 5% of the children who suffer from meningitis are deafened by it.

Prematurity

The World Health Organization (WHO) rejects the use of the term "prematurity." They indicate that there are actually two types of abnormal conditions that may be related to later problems: (1) *Low birth weight* infants weigh less than the low end of normal birth weight. A short gestation period, genetic abnormalities, or prenatal nutrition problems may be responsible. (2) *Short gestation period* infants are born somewhat earlier than the usual 9-month gestation period regardless of physical size or weight at birth.

COMPREHENSION CHECK 14.6

Enumerate the causes of hearing impairments and explain how incompatibility in blood groups of the parents can give rise to a severe hearing loss in the child.

PREVALENCE OF HEARING LOSS

Perhaps 14,000,000 Americans have some form of hearing impairment (Moores, 1982). This represents about 6% of the total population and includes elderly people whose hearing acuity is diminishing, individuals with mild hearing losses, and those with reduced functioning in one ear and normal hearing in the other. Most hearing loss is acquired in adulthood after a person has speech and language skills, and most hearing loss is relatively mild. Prelingually deaf Americans, on the other hand, represent only a small part of the American hearing-impaired population. Where one person in 16 may be hearing impaired, only on in 1000 is prelingually deaf.

In a school population of 50,000,000 we would expect 50,000 deaf children with perhaps 3000 to 4000 young deaf children entering the educational system each year. This number can be dramatically higher as a result of the consequences of epidemics. For example, the rubella epidemic of the early 1960s more than doubled the incidence of deafness over roughly a 2-year period. Except for unusual situations like this, a figure of 1 case per 1000 population seems to hold consistently in the United States.

ASSESSMENT OF HEARING CAPABILITIES

Indications of hearing impairment

Although it will be necessary to employ the services of a certified audiologist to measure precisely the hearing loss of a given child, there are some indications that can be observed by people who are not familiar with hearing-impaired children. One telling characteristic of hearing-impaired children is their lack of attention to spoken words and sounds. Many times it seems like the children are not paying attention when, in fact, they are not able to hear what is happening in the environment. In a school situation, for example, the child may seem to be daydreaming when the teacher is talking. This problem is likely to worsen in large groups as opposed to individual situations. In groups the child is less likely to hear what is happening because of not always being next to the teacher. In addition, the child may have some lipreading skills that cannot be used when the teacher turns. It is not uncommon for hearing-impaired children to be able to adjust well to speech when they see the person's face. The deaf child may say "Huh?" to questions but may be able to manage. When the speaker turns away, however, the child is totally lost.

Another indication of hearing loss is language delay. Children possessing hearing loss of any magnitude will exhibit problems in trying to use words. Whereas most children begin the use of words at approximately 12 months of age, the hearing-impaired child is most likely to start using words much later. Generally speaking, the more significant the hearing loss, the later in life the child will begin the use of words for functional purposes. Parents having other children are usually well aware of when their other children begin using words and are able to recognize language delay with remarkable facility. It should be added that parents are usually quite aware that there is something "different" about their child who has impaired hearing.

In addition to language delay, any child with a significant hearing loss will have speech problems. Hearing-impaired children start pronouncing words later in life than normal-hearing children. Likewise, these hearing-impaired children make many mistakes when trying to say words. The speech problems encountered by hearing-impaired children generally deal with consonant sounds. Therefore, any child who has speech problems should have their hearing tested to ensure that the problem is not caused by deficient hearing.

Another problem hearing-impaired children have is associated with inappropriate responses to questions. For example, a person may ask a hearing-impaired child, "How are you?" The child may respond, "I am 5 years old." The response is obviously inappropriate but is caused by the child's inability to hear the question correctly.

A final indication of hearing loss is a child's response to television, radio, stereos, and other equipment that has auditory production. A child may not understand what is being said by the people on television and may try to increase the volume when given the opportunity. It is also common for the hearing-impaired child to miss much of the information that is presented over television, video recorders, or motion-picture projectors. This can be a problem in classroom or day-care environments.

Teacher interaction with hearing loss

It is important that teachers be able to recognize hearing loss and interact with it as best as possible. The preceding section outlined some of the ways that a teacher can recognize hearing loss. It is important for the teacher to know that hearing-impaired children do better in individual settings than in groups. Similarly, hearing-impaired children are able to respond better in small groups than in larger groups. This happens because a hearing-impaired child will need to watch people better than normal-hearing children. The hearing-impaired child may lip-read to get information or may evaluate facial gestures or expressions.

It is important for the teacher to make certain modifications when there is a hearing-impaired child in the room. The teacher should ensure that there is adequate lighting in all areas of the room. The child should be placed in front of the class as close to the teacher as possible. When speaking, people should face the hearing-impaired child directly. The teacher must be careful to avoid talking with her back turned to the class. When there is a movie/television program to be viewed, the child should be placed as close to the speaker as possible. If necessary, the teacher should be prepared to give extra instructions and information to help in guiding the hearing-impaired child.

Problems in early detection

The discovery of hearing loss in a child can be elusive. As previously mentioned, children with only slight losses are sometimes able to function so well that it is only on entry into school that the problem is discovered. One major problem in detecting hearing loss is that deaf children do go through a stage of normal babbling between 3 and 6 months of age (Lenneberg, 1967). Most parents will assume that a child who is babbling has at least some hearing because they seem to be imitating sounds. To further compound the problems of early identification of hearing loss, many children who have profound hearing losses will react to loud noises, such as the slamming of doors. The reason for this is that loud noises may produce enough vibrations to cause the child to feel the noise. Parents can misconstrue this as the ability to hear. A final problem with the early indentification of hearing loss rests with the pediatrician who encounters few young hearing-impaired patients. Some pediatricians simply do not have the background or experience to recognize a hearing loss in a young child. As a result, many doctors tell parents that their concern about their child's hearing is not warrranted. Parents are told to be patient and that, in time, the child will start paying attention and will be able to hear better when he/she is older. It must be noted that even audiologists are not always accurate in their appraisal of hearing problems in young children.

The assessment of hearing is a complex process; therefore, a complete description is beyond the scope of this chapter. The brief description that follows may be augmented with the help of a basic audiology text such as that written by Newby (1978).

The usual procedure for testing hearing involves placing a set of headphones on a child and presenting sound of varying intensities (measured in decibles) and varying frequencies (measured in cycles per second, also called hertz). The sounds presented to young children are usually pure tones, that is, sounds consisting of one frequency. The range of frequencies is commonly from 25 hertz (Hz) to 8000 hertz (Hz). The machine that produces the sounds is called an audiometer.

The child is usually required to make a deliberate, clear response. To do definitive testing, this procedure works best for children at least 3 years old.

For younger children (ages 3 years and younger), other procedures are used for testing hearing. Using conventional audiometric procedures (using a standard audiometer), a young child is placed in a sound-deadened room where sounds will be presented to the child through speakers. This is done because most young children will not allow headphones to be placed on them. Another adaption that is made is concerned with response. A child who is older than 3 years can be instructed to raise her hand or make some other type of overt response. Many times the sounds are presented to children (younger than 3 years) and the audiologist waits for some type of spontaneous response by the child. This is done because it may not be possible to instruct the child to make some definite type of response. The skilled audiologist can see a child's reaction to sound in a reliable fashion, however.

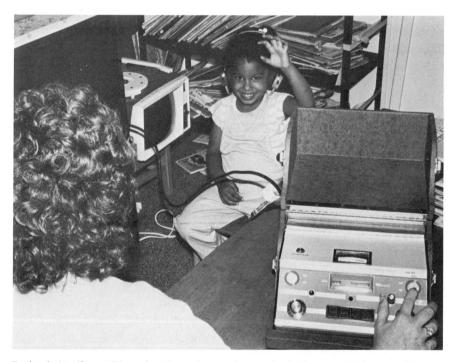

Early detection of hearing impairments can help to avert later problems in language development.

Another procedure that is used with young children is called brain-stem evoked response (BSER) audiometry. This method consists of placing harmless electrodes on the child's scalp. Sounds are then presented to the child, and the brain's electrical responses to the sounds are gathered and measured by the BSER audiometer. BSER audiometry is 95% effective in testing frequencies between 1500 and 4000 Hz (Stein, 1976). BSER audiometry is ideal for neonates and other children who may be difficult to test using the conventional procedures. Because BSER is a heavily researched area, improvements in testing seem to be only a matter of time.

COMPREHENSION CHECK 14.7

Describe the problems associated with early identification of hearing-impaired preschoolers.

Describe a procedure effective for assessing hearing loss in infants.

Educational assessment

Deaf children are usually asessed in a variety of areas of functioning before their educational placement. This assessment has been strengthened by the mandate of Public Law 94–142 that all handicapped children must receive an individual education plan. Before entering school, young hearing-impaired children are usually assessed in terms of hearing loss, general intellectual functioning, language, speech, speech-reading, and social skills. The testing of hearing-impaired children and interpretation of test results are often a problem because of the lack of testing materials specifically developed and standardized for these children.

Hearing loss, as mentioned previously, is assessed by an audiologist. After the child's hearing is assessed, the audiologist usually checks the child's hearing aid to assure its proper functioning. If the hearing aid has a minor problem, such as a dead battery or dirty ear mold, the aid is repaired and the child is tested.

In a comprehensive review of psychological assessment of deaf children, Sullivan and Vernon (1979) report that only a small minority of school psychologists have had any contact with deaf children. Even fewer have been trained to work with the deaf or have satisfactory communication skills to do so. The implications for the reliability and validity of most psychological evaluations of deaf children are clearly of concern.

The area of socioemotional development has been well researched using relatively large numbers of young deaf children. Meadow has developed the Meadow-Kendall Social-Emotional Inventory, which provides norms for deaf children by age and sex. The inventory includes a preschool scale (Meadow, 1982). The inventory is available through the Kendall Demonstration Elementary School and its Outreach Program (see the Appendix A).

Assessing the intelligence of a hearing-impaired child should only be done by a certified psychologist who is experienced in working with hearing-impaired children. It is easy to underestimate a hearing-impaired child's intellectual potential if inappropriate tests are used. For example, deaf children almost always do poorly on vocally administered tests. This is simply because a child who cannot hear the directions for a test will probably do very poorly on it. A hearing-impaired child should be given *nonverbal* tests of intelligence. The Nebraska Test of Learning Aptitude (NTLA) (sometimes called the Hiskey-Nebraska Test of Learning Aptitude) is an intelligence test providing norms for deaf children from 3 to 16 years. The instructions can be given through pantomime so that a child can understand the test requirements.

Another test commonly used with deaf children is the Leiter International Performance Scale, which is an untimed, nonverbal scale containing 60 items ranging from the 2-year to the 12-year level. Instructions can be given nonverbally.

The Weschler Intelligence Scale for Children (revised edition), or more commonly called WISC–R, is also used frequently with deaf children. Although the WISC–R has a verbal and a nonverbal scale, hearing-impaired children are only given the nonverbal scale. Norms for deaf children are now available on the performance subtests of the WISC–R.

Although there are problems with all these tests (see Salvia and Ysseldyke, 1978, for a complete discussion), they are the most preferable of those available. Tests such as the Stanford-Binet and Peabody Picture Vocabulary Test–Revised produce consistently low estimates of the ability of deaf children because of the dependence of the tests on spoken language.

Even though language is such an important area, there are no comprehensive standardized tests for testing language in hearing-impaired children. Often, informal measures that have been devised by staff members of school programs are administered. These tests, although providing some information, do not give norms for comparative purposes.

There is probably no achievement test more widely used with hearing-impaired children than the Stanford Achievement Test. This test has the advantage of possessing norms for hearing-impaired students. The major disadvantage of this test is that it is restricted to use with children who are more than 5 years old. Although some younger hearing-impaired children may be capable of performing on the Stanford Achievement Test, the norms are not designed for these children.

The speech of hearing-impaired children is generally assessed by a speech therapist. Again, there are few standardized measures that can be used. Most speech therapists use a test designed for children with normal hearing. Any of the currently available standardized articulation tests will yield valuable information regarding the speech of a hearing-impaired child.

COMPREHENSION CHECK 14.8

Scores on intelligence tests are a function of the nature of the test. Explain this statement with reference to hearing-impaired children.
Mention two intelligence tests that consider the characteristics of the hearing-impaired population.

TREATMENT OF HEARING LOSS

The most common method for the treatment of hearing losses is the use of hearing aids. Hearing aids come in a variety of sizes and styles. One type, the *body aid,* looks like a small transistor radio and is placed in a harness that is worn on the chest. The body aid is common for children who have severe to profound losses. Another type of hearing aid is the *behind-the-ear (postauricular) aid.* This is a small aid that wraps around the back of the ear. These postauricular aids are used most frequently for children with less severe losses.

Another type of hearing aid is the *auditory trainer.* Auditory trainers come in a variety of shapes and sizes. Until recently, many auditory trainers were quite bulky, having a variety of wires and attachments. Within the last 10 to 15 years, however, advances have been made so that these devices now look like large body hearing aids. Some of these auditory trainers now have wireless transmitting microphones that can be worn by the teacher. The microphone actually broadcasts, via an FM frequency, directly to each child's auditory trainer. The child is able to hear the teacher clearly no matter where the teacher is standing in the room. Each classroom is given a set of auditory trainers so that every child can hear the teacher clearly. Each set of classroom auditory trainers has a different frequency so that children will not be able to hear the voice of the teacher in the adjoining room.

Another potential extra educational tool is the cochlear implant. This is a procedure that is still in the experimental stage. In this procedure, a surgeon

Teachers can communicate with children who have significant hearing impairments by using auditory trainers.

implants an artificial cochlea (inner ear) in the patient. Because the procedure is still in the experimental stage, it is not often used on children. The procedure is also a very expensive one. To date, cochlear implants have been unable to produce normal hearing in a deaf person. It is a matter of conjecture whether or not this procedure will be successful in the future.

COMPREHENSION CHECK 14.9

Discuss the relative merits of hearing aids and cochlear implant in the treatment of hearing loss.

EDUCATION OF HEARING-IMPAIRED CHILDREN

Historical roots

Historically, the education of the hearing impaired has been labeled "education of the deaf." The reason for this is that, before the invention of hearing aids, many hard-of-hearing people were thought to be deaf. Therefore, in this section, reference will be made to education of deaf when considering all hearing-impaired individuals.

The first known teacher of deaf children was a Spanish monk named Pedro Ponce de Leon (not to be confused with Juan Ponce de Leon whose quest for the fountain of youth lead him to Florida). Teaching in the middle of the sixteenth century, Ponce de Leon worked with children of noble birth. Because his manuscripts were later burned, there is no direct knowledge of the methods he used. It is believed that he emphasized reading and writing and used a manual alphabet (Moores, 1982).

Another Spanish teacher was Juan Pablo Bonet. Bonet published a book in 1620 entitled *Simplification of the Alphabet and the Method of Teaching the Mute to Talk*. This book is generally regarded as the literary cornerstone of deaf education (Deland, 1931). In this book, Bonet illustrated a manual alphabet that is still used today with minor modification. It also forms the basis for the American Manual Alphabet (Moores, 1982).

In 1755, a French priest, Abbe Charles Michael de l'Epee, founded a school from deaf children in Paris. This was the first school founded for deaf children who were not from affluent backgrounds (Bender, 1970). Abbe de l'Epee adopted the Spanish manual alphabet used by Ponce de Leon and Bonet. He also was, apparently, the first person to introduce the use of a sign language for teaching deaf children. During the last quarter of the eighteenth century, a controversy regarding methodology in teaching deaf children developed and became intensified. In an exchange of letters, Samuel Heincke (a German educator of deaf children) debated the virtues of teaching speech to deaf children with del l'Epee, who believed that speech should never be emphasized over the use of sign language (Garnett, 1968). This was the first formal exchange in what would be regarded as the "oral-manual controversy," which has persisted for more than 200 years.

The first significant development in the education of the deaf in the United States came when Dr. Mason Cogswell searched for a teacher for his young deaf daughter, Alice. Dr. Cogswell and his friends raised enough money to send Thomas Gallaudet to Europe to study the methods of deaf educators and bring the knowledge back to America.

Gallaudet sailed to England where he was to study with the Braidwood family, famous for its advances in teaching deaf children. Gallaudet wanted to study first with the Braidwoods and then journey to France to study with Abbe de l'Epee's successor, Roche Sicard. When both methods had been studied, Thomas Gallaudet would combine the best of both systems and implement that knowledge in the United States. This arrangement, however, was not agreeable to the Braidwoods. They saw no reason for young Gallaudet to learn any system except the one that they were using. They insisted that Gallaudet use only the English system to the exclusion of the French method. The problem could not be resolved, and Gallaudet left England without studying with the Braidwoods. After arriving in France, Gallaudet studied with Sicard. When his studies were complete, Gallaudet returned to America with a deaf teacher from Sicard's school, Laurent Clerc. A man of remarkable talents, Clerc learned English rapidly. Gallaudet opened the first school for the deaf in the United States at Hartford, Connecticut, in 1817, with Clerc as the first teacher.

Because Gallaudet studied in France, he returned to the United States with the French method based on French Sign Language. Using the French Manual Alphabet (which came from the Spanish) and French Sign Language as a base, Clerc developed an instructional system designed to teach English. In the case of finger-spelling, of course, there was no difficulty in making the transition. Using the same alphabet, one could either write or finger-spell *B-O-N* or *G-O-O-D* as needed. The use of signs presented a different situation. Many could be used regardless of the spoken or written language. Others had been developed with handshapes to signify the initial French letter for the word. Clerc solved this problem by changing the handshape for many signs. For example, the American sign for *green* is the same as the French sign for *verde,* except a *G* handshape has been substituted for *V.* In the same way, the days of the week, except Sunday, are signed in the same way with only the handshape differing; *M* is used for Monday, *T* for Tuesday, and so on, with *H* for Thursday to differentiate it from Tuesday.

Although some of the signs of American Sign Language (ASL) are still close to their French Sign Language roots, the two languages are now separate and mutually unintelligible. Most of the vocabulary is now different, and there is a different word order and grammar. This form is analogous to spoken language. For example, Spanish and French (or Portuguese and Italian) have the same roots but are clearly different languages.

The education of the deaf was predominantly manual, that is, stressed sign language, from 1817 until the 1870s. Gradually, however, the United States became more and more oriented to oral-only education. During the twentieth century, virtually all the education for young deaf children became oral only. This trend started to change in the 1960s with the work of several researchers indicating that profoundly deaf children with deaf parents who used sign language had speech skills equal to children who had been enrolled in intensive oral-only preschool programs. Furthermore, not only their speech, but the language skills of the children who used sign language were far superior to those children who had been trained only in speech. It must also be pointed out that the children with deaf parents had no preschool experience in comparison with the children in speech-only programs who had 2 to 3 years of preschool.

The findings of academic and linguistic superiority of deaf children of deaf parents over deaf children of hearing parents by a wide range of professionals in such fields as psychology, education, sociology, and speech sciences (Brasel, 1975; Meadow, 1967; Stuckless and Birch, 1966; Vernon and Koh, 1970) were shocking to many educators of the deaf, especially those working with young children. Programs in the United States had been established in the belief that the use of signs would hinder the development of spoken and written language, academic achievement, and socialization. As a matter of policy, programs would punish children for using signs or gestures. Deaf teachers were not hired in the belief that they would hurt the speech development of deaf children. As the evidence piled up that deaf children who used signs from infancy were academically, linguistically, and socially *superior,* it became clear to more and more hearing educators that a great disservice had been done to deaf children—and to deaf individuals who might have been teachers.

These findings lead to a virtual revolution in the use of communication modes in the classroom, with oral-only education yielding to a combined oral-manual approach. Most programs now endorse a philosophy called *total communication,* which calls for the use of all components necessary to meet a child's needs, for example, speech, auditory training, signs, speech-readings, finger-spelling, reading. During a 10-year period from 1968 to 1978, 538 programs in the United States turned to total communication (Jordan, Gustason, and Rosen, 1979). This system was used in a majority of programs in the United States by 1978 with all ages—preschool, elementary, and secondary.

One long-term study has been conducted to study the effectiveness of different types of early-intervention programs, that is, those that serve deaf children and their families from the time of identification of a hearing loss through age 8 (Moores, 1986). The children were enrolled in eight programs in eight states across the United States and data were gathered over 4 years. Several interesting findings were obtained. First, the most successful programs had well-structured curricula emphasizing the coordinated use of auditory training, speech, and manual communication from the beginning. It was concluded that the past tendency of educators of the deaf to wait for a child to "fail" orally was a mistake. Manual communication can be used effectively at a very early age. A second major finding was that the most successful programs tended to have strong congnitive/academic components. In addition to communication and socialization experiences, children were trained in such areas as prereading and premath skill development. There were a number of other important findings. The children in the study were intellectually on a par with the norms for hearing children. Also, their scores in the five visual-motor subtests of the Illinois Test of Psycholinguistic Abilities were almost identical to those of hearing age peers, with the exception of Manual Encoding, where the deaf children were superior. (It should be noted that Manual Encoding has nothing to do with manual communication or the manual alphabet.) Also, communication mode was related to communication effectiveness. As might be expected from children with an average hearing loss of 99 dB, they received relatively little information through listening alone. With the addition of each element, comprehension improved. Thus, sound plus speech-reading (lipreading) was better than sound alone. Sound plus speech-reading plus signs was the most effective of all modes tested. The children were able to use their residual hearing while speech-reading and understanding signs at the same time.

Interestingly, none of the total communication programs in the study used ASL per se, rather they used systems that may be considered manual codes of English. The distinction between a *full* language method and an *instructional system* is presented in detail in the next section.

COMPREHENSION CHECK 14.10

How would you account for the resemblance between American Sign Language and French Sign Language?
Develop a program of total communication that, in your opinion, will be effective with hearing-impaired children. Point out the salient features of your program.

Service delivery systems

The education of hearing-impaired children depends, to a great degree, on the hearing loss of an individual child. Children with mild losses are usually served by neighborhood schools. These children are frequently given support services such as speech therapy and tutors and are in regular classrooms with hearing children for most or all of their school day. Public Law 94–142 requires that handicapped children are to be educated with nonhandicapped children as much as feasible ("least restrictive environment" clause).

The placement of children who have greater hearing losses involves some different considerations, however. When a child has a severe or profound hearing loss, it is usually difficult for that child to communicate with children who have normal hearing. Such hearing-impaired children often have poor speech and frequently are difficult to understand. Speech-reading is a poor method of communication because 40% to 60% of the sounds look the same on the lips. An example of the difficulty children may have in speech-reading is the fact that all the words that follow look similar on the lips:

$$\begin{array}{lll} \text{MOM} & \text{BOMB} & \text{POP} \\ \text{MOP} & \text{BOB} & \text{POMP} \\ \text{MOB} & \text{BOP} & \end{array}$$

Frequently, children with profound hearing losses are not able to understand what people are saying through speech-reading and are not able to make their wants known because of their poor speech. When placed in regular school programs, many young children with profound hearing losses find themselves socially isolated because of their communication problems. These children must compete with children who have the decided advantage of hearing all that happens in the classroom. Deaf children are in a far different position than are hearing children in their educational endeavors. A good example of this is reading. Reading is based on the assumption that a person is conversant in a given language. After knowing a language in its spoken form, reading that language is a logical extension. The normal-hearing child is able to use the language base in order to be able to decode the reading process. This is not true with the deaf child, however. A deaf child often has no language base from which to work. When the deaf child learns to read, often they are learning not only how to read but also learning the meaning of words. The deaf child is placed into a situation where twice as much must be learned as the hearing child on entering school. Not surprising, the deaf child starts behind normal-hearing counterparts and continues to get more and more behind.

Children with severe and profound hearing losses usually do best when placed in classrooms designed specially for hearing-impaired children. Such classrooms are small in size (usually 6 to 8 students) and usually have a teacher who is trained in all aspects of communications, including sign language. The hearing-impaired child is able to communicate with classmates as well as with the teacher. Classrooms for deaf children occur in three basic settings: public schools, special schools, and residential schools. Many public schools have classrooms that are designed to serve hearing-impaired youngsters. Unless the community is fairly large (population of 150,000 or more), the children are usually placed with other hearing-impaired children of various ages and hearing impairment. The incidence of hearing impairment makes educational programming difficult in areas of small population. For this reason, many hearing-impaired children have been placed together in special schools.

Special schools are designed to teach only hearing-impaired children. These schools operate quite similarly to regular public schools with the exception that all their students have difficulty in hearing spoken messages.

The final type of school is the residential school. Most states in the 48 contiguous United States possess at least one state residential school for the deaf. These schools are usually funded by the state to provide free public education. Many of the children in these programs live in dormitories that are on the campus of the school. If a child's parents live nearby, the child is usually transported to and from school on a daily basis much the same as taking the bus to school. Other children, however, live at the school during the school week. Some schools in larger states stay open during the weekend, and the children are in residence at that time.

On the surface, it may seem cruel to place children with severe and profound hearing losses in an educational setting removed from their parents and family. Many parents experience serious trauma when deciding on a school placement. On the other hand, these children are the ones who have greatest difficulty in communicating with hearing people. The lack of communication causes problems with social, personal, and educational development when these children are placed among people who cannot use a sign language or sign system. The effect is that the young child with a profound hearing loss seems isolated and literally has no one to talk with. The special school for hearing-impaired children gives children a chance to interact with

Kendall Demonstration Elementary School (KDES) in Washington, D.C. offers a model preschool program as well as school for hearing-impaired students up to the age of 15. KDES is on the campus of Gallaudet College. *Source:* Gallaudet College.

a variety of people ranging from students to teachers. Because most of the staff working on the campus of a school for the deaf are able to communicate through signs, the children are less likely to feel a sense of isolation. The children also are more likely to feel that they "fit in" well with the other children. Sometimes deaf children feel different when placed in integrated classroom settings because they are the only ones who cannot hear. In a school for the deaf, the children can identify with all the children in the school, and it becomes much easier to adjust to their deafness.

Another important fact about life in a residential school concerns the role models that are present for young hearing-impaired children. Children in residential schools see deaf adults in a variety of functions that helps make it possible for the deaf child to realize that deaf people do grow up and can function effectively in the world. A child who is in a school that has no deaf adults lacks appropriate adult role models.

The placement of a hearing-impaired child is dependent on a variety of factors, one of the most important being the hearing loss itself. Children with greater hearing losses need educational programming that is more specific than do children with mild losses. Most of the children encountered on campuses of residential schools for the deaf are either severely or profoundly hearing impaired. The age of onset of the hearing loss also is an important factor in considering educational placement. Children who are *adventitiously* deaf, that is, deaf owing to some accident or disease after birth, can be quite different from congenitally deaf children. Children born deaf never hear language and never gain linguistic information through hearing. Children who hear normally for the first 5 years of life will have a good understanding of their language and will have good speech skills. After 5 years of normal hearing, children will usually be able to function better in a hearing environment. These adventitiously deaf children are often better candidates for intergrated placement than are children who are born deaf.

Parents are often troubled about the placement of their deaf child. Some parents are very opposed to having their child placed in a deaf "institution." In some cases, they fight placement in a deaf school with great vigor. On the other hand, some deaf parents of deaf children insist that their children must be placed in special schools for the deaf so their children can have the opportunity to interact with other hearing-impaired children and hearing-impaired adults.

COMPREHENSION CHECK 14.11

Describe the impact of PL 94–142 on the educational placement of hearing-impaired children.

The least restrictive environment for children with severe and profound hearing losses may actually be special schools. Does this violate PL 94–142? Give reasons for your answer.

Deciding on the educational placement

Educational placement for the hearing-impaired child is determined by the geographic area in which the student resides, the extent of the hearing loss, and any additional problems the child may possess. A child with a loss less than severe is generally better suited for a public elementary school. A child with severe or profound loss is generally served by specialized programs for the deaf. Placement decisions usually are determined largely on the basis of functioning. The child that is able to function as a hearing child will be placed in those environments that have few specialized services. That child can use the services of the same speech therapist who works with children who have normal hearing, and, when facing academic problems, is able to seek the help of the same resource people that are available to the general student population.

Children with severe and profound hearing losses usually need services that are specialized to a degree greater than can be provided by the regular school program. These children usually need trained teachers of the hearing impaired, access to sign language and/or a sign system, and specialized resource people such as speech therapists, psychologists, and reading specialists.

There are basically seven placements that are available to hearing-impaired children under the age of eight. These are:

1. *Regular school placement.*   These schools may or may not have additional services other than what is provided to the hearing children. In some cases, these programs provide sign-language interpretation, a tutor for part of the class day, or supplemental work on speech and language. These programs are generally most effective with children who have losses that are less than severe.

2. *Private preschools.* Located almost exclusively in large urban areas, these schools serve a wide range of hearing-impaired children. The minimum age for acceptance into the program varies widely among programs. Some of these schools require that the children be toilet-trained before entering the program, but other programs will accept the child as soon as the hearing loss has been identified. The range of services of each program depends on the resources available.

3. *Speech and hearing centers.* Speech and hearing centers may offer schools, classes, or individual training for hearing-impaired children. As public education has accepted more and more responsibility for education of handicapped children, the role of speech and hearing centers in education of the deaf has diminished.

4. *Hospitals.* In some areas, hospitals operate preschools for hearing-impaired children. Some have made significant contributions to educational progress with young hearing-impaired children. Among the more notable are preschool programs operated by St. Christopher's Hospital in Philadelphia and Michael Reese Hospital in Chicago.

5. *Special schools.* These schools may enroll children beginning at ages 2 to 5 years, depending on the particular school. These schools are either for hearing-impaired children exclusively or are designed to serve the needs of different types of handicapped children.

6. *Residential schools for the deaf.* The majority of residential schools for the deaf in the country provide at least some service to hearing-impaired children under the age of 5 years (Craig and Craig, 1982). These schools serve wide ranges of hearing losses, and each school has its own set of criteria for admission into its program.

7. *Home service.* Many areas provide services to their hearing-impaired children on a preschool level by sending teachers to the homes of the children. These teachers work with parents as well as children. The children served are quite heterogenious when considered as a group.

Placement for children with multihandicapping conditions

Hearing-impaired children can be affected by additional handicapping conditions. Many of the causes of deafness can also cause other problems. A hearing-impaired child can also be mentally retarded, blind, emotionally disturbed, psychotic, or manifest behavior problems. Children with multihandicapping conditions present a substantial challenge to educators. Educators must be able to address other needs of the children in addition to their hearing impairment. Multihandicapped children represent a range that defies simple description. To say a child is both deaf and retarded may indicate an IQ of 45 and a hearing loss of 75 dB or an IQ of 75 and a hearing loss of 100 dB. The categories are so inclusive as to make many of the classifications, in effect, useless. What is more important is how the child is able to function. The most important consideration is what the child can do and what the child is potentially capable of doing with proper instruction.

It is difficult to find individuals who can teach hearing-impaired children with facility. It is even more difficult to find teachers who can teach multihandicapped, hearing-impaired children. When a hearing-impaired child has an additional handicap, a teacher is expected to be expert both in hearing impairment and in working with the additional handicap. Clearly, this places an extra burden on the teacher. To compound the problem of additional handicaps, some of these children do not make high rates of progress in the classroom. As a result, teachers can become frustrated and discouraged. It is important that the administrative staff of any school serving multihandicapped children be aware of the frustrations involved in teaching such children. The administration should be ready to provide extra support for teachers of multihandicapped hearing-impaired children.

COMPREHENSION CHECK 14.12

Explain the factors that merit consideration before educational placement for a hearing-impaired child is finalized.
The problem of hearing loss in the child is often compounded by other problems. Mention some handicapping conditions that may be associated with hearing loss.

Educational materials and tools

As discussed in an earlier section, there are many resources for parents of very young children. However, there is little material designed for the children themselves. Moores (in press) noted that many of the materials and techniques used with young deaf children represent modifications of materials originally developed for older deaf children or for hearing children. Many teachers are very creative in modifying materials to fit the needs of young deaf children.

There have been promising developments, however. Ewoldt has taken a leadership role in developing a language-arts curriculum for young deaf children with attention to early reading instruction and early writing. This work forms the foundation for the Kendall Demonstration Elementary School Language Arts Curriculum (see the resources list in the Appendix).

Bornstein has developed several sets of signed English readers designed for parents and teachers to use with young deaf children. The readers contain material of interest to children such as nursery rhymes and fairy tales. Printed materials, illustrations, and sign depictions are presented in an integrated manner. The readers are designed to introduce the children to signs in a relaxed, informative environment. The materials are available through the Gallaudet College Press (see the Appendix).

Clark, Moores, and Woodcock (1975) developed the Minnesota Early Language Development System (MELDS), which was designed to introduce young deaf children to print, sign, and rebus material. This was later expanded into the Clark Early Language Program (Clark and Moores, 1981) for use with a wide range of language-delayed children. Like the signed English material, it can be used by adults who are not proficient in the use of signs.

Another educational tool that was designed for use with hearing-impaired children is Project LIFE (Language Improvement to Facilitate Education). Project LIFE was marketed commercially starting in 1973 (Pfau, 1974) and has been used extensively in classrooms teaching hearing-impaired children. Project LIFE is a programmed instruction method for teaching language, visual perception, and nonverbal thinking activities to hearing-impaired children. The student is given four alternatives to select when working at a project LIFE machine. By pushing the correct button, the machine advances automatically to the next question. If a mistake is made, the student is required to select until the proper reponse is made.

A recent development that may have a profound effect on the way we educate hearing-impaired children is the microcomputer. Programs are being developed at a feverish rate to meet the needs of many different groups of handicapped children. Likewise, there are currently many schools for the deaf that are involved with the use of a computer in the classroom for the hearing-impaired child. The changes in this field are so rapid that extensive discussion here is not warranted.

American Sign Language (ASL) and Signed Systems

As previously mentioned, ASL has ben heavily influenced by the French Sign Language, which was the basis for the first instructional system used with deaf children in the United States more than 160 years ago. There has been speculation that this imported language might have merged with one or more sign languages used by deaf Americans among themselves before establishment of schools for the deaf (Moores, 1982).

Ever since the establishment of schools for the deaf, there have been differences in America between the sign systems used in the classroom and in social situations, just as there have been differences between spoken systems in different situations. In the nineteenth century the terms "natural" signs and "methodical" signs were used to differentiate two district systems (Stedt and Moores, 1983). The methodical sign system was designed to express English exactly. Natural signs, as the name implies, were not designed, but developed naturally as the language used by deaf Americans. The same situation exists at present. American Sign Language is used by deaf people in the United States and Canada today in much the same way. It serves the same functions for deaf people that a spoken language serves for hearing people.

A number of systems, which we might call manual codes in English, have been designed for classroom conditions, to be used in coordination with speech. These systems, of course, have much in common with the nineteenth-century methodical sign systems. Although the contemporary systems vary, they have some elements in common. They follow standard English word order and are designed to be used in coordination with speech. Most of the signs in each system are borrowed from ASL vocabulary. The most widely used pedagogical system in classroom use is Signing Exact English developed by Gustason, Pfetzing, and Zawolkow (1972). This system, known as SEE$_2$ has signs for elements such as pronouns (he, she, it), and suffixes (-ly, -ness, -ment), which in the past would have been finger-spelled in the classroom.

There has been interest lately in the use of ASL itself in classroom situations with young deaf children. Wilbur (1979) has supplied an in-depth analysis of ASL and the various instructional systems. Although there has been resistence to its use in the past, we believe that the use of ASL in the classroom deserves the same type of objective trial as other systems.

COMPREHENSION CHECK 14.13

How can computer technology contribute to the education of hearing impaired children?

SUMMARY

Hearing impaired is a term that covers a wide variety of individuals. There are two categories for legally classifying hearing losses: *hard of hearing* and *deaf*. The hard of hearing individual has a hearing loss of 35 to 69 dB, and the deaf individual a loss of 70 dB or greater. The categories of hearing loss used by the audiologist include mixed, moderate, severe, and profound.

Stress is placed on the family as well as the child when the child is coping with a hearing impairment. Financial burdens and psychological problems may be associated with raising a hearing-impaired child.

Five major causes of hearing impairment result in conductive sensory-neural or mixed hearing losses. Hearing losses are most commonly treated with hearing aids, which come in a variety of sizes and styles.

The education of the hearing-impaired child has been traced back to the sixteenth century, and today incorporates a system of total communication. Hearing impaired children are placed in one of seven educational settings based on the degree of hearing loss, geographic area, and any additional problems of the child.

SUGGESTED READINGS

Blackman, J. A. (1984). Middle ear disease (otitis media). In James A. Blackman, (Ed.), *Medical aspects of developmental disabilities in children, birth to three*. Rockville, MD: Aspen Systems Corporation.

Dubose, R. F. (1979). Hearing impairments. In S. Gray Garwood (Ed.), *Educating young handicapped children: A developmental approach*. Germantown, MD: Aspen Systems Corporation.

Robert Sheehan
John Lasky

CHAPTER OUTLINE

Colleen Martin has 11 infants in her early-intervention program who range in age from 8 to 18 months. Five are developmentally delayed; two have been diagnosed as failure to thrive (FTT); and four are infants with cerebral palsy. In the center, Ms. Martin and her two aides work individually and in groups with each mother and infant; her goal is to increase each infant's skill in exploring objects and in interacting with others by modeling specific teaching and therapy techniques for the mothers. With so much time spent on teaching these mothers and their infants with various problems, Ms. Martin wants to be sure that her subjective impressions about the positive gains that the infants are making can also be documented on more objective measures so that she can be confident about the effectiveness of her teaching methods and the appropriateness of her goals. So, she has begun to use an ongoing assessment system that allows both the mothers and the teachers and aides to record each infant's progress on a daily, weekly, and monthly basis. She wants to be able both to record progress and to highlight areas of little progress; this may alert her to possible changes that may be needed in her methods or goals for particular infants and also her entire center, in general.

Colleen has wisely combined several different methods in her evaluation system. For example, parents and teachers write daily anecdotal narratives about the infant's changes in behavior or temperament. Each week Colleen and her aides complete developmental and behavioral rating scales as well as update their specific behavioral and developmental goals for each infant. Monthly, Colleen works closely with other team members to assess each infant more objectively on a developmental curriculum that allows her to obtain developmental age estimates and to then assess changes in each infant's rate of development during intervention over the past month. Colleen is able objectively to document change resulting from treatment and can now more effectively communicate her goals and the impact of her program to parents and professionals.

Evaluation is really quite simple. It is a process of measuring characteristics of programs so that decisions can be made affecting those programs. In a very real sense, every person participating in an educational program is a decision maker. Parents make a choice of a program for their child and their family. They continue to make choices about their child's attendance and activity in an educational program and they make choices about their own continued involvement in a program.

Teachers are decision makers as they plan children's educational programs, arrange educational environments, make materials available to children, and choose appropriate ways to interact with children and families. Teachers also make decisions about referrals and follow-up of children who leave their programs, and they modify their programs based on children's and family members' success in the programs and in later placements.

Administrators make decisions about the allocation of funding, supervision of staff, and determination of program guidelines and policies. This need to make decisions, a need shared by all participants in an educational setting, is what prompts educators' involvement in program evaluation. Program evaluation is simply a process of informed decision making. If there is anything that differentiates program evaluation and the type of decision making commonly found in current programs, it is that that many such decisions are made in the absence of supportive information or data, resulting in decisions being made poorly or in error. Thoughtful use of program evaluation leads to informed and accurate decision making in educational settings.

DEFINITION AND DESCRIPTION OF PROGRAM EVALUATION

Program evaluation versus research

In some respects evaluation and research are similar. Both involve the collection of data in careful, systematic fashions. One difference is that an evaluation is performed to gather information for specific decisions regarding an existing program. A research study is usually conducted to obtain more basic information useful in decision making that extends beyond existing programs. For example, research may indicate the relative effectiveness of home-based versus center-based early intervention whereas evaluation might indicate the absolute usefulness of one or another of these intervention types. For example, if the director of a day-care program serving typical and atypical preschool children wanted to know how to modify an in-service training program to best meet the needs of her particular staff, she would be requesting an evaluation. The director did not want to know about staff training needs in *general* or training strategies that might be *generally* useful. Such interests might be viewed as a request for research. Nevertheless, research and evaluation share many common features (Hodges and Sheehan, 1978).

Program evaluation versus statistics

Evaluation should not be viewed as synonymous with statistics. Although almost all types of evaluation do employ the use of numbers and scales, such numerical manipulation usually exists only at the level of counting, averaging, examination of frequencies, and so forth. An example of this is evident in a trick examination question sometimes asked of graduate students in a research comprehensive examination. The question is as follows:

> *Mr. Brown, a principal, is interested in knowing whether the students in teacher A's class have higher test scores than the students in teacher B's class. What statistical test should Mr. Brown use for this purpose?*

The answer to this trick question is that no statistical test is necessary at all! Mr. Brown can average the scores if he likes, look at the two averages and then make a decision based on those averages. Mr. Brown does not need a statistical test because he is not attempting to generalize or infer to any larger population, hence no need for an inferential statistical test. As we have pointed out in distinguishing between evaluation and research, most evaluators are not attempting to generalize beyond a particular program, hence a lessened emphasis on particular statistical testing.

Program evaluation versus child evaluation

A distinction must also be made between program evaluation and child evaluation. Child evaluation is the collection of information about a child's performance for the purpose of research or decision making about that particular child. When program evaluation is directed at decision-making about children, it often requires child evaluation data. However, in many instances program evaluation efforts are directed at decisions other than those that are child-related. For example, a program evaluation might be directed at the impact of a new sliding-fee scale on family involvement. This evaluation might never include examination of child data.

Most program evaluators are knowledgeable about research, statistics, and child-assessment tools. They use their background in these areas to facilitate successful program evaluation. It is recommended for early educators who are interested in program evaluation to have training in these areas. This chapter draws the readers' attention to the decision-making aspects of program evaluation based on the belief that the factors most often mediating successful program evaluation are to be found in the nature of the evaluation questions being asked, and the usefulness of those questions, rather than in the specific technology used in the conduct of an evaluation.

Program evaluation as informed decision making

Program evaluation is simply informed decision making. Although this definition of program evaluation is not new, very few instances have been encountered in which program evaluation efforts have contributed to informed decision making. It is argued that program evaluations must surely have a dramatic effect on decisions to fund or not fund a program. Such arguments, unfortunately, find little support in actual evaluation practice. Recently, Cook (1981) suggested a number of propositions about program evaluation in social programs. Two of these relate specifically to decisions about the funding of projects. The two propositions are:

> Ongoing programs rarely die . . . . *Certainly to our knowledge, it is currently impossible for negative evaluation results to lead to the termination of programs. (pp. 261–262)*

> While program budgets are sometimes marginally affected by evaluations, typically they are not . . . *evaluations tend not to be used at all or to be used in more diffuse ways that influence the thinking of decision makers without affecting funding decisions. (pp. 262)*

Cook's (1981) propositions and the belief stated earlier that few evaluations lead to informed decision making should *not* suggest that evaluation *cannot* lead to such decision making. Rather, they support the fact that evaluators and indeed all participants in early-education settings must give serious thought at the beginning of an evaluation to its likely impact on decision making. For example, it is often useful to talk with program administrators and to ask what they would do if the evaluation confirmed that the program was having a positive effect on client populations. The administrators usually responded that they would continue functioning in the same manner.

When asked how they would respond to the conclusion that their efforts have no effect, the more candid administrators admitted that they would look for flaws in the evaluation—weak designs, insensitive measures, incorrect analyses, and so forth.

In essence, a decision to fund or not to fund a program is usually not relevant to the functioning policies of most programs. In response to this discussion, an evaluation is designed that builds on the policy-relevant variables that can and, if necessary will, be changed or modified within a program rather than focusing on variables that will have little effect on actual decision making in early-education settings. This theme, emphasizing the decision-making aspects of program evaluation, will be sounded repeatedly throughout this chapter.

COMPREHENSION CHECK 15.1

How can early-childhood teachers and other team members ensure that their evaluation efforts will result in program changes that can directly benefit the parents and their handicapped preschoolers?

How can a teacher evaluate whether the selection of toys in the preschool fills the needs of her preschoolers?

TYPES OF PROGRAM EVALUATION

Program evaluations can lead to a variety of decisions within early-childhood special-education settings. Although many groups have a stake in any evaluation (Cook, 1981), it is useful to identify those groups who have special program-evaluation goals and objectives. To place these decisions within the context of actual intervention settings and to introduce the different types of program evaluation, the organization of a typical early-education program will be discussed.

Program evaluation within the context of early-childhood special education programs

Many early-education settings can be viewed as having six distinct levels of function or activity. These six different functions are separate levels of an organizational structure that usually have ben added one at a time to start the program and keep it running. Figure 15.1 depicts these six functional levels of an early-intervention program.

At the top of this typical structure is the funding source. Such sources vary greatly from program to program. For example, some states provide funding for early-intervention programs through their legislature. These funds are usually channeled through a state department, bureau, or division and then disbursed to intervention programs. Educators in other states must rely on private funding sources or depend entirely or in part on tuition paid by parents. The function of this level of early-childhood special education is

Figure 15.1
Structure of a Typical Early-Intervention
Program

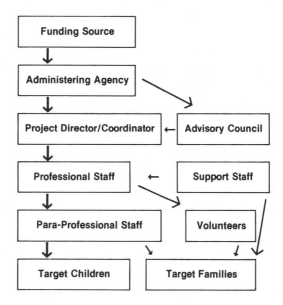

to ensure that adequate funding is provided to an intervention program or to a number of intervention programs.

The second level of the proposed structure, the administering agency, may be a public or private school, a community service agency, a day-care center or nursery school, a research firm, or some other type of agency. Administering agencies for early-childhood special education programs might loosely be called local education agencies. Individuals at this level, agency administrators, monitor program spending, ensure that services are not redundant, and assume responsibility that a program's goals and objectives are appropriate.

The third level consists of a project director, coordinator, or principal, and an advisory council. The advisory council is placed on the same level as the project director because the function of the advisory council is *to advise* rather than to direct. Project directors, coordinators, or principals oversee implementation of a program. They bear the responsibility of ensuring that goals and objectives of a program are being accomplished, and they are usually most concerned to demonstrate the effectiveness of a program and its benefit to a community.

Level four consists of the professional staff who operate the early-intervention program and serve the need of children and events. This group includes the entire interdisciplinary early-intervention team but particularly the core staff of preschool teachers, physical and occupational therapists, and speech/language clinicians.

The fifth level of a typical early-education setting is composed of paraprofessional staff and volunteers. These are individuals who function mainly under the direction and guidance of professional staff members and help implement the day-to-day functioning of a program.

Finally, the client population is conceptualized as the sixth level of an educational program. These are the target children and the target families. We emphasize the inclusion of families at this level in recognition that more and more early-childhood special education programs are including family goals and objectives as direct targets of their intervention efforts. The client population is concerned with the rewards that they and others realize as a result of the program. Additionally, they are concerned with other needs related to an education program, needs such as cost, transportation, availability of services, and hours of operation.

Although overlap of concerns does exist among the six levels of activity in an early-education program, numerous distinctions also exist among these levels related to the types of decisions of interest to individuals at each level. Evaluations directed at certain decisions will be of greater interest to individuals at one level than another. For example, funding agencies are rarely concerned about a data-based choice of one instructional strategy rather than another (e.g., grouping by chronological age versus grouping by developmental level). Similarly, interventionists are rarely concerned about a data-based choice of one method of cost accounting rather than another whereas such a question would be of prime interest to a funding source or an administering agency. Another example is that family members are not likely to show much interest in an evaluation designed to improve the effectiveness of a project coordinator's supervision of a professional staff. Family members may be interested in an evaluation addressing the magnitude of gains shown by their individual children or even groups of children during the period of intervention.

An important first step, therefore, to understanding the various types of evaluations is to understand the organizational structure under question and to probe the source of evaluation questions. It is useful to obtain and/or develop job descriptions from all educators in an educational program to help understand the differing and complimentary concerns of those educators as a first step to designing a program evaluation.

Understanding the organizational structure of a program provides some initial answers to the following questions: Who in the organization wants an evaluation to be conducted; who in the program might not want an evaluation to be conducted; who is the target audience for the evaluation; and who wants to (or can) make decisions in a program based on an evaluation?

COMPREHENSION CHECK 15.2

Identify the possible child and program evaluation needs of a university-based normal day-care center that has also integrated a few handicapped young children into their program.

Once an understanding is reached about an organizational structure to be evaluated and the source of evaluation questions, it is possible to categorize evaluations as one of five general types: (1) evaluability assessment, (2) program monitoring, (3) needs assessment, (4) formative evaluation, and (5) outcome evaluation. Although all five of these evaluation types are of interest to educators, we will discuss the last three of them; needs assessment, formative, and outcome evaluation in more detail than the others because of their direct relevance to training early-childhood special educators.

Each of these five evaluation types addresses certain decisions of interest to educators. Although the decisions leading to different types of evaluation differ in focus, there is no limit to the exact questions appropriate for any type of evaluation. Therefore, the examples in this chapter are only suggestive and are in no sense a complete listing.

Evaluability assessment

Evaluability assessment is an evaluation directed at decisions about the viability of evaluations. Simply, evaluability assessment is an evaluation of whether or not an evaluation can (or should) be conducted. This type of an assessment is an important first step to the conduct of any successful evaluation. It is usually implemented by carefully reviewing existing literature about the decisions under question and by conducting a number of interviews with other educators to determine whether the evaluation under question is feasible.

One important area in which this type of evaluation activity would be particularly useful for early-intervention programs is parental stress. Numerous programs have been encountered that have as one of their stated objectives the reduction of stress experienced by parents of handicapped children. Few adequate general measures of stress exist, and no adequate measures specifically relating to the parenting of handicapped children have been encountered.

A second example of the potential usefulness of evaluability assessment can be found in the many early-childhood special education programs serving infants diagnosed as at-risk. All too often evaluations are hastily conducted with this population directed at an understanding of the short-term gains shown by these children. Evaluability assessment questioning might indicate that such an evaluation is premature and must be delayed until a later date (e.g., until the children's entry to preschool or public school). In such instance, alternative decisions or questions might be more fruitfully addressed by other types of evaluation efforts.

The following is a listing of questions that might be addressed during the conduct of an evaluability assessment:

1. Do adequate measures exist to conduct a proposed evaluation?

2. Is the timing of the proposed evaluation reasonable and appropriate given the expected accomplishment of objectives?

3. Does the cost of the proposed evaluation, in time and money, appear reasonable in light of the expected results of the evaluation?

4. To what extent do the questions posed by an evaluation lead to genuine decisions that can be made affecting the educational program?

Program monitoring

Program monitoring is a type of evaluation usually concerned with fiscal and management concerns of an administering agency. This type of evaluation can best be viewed as a "looking over the shoulder of management" or to put it more objectively, a "careful data based scrutiny of management."

Program monitoring is usually initiated by a funding source, although it can be requested by individuals or groups within an administering agency as well. Program monitoring is sometimes called program auditing and addresses the following types of questions:

1. Are employee records accurate and complete?

2. Are agency standards being enforced? If not, why not?

3. Are the number of clients being served in accordance with predetermined expectations?

4. Are funds being spent as proposed?

5. Do all children have required immunization records on file?

6. Are individual educational plans developed and updated regularly for each handicapped individual?

Needs assessment

Needs assessment is an evaluation directed at understanding the needs of any program under consideration. The important characteristic of this type of evaluation is that it is directed at *needs* rather than at processes or outcomes. In its earliest use, this type of evaluation may be focused on an unserved target population to determine whether a program is necessary at all. Such an evaluation might involve a process as laborious as a house-to-house search for handicapped children who are not receiving educational services. It could also involve a survey mailed or otherwise disseminated to families to inform them of available services and requesting that they respond if such services are needed. Currently, a survey is being conducted to determine the needs of families in one community for day care to be located in the public schools. A survey was sent out with all employee paychecks of local companies and sent home with all schoolchildren. In addition a question box was placed in local newspapers. The questions are as simple as follows:

Do you anticipate a need for: (check all that apply)
Infant Child Care _____ Half day _____ Part week _____
Toddler Child Care _____ Full day _____ Full week _____
Preschool Child Care _____ After school _____

Needs assessments might also be conducted by reviewing the incidence figures for a given state or country to determine likely percentages of handicapped children. Such data can be compared with the known number of children currently receiving services to obtain an estimate of the number of children and families not receiving appropriate services for a particular area.

Needs assessment can begin once a program is in operation. Table 15.1 presents a number of questions posed in a needs-assessment instrument

TABLE 15.1
Needs-Assessment Questions Related to Services to Children

Step 2: (A) Administration and Management Needs
•Please answer the following questions:
1. Does your program have pressing needs in the development of written program guidelines?   Yes _____ No _____
•If so, do you need our technical assistance to meet these needs?   Yes _____ No _____

2. Does your program have pressing needs in handling personnel issues? (i.e., identifying staffing needs, recruitment, development job descriptions)   Yes _____ No _____
•If so, do you need our technical assistance to meet these needs?   Yes _____ No _____

3. Does your program have pressing needs in keeping records and/or preparing reports?   Yes _____ No _____
•If so, do you need our technical assistance to meet these needs?   Yes _____ No _____

4. Does your program have pressing needs in monitoring the activities of intervention program staff?   Yes _____ No _____
•If so, do you need our technical assistance to meet those needs?   Yes _____ No _____

5. Does your program have other pressing needs related to administration and management?   Yes _____ No _____
•Please specify those needs: _____

_____

•If so, do you need our technical assistance to meet those needs?   Yes _____ No _____

Source: Reprinted with permission from Project Transition Outreach Services Replication Site Profile II: A Needs Assessment Instrument. Houston, Texas: Project Transition, Harris County Mental Health Retardation Center, 1982.

developed recently for an early-childhood special education program in Houston, Texas. The entire needs assessment instrument discussed in Table 15.1 is nine pages in length. Early-childhood special educators completing the measure go through a two-step process: first determining whether they have needs in general areas such as providing services to children, and then determining their specific needs in those areas as well as indicating whether technical assistance can be initiated.

Needs-assessment evaluation may also provide early educators with a useful training process. For example, Black, Prestridge, and Anderson (1981) published a paper describing the development of a needs assessment process. A summary page from one of their measures is found in Figure 15.2. This summary page contains a number of items grouped into three areas: conceptualization, implementation, and evaluation. An inexperienced early educator completing this needs-assessment measure would learn a great deal about developing an early-education model simply by completing the instrument!

Figure 15.2
Items of a Needs Assessment Profile

Sample Summary Page from the Profile

STAFF DEVELOPMENT COMPONENT

This component identifies tasks that relate to the professional development of project staff. It includes determining staff development needs, resources, and plans to meet those needs.

Task	CURRENT PROJECT STATUS				Desired Change in Status During This Year	Technical Assistance Need
	Not Relevant to The Project	Must Be Considered and Planned	Task Partially Completed	Task Completed/in Operation		

Conceptualization

1. The project has a written statement of goals and objectives for the Staff Development Component.
The project has a written statement of and/or clearly delineated plans and procedures for . . .

Task	Not Relevant	Must Be Considered	Task Partially Completed	Task Completed	Desired Change	Technical Assistance
. . . statement of goals and objectives	0	1	2	3	___	___
2. . . . orienting staff to the project and the Handicapped Children's Early Education Program.	0	1	2	3	___	___
3. . . . identifying the competencies necessary to fulfill each staff role.	0	1	2	3	___	___
4. . . . determining staff development/training needs.	0	1	2	3	___	___
5. . . . a staff development/training program that addresses the currently identified needs.	0	1	2	3	___	___
6. . . . assigning staff responsibilities within the Staff Development Component.	0	1	2	3	___	___
7. . . . maintaining records on the activities of the Staff Development Component.	0	1	2	3	___	___
OTHER CONCEPTUALIZATION TASKS: ___	0	1	2	3	___	___
___	0	1	2	3	___	___

Implementation

Task	Not Relevant	Must Be Considered	Task Partially Completed	Task Completed	Desired Change	Technical Assistance
8. Current staff have been oriented to the project and to the Handicapped Children's Early Education Program.	0	1	2	3	___	___
9. Staff development/training needs have been identified.	0	1	2	3	___	___
10. Resources needed for implementing the staff development/training program have been acquired.	0	1	2	3	___	___
11. Staff development activities are ongoing and/or completed.	0	1	2	3	___	___
12. Records on the activities of the Staff Development Component are being maintained.	0	1	2	3	___	___
OTHER IMPLEMENTATION TASKS: ___	0	1	2	3	___	___
___	0	1	2	3	___	___

Evaluation

Data are being collected to

Task	Not Relevant	Must Be Considered	Task Partially Completed	Task Completed	Desired Change	Technical Assistance
13. . . . document the existing staff development needs of project staff.	0	1	2	3	___	___
14. . . . document the extent to which all planned staff development activities were provided.	0	1	2	3	___	___
15. . . . document the extent to which goals and objectives of the Staff Development Component have been attained.	0	1	2	3	___	___
16. . . . document the extent to which staff members were satisfied with the staff development program.	0	1	2	3	___	___
17. . . . document the extent of progress or change in staff knowledge/skills as a result of staff development activities (where appropriate).	0	1	2	3	___	___
18. . . . document the extent to which project staff have acquired the competencies necessary to fulfill their respective staff roles.	0	1	2	3	___	___

*Reprinted with permission from Black, T., Prestridge, S., Anderson, J. (1981) *The development of a needs assessment process.* Occasional Paper 3. Chapel Hill, NC. Technical Assistance Development Systems.

Needs-assessment evaluation is not only useful for direct service professional staff. Administrators of programs must periodically assess their own needs, although the specific items or questions addressed by their needs assessment will be different from those already discussed. Table 15.2 presents needs-assessment questions pertaining to administration and management in the needs-assessment instrument that was recently developed for an

TABLE 15.2
Needs Assessment Questions Related
to Administration and Management

Step 2: (D) Providing Services to Children
- Please answer the following questions:

1. Does your program have pressing needs in the areas of developing and/or using individual educational programs (IEPs)?   Yes _____ No _____
   - If so, do you need our technical assistance to meet those needs?   Yes _____ No _____

2. Does your program have pressing needs in the selection of an overall curriculum?   Yes _____ No _____
   - If so, do yu need our technical assistance to meet those needs?   Yes _____ No _____

3. Does your program have pressing needs in implementing an overall curriculum?   Yes _____ No _____
   - If so, do you need our technical assistance to meet those needs?   Yes _____ No _____

4. Does your program have pressing needs in coordinating and/or delivering ancillary services to children (i.e., speech therapy, occupational therapy, etc.)?   Yes _____ No _____
   - If so, do you need our technical assistance to meet those needs?   Yes _____ No _____

5. Does your program have pressing needs in conducting and/or using ongoing data with children?   Yes _____ No _____
   - If so, do you need our technical assistance to meet those needs?   Yes _____ No _____

6. Does your program have pressing needs in following up on children whose have left programs?   Yes _____ No _____
   - If so, do you need our technical assistance to meet those needs?   Yes _____ No _____

7. Does your program have other needs related to services to children?   Yes _____ No _____
   - Please specify those needs: _____

   - If so, do you need our technical assistance to meet those needs?   Yes _____ No _____

Source: Reprinted with permission from Project Transition Outreach Services Replication Site Profile II: A Needs Assessment Instrument. Houston, Texas: Project Transition, Harris County Mental Health Mental Retardation Center, 1982.

early-childhood special education program. As the table indicates, questions related to administration have more to do with personnel, record keeping, and so forth than with direct services to children.

Needs assessment of program functioning can be completed in a variety of fashions. Such assessment can be conducted by having a trained needs assessor review project functioning at a site or by telephone. Needs assessment can also be completed in a self-reporting fashion with the results then being sent elsewhere or used internally by a project coordinator or director to plan in-service training objectives.

As the examples presented in the preceding tables indicate, needs-assessment evaluation can be a simple, yet an extremely useful process for educators. Educators should be encouraged to develop their own needs-assessment measures, although they must be cautioned to avoid development or adoption of a system that involves too much paperwork. In a recently complete third-party evaluation (Sheehan, Gallagher, and Robson, 1982) of special education programs, educators were found to be frustrated with the amount of needs-assessment paperwork necessary to obtain technical assistance or communicate their needs to others. Such frustration can quickly undermine any attempt to systematically and empirically assess the needs of any part of an early-education program.

COMPREHENSION CHECK 15.3

How can an early-intervention program in a small, rural town identify the needs of all single teenage mothers and their at-risk infants so that effective support services can be planned and implemented?

Formative evaluation

Formative evaluation is somewhat similar to program monitoring in that information is gathered during the ongoing operation of a program. A distinction can best be made between these types of evaluation by recognizing that formative evaluation focuses more on the processes of a program as they relate to the delivery of objectives rather than the administrative concerns of an agency.

Formative evaluation is implemented and used during the conduct of a program focusing on the process of program delivery and attainment of short-term objectives. This definition is more specific than Baker's (1974), who suggests that formative evaluation consists of information and judgments to assist in the revision and imporvements of instructional programs.

Formative evaluations are data based. They rarely, however, involve the use of experimental research designs. One reason is that formative evaluation usually involves data collection on children, families, or staff *within a program* whereas most experimental research designs emphasize comparisons between clients or staff within a program and similar individuals receiving no services or an alternative form of services.

Regular examination of children's educational plans might constitute a form of formative evaluation. Maintaining a log of parent requests for infor-

Teachers can monitor children's learning with simple devices to help in formative evaluation.

mation and recording the instances in which those requests were successfully and unsuccessfully met provides valuable formative data.

Programs placing strong emphasis on formative evaluation usually have well-developed data collection systems on children, families, and staff. Information generated by these systems is then periodically reviewed, and programs are consequently modified based on the formative evaluation data. For example, Bricker, Sheehan, and Littman (1981) describe one formative-evaluation system for infants. To ensure consistency and continuity in monitoring child progress, systematic data collection activities were necessary. To assist the instructional staff, three types of data-recording forms were devised. These forms were designed to collect trial-by-trial data, muiltiple targets or subject's data, and continuous data.

The data-recording form contained in Figure 15.3 was designed to collect trial-by-trial data and also to provide space for indicating the following information:

Target area: The general area within which the objectives are located, such as gross motor.

FIGURE 15.3
Sample Recording Form for Trial by Trial Data

Target Area ___ Fine Motor

Original STO: ___ Infant will track from mid-line to right.

Program Objective: ___ Infant will track 30°, 60°, and 90° from mid-line to right.

LTO: ___ Infant will track a slowly moving object 180° in both directions.

Data collection Specifications: ___ Ten trials per day; criteria 8/10 trials correct for two consecutive days

Child: ___ A

Teacher: ___ Jones

Date	Step-1 Tracks 30° to right										Step-2 Tracks 60° to right										Step-3 Tracks 90° to right										Step-4										Comments
6/5	I
6/6	I	I
6/7	.	.	I
6/8	.	.	.	I
6/9	.	.	.	.	.
6/12											I	.	.
6/13											I	I	.	.
6/14											.	.	.
6/15																					I	I	.	.
6/16																					I	I	I	.	.
6/17																					I	I	I	I	.
6/18																					.	I	I	.	.
6/19																					.	.	.	I	.
10
9
8
7
6
5
4
3
2
1

Source: Reprinted with permission from Bricker, D., Sheenan, R., Littman, D. (1981). *Early interventions: A plan for evaluating program impact.* Series Paper 10, Monmouth, OR: Western States Technical Assistance Resource.

LTO: The long-term objective.

Original STO: The original short-term objective from the programming training targets (in the event that a teacher must branch from the STO in the skill sequence, this space specifies the STO from the sequence. In this way, the data records always relate to the core skill sequences, despite necessary variations by each teacher).

Program objectives: Either the STO from the skills sequence (if it was appropriate) or the objective that was branched from the original STO.

Data collection: The specific data-collection procedures (e.g., 15-minute time sample, frequency data).

The data recording form is composed of three sections: a space to indicate the data, a series of columns to record trial-by-trail data, and a space for comments. Data columns are divided into four sections, each composed of 10 squares. The space above the recording squares is for specifications of the behavior, cues, and criterion for that particular target step in the training program. Moving from left to right, steps targeted should more closely approximate the program objective. This form can be used to record a variety of data, such as frequency, correct/incorrect, rate or interval.

Figure 15.4 contains a form for recording data on multiple subjects or multiple targets for one child. This form is particularly useful for collecting simultaneous information on small groups of children or for comparing an individual child's progress across four different targets. If a teacher wants to increase the number of trials per session, the form is easily modified.

The recording form contained in Figure 15.5 was developed to accommodate the collection of continuous data in which it is important to specify the context, antecedent, and consequences for a targeted behavior, as when monitoring the occurrence of productive language during a free play period.

In general, data were collected on a child's progress toward targets on a daily or weekly basis (Bricker, Sheehan, and Littman, 1981, pp. 12–18). The formative data on infant progress are collected for the purpose of developing and modifying educational goals for children—data collection for decision-making purposes. A recent text by Bagnato and Neisworth (1981) provides extensive useful discussion of this type of formative evaluation for planning and modifying children's educational programs. Perhaps similarly refined systems of formative evaluation for families and staff will also soon be developed and disseminated.

One serious limitation of formative evaluation is that the systems established to conduct such evaluations at times become viewed as an end goal. Because of the multiple demands in their job, many teachers fill out individual educational plans in a grudging fashion and view them as time-consuming and often irrelevant paperwork. For example, recently work was done with the staff of one early-intervention program to assist them in their formative evaluation efforts. The staff members had developed an extensive assessment-based curriculum and were faithfully plotting each acquisition of new preschooler's behavior. When the staff were asked how they used data, they were unable to respond. When they were asked what decision rules had been

FIGURE 15.4
Sample Recording Form for Multiple Subject or Targets

Sample Recording Form for Multiple Subjects or Targets

Name: __A__

Target: __Answering questions appropriately__
__during small group time__

Steps: __¹Sitting in chair; ²Attending to teacher; ³responds__
__appropriately when asked a question.__

	6/2	6/3	6/4	6/8	6/10	6/11	6/12	6/14	6/15	6/16	6/17	6/18
	5	5	5	5	⑤	⑤	⑤	⑤	⑤	⑤	⑤	⑤
	4	4	③	4	4	4	4	4	4	4	4	4
	3	3	2	3	3	3	3	3	3	3	3	3
	2	2	2	②	2	2	2	2	2	2	2	2
	①	①	1	1	1	1	1	1	1	1	1	1
	0	0	0	0	0	0	0	0	0	0	0	0

Baselines: _____

Name: __B__

Target: __same__

Steps: _____

	6/2	6/3	6/4	6/8	6/10	6/11	6/12	6/14	6/15	6/16	6/17	6/18
	5	5	5	5	5	5	5	⑤	⑤	⑤	⑤	⑤
	4	4	4	4	4	④	④	4	4	4	4	4
	3	3	③	3	③	3	3	3	3	3	3	3
	②	②	2	②	2	2	2	2	2	2	2	2
	1	1	1	1	1	1	1	1	1	1	1	1
	0	0	0	0	0	0	0	0	0	0	0	0

Baselines: _____

Name: C
Target: same
Steps: _____

	6/2	6/3	6/4	6/8	6/10	6/11	6/12	6/14	6/15	6/16	6/17	6/18
	5	5	5	5	5	(5)	(5)	(5)	(5)	(5)	(5)	(5)
	4	4	4	(4)	(4)	4	4	4	4	4	4	4
	(3)	(3)	(3)	3	3	3	3	3	3	3	3	3
	2	2	2	2	2	2	2	2	2	2	2	2
	1	1	1	1	1	1	1	1	1	1	1	1
	0	0	0	0	0	0	0	0	0	0	0	0

Baselines: _____

Name: D
Target: same
Steps: _____

	6/2	6/3	6/4	6/8	6/10	6/11	6/12	6/14	6/15	6/16	6/17	6/18
	5	5	5	5	5	5	5	5	5	5	5	(5)
	4	4	4	4	4	4	4	4	(4)	4	(4)	4
	3	3	3	3	3	3	3	(3)	3	(3)	3	3
	2	2	2	2	2	2	(2)	2	2	2	2	2
	1	1	(1)	1	(1)	(1)	1	1	1	1	1	1
	(0)	(0)	0	(0)	0	0	0	0	0	0	0	0

Baselines: _____

*Circled number indicates number of correct responses.
Source: Reprinted with permission from Bricker, D., Sheehan, R., Littman, D. (1981). *Early intervention: A plan for evaluating program impact. Series Paper 10.* Monmouth, OR: Western States Technical Assistance Resource.

FIGURE 15.5
Sample Recording Form for Multiple Subjects or Targets

Sample Recording Form for Continuous Data

Domain: ___Communication___   Child: __A__

LTO: ___Expresses linguistic functions of labeling of objects___   Teacher: ___Dan___

Program Objective: ___responds when asked to label object___

DATE	CONTEXT	ANTECEDENT	BEHAVIOR						CONSEQUENCE
			Vocalize	Gesture	Word				
1/20	Play area/peer	Peer points			ball				Peer takes ball
1/20	Play area/peer	Ball rolls away			go				Peer looks at ball
1/20	Play area/peer	Ball rolls away		points	ball go				Peer looks at ball
1/20	Play area/peer	Ball rolls away		points	ball go				Peer retrieves ball
1/20	Play area/peer	Peer holds ball		points	ball				Peer gives ball to Kevin

Source:

Reprinted with permission from Bricker, D., Sheenan, R., Littman, D. (1981). *Early interventions: A plan for evaluating program impact.* Series Paper 10, Monmouth, OR: Western States Technical Assistance Resource.

developed to choose when to abandon a developmental item and either move on or drop back in their curricular planning, the staff also were unable to respond. When the staff were asked how often they had incorrectly chosen a developmental item to work on with children or families, they were confused about the necessity of evaluating this factor. Is the formative evaluation data really providing any information useful for decision making or are the data being collected simply to provide a post hoc rationale for the decisions that they were already making? The measure of success of any program evaluation is to be found in its usefulness for program functioning.

Outcome (summative) evaluation

Outcome or *summative evaluations* are the most commonly used evaluations, and many educators think only of this type in connection with an evaluation. The commonly perceived purpose of outcome evaluation is to assess the overall outcome of an educational program on one or more client populations. Recall the example given earlier in this chapter of a discussion with an administrator who has been informed that a program is having a positive impact. The response of the administrator was "Fine, keep it going." The same administrator when informed that a program was not having a positive impact usually responds "What is wrong with your evaluation?" As a result of these responses, the following alternative definition of outcome evaluation is suggested:

> *Outcome evaluation is (or should be) an evaluation implemented throughout the conduct of a program and used toward the end of one cycle of a program to make major changes in one or more aspects of the program.*

The decision-making nature of this definition should be obvious to readers. Educational programs should be viewed in the same developmental fashion as children. Educational change in such programs is always possible (and is necessary), and such change should be guided by data.

As indicated earlier, outcome studies in education sometimes involve the use of experimental designs involving random assignment of children and/or families to control groups or matched comparison groups (Cook and Campbell, 1979) for comparison purposes (see Dunst, 1979, for a discussion of such designs being used in special education). Designs such as these are used less often in early-childhood special education because of the ethical problems associated with assigning children and/or families to "no treatment" groups or the absence of "alternate treatment" groups.

As stated earlier, the field of intervention research with handicapped children is still in its own infancy. Thus, the best way of demonstrating and comparing progress is not yet known. In light of this, an intervenor must make several comparisons and choose that one that seems to have the most logic and credibility.

The qualifications that have just been cited are actually common in applied research efforts. Rather than minimize the value of applied research, these qualifications suggest caution, and they also suggest that the role of the intervention evaluator is to pay careful attention to the logic implied in any evaluation effort.

In determining whether the intervention with infants may be influencing their progress, one approach (Sheehan, 1979b) is to examine whether the estimates of developmental progress exceed any of several expectations of how the infants would have fared in the absence of intervention. Based on the position stated earlier in reference to a subset, these examinations must be made for all children and, in particular, for those children who show evidence of progress.

At least three types of comparisons might be used as a standard for the progress shown by infants in a case-study intervention program. The first of the comparisons, the most liberal one, is a simple comparison of the progress of infants to a hypothesis of no progress. The essence of this argument is the assumption that handicapped or at-risk infants who are not cared for in intervention programs are likely to show no progress. Thus, the comparison tests whether this expectation is exceeded.

A second comparison is whether the progress of infants exceeds an estimate of their own initial rate of progress. The essence of this argument is the progressive decrement hypothesis. This hypothesis suggests that while some growth may occur, it is declining in rate. Thus, a viable test is to determine whether the progress of the infants in the intervention program equals or exceeds this initial rate.

There are many difficulties inherent in identifying any measure of infant progress as their "rate" (Sheehan, 1979a, 1979b). This difficulty pertains to the stability of rate of progress and also the number of data points necessary to define rate. Despite this difficulty and because of some measurement problems that occur with low functioning infants, a proportional measure of developmental age/chronological age (DA/CA x 100) is sometimes used. Thus, this measure assesses changes in developmental age relative to chronological age.

A third, and most conservative argument, is whether the progress of infants in one intervention program exceeds the progress of normal infants during a similar 6-month period. It is clear that this most conservative comparison might never be exceeded by very seriously involved infants.

Outcome evaluation studies such as those just discussed represent notable attempts to conduct outcome-oriented program evaluation in early-childhood special education. They have, however, only a limited influence on the decision making of educators working with young handicapped children and their families. The most significant influence is in confirming that early-childhood special education is an activity that is worthwhile. However, such confirmation either may not be necessary or may be necessary only at infrequent intervals. Rather than suggesting that emphasis on outcome evaluation studies should be diminished, it is suggested that continued outcome-evaluation activity can be useful, *provided that the focus of outcome-evaluation questioning be somewhat redirected.*

In the definition of outcome evaluation, it was stated that outcome evaluation should be conducted throughout the course of a program and used toward the end of one cycle of a program to make major changes in one or more aspects of the program. *Before the start of an outcome evaluation, educators must identify specific ways in which they are willing to change their programs, if such changes are supported by evaluation data.* Outcome evaluations should then be directed toward those areas of suggested change. In rare instances in which educators are willing to totally terminate a program showing null effects, evaluation studies such as those already mentioned might be conducted. In other instances, educators may prefer to consider less dramatic program changes. For example, educators may be willing to restrict their intervention to similar populations of children and families if it can be shown that heterogeneous grouping is less effective than homogeneous grouping. Or educators may be willing to accept younger children into a program if subsequent data indicate that those children do benefit from earlier intervention. Early educators who are using a behavioral curriculum may be unwilling to adopt a more cognitive strategy even if evaluation data supported the cognitive approach. In such instances, outcome evaluation studies should not be directed at the efficacy of behavioral versus cognitive strategies. Clients must first be supportive of change before they can be assisted in that change process. Otherwise, they will be resistant and reluctant to accept therapeutic suggestions.

A refocusing of the questions to be answered by outcome evaluation does not change the methodology to be used. Experimental and quasiexperimental research designs can still be used, provided that educators ask questions leading to their use. Standardized measures, rating scales, and parental reports may still be appropriate, as will be a wide variety of data analytic tools. The only deviation from traditional outcome evaluation is for educators to specify in advance ways in which evaluation data will be used, rather than waiting until the data are collected to ponder and act on their implications. "How will we use this information?" is the question that should be asked at each stage of the evaluation process. This alternative approach will result in more useful outcome evaluations in early-childhood special education.

COMPREHENSION CHECK 15.4

Explain the primary differences between *formative* and outcome or *summative* evaluation methods and give clear examples of each that teachers could use in their preschools.

SUMMARY

This chapter has provided a brief overview of program evaluation in early childhood special education. Numerous volumes exist pertaining to program evaluation. The concern, however, of this chapter has been to provide readers with the necessary encouragement to become involved in program-evaluation efforts.

Program-evaluation specialists with backgrounds in research design, measurement, and statistics play an important role in the conduct of evaluation in clinical early-education settings. Of equal importance is the role played by parents, aides and teachers, program directors, coordinators, and principals, administrators, and funding agents, for it is these other groups of individuals who must provide the substance of a good evaluation. This substance is composed of the evaluation questions, reflecting genuine decisions that the parents and educators are willing to make in early-intervention programs.

A high quality program evaluation is based on an accurate understanding of the structure of an early-childhood special education program. It reflects a clear statement of the target audience of an evaluation, the evaluation questions being asked, and the ways in which answers to evaluation questions can be translated into decisions affecting the quality of educational programs for children and families. A number of evaluation types exist to assist the information decision making of educators, each type contributing in a unique way to that decision making.

Early-intervention efforts can and should be based on a sound foundation of empirical support; program evaluation, when conducted well, provides that empirically-based foundation. Early-childhood educators at all levels can ensure and enhance the quality of program-evaluation efforts by becoming involved in evaluating their programs.

SUGGESTED READINGS

Berk, R. (1981). *Educational evaluation methodology: The state of the art.* Baltimore: Johns Hopkins University Press.

Cook, T. (1981). Dilemmas in evaluation of social programs. In M. Brewer and B. Collins (Eds.), *Scientific inquiry and the social sciences.* San Francisco: Jossey-Bass.

Garwood, S. G. (Ed.). (1982). *Program evaluation: Topics in early childhood special education, 1*(4).

Sheehan, R., and Gallagher, R. J. (1983). Conducting evaluations of infant intervention programs. In S. G. Garwood and R. R. Fewell (Eds.), *Educating handicapped infants.* Rockville, MD: Aspen.

Journals of relevance for this topic are *Educational Evaluation and Policy Analysis, Journal of the Division of Early Childhood,* and *Topics in Early Childhood Special Education.*

16

Evolving Themes in Theory, Training, and Practice

Stephen J. Bagnato
John T. Neisworth

CHAPTER OUTLINE

The field of early childhood special education is growing and changing rapidly. Eight themes or dimensions of change can be identified that reflect progress within the profession; these are described in this closing chapter.

PROFESSIONAL STATURE

The increasing stature and respect for the field of early intervention and for the early-childhood special educator in particular is reflected in changes within professional organizations that represent the field. One of the largest and most active subdivisions of The Council for Exceptional Children is the Division for Early Childhood (DEC). The organization sponsors annual interdisciplinary conferences that serve as a vehicle for the presentation of applied research and clinical methods for working with handicapped infants, preschoolers, and their families. In addition, DEC publishes its own journal to disseminate such early-intervention research and methods.

The rapidly increasing validity of early-intervention practices is reflected also in the number of other disciplines that have special interest groups that focus on issues relevant to young exceptional children. These include the American Educational Research Association, Society for Research in Child Development, American Psychological Association-School Psychology Division 16, and the National Association of School Psychologists. In addition, various medical groups sponsor symposia and journal research issues that attest to the wide interest and importance attached to early intervention concerns. Annual conferences are sponsored by the National Center for Clinical Infant Programs in Washington, D.C. Such organizations as the World Association of Infant Psychiatry and the Society for Developmental and Behavioral Pediatrics are also active in this regard.

TRAINING PROGRAMS

The recent development and expansion of university programs in early-childhood special education also dramatically signals the increased training emphasis in early intervention. Departments of special education, human development, and even school psychology have created specializations for graduate students in this area. In fact, the trend toward interdisciplinary training has resulted in interdepartmental course work that more comprehensively prepares the student for a career in early intervention.

Interdisciplinary training programs include course work in such areas as developmental assessment, normal and atypical child development, developmental disabilities, parent counseling and education, behavior-modification strategies, program administration, program evaluation, and curriculum planning and intervention. This academic preparation is effectively coupled with practicum and internship experiences in a variety of interdisciplinary settings such as community agencies (e.g., Easter Seals, United Cerebral Palsy), schools, day-care centers, Head Start programs, rehabilitation centers, and pediatric hospitals and medical centers. Direct, cooperative work experience with both handicapped children and the various specialists who serve them forges a strong link between theory and practice for the infant and preschool specialist. With specific credentialing as a child development associate, early-childhood special educator, or a preschool or developmental school psychologist, training programs have translated the need for training in early intervention into practical outcomes.

EARLY-INTERVENTION EFFICACY RESEARCH

During the past 5 years, the field of early intervention has shown a growing maturity in that it now is confident enough about its status and worth to address crucial questions regarding the effectiveness of its diverse treatment approaches. This focus is also coupled with practical questions about the cost benefits of treating young handicapped children early in life in order to prevent, remedy, or compensate for developmental disabilities that would more severely compromise adaptive functioning in middle childhood without the positive impact of such treatment. With increased sophistication in methods of monitoring child progress and program effectiveness, researchers are now beginning to demonstrate the long-term benefits of early intervention for mildly handicapped children in terms of increased adaptive and social skills, increased learning readiness, and less frequent placement for special-education services at school entrance.

Although clinical research is just emerging, studies demonstrate that intensive early treatment for severely developmentally disabled children can be effective in teaching compensatory skills for visual, auditory, and neuromotor disabilities. Many severely impaired children show dramatic improvement during phases of intensive interdisciplinary treatment that exceed the gains one would expect based on their rate of maturation alone. Such interdisciplinary intervention appears to be the factor that accounts for such gains, although much more research is needed concerning the long-term generalization of these gains.

Comparisons among different types of service-delivery models (e.g., home, center, hospital, combination) are beginning to help professionals in the field to address the issue of most impact for the least cost. More importantly, such research is only beginning to provide information on the most effective matches between child needs and treatment strategies. This promises to be one of the most exciting avenues of research for the future.

PARENT-CHILD INTERACTION AND
INTERVENTION STRATEGIES

The study of styles of the nature of parent-child interactions and ways to facilitate the development of these attachment relationships is beginning to revolutionize early-intervention methods. Research in developmental psychology has demonstrated that parents and infants influence the behavior of each other in distinct, reciprocal ways. Through these interactions parents learn how to elicit certain social and affective behaviors from their infants and consequently gain greater confidence about their personal competence; similarly, infants learn that their behavior leads to predictable outcomes, thus their patterns of smiling, crying, activity, vocalizing, and visual gazing are reinforced. This clinical research is beginning to have a dramatic and practical impact on our treatment strategies. The content of infant and preschool curricula is changing to include a greater emphasis on promoting the development of social and affective behaviors that encourage attachment and bonding. Similarly, this research has facilitated the design of teaching and "coaching" strategies used to help parents read the behavioral cues of their infants and to alter their styles of interaction to encourage social and affective development.

Early-intervention programs now place great emphasis on the involvement of parents in the classroom and in their young child's therapy. Parent involvement not only emphasizes the learning of how to develop skills for their handicapped infants but also addresses the parents' emotional needs in adjusting to a child with special needs and the stresses that entails. The use of interactive and systems approaches in working with parents and children is the next major development in early-intervention treatment techniques.

SERVICE-DELIVERY MODELS

A wider array of service-delivery models are becoming available so that young handicapped children and their parents can be helped through approaches that can match their individual needs. The traditional models for home-based, community center-based, and hospital programs are now supplemented by models that stress innovative combinations of these to provide services in various regional and local settings. Many hospital programs serve chronically ill children but work effectively with community programs to promote integration into those settings as children stabilize in adjusting to their conditions. Great emphasis is now placed on "transitioning" severely handicapped children from preschool settings into public school contexts.

Cooperative links between the schools and various agencies serving young exceptional children are being developed for children at younger ages so that the schools know these children and can anticipate future programming needs and trends. Rehabilitation programs for children with both acquired and congenital brain injuries emphasize a high level of parent involvement in the care and teaching of their children. A combined focus on intensive hospital-based rehabilitation with gradual furloughs of the parents and children to home for extended weekends or in transitional living quarters effectively ensures that parents can meet their child's needs. Finally, more day-care centers and Head Start programs are including handicapped children to form integrated programs that will encourage normalization by allowing the handicapped children to model the more appropriate language and social behaviors of their peers and by developing attitudes of acceptance in normal children for individual differences in their peers.

LINKAGES BETWEEN DEVELOPMENTAL
ASSESSMENT AND INTERVENTION

Various early-intervention researchers have designed comprehensive models that allow interdisciplinary specialists to assess young handicapped children in a manner that targets individualized goals and strategies for treatment. This is a significant development that is a key to treatment efficacy. Most such models integrate screening, assessment, program linkage, and evaluation into one continuous approach that matches child needs with programming goals. Recent advances in assessment-intervention models have broadened this conceptualization to include such critical variables as infant temperament, the use of clinical judgment in diagnosis, systematic observation of parent-child interaction patterns, parent stress and attachment, and adaptive modifications for multihandicapped children. Two of the most recent developments in assessment research focus on affect as an indicator in infant cognitive abilities and structured measures to assess play patterns in young exceptional children. Further refinements in these approaches and methods using computer-based strategies will allow the early-intervention specialist to merge diagnosis and treatment of young handicapped children more accurately.

CURRICULUM AND INSTRUCTIONAL
MATERIALS DEVELOPMENT

Curriculum packages have always been one of the common products of early-intervention programs for handicapped infants and preschoolers. However, three recent developments in this area signal a new era of research and practice: adaptive modification for specific impairments, the design of response-contingent toys, and parent materials that stress socioemotional interactions. Newly developed early-intervention curricula are now routinely including standardized modifications of how to teach specific functional skills to young children suffering various sensory and neuromotor, and affective disorders. This standardized alternative teaching strategies helps to ensure consistency in the teaching of children by both parents and interdisciplinary specialists. Also, the modifications help to circumvent the child's impairment to some degree and facilitate the learning of compensatory methods of adaptive functioning.

One of the most exciting areas of research is the design and commercial production of toys that can be used with young exceptional children. Toys are being developed that can be used with both nonhandicapped and handicapped children but that have stimulus-and response-sensitive characteristics that mark their effective use with special-needs preschoolers. For example, Johnson and Johnson Child Development Toys discussed and illustrated in an earlier chapter are based on developmental researach that has heightened their stimulus value and increased the chances of a child's interacting with them. Parallel developments in toy research involve the design of prosthetic devices such as pressure and heat sensitive switches and plates that allow the severely impaired child to learn that his actions have a direct and immediate impact on objects in his environment. This series of toys promotes the child's sense of personal competence and decreases the common problem of "learned helplessness," a form of depression, seen in many severely disabled infants and preschoolers.

Finally, curriculum materials now stress the development of socioemotional behavior patterns that promote healthier and more appropriate interactions between parents and their young children. Such materials also use a variety of group and individual behavioral techniques to facilitate such patterns. In the future, early-childhood special educators will have increased opportunities to consult with and work for the companies that recognize the commercial and social benefits of developing and distributing these curriculum materials and toys.

TECHNOLOGY IN EARLY INTERVENTION

The use of computers in the assessment of and intervention with young handicapped children is a relatively uncharted area. Researchers have only recently begun to tap the possibilities in this area. Early-intervention specialists will use computer-based methods to assess the cognitive abilities of young children who cannot respond with their hands and arms. Alternative communication systems using voice synthesizers will promote communication skills for some of these children. Computers will be used with disabled infants both at home and in the preschool to teach and reinforce various types of learning skills that depend on strong visual abilities. On a program administration level, computers will aid in the identification and tracking of large groups of infants at risk from various causes. This capability will guide the allocation of funding and resources for such groups of children.

SUMMARY

Creative developments are in the works for professionals who will serve young exceptional children and their families. Refinements in validated theories and methods will serve as the springboard for more effective approaches. The early-childhood special educator is in a central position to advance new approaches guided by broad-based programs of preparation that have scientific, creative, pragmatic, and humanitarian means and goals.

APPENDIX: RESOURCES

Alexander Graham Bell Association for the
Deaf
3417 Volta Place, NW
Washington, DC 20007
American Academy of Pediatrics
1801 Hinman Avenue
Evanston, IL 60204
American Council of the Blind
Suite 506
1211 Connecticut Avenue, NW
Washington, DC 20036
American Foundation for the Blind
15 West 16th Street
New York, NY 10011
American Printing House for the Blind, Inc.
PO Box 6085
Louisville, KY 40206-0085
American Speech-Language-Hearing Associa-
tion (ASHA)
10801 Rockville Pike
Rockville, MD 20852
Association for Childhood Education Interna-
tional (ACEI)
3615 Wisconsin Avenue
Washington, DC 20016
Association for Children with Learning Disa-
bilities
5225 Grace Street
Pittsburg, PA 15236
Association for Education of the Visually Han-
dicapped
919 Walnut Street, 7th Floor
Philadelphia, PA 19107
Association for Retarded Citizens (ARC)
National Headquarters
2501 Avenue J
Arlington, TX 76011
Association for the Gifted (TAG)
Council for Exceptional Children
1920 Association Drive
Reston, VA 22091
Children in Hospitals (CIH)
31 Wilshire Park
Needham, MA 02192
Committee for Single Adoptive Parents
PO Box 4074
Chevy Chase, MD 20815
Conference of Educational Administrators
Serving the Deaf
5034 Wisconsin Avenue, NW
Washington, DC 20016
Convention of American Instructors of the
Deaf

5034 Wisconsin Avenue, NW
Washington, DC 20016
Council for Exceptional Children (CEC)
1920 Association Drive
Reston, VA 22091
Cystic Fibrosis Foundation
Suite 309
6000 Executive Boulevard
Rockville, MD 20852
Division for Children with Communication
Disorders (DCCD)
Council for Exceptional Children
1920 Association Drive
Reston, VA 22091
Division for Early Childhood (DEC)
Council for Exceptional Children
1920 Association Drive
Reston, VA 22091
Division for the Physically Handicapped (DPH)
Council for Exceptional Children
1920 Association Drive
Reston, VA 22091
Division for the Visually Handicapped (DVH)
Council for Exceptional Children
1920 Association Drive
Reston, VA 22091
Division on Mental Retardation (CEC-MR)
Council for Exceptional Children
1920 Association Drive
Reston, VA 22091
Epilepsy Foundation of America
Suite 405
1828 L Street
Washington, DC 20036
Gallaudet College Press
Gallaudet College
Washington, DC 20002
Gesell Institute of Child Development
310 Prospect Street
New Haven, CT 06511
Head Start
Adminstration for Children, Youth and Fam-
ilies
Office of Human Development Services
U.S. Department of Health Human Services
PO Box 1182
Washington, DC 20013
International Association of Parents of the
Deaf
814 Thayer Avenue
Silver Springs, MD 20910
International Institute for Visually Impaired
0-7, Inc.

Rutgers Circle
East Lansing, MI 48823
John F. Kennedy Institute
707 North Broadway
Baltimore, MD 21205
Kendall Demonstration Elementary School
Outreach Program
Gallaudet College
Washington, DC 20002
March of Dimes Birth Defect Foundation
1275 Mamaroneck Avenue
White Plains, NY 10605
National Academy for the Deaf
Gallaudet College
Washington, DC 20002
National Association for Down's Syndrome
Box 63
Oak Park, IL 60303
National Association for the Education of
Young Children (NAEYC)
1834 Connecticut Avenue, NW
Washington, DC 20009
National Association for the Parents of the
Visually Impaired, Inc.
PO Box 180806
Austin, TX 78718
National Association for the Physically Handi-
capped
76 Elm Street
London, OH 43140
National Association of the Deaf
814 Thayer Avenue
Silver Springs, MD 20910
National Center for Clinical Infant Programs
Suite 912
733 15th Street, NW
Washington, DC 20005

National Committee for Prevention of Child
Abuse (NCPCA)
332 S. Michigan Avenue
Chicago, IL 60604
National Easter Seals Society
2023 W. Ogden Avenue
Chicago, IL 60612
National Information Center on Deafness
Gallaudet College
Washington, DC 20002
National Institute for Autistic Children
(NSAC)
Suite 1017
1234 Massachusetts Avenue, NW
Washington, DC 20005
The National Newspatch
Oregon School for the Blind
700 Church Street SE
Salem, OR 97310
National Single Parent Coalition
16 W. 23rd Street
New York, NY 10010
National Society for Prevention of Blindness,
Inc.
79 Madison Avenue
New York, NY 10016
Parents Without Partners
7910 Woodmont Avenue, Suite 1000
Bethesda, MD 20814
Registry of Interpreters for the Deaf
814 Thayer Avenue
Silver Springs, MD 20910
Single Dad's Hotline
PO Box 4842
Scottsdale, AZ 85258
United Cerebral Palsy Association, Inc.
66 East 34th Street
New York, NY 10016

GLOSSARY

Abuse: An active form of maltreatment through which the child is physically or psychologically injured, regardless of whether or not the injury was intended.

Accommodation: Changing behaviors and knowledge to match perceptions of the world.

Adaptive Behavior: Extent to which a child demonstrates age- appropriate social and self-care skills.

Adventitiously Deaf: Deafness caused by some accident or disease after birth.

Affective Behavior Disorder: Any significant problem related to excessive or inadequate emotional expression, especially in interpersonal and other social situations.

Amblyopia: Dimness of vision without any apparent disease of the eye. Usually the result of not using an eye ("lazy eye") to avoid the discomfort of double vision caused by a muscle problem.

Assimilation: Piagetian concept dealing with how people change the world to match their present cognitive abilities.

Asthma: A chronic respiratory condition in which the indiviual experiences repeated episodes of difficulty in breathing.

Athetosis: Body movement characterized by fluctuating tone.

At risk: Infants who, because of biological or environmental complications, have a high likelihood of exhibiting developmental delay or deficiencies later in life.

Audiogram: Precise information regarding the hearing loss of an individual based on audiometric measures.

Audiologist: A professional who measures and studies hearing and develops remedial procedures, such as prescribing hearing aids.

Audiometer: Device used to test hearing.

Auditory Impairment: Deficit in the ability to receive auditory input because of a hearing loss.

Auditory Processing: Ability to comprehend information presented auditorially.

Autism: An early childhood socioemotional disorder characterized by extreme isolation, withdrawal, lack of communication, and sometimes accompanied by bizarre and stereotypic behavior.

Behavioral Management: Training to help a child control his or her own behavior.

Biological risk: A category of children with early developmental histories that suggest a strong probability for neurodevelopmental problems.

Blindisms: Mannerisms common to most blind people,—rocking, eye poking, finger flicking.

Blood Incompatibility: Rh incompatibility, which results in agglutination of blood with serious consequences for the baby and the mother.

Brain Stem Evoked Response (BER): Audiometry procedure putting harmless electrodes on the child and presenting a series of sounds at a rapid rate. Electrical responses of the brain are then measured.

Catheterization: Insertion of a tube into the body, as for example into the bladder for the release of urine.

Center-Based Program: Programs designed for older preschool children and delivered through day-care centers, group centers, or nursery schools.

Cephalocaudal: Development of sensorimotor patterns from head to foot.

Cerebral Palsy: Brain injury that results in problems in motor control; almost always present at birth.

Child Find Procedures: Systematic activities within a community designed to locate handicapped or at-risk children for more detailed assessment and programming.

Chronic Illness: A health problem that is long term and that requires some type of special care.

Cognition: The ability to relate bits of information, attend to and remember information, and to process, organize and relate it to past information.

Cognitive Disability: Any significant problem related to intellectual function, including disorders of learning, recall, generalization, and concept development.

Communication Sense: Showing anticipatory behavior and reciprocity in interaction.

Conductive Hearing Loss: An impairment of hearing caused by damage or obstruction of the ear canal, the drum membrane, or the ossicular chain in the middle ear.

Congenital: Present at birth.

Cystic Fibrosis: An inherited disease characterized by chronic respiratory and digestive problems.

Deaf: Hearing limited to an extent that precludes the understanding of speech through the ear alone, with or without a hearing aid.

Decibel: A standard unit that measures sound intensity.

Developmental Assessment: Comprehensive analysis of a child's developmental capabilities, delays, and deficits.

Developmental/Diagnostic-Prescriptive Approach: The series of steps professionals use to detect developmental problems, assess developmental status, specify objectives and methods for treatment, and evaluate treatment effectiveness.

Developmental Disability: Any severe and/or chronic dysfunction that is discovered before the age of 22 years, is likely to continue indefinitely, and will result in substantial limitations in functioning.

Developmental Interactionism: Developmental perspective that stresses the crucial importance of the child's environmental transactions for promoting progress.

Developmental Programming: Establishing individualized instructional activities and strategies adapted for teaching young children.

Developmental Psycholinguistics: A theory regarding language acquisition concentrates on the achievement of competence in language and communication.

Developmental Retardation: Delays in developmental areas: motor skills, speech and language skills, cognitive skills, perceptual-motor skills, and social and emotional behaviors.

Differential Reinforcement of Incompatible Behaviors (DRI): Reinforcing a response that competes with the target behavior to be eliminated or reduced.

Diplegia: Paralysis of any two limbs.

Disability: An actual loss of function resulting from some physical disorder.

Dysnomia: Word retrieval deficits.

Early-Childhood Special Education: The branch of education concerned with programmatic developmental instruction of preschool exceptional children.

Echolalia: Meaningless repetition of words or sentences initially spoken by others.

Empathetic Caring: Sensitivity to children's needs and an ability to meet those needs.

Environmental Risk: A category of children who appear to be stable from a neurophysiological standpoint, but who have impoverished environments that limit their ability to profit from important learning experiences.

Established Risk: Handicapped children whose developmental disorders result from medically diagnosed conditions or syndromes, which may have specific causes.

Eugenics: The deliberate control of mating and the elimination of those that are judged to be defective. Practiced during the third century A.D. in Greece.

Evaluability Assessment: An evaluation directed at decisions about the viability of evaluation.

Evaluation: A process of measuring characteristics of programs so that decisions can be made affecting those programs.

Exceptional: A condition that is so different from the average or the expected that special methods, materials, and settings must be employed to promote child progress.

Expressive Disorders: Problems in coordinating oral muscles to produce fine movements required to form a variety of speech sounds.

Extension: Unfolding from a flexed position.

False Positives: Cases of children identified as having developmental delays or deficits when in reality none exist.

Fetal Alcohol Syndrome: Disorder that includes mental retardation, poor motor development, hyperactivity, and short attention span; associated with a history of maternal alcoholism.

Formative Evaluation: Information gathered during the ongoing operation of a program; focuses on the process of program delivery and/or attainment of short-term objectives.

Gifted: Children and youth who are identified at the preschool, elementary, or secondary level as possessing demonstrated or potential abilities that give evidence of high performance capabilities in areas such as intellectual, creative, specific academic or leadership abilities, or in the performing or visual arts, and who by reason thereof require service or activities not ordinarily provided by the school.

Handicap: The burden imposed on a child as a result of the interaction of a deviant characteristic within an environment.

Hard of Hearing: Hearing limited to an extent that makes difficult but does not preclude the understanding of speech through the ear alone, with or without a hearing aid.

Hearing Impaired: A decrement in hearing to the extent that the individual experiences some handicap in communication or in sensing normal auditory signals.

Hemiplegia: Paralysis of one side of the body.

Hemophilia: A rare, sex-linked blood disorder, characterized by sudden, uncontrolled bleeding.

Hip Dysplasia: Skeletal problem in which the thigh bone fits improperly into the hip socket.

Home-Based Program: The delivery of educational services to the disabled by specialists making home visits. In addition, they train parents to understand and work with the child's handicapping conditions.

Home-Center-Based Programs: Approach combining the advantages of both models by combining center-based activities with home visits.

Hyaline Membrane Disease: A disorder in breathing common in premature infants.

Hydrocephalus: An increase in cerebral spinal fluid pressure in the brain.

Hyperactivity: Overactivity, excessive talking, fidgeting, distractibility, and almost continuous motor activity.

Hypertonia: Exaggerated muscle tone, spasticity, excessive tightness.

Hypotonia: Poor, weak, "floppy" muscle tone.

Infant Stimulation: Organized programs of sensory and/or physical enrichment designed to provide developmentally appropriate activities to infants and toddlers who either have or are at risk for a variety of conditions that may eventually interfere with their ability to lead a full and productive life.

Interdisciplinary Team: A group of specialists who work together to determine the cause of a child's disorder and develop behavioral strategies in the intervention process.

Interpersonal Differences: Differences among individuals.

Intracranial Hemorrhage: Bleeding in the brain.

Intrapersonal Differences: Differences within the same person.

Juvenile Diabetes Mellitus: A problem of sugar metabolism caused by a failure of the pancreas to produce enough insulin, usually with hereditary or developmental origins.

Learned Helplessness: A developmental disorder in infancy and early childhood characterized by passive behaviors caused by lengthy exposure to unavoidable aversive events.

Learning and Perceptual Disorders: Problems in developing an understanding of linguistic concepts because of difficulties in perceiving and interpreting the speech of others.

Learning Disability: A disorder in one or more of the basic psychological processes involved in understanding or using language, spoken or written, which may manifest itself in an imperfect ability to listen, think, speak, read, write, spell, or do mathematical calculations.

Legal Blindness: Visual acuity of 20/200 or less in the better eye after the best possible correction.

Leukemia: A disorder of the blood system causing healthy blood cells to become reduced in number. Results in anemia, increased vulnerability to infection, and decreased blood-clotting abilities.

Memory: Capacity to recall and retain chunks of information for varying lengths of time.

Meningitis: A bacterial infection of the membranes encasing the brain and spinal cord.

Mental Retardation: Intellectual functioning that is significantly below average for age (IQ below 70) concurrent with comparable deficits in adaptive behavior or social competence.

Mixed Hearing Loss: The combination of a conductive and sensorineural hearing loss.

Motor Control: The process by which the brain and the muscles work together to produce coordinated, skilled movement.

Multidomain: Coverage of a wide range of functional skills across many behavioral areas.

Multisource: Combining information about a child's functioning from a variety of perspectives: parent-teacher ratings, interviews, actual child performance, and curriculum- based records.

Muscular Dystrophy: A progressive weakness of all muscle groups.

Musculoskeletal Disorders: Acquired or hereditary conditions usually affecting the limbs, spine, or joints.

Needs Assessment: An evaluation directed at understanding the needs of any program under consideration; directed at needs rather than processes or outcomes.

Negative Reinforcement: The contingent removal of an aversive stimulus immediately following a response, leading to an increase in the future rate of probability of the response.

Neglect: A passive form of maltreatment through which the child suffers from the omissions of the parent or caretakers.

Neonatal Asphyia: A lack of sufficient oxygen often as a result of complications during the birth process.

Neurological Disorders: Damage, defect, or deterioration of the brain or spinal cord. Most common cases are heredity, maternal infection, lack of oxygen to the fetus, Rh imcompatibility, or prematurity.

Norm-Referenced: Compares an individual's performance to the performance of his/her peers.

Obesity: The condition of being more than 20% heavier than that considered appropriate for age and height.

Object Permanence: The knowledge that an object exists even though the object can be neither seen nor heard.

Ophthalmologist: A physician who assesses vision, fits corrective lenses, prescribes medication, and performs surgery for the visually impaired.

Optometrist: A specialist who fits corrective lenses.

Organizational/Sequential Skills: Capability to synthesize, order, and relate information in an organized fashion to aid problem solving.

Ossicle: Cavity within the middle ear containing three small bones; the hammer (malleus), anvil (incus), and the stirrup (stapes).

Osteogenosis Imperfecta: Brittle bone disease; the result of loosely woven bone fibers and protein-deficient bones.

Otitis Media: The most common type of hearing loss, caused by fluid in the middle ear cavity, resulting from infection.

Outcome (Summative) Evaluation: An evaluation implemented throughout the conduct of a program and used toward the end of one cycle of a program to make major changes in one or more aspects of the program.

Parent Therapy: Approach that focuses on helping the parent adjust emotionally to having a handicapped child.

Partially Sighted: Visual acuity of between 20/70 and 20/200 in the better eye after maximum correction.

Phonologic Disorders: Speech problems in how to produce and relate different sounds to produce words.

Phonology: Rule system that governs the actual ordering of specific sound units to form individual words.

Positive Reinforcement: The presentation of a desired stimulus, immediately following a response, that lead to an increase in the future rate or probability of the response.

Postlingual Deafness: Hearing loss after speech and language were obtained.

Postural Drainage: Placement of the body into special positions to encourage drainage of mucus.

Pragmatics: Understanding and using the purposes or functions of language when communicating with others.

Prelingual Deafness: Hearing loss before acquiring speech.

Primary Reinforcer: Satisfier of a basic biological need (for example, food, warmth).

Program Monitoring: Evaluation of a program's impact, administration, cost/benefit analysis, or other dimensions of educational, staff, or fiscal concern.

Prone Position: Positioning a child on the stomach.

Proximal To Distal: Development of sensorimotor patterns from trunk to extremities.

Quadriplegia: Paralysis involving all four limbs.

Reflex : A stereotyped movement produced in response to particular sensory input.

Repetitive Verbalizations: Repetitions of an utterance already spoken.

Retinopathy Of Prematurity: Visual impairment in premature infants caused by too much oxygen.

Retrolental Fibroplasia: Loss of sight resulting from the formation of scar tissue behind the lens of the eye, caused by the administration of high concentrations of oxygen to a child at birth.

Righting Reaction: Early component that assists in the control of the head and trunk.

Rubella: German measles, especially hazardous to the fetus during the first three months of pregnancy.

Screening: A detection process that highlights possible problems in development requiring more detailed assessment.

Secondary Reinforcer: Acquisition of reinforcing qualities through frequent association with a primary reinforcer (for example, social praise, money).

Self-Injurious: Compulsively repetitive behaviors that present a constant threat to the health and well-being of an individual (for example, head banging, hitting body with fists, biting one self).

Self Stimulation: Repetitive behaviors that have no apparent utility (for example, body rocking, hand flapping, head weaving); common to severely retarded individuals, especially those who are institutionalized.

Semantics: Vocabulary development and the conceptual understanding of how different words relate to one another to express meaningful thoughts.

Sense Empiricism: Changing a child's development by providing information about the world through the child's various senses.

Sensorineural Impairment: Hearing loss resulting from a pathologic condition in the inner ear, in the eighth cranial nerve, or both, which cannot be restored.

Sexual Abuse: Contact or interactions between a child and an adult when the child is being used as an object of gratification for adult sexual needs or desires.

Short Gestation Period: Infants born somewhat earlier than the usual 9-month gestation period, regardless of physical size or weight at birth.

Sickle Cell Anemia: An inherited abnormality of the red blood cells resulting in severe anemia.

Social/Curtural Retardation: A category of at-risk infants born into extremely deprived social and economic circumstances.

Social Isolation/Withdrawal: Low rates of interaction, with skill deficits and motivational deficits.

Spasticity: Body movement characterized by increased tone.

Spina Bifida: A group of disabilities characterized by open defects in the spinal cord.

Stretch Reflex: Basic postural reaction that involves the passive stretch of a muscle followed by its contraction.

Supine Position: Positioning a child on the back.

Surface Structure: Elements of language that can be heard or seen in writing.

Syntax: The precise sequence in which words are ordered in a sentence so that they convey meaning.

Tactile Defensiveness: Inability to tolerate certain textures, touch, or stimulation.

Tonic Relex: Extension of the arms and a flexion of the legs when the head is bent backward.

Tympanogram: A graphic record of the pressure of the middle ear.

"Verbalism": Stereotyped verbal behavior including repetition of meaningless phrases characteristic of deaf children, especially those in institutionalized settings.

Visual Impairment: Visual acuity of 20/200 or less in the better eye after the best possible correction with glasses or contact lenses.

Vulnerable: A term used to describe an infant who by reason of physical makeup is at risk for developmental disorders.

REFERENCES

Abrams, B. R., Schultz, S. R., Margen, S., and Ogar, D. A. (1979). Perspectives in clinical research: A review of research controversies surrounding the Feingold diet. *Family and Community Health,* 4:93–113.

Adler, B. A. (1984). *Zero-five: Do early intervention programs really prevent child abuse?* The Fifth International Congress on Child Abuse and Neglect, Montreal, September 16–19.

Ainsworth, M. S. (1973). The development of infant-mother attachment. In B. Caldwell and H. Ricciuti (Eds.) *Review of child development research,* Vol. 3, pp. 113-139. Chicago: University of Chicago Press.

Allen, E., Holm, J. T., and Schiefelbusch, R. (1978). *Early intervention: A team approach.* Baltimore: University Park Press.

Allen, K. E. (1980). *Mainstreaming in early childhood education.* Albany, NY: Delmar Publishers.

Alpern, G. D., Boll, T. J., and Shearer, (1981). *The developmental profile.* Aspen, CO: Psychological Development Publications.

Als, H., Lester, B. M.,Tronick, E. C., and Brazelton, T. B. (1982). Toward a research instrument for the Assessment of Preterm Infants Behavior (APIB). In H. E. Fitzgerald, B. M. Letter, and M. N. Young (Eds.) *Theory and research in behavioral pediatrics,* Vol. 1 New York: Plenum.

Altschuler, A. (1974). *Books that help children deal with a hospital experience.* Baltimore: U.S. Department of Health, Education and Welfare (Publication No. HSA 74–5402).

American Humane Association. (1980). *Highlights of the 1978 National Reporting Data.* Englewood, CO.

Anastasiow, N. J. (1981). Socioemotional developmental: The state of the art. In N. J. Anastasiow (Ed.). *New directions for exceptional children: Socioemotional development,* Vol. 5, pp.65-81. San Francisco: Jossey-Bass.

Apgar, V. (1983). A proposal for a new method of evaluation of the newborn infant. *Current researches in Anesthesia and Analgesia, 32:*260–267.

Ayres, A. J. (1972). *Sensory integration and learning disorders.* Los Angeles: Western Psychological Services.

Badger, E., Burns, D., and Deboer, M. (1982). An early demonstration of educational intervention beginning at birth. *Journal of the Division for Early Childhood,* 12:19–30.

Bagnato, S. J. (1981). Developmental scales and developmental curricula: Forging a linkage for early intervention. *Topics in Early Childhood Special Education,* *1*(2):1–8.

Bagnato, S. J., and Neisworth, J. T. (1980). The intervention efficiency index: An approach to preschool program accountability. *Exceptional Children,* *46*(4): 264–269.

Bagnato, S. J., and Neisworth, J. T. (1981). *Linking developmental assessment and curricula: Prescriptions for early intervention.* Rockville, MD: Aspen Systems.

Bagnato, S. J., and Neisworth, J. T. (1985). Efficacy of interdisciplinary assessment and treatment for infants and preschoolers with congenital and acquired brain injury. *Analysis and Intervention of Developmental Disabilities,* 5:81–102.

Bailey, D. B., Jens, K. G., and Johnson, N. (1983). Curricula for handicapped infants. In S. G. Garwood and R. R. Fewell (Eds.) *Educating handicapped infants,* pp. 387–415. Rockville, MD: Aspen Systems.

Bailey, D. B., and Simeonsson, R. J. (1984). Critical issues underlying research and intervention with families of young handicapped children. *Journal of the Division for Early Childhood,* *9*(1):38–48.

Bailey, D. B., and Wolery, M. (1984). *Teaching infants and preschoolers with handi-caps.* Columbus, OH: Merrill.

Baker, E. (1974). Formative evaluation of instruction. In J. Pophams (Ed.) *Evaluation in education: Current applications.* pp. 127–151. Berkeley, CA: McCutcheon.

Baldwin, A. (1977). Identification matrix combines 11 testing scores. *N/S-LT1-G/T Bulletin, 3.*

Bandura, A. (1969). *Principles of behavior modification.* New York: Holt, Rinehart and Winston.

Bandura, A. (1977). *Social learning theory.* Englewood Cliffs, NJ: Prentice-Hall.

Barnes, K. J., Murphy, M., Waldo, L., and Sailor, W. (1979). Adaptive equipment for the severely, multiply handicapped child. In R. York and E. Edgar (Eds.) *Teaching the severely handicapped,* pp. 79–97. Columbus, OH: Special Press.

Barraga, N. (1964). *Increased visual behavior in low vision children.* New York: American Foundation for the Blind.

Barraga, N. (1970). *Teacher's guide for the development of visual learning abilities and utilization of low vision.* New York: American Foundation for the Blind.

Barraga, N., and Morris, J. (1980). *Program to develop efficiency in visual functioning.* Louisville, KY: American Printing House for the Blind.

Bayley, N. (1969). *Manual for the Bayley scales of infant development.* New York: Psychological Corporation.

Beckman-Bell, P. (1981). Child-related stress in families of handicapped children. *Topics in Early Childhood Special Education, 1,* 45–55.

Belsky, J. (1981). Early human experience: A family perspective. *Developmental Psychology, 17:*3-23.

Bemelmans, L. (1939). *Madeleine.* New York: Viking Press.

Bender, R. (1980). *The conquest of deafness.* Cleveland: Case Western Reserve.

Bergen, A. (1979). Sidelyer with positioning blocks. *Physical Therapy, 59:*303.

Bettleheim, B. (1950). *Love is not enough.* Glencoe, IL: Free Press.

Beuf, A. H. (1979). *Biting off the bullet: A study of children in hospitals.* Philadelphia: University of Pennsylvania Press.

Bijou, S. W., and Baer, D. M. (1981). *Child development I: A systematic and empirical theory.* New York: Appleton-Century-   Crofts.

Blacher, J. (1984a). Attachment and severely handicapped children: Implications for intervention. *Journal of Developmental and Behavioral Pediatrics, 5*(4):178–183.

Blacher, J. (1984b). Sequential stages of parental adjustment to the birth of a child with handicaps: Fact or artifact? *Mental Retardation, 22*(2):55–68.

Black, R., and Mayer, J. (1979). *An investigation of the relationship between substance abuse and child abuse neglect.* Final report to the National Center on Child Abuse and Neglect. Washington, DC: U.S. Department of Health, Education and Welfare (DHEW).

Black, T., Prestridge, S., Anderson, J. (1981). *The developement of a needs assessment process.* Occasional Paper 3. Chapel Hill, NC: Technical Assistance Development Systems.

Blair v. *Union Free School District Number 6, Hauppauge,* 324 N.Y.S. 2d 222 (1971).

Bleck, E. E. (1975a). Cerebral palsy. In E. E. Bleck and D. A. Nagel (Eds.) *Physically handicapped children: A medical atlas for teachers* pp. 70–86 New York: Grune & Stratton.

Bleck, E. E. (1975b). Osteogenesis imperfecta and cerebral palsy. In E. E. Bleck and D. A. Nagel (Eds.) *Physically handicapped children: A medical atlas for teachers* pp. 87–96 New York: Grune & Strattton.

Bloom, B. (1956). *Taxonomy of educational objectives: The classification of educational goals.* New York: Longmans, Green.

Bloom, B. S. (1964). *Stability and change in human characteristics.* New York: Wiley.

Bloom, L., and Lahey, M. (1978). *Language development and language disorders.* New York: Wiley.

Blos, P., Jr. (1978). Children think about illness: Their concepts and beliefs. In E. Gellert (Ed.) *Psychosocial aspects of pediatric care,* pp. 37–49. New York: Grune & Stratton.

Bluma S. M., Shearer, M. S., Frohman, A. H., and Hillard, J. M. (1976). *Portage guide to early education.* Portage, WI: Cooperative Educational Service Agency 12.

Bobath, B. (1967). The very early treatment of cerebral palsy. *Developmental Medicine and Child Neurology, 9:*373–390.

Bobath, B., and Bobath, K. (1975). *Motor development in the different types of cerebral palsy.* London: Heinemann Medical Books.

Bonet, J. (1620). *Reduction de las letras y arte para ensenar a hablar los mundos.* Madrid: Par Francisco Arbaco de Angelo.

Bornstein, H., Hamilton, L., Saulnier, K., and Roy, H. (1975). *The Signed English dictionary for preschool and elementary levels.* Washington, DC: Gallaudet College Press.

Bower, T. G. R. (1971). The object in the world of the infant. *Scientific American, 225:*30–38.

Bower, T. G. R. (1974). *Development in infancy.* San Francisco: Freeman.

Bowerman, M. (1978). Semantic and syntactic development. In R. L. Schiefelbusch (Ed.) *Language intervention series; Vol. 1, Basis of language intervention.* pp. 63–89. Baltimore: University Park Press.

Bowlby, J. (1961). Separation anxiety: A critical review of the literature. *Journal of Child Psychology and Psychiatry, 1:*251–269.

Boyd, R. D. (1974). *Boyd developmental progress scale.* San Bernardino, CA: Inland Counties Regional Center, Inc.

Brackman, B., Fundakowski, G., Filler, J. S., and Peterson, C. (1977). Total programming for severely/profoundly handicapped young children. In B. Wilcox (Ed.) *Proceedings of the Illinois Institute for Educators of the Severely/Profoundly Handicapped,* pp. 51–67 Springfield: Illinois Office of Education.

Brandwein, H. (1973). The battered child: A definition and significant factor in mental retardation. *Mental Retardation, 11*(5):50–51.

Brasel, K. (1975). *The influence of early language and communication environments on the development of language in deaf children.* Unpublished doctoral dissertation, University of Illinois, Urbana.

Brazelton, T. B. (1973). *Neonatal behavioral assessment scale.* Philadelphia: Lippincott.

Brazelton, T. B. (1976). Early parent-infant reciprocity. (71–77), In V. C. Vaughan and T. B. Brazelton (Eds.) *The Family-Can it be saved,* Chicago, IL: Yearbook Medical Publishers, Inc.

Brazelton, T. B. (1982). Assessment as a method of enhancing infant development. *Zero to Three, 2*(1):1–8.

Brazelton, T. B. (1984). *Neonatal behavioral assesesment scale,* 2nd Ed. Philadelphia: Lippincott.

Bricker, D. (Ed.). (1981). *Intervention with at-risk and handicapped infants: From Research to Application.* Baltimore: University Park Press.

Bricker D., and Casuso, V. (1979) Family involvement: A critical component of early intervention. *Exceptional Children, 46:*108–116.

Bricker, D. and Dow, M. (1980). Early intervention with the young severely handicapped child. *Journal of the Association for The Severely Handicapped, 5:*130–138.

Bricker, D., Seibert, J., and Scott, K. (in press). Early intervention: History, current status and the problems of evaluation. In D. Doleys, T. Vaughn, M. Cantrell (Eds.) *Interdisciplinary assessment and treatment of developmental problems.* New York: Spectrum.

Bricker, D., Sheehan, R., and Littman, D. (1981). *Early intervention: A plan for evaluating program impact.* Seattle: Western States Technical Assistance Resource (WESTAR), Series Paper No. 10.

Brigance, A. H. (1978). *Inventory of early development.* Woburn, MA: Curriculum Associates.

Brigance, A. (1983). *BRIGANCE Diagnostic inventory of early development.*, Allen, TX: Teaching Resources/Developmental/Learning Materials.

Brinker, R. P., and Lewis, M. (1982). Discovering the competent infant: A process approach to assessment and intervention. *Topics in early childhood special education, 2*(2):1–16. Brinker, R. P., and Lewis, M. (1983). Contingency intervention. In J. Anderson (Ed.) *Curricula for high-risk and handicapped infants.* pp. 49–62. Chapel Hill, NC: TADS.

Bromwich, R. (1981). *Working with parents and infants: An interactional approach.* Baltimore: University Park Press.

Bronfenbrenner, U. (1975). Is early intervention effective? In B. Z. Friedlander, G. M. Sterritt, and G. E. Kirk (Eds.) *Exceptional infant, Vol. 3 Assessment and intervention,* pp. 449–475. New York: Brunner/Mazel.

Brooks-Gunn, J., and Lewis, M. (1981). Assessing young handicapped children: Issues and solutions. *Journal of the Division for Early Childhood,* 84–95.

Brooks-Gunn, J. and Lewis, M. (1982). Affective exchanges between normal and handicapped infants and their mothers. In T. M. Field and A. Fogel (Eds.) *Emotion and early interaction,* pp. 161–188. Hillsdale, NJ: Earlbaum.

Brown, D., Simmons, V., and Methvin, J. (1978). *Oregon project for the visually impaired and blind preschool children.* Medford, OR: Jackson County Education Service District.

Brown, J., and Hepler, R. (1976). Stimulation—a corollary to physical care. *American Journal of Nursing, 76*:578–581.

Brown, L., Nietupski, J., and Hamre-Nietupski, S. (1976). Criterion of ultimate functiong. In M. A. Thomas (Ed.) *Hey don't forget about me!*, pp. 37–45. Reston, VA: Council for Exceptional Children.

Bruder, M. B. and Bricker, D. (1975). Parents as teachers of their children and other parents. *Journal of the Division of Early Childhood, Spring*:136–150.

Bruner, J. S. (1982). The organization of action and the nature of the adult-infant transaction. In E. Z. Tronick (Ed.). *Social interchange in infancy: Affect, cognition and communication.* Baltimore: University Park Press.

Bulkhart, J. A., Rutherford, R. B., and Goldberg, K. E. (1978). Verbal and nonverbal interaction of mothers with their Down's Syndrome and nonretarded children. *American Journal of Mental Deficiency, 79*:52–58.

Bumbalo, J. (1978). The clinical nurse specialist. In K. E. Allen, V. Holm, and R. Schiefelbusch (Eds.) *Early intervention: A team approach,* pp. 123–145. Baltimore: University Park Press.

Bzoch, L., and League, R. (1970). *Receptive-expressive emergent language scale.* Gainesville, FL: Tree of Life Press.

Caldwell, B., and Bradley, R. H. (1979). *Home observation for measurement of the environment.* Little Rock: University of Arkansas.

Campbell, P. H., Green, K. M., and Carlson, L. M. (1977). Approximating the norm through environmental and child-centered prosthetics and adaptive equipment. In E. Sontag, J. Smith, and N. Certo (Eds.) *Educational programming for the severely and profoundly handicapped.* Reston, VA: Council for Exceptional Children.

Cantrell, R. R., and Cantrell, M. L. (1970). *Systematic decision-making and children's problems: A heuristic attempt.* University of Illinois, Urbana: Prevention-Intervention Project Working Paper.

Carey, W. B., and McDevitt, S. C. (1978a). Ability change in individual temperament diagnoses from infancy to early childhood. *Journal of Child Psychiatry, 17*:331–337.

Carey, W. B. and McDevitt, S. C. (1978b). *Infant temperament questionaire.* Media, PA: Carey Associates.

Carr, E. G. (1977). The motivation of self-injurious behavior: A review of some hypotheses. *Psychological Bulletin, 84*:800–816.

Cartwright, C. A. (1981). Effective programs for parents of young handicapped children. *Topics in Early Childhood Special Education, 1*(3):1–9.

Cartwright, G. P., Cartwright, C. A., and Ward, M. E. (1984). *Educating Special Learners,* 2nd Ed. Belmont, CA: Wadsworth.

Castle, W. (1980). Deafness and rubella: Infants in the 60's, adults in the 80's. *American Annals of the Deaf, 125*(7):961–963.

Cataldo, M. F., and Risley, T. R. (1974). Infant day care. In R. Ulrich, T. Stachnik, and J. Mabry (Eds.) *Control of human behavior: Behavior modification in education,* pp. 127–145. Glenview, IL: Scott, Foresman.

Chapman, R. S. (1981). Exploring children's communicative intents. In J. F. Miller, *Assessing language production in children–experimental procedures,* pp. 117–132. Baltimore: University Park Press.

Chess, S. (1978). The plasticity of human development: Alternative pathways. *Journal of the American Academy of Child Psychiatry, 6*:80–91.

Cicchetti, D., and Stroufe, L. (1978). An organizational view of affect: Illustration from the study of Down syndrome infants. In M. Lewis and L. Rosenblum (Eds). *The development of affect,* Vol. 1, pp. 58–74. New York: Plenum.

Clark, C., and Moores, D. (1981). *Clark Early Language Development Program.* Highham, MA: Teaching Resources.

Clark, C., Moores, D., and Woodcock, R. (1975). *Minnesota Early Language Development Sequence.* Minneapolis: University of Minnesota Research Development and Demonstration Center in Education of Handicapped Children.

Cohen, M. A., and Gross, P. J. (1979). *The development resource. Behavioral sequence for assessment and program planning, Vols. I and II.* New York: Grune & Stratton.

Cohn, A. H., and Garbarino, J. (1981). *Toward a refined approach to preventing child abuse.* Chicago: National Committee for Prevention of Child Abuse.

Collins, M., and Barraga, N. (1980). Development of efficiency in visual functioning: An evaluation process. *Journal of Visual Impairment and Blindness, 74* (March):93–96.

Congressional Record. (1978, October 10). H-21279.

Connolly, B., and Russell, F. (1976). Interdisciplinary early intervention program. *Physical Therapy, 56*:155–159.

Connor, F. P., Williamson, G. G. and Siepp, J. M. (1978). *Program guide for infants and toddlers with neuromotor and other developmental disabilities.* New York: Teachers College Press.

Connors, E. T. (1981). *Educational tort liability and malpractice.* Bloomington, IN: Phi Delta Kappa.

Conrad, R. (1979). *The deaf school child.* New York: Harper & Row.

Consortium for Longitudinal Studies. (1978). Lasting effects after preschool. (Final report of HEW grant 90c–1311. Denver: Education Commission of the States.

Cook, R. E., and Armbruster, V. B. (1983). *Adapting early childhood curricula: Suggestions for meeting special needs.* St. Louis Mosby.

Cook, T. (1981). Dilemmas in evaluation of social programs. In M. Brewer and B. Collins (Eds.). *Scientific inquiry and the social sciences.* San Francisco: Jossey-Bass.

Cook, T., and Campbell, D. (1979). *Quasi-experiementation: Design and analysis issues for field settings.* Chicago: Rand McNally.

Council for Exceptional Children. (1983). Code of ethics and standards for professional practice. *Exceptional Children*, *50*(5):205–209.

Craig, W., and Craig, H. (1982). Directory of services for the deaf. *American Annals of the Deaf*, *127*(3).

Cratty, B. J. (1979). *Perceptual and motor development in infants and children*. (2nd Ed.) New York: Macmillian.

Crocker, E. (1980). Reactions of children to health care encounters: Programs that can make a difference. In G. C. Robinson and H. F. Clarke, *The hospital care of children*. pp. 47–59. New York: Oxford University Press.

Cross, L., and Goln, K. (1977). *Identifying handicapped children*. New York: Walker.

Croft, N. B., and Robinson, L. W. (1976). Project Vision-Up. Boise, ID: Educational Products and Training Foundation.

Dale, P. S. (1979). *Language development: Structure and function*. Hinsdale, IL: Dryden.

Daragassles, S. (1977). *Neurological development in the full-term and premature neonate*. New York: Excerpta Medica.

Decarie, T. (1969). A study of the mental and emotional development of the thalidomide child. In B. M. Foss (Ed.). *Determinants of infant behavior*, Vol. 4. London: McThuen.

Deland, F. (1931). *The story of lipreading*. Washington, DC: Volta Review.

DeMeyer, M. K. (1975). The nature of neuropsychological disability in autistic children. *Journal of Autism and Childhood Schizophrenia*, *5*:109–128.

DeVine, R. A. (1980). Sexual abuse of children: An overview of the problem. In B. Jones, L. Jenstrom, and K. MacFarlane (Eds.) *Sexual abuse of children: Selected readings*, pp. 3–7. DHHS Pulbication 78–30161. Washington, D.C.: U.S. Department of Health and Human Services.

DeVita, V.T. (1982). *Cancer: Principles and practice of oncology*. Philadelphia: Lippincott.

Dougherty, N. J. (1983). Liability. *Journal of Physical Education, Recreation and Dance*, *54*:52–54.

Douglas, J. W. B. (1975). Early hospital admission and later disturbances of behavior and learning. *Developemental Medicine and Child Neurology*, *17*:456–480.

Downey, J. A., and Low, N. L. (1974). *The child with disabling illness: Principles of rehabilitation*. Philadelphia: Saunders.

DuBose, R. F. (1979). Assessment of visually impaired infants. In B. L. Darby and M. J. May (Eds.) *Infant assessment: Issues and applications*. Seattle: WESTAR.

DuBose, R. F. (1981). Assessment of severely impaired young children: Problems and recommendations. *Topics in Early Childhood Special Education*, *1*(2):9–21.

DuBose, R. F., and Deni, K. (1980). Easily constructed adaptive and assistive equipment. *Teaching Exceptional Children*, *12*:116.

DuBose, R. F., and Langley, M. B. (1977). *The developmental activities screening inventory*. New York: Teaching Resources.

DuBose R. F., Langley, M. B., and Staff, V. (1979). Assessing severely handicapped children. In E. L. Meyen, G. A. Vergason, and R. L. Whelan (Eds.) *Instructional planning for exceptional children*, pp. 38–59. Denver: Love Publishing.

Dubowitz, L., Dubowitz, V., and Goldberg, C. (1970). Clinical assessment of gestational age in the newborn infant. *Journal of Pediatrics*, *77*:1–10.

Dunn, J. (1982). Comment: Problems and promises in the study of affect and intention. In E. Z. Tronick (Ed.) *Social interchange in infancy: Affect, cognition and communication*. Baltimore: University Park Press.

Dunn, L. M., and Markwardt, F. C. (1970). *Manual for the Peabody Individual Achievement Test*. Circle Pines, MN: American Guidance Serivce.

Dunst, C. (1979). Program evalulation and the education for all handicapped children act. *Exceptional Children, 46*(1):24–33.

Dunst, C. (1981). *Infant learning a cognitive-linguistic intervention strategy.* Austin, TX: Pro-ED.

Dunst, C. (1983). Evaluating trends and advances in early intervention programs. *New Jersey Journal of School Psychology, 2*:26–40.

Durkin, R. (1984). *The evaluation of Seattle by nursery associations care and treatment program for abused children and their families: And its implications.* The Fifth International Congress on Child Abuse and Neglect, Montreal, September 16–19.

Educational Testing Service. (1976). *Circus assessment system.* Princeton, NJ.

Education For All Handicapped Children Act of 1975, 20 United States Congress 1401 (1975).

Efrom, M., and DuBoff, B. (1975). *A vision guide for teachers of deaf-blind children.* Raleigh, NC: State Department of Public Instruction.

Ehly, S. W., Conoley, J. C., and Rosenthal, D. (1985). *Working with parents of exceptional children.* St. Louis: Times/Mirror, Mosby.

Eimas, P. D. (1975). Speech perception in early infancy. In L. B. Cohen and P. Salapatek (Eds.) *Infant perception: From sensation to cognition,* Vol. 2. New York: Academic Press.

Elardo, R., Bradley, R., and Caldwell, B. M. (1975). The relation of infants' home environment to mental test performance from six to thirty-six months: A longitudinal analysis. *Child Development, 46*(1):71–76.

Ellis, D. (1978). Methods of assessment for use with the visually and mentally handicapped: A selective review. *Child: Care, Health & Development, 4*:397–410.

Elmer, E., and Gregg, G. S. (1967). Developmental characteristics of abused children. *Pediatrics, 40*:596–602.

Emde, R. N., and Harmon, R. J. (1972). Endogenous and exogenous smiling systems in early infancy. *Journal of the American Academy of Child Psychiatry, 11*:177–200.

Epstein, A. S., and Weikart, D. P. Changed Lives: The effects of the Perry Preschool Program as youths through age 19, Monograph 8, Ypsilanti, MI: HIGH/SCOPE Press.

Epstein, L. H. Doke, L. A., Sajwaj, T. E. Sorrell, S., and Rimmer, B. (1974). Generality and side effects of overcorrection. *Journal of Applied Behavior Analysis, 7*:385–390.

ERIC Clearinghouse on Handicapped and Gifted Children (1985). Council for Exceptional Children. 1920 Association Drive, Reston, VA: 22091-1589.

Erickson, E. H. (1968). *Identity, youth, and crisis.* New York: Norton.

Erikson, E. H. (1963). *Childhood and society.* New York: Norton.

Fallen, N. H., and Umansky, W. (1985). *Young children with special needs,* 2nd ed. Columbus, OH: Merrill.

Faller, K. C., and Russo, S. (1981). Definition and scope of problem of child maltreatment. In K. C. Faller (Ed.) *Social work with abused and neglected children,* pp. 3–11. New York: Free Press.

Fantz, R. L., Fagin, J. F., and Mirarda, S. B. (1973). Early visual selectivity. In L. B. Cohen and P. Salapatek (Eds.) *Infant perception: From sensation to cognition.* New York: Academic Press.

Fetters, L. (1982. The development of object permanence in infants with motor handicaps. *Physical Therapy. 61*:327–332.

Fewell, R. R. (1983). The team approach in infant education. In S. G. Garwood and R. R. Fewell (Eds.) *Educating handicapped infants,* pp. 232–254. Rockville, MD: Aspen Systems.

Fewell, R. R., and Sandall, S. R. (1983). Curricula adaptions for young children: Visually impaired, hearing impaired, and physically impaired. *Topics in Early Childhood Special Education*, 2(4):51–66.

Field, T. (1983). High-risk infants "have less fun" during early interactions. *Topics in Early Childhood Special Education*, 3(1):77–87.

Field, T., Widmayer, S., Greenberg, R. and Stoller, S. (1982). Effects of parent training on teenage mothers and their infants. *Pediatrics*, 69(6):703–707.

Filler, J. W., Jr. (1983). Service models for handicapped infants. In S. G. Garwood and R. R. Fewell (Eds.), *Educating handicapped infants*, pp. 369–386.

Filler, J. W., and Kasari, C. (1980). *Implementing a data based program for infants in the public schools*. Paper presented at the Annual Meeting of the Association for the Severly Handicapped, Los Angeles.

Finnie, N. (1975). *Handling the young cerebral palsied child at home*. New York: Dutton.

Fleck, S. (1972). An approach to family pathology. In G. D. Erickson and T. P. Hogan (Eds.). *Family therapy: An introduction to theory and technique*. Monterey, CA: Brooks/Cole.

Foxx, R. M., and Azrin, N.H. (1972). Restitution: A method of eliminating aggressive-disruptive behavior of retarded and brain-damaged patients. *Behavior Research and Therapy*, 10:15–27.

Foxx, R. M., and Azrin, N. H. (1973). The elimination of autistic self-stiumlating behavior by overcorrection. *Journal of Applied Behavior Analysis*, 6:1–14.

Fraiberg, S. (1974). Blind infants and their mothers: An examination of the sign system. In M. Lewis and L. Rosenblum (Eds.) *The effect of the infant on its caregiver*. New York: Wiley.

Fraiberg, S. (1977). *Insights from the blind*. New York: Basic Books.

Fraiberg, S., Siegal, B., and Gibson, R. (1966). The role of sound in the search behavior of a blind infant. *Psychoanalytic Study of a Child*, 71:327–357.

Frankel, F., and Simmons, J. Q. (1976). Self-injurious behavior in schizophrenic and retarded children. *American Journal of Mental Deficiency*, 60:512–522.

Frankenberg, W. K., Dodds, J., and Fandal, A. (1975). *Denver developmental screening test*. Denver: LADOCA Project and Publishing Foundation.

Frankenburg, W. K. Dodds, J., and Fandal, A. (1975). *Denver developmental screening test*. Denver, CO: LADOCA Project and Publishing Foundation.

Freeman, R. D. (1967). Controversy over "patterning" as a treatment for brain damage in children. *Journal of the American Medical Association*, 202:83–86.

Freeman, R., Carbin, C., and Boese, R. (1981). *Can't your child hear?* Baltimore: University Park Press.

Freud, A. (1979). *Psychoanalysis for teachers and parents*. New York: Norton.

Friedlander, S., Pothier, P., Morrison, P., and Herman O. (1982). The role ofneurological developmental delay in childhood psychopathology. *American Journal of Othopsychiatry*, 52:102–108.

Frisina, R. (1974). *Report of the committee to redefine deaf and hard-of-hearing*. Silver Springs, MD: Conference of Executives of American Schools for the Deaf.

Fullard, W., McDevitt, S. C., and Carey, W. B. (1978). *Toddler temperament scale*. Media, PA.

Furuno, S., O'Reilly, K. A., Hosaka, C. M., Inatsuka, T. T., Allman, T. L., and Zeisloft, B. (1979). *Hawaii Early Learning Profile and Activity Guide*. Palo, Alto, CA: VORT Corporation.

Gabel, H., McDowell, J., and Cerreto, M. C. (1983). Family adaptation to the handicapped infant. In S. G. Garwood and R. R. Fewell, *Educating Handicapped Infants*, pp. 455–486. Rockville, MD: Aspen Systems.

Gagne, R. (1970). *Conditions of learning*. New York: Holt, Rinehart and Winston.

Gagne, R. (1974). *Essentials of learning*. New York: Holt, Rinehart and Winston.

Gallagher, R. J. Jens, K. G., and O'Donnell, K. E. (1983). The effect of physical status on the affective expression of handicapped infants. *Infant Behavior and Development, 6*:73–77.

Gargiulo, R. M. (1985). *Working with parents of exceptional children.* Boston: Houghton Mifflin.

Garmezy, N. (1974). Children at risk: The search for the antecedents of schizophrenia. Part I. Conceptual models and research methods. *Schizophrenia Bulletin, 8*:14–89.

Garnett, C. (1968). *The exchange of letters between Samuel Heinicke and Abbe Charles Michael de l'Epee.* New York: Vantage.

Garwood, S. G. (1983). *Educating young handicapped children: A developmental approach,* 2nd ed. Rockville, MD: Aspen Systems.

Garwood, S. G., Fewell, R. R. (1983). *Educating handicapped infants.* Rockville, MD: Aspen Systems.

Gerber, A., and Bryen, D. (1981). *Language and learning disabilities.* Baltimore: University Park Press.

Gesell, A. (1949). *Vision—Its development in infant and child.* New York: Harper & Row. ms pp.829-831

Gil, D. (1969). What schools can do about child abuse. *American Education, 5*:2–5.

Glover, M. E., Preminger, J. L., and Sanford, A. R. (1978). *Early Learning Accomplishment Profile.* Winston-Salem, NC: Kaplan Press.

Goetz, E. M. (1982). Behavior principles and techniques. In K. E. Allen and E. M. Goetz (Eds.) *Early childhood education: Special problems, special solutions,* pp. 31–76. Rockville, MD: Aspen Systems.

Goldberg, S. (1977). Social competence in infancy: A model of parent-infant interaction. *Merrill-Palmer Quarterly, 23*:163–177.

Goodwin, J. (1982). *Sexual abuse incest victims and their families.* Boston: John Wright.

Gray, S. W., Ramsey, B. K., and Klaus, R. A. (1982). *From 3 to 20: The early training project.* Baltimore: University Park Press.

Graziano, A. M., and Mooney, K. C. (1984). *Children and behavior therapy.* New York: Aldine.

Greenberg, M. (1983). Family streses and child competence: The effects of early intervention for families with deaf infants. *American Annals of the Deaf, 128*:407–417.

Greenspan, S. I., and White, K. R. (1985). The efficacy of preventive intervention: A glass half full? *Zero to three, Bulletin of the National Center for Clinical Infant Programs. 5*(4).

Greenspan, S. I., Wieder, S., Lieberman, A., Nover, R., Lourie, R., and Robinson, M. (1985). *Infants in multi-risk families: Case studies of preventive intervention.* New York: International Universities Press.

Grollman, E. A. (1976). *Talking about death: A dialog between parent and child.* Boston: Beacon Press.

Grossman, H. J., (Ed.) (1973). *Manual on terminology and classification in mental retardation.* Washington, DC: American Association on Mental Deficiency.

Growing Up: A developmental curriculum. (1985). Austin, TX: Parent Consultants.

Guess, D., and Noonan, M. J. (1982). Curricula and instructional procedures for severely handicapped student. *Focus on Exceptional Children, 14*(5):1–12.

Gustason, G., Pfetzing, D., and Zawolkow, E. (1972). *Signing exact English.* Rossmoor, CA: Modern Signs Press.

Haeussermann, E. (1958). *Developmental potential of preschool children: An evaluation in intellectual, sensory, and emotional functioning.* New York: Grune & Stratton.

Haeusserman, E. (1969). Evaluating the developmental level of cerebral palsy preschool children. In J. M. Wolf and R. M. Anderson (Eds.) *The multiply handicapped child*. Springfield, IL: Thomas.

Hagan, C., Porter, W., and Brink, J. (1973). Nonverbal communication: An alternate mode of communication for the child with severe cerebral palsy. *Journal of Speech and Hearing Disorders, 38*:448–454.

Hall, C.S., and Lindzey, G. (1978). *Theories of personality*, 3rd ed. New York: Wiley.

Hall, E., and Skinner, N. (1980). *Somewhere to turn: Strategies for parents of the gifted and talented*. New York: Teachers College Press.

Hallahan, D., and Kauffman, J. (1978). *Exceptional children: An introduction to special education*. Englewood Cliffs, NJ: Prentice-Hall.

Hanson, M. J. (1978). *Teaching your Down's syndrom infant: A guide for parents*. Baltimore: University Park Press.

Hanson, M. J. (1981). A model for early intervention with culturally diverse single and multiparent families. *Topics in Early Childhood Special Education, 1*(3):37–44.

Hanson, M. J. (Ed.). (1984). *Atypical infant development*. Baltimore: University Park Press.

Hanson, M. J., and Bellamy, G. T. (1977). Continuous measurement of progress in infant intervention programs. *Education and Training of the Mentally Retarded, 12*:52–58.

Hanson, J. W., Jones, K. L., and Smith, D. W. (1976). Fetal alcoholism syndrome: Experience with 41 patients. *Journal of American Medical Association, 235*:1458–1460.

Hanson, M. J., and Schwarz, R. (1978). Results of a longitudinal intervention program for Down's syndrome infants and their families. *Education and Training of the Mentally Retarded, 13*:403–407.

Hardgrove, C. B., and Dawson, R. B. (1972). *Parents and children in the hospital: The family's role in pediatrics*. Boston: Little, Brown.

Hare, B. A., and Hare, J. M. (1979). Learning disabilities in children. In S. G. Garwood (Ed.) *Educating young handicapped children: A developmental approach*. Germantown, MD: Aspen Systems.

Haring, N. G., Liberty, K. A., and White, O. (1980). Rules for data-based strategy decisions in instructional programs: Current research and instructional implications. In W. Sailor, B. Wilcox, and L. Brown (Eds.). *Methods of instruction for severely handicapped students*. Baltimore: Paul H. Brookes.

Haring, N. G., and Phillips, E. L (1962). *Educating emotionally disturbed children*. New York: McGraw-Hill.

Harper, G. F. (1980). Teaching and child abuse. *Educational Forum, 44*(3):321–327.

Harris, S. R. (1981). Relationship of mental and motor development in Down's syndrome infants. *Physical and Occupational Therapy in Pediatrics, 1*:13–18.

Harris-Vanderheiden, D., and Vanderheiden, G. (1977). Basic considerations in the development of communicative and interactive skills for non-vocal severely handicapped children. In E. Sontag, J. Smith, and N. Certo (Eds.). *Educational programming for the severely and profoundly handicapped*. Reston, VA: Council for Exceptional Children.

Hart, V. (1974). *Beginning with the handicapped*. Springfield, IL: Thomas.

Hawkins, D. R., and Pauling, L. (1973). *Orthomolecular psychiatry*. San Francisco: Freeman.

Hayden, A. H., and Dmitriev, V. (1975). The multidisciplinary preschool program for Down's syndrome children at the University of Washington Model Preschool Center. In B. Z. Friedlander, G. M. Sterritt, and G. E. Kirk (Eds.) *Exceptional infant*, Vol. 3, *Assessment and intervention*, pp. 193–221.

Hayden, A. H., and Edgar, E. B. (1977). Identification, screening and assessment. In

J. B. Jordan, A. H. Hayden, M. B. Karnes, and M. M. Wood, *Early childhood education for exceptional children. Reston, VA: The Council for Exceptional Children.*

Hetherington, E. M., and Parke, R. D. (1979). *Child psychology: A contemporary viewpoint,* 2nd ed. New York: McGraw-Hill.

Heward, W. L., and Orlansky, M. D. (1984). *Exceptional children: An introductory survey of special education,* 2nd ed. Columbus, OH: Charles E. Merrill.

Hobbs, N. (1966). Helping the disturbed child: Psychological and ecological strategies. *American Psychologist, 21:*1105–1115.

Hodges, W. L., and Sheehan, R. (1978). Evaluation: Strategies for generating knowledge. In C. C. Rentz and R. R. Rentz (Eds.) *New directions in program evaluation.* San Francisco: Jossey-Bass.

Holm, V. (1978). Team issues. In K. E. Allen, V. Holm, and R. Schiefelbusch (Eds.) *Early intervention—A team approach,* pp. 99–115. Baltimore: University Park Press.

Holmes, T. H., and Rahe, R. H. (1967). The social readjustment rating scale. *Journal of Psychosomatic Research, 11:*213–218.

Hughes, P. R. (1978). *Dying is different.* Mahomet, IL: Mech Mentor Educational Publishers.

Hunt, J. McV. (1961). *Intelligence and experience.* New York: Ronald Press.

Institute of Medicine. (1985). Preventing low birthweight. Washington DC: National Academy Press.

Jackson, N. E., and Robinson, H. B. (1977). Early indentification of intellectually advanced children. Paper presented at the Annual Convention of National Association for Gifted Children, San Diego. Jacobs, J. C. (1971). Effectiveness of teacher and parent identification of gifted children as a function of school level. *Psychology in the Schools, 8:*140–142.

Jacobs, L. (1980). *A deaf adult speaks out.* Washington, DC: Gallaudet College Press.

Jens, K. G. , and O'Donnell, K. E. (1982). Bridging the gap between research and intervention with handicapped infants. In D. D. Bricker (Ed.) *Intervention with high-risk and handicapped infants: From research to application.* Baltimore: University Park Press.

Jensema, C. (1974). Post-rubella children in special education. *Volta Review, 76:*466–573.

Johnson, N. M., Jens, K. G., and Attermeier, S. A. (1979). *Carolina curriculum for handicapped infants.* Chapel Hill, NC: Frank Porter Graham Child Development Center, University of North Carolina.

Johnson, N. M., Jens, K. G., Gallagher, R. J., and Anderson, J. D. (1980). Cognition and affect in infancy: Implications for the handicapped. *New Directions for Exceptional Children, 3:*21–36.

Jones, M. H. (1975). Habilitative management of communicative disorders in young children. In D. B. Tower (Ed.). *The nervous system: Human communication and its disorders,* Vol. 3. New York: Raven Press.

Jones, C. O. (1981). Characteristics and needs of abused and neglected children. In K. C. Faller (Ed.). *Social work with abused and neglected children,* pp. 79–83. New York: Free Press.

Jones, B., MacFarlane, K. and Jenstrom, L. (Eds.). (1980). *Sexual abuse of children: Selected readings.* DHHS Publication 78–30161. Washington, DC: U.S. Department of Health and Human Services.

Jordan, I., Gustason, G., and Rosen, R. (1979). An update on communication trends in programs for the deaf. *American Annals of the Deaf, 124*(3):350–357.

Karnes, M. B. (1977). Exemplary early education programs for handicapped children: Characteristics in common. *Educational Horizons, 56*(1):47–54.

Karnes, M. B. (1979). *Small wonder! User's guide*. Circle Pines, MN: American Guidance Service.

Karnes, M. B., Linnemeyer, S. A., and Shwedel, A. M. (1981). A survey of federally funded model programs for handicapped infants: Implications for research and practice. *Journal of the Division of Early Childhood, 2:*25–39.

Karnes, M. B., and Teska, J. A. (1980). Toward successful parent involvement in programs for handicapped children. In J. J. Gallagher (Ed.). *New directions in exceptional children: Parents and families of handicapped children*, pp. 85–111). San Francisco: Jossey-Bass.

Kasari, C., and Filler, J. W. (1981). Using inflatables with severely motorically involved infants and preschoolers. *Teaching Exceptional Children, 14:*22–26.

Kauffman, J. M. (1981). *Characteristics of children's behavior disorders*. Columbus, OH: Merrill.

Kazdin, L. (1975). *Behavior modification in applied settings*. Homewood, IL: Dorsy Press.

Kelly, J. F. (1980). *Analysis of service delivery to children birth to three years and their families*. Olympia: Washington State Education Agency.

Kirk, S., and Gallagher, J. *Educating exceptional children*. Boston: Houghton Mifflin.

Kleinberg, S. B. (1982). *Educating the chronically ill child*. Rockville, MD: Aspen Systems.

Knapp, S. (1983). Counselor liability for failure to report child abuse. *Elementary School Guidance and Counseling, 17:*177–179.

Knobloch, H., and Pasamanick, B. (1974). *Developmental diagnosis*. New York: Harper & Row.

Knobloch, H., Pasamanick, B., and Sherard, E. S. (1966). *A developmental screening inventory*. Albany, NY: Albany Medical College.

Knott, M. (1966). Neuromuscular facilitation in the child with central nervous system deficits. *Journal of the American Physical Therapy Association, 46:*721–724.

Koegel, R. L., and Covert, A. (1972). The relationship of self- stimulation to learning in autistic children. *Journal of Applied Behavior Analysis, 5:*381–387.

Koegel, R. L., Egel, A. L., and Dunlap, G. (1980). Learning characteristics of autistic children. In W. S. Sailor, B. Wilcox, and L. J. Brown (Eds.), *Methods of instruction for severely handicapped students*. Baltimore: Brookes.

Koegel, R. L., Firestone, P. B., Kramme, K. W., and Dunlap, G. (1974). Increasing spontaneous play by suppressing self- stimulation in autistic children. *Journal of Applied Behavior Analysis, 7:*521–528.

Kogan, K. L., Tyler, N., and Turner, P. (1974). The process of interpersonal adaptation between mothers and their cerebral palsied children. *Developmental Medicine and Child Neurology, 16:*518–527.

Kopp, C. B. (1982). Antecedents of self-regulation: A developmental perspective. *Developmental Psychology, 18*(2):99–214.

Kopp, C. B., and Simeonsson, R. J. (Eds.). (1982). Young handicapped children: Research findings. *Topics in Early Childhood Special Education, 2*(2).

Kounin, J. S. (1977). Some ecological dimensions of school settings. Paper presented at American Educational Research Association Conference, New York, April.

Kurtz, P. D., Neisworth, J. T., and Laub, K. W. (1977). Issues concerning the early identification of handicapped children. *Journal of School Psychology, 15*(2):136–140.

Langley, B. (1980a). *Functional vision inventory for the multiple and severely handicapped*. Chicago: Stoelting.

Langley, B. (1980b). *The teachable moment and the handicapped infant*. Reston, VA: The Council for Exceptional Children.

Langley, B., and Dubose, R. (1976). Functional vision screening for severely handicapped children. *New Outlook for the Blind, 70*(8):346–350.

Lasky, E., and Chapandy, A. (1976). Factors affecting language comprehension. *Language, Speech, and Hearing Services in Schools, 7:*159–168.

LeBow, M. D. (1984). *Child obesity: A new frontier in behavior therapy.* New York: Springer.

Leib, S. A., Benfield, G., and Guidubaldi, J. (1980). Effects of early intervention and stimulation on the preterm infant. *Pediatrics, 66:*83–90.

LeMay, D. W., Griffin, P. M., and Sanford, A. R. (1978). *Learning accomplishment profile: Diagnostic edition,* Rev. ed. Winston-Salem, NC: Kaplan School Supply.

Lenneberg, E. (1967). *Biological foundations of Language.* New York: Wiley.

Lerner, J., Mardell-Czudnowski, C., and Goldenberg, D. (1981). *Special education for the early childhood years.* Englewood Cliffs, NJ: Prentice-Hall.

Lewis, M., and Fox, N. (1980). Predicting cognitive development from assessment in infancy. In B. W. Camp (Ed.), *Advances in behavioral pediatrics,* vol. 1. Greenwich, CT: JAI Press.

Lillie, D. L. (1976). *Carolina Developmental Profile.* Winston-Salem, NC: Kaplan Press.

Linder, T. W. (1983). *Early childhood special education–Program development and administration.* Baltimore: Brookes.

Lovaas, O. I., Schreibman, L., Koegel, R., and Rehn, R. (1971). Selective responding by autistic children to multiple sensory input. *Journal of Abnormal Psychology, 77:* 211–222.

Lowenfeld, B. (1971). *Our blind children.* Springfield, IL: Thomas.

Lyons, D. F., and Powers, V. (1963). Follow-up study of elementary school children exempted from Los Angeles city schools during 1960–1961. *Exceptional Children, 30:*133–162.

McCall, R. B., Hagarty, P. S., and Hurlburt, N. (1972). Transitions in infant sensorimotor development and the prediction of childhood IQ. *American Psychologist, 27:*728–748.

McCollum, J. A., and Strayton, F. D. (1985). Infant/parent interaction: studies and intervention guidelines based on the SIAI model. *Journal of the Division of Early Childhood,* Spring:125–135.

McLean, J. E., and Snyder-McLean, L. K. (1978). *A transactional approach to early language training.* Columbus, OH: Merrill.

McCartin, R. (1978). Training in interdisciplinariness. In K. E. Allen, V. Holm, and R. Schiefelbusch (Eds.), *Early intervention–A team approach,* pp. 115–122. Baltimore: University Park Press.

McMurtry, S. L. (1985). Secondary prevention of child maltreatment: A review. *Social Work, 30:*42–48.

Mager, R. F. (1975). *Preparing instructional objectives,* 2nd ed. Belmont, CA: Fearon Publishers.

Mallory, B. (1983). The preparation of early childhood special educators: A model program. *Journal of the Division of Early Childhood, 7:*32–40.

Mardell, C., and Goldenberg, D. (1975). *Developmental indications for the assessment of learning—Manual.* Edison, NJ: Childcraft.

Martin, E. W. (1970). A new outlook for education of handicapped children. *American Education, 66*(3):7–10.

Martin, H. P. (1972). The child and his development. In C. H. Kempe and R. E. Helfer (Eds.). *Helping the battered child and his family.* Philadelphia: Lippincott.

Martin, H. P. (1980). The consequences of being abused and neglected: How the child fares. In C. H. Kempe and R. E. Helfer (Eds.), *The battered child,* 3rd ed., pp. 347–365. Chicago: University of Chicago Press.

Martin, H. P., Beezley, P., Conway, E. F., and Kempe, C. H. (1974). The development of abused children. *Advances in Pediatrics, 21:*25–73.

Martini, L. M., and Macturk, R. H. (in press). Issues in the enumeration of handcapping conditions in the United States. *Mental Retardation.*

Martinson, R. A., and Seagoe, M. V. (1967). *The abilities of young children.* Washington, DC: The Council for Exceptional Children.

Massie, N. H. and Campbell, B. K. (1983). The Massie-Campbell scale of mother-infant attachment indicators during stress (AIDS scale) (394-412). In J. D. Call, E. Galerson, and R. L. Tyson, (Eds.).

Mattsson, A. (1972). Long-term physical illness in childhood: A challenge to psychosocial adaptation. *Pediatrics, 50:*801–811.

Meadow, K. (1967). *The effect of early manual communication and family climate on the deaf child's environment.* Unpublished doctoral dissertation, University of California, Berkeley.

Meadow, K. (1981). *Deafness and child development.* Berkely: University of California Press.

Meadow, K. (1982). *Meadow-Kendall Social Emotional Assessment for deaf and hearing impaired children, preschool form (research edition).* Washington, DC: Gallaudet College, Kendall Demonstration Elementary School, Outreach Programs.

Meichenbaum, P. H. and Goodman, J. (1971). Training impulsive children to talk to themselves: A means of developing self-control. *Journal of Abnormal Psychology,* 77:115–126.

Meier, J. (1976). Screening, assessment, and intervention for young children at developmental risk. In N. Hobbs (Ed.), *Issues in the classification of children,* vol. 2. San Francisco: Jossey-Bass.

Meier, J. H. and Malone, P. J. (1979). *Facilitating children's development.* Baltimore: University Park Press.

Meisels, S. J., Jones, S. N., and Stiefel, G. S. (1983). Neonatal intervention: Problems, purpose and prospects. *Topics in Early Childhood Special Education, 3*(1):1–13.

Mercer, C. P., Algozzine, B., and Trifilett, J. J. (1979). Early identification: Issues and considerations. *Exceptional Children, 21* 52–54.

Mian, M., Wehrspann, W., Klajner-Diamond, H., LeBaron, D., and Winder, C. (1984). *Review of 125 children 6 years of age and under who were sexually abused.* The fifth International Congress on Child Abuse and Neglect, Montreal, September 16–19.

Miller, J. F. (1981). *Assessing language production in children—experimental procedures.* Baltimore: University Park Press.

Mindes, G. (1982). Social and cognitive aspects of play in young handicapped children. *Topics in Early Childhood Special Education, 2*(3):39–52.

Moersch, M. S. and Schafer, D. S. (1981). *Developmental programming for infants and young children,* vol. 3, Stimulation activities. Ann Arbor: University of Michigan Press.

Moores, D. (1982). *Educating the deaf: Psychology, principles and practices.* Boston: Houghton Mifflin.

Moores, D. (1985). Early intervention programs for hearing impaired children: A longitudinal assessment. In K. Nelson (Ed.), *Children's language: Volume V,* 159–196. Hillsdale, NJ: Earlbaum Associates.

Morales v. *Turman,* 364 F. Supp. 166 (1973). U.S. Supreme Court.

Mordock, J. (1979). The separation-individuation process and developomental disabilities. *Exceptional Children, 20:*176–184.

Mori, A. A., and Neisworth, J. T. (1983). Curricula in early childhood education: Some generic and special considerations. *Topics in Early Childhood Special Education,* 2(4):1–8.

Morris, H. H. (1956). Aggressive behavior disorders in children: A follow-up study. *American Journal of Psychiatry, 112:*991–997.

Morris, S. E. (1978). Sensorimotor prerequisites for speech and the influence of cerebral palsy. In J. M. Wilson (Ed.), *Oral-motor function and dysfunction in children*. Chapel Hill: University of North Carolina Physical Therapy Department.

Moyer, J. R., and Dardig, J. D. (1978). Practical task analysis for special educators. *Teaching Exceptional Children, 11:*16–18.

National Center on Child Abuse and Neglect. (1981). *National study of the incidence and severity of child abuse and neglect.* DHHS Publication 81–30325. Washington, DC: U.S. Department of Health and Human Services.

Neisworth, J. T., Willoughby-Herb, S. J., Bagnato, S. J., Cartwright, C. A., and Laub, K. W. (1980). *Individualized education for preschool exceptional children.* Rockville, MD: Aspens Systems.

Newby, H. A. (1978). *Audiology,* 4th ed. Englewood Cliffs, NJ: Prentice-Hall.

Northern, J. L., and Downs, M. P. (1978). *Hearing in children.* Baltimore: Williams & Wilkins.

Nurcombe, B., Howell, D.C., Rauh, V. A., Tetl, D. M., Ruoff, P., and Brennan, J. (1984). An intervention program for mothers of low birthweight infants: Preliminary results. Journal of developmental and behavioral pediatrics, 3(2): 34–43.

O'Brien, R. (1976). *Alive . . . aware . . . a person.* Silver Springs, MD: Montgomery County Schools.

Oregon Project for Visually Impaired and Blind Preschool Children. (1978). Bedford, OR: Jackson County Intermediate Education District.

Paget, K. D., and Bracken, B. A. (1983). *The psychological assessment of preschool children.* New York: Grune & Stratton.

Parten, M. B. (1932). Social play among preschool children. *Journal of Abnormal Social Psychology, 27:*243–269.

Pate, J. (1963). Emotionally disturbed and socially maladjusted children. In L. Dunn (Ed.). *Exceptional children in the schools.* New York: Holt, Rinehart and Winston.

Paul, J. L., and Epanchin, B. C. (1982). *Emotional disturbance in children.* Columbus, OH: Merrill.

Pauling, L. (1968). Orthomolecular psychiatry. *Science,* 160:265–271.

Peterman, R. H., and Goodhart, R. S. (1954). Current status of vitamin therapy in nervous and mental disease. *Journal of Clinical Nutrition, 2:*11–21.

Peters, D., Neisworth, J., and Yawkey, T. (1985). *Early childhood education: From theory to practice.* Monterey, CA: Brooks/Cole.

Peterson, N. L. (1982). Early intervention with the handicapped. In E. Meyen (Ed.). *Exceptional children and youth: An introduction,* 2nd ed., pp. 103-128. Denver, CO: Love Publishing.

Piaget, J. (1973). *The child and reality: Problems of genetic psychology.* New York: Grossman.

Piaget, J. (1952). *The origins of intelligence in children.* New York: International Universities Press.

Piaget, J., and Inhelder, B. (1969). *The psychology of the child.* New York: Basic Books.

Pierce, L. H., and Pierco, R. L. (1984). Race as a factor in the sexual abuse of children. *Social Work Research and Abstracts, 20,* 9–14.

Pless, I., Satterwhite, B., and Van Vechten, D. (1976). Chronic illness in childhood: A regional survey of care. *Pediatrics, 58:*37–46.

Popovitch, D., and Latham, S. L. (1981). *The adaptive behavior curriculum.* Baltimore: Brookes.

Potter, C. A. (1983). Professional liability: And how to protect yourself against acts of nature. *School and Community, 69:*1—12.

Project vision-up curriculum. Boise, ID: Educational Products and Training Foundation.

Prugh, D. G., Staub, E. Sands, H. H., Kirschbaum, R. M., and Lenihan, E. A. (1953). A study of the emotional reactions of children and families to hospitalization and illness. *American Journal of Orthopsychiatry, 20:*70–106.

Rainforth, B. and Thompson, Z. (1978). *If you don't know where "relaxation" is, how will you know when you've arrived?* Paper presented at the Annual Meeting of the Association for the Severely Handicapped, Baltimore.

Raynor, S., and Drouillard, R. (1977). *Get a wiggle on.* Mason, MI: Ingham Intermediate School District.

Redl, F. (1959). The concept of the life space interview. *American Journal of Orthopsychiatry, 29:*721–734.

Resource Materials: A Curriculum on Child Abuse and Neglect. (1979). DHEW Publication 79–30221. Washington, DC: U.S. Department of Health, Education and Welfare.

Rey, M., and Rey, H. A. (1966). *Curious George goes to the hospital.* Boston: Houghton-Mifflin.

Reynolds, M. (Ed.). (1962). *Early school admission for mentally advanced children.* Washington, DC: The Council for Exceptional Children.

Ribble, M. (1944). Infantile experience in relation to personality development. In J. McV. Hunt (Ed.). *Personality and the behavior disorders,* pp. 621–651. New York: Ronald Press.

Rich, H. L. (1982). *Disturbed students: Characteristics and educational strategies.* Baltimore: University Park Press.

Richardson, S. (1976). The influence of severe malnutrition in infancy on the intelligence of children at school age: An ecological perspective. In R. N. Walsh and W. T. Greenough (Eds.). *Environments as therapy for brian dysfunction: Advances in behavioral biology,* No. 17. New York: Plenum.

Rimland, B. (1978). A risk/benefit perspective on the use of aversives. *Journal of Autism and Childhood Schizophrenia, 8:*100–113.

Risley, T. R. (1968). The effects and side-effects of punishing the autistic behaviors of a deviant child. *Journal of Applied Behavior Analysis, 1:*21–34.

Ritchey, D. D. (1980). Educators and the primary prevention of child abuse. *Educational Forum, 44*(3):329–337.

Roach, J. L. (1958). Some social-psychological characteristics of child guidance clinic caseloads. *Journal of Consulting Clinical Psychology, 22:*183–186.

Robertson, J. (1952). *A two-year-old goes to the hospital.* (Film). New York: New York University Film Library. (16 mm, sound, 45 min).

Robertson, J. (1953). Some responses of young children to the loss of maternal care. *Nursing Times, 49:*382–386.

Robertson, M. E. (1972). *Psychological impact of illness and hospitalization on the child: Birth through 12 years.* Paper presented at a meeting of the Metropolitan Washington Affiliate of the Association for the Care of Children in Hospitals.

Robins, L. N. (1966). *Deviant children grown up: A sociological and psychological study of sociopathic personality.* Baltimore: William & Wilkins.

Robinson, C. C. (1982). Questions regarding the effects of neuromotor problems on sensorimotor development. In D. D. Bricker (Ed.), *Interaction with high risk and handicapped infants: From research to application.* Baltimore: University Park Press.

Robinson, C. C., and Robinson, J. H. (1978). Sensorimotor functions and cognitive development. In M. E. Snell (Ed.), *Systematic instruction of the moderately and severely handicapped.* Columbus, OH: Merrill.

Robinson, S. and Smith D. (1981). Listening skills: Teaching learning disabled students to be good listeners. *Focus on Exceptional Children, 13*(8):1–15.

Roedell, W. C., Jackson, N. E., and Robinson, H. B. (1980). *Gifted young children.* New York: Teachers College Press.

Rogers, C. R. (1961). *Personality adjustment inventory*. New York: Association Press.

Rogers, S. (1977). Characteristics of the cognitive development of profoundly retarded children. *Child Development, 48:*837–843.

Rogow, S. M. (1978). Considerations in assessment of blind children who function as severely or profoundly retarded. *Child: Care, Health and Development, 4:*327–335.

Rose, D. E., and Tompkins, J. (1978). Physics of sound. In D. E. Rose (Ed.), *Audiological assessment*. Englewood Cliffs, NJ: Prentice-Hall.

Ross, A. D. (1981). *Child behavior therapy: Principles, procedures, and empirical basis*. New York: Wiley.

Ross, D. D. (1982). Selecting materials for mainstreamed preschools. *Topics in Early Childhood Special Education, 2*(1):33–42.

Ross, Conference Task Force (1982). Report of the fourth Canadian Ross Conference on pediatric research: Childhood antecedents of adult disease. Vancouver, B.C.: National Press.

Rothberg, A., Maisels, M. J., Bagnato, S. J., and Murphy, J. P. (1981). Outcome for mechanically ventilated prematures weighting less than 1250 g. at birth. *Journal of Pediatrics, 98*(1):106–111.

Rothberg, A., Maisels, M. J., and Bagnato, S. J. (1983). Infants weighing 1000 grams or less at birth: Developmental outcome for ventilated and nonventilated infants. *Pediatrics, 71:*599–602.

Rutter, M. (1972a). *Maternal deprivation*. London: Penguin Books.

Rutter, M. (1972b). Childhood schizophrenia reconsidered. *Journal of Autism and Childhood Schizophrenia, 2:*315–337.

Rutter, M., and Bartak, L. (1973). Special educational treatment of autistic children: A comparative study—II. Follow-up findings and implications for services. *Journal of Child Psychology and Psychiatry, 14:*241–270.

Rutter, M., Tizard, J., and Whitmore, K. (1970). *Education, health, and behavior*. New York: Wiley.

Safford, P. L. (1978). *Teaching young children with special needs*. Saint Louis: Mosby.

Salvia, J. and Meisel, C. (1980). Observer bias: A methodological consideration in special education research. *Journal of Special Education, 14*(2):261–270.

Salvia, J., and Ysseldyke, J. E. (1985). *Assessment in special and remedial education*, 3rd ed. Boston: Houghton-Mifflin.

Salzen, E. A. (1963). Visual stimuli eliciting the smiling response in the human infant. *The Journal of Genetic Psychology, 102:*51–54.

Sameroff, A. J. (1973). Early influences on development. *Merrill-Palmer Quarterly, 21:*267–294.

Sameroff, A. J. (1979). The etiology of cognitive competence: A systems perspective. In R. B. Kearsley and I. E. Sigel (Eds.). *Infants at risk: Assessment of cognitive functioning*. Hillsdale, NJ: Elbaum.

Sandgrund, A. (1974). Child abuse and mental retardation: A problem of cause and effect. *American Journal of Mental Deficiency, 43* 327–330.

Scarr-Salaptek, S. and Williams, M. (1973). The effects of early stimulation on low-birth weight infants. *Child Development, 44:*94–101.

Schaefer, D. S., and Moersch, M. (1981). Developmental programming for infants and young children. Ann Arbor: University of Michigan Press.

Schiefelbusch, R. L. (Ed). (1978). *Language intervention series Vol. 1, Basis of language intervention*. Baltimore: University Park Press.

Schiefelbusch, R. L. (Ed). (1980). *Language intervention series, Vol. 4. Nonspeech language and communication—analysis and intervention*. Baltimore: University Park Press.

Schlesinger, H. and Meadow, K. (1972). *Sound and sign: Childhood deafness and mental health*. Berkeley: University of California Press.

Schloss, P. J. (1984). *Social development of handicapped children and adolescents.* Rockville, MD: Aspen Systems.

Schloss, P. J., and Johann, M. (1982)., A modeling and contingency management approach to pacifier withdrawal. *Behavior Therapy, 13:*254–257.

Schweinhart, L. J. and Weikart, D. P. (1980). Young children grow up: The effects of the Perry Preschool Program on youths through age 15. Ypsilanti, MI: High Scope Educational Research Foundation.

Scott, J. P. (1968). *Early experience and the organization of behavior.* Belmont, CA: Wadsworth.

Scott, K. G., and Hogan, A. E. (1980). Methods for identification of high-risk and handicapped infants. In C. T. Ramey and P. L. Trohanis (Eds.), *Finding and educating the high-risk and handicapped infant.* Chapel Hill, NC: Technical Assistance Development System.

Seligman, M. E. P. (1975). *Helplessness: On depression, development, and death.* San Francisco: Freeman.

Semans, S. (1967). The Bobath concept in the treatment of neurological disorders. *American Journal of Physical Medicine, 46:*732–785.

Serunian, S. A. and Broman, S. H. (1975). Relationship of Apgar scores and Bayley mental and motor scores. *Child Development, 46:*694–700.

Shearer, M. A., and Shearer, D. E. (1976). The Portage Project: A model for early childhood education. *Exceptional Children, 43:*210–219.

Sheehan, R. (1979a). Documenting the progress of children: Implications for data collection designs second instrument selection. In T. Black (Ed.). *Perspectives in measurement: A collection of readings for educators of young handicapped children,* pp. 42-54. Chapel Hill, NC: Technical Assistance Development System.

Sheehan, R. (1979b). Measuring progress in the mild to moderately handicapped preschooler. In T. Black (Ed.), *Perspectives in measurement: A collection of readings for educators of young handicapped chilren.* Chapel Hill, NC: Technical Assistance Development System.

Sheehan, R. (1985). Efficacy research in early childhood (Research Forum) *DEC Communicator, 11:*(4)4.

Sheehan, R., Gallagher, K., and Robson, D. (1982). *Technical assistance for demonstration programs: An evaluation of the Program Development Assistance System (Vol. 1) — The evaluation report.* Submitted to the U.S. Department of Education, Office of Special Education and the University of Washington.

Shenfeld, M. (1980). *The behavioral treatment of social withdrawal and isolation in children.* Unpublished manuscript, State University of New York of Buffalo.

Shere, E., and Kastenbaum, R. (1966). Mother-child interaction in cerebral palsy: Environmental and psycho-social obstacles to cognitive development. *Genetic Psychology Monographs, 73:*255–335.

Shorr, D. N., and McClelland, S. P. (1980). Assessing general intellectual status in bright preschool children. In W. C. Roedell, N. E. Jackson, and H. B. Robinson, *Gifted young children.* New York: Teachers College Press.

Showman, J. C. (1962). The rationale of patterns and techniques of proprioceptive neuromuscular facilitation. *Australian Journal of Physiotherapy. 8:*1–10.

Sigel, I. E. (1979). Application of research to psychoeducational treatment of infants at risk. In R. B. Kearsley and I., E. Sigel (Eds.). *Infants at risk: Assessment of cognitive functioning,* pp. 121–147. Hillsdale, N.J.: Erlbaum.

Simeonsson, R. J. (1977). Infant assessment and developmental handicap. In B. M. Caldwell and D. J. Stedman (Eds.). *Infant education: A guide to helping handicapped children in the first three years of life.* New York: Walker.

Simeonsson, R. J., Cooper, D. H., and Scheiner, A. P. (1982). A review and analysis of the effectiveness of early intervention programs. *Pediatrics, 69*(5):635–641.

Simeonsson, R. J., Huntington, G. S., and Parse, S. (1980). Expanding the developmental assessment of young handicapped children. In J. J. Gallagher (Ed.). *New Directions for Exceptional Children: Young Exceptional Children.* San Francisco: Jossey-Bass.

Simeonsson, R. J., Huntington, G. S., Short, R. J., and Ware, W. B. (1982). The Carolina record of individual behavior: Characteristics of handicapped infants and children. *Topics in Early Childhood Special Education, 2*(2):43–55.

Simeonsson, R. J., and Wiegerink, R. (1975). Accountability: A dilemma in infant intervention. *Exceptional Children, 41:*474–481.

Sisk, D. A. (1978). Education of the gifted and talented: A national perspective. *Journal for the Education of the Gifted, 1:*5–24.

Siva-Sankar, D. V. (1979). Plasma levels of folaters, riboflavin, vitamin B_6 and ascorbate in severely disturbed children. *Journal of Autism and Developmental Disorders, 9:*73–82.

Skeels, H. (1966). Adult status of children with contrasting early life experience. *Monographs of the Society for Research in Child Development, 31*(3).

Skeels, H. and Dye, H. (1939). A study of the effects of differential stimulation on mentally retarded children, *Preceedings of the American Association on Mental Deficiency, 44:*114–136.

Skipper, J. K., and Leonard, R. C. (1968). Children, stress, and hospitalization: A field experiment. *Journal of Health and Social Behavior, 9:*274–287.

Skodak, M. and Skeels, H. (1949). A final follow-up of one-hundred adopted children. *Journal of Genetic Psychology, 75:*85-125.

Sleator, E. K., and Sprague, R. L. (1978). Pediatric pharmacotherapy. In W. G. Clark and J. del Guidice (Eds.). *Principles of psychopharmacology,* 2nd ed. New York: Academic Press.

Smith, A., and Cote, K. (1982). *Look at me.* Philadelphia: Pennsylvania College of Optometry Press.

Smith, R. (1974). *Clinical teaching.* New York: McGraw-Hill.

Snell, M. E., and Smith, D. D. (1983). Developing the IEP: Selecting and assessing skills. In M. E. Snell (Ed.), *Systematic instruction of the moderately and severely handicapped,* 2nd ed., pp. 76–112. Columbus, OH: Merrill.

Solnick, J. V., Rincover, A., and Peterson, C. R. (1977). Determinants of the reinforcing and punishing effects of time-out. *Journal of Applied Behavior Analysis, 10:*415–428.

Sontag, L., Baker, C., and Nelson, V. (1958). Mental growth and personality development: a longitudinal study. *Monograph of the Society for Research on Child Development, 23*(2): whole no. 68.

Sontag, E., Burke, P. J., and York, R. (1973). Considerations for serving the severely handicapped in public schools. *Education and Training of the Mentally Retarded, 8:*20–26.

Sorce, J. F., and Emde, R. N. (1982). The meaning of infant emotional expressions: Regularities in caregiving responses in normal and Down's Syndrome infants. *Journal of Child Psychology and Psychiatry, 23:*145–158.

Sparrow, S., and Zigler, E. (1978). Evaluation of a patterning treatment for retarded children. *Pediatrics, 62:*137–150.

Spates, D. B., Alessi, G. J., Gutmann, A., Ellsworth, S., Mueller, K. L., and Ulrich, R. E. (1974). An educational day-care program for infants. In R. Ulrich, T. Stachnik, and J. Mabry (Eds.). *Control of human behavior: Behavior modification in education,* pp. 226–243. Glenview, IL: Scott, Foresman.

Spinnetta, J., and Rigler, D. (1972). The child abusing parent: A psychological review. *Psychological Bulletin, 77*(7):296–314.

Spitz, R. (1945). Hospitalism, An inquiry into the genesis of psychiatric conditions in early childhood. *Psychoanalytic Studies of Childhood, 1:*53–74.

Spitz, R. (1965). *The first year of life.* New York: International Universities Press.

Sprinthall, R. C., and Sprinthall, N. A. (1981). *Educational psychology: A developmental approach,* 3rd ed. Menlo Park, CA: Addison-Wesley.

Sroufe, L. A. (1979). The coherence of individual development: Early care, attachment, and subsequent developmental issues. *American Psychologist, 34*(10):834–841.

Stedman, D. (1973). The need for getting it all together. In J. B. Jordan and R. F. Dailey (Eds.). *Not all little wagons are red: The exceptional child's early years.* Reston, VA: Council for Exceptional Children.

Stedt, J. D., and Moores, D. F. (1983). American Sign Language and Signed English Systems contemporary issues. In F. Solano, S. Egelston-Dodd, and E. Costello (Eds.). *Focus on infusion, Vol. 2,* pp. 98–128. Silver Springs, MD: The Convention of American Instructors of the Deaf.

Steele, B. (1980). Psychodynamic factors in child abuse. In C. H. Kempe, and R. E. Helfer (Eds.). *The battered child,* 3rd ed., pp 49–85. Chicago: University of Chicago Press.

Stein, L. K. (1976). An electrophysiological test of infant hearing. *American Annals of the Deaf, 121:*322–326.

Steinmetz, S. K., and Strause, A. (Eds.). (1974). *Violence in the family.* New York: Mead.

Stockmeyer, S. (1967). An interpretation of the approach of Rood to the treatment of neuromuscular dysfunction. *American Journal of Physical Medicine, 46:*900–966.

Stokes, T. F., and Baer, D. M. (1977). An implicit technology of generalization. *Journal of Applied Behavior Analysis, 10:*349–367.

Stone, F. B., and Rowley, V. N. (1964). Educational disability in exceptional children. *Exceptional Children, 31:*423–426.

Strain, P. S., Kerr, M. M., and Alpher, R. (1979). Child-child and adult-child interaction in a preschool for physically-abused and neglected children. *Reading Improvement, 16*(2):163–168.

Straus, M. (1978). *Family patterns and child abuse in a nationally representative American sample.* Paper presented at Second International Congress on Child Abuse and Neglect. London, England.

Stuckless, E., and Birch, J. (1966). The influence of early manual communication on the linguistic development of deaf children. *American Annals of the Deaf, 111*(4):425–460, 499–504.

Sullivan, P., and Vernon, M. (1979). Psychological assessment of hearing impaired children. *School Psychology Digest, 8*(4):271–290.

Sutton-Smith, B. (1970). *A descriptive account of four modes of children's play between one and five years.* New York: Columbia University Teachers College.

Taitz, L. S. (1983). *The obese child.* Oxford: Blackwell Scientific.

Talbutt, L. C. (1983). Libel and slander: A potential problem for the 1980s. *The School Counselor, 30:*164–168.

Telford, C. W., and Sawrey, J. M. (1977). *The exceptional individual.* Englewood Cliffs, NJ: Prentice-Hall.

Thoman, E. B. Acebo, C., Dreyer, C. A., Becker, P. T., and Freese, M. P. (1979). Individuality in the interactive process. In E. B. Thoman (Ed). *Origins of the infants social responsiveness,* pp 76–91. Hillsdale, NJ: Erlbaum.

Thomas, A. (1981). Current trends in developmental theory, *American Journal of Orthopsychiatry, 51*(4):580–609.

Thomas, A., and Chess, S. (1977). *Temperament and development.* New York: Brunner/Mazel.

Thompson, R. H. (1985). *Psychosocial research on pediatric hospitalization and health care: A review of the literature.* Springfield, IL: Thomas.

Thompson, R. J., Coppleman, M. W., Conrad, H. H., and Jordan, W. B. (1982). Early intervention program for adolescent mothers and their infants. *Developmental and Behavioral Pediatrics, 3*(1):18–21.

Thurston, P. W. (1982). Torts. In P. K. Piele (Ed.). *The yearbook of school law,* pp. 182–208. Topeka, KA: National Organization of Legal Problems of Education.

Tjossen, T. (1976). *Intervention strategies for high-risk infants and young children.* Baltimore: University Park Press.

Travis, G. (1976). *Chronic illness in children: Its impact on child and family.* Stanford, CA: Stanford University Press.

Turnbull, A. P. (1983). Parent professional interactions. In M. E. Snell (Ed.). *Systematic instruction of the moderately and severely handicapped,* 2nd ed., pp. 18–43. Columbus, OH: Merrill.

Turner, K., and Wade, G. C. (1982). Learning disabled, birth to three: Fact or artifact? *Journal of the Division for Early Childhood, 5:*79–86.

Ulrey, G. (1981). Emotional development of the young handicapped child. In N. J. Anastasiow (Ed.). *New directions for exceptional children: Socioemotional development, Vol. 5.* San Francisco: Jossey-Bass.

Ulrey, G., and Rogers, S. J. (1982). *Psychological assessment of handicapped infants and young children.* New York: Thieme-Stratton.

U.S. Department of Health Education and Welfare. (1980). The Status of handicapped children in Head Start programs. Washington, D.C.: Office of Human Development Services. Administration for Children, Youth, and Families. Head Start Bureau.

Uzgiris, I., and Hunt, J. (1975). *Infant assessment: Toward ordinal scales of psychological development.* Champaign: University of Illinois Press.

Van Blankenstein, M., Welbergen, U. R., and de Haas, J. H. (1975). *The development of the infant.* London: Heinemann Medical.

Vernon, M., and Koh, S. (1970). Effects of manual communication on deaf children's educational achievement, linguistic competence, oral skills, and psychological development. *American Annals of the Deaf, 115*(5):527–536.

Vincent, L. J., Brown, L., and Getz-Sheftl, M. (1981). Integrating handicapped and typical children during the preschool years: The definition of best educational practice. *Topics in Early Childhood Special Education, 1*(1):17–24.

Vincent, L., Salisburg, C., Walter, G., Brown, P., Gruenewald, L. and Powers, M. (1980). Program evaluation and curriculum development in early childhood/special education. In W. Sailor, B. Wilcox, and L. Brown (Eds.). *Instructional design for the severely handicapped.* Baltimore: Brookes.

Visintainer, M. A., and Wolfer, J. A. (1975). Psychological preparation for surgical pediatric patients: The effects on children's and parents' stress responses and adjustment. *Pediatrics, 56:*187–202.

Vygotsky, L. S. (1962). *Thought and language.* Cambridge, MA: MIT Press.

Walker, J. (1982). Social interactions of handicapped infants. In D. Bricker (Ed.). *Intervention with high-risk and handicapped infants: From research to application,* pp. 217–232. Baltimore: University Park Press.

Walker, J., and Hallan, M. (1981). Why the "H" in ECEH? Considerations in training teachers of young handicapped children. *Journal of the Division for Early Childhood, 2:*61–66.

Warren, D. (1984). *Blindness and early childhood development,* 2nd ed., revised. New York: American Foundation for the Blind.

Wass, H., and Corr, C. A. (Eds). (1984). *Helping children cope with death: Guidelines and resources,* 2nd ed. Washington, DC: Hemisphere Press.

Weber, C. U., Foster, P. W., and Weikart, D. P. (1978). *An economic analysis of the Ypsilanti Perry Preschool Project.* Ypsilanti, MI: High Scope Educational Research Foundation.

Wechsler, D. (1967). *Manual for the Preschool and Primary Scale of Intelligence.* New York: Psychological Corporation.

Wechsler, D. (1974). *Manual for the Wechsler Intelligence Scale for Children–Revised.* New York: Psychological Corporation.

Weikart, D., Bond, J., and McNeil, J. (1978). *The Ypsilanti preschool project.* Monograph no. 3. Ypsilanti: High Scope Educational Research Foundation, 1978.

Weikart, D., Rogers, L., Adcock, C., and McClelland, D. (1970). The cognitively oriented curriculum: A framework for preschool teachers. Washington, DC: National Association for the Education of Young Children.

Weisler, A., and McCall, R. B. (1976). Exploration and play: Resume and redirection. *American Psychologist, 31:*492–508.

Welsh, M. M., and Odum, C. S. H. (1981). Parental involvement in the education of the handicapped child: A review of the literature. *Journal of the Division for Early Childhood, 3:*15–25.

Werner, E., and Smith, R. (1981). *Vulnerable but invincible: A longitudal study of resilient children and youth.* New York: McGraw-Hill.

Westinghouse Learning Corporation (1969). *The impact of Head Start: An evaluation of the effects of Head Start on children's cognitive and affective development.* Columbus, OH: Ohio University.

Wherry, J. N. (1983). Some legal considerations and implications for the use of behavior modification. *Psychology in the Schools, 20:*46–51.

White, K. R., and Casto, G. (in press). An integrative review of early intervention efficacy studies with at-risk children: Implications for the handicapped. *Analysis and Intervention in Developmental Disabilities.*

White, O., Edgar, E., Haring, N., Affleck, J., Hayden, A., and Bendersky, M. (1981). *Uniform performance assessment system.* Columbus, OH: Merrill.

Wiig, E. H., and Semel, E. M. (1976). *Language disabilities in children and adolescents.* Columbus, OH: Merrill.

Wiig, E. H. Semel, E. M., and Nystrom, L. (1982). Comparison of rapid naming abilities in language learning disabled and academically achieving 8-year-olds. *Language, Speech and Hearing in Schools, 13:*11–23.

Wilbur, R. (1979). *American Sign Language and Sign Systems.* Baltimore: University Park Press.

Williams, J. (1980). *Red flag green flag people.* Fargo, ND: Rape and Abuse Crisis Center of Fargo–Moorhead.

Williams, G. F. (1981). *Children with chronic arthritis: A primer for patients and parents.* Littleton, MA: PSG

Willoughby-Herb, S. J., and Neisworth, J. T. (1983). *HICOMP Preschool Curriculum.* Columbus, OH: Merrill.

Wilson, J. M. (1978). *Oral-motor function and dysfunction in children.* Chapel Hill: University of North Carolina Physical Therapy Department.

Wilson, E. O. (1979). *On human nature.* New York: Bantam Books.

Witty, P. (1940). Some considerations in the education of gifted children. *Educational Administration and Supervision, 26:*512–521.

Wolfensberger, W. (1972). Normalization: The principle of normalization in human services. Toronto: National Institute on Mental Retardation.

Wolfensberger, W. (1983). Social valorization: A proposed new term for the principle of normalization. *Mental Retardation, 21:*234–239.

Wolinsky, G. F. (1983). Cognitive curricula: Theory, models, and implementation. *Topics in Early Childhood Special Education, 2*(4):34–42.

Wood, M. M. (1981). Costs of intervention programs. In C. Garland, N. W. Stone, J. Swanson, and G. Woodruff (Eds.), *Early intervention for children with special needs and their families,* pp. 79–97. Monmouth, OR: Westar.

Wyatt, v. *Stickney,* 325 F. Supp. 781 (1971). U S Supreme Court.

Zehrbach, R. (1975). Determining a preschool handicapped population. *Exceptional Children, 42:*76–83.

Zelazo, P. R. (1979). Reactivity to perceptual-cognitive events: Application for infant assessment. In R. B. Kearsley and I. E. Sigel (Eds.). *Infants at risk: assessment of cognitive functioning. Hillsdale, NJ: Erlbaum.*

Zelazo, P. R. (1982). Alternative assessment procedures for handicapped infants and toddlers: Theoretical and practical issues. In D. D. Bricker (Ed.). *Intervention with high-risk and handicapped infants: From research to application.* Baltimore: University Park Press.

Ziai, M. (Ed.). (1975). *Pediatrics,* 2nd ed. Boston: Little, Brown.

Zigler, E., and Berman, W. (1983). Discerning the future of early childhood intervention. *American Psychologist.* August 1983:894.

Zigler, E., and Trickett, P. K. (1978). IQ, Social competence and evaluation of early childhood intervention programs. *American Psychologist,* September 1978:789.

Author Index

Indexes prepared by Mary Pratt, with Angela Capone and Elaine Cutler.

Subject Index